ARMY SERVICE CORPS

1902-1918

ARMY SERVICE CORPS
1902-1918

by

MICHAEL YOUNG

With a Foreword by
PROFESSOR RICHARD HOLMES

LEO COOPER

First published in Great Britain in 2000 by
LEO COOPER
an imprint of
Pen & Sword Books
47 Church Street
Barnsley
South Yorkshire
S70 2AS

Published on behalf of
The Institution of The Royal Army Service Corps
and The Royal Corps of Transport

ISBN 085052 730 9

A catalogue record for this book
is available from the British Library

Typeset in 11/12pt Garamond by
Phoenix Typesetting, Ilkley, West Yorkshire

Printed in England by
Redwood Books Ltd, Trowbridge, Wilts.

Contents

Foreword ix

Prologue 1

Chapter 1: 1902-1914: A Modern Army for Europe 5

Chapter 2: 1914: Baptism of Fire 41

Chapter 3: 1915: Increasing Responsibilities 71

Chapter 4: 1916: New Challenges 88

Chapter 5: 1917: A Year of Contrasts 103

Chapter 6: 1918: Ebb and Flow 118

Chapter 7: The Home Front: Springboard for Success 131

Chapter 8: Italy 150

Chapter 9: Egypt and Palestine 153

Chapter 10: Mesopotamia (Iraq) 159

Chapter 11: The Balkans (Salonika) 164

Chapter 12: The Dardanelles 171

Chapter 13: East Africa 180

Chapter 14: Russia 183

Epilogue 189

Annexes 195

Index 392

List of Annexes

A	ASC Company Locations 1902–1914	195
B	Establishment of ASC Horse Transporter Company 1902	204
C	Key ASC Officers 1902–1918	205
D	Territorial Force Transport and Supply Columns 1908	212
E	Wagon Mounting and Dismounting Competition	217
F	ASC Vehicles in 1910	220
G	Expeditionary Force Tables November 1912	226
H	Remounts	227
I	ASC Vehicles in August 1914	230
J	Ambulance Donors 1914–1918	231
K	Labour Companies ASC	236
L	Resupply Chain	238
M	Regimental Prefixes and Numbers	239
N	Unit Establishments	243
O	ASC Tank Drivers Flers-Courcelette 1916	259
P	Unit Signs	261
Q	ASC Company Information 1914–1918	269
R	Units in Formations/Theatres of War	334
S	Honours and Awards	368
T	Military Growth of the ASC	383
U	Supply Statistics	389

Sources and Acknowledgements

The following sources are gratefully acknowledged:

The Royal Corps of Transport Archives in the Royal Logistic Corps Museum.

The Public Record Office Kew: QMG and ASC Company files.

The London Transport Museum.

The RASC. A History of Transport & Supply in the British Army Volume 2 by Colonel R H Beadon.

With the MT in Mesopotamia by Lieutenant Colonel F W Leland CBE DSO.

Citizen Soldiers by Colonel G Williams OBE.

Tanks in the Great War 1914-1918 by Colonel J F C Fuller DSO.

The Tanks at Flers by Trevor Pidgeon.

The author's thanks go to the Trustees of the Imperial War Museum for allowing access to the papers of the following: Major H N G Watson, Captain C A Cooke, Captain A Gibbs MC, Lieutenant F Howitt, Sergeant D Clark, Sergeant E C H Rowland; also to the copyright holders for permission to publish extracts from the papers of Captain Gibbs, Lieutenant Howitt, Sergeant Clark and Sergeant Rowland. Every reasonable effort has been made to contact the copyright holders for Major Watson and Captain Cooke, regrettably with no success.

Every reasonable effort has also been made to trace the owners of other possible copyright material in this book, but this has been impossible in some instances. The author will be glad to receive information leading to more complete acknowledgements in any subsequent printing of this book and in the meantime extends his apologies for any omissions.

Foreword

by

PROFESSOR RICHARD HOLMES

The military thinker Clausewitz called war a passionate drama, and historians and their readers have certainly been fascinated by its stars. They all too often fail to pay proper attention to the tireless stagehands of war, the logisticians who ensure that armies are supplied with everything they need, from bullets to blankets, petrol to plasma, tanks to tourniquets. In the past twenty years only two major histories of military logistics have appeared, and it was not until 1998 that we saw Ian Malcolm Brown's scholarly study of British logistics on the Western Front. Practical soldiers usually know better. Field Marshal Lord Wavell wrote that: 'The more I see of war, the more I realise how it all depends upon administration and transport.'

Michael Young's history of the Army Service Corps 1902–1918 is not simply a standard corps history, charting the remarkable achievements of a corps in whose successors he served. It goes much, much further, and fills a recognizable gap in the historiography of the First World War, providing its students – professional historians as well as that growing band of amateur enthusiasts for whom the conflict exercises such a bitter-sweet appeal – with the first modern history of the British army's transport service, the Army Service Corps.

The book falls into two parts. The first charts the history of the ASC from 1902, when it was re-establishing itself after the Boer War, until the end of the First World War – when its numbers peaked at an extraordinary 10,547 officers and 315,334 men, greater than the total strength of the British armed forces, regular and reserve, at the time of writing. It examines not only the ASC's activities on the Western Front, but also its performance in the war's numerous 'sideshows', like Gallipoli and Palestine. In the process it touches on dozens of fascinating topics from the organization of the ASC-badged Women's Forage Corps, and the Mesopotamian Expeditionary Force's canteen aboard the barge SS *Masoodi* on the River Tigris, to the duties of the senior transport officer at corps headquarters. The second part, which will prove invaluable to serious researchers and genealogists, consists of annexes, culled from archival research, which provide a wealth of detail on matters as diverse as ASC company locations at home and abroad, unit signs and establishments, key personalities, and honours and awards. My own life would have been a good deal simpler had Annex Q, a list of transport companies, been available when I first started to write about the First World War.

Yet this is no bloodless compilation of dates and statistics. Michael Young has used a wide range of personal accounts which put flesh on the statistical bones, and there are plenty of surprises. Sergeant John Jackson tells us of his narrow escape from German Uhlans on the retreat from Mons in 1914, where his drivers emptied a good few saddles, and Private White drove his truck through German lines, so transformed by the experience that his hair had changed colour and he was known thereafter as 'Snowy White'. Captain Watson identified the strange knocking sounds in his truck not as the stones thrown up against the mudguards, as his driver suggested, but as rifle-fire from a

German aircraft flying low overhead in one of the earliest examples of ground attack. Sergeant Douglas Clark's account of taking ammunition to a siege battery, Royal Garrison Artillery, during the terrible fighting at Passchendaele in 1917 reminds us just how dangerous it was to drive, along routes well-known to German artillery observers, with a dangerous cargo.

There was the ever-present problem of horse-management in hellish conditions. While men could take cover in trenches or dugouts, horses could not, and many a driver stuck bravely to his box seat under shellfire to steady his terrified team. A journalist noted that drivers' orders specified that 'A driver will under no circumstances leave his horses and wagon unattended,' but thought that 'the regulation was not needed to ensure that,' for a driver became warmly attached to 'his pair'.

And there is a lighter side. Sergeant 'Red' Rowland ASC wrote the words to 'Mademoiselle from Armentières', commemorating the rebuff of an amorous officer by a determined young widow. 563 Company ASC, equipped with the London buses which made their incongruous appearance on the Western Front in 1914, took as its badge the figure of Britannia, from the penny, to make the point that its buses had once taken passengers about London at 'a penny all the way'. The photographs, most of them never published before, are a delight. They include what is perhaps the army's first ever 'work ticket' – signed by a major general – and a wonderful shot of a pre-war barrack room, got up in the best of Edwardian style. But the photograph that makes the point about the ASC's wartime performance is, for me, that of a supply column on the Merville road in April 1918, during the German spring offensive. An exhausted corporal lies asleep at the roadside while his tired horse rests its head against a tree.

Of course no book on a subject this huge can claim to be comprehensive. But Michael Young covers his vast canvas with enormous skill. His is a remarkable achievement and a fitting tribute to the men who drove their horses or trucks, wore the brass shoulder-title ASC and risked, and so often lost, their lives:

. . . to drive a load of shell
of fodder, kit and rations – from rail'ead up to 'ell.

Richard Holmes

Prologue

After a lifetime of service in the army, either in the Royal Army Service Corps or Royal Corps of Transport, I became Curator of the RCT Museum in Aldershot in 1987 and my particular interest focused on the Army Service Corps (ASC) during this century – the ASC in the Victorian period up to the end of the Boer War in 1902 is really a separate subject. The artefacts in the museum and the wealth of material hidden away in the archives were a constant source of interest, let alone a means of answering the regular stream of inquiries that came in from researchers or the descendants of soldiers who had served in the First World War. Their sole knowledge of, say, a grandfather was only what could be gleaned from a tatty postcard or uninformative discharge papers and they had no opportunity or time to visit the few places where research material was available, even if they knew where those places were.

As I read more into our history I realized that the otherwise wholly admirable history by Colonel R H Beadon, *The RASC. A History of Transport & Supply in the British Army,* Volume 2, published in 1931, neither contained any photographs nor provided the sort of information that people seem to want today; in any event the book is an expensive collector's item, even if it can be found. As a result, there are few people who know anything about the ASC during this century. This strikes me as disappointing, as not only was the Corps overwhelmingly the largest and most successful logistic Corps of its day but its officers and men also achieved wonders for which they have still never been given full credit. There can be no doubt that the subsequent success of the RASC and RCT was based on the performance of the ASC in the early years of the 20th century.

The idea of writing a history of the ASC gradually developed, but for some time the awareness that most military history *aficionados* are only interested in bayonets, trenches, guns and cavalry discouraged me. The general perception is that, whatever major contribution it makes to the war, a logistic Corps lacks glamour, is not politically important, has no leaders who were influential in the war, is not seen as heroic and, frankly, is not as interesting as those cap badges with exciting tales to tell – but, in spite of this, I believe that it is people who are interesting and the ASC, with almost a third of a million people in uniform, provides a huge source of interest for anyone who is prepared to consider the possibility. So, with archive sources easily available to me but not generally to others, I began my task. That was the easy bit.

My impression when I started to look at how to achieve my aim was like standing on a precipice and looking down into a large bottomless hole, facing the task of digging away like a field archaeologist and building up a jigsaw puzzle that I soon realized could never be completed. I would not wish to make excuses, but the history of a large Corps is virtually impossible to write, bearing in mind the number of people, functions and theatres of war involved – anything definitive would be totally out of the question, unless a large team of researchers were to produce a multi-volume work. There is no single story line as there is with an infantry battalion or Division, yet one has to tell as much about the Corps as possible while at the same time providing interest and information; furthermore there are no locations peculiar to the ASC on the Western Front or in other theatres of war which can be considered to be of interest to the military tourist. One realization was clear from the beginning: it would be impossible to tell the story of the war and the Army as well as that of the ASC, so, on the assumption that those who read this book will also know the story of the war, this history unashamedly concentrates on the ASC only. There are thousands of other books to read about other regiments and Corps, let alone books with a more general approach, so I hope readers will bear with me on this matter.

The result of my labours is a book which, so far as I am aware, is like no other regimental history. This might be a fatal weakness, but it might have an appeal because of that. Hopefully, the reader will follow with ease the glimpses of life in the ASC over the years, with separate small chapters on campaigns outside mainland Europe. The introductory chapter for the period 1902 to 1914 covers an essential period, seeing as it does the introduction of mechanical transport in the army (in conjunction with pioneer work by the Royal Engineers), the early development of ASC Volunteer units and modernization following the Boer War, all of which put the ASC in an incomparable position for the start of the war in 1914.

The photographs, variously from the RCT archives (annotated (A)) or my own postcard collection (annotated (B)), should provide much of interest to both the casual reader and serious military historian. Fortunately the ASC was easier to photograph than the fighting arms, and there were so many men in so many places doing so many different things. The Annexes at the back provide a considerable amount of information that was impossible to incorporate within the main body of the narrative. Indeed they provide a mini-archive which would have provided answers to many of the queries that came to me as RCT Curator (and still come in to the Curator of The Royal Logistic Corps, the Corps into which the successor of the RASC, the RCT, was amalgamated in 1993).

The huge tapestry and the large amount of material available mean that only outline information can be given on many subjects; and yet, ironically, there is a dearth of material on some aspects of the history and individuals concerned. There was no Corps Museum to be the focus of archive material until after the Second World War and most members of the Corps did not think their work was of sufficient interest or importance to make extensive records at the time. Their modesty and self-effacement are no grounds, however, for historians to ignore them.

I am unhappily aware that I have come to this history fifty years too late – all the senior participants died long ago and the handful of gallant survivors still alive today have few clear recollections of value to me; I am equally conscious that not many individuals are represented, particularly in their correspondence home, but I have tried to include anecdotal pieces which go some way to compensate for this. The result, however, is an incomplete and patchy account that no perfectionist should even start reading, a history which has no real balance, but which, with a little luck, will provide an impression of a large Corps over a period of seventeen years or so. As ever, in a large landscape with much detail to discern, it is difficult to 'see the wood for the trees'. At the very least, I would hope to increase the level of information in the public arena and, in so doing, contribute my bit to the memory of a large number of good men and women.

What can one say in general terms about the ASC? Much of what they did was pioneer work. After all, the 1914-18 war was the first war in which mechanical transport played an important, even decisive, part, and it would not be too much of an exaggeration to say, when comparing the situations in 1902 and 1918, that a quiet revolution had taken place. Behind the army of men in the trenches on the Western Front was another army which was no less important. Theirs was not the task of person-to-person combat with the enemy, but it was theirs to support, largely unseen and unsung, the men who had that task. And if you doubt that their work was unsung, you only have to look at the indexes to the Official History of the Great War. It is shameful that the ASC is listed on only four occasions in the fourteen volumes. The ASC may not have been seen as front-line troops, but in practice they were always up behind the front trenches, either with essential supplies, ammunition, water or the ubiquitous ambulance; and any Gunner will tell you that a good proportion of their targets are formation administrative areas or key crossroads where moving traffic on replenishment duties is bound to concentrate (ie the enemy's transport and supply organization).

Any book on logistic support has a wider view than most regimental histories. It has a bigger and more important story to tell. The problem, though, is the general perception of the ASC in the minds of historians and the general public. This inevitably leads one to question what popular interest is based on and what heroism is. The thousands of books that have been written about war often highlight the courage needed to survive in the front line, the bravery needed to leave the relative safety of a trench and assault an enemy position, as well as the excitement of hand-to-hand combat or the occasional VC actions. Is that the only form of heroism? What of the man who has no trenches to protect him? What of the man who sits on a GS wagon or in a lorry as he goes up to forward positions day after day, night after night, on roads which are regularly shelled? Does not the man who has no officer to lead him or Sergeant Major to 'put the fear of living daylight' into him show a particular kind of courage, especially with no regimental *esprit de corps* or regimental family to provide the sort of backbone for which the British Army is famous?

What of the officers and soldiers of the ASC? The overwhelming majority, sadly, remain faceless and unknown. The information needed for a serious analysis is simply not available today, if ever it was in the past. A few generalizations based on impressions gleaned by looking at many papers and photographs, however, might be of value. The Corps as a whole had no particular social status. No self-respecting public schoolboy would volunteer for the ASC, when other regiments had more class and style, regiments in which their chums were to be found and where their socially-sensitive feelings would find a comfortable home. You did not need, however, money or 'family' to be commissioned in the ASC, but you did at least have easy access to horses and riding, which was certainly not the case in most regiments. The opportunity to ride was undoubtedly an attraction to many officers who could not quite afford the life of a fashionable regiment. You did, however, need to be efficient at your job, which would have been a discouraging thought for many. On balance, most ASC officers had a particular skill when they joined, perhaps the sort of background or ability in practical matters of life which was easy to sneer at but which, nevertheless, was essential to the efficiency of the army.

Soldiers of all regiments and Corps come from a wide variety of backgrounds. The fighting arms and Volunteers in the Territorial Force were recruited more on a territorial basis than in the ASC. A glance at the pre-war occupations of one of the MT Companies, which are to be seen in the 1916 chapter, will show a higher skills background than would probably have been found in any other regiment; on the other hand, a similar list for a Horse Transport Company would undoubtedly have shown a different picture. Unfortunately, no suitable list is available.

What held them together in their work during the war, in conditions often just as intolerable as in the front line? Certainly not *esprit de corps*. The ASC was too large and too dispersed for any concentration of regimental consciousness. I believe there were two reasons why the ASC soldier did well: firstly he wanted to help the fighting units as best he could. He saw enough dead and wounded to know that those units needed his personal support, and he was not going to let them down; and, secondly, he had great pride in his work, often as a skilled tradesman, doing a job he knew no one in an infantry battalion could do. Yes, he had his leg pulled as a 'Jam Stealer'; yes, he did not have to shelter in a trench being shelled by an unseen enemy; yes, he did not attract media attention as a hero, but he knew his work was part of a team effort which contributed just as much to the success of British arms as the efforts of any infantryman. Together they made it work. The position of the ASC in supporting the army during the First World War was second to none and the result of their work was that the British soldier was not only better looked after than he had been at home but also had the best administrative support of all the armies in the western alliance.

On a personal note, one of the most memorable moments of my research was visiting an old soldier of the ASC in a London Transport Residential Home in Wembley, through the good offices of the London Transport Museum. He was just approaching his hundredth birthday and sadly was wheelchair bound; although he could not talk he understood what I was saying to him and was able to indicate agreement and interest. The reason I went to see him was that he was almost certainly the last of the London bus drivers alive who drove omnibuses on the Western Front, the story of which is one of the jigsaw pieces of this history. Mr Alfred Cummings was a big man who was forever proud of 'doing his bit' in the war. His son, who was present and had himself served in the RASC, confirmed the tales his father used to tell. As I said farewell, I shook hands with this man who was the last of an outstanding group of characters and I felt I was touching history, reaching out to the past; his large strong hand, not at all old or gnarled, seemed to impart a power to me that is difficult to describe. His were the hands that had steered a London omnibus through the war, eventually, with many others behind the scenes, helping to stop the German attack in March-April 1918. I felt a better person, a more empowered person, having shaken the hand of such a man. In the same way, albeit not with a handshake, I hope that readers of this book will have a sense of reaching out into the past, of touching an unknown part of our history and feeling a sense of identity with the men of the ASC. If these faceless men could talk they would be pleased to be the subject of our interest, modestly of course.

CHAPTER 1

1902-1914: A Modern Army for Europe

In 1902 the ASC was in the process of re-establishing itself after the war against the Boers in South Africa, where it had performed magnificently, forging a reputation and sense of unity that was going to stand it in good stead over the coming years. Most members of the Corps served there and few were left in the United Kingdom. Gradually, though, with peace, most of the army in the southern hemisphere was returning home, among them companies of the ASC (see Annex A for company locations over the period 1902-1914).

At this point the Corps consisted of sixty-five Horse Transport (HT) Companies, five Supply Companies and two Remount Companies, with 467 officers and some 7,000 men. The two main depots of the Corps were in Aldershot (Horse Transport and Supply) and Woolwich (Horse Transport). Command and leadership was in the hands of the Assistant Quartermaster General (AQMG) ASC based in the Quartermaster General's Department in the War Office. There was no head of Corps, as was to be the case until 1914.

The duties of the ASC were to provide transport and supplies for all branches of the army and to allot barracks and quarters and their equipment. Transport Companies were stationed in the large garrisons at home and at a few stations in the colonies, transport services being carried out by those companies or by civilian transport hired from contractors, under the supervision of the ASC officer in charge of transport.

It was not until January 1905 that ASC District Barrack Officers were appointed to Commands, with four Quartermasters being cut from the Corps establishment in compensation. They supervised all duties concerned with barrack accommodation and furniture, with each Command divided into areas and an ASC officer appointed to each area as officer in charge of barracks. He issued barrack furniture to the troops, the stores having been drawn from the Army Ordnance Department.

The Supply Companies were stationed at Aldershot and other large garrisons. All the men of the Supply Branch of the ASC belonged to these companies, but they were scattered in small detachments of varying strength, according to the size of the garrison, at nearly all the military stations at home and abroad, except in India. 'Supplies' essentially meant food and forage, but included other consumable items such as fuel and light. At large stations the rations were supplied by the ASC direct from their own bakeries and abattoirs, which not only served to train the men of the Corps in their trade but also accustomed units to draw their supplies in peace in the same way as they would in the field or at war. At small stations the ASC arranged civilian contract for delivery direct to units. The Supply Branch also included staff clerks employed in the various staff offices. These had until 1893 been members of the Corps of Military Staff Clerks (a Corps which had no officers, so they tended to be 'nobody's children'; they had been absorbed into the Supply Branch of the ASC in November 1899).

In 1902 7, 9, 12, 19, 21, 24, 28, 30, 31, 33 and 37 Companies were still in South Africa; 6, 10, 11, 17, 25, 29, 34, 35, 40 and 42 Companies arrived back in England from South Africa during the year; 15 and 22 Companies were in South Africa too, but were about to go to Somaliland; 68 Company was in Gibraltar, 69 Company in Malta and 70 Company in Egypt. In addition to the companies listed above, the Corps had small detachments in a variety of stations throughout the world, in Bermuda, Cyprus, Jamaica, Mauritius, North and South China, Sierra Leone and Singapore.

Many Horse Transport Companies were on lower establishment. A typical establishment was of two officers, one Warrant Officer, one Company Sergeant Major and Company Quartermaster Sergeant, two Sergeants, two Corporals, a second Corporal, one Trumpeter, two Lance Corporals, fifteen Drivers and a Wheeler, Saddler and Farrier Staff Sergeant or Corporal, a total of some thirty men (see Annex B). There were no regimental organizations as we know them today. Companies were allocated as required to formations only on annual manoeuvres, until war was on the horizon. Over the next few years a good number of Horse Transport Companies in England were mechanized, converting at Aldershot before they returned to their various stations around UK, 'spreading the gospel' of a new form of locomotion.

Supply Companies, previously identified with numbers, were re-designated with letters in 1902 and we see A and C Supply Companies in Aldershot, B Supply Company in South Africa, D Supply Company in Dublin and E Supply Company in Woolwich. In 1906 an additional F Supply Company was formed in Tidworth.

* * *

In recognition of the Corps' services in South Africa, HM King Edward VII appointed his brother, Field Marshal HRH The Duke of Connaught and Strathearn, to be Colonel of the ASC in 1902, which announcement appeared in the London Gazette of 2 September 1902. He was a frequent visitor to Corps functions and held this appointment until his death in 1942.

The Assistant Quartermaster General ASC in the War Office, Colonel F T Clayton, sent the following telegram to His Royal Highness: "The Army Service Corps are deeply sensible of the great honour conferred on the Corps by His Majesty and respectfully salute Your Royal Highness on your appointment as their first Colonel-in-Chief." To which the reply was received: "Duke of Connaught thanks you for your congratulations on his appointment as Colonel of Army Service Corps. Military Secretary." In communicating the above to the Corps in the *ASC Journal*, the Assistant Quartermaster General ASC said that "he is sure that all ranks will join him in the expression of thanks to His Majesty for the great honour conferred on the Army Service Corps, and congratulations to His Royal Highness on his appointment as Colonel of the Corps."

* * *

The year 1902 also saw a blossoming of regimental activities as the confidence gained from successful operations in South Africa took hold. In St George's Church, Stanhope Lines, Aldershot, the ASC South African Memorial East Window was unveiled and dedicated in April; and on a wet and rainy day in June the first general Corps gathering took place, the forerunner of subsequent Corps Weeks. Cricket matches were played against the Royal Artillery and Royal

Engineers and on the last day of the sports a luncheon was served in the Corps Theatre next to the Recreation Ground for all officers in station and their ladies. On the Saturday an Officers' Ball took place in the Corps Theatre, with a special train running between Aldershot and London for guests; even an Ascot Day was instituted, not forgetting a 'Nil Sine' Lunch Club.

*　　*　　*

The Corps Masonic Lodge (No. 2736) had been formed in London on 23 July 1898, with Lieutenant Colonel G J Parkyn as the first Worshipful Master and Colonel J A Boyd and Lieutenant Colonel F T Clayton as the first Wardens; on 22 October 1903 in the ASC Theatre, Stanhope Lines, Aldershot, Field Marshal HRH The Duke of Connaught was elected as Worshipful Master and Colonel F W B Landon, Commanding ASC, Aldershot as Worshipful Deputy Master. The first Secretary of the Corps Lodge, Major G McFarlane, was a well-known personality: he had joined the ASC in 1878 as a Private, being commissioned in 1898 as Honorary Lieutenant and Quartermaster, taking out the first detachment of the ASC to serve in the Boer War in South Africa. While stationed in London in 1892 he had instituted a campaign for the introduction of shorthand in the Army.

*　　*　　*

The Corps Band, which had started life as a Voluntary Mounted/Marching Band in 1891 to play on church parades, was now an essential (though still voluntary) part of the life of the Corps, paid for as usual in those days by the officers. In 1903 a new Bandmaster, H J Cook, late of The Wiltshire Regiment, took over from Staff Sergeant Bryce, staying until 1922. During this period the Band numbered anything from thirty-two to thirty-seven, playing on occasions at the Royal Naval & Military Tournament at Olympia.

The Band, however, always seemed to have financial problems, almost inevitable when considering the apparent unwillingness of officers in stations abroad or far from Aldershot voluntarily to pay a subscription to support it; there were even difficulties in the attendance of musicians, since some of them were clerks in the local Command Headquarters and staff officers were reluctant to release them. This situation was a running sore right up to the period preceding the outbreak of war in 1914, but the Corps Club in the end appears to have voted money to help.

*　　*　　*

The ASC had considerable influence in the foundation of the Union Jack Club in London, the brainchild of Miss McCaul, through two officers late of the ASC, Colonel Sir Edward Ward KCB (Chairman of the Executive Committee) and Major Arthur Haggard (Club Secretary). It was proposed in 1902 that a social club be established in London in memory of sailors and soldiers who had died in South Africa and China, since other Soldiers' 'Homes' in London did not sufficiently meet the needs of the day. It was intended that the club was open to all sailors and soldiers, and to Reservists on production of their papers, to provide close to Waterloo Railway Station a place where they could meet their comrades, procure a good bed, a comfortable meal, where their interest would be safeguarded and where they could "avoid the many temptations and pitfalls which await them". The ASC supported the formation of such a club, not least through financial support, since the Corps' two largest stations, Aldershot and Woolwich, were close to the capital and many recruits for the Corps came from London.

*　　*　　*

The *Corps Journal* had first been published in April 1891, one of the earliest Journals in the Army, its stated aim to enable members of the Corps throughout the world to stay in touch with one another. The editorial of the April 1902 issue stated:

> "In reviewing the work of the Journal during the past eleven years, we think that it has been an instrument towards the encouragement of 'Esprit de Corps.'
>
> "Thus it is our desire to encourage in every way with the motto 'The Army Service Corps for the Army Service Corps.' Never was this spirit more needed than at present. The 'three thousand strong' of Lieutenant Colonel Grattan's days (ie 1891) has now become seven thousand and further increases appear to be inevitable. Let all ranks stick together and 'Gang forward.' Our monthly issue at present averages 1,150 to 1,200 copies. We would again take the opportunity of asking subscribers to inform us of any change of address. This is sometimes forgotten."

The first ASC Quarterly was published in 1905, devoted to professional papers on general military subjects. Subsequent issues not only continued to inform ASC officers of military matters of importance but also provided an opportunity for the more serious and ambitious officers to publish their views on ASC and other matters for the education of their fellow officers.

*　　*　　*

In 1901 mechanical road transport had come onto the military scene, with the army taking advantage of civilian technology and keeping abreast of developments in continental armies. The Royal Engineers had used steam traction engines in the Boer War, but the lack of water and coal, dust and low speeds led to limited success; two lorries had even been trialled there in the closing months of the war. Die-hards in the army, however, did not consider MT had any place in 'real soldiering', although some in South Africa took notice when a traction engine recovered a bogged-in wagon which eighty oxen had failed to move.

General Sir Redvers Buller, who had been so influential in the formation of the second ASC in 1888, was well aware that steam engines had been used in South Africa and the advantages of cars. Back in England in 1901, he asked the Automobile Association whether he could hire a car for his use during army manoeuvres that year. Several members agreed to help him. The weather was terrible but the three cars concerned performed well, which led to four cars being used by General Sir Evelyn Wood's staff during the Volunteer manoeuvres in August the same year, the Honourable C S Rolls being one of the drivers.

*　　*　　*

During the Boer War the War Office had established a Mechanical Transport Committee, which included Royal Artillery, Royal Engineers and ASC representatives (Colonel C E Heath and Lieutenant Colonel F T Clayton were the ASC members). There were four sub-committees: Experimental, Royal Artillery, Royal Engineers and ASC. The Committee, which was to have a powerful influence on the development of MT in the army over the next thirty years or so, set up War Office trials in 1901 in the search for lighter vehicles with a radius of more than thirty miles suitable for British and European roads. Prizes of £500, £250 and £100 were awarded and the War Office had the option of buying any of the vehicles for its own use.

The 1901 trials in Aldershot were followed in subsequent years by other trials, but it might be of interest to look at the early mobility requirements in these first trials. Specifications included a need to be able to work on rough roads, go where country carts could go (including through a 7 foot 6 inch gate), carry 5 tons (3 tons on board the prime mover and 2 tons in a trailer), capable of a maximum speed, fully laden, of 8 mph and an average speed of 5 mph, able to climb a gradient of 1 in 8 without assistance, and run for forty-eight hours without overhaul or cleaning, with a crew of one. There were eleven entrants, all except the Milnes-Daimler being steam-driven, of which only five started. With a maximum speed of 10 mph on the level, the Straker was considered very fast, but a Thornycroft steam lorry won first prize (£500), a Foden second (£250) and a Straker third (£100). The Thornycroft and Foden were purchased, sent to South Africa in February 1902 and trialled for four months. The Thornycroft was the most reliable of the two and Lord Kitchener's report to the Royal Commission on the war in South Africa stated that "Thornycrofts are the best". Two vehicles would have had no impact on logistic efficiency in South Africa and the period of the trial was relatively short, but the success of these two makes had long-term implications on subsequent contracts for the Army.

The report issued by the MT Committee in 1902 stated:

> "The trials at Aldershot have shown that these steam lorries are good and serviceable machines suitable for present supply, and likely to be of great advantage to the transport service in countries where fuel and water in sufficient quantity is available. The Committee would, however, desire to call attention to the great possibilities for military purposes of the internal combustion lorry burning heavy oil, as shown by the small combustion of fuel and practical independence of water of the one which was tried. They strongly recommend that steps to develop such lorries be proceeded with.
>
> Compared with draught horses, these trials have shown that self-propelled lorries can transport 5 tons of stores at about six miles an hour over very considerable distances on hilly average English roads under winter conditions. The load transported by each single lorry (five tons) if carried in horse waggons of serving pattern would overload three GS waggons, requiring twelve draught horses besides riding horses, whose

pace would not ordinarily exceed three miles an hour. Moreover, the marching of 197 miles in six consecutive days over hilly roads would not have been accomplished by horses even at that speed without the assistance of spare horses.

The Committee are of the opinion that it has been demonstrated that mechanical transport of this nature has many advantages, and that it is well worth a much more extended trial.

Regarding the type of lorry, the experience gained at these trials has caused the Committee to somewhat modify their original views. On more than one occasion the disadvantage of the trailer in preventing the lorry from moving freely backwards when required was clearly noticeable. On the whole the Committee consider that a lorry drawing a single waggon, while having the disadvantages accruing from the use of a trailer, does not obtain, owing to there being only one of these vehicles, the full advantages which should belong to the system, and they consider that for handy and rapid work of distribution among troops and near the front of an army, a lorry without a trailer is preferable. At the same time, they consider that for the heavier work of moving stores in large quantities to the depots, a powerful tractor, drawing a train of waggons behind it, will be found most suitable.

The Committee therefore recommend that they be empowered to take steps to obtain for trial a lorry or lorries on the following lines: to carry three tons, driven by an internal combustion engine burning heavy oil; weight as light as consistent with due adhesion; wheels large and broad and fitted with a means for rapidly applying numerous spuds for use on boggy ground. Speed up to eight miles an hour; large platform area.

Finally the Committee beg to call special attention to the demonstration afforded by these trials of the entire harmlessness to roads of vehicles considerably exceeding in weight and road speed the limits allowed by the present regulations on the subject, and also fitted with wheels to which road strips have been fixed, so long as these wheels are of large diameter and have tyres of considerable width. It has now been proved that the existing regulations are unnecessarily restrictive, whilst they stand in the way of the development of a most important method of transport and branch of industry. The Committee strongly recommend that this matter be brought to the notice of the proper authorities, feeling confident that the removal of these restrictions will tend to assimilate the commercial and military types of vehicles, and is not only important therefore from a Service point of view, but also will have a most beneficial effect on the manufacturing industries of the country and its commercial development generally."

The matter of trailers behind primer movers was subsequently a subject of considerable trial and it is significant that in due course, in the 1914-18 war, trailers were not used.

At the same time a few motor cars were purchased by the War Office for the Royal Engineers in Chatham and for the ASC in Aldershot for experimental work. A letter of 21 January 1902 from the War Office informed the General Officer Commanding 1st Army Corps in Aldershot that "it is proposed to purchase a motor car for your use in order to facilitate the inspection of works in progress in the district under your command and also in order that this class of vehicle may be tried as to its suitability for aiding, by its capabilities of rapid locomotion, the command of troops in the field." (The 1st Army Corps, the Field Army, was renamed 'Aldershot Command' on 21 October 1904.)

With senior officers becoming more interested in a convenient and speedy form of transportation which required no effort from them as passengers, trials in 1902 and 1903 were carried out with internal combustion engines, with most attention being paid to the acquisition of cars.

*   *   *

In September 1902 Colonels' appointments were established in the ASC and the October Army List shows Colonels H N Bunbury, F F Johnson CB, C E Heath and F T Clayton CB, W A Dunne CB, R A Nugent CB, M E R Rainsford CB removed from the Corps as Colonels but still on the Active List. There were otherwise thirty-six Lieutenant Colonels, fifty Majors, 130 Captains, 103 Lieutenants, sixty-five 2nd Lieutenants, seventy-six Quartermasters, sixty Retired Officers temporarily employed, three officers attached, and ten 2nd Lieutenants from the Infantry on probation prior to transfer. The large number of Retired Officers were almost certainly employed as replacements for officers who went to South Africa but whose appointments still needed to be filled.

In the War Office Colonel Sir Edward Ward KCB late ASC was serving as Permanent Under Secretary of State. Colonels Dunne, Becket, Heath and Clayton were serving on the Quartermaster General's staff as Assistant Quartermaster Generals and Major E E Carter CMG MVO was one of two Deputy Assistant Quartermaster Generals. One will search in vain in Army Lists for other ASC officers, other than Temporary Captain A E W Harman, who was a Staff Captain in Cairo. There were certainly no officers of the Corps listed as Professors or Instructors at the Royal Military College or any of the Army Schools. The ASC at this time was alone among the major army organizations not to have its own school. There were a number of other ASC officers on the staff of various Headquarters in South Africa and Egypt, not to mention oddments such as two Captains employed in the Uganda Protectorate, a Quartermaster employed with the South African Constabulary and a Captain with the Transvaal Government. Other senior Corps appointments in 1902 can be seen in Annex C.

*   *   *

In spite of some of its officers showing enthusiasm for all things motor transport, the *Corps Journal* of June 1903 was a little 'sniffy':

'The number of fatal accidents which attended the recent Paris to Madrid Motor Race ought surely to convince the public that motor racing has very little to recommend it.

'Whilst Englishmen will ever continue to admire the professional or amateur jockey who rides a horse to victory either in a flat race or especially in a steeple-chase, there can be very little enthusiasm excited for the man who wins a motor race simply because he is rich enough to own a machine of the very latest pattern.

'On the subject of motors it was quite refreshing to read the other day of a member of the House of Lords who had the courage to protest against the introduction of the intolerable word "chauffeur" into our language. English is quite good enough for us, and as the words cab-driver and bus-driver are of every day use, why not "motor-driver?" '

*　　*　　*

Only a few Corps Officers went to the Staff College in this period, not that it was then as well regarded as it later became. Those officers were:

Captain C F Moores (8 February 1901-21 December 1902)

Captain W W Molony (22 January 1903-21 January 1904 (withdrawn))

Major L W Atcherley (22 January 1906-2 March 1906 (retired)) (later Colonel (Honorary Major General) Sir Llewellyn Atcherley Kt, CMG CVO)

Captain C H M Bingham (16 May 1908-21 December 1909)

Captain R D Barbor (22 January 1909-21 December 1911)

Captain D C Cameron (22 January 1910-21 December 1911)

Captain M N G Anderson DSO (16 May 1910-21 December 1911) (later Major General M N G Anderson CB CMG DSO)

There were four places each year for nominated officers (ie for those whose performance, generally in the field, was such that senior commanders nominated them, or those who failed the entrance examination (like Douglas Haig) but still deserved a nomination). Of the ASC officers listed above, Moores, Molony, Bingham and Anderson were nominated. Major Atcherley must have been a man of remarkable abilities: he retired from the army while he was at the Staff College to take up the appointment of Chief Constable of Shropshire; during the war he became Controller of Salvage with the honorary rank of Major General, subsequently being appointed as Chief Constable of West Riding and HM Inspector of Police.

As a result of high level concerns that Staff College students were not learning the administration side of war (a problem that continues to this day), the Commandant, Brigadier General (later Field Marshal) Henry Wilson, had an ASC officer added to the Directing Staff, Lieutenant Colonel Harold Franz Passauer Percival DSO, who stayed from 1 October 1912 to 5 August 1914. Like other members of the Directing Staff and all students, he left immediately for the war. This remarkable man, half-Austrian, was appointed an official German interpreter at the peace treaty negotiations in Versailles in 1919, for which work he was knighted.

In the Quartermaster General's Department, Colonel F T Clayton became the Assistant Director of Transport in the Directorate of Transport & Remounts, with Brevet Major A R Crofton Atkins as his Staff Captain; Major A Phelps became the Deputy Assistant Director of Movements in the Directorate of Movements & Quartering; and Colonel W A Dunne became the Assistant Director of Supplies in the Directorate of Supplies & Clothing. In the Headquarters of the 1st Army Corps in Aldershot, Colonel J C Oughterson became the Director of Supplies & Transport.

Widespread recognition of the worth of the Corps' officers and further pressure by Colonel Clayton ensured that the Army Council accepted in 1904 that ASC officers "would be eligible equally with officers of other arms, thus giving opportunities of promotion to general officer's rank." This important decision soon bore fruit: Colonel C E Heath was promoted in 1905 to Brigadier General in Aldershot; Colonel H N Bunbury was promoted in 1906 as Major General Administration in Ireland; Brigadier General Heath moved in 1908 to the War Office as Major General, Director of Transport & Remounts; and Colonel C A Hadfield was appointed in 1908 as Major General Administration in South Africa, to be succeeded in 1909 by Colonel Clayton himself. It can thus be seen that, within four years of the 1904 Army Council decision, the ASC could boast of four Major Generals, which much strengthened the position of the Corps in the army and enabled it to develop along practical lines, not those dictated by staff officers from other arms with limited knowledge and vision.

* * *

The year 1902 was a key one in the history of MT in the army: the formation of a section of MT was authorized from 1 April 1902, consisting of four Sergeants and 30 Rank & File; and the establishment of MT companies was authorized by Royal Warrant of 30 August 1902 (GRO 230 of 1902). Two MT companies were subsequently approved with effect from 1 April 1903, the total manpower of 22 Sergeants, two Trumpeters and 194 Rank & File being provided by the reduction of four Horse Transport Companies. The War Office decided that mechanical transport should be the responsibility of the ASC, which was probably not seen as a major decision in its day, since the horse lobby still held tremendous sway throughout the army; in any event it was believed that petrol was too dangerous a fuel for military use and steam vehicles had been seen to have their limitations in South Africa.

* * *

At the end of January 1903 Brevet Major C E I McNalty visited Chatham with a view to making arrangements for the formation of the first ASC MT unit, including the transfer of steam engines and experimental cars and lorries held by the Royal Engineers. (As a Captain, McNalty had served in the Boer War and was present at the Siege of Ladysmith, being credited as the 'inventor' of the famous 'Chevril', a sort of meat paste made from horse flesh which was issued to hospitals in the garrison.)

A number of Sapper Steam Engine Corporal Instructors reported to the workshop in Brompton Barracks, Chatham and were briefed on the formation of the ASC MT Section. With the promise of promotion to Sergeant, they were invited to transfer, with excellent promotion prospects in the future. When Major McNalty stopped talking there was a dead silence, until one brave soul asked the critical question: "What about the rates of pay, sir?" The problem was that the Corporals received more pay in their trade with the Royal Engineers than they would as Sergeants in the ASC.

A few days later, having referred the matter to the War Office, Major McNalty returned to Chatham with the agreement that he had authority to state that the rate of pay and Corps pay for the ASC would be similar to those in the Royal

Engineers. Twelve men agreed to transfer and were posted on 16 February 1902 (other than the first named, who was posted on 11 February): 22 Corporal A Langley*, 25663 Corporal J C Moins*, 26716 Corporal A G Woodhams*, 10563 Corporal T Cook*, 19 Corporal G W Martin*, 29196 2nd Corporal A S Brunton*, 1343 2nd Corporal C Bennett, 407 Lance Corporal T Barber, 3865 Lance Corporal J Jack, 3490 Lance Corporal E Wingate, 2405 Sapper W Cossey, 1816 Sapper G H Jones (*posted as Sergeants). In the predominantly horse transport world of the ASC they became known as 'the Mucky Dozen'.

Some days later Major McNalty returned to Chatham with Company Quartermaster Sergeant R Doherty and about a dozen other NCOs and men, mainly ASC but with a few Gunners. This party, with those already transferring from the Sappers, was the nucleus of 77 MT Company ASC and the core from which mechanization in the British Army developed in the twentieth century.

In a short while other men arrived, transfers from other units and men specially enlisted for the task, including Privates Nicholson and Way, as well as several officers, Major Cochrane and Captain Butcher-Hill of the Dublin City Artillery (Militia), Lieutenant C S Lyons RA and Lieutenant Saunders, 5th Dragoons (complete with metal helmet and plume). The new unit was housed in the corrugated iron sheds near the Royal Engineers workshop, bitterly cold buildings that survived past the Second World War.

When the unit moved to Upper Chatham Barracks (later Kitchener Barracks) their 'new' (but very part-worn) vehicles arrived:

a 20 ton Burrell traction engine equipped with a crane

four internal combustion lorries (German Milnes-Marienfeldt and Milnes-Neustadt)

two small traction engines (Tasker and Wallis & Stevens)

a 10 hp Wolseley car (horizontal twin engined), and

a 3 cylinder Brooke car

Concurrently a small detachment was sent to Aldershot to take over several Lion-type Fowler tractors from the Royal Engineers, and detachments were sent to London for staff car work and to the Curragh. There was also a detachment in Shoeburyness consisting of Corporal Bradburn and a Private who operated a motor launch. Traction engines of the Royal Engineers in Gibraltar and Malta were also transferred to the ASC.

*   *   *

Private John Jackson, under age at sixteen, joined the ASC in 1904. Fortunately for him he had been apprenticed in 1901 as a fitter and had driven steam engines at the Jesse Ellis Works in Maidstone; he was therefore in his element when he reported for duty in Chatham. "I found on arrival that the transport consisted of two large Fowler engines taking three trucks and a water barrel, two small Taskers, one truck outfit, six solid iron tyred Daimler lorries and a Wolseley car. There were six of us recruits, and none of us had driven any of these types.

"Three days later I was detailed to take a Fowler, three trucks etc, load up with camp equipment and deliver to the barracks at Gravesend. It took us two days to get there, water being our main trouble. Whilst the trucks were being unloaded I thought this would be a good opportunity to visit Aunt Annie. Living in a large house in Gravesend, she was entertaining the vicar when I was shown in, as black as ink and covered in oil. In fifty seconds flat I was out again. My cousin May, about my age, showed me out and was highly interested in the big black road engine; my steersman was using the injector for water, steam and noise all over. I asked May if she would like a ride, warned my steersman, a big burly ex-circus driver, to mind his language, swamped the big ends with oil and we were off.

"May had a summer frilly white frock on and a 'picture' hat; the oil from the big end threw a shower [of oil] over both of us, coal dust from the bunker helped and she was a picture when she arrived back. We got back to Chatham OK but nobody expected us to.

"After a month's bull and square-bashing [in Aldershot] I was posted to Tidworth as driver of the government car allotted to Sir Ian Hamilton, GOC Southern Command. This was in 1906 and the car [was] a two-cylinder Siddeley, with a single seat in front and a bench seat at the back for two, no doors. For some reason the big ends were set eccentric, so that at slow speeds we jerked along like a fast crab. Sir Ian soon had this replaced by a four-cylinder Wolseley saloon, and I found plenty to do.

"About two weeks later I returned to camp after driving a Fowler over Salisbury Plain, and saw a hell of a commotion on the square. My kit was packed in the Company car and the OC of the Company was getting a real dressing-down about discipline. I was rushed into the wash-house, my dirty dungarees taken off, washed, the Company barber trimmed my hair whilst a Subaltern asked me questions and finally said I had passed the test and was going back to Salisbury.

"It appeared that, hanging over the front seat, were two leather lined knee rugs for the use of the rear passengers. Archie [an ASC friend] had been out all day with Sir Charles and staff on a wet muddy Salisbury Plain, the General and staff getting in and out of the car all day. On return to Salisbury Archie, who was wondering how he was going to get the car clean, opened the rear door and saw both rugs on the floor, covered in mud from his passengers' boots. Without thinking he said to the general, "Excuse me, Sir, those rugs are to put round your knees, not to wipe your boots on." Archie didn't remember much after that, except being carried by two of the escort to the Provost Sergeant's office. It was all quietly forgotten and he was not court-martialled, hung, drawn and quartered as expected."

*   *   *

It was not long before vehicles were seen on the roads around Aldershot. Convoys of three or four Lion-type Fowlers, each with 3 or 5 ton trailers carrying hay or oats, presented a considerable change from what people were used to, quiet GS wagons drawn by quiet horses. These noisy vehicles had to travel at a walking pace (the man with the red flag walking in front had only recently been declared unnecessary). Complaints were constantly being received: local authorities objected to having army vehicles with two or three 5 ton trailers crossing their bridges and water being taken from streams and cress ponds. Horse owners (especially retired Colonels) raged that their horses were terrified, shopkeepers complained that their sun blinds were being damaged and one old lady even made a claim because she said the vibration of the passing vehicles had caused her wedding presents to fall off a shelf.

An *ASC Journal* of the day provides a colourful impression of the ponderous nature of these lumbering beasts: "The cleaner is the man who sits in the last truck when the engine is on the road – he applies the brakes to the truck, notifies the driver of overtaking traffic and generally makes himself useful. The cleaner lights the fire while the driver and steersman are having their breakfast. When finished they relieve the cleaner who, in turn, has his meal."

* * *

Officers who were among the early pioneers of MT in the Army were Major W E Donohue (later promoted Colonel), Captain H N Foster (promoted Major General in 1931), Captain H R Lever, Lieutenants T M Hutchinson (promoted Lieutenant Colonel in 1917), E F Unwin and G C G Blunt. The latter officer was a remarkably interesting man: quite apart from attending a Straker course in Brazil of all places, he attended a month-long Balloon & Cody Kite course at the School of Ballooning in Aldershot in November 1906. He wryly wrote that the course had to be counted against his annual leave. The famous Colonel Cody instructed on the course. Afterwards, students went on a 180-mile flight via Marlborough, Birmingham and Derby, photographing Stonehenge from the air *en route*. They returned by train to Aldershot, with the balloon in its wicker basket loaded in the goods van.

* * *

78 MT Company was also formed in 1904 in Aldershot as the second MT company of the Corps, commanded by Captain H R Hayter, and 52 HT Company converted to be 52 (Depot) Company as the first Driving School, Heavy Repair Shop and MT Stores Depot all in one. To provide the manpower for 77 and 78 MT Companies, four HT Companies were reduced in establishment. These were momentous times.

Corps Order No. 25 in 1903 notified for general information that, on the formation of the MT Section of the ASC, the following would be adopted:

Carpenters, in future to be called "Wheelers", will be selected from the present qualified Wheelers; their future promotion will be in the Transport Companies as Wheeler Corporals and Wheeler Staff Sergeants.

Smiths and Fitters for wagons and trailers will in future be called "Carriage Smiths" and will be selected from Shoeing Smiths who have qualified as Carriage Smiths. Their future promotion will be in the Transport Companies as Farrier Corporals and Carriage Smiths and Farrier Staff Sergeants.

Engine Cleaners and Traction Engine Firemen will be selected from men of the Corps now under instruction at Woolwich and from men enlisting for the Mechanical Transport Section. Their future will be promotion to Lance Corporal, 2nd Corporal, Corporal and Sergeant as "Lorry and Engine Drivers."

Lorry Drivers will be selected from men of the Corps now under instruction at Woolwich etc, and from other branches of the service.

In 1903 15 and 22 Companies of the Corps, commanded by Captains C E Watling and E W W Scott respectively, saw active service on a small scale in Somaliland, where the Indian Army in operations five years earlier had undertaken the supply and transport work. They arrived in Berbera on 30 July on board the SS *Drayton Grange* and were employed on the Line of Communication on the Berbera-Bohotle road to the foot of the Sheikh Pass. The strength of the two units totalled six officers, two Warrant Officers, sixty NCOs and men, eleven Conductors, 211 natives, forty-five horses, 899 mules, eighty wagons and four water carts.

Repair materials for six months were taken, along with supplies and forage for three months. The carriage of all stores, including water, was by camel, but it is of interest that a steam tractor was used, although it only proved itself unsuitable for those conditions. Of further interest is that the War Office was persuaded to buy several Stirling lorries (they were manufactured in Edinburgh) for use in Somaliland, where the use of petrol was considered an acceptable risk, as opposed to its total ban at that time on the roads of England. The ASC contingent left Somaliland on 26 June 1904, drawing praise in the *Army and Navy Gazette* for "the excellent work the two units had done and the splendid example of devotion to duty which has been set by all ranks during one of the most arduous small wars ever undertaken by British troops". Little or nothing is recorded, however, of what they did.

In the event the Stirling lorries did not go to Somaliland and were shortly afterwards converted to paraffin fuel, clearly not successfully, as the nine-day journey by one of them from Chatham to Aldershot, full of accidents and breakdowns, showed. The lorry concerned was nicknamed "spit and cough machinery".

*   *   *

By 1903 the ASC thus had several forms of mechanical transport, cars, lorries and traction engines to complement the Horse Transport Companies around the world. All MT, however, was initially held on an experimental basis and was not seen as part of the real army, the Field Force. In the 1903 manoeuvres, for example, horse-drawn omnibuses were used for the movement of troops, but there was only a limited use of MT, in the form of steam lorries and traction engines.

Horse-dominated though they were, the 1903 manoeuvres by the 1st Army Corps were important for the ASC and deserve some attention. For the first time since 1876 grocery rations were issued on manoeuvres, with separate items such as sausages, bacon, cheese, jam and milk being packed in parcels variously for five, ten, twenty or fifty men. The general system adopted was that troops carried a 'haversack ration' of five biscuits and 2½ ounces of cheese, with a day's supply of biscuits, preserved meat, groceries (with jam), fuel and forage carried in the regimental wagons, one day's rations in the Supply Column and one day's in the Supply Park. The Supply Park replenished the Supply Column when needed, and the Supply Park was topped up from special trains. In addition, four days' rations were loaded onto special trains for the various parts of the Force, each of these being stabled at convenient railway junctions (Andover, Basingstoke, Didcot, Newbury and Reading), able to be redirected at short notice to other railway stations near where troops were encamped.

While this appears to have been an adequate though slightly unwieldy system, it was a great improvement on previous outings, when Manoeuvres Supply Depots were established by the ASC beforehand and the tactical movement of troops had to conform to the location of those depots. This was not only the death knell of imagination and flexibility, not that senior commanders and Staffs were noted for these qualities, but it was also of minimal practicality for units and the ASC.

The Supply Park for the Army Corps on manoeuvres in 1903 consisted of traction engines and steam lorries, under the command of a Steam Transport Officer, with a Supply Officer in charge of the contents. The allocation of transport was:

Cavalry Brigade:	three steam lorries
1st Division:	two traction engines with four trucks each and three steam lorries
2nd Division:	as with the 1st Division
Corps Troops:	two traction engines
Detached Force:	two traction engines (Each of the traction engines could tow twelve tons on a trailer and the steam lorries could carry three-and-a-half tons.)

Transport for these 1903 manoeuvres was provided by a mixture of ASC, civilian-hired and unit first line (the latter only in the case of the Cavalry). Some statistics for these manoeuvres might be of interest:

814 officers and 16,714 Rank & File made up the 1st Army Corps

The 1st Army Corps deployed with 6,065 horses, 147 guns and 708 wagons or carts

1,250 horses were hired for their use

18 officers and 704 Other Ranks ASC, along with 272 hired civilian drivers, supported the Army Corps

The total of ASC horsed wagons used was:

333 GS wagons

27 ambulance wagons

20 light forage wagons

9 forage GS wagons

4 post carts

80 water carts

9 squadron carts (horsed by the Cavalry)

25 small arms ammunition carts furnished by battalions, supplemented by ASC horses (including some light experimental carts)

21 machine-gun carts

Commenting subsequently on harness traces used in the manoeuvres, Colonel C H Bridge highlighted what today would be called lack of interoperability (or harmonization): Artillery horses could not be harnessed to ASC or civilian wagons, ASC and Royal Engineers horses could not be attached to guns and Artillery or civilian wagons and civilian harness could not be used with GS, Artillery or Engineers wagons. (Similar problems still exist today, although in a different form.) Thinking ahead to mobilization for a future war, he recommended that a large building or partially covered-in shed which could shelter 1,000 horses should be taken in for use by the army, but nothing came of it.

There was already a division of opinion between the relative virtues of steam traction and internal combustion in these early days, which would take some time to resolve; indeed the years until 1905 were occupied in consolidating ground won in the fight for recognition of mechanical transport at the same time as deciding the relative advantages of tractor and lorry. Horse transport, though, still held an unassailable position in the ASC world, its senior officers knowing that the War Office would not countenance the wholesale, expensive replacement of a well-proven, familiar form of transport, especially in the absence of a pool of drivers qualified in this new and little understood form of locomotion.

*   *   *

Encouraged by the successful first time use of cars for military purposes in 1901, a Motor Volunteer Corps was established in 1903, the *London Gazette* of 3 March announcing:

"His Majesty has been graciously pleased to approve the formation of a Volunteer Corps, to be designated 'The Motor Volunteer Corps'."

At its inception the Honorary Colonel was Colonel The Right Honourable Sir John Macdonald KCB VD and the Commanding Officer Lieutenant Colonel M J Mayhew. The latter had been, as Mr Mark Mayhew with his 7 hp Panhard, one of General Buller's drivers along with the Honourable C S Rolls during the earlier manoeuvres in 1901. The Corps was organized into six sections, each to support one of six notional Army Corps areas, and was officered by five Majors, twelve Captains and fourteen Lieutenants. The drivers had to complete a certain number of hours in support of the army, for which they received a small amount of money and the cost of their fuel.

The idea caught on and forty-three cars and thirty-one motor cycles turned out for the August 1903 manoeuvres in the Borders and in Savernake Forest. A contemporary report states:

"On leaving camp the members would then drive the umpires distances varying perhaps from ten to fifteen miles to the foot of some hill. The officer would then leave the car and very often mounted his horse, which would be waiting for him, and ride up the hill. The driver of the car would then wait at the bottom of the hill until his return.

"The car drivers would seem to have had a reasonably easy time, not so the motor cyclists. One report said 'one cannot exaggerate the importance of the role which the motor cyclists played in the manoeuvres'. They were often up all night in camp waiting to receive dispatches. To show their usefulness, I quote one instance. It was discovered that a certain general's position was not exactly where it was supposed to have been at the close of the operation for the day, and at the last moment this necessitated all other commanding officers in various camps being informed. The telegraph after ten o'clock was not in working order, and therefore six motor cyclists were sent round to all other camps with new instructions for the morning's operations. Some idea of the motor cyclists' difficulties can be obtained if we remember that their machines were fitted with poor brakes and lights and very often had no springs at all. These machines were ridden at breakneck speeds (30 mph!) on heavily rutted dust roads which were liberally strewn with sharp flints and nails from discarded horse shoes, making punctures the rule and not the exception. The work of both the cars and motor cycles impressed the General Staff so much that Lord Roberts was moved to say that 'the manoeuvres would not have been so successful but for the work of the Motor Volunteers'."

In 1904 a further step in the introduction of MT in the army was taken by the War Office when forty motor cycles were added to the MVC establishment (several years before the Regular Army had them) and extensive support was provided for the manoeuvres in Essex in September, when the Blue Force under General French landed from ten troop ships on the coast between Frinton and Clacton, opposed by the Red Force based on Colchester. MVC duties consisted of carrying despatches and conveying umpires, foreign attachés and other officers.

The 'neutral' drivers lived in a tented camp beside Meanee Barracks in Colchester:

"The accommodation for the motors was excellent, a long gun-shed being provided for the purpose. Assistance was also available for cleaning and washing down, while in many cases, car drivers brought their chauffeurs with them . . . the mess marquee was universally acknowledged to surpass anything on either side. The catering was excellently carried out, and every possible convenience provided, not forgetting a plentiful supply of literature. Each member had a separate tent, fully equipped with tent furniture and floor boards."

On the other hand the motor cycle riders seem to have been second-class gentlemen, and the twelve who were attached to the Red and Blue Force had to find their own accommodation.

"Some were on duty for two days on end with little or no sleep, in pouring rain all the time and riding over practically impassable roads, often pushing the machine for miles where it was impossible to ride."

At the end of the Essex manoeuvres HRH The Duke of Connaught congratulated members of the MVC on their contribution, an encouragement which may well have led to the Corps rising in strength to 155 by the end of the year.

Another notable MVC occasion took place on Thursday 8 June 1905, when a Royal Review was held on Laffan's Plain in Farnborough. HM King George V was accompanied by HM The King of Spain, HM Queen Alexandra, The Prince and Princess of Wales, Princess Victoria, The Duke and Duchess of Connaught and Field Marshal Lord Roberts. After the 'present arms', Their Majesties rode to the right of the line, where twenty-two cars of the Motor Volunteer Corps were drawn up in line under the command of Lieutenant Colonel M J Mayhew. Each car was driven by an officer of the Motor Volunteer Corps, with a full complement of passengers provided by Warrant Officers, NCOs and men of the ASC. After inspecting the Corps, His Majesty's party then proceeded to inspect the rest of the parade, starting with 2,000 men of the Naval Brigade. After the inspection all troops on parade marched past – with the 1st Division were 27 Company ASC (Captain F J Delavoye), 40 Company ASC (Captain F J Reid) and 51 Company ASC (Captain C G E Hughes); with the 2nd Division were 4 Company ASC (Captain W K Bernard), 55 Company ASC (Captain F I Day) and 58 Company ASC (Captain H A Boyce); and with the 3rd Division were 13 Company ASC (Captain J D Buller), 16 Company ASC (Captain C E Watling) and 59 Company ASC (Brevet Major Burrows).

Success, however, was leading to dissatisfaction and mid-1905 saw a good many resignations and few new recruits, partly because the allowances were considered to be inadequate and partly because many car owners did not wish to join as Privates. To keep this sense of importance satisfied it was proposed that, in addition to allowances being increased, all car owners should have commissions and that motor cyclists should be Sergeants, with the rank of Private abolished.

The year 1905 saw, perhaps, the high point in the life of the MVC when twelve cars under the command of Major G Macmillan were inspected by HM King Edward VII at the Great Royal Review near the Palace of Holyrood House in Edinburgh before driving past the saluting dais in two lines. During the inspection the King said, with a suspicion of a wink, to the Commanding Officer in the leading car, "Take care you do not exceed the regulation speed." The spectators apparently followed proceedings 'with bated breath'.

In September that year further transport support was provided for the annual manoeuvres in the Upper Thames Valley. The development of MT in the army, however, meant that there was really no further use for the MVC and it was officially disbanded on 26 July 1906. Some members subsequently joined the Army Motor Reserve as part of the Special Reserve of the ASC on the formation of the Territorial Force under Mr Haldane's 1908 reforms.

Information on MVC dress regulations is scanty. Army Lists merely note that the uniform was 'drab' (ie khaki) with olive-green facings. More is known of the uniform of the Army Motor Reserve: normal service dress was worn, with full dress of olive-green with gold accoutrements, examples of which are held in the RCT museum collection.

*　　*　　*

In 1903 an Inspectorate of Mechanical Transport was established within the ASC, which not only dealt with all technical aspects of MT but also gave technical advice to the War Office. Major W E Donahue, who transferred to the ASC from the Army Ordnance Corps, was Chief Inspector of this organization, initially with two inspectors (five by 1914), their pay varying from 13 shillings to 23 shillings a day. They acted as a focal point within the ASC for the slowly growing group of officers who saw a bright future in this new form of mobility. The Inspectorate of MT was under the command of the Commandant ASC Training Establishment in Aldershot. They were responsible for the biennial inspection of all MT vehicles, machine tools and non-accountable stores. Initially, with a relatively small number of vehicles, this was not too much of a problem.

With the few MT Companies spread around the country, unit and running repairs were carried out by the MT Companies themselves and by the Depot & Training Company, Aldershot. Overhauls were carried out by the Depot & Training Company at Aldershot, by the Army Ordnance Department in their shops, or by civilian contractors, the work required to be done being specified by the OC of the company, who was also present during the final tests. The Inspectorate arranged for the insurance and inspection of all boilers for MT steam vehicles at home and abroad.

The Chief Inspector of MT also submitted specifications for mechanically propelled vehicles, tools and stores for the ASC to the Technical MT Committee in the War Office, who arranged for their manufacture and testing. He or his representative was responsible for testing the materials used in their construction at the factory and for their ultimate road trials before being taken into service. Officers were considered highly technical and were paid accordingly.

*   *   *

The War Office trials of 1903 were won by a 13 ton Hornsby-Ackroyd tractor, which, being too heavy for army use, was later converted with caterpillar tracks, but was dismantled in 1914. The Secretary of State for War, Mr Haldane, saw it in action at the MT Depot in Aldershot on 1 November 1908, expressing satisfaction at the performance of the engine when he saw it run at 8 mph and cross a large bank.

A smaller version, the 'Little Caterpillar', was purchased in 1910 from Hornsby in Grantham. Towing an 8 ton trailer, it took ten days to reach Aldershot. The speed limit had been raised to 20 mph in 1903, up from 14 mph, with 10 mph allowed in towns, so it was not the national speed limit which made it take so long. Its slow progression apparently resembled the corkscrew action of a small ship in rough seas and the vehicle was at once christened 'Rock and Roll'. The funnel was an oddity as it was not required for an internal combustion engine, but it was incorporated in the design since it was said that horses were accustomed to steam-driven tractors with funnels and it was considered that they would react badly to noisy vehicles without funnels. These vehicles were the early forerunners of the tank. (This vehicle, which took part in the Royal Tournament in 1933, driven by the son of one of the original drivers, is the first exhibit a visitor to the Tank Museum in Bovington sees today, as it was unfortunately given to that museum in the 1950s by the then Director Supplies & Transport.)

*   *   *

The 1904 manoeuvres involved the embarkation of a force at Southampton and its disembarkation at Clacton-on-Sea in Essex, so there was little opportunity

Mechanical Transport - Army Service Corps.
Essex Manoeuvres 1904

Vehicles gathered together, probably in Colchester, for the 1904 manoeuvres. In the rear can be seen a number of Fowler steam traction engines, including a recovery version, seven Thornycrofts, a variety of cars, a motor cycle and two flat-bed lorries (probably hired) (A).

CASTLE SERIES

The Royal Volunteer Review, Edinburgh on 18 September 1905. The Motor Volunteer Corps are driving onto the parade ground at the rear of the Palace of Holyrood House (B).

LORD KITCHENER Says:

"The Motor Lorries sent to South Africa did well;
THORNYCROFT'S ARE THE BEST" (Vide War Commission Report)

Thornycroft wagons of the type that won the first prize of £500 in the 1901 War Office trials (B).

Four early vehicles of the ASC in Kensington Barracks, London, 1904. Left to right they are: a 12 hp Wolseley used by members of the Army Council; a 12 hp Lanchester used by the Chief Royal Engineer; a 6 hp Wolseley used by HQ 1st Army; and a 12 hp Siddeley used by HQ 4th Army (B).

Motor Car Itinerary.

(To be filled in by the Officer using Car.)

N° 7

Date 7 - 8 - 1905.

Left _Salisbury_ at 9·30 am

Proceeded to _Nunton Tidworth & District & Nunton_

(Name roads and towns.)

Nature of journey _To Inspect Barracks Tidworth &c with C.E. S.C._

Returned to _Salisbury_ at 2 pm

Miles run 50 (approximately).

weight.

Carried { passengers, **3**
          { baggage. —

Any special remarks on journey _Car went well & Smoothly (though road v. wet) no breakdown_

E O Strong.

Signature of Officer.

MAJOR GENERAL I/C ADMINISTRATION.

H W V 2500 9—02

A 1905 'Motor Car Itinerary' (nowadays called a work ticket). Major General E O
Strong went from Salisbury to visit barracks in Tidworth with his Chief Engineer and
Staff Captain. Fortunately the "car went well and smoothly (though road very wet)" (A).

Lieutenant General Sir John French in a 1905 Wolseley (ASC 17) visiting manoeuvres in the Aylesbury area in September 1907 (See Annex F) (B).

Two Captains and members of the Motor Volunteer Corps at camp in the Farnham area, August 1904 (B).

The Guard Room and HQ ASC building in Woolwich, c. 1905 (B).

The ASC Band in front of the Officers' Mess in Woolwich. The Bandmaster is
Warrant Officer H J Cook LRAM, who led the band from 1903 to 1922 (B).

Four-in-hand covered GS wagon in the ASC lines in Woolwich, c. 1905 (B).

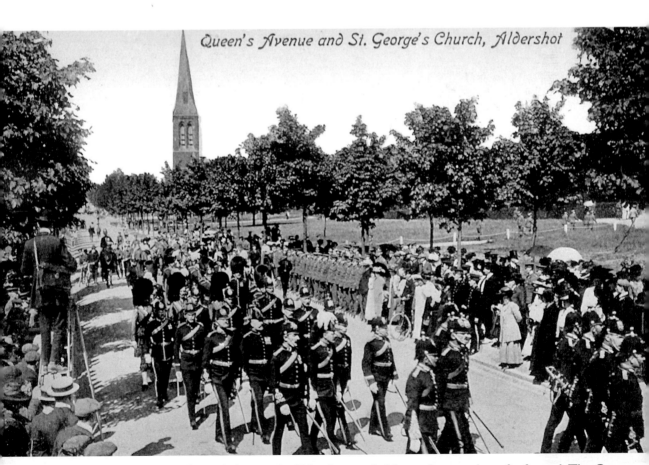

ASC officers marching up Queen's Avenue in Aldershot, probably on the occasion of a funeral. The Corps church of St George is in the background (B). Note the photographer on his stepladder on the left.

Wagon Mounting and Dismounting competition (a preliminary for Olympia) on Stanhope Lines Recreation Ground on 28 April 1904. The judges were Colonel T J O'Dell and Lieutenant Colonels F C A Gilpin and H G Morgan CB DSO. This winning team was probably 16 Company from Woolwich (B).

ASC teams from Aldershot and Woolwich at the Royal Naval & Military Tournament in Olympia c. 1908 (B).

Staff of the Reserve Supply Depot ASC of the North Midlands Division (B).

Cattle about to be slaughtered in the Aldershot Supply Depot, whose OC sent this card in 1904 with the message: "These animals have long since been duly sampled by Thomas Atkins." The scrub area to the immediate rear is now occupied by St Omer Barracks (B).

to demonstrate the advantages of MT, but it was used for the first time on manoeuvres for the supply of bread and groceries to supplement the work of 26 and 52 Horse Transport Companies based in Aldershot. The year 1904 also saw the introduction of red crosses painted on the sides of ambulance wagons and carts of a medical unit, which would hopefully provide clearer identification and therefore protection than had been the case in South Africa.

*   *   *

The ASC enjoyed an excellent rapport with its sister Corps in the Empire and assistance was readily given when it was required in their early days.

In 1903 Lieutenant Colonel J Lyons Biggar, Assistant Quartermaster General Canadian Forces, visited the ASC School of Instruction in Aldershot to see how supply and transport was run in the British Army. He lost no time and officers of the newly-formed Canadian ASC were sent in 1904 to UK for training. To cement the link between the two countries Colonel Sir Edward Ward was appointed Honorary Colonel of the Canadian ASC on 15 April 1904. Starting in 1903 with one officer and fourteen men, the Canadian ASC had expanded to thirteen officers and 151 men by 1906, with units located on a garrison basis. There were also regular attachments from the ASC to Australia, India and New Zealand.

The year 1887 had seen the start of the Australian ASC when an Ordnance, Commissariat and Transport Company was formed. Initially, the states had raised and maintained the companies but federal control was exercised in 1901 with garrison and Field Force units.

The New Zealand ASC was authorized in 1912 and several members of the ASC were sent to New Zealand to help establish their new Corps: Captain H O Knox, Staff Sergeant Major J W F Cahill (HT), Company Quartermaster Sergeant J J Wass (HT), Staff Quartermaster Sergeant P M Petty (Supply) and Staff Sergeant F E Ostler (Supply). Captain Knox was appointed Director Supplies & Transport of the New Zealand ASC in the rank of Lieutenant Colonel in 1911 and Quartermaster General in 1912, retiring eventually as a Brigadier General; Staff Sergeant Ostler was commissioned and became the Director Supplies & Transport New Zealand ASC from 1917 until 1919, being the only one of the original four who remained in New Zealand for the duration of the war. Staff Sergeant Major Petty was also commissioned in the war, like Staff Sergeant Major Cahill and Company Quartermaster Sergeant Wass, all three serving with the New Zealand Expeditionary Force overseas before returning to the UK after the war. The South African Service Corps was also raised in 1912. The Supply & Transport Corps in the Indian Army traces its predecessors back to the Commissariat of the Honourable East India Company, but effectively dates from 1895.

*   *   *

Three new ranks were published in Army Order No 1 for the MT Section of the ASC: Mechanist Sergeant Major (seven shillings a day), Mechanist Quartermaster Sergeant (six shillings a day) and Mechanist Staff Sergeant (five shillings and three pence a day). The *ASC Journal* of May 1905 instituted a fascinating series of informative pieces entitled 'Automobile Notes':

"A slight innovation has been made in this number of the 'Journal' by the introduction of 'Automobile Notes.' Now that the Army Service Corps has taken over the general direction, as well as the executive work of the Mechanical Transport of the Army, it would seem that everyone belonging to the Corps should take an intelligent interest in this branch of transport work – a branch which has undoubtedly a great future in front of it."

A year later the following were published under the same heading:

"The 12 hp 'Wolseley' car employed by General French has lately been fitted with a new form of mileage recorder. It is attached to the off front hub cap, and rotates with the wheel. The mechanism is actuated by the rotation of the instrument round its central spindle, which is held by the axle of the car.

"The petrol tank of a motor car should never be filled while lamps are burning, as there is great danger of the vapour igniting and communicating the flame to the open petrol tank.

"One of the instructional motor cars will shortly be fitted with a new type of pneumatic tyre protector, the invention of an officer at the Staff College.

"In a few years, when automobiles of all kinds become very plentiful, the danger of collision with another motor car round blind corners will be a very real one indeed, and such a contingency can only be avoided by each car keeping strictly to its own side of the road, and slackening speed. Curves to the left can be taken somewhat faster than those to the right."

*   *   *

An early decision was made concerning the repair of vehicles. The Army Ordnance Department was made responsible for base overhauls, but otherwise the ASC was responsible for all running repairs, training and provision. In 1905 the first static workshop was built at Thornhill Road, Aldershot (the present site of Travers Barracks and Buller Barracks) which served mainly 77 MT Company and its sister 78 MT Company. The division of responsibility between the two companies was that OC 77 MT Company held on his charge all motor cars, MT vehicles and trucks in Ireland, Bulford, Chatham, Portsmouth and Woolwich, while OC 78 MT Company was responsible for all vehicles and trucks in the Aldershot Command (but not cars).

*   *   *

Every war has its post-mortem and the period following the end of the Boer War was no exception. The Esher Report of 1904 made major recommendations for reform of the army's organization, including the formation of a General Staff and the re-organization of the responsibilities of two key posts which impacted on the ASC, the Adjutant General and the Quartermaster General. Transport and Supply were to be separated under different Directorates in the War Office, and the Director of Transport & Remounts was to have the Director General of Army Veterinary Services under him. A new Director of Movements & Quartering took over responsibility for railways in war as well as the custody and equipping of barracks and a Directorate of Clothing & Supplies was created. From a Corps point of view, the separation of Supply and Transport functions, which had always worked well when in close co-ordination, was a difficult pill to swallow; furthermore the duplication inherent in 'Transport & Remounts' and 'Movements & Quartering' prohibited any possible co-ordination in the use of rail, road and water transport by one Director. The end result was that ASC duties were split between several Directorates, Transport & Movement under one, Supply & Quartering under another. This was not the way to achieve efficiency. After the mistakes of the previous century and developments in the Boer War this split, while following the example of continental armies, was less than practical.

The 1888 stipulation that the ASC should fill thirty staff appointments was effectively cancelled by the Esher Committee, much to the disappointment of the Corps, although it has to be admitted that the ASC did not possess thirty qualified officers in 1904. Colonel F T Clayton wisely did not press the matter but persuaded the Staff that the lack of staff vacancies was inherently unfair and obtained approval for the creation of Assistant Directors as well as Deputy Assistant Directors of Supplies & Transport at the various Command Headquarters, in which there had been no Supply or Transport representatives until 1903. The Assistant Director Supplies & Transport appointments ensured at least that the best ASC officers would be promoted to Colonel, the most senior rank available to them at the time.

*   *   *

Until 15 May 1904 all members of the ASC in Aldershot came under the command of 'OC ASC Aldershot', who probably had the largest Lieutenant Colonel's command in the British Army, never under 1,000 men and often as high as 1,500 or 1,600. There was now a rationalization, which placed trained soldiers (ie those in working Supply and Transport Companies) under a 'Commanding Officer Service Companies ASC' and soldiers under training under a 'Commanding Officer Training Establishment ASC' for the Depot Companies, Station Staff Unit, Instructional Staff and the Riding Establishment. The officers concerned were respectively Brevet Colonel F W B Landon and Brevet Lieutenant Colonel F A Gilpin.

*   *   *

When MT was involved in manoeuvres for the first time in a general role in 1905 mobile workshop trailers were designed, which contained a lathe, drilling machine, tool-grinding machine, a fitter's bench and vices, driven by a dynamo from the towing traction engine. A mobile MT Repair Depot was located at Hurley (near Henley on Thames), the Depot consisting of two trains of three vehicles drawn by oil-fired engines. Apart from carrying out running repairs, including repairing a broken steel shaft, the Depot provided electric lighting for the field bakery located nearby. The Repair Train, commanded by Major W E Donohue, Chief Inspector of MT, and supported by Lieutenant C S Lyon and sixty men, consisted of a Rescue Section (a crane and breakdown trucks) and a Workshop Section (a traction engine and wagons containing repair machinery, stores and a dynamo). It was not long before these mobile workshops were built onto lorries, which not only did excellent service during the 1914-18 war but also saw service long after the end of the war.

* * *

The Curragh was one of the major garrisons of the British Army, best known perhaps as a training area and a source of livestock for mounted units. The 14th Infantry Brigade went on exercise in the Wicklow Mountains in August 1905, accompanied by 42, 47 and 57 Companies ASC, with two trains of MT taking the place of 61 and 66 Horse Transport Companies from Dublin. Glen Imaal was the camp location, where hill operations and night attacks took place. Of interest was the use of pack animals for work in the mountains, not a normal feature of manoeuvres in the rest of Great Britain. Thirty-two donkeys and sixteen horses were hired locally. Each donkey carried five picks and five shovels in a specially designed saddle made of canvas and stuffed with hay, the horses carrying double that load. The saddles and fittings were made by ASC artificers and proved very satisfactory, the pattern coming from the War Office. During the first march, however, the donkeys gave trouble. Near Newbridge they broke away from their drivers and galloped down the road, shedding picks and shovels right and left, much to the amusement of the troops and assembled locals. That evening the OC spent several hours devising a better way to pack the saddles, with the result that the donkey pack transport was an acknowledged success for the rest of the manoeuvres.

* * *

After the 1905 manoeuvres it was evident that MT was now a regular feature of movement in the army. The ASC Training Establishment in Aldershot took steps to train all its officers in MT duties, with the most promising being selected for further training as workshop officers. The first MT instructor was Captain T M Hutchinson, who was to be a member of the War Office MT Committee after the Great War. Illustrating what advances were being made, a scheme was instituted in 1906 for a small amount of MT to be incorporated into mobilization plans, on the basis that MT could travel twice the distance of horse drawn transport in a day. Light steam tractors were allocated to the third echelon of supply in the field (ie the Parks).

Practical demonstrations of the efficacy of MT were still needed, however, and these were given in 1906, the year in which the London General Omnibus Company invested £1 million on converting their horse-drawn buses to MT, predominantly with Dennis, Leyland, Maudslay and Thornycroft vehicles. The March 1905 *ASC Journal* contained a note on this development, which had other implications for the ASC: "A very significant letter appeared in *The Times* of 15th February from the solicitors to the London Omnibus Owners Federation, pointing out that the leading London Omnibus Companies, headed by the London General Omnibus Company and the London Road Car Company 'have at this moment a very large number of motor omnibuses under construction and that they will be in actual work during the next few months, and, further, that it is their intention to cover the whole of the roads with motor vehicles at an early date.'

"It is quite sad to think of the possible disappearance of that characteristic race of bus drivers and the thick-set, short-legged pairs of stout-hearted horses which most of them drive so well.

"The box seat, which was the joy of childhood, has long disappeared from the vehicle and the hideous but utilitarian "garden roof" has taken the place of the old cry of "off side down." Now we shall have the smell of the motor bus always with us.

"But stay, one man will surely rejoice – will it not possibly be he who is charged with buying transport remounts, because soon he will have no 'Bus Companies' to bid against? On the other hand, where are our 20,000 registered horses to come from when the omnibuses start 'motorizing'?"

Except when using ships or railways, the mass movement of troops had always been on foot. Buses provided a new opportunity, but clearly the army was not going to buy them for occasional use on manoeuvres in peacetime when they could be hired from civilian firms.

*   *   *

It was on 1 July 1905 that the regimental work (ie postings, promotions etc) of Warrant Officers, NCOs and men of the ASC was transferred to the recently instituted appointment of 'OIC ASC Records and Commanding Depot ASC' in Woolwich Dockyard, otherwise the ASC staff under the Assistant Quartermaster General ASC in the War Office continued to deal with all questions affecting officers, changes of station of ASC companies, all MT matters and Corps Memoranda. The telegraphic address changed from 'Transcom, Woolwich' to 'Attest Army Service Corps, Dockyard Woolwich' with effect from August 1905. The Record Office staff in Woolwich at this time consisted of a Colonel, an officer assistant and fourteen clerks. In 1906 five Retired Officers were permanently employed at ASC Records in place of serving officers.

The ASC clerks in staff headquarters in the army contributed greatly to the efficiency of the staff they served. This in itself proved something of a problem, as can be seen by the following Corps Order of 22 September 1906 signed by Colonel F W B Landon, OIC Records and Commanding the ASC Depot in Woolwich Dockyard (he had taken over the appointment in 1904 and handed over to Brevet Colonel G R C Paul CMG in January 1908; he in turn handed over to Colonel F Horniblow in July 1908):

> "Careful examination of the records has shown that clerks throughout the United Kingdom have been retained at their several stations in many cases for three years and in extreme cases up to five and six years, and have been employed the whole time in the same offices and engaged at the same class of work.
>
> "Changes of station either to other home stations or to stations abroad must in time necessarily occur, when such clerks are liable to find themselves put to a class of work which is entirely strange to them for which at first they show little or no aptitude, thus getting bad reports and losing heart in their work. This state of affairs cannot be entirely remedied by orders from this office, and Officers Commanding, Army Service Corps, of Commands must make such changes in the work at which their Army Service Corps clerks are engaged – even if such changes may involve temporary inconvenience in offices – as will render a clerk proficient in

any branch of this calling. Sometimes to effect this, change of stations will, no doubt, be necessary within the Commands, but great care should be taken that such changes are not carried to excess, in order to avoid expense to the public.

"A review of Corps History Sheets once a year by the Officer Commanding, Army Service Corps, of the Command etc would show the clerks whom it would be desirable to give a chance of work to. The Corps History Sheets reviewed to be those of Sergeants and downwards as it would cause too much inconvenience to frequently change Non-Commissioned Officers who may be in charge of an office or occupying such other positions of importance as generally falls to the lot of a clerk of the rank of Staff Sergeant or Staff Quartermaster Sergeant. Besides, with the stringent conditions now exacted before a man can be classified as "Chief Clerk", it may be taken that once a clerk is so classified he will require no other training beyond that which he gains in the office where he is employed, and one of the objects in issuing these instructions is to ensure that the training of clerks is sufficiently varied to fit them for the post of 'Chief Clerk' in any branch.

"Before moving a Sergeant from an office to give him a change of work, the Officer Commanding, Army Service Corps should refer the matter to this office to see if there is any reason which would render his move undesirable, such as his proximity to foreign service, or the Chief or other senior clerk in the same office being near foreign service, or a move to some other position elsewhere.

"Corps History Sheets should be called up for review in each Command on the 1st February in each year."

*　　*　　*

In May 1907 a web girdle (nowadays called a stable belt) was issued to all mounted Warrant Officers, NCOs and men of Horse and Remount Companies, the girdle being provided by the Chief Ordnance Officer in Pimlico. The buff waist belt in use was still retained, however, and Warrant Officers, Staff Sergeants and Trumpeters wore them under their tunics when wearing a sword, with the web girdle on the outside. Clearly someone abroad stepped enthusiastically out of line as an order was issued two months later that the web girdle was not to be worn with the foreign service frock coat. A full page cartoon in a 1907 *ASC Journal* shows a smart soldier walking out in his blue uniform, showing off his new blue and white belt. A paper boy, something of an urchin, shouts, "Hie! Tommy, you've got your braces round yer waist."

*　　*　　*

The post of Inspector of the ASC was created in early 1907, the first officer to be appointed being Colonel C A Hadfield (he was promoted to Major General that year). Subsequent Inspectors were of one or two star rank. (This post continued until April 1993, when the Royal Corps of Transport was subsumed in The Royal Logistic Corps.) He worked on the staff of the Inspector General of the Forces, a move which was seen as a step towards increased efficiency and raising of standards in the ASC. The year 1908 saw the creation of the post of Commandant of the ASC Training Establishment in Aldershot, which brought the Corps in line with the rest of the training establishments in the army. The first Commandant was Colonel S S Long, with Captain A R Liddell as Adjutant, Major A R Crofton Atkins as Chief Instructor and Captains H F C Cumberlege and O Striedinger as Instructors.

Officer education was well attended to. For instance, a number of officers attended special courses for procurement at the London School of Economics and officers were attached to industry for specialized training or instruction (eg attending a course in Birkenhead for judging the quality of meat). MT Courses at engineering works were arranged for the more promising ASC officers, although there was still a general feeling that horses were still the main means of locomotion. Certainly, the training of officers focused on horse transport training, but officers were given sufficient instruction to enable them to understand the use and administration of mechanical transport; the more promising and interested ones were sent on long transport courses. The main reason many officers joined the ASC was, in fact, because they were keen to ride but could neither afford their own horse nor had the private income necessary to join a cavalry regiment. At least in the ASC an officer was allocated his own horse even if the Corps was low down in the social scale. Partly because the ASC attracted good horsemen and administrators, and took their profession seriously, unlike some, the Corps had a high reputation in the equestrian world and was constantly consulted.

At first officers were attached to firms producing steam vehicles but later, in 1911-12, arrangements were made to send them to firms manufacturing internal combustion lorries. Two officers were with the London General Omnibus Company for a short period, for example, to obtain an insight into garage management, which was considered to be essential in the near future when MT vehicles would have to be handled on a large scale. Only one course a year at a steam engine works was planned from 1912 on, which gives an indication of how the ASC was viewing this means of road transport.

*   *   *

A small Cookery School was established in Stanhope Lines, Aldershot, in 1907, since messing was the responsibility of the ASC, largely because the Corps was responsible for rations. Cooks at that time were regimental soldiers but courses were run by the ASC, not the more sophisticated training given after the 1960s but on how to cook in centralized kitchens, from which soldiers from each barrack room collected boiled potatoes and meat stew.

The first full-time Messing Adviser was appointed in 1911, Lieutenant Colonel H O Morgan (Retired Pay), who held the post until 1919, when the appointment lapsed. During the 1914-18 war other Cookery Schools were established in major garrison towns in UK, still under the direction of the ASC. An Inspector of Catering was appointed in 1914 and progressively more attention was paid to cooking in the army until just before the Second World War. (On advice from Mr Hore Belisha, Secretary of State for War, and Sir Isidore Salmon, Chairman of Lyons, the Army Catering Corps was formed in 1941.)

*   *   *

Having seen the earlier introduction and disbandment of the Motor Volunteer Corps, we need, at this stage, to look at the Territorial side of the army.

The Boer War of 1899-1902 had exposed the inadequacies of the Militia and exploded the myth that Volunteers could be maintained in a state of readiness for war. A total of 45,566 Militia went to serve in South Africa, but it was found that Volunteers' terms of service did not permit them to be embodied for a war outside the UK. There was no way the action of the Boers could be considered as a prelude to an invasion of Britain. There was a let-out, however, for Volunteers in that individuals were permitted to volunteer for service and a great number did so. In all, a total of 19,856 Volunteers went to South Africa, of which a good representation were from the ASC.

Some Volunteer regiments, long before the war, had realized the necessity for efficient administrative support. Some of them ran their own administrative services through the medium of their Engineers, as did the Cheshires and Gloucesters. The Hampshires provided the first effective Transport Company, which became the Hampshire Company ASC. The Herefords also created a separate Transport Company called 'The Weobley Company'. The West Kent Infantry Brigade ASC, the 3rd Lancashire ASC Company and the 4th London Brigade Company ASC were all formed long before the South African war.

It will be no surprise to hear that the main ASC problem of the time was a general shortage of horses and equipment; few units had their own. Equestrian training was carried out normally on wooden horses and horses and wagons were hired for annual camps. County Associations had to budget for annual training costs: £115 for the No 1 (HQ) Company and £40 each for the other three companies. These grants had to cover the hire of horses, wagons and transport, harness and saddlery, insurance costs and the cost of veterinary services. The hire of a wagon and two horses was £1 a day, while a single horse and cart cost 10 shillings a day. The average camp requirement for a Transport & Supply Column was twenty pair-horsed wagons and five single-horsed carts. A lorry and trailer, without driver, however, was expensive: £2 10s 0d a day, excluding fuel costs, but few people were qualified to drive.

Volunteer officers were obliged to undergo two courses, each of fifteen days, a transport course at one of the Regular Transport Depot Companies ASC or a local MT Company, and a Supply Course at Aldershot. There was no pay for training nights and weekends, only for attendance at annual camp, but a retainer of 10 shillings a year was paid to those who volunteered for the Special Service Section, which imposed the obligation to serve in case of a national emergency.

A recruit had to be between 17 and 35 years of age; retiring age was 40 for soldiers and 50 for senior ranks. Annual training obligations for the Rank & File of the ASC were:

20 mounted drills (riding and driving)

8 foot drills

Annual camp

and a course in weapon training

Training bounties were introduced after the 1913 camps, a departure which not only indicated that the worth of the Territorial had been recognized but also provided an added incentive to raise the standard of efficiency. The bounties were:

Commanding Officer:	£60
Field Officers:	£40
Captains:	£30
Subalterns:	£20
NCOs and Men:	£2

In order to qualify for their bounties, however, NCOs and men had to attend 30 drills and attend a fifteen-day camp. The disparity in bounty levels might not be quite so acceptable these days.

The Territorial Force (as it was renamed) was reorganized on 1 April 1908. It consisted of fourteen Divisions and thirteen Mounted Brigades, one for each of the military districts (two for London, except that there was only one Mounted Brigade), each with its own Transport & Supply Column, the first regimental-sized Transport & Supply units since Colonel McMurdo's Land Transport Corps in the Crimean War during the period 1855-56.

An *ASC Journal* of the day cast a wary eye on the embryo organization: "It is early yet to speak of the Territorial Army. Beyond the fact that it is to be complete in Transport and Supply Services, we have been able to ascertain little concerning its effect on the ASC. Provided that sufficient recruits are forthcoming, the system cannot fail to be an improvement on the somewhat sketchy organization of some of the ASC companies of the present volunteer brigades. This time next year we might have something more definite to say on the Territorial ASC." In the event, he had nothing more to say, as the Territorial ASC's bustling success was self-evident.

The Territorial Divisional Column, each with a No 1 (HQ) Company and three 'County' Brigade Companies, had a strength of nineteen officers and 450 men (plus a Regular Adjutant and four Warrant Officer Permanent Staff Instructors ASC), while the Mounted Brigade Column was of company strength. In addition to ASC units for both Regular and Territorial Divisions, there were additional ASC units for Army Troops and for specialist purposes (eg wireless, cable, airline, field HQs and medical units). (See Annex D for 1908 details of the Transport & Supply Columns.) The Lowland Division Transport & Supply Column had the distinction of being the first Territorial unit of the ASC to report that it had reached 30% of its establishment, while the Column of the 2nd South Midland Mounted Brigade (a company-sized unit) was one of two units to report to the War Office on 30 June that it had reached full strength.

* * *

In December 1908 twenty-four omnibuses of the London General Omnibus Company were used on army manoeuvres for the first time, moving troops from Hounslow to Shoeburyness. An *ASC Journal* of the day commented: "The drivers of the LGOC set an excellent example by their faultless discipline. In their desire to make the work of the ASC columns successful they took off their coats and voluntarily assisted in loading and unloading, and in fatigue work in camp. It was a pleasure to deal with such men."

Lieutenant General Sir Arthur Page, GOC-in-C Eastern Command, commented on the trials and noted that two officers and twenty-four men with equipment could be carried in each vehicle. The evacuation of casualties was suggested by the medical authorities as a possible means of employment.

Army records appear to show little or no further use of omnibuses before 1914; London Transport Museum's records, however, indicate that many of the LGOC drivers who volunteered for service in the first months of the war had been in the Special Transport Reserve, for which they received a retainer of £4 a year.

*   *   *

The following year, on a freezing March day, a composite battalion of Guards was moved from London to Hastings by 316 privately-owned cars, all organized by the Automobile Association. Crowds greeted them *en route* and the resultant publicity reinforced the potential of transport for war, providing a much-needed fillip for ASC transport enthusiasts in the War Office and visionaries in the automotive industry.

No doubt influenced by the success of these demonstrations, Colonel G R C Paul, the Assistant Director of Transport in the War Office, obtained approval for 900 vehicles to be written into mobilization plans over and above those already held in units. Needless to say, the army did not possess this number of vehicles, so the problem was solved by introducing a Registration Scheme. (Colonel Paul must have been a remarkable man: he had returned to Chatham in 1904 from special service in Somaliland, where he went to considerable pains to gather together a complete set of camel mouths showing the condition of teeth at the various ages. By this means, the dentition of camels could be studied at the ASC School of Instruction.)

*   *   *

In 1908, £2 a year was paid to owners of steam lorries of approved pattern if they agreed to be incorporated into the Registration Scheme for call-up "in the event of unpleasant developments" (ie war). In 1911 its successor, the Subsidy Scheme, included mainly petrol-driven lorries, with the amount paid rising to a sum varying from £38 to £52. The aim of the subsidy-type vehicles was not only to provide vehicles in war for an army that could not afford them in peace, but also to standardize the controls and to minimize the variety and number of spare parts which had to be carried. Captain H N Foster was appointed Inspector of Subsidized Transport at the War Office.

There were two classes of subsidy vehicle: Class A lorries of 3 ton load capacity and Class B of 30 cwt. Among other requirements, they had to be capable of carrying two men on the front seat on the driver's left as well as a fair kit of tools and spare fuel cans; all engines had to be governed so as not to exceed 1,000 rpm; all vehicles had to have 30 gallon tanks, with four forward gears and one reverse. Chain drive to the rear axle was not permitted and wheels were to be fitted with solid rubber tyres of the band type; the clutch pedal was to be on the left, the brake on the right, to be marked 'C' and 'B' respectively; the clutch and brake pedals had to be fitted with springs of such a strength that the driver could keep his feet on them continuously if desired, the accelerator pedal, if required, to be on the right of the brake pedal; the hand brake lever to be well away from and to the right of the gear lever, the former to have a cylindrical knob, the latter a circular one. The driver had to be adequately protected from the weather; and petrol consumption had to be no worse than 40 miles per gallon. In 1912 1,000 vehicles were registered, the amount paid now being £110 a year. Times were changing.

Many manufacturers and owners were keen to register under the Subsidy Scheme as the sums paid were a real bonus for their businesses. There was a catch, of course: on the owner's side he hoped that war would not be declared, and on the army's side there was an insistence on certain standardization measures, essential in a newly developing industry in which all makers went their own way. A live axle was also considered essential but the manufacturers could not provide at the time, so in the event a good number of chain-driven Albions, Commers, Guys, Halleys and Hallfords were requisitioned for war use.

* * *

The Somaliland expedition of 1909 was a small affair in which little appeared to happen. On the ASC side, 15 Company was involved, along with Major G E Pigott DSO, Capt M N G Anderson DSO and two other Captains, three Lieutenants, six NCOs for Supplies and six NCOs for Transport. Captain B L Beddy arrived in July 1909 to take over as OC ASC. They gathered at Kensington Barracks in London and embarked on the P & O SS *Palma* on 16 January, arriving in Berbera on 5 February. The heat, troublesome camels and lack of water seemed to be their major problems. The force consisted of an Infantry Brigade of the Indian Army and four battalions of the King's African Rifles. The ASC Headquarters was established in Burao, along with the Camel Depot, and the Base was in Berbera. The ASC disembarked in early 1910. The only point of interest is that a steam tractor was landed at Berbera, with two ASC drivers and a fitter, for experimental purposes, but the lack of water must have inhibited its use anywhere but in the Base.

* * *

The ASC Old Comrades Club was initiated in July 1910. Among the earliest to join were Assistant Commissary General E Kitchfield, who had served in the Crimean War 1854-56, and Major T W Reynolds, who had served in the Military Train in the 1860s. The first annual dinner was held in the Holborn Restaurant in London on 20 October 1910, with some 260 members present, the chair being taken by Major General H N Bunbury CB. Also in the same year was formed the Corps Club, in order to control the various other clubs and activities which had developed in recent years (ie the ASC point-to-point, cricket, dinner, the Band, the Ascot Lunch, the Journal, Quarterly and the Seniority List). The stated aim was that "The Corps, past and present, be a united family and work together for the general benefit of the Corps".

* * *

The close links with the Royal Artillery were given a boost in 1910 when gun-towing was started by the ASC on an experimental basis. Using caterpillar tractors, the trials in Yorkshire were surprisingly successful, but this function did not become a routine part of the ASC's duties until the war.

*   *   *

The Corps Band made its first appearance at the Royal Navy & Military Tournament in Olympia in July 1910 and is recorded as having acquitted itself with credit. During this period two company teams each from Aldershot and Woolwich, the two main ASC centres, competed keenly in wagon mounting and dismounting competitions, precursors of the naval gun races at the Royal Tournament. The competitions took place in the arena during three mornings or at other convenient times out of performance hours. Perhaps surprisingly, there was good crowd support for these events, but they were discontinued after 1914.

The last tournament before the war could justifiably be described as the ASC's best ever, organized as it was by Lieutenant Colonel (later Major General) R Ford, OC ASC Service Companies in Aldershot. The normal mounting and dismounting of GS wagons was combined with an exhibition of entraining and detraining at an imaginary railhead in the desert. Railway lines into the arena were rapidly laid by men of the MT Branch and South Western Railway trucks rolled in, disgorging horses which were then harnessed into the wagons. At the end of the display the horses scampered back into the trucks, reflecting much time spent on rehearsals in Aldershot. Fifty-four ASC men made up the arena party, appearing sometimes as arena party, at others as Ancient Britons in the pageant; the Roman Wall which moved down the arena in a stately fashion was propelled (unseen of course) by ASC brawn and muscle, the Roman chariot was driven by another ASC man and even the two 'sacred' oxen with gilded horns in the Roman pageant procession were enjoying a change of air from the Supply Depot in Stanhope Lines, Aldershot, before they became tasty morsels in someone's ration scale.

The rules for these competitions can be seen in Annex E. Their rewrite for 1908 reflected concerns in a letter published in the May 1907 *Journal* that "numerous dodges and artifices [are] at present perpetrated", among which were: dummy buttons on the tunic, belts sewn on the back and sides, wagon cover ropes too loose, slits cut in straps between holes and stirrups too long (enabling a short driver to mount more easily).

In spite of the rules being tightened up, however, there were evidently still ways of gaining advantage, ways which appear to have been obvious to soldiers taking part but not to the officers judging, as evinced by a postcard in the author's collection sent in June 1910 by Private A Triggs to his sister in Patching near Worthing. On the reverse is the message: "Dear Mag, Just a line hoping this will find you quite well as it leaves me, the same. Well we came back from the Olympia last night Friday we got done out of the cup again, of course Woolwich won again, and both of the judges came from Woolwich, well I would not go in the team another year after this lot."

*   *   *

Uniforms for the ASC were the essence of simplicity: the basic colours were dark blue with white facings, colours which had originated with the Land

Transport Corps and Military Train in the middle of the nineteenth century. Members of the Corps were highly recognizable in their best uniform with white collars and two white stripes on their netherware. Regular officers wore gold braid, while their Territorial brothers wore silver. Badges were developments of those in Victorian times. Details of officers' dress regulations and soldiers' dress details can be seen in Army Dress Regulations. ASC ceremonial dress was authorized until the outbreak of war in 1939.

When looking at photographs of ASC rank & file it should be remembered that there were certain differences between the mounted trades and those in MT and Supply. Horse Transport men wore on the left shoulder the distinction of all mounted regiments, the white lanyard (nothing to do with saving the guns at Colenso, a false belief that will not go away), the leather bandolier and riding breeches, with long puttees or boots and spurs; the greatcoat was double breasted. Supply personnel were not entitled to wear a lanyard, but many soldiers seemed to enjoy sporting a khaki or brown one and some risked incurring the wrath of the Sergeant Major by wearing a plaited leather chinstrap. MT and Supply wore a leather belt, trousers, with or without puttees, and a single-breasted overcoat. MT personnel often made a point of wearing goggles on their hats to indicate they were of a superior trade; another tell-tale for MT was the hat with ear muffs (although horse transport drivers' ears must have got equally cold).

Territorials can invariably be identified by the 3-bar shoulder titles, a different one for each TA Association area, as well as, occasionally, a silver-coloured 'Volunteer' badge above the right breast pocket of their serge jacket. (Comprehensive details of the shoulder titles can be seen in Ray Westlake's *Collecting Metal Shoulder Titles,* Second Edition 1996, published by Pen & Sword.) Volunteers' collar badges in blues were silver-coloured instead of the gold-coloured ones worn by the Regulars. The Brodrick Cap was worn from immediately after the Boer War until 1907. It goes without saying that enormous variations in standards and accuracy of dress are to be seen in photographs; large Corps are not known for standardization.

*   *   *

An admirable entry on flying appeared in the December 1910 *ASC Journal,* which is worth quoting in full:

> "About a quarter past nine on Tuesday, 29th November the mighty humming of an aerial engine was heard over Buller Barracks. Conjecture ran high as to the identity of the intrepid airman. The appearance of the aeroplane as she sailed into sight dispelled the idea that it might be Cody. A few experts recognised the Farman biplane and guessed that Lieutenant Snowden-Smith had come to pay us a visit. After circling once or twice round Buller Barracks, he landed easily on the Queen's Parade rugby football ground. He was soon the centre of a large admiring crowd. It was a cold frosty morning, and of all the cold people collected round the aeroplane the airman was the coldest.
>
> "He had started from Brooklands in a slight fog, but had no difficulty in finding his way to Aldershot, following the line of the L & SW Railway as far as Frimley, and then, turning towards Farnborough, he circled over the

Cove Balloon School, and thence to Buller Barracks and back again to the Queen's Parade.

"Shortly after his arrival, air friends, one of whom was the wife of a celebrated motorist, arrived in a motor and carried him off to breakfast at the Queen's Hotel.

"The news quickly gained ground that he intended to make the return flight after breakfast, and an eager crowd patiently awaited his return. Their patience was rewarded, for Lieutenant Snowden-Smith returned in the car and with a smile donned goggles and helmet. He coolly took his seat, and with a final word to the spectators in front of the machine to stand clear, gradually soared away, and, as we afterwards heard, landed quite comfortably in Brooklands." (Lieutenant Snowden-Smith was promoted to Major General in 1938 and was Director of Supplies & Transport in 1940.)

It was the custom before the 1914-18 war to attach officers to foreign armies to observe developments and for liaison. A number of Corps officers enjoyed such visits, particularly in Austria, France and Germany. An Austrian petrol-engined Saurer lorry was imported into Aberdeen from the Continent in 1910, even though petrol was still banned for private users. This vehicle was trialled extensively between Elgin and London and, as a result, the army bought a batch of petrol-driven Thornycrofts. At the same time ninety steam tractors were hired for the 1910 manoeuvres to test MT at Divisional level, although their use merely illustrated that the vehicles did not have the necessary eighty mile radius envisaged for MT in war. The vehicles owned and operated by the ASC in 1910 can be seen in Annex G, details which were fortunately recorded in a little black book by Lieutenant J C Mackie of the Inspectorate of MT.

This limitation in radius had a considerable influence on the method of supply. There were no manoeuvres in 1911 (reportedly due to the exceptionally dry summer causing a serious shortage of water in the area to be used, although the shortage of funds to hire so much civilian road transport was a more likely reason) and the time was used to redesign the supply system. Petrol-engine lorries were to distribute supplies from a forward railhead, from which point ASC second line or regimental transport would take over. This was a radical introduction, a new idea, which was then successfully trialled in 1912, albeit with only twenty vehicles from Gosport, and immediately written into operations manuals. The ASC was thus in a position in 1914 to provide the army's needs with up-to-date equipment and a new method of supply, which obviated the problems of time and distance experienced in South Africa and provided a flexibility never before available to the British Army. At the same time Divisional Ammunition Parks ASC were created, with steam tractors earmarked, to carry third line artillery stocks under the Inspector General Line of Communication, and a Royal Artillery Officer was allotted to each Ammunition Park to ensure that the lorries sent up to the various refilling points contained the natures of ammunition required. The supply of artillery ammunition and small arms ammunition otherwise remained the responsibility of the Royal Artillery. An important decision was also made to equip sixteen sets of mobile workshops, one for each MT unit, a great step forward.

*   *   *

Two-wheeled locomotion has not yet been mentioned. The *ASC Quarterly* of 1909 had opined:

> "At present, section sergeants are mounted on bicycles. No mounts [ie horses] are provided for Staff Sergeants who might, with advantage, ride the motor cycles allotted to the company. For working with traction engines nothing can be equal to a steady horse, as the average speed of a loaded engine is about 4 mph. For fast lorries a motor car is best, while motor bicycles are useless for accompanying convoys. If they take it into their heads to run well, one gets miles ahead; if they run badly one is soon left behind trying to make the necessary adjustments. They are not an officer's mount." Quite!

In 1911 Olympia staged a Motor Cycle Show, which was visited by army representatives, who then invited various manufacturers to send their machines to Brooklands in Surrey for trial. The average speed of the motor cycles sent was extremely high for those days, 40 mph. Ten machines were bought for field trials with ASC units, among them two Douglas (2¾ hp), two Phelon & Moores (3½ hp), one Premier (3½ hp), two Rudge-Whitworths (3½ hp), two Triumphs and one Zenith (3½ hp).

When the machines were sent to stations in England the Director of Transport directed: "They are primarily for use in connection with the supervision and control of MT services. As a considerable number of motor bicycles are allotted for use by officers of the Supply Columns of the Expeditionary Force on mobilization . . . instruct all ASC officers serving with MT Companies in their care and management . . . the bicycles should only be used in connection with the military duties for which they are primarily provided and should be regarded as auxiliaries to the motor cars already allotted to MT Companies."

One subsequent report from a unit stated: "The motor cycle takes the place of a horse rather than of a car. Reports are favourable. Side cars should be left out of the question – there are no points in its favour when there are small cars available as these would be. It only makes the motor bicycle into a very indifferent small car and hampers its proper use as a single man's machine."

As for tracked vehicles, the War Office decided in 1911, as part of the general review and reorganization of both HT and MT in the Corps, that there was no future for them in the army; although caterpillar vehicles continued in use, they were not trialled or developed further by the army until the war, when tanks first appeared.

*   *   *

On 16 May 1912 a great boost was given to the MT Section of the Corps when Their Majesties The King and Queen, King George V and Queen Mary, inspected the MT of the ASC on parade in Aldershot. On view was the Supply Column for three Brigades, complete with first aid lorries, spare lorries and workshops. Lieutenant Colonel R Ford DSO (promoted to Major General in 1918) was in command of the whole parade, which had been called at short notice, with Major H C Wilder in command of the Supply Column. His Majesty was accompanied by General Sir John French and Lieutenant General Sir Douglas Haig, while Colonel T J O'Dell, late ASC, guided the royal party round the parade. Particular attention was paid to the Repair Train and to the new meat van, which had been modified to carry 2,000 rations of bread and meat for camp work during the summer. Even Her Majesty The Queen, accompanied by Lady Stamfordham and her ladies-in-waiting, inspected the workshop vehicles and the motor ambulance, which was opened for inspection.

*　*　*

With war on the Continent increasing in likelihood, serious attention was now clearly paid to allocating ASC units to task. Expeditionary Force Tables of November 1912 allocated ASC units to formations (see Annex G), but wholesale changes were made in due course when it came to mobilization. Apart from the Transport Companies shown in the Annex, the following units were allocated in the order of battle: Nos. 1-6 Field Butchery, Nos. 1-6 Field Bakery, Nos. 1-8 Railway Supply Detachment, a Central Requisition Office, Nos. 1-30 Depot Units of Supply, Nos. 1-8 Bakery Sections, 1 and 2 Advanced Remount Depots and a Base Remount Depot.

*　*　*

The MT Committee in 1912 consisted of the following: Colonel H C L Holden RA (President), Lieutenant Colonel A Slade Baker, Major W E Donohue (Chief Inspector MT ASC), Major A G Stevenson DSO (War Office), Major H C F Cumberlege (OC 52 (MT) Depot Company ASC), Captain H N Foster (Chief Inspector Subsidized Transport) and Captain A E Davidson RE Secretary. The record of their meetings in the years before the war reflects not only a massive amount of work but also a dazzling array of developing technology which would surprise most readers.

During 1911-12 , in addition to the motor cycles tested at Brooklands, the Committee purchased the following vehicles for trial purposes:

16	3 ton Leylands (new WD subsidy specifications)
3	3 ton Hallfords
4	30 cwt Leylands
5	30 cwt Commercial Cars Ltd
1	30 cwt Leyland motor ambulance
6	Special workshop trucks with steel frames
2	4-seater open motor cars – Deasy (including the Commandant Staff College)
2	5-seater limousine bodies – Deasy (GOC Eastern Command and the Army Council)
3	4-seater Arrol Johnstones (Cork, Malta and Southern Command)
7	2-seater Vulcan cars (use in MT Companies)

*　*　*

In April 1912 a new category of Special Reserves was introduced: Category C. MT Drivers ASC were enlisted in this category, with the number at first authorized at 1,000 men. In December a limited number of ASC Horse Transport NCOs and Drivers were also enlisted into Category C, to be graded as Roadmasters (Staff Sergeants), Foremen (Corporals) and Wagoners (Drivers). They were a remarkable organization, initially known as the Wagoners Special Reserve but later as the Wolds Wagoners, the brainchild of Lieutenant Colonel Sir Mark Sykes Bt, MP of Sledmere in Yorkshire. (The single 'g' of Wagoner' was used on the original membership badge and, although it was incorrect, this spelling was retained. Since the formation of the Royal Waggoners in 1794 the double 'g' has been used by the Corps in subsequent titles (ie Royal Waggon Train)).

Seeing war on the horizon, Sir Mark realized that the skills of Wagoners in the Wolds of Yorkshire would prove invaluable to the army, since they would need no training when it came to mobilization, unlike most others who in due course would be involved with horses during the war. His proposal to the War Office that a special Corps be formed and the men paid a small amount in exchange for a commitment to enlist as drivers for service at home or abroad in the event of war was accepted.

Captain S E Sykes (not related to Sir Mark Sykes), who was stationed with the ASC in York, went around the Wolds encouraging farm-hands to join; against an original target of 1,200 men, 200 had enrolled by January 1913 and 400 by July that year. Further recruiting continued, the final total reaching 1,127. Each recruit received £1 when he signed on, with a promise of £1 for every subsequent year, and Foremen received £2, Roadmasters £4. Among other places recruiting took place at Fimber, where annual wagon-driving competitions took place. In July 1913, Brigadier General F W B Landon CB, Director of Transport & Movements at the War Office, accompanied by Colonel A Phelps, Assistant Director of Supply & Transport in Headquarters Northern Command in York, presented prizes at the Fimber meeting.

*   *   *

Sport has always played an important part in the life of the Corps and a fair amount of space was allocated to sports results in the *Corps Journal*. April 1913 had seen the first ASC golf meeting take place at Worplesdon golf club near Woking, some fifty officers taking part. January 1914 saw the new football ground opposite the Aldershot Supply Depot opened for play, taking over from the old pitch on the Recreation Ground in Stanhope Lines (later to be called 'God's Acre'). New Year's Day saw the inaugural match between the eleven oldest ASC officers in Aldershot and members of the ASC Sergeants' Mess, the latter winning 2-1 in a boisterous, memorable match.

Real success was achieved, however, on Easter Monday, 13 April 1914 at the Army Football Ground on Queen's Avenue in Aldershot, when, after years of unsuccessful effort, the ASC Woolwich football team beat the 1st Battalion Hampshire Regiment for the Army Football Cup, the army's premier sports trophy. Sergeant Williams scored the only goal of the match after 38 minutes. Well over 12,000 uniformed men watched a thrilling match along with Their Majesties The King and Queen, HRH The Prince of Wales, HRH Princess Mary and HRH Prince Arthur, Duke of Connaught. After the silver Warwick Vase was presented by the Queen to Lieutenant Colonel C S Dodgson, Commanding ASC Woolwich, the GOC-in-Chief Aldershot Command, Lieutenant General Sir Douglas Haig, called for three cheers for Their Majesties. (Corps teams subsequently won the Army Cup on five occasions, finally in 1989, when 10 Corps Transport Regiment Royal Corps of Transport beat the School of Signals 5-0.)

*   *   *

The early recruitment of Volunteers for the Territorial Force from 1908 had been slow, with critics hurling taunts and nicknames at every opportunity, but "Haldane's Horse" or "The Saturday Night Soldiers" carried on, encouraged by King Edward VII's personal intervention through Lord Lieutenants of the counties. Because their establishments were small and they were able to recruit from civilian sources where occupations generally matched military functions, Volunteer ASC units had quite the best recruiting results in the entire Territorial Force. By 1913 every ASC unit had experienced more than once the duties of Transport and Supply in support of its formation on manoeuvres or at camp. The summer camps of 1914 saw all units on collective training with their formations, so that they too, like their Regular counterparts, were as ready as they could be for war.

*   *   *

King's Regulations and Orders for the Army 1912 (which were later reprinted with amendments published in Army Orders up to 1 August 1914) laid down the duties of the ASC, hardly changed from 1902: "The officers of the ASC are entrusted with furnishing transport, provisions, fuel, light and supplies, for the use of all branches of the army, and with the allotment of barracks and quarters and their equipment, as laid down in the Regulations for Supply Transport and Barrack Services." This fine, almost simple theory was shortly to be tested in the heat of war, during which many new tasks would accrue and major responsibilities would develop, to the extent that the Corps of pre-war days would not have recognized the Corps it was soon to become. In the process of all the change that took place in the period 1902-1914, an important development had taken place, almost imperceptibly to many: the British Army moved away from fighting Colonial wars in Africa and was fast becoming a modern army for Europe.

40

CHAPTER 2

1914: Baptism of Fire

For all nations participating in the war, 1914 was a year of high hopes and illusion. When Germany mobilized and declared war on France on 3 August, they had full confidence in the success of the Schlieffen Plan to scythe through Belgium and capture Paris, in the process annihilating the French Army, not to mention Britain's 'contemptible little army', before Russia could mobilize and enter the field against them. German military and political leaders grossly under-estimated the time it would take to achieve success and the consequences of their actions.

Strong German forces entered Belgium on 4 August, sweeping aside brave but ineffective Belgian resistance before they were opposed by the British Expeditionary Force, which had landed in France over the period 7-16 August, led by Field Marshal Sir John French. The immortal retreat from Mons started on 23 August, with British forces fighting a difficult withdrawal, until the Germans were held at the Battle of the Marne on 5-10 September. The counter-offensive subsequently pushed the German Army north-eastwards to positions which varied little over the next few years. Both sides dug in, developing trench positions. The only major battle in 1914 was at Ypres in October and November, an indecisive conflict given the title 'First Battle of Ypres'.

On the one hand the well-trained German soldier crossing into Belgium or France was confident of Germany's right to establish its proper status as a major trading nation on the world stage; on the other, the British soldier, entering mainland Europe for the first time since the Napoleonic war 100 years before, was confident of his ability to stop superior forces, something the British Army had been doing since time immemorial. 'Home by Christmas' was the general cry, more through hope than anything else. Illusion can be a fine thing.

On 31 August the Government issued orders for raising the first of the New Army Divisions, with volunteers rushing to join, their sense of patriotism matching the high hopes of the all-Regular Divisions that were already in France. On 11 September orders were issued to raise the second batch of six Divisions for the New Army, with encouragement provided by the famous recruiting poster of the Minister for War, Field Marshal Lord Kitchener, pointing his finger at all Britons: 'Join Your Country's Army. God Save the King'.

In trying to stop the German offensive, the British Army's losses were considerable but the small, experienced, pre-war Regular Army remained intact as a fighting force, retreating as best it could, almost to the gates of Paris. The 'Old Contemptibles', as they were called, became the nucleus of Kitchener's New Armies, providing experience and training to a new generation of soldiers. Having been stopped and pushed back almost to the borders of France, the Germans realized by the end of 1914 that their gamble had failed. Their lightning success of 1870 was not be repeated. The next time they would succeed would be in 1940.

The flexibility, versatility and imagination of the ASC were tested to the full with mobilization and the application of pre-war plans. Only the British could go to war with vehicles displaying the names of commercial firms and London

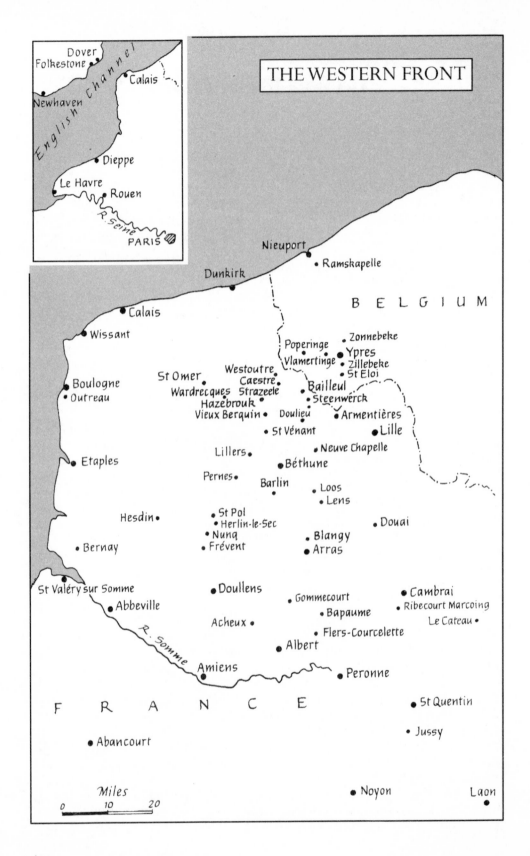

THE WESTERN FRONT

Dover
Folkestone
English Channel
Calais
Newhaven
Dieppe
Le Havre
Rouen
R. Seine
PARIS

Nieuport
Ramskapelle
Dunkirk
BELGIUM
Calais
Zonnebeke
Poperinge
Ypres
Wissant
Vlamertinge
Zillebeke
St Eloi
St Omer
Westoutre
Caestre
Boulogne
Wardrecques
Strazeele
Bailleul
Outreau
Hazebrouk
Steenwerck
Vieux Berquin
Doulieu
Armentières
St Vénant
Lille
Lillers
Neuve Chapelle
Etaples
Béthune
Pernes
Barlin
Loos
Lens
Hesdin
St Pol
Herlin-le-Sec
Douai
Nunq
Blangy
Bernay
Frévent
Arras
St Valéry sur Somme
Doullens
Cambrai
Abbeville
Gommecourt
Ribecourt Marcoing
R. Somme
Bapaume
Le Cateau
Acheux
Flers-Courcelette
Albert
Amiens
Peronne
F R A N C E
St Quentin
Jussy
Abancourt
Miles
0   10   20
Noyon
Laon

omnibuses advertising shows in the West End of London. The organization may have looked amateur to continental eyes, but it worked. New Army Divisions increased the pressure on the training and testing organizations of the ASC, leading to expansion in the Grove Park, Osterley Park and Bulford areas.

*   *   *

On the eve of war the ASC was scattered throughout the world, in every army garrison except India. On 1 August 1914 it numbered 498 Regular officers and 5,933 men, largely in seventy-three companies as follows: five Depot Companies (three HT and one each for MT and Supply), thirty-three HT companies and twenty MT companies, two Station HT companies at lower establishments, four Service Companies for Supply, four Remount companies and five HT companies in the Middle East or in South Africa. The position was about to change.

The officer strength consisted of three Generals, fifteen Colonels, twenty-three Lieutenant Colonels, sixty-two Majors, 184 Captains, 115 Lieutenants, fifty 2nd Lieutenants, seventy Quartermasters, seven District Barrack Officers and one Retired Officer.

The split in responsibilities between Supply and Transport were:

Director of Supplies: the provision and administration of all food, forage, fuel, light and disinfectants

Director of Transport: the provision, administration and distribution of all transport (except technical vehicles under the Director of Ordnance Services), excluding railways and sea transport but including inland water transport

When the realities of war took hold, the separation of Supplies and Transport in the War Office was ended in September with the creation of the appointment of Director of Supplies & Transport, the first incumbent being Brigadier General S S Long. In support he had Lieutenant Colonel F W Stringer as Assistant Director of Transport and Colonel H C L Holden (retired Gunner) as Assistant Director of Mechanical Transport. Above all, the Corps was fortunate in having as Quartermaster General Lieutenant General Sir John Cowans, late Rifle Brigade, who served in that post from 1912 to 1918. He was the ideal man for the job and the army and ASC have cause to be grateful to him.

*   *   *

The following telegram was sent to all Commands at 7.50 pm on 2 August: "All troops out for training at places other than their peace stations, whether Regulars, Special Reserve, OTC or Territorial, are to return to their peace stations forthwith, except troops employed during the precautionary period." Mobilization in August 1914 provided a mixed bag of problems for the ASC. The supply and transport plans were well thought out and in place, but the manpower difficulties were enormous and soon worsened as the army grew ever larger.

Most Regular units were in barracks carrying out their usual routines or, like 12 HT Company from Colewort Barracks in Portsmouth, were at annual camp on Salisbury Plain, attached to the RAMC School of Instruction in Tidworth. For them life was moderately easy, with the officers and NCOs enjoying rambles over the hills towards the end of the day, keeping their respective messes well supplied with mushrooms and raspberries.

There had been early signs of something unusual happening, but no one took much notice: in July half-a-dozen lorries had passed their camp at speed, full of armed soldiers cheerily singing 'Tipperary'. Newspapers were full of the troubles in Ireland (nothing new) and they thought the troops were probably on their way there. The next day several large farm-carts trekked slowly towards the barracks in Tidworth, a curious sight. One old carter volunteered the information that they were moving baggage to Ludgershall Railway Station. Then, within days, information came in that the permanent staff and cooks of the Public Schools Officer Training Corps at Tidworth Pennings had been sent back to their units and the RAMC School of Instruction suddenly closed. Something was clearly up.

Finally 12 HT Company received orders to return to Portsmouth as quickly as possible. Normally the return trip took two days, with an overnight stop in Romsey, but the choice was either to return in one day by train or complete the 55-mile march by road. Movement by train would have been very unprofessional (if not ignominious), so the return trip by road was completed in one long day with no mishap, other than one horse which went badly lame and had to complete the journey from Romsey by train.

Life became somewhat hectic on their return. Rumours of war were in the air and excitement was intense. On the evening of 4 August all members of the company had to present themselves for medical inspections. An immediate problem arose when the Company Sergeant Major and one of the company cooks were found to be unfit for active service. After a late night the company marched out of barracks to mobilize at Hilsea, where they occupied a large field next to the Ordnance Mobilization Sheds. The Officers Mess, though, was located in the 'Coach and Horses' inn, highly suitable for a horse transport unit.

In the ten days the company was allocated in which to complete their mobilization schedule, life became more strenuous than ever as stores of all description, but mainly wagons and harness, were drawn from Ordnance, and reservists and specially enlisted men began to roll in from all over the country, with officers and several men regularly going to Portsmouth Town Station to meet incoming trains, which frequently did not arrive on time. Suddenly fifty or sixty heavy draught horses arrived by rail, day after day, chiefly from the principal horse centres of England, not always amenable to military discipline.

In no time at all, it seemed, a pre-war HT Company on the lower establishment of about thirty men and forty horses, 12 HT Company emerged as the 5th Reserve Park, with seven officers, 289 men, 153 wagons and 358 horses. The Corps mobilization plans had worked well, except that a few teething faults surfaced: the neck collars and nose bags issued were too small for the

Shire and Clydesdale horses with which the company was largely equipped and there was a real problem in the supply of water for such a large number of horses.

In the end, mobilization was completed a day early and the unit shook down with local treks to accustom a variegated collection of men and horses to convoy duties and march discipline. Even when the company moved to Southampton by train later in August they did not know their destination, but they were at least heartened by Lord Kitchener's sound advice on how to treat their allies, especially the women. It was only after they had sailed that sealed orders were opened: they were *en route* for Le Havre in France. For them the war had started.

* * *

It was not only manpower that was a problem on mobilization; supplies too provided a headache, but fortunately ASC planning had been good. 125,000 men had been rationed before mobilization (bread and meat only) whereas suddenly 300,000 complete rations were required for Regulars and 300,000 for Territorials. In the event, supplies were obtained with a minimum of interference to the general supplies of the country as a whole, and more economically than in any previous war. Due to the valuable assistance provided by the Food Inspection staffs of the Local Government Board, Health Officers and Inspectors throughout the country, the quality was excellent.

Thanks to Brigadier General S S Long, who had progressed from the Officers' Training Establishment in Aldershot to the Supply Reserve Depot in Woolwich and then to the position of Director of Supplies & Quartering, the army at least had sufficient supplies for its immediate commitments. With war imminent, contracts had been placed and plans were even complete to use refrigerated ships as cold stores for frozen meat from overseas. In the transport field, previously under Major General F W B Landon, Director of Transport & Movement, establishments had been revised, vehicle provision and issue planned, spares and equipments were earmarked, repair workshops allocated and mobilization plans drawn up. It had never been possible, however, to practise mass mobilization, although plans had been made by the Assistant Director of Transport, Lieutenant Colonel F W Stringer, and a location in London earmarked.

In September 1914 Major General Landon was appointed Inspector of QMG Services and Brigadier General Long became the Director of Supplies & Transport in the War Office. Quartering remained an ASC responsibility under Major General C E Heath.

* * *

The personality of Brigadier General Long as the first Director of Supplies & Transport is worth highlighting at this stage, since much of the success of the ASC during the war resulted from his achievements before and during the early years of the war. He tolerated no fools and was able to get things done quickly, showing little respect for long-winded arguments from finance branches or government departments. Without obtaining financial agreement, he made contracts at the price he personally considered fair to both supplier and the army. He thus saved the army much money and pain before trade suppliers greedily raised their prices and hoarded precious food.

Brigadier General Long is the only officer ever who caused a Bill to pass through both Houses of Parliament and receive the King's assent in one day. The cause was that suppliers argued about the price of sugar, claiming that civilian consumption was more important than the army's, and they were reluctant to provide the amount required. He gave the contractors the option of making contracts on his terms or face requisition. Equally improperly, he sent instructions for meat stores in Bristol and Liverpool to be taken over by ASC units until the army's needs were met. He then informed the Parliamentary Financial Secretary at the War Office that an Act of Parliament must be passed to enable military authorities to seize foodstuffs essential for the army. The MP concerned said this was impossible but Brigadier General Long informed him that this had already been done and if the Act were not passed the Government would face a claim for millions of pounds. The Act was passed that night. Impetuous, direct, irascible and demanding though he was, Brigadier General Long was the right man for the job at the right time.

*　　*　　*

At 4 pm on 4 August 1914 the order for the mobilization of the Expeditionary and Territorial Forces was issued by the Government. Barracks and quarters were emptied, tented camps blossomed, buildings were hired and men were billeted on the local population. All garrisons were recalled from Egypt, Gibraltar, Malta and South Africa. The previous day had been a Bank Holiday and most Territorial units were on the move to camps for their annual training. Nevertheless mobilization went smoothly and 120,000 horses were collected.

*　　*　　*

The Remount service, which had the responsibility for providing remount horses to regiments and units in UK, had become the responsibility of the ASC in 1891. After a searching examination of its performance in the Boer War, it found itself in 1914 under the Director of Transport & Remounts in the War Office, where Colonel C H Bridge CB CMG was Assistant Inspector of Remounts. Each Command Headquarters contained a Deputy Assistant Director of Remounts, who was responsible for collecting information on the horse population in his Command area, having the authority by law to enter stables and classify animals. Remount Purchasing Officers were appointed to each District in the Command.

There were four Remount Depots in UK before the war and the increased demand for horses saw a number more established during the war (see Annex H). Men came from a variety of regiments, but were essentially ASC. The Remount Squadron was generally commanded by a Major, and he had a strength of some 200 all ranks to train 500 horses, with an officer from the Army Veterinary Corps to attend to their health.

A Base Remount Depot (with 2,600 animals) and two Advanced Remount Depots (each with 300 animals) went to France with the British Expeditionary Force. As the campaign continued, further Base Remount Depots of the same size opened at the Base Ports and one of the Advanced Depots was discontinued, leaving the other co-located with the Advanced Horse Transport Depot in Abbeville.

It had been hoped that French civilians could be obtained to assist with the manning of the depots, but this proved impossible and a number of ex-Cavalry Reservists were employed. The number of animals received in Remount Depots from overseas were:

As at	Horses	Mules
31 December 1914:	38,867	109
31 December 1915:	55,113	10,695
31 December 1916:	52,258	21,520
31 December 1917:	93,847	36,613
31 December 1918:	76,404	26,567
Totals:	316,489	95,504

Remount Purchasing Officers went to North and South America, New Zealand, Spain, Portugal, India and China.

* * *

The effectiveness of the pre-war Registration Scheme, which had been introduced to obtain 14,000 horses by compulsory purchase on the outbreak of war for the anticipated Expeditionary Force, was amply illustrated by the success of the scheme in 1914 when it obtained ten times that number.

During the first month of the war the wastage of horses ran at twenty per cent, twice the pre-war estimate. By mid-September 1914 55,000 horses had sailed with the British Expeditionary Force (5,000 had gone as reinforcements in the first month), 21,000 had been issued to the Regular Army at Home and 83,830 had been issued to the Territorial Force, all this against a peace establishment of 20,000. There is no doubt that the supply of horses was not a happy situation, since a large number of animals were quite unsuited for the hard work demanded of them by the army. One of the reasons put forward for this was that the breeding of horses was being adversely affected by the increase in motor transport. The most suitable for military purposes were Clydesdales, Suffolks and Welsh cart horses as well as the American Percherons. Later, in August 1915, the War Office established a committee to consider and advise what steps should be taken in England and Wales to secure an adequate supply of horses for military purposes.

* * *

As part of the mobilization process MT Mobilization Depots were opened at Avonmouth and Seaforth on 4 August and Numbers 1 and 2 Reserve HT Depots were formed at Deptford and Islington, also in August. Numbers 1 and 2 Labour Companies were formed at Aldershot on 24-25 August.

* * *

To speed up communication within the Corps, Registered Telegraphic Addresses were laid down for use in telegrams:

Director of Supplies & Quartering:	Jauntiness
Transport & Movements:	Packsaddle
Inspector of the ASC:	Kit
Assistant Director of Supplies & Transport (In London District):	Suppleons
Assistant Director (London District):	Duellum
OIC ASC Records:	Attest Commissariat
Commandant ASC Training Establishment:	Micrometer

*   *   *

On 4 August the order to requisition vehicles was signed. Initially the army needed 900 vehicles. In London, for instance, as a small part of the whole process, Captain T M Hutchinson at the Kensington Gardens Barracks was authorized "to procure from civilian owners, by impressment or otherwise, the following minimum number of Motor Transport Vehicles: 12 powerful motor cars, Laundulette Daimlers or Napiers preferred, 50 moderate powered motor cars, Panhard or Napier taxicabs preferred, 3 vans fitted with pneumatic tyres and one motor charabanc seating 22-27 persons, to arrive in any case not later than 12 midnight at the end of the first day of Mobilization. You should endeavour to persuade the driver of each vehicle to enlist. Pay 6/= per diem. Period 1 year." The War Office return in August 1914 shows that 507 vehicles were held by ASC units (see Annex I), including thirty-five abroad; the remainder of the 900 were requisitioned so that HQ Staffs and the first six Infantry Divisions and the Cavalry Division were up to strength. This was, of course, only an initial requirement.

Mobilization for the Territorials did not go well. Personnel for Territorial units were called up by Officers Commanding as soon as they received orders to mobilize, but their equipment was not held ready as it was for Regular units. It had to be obtained. Some of this equipment was provided by the Army Ordnance Department, but the great bulk was obtained by local purchase under arrangements made by County Associations. In some Districts vehicles and equipment were not available and considerable delays were incurred by most Territorial units. This was unsatisfactory but was the inevitable result of the policy in force for Territorials, ie that they were for Home service only.

*   *   *

In the event the pre-war planning figure for MT was quite inadequate since a field force of only six Divisions had been contemplated and this is when the pre-war Vehicle Subsidy Scheme bore fruit. Some 1,200 vehicles were called in, also private cars and motor cycles. This was still not enough, if only because there had been no motor transport planned for the Territorial divisions.

Contracts were placed in the USA, including contracts for 13,000 horse-drawn GS wagons; previously rejected steam and chain driven vehicles were taken, more vehicles were impressed and the army took over much of the factory output throughout the land. It was not only MT vehicles and GS wagons that were ordered from America. Officers were sent to buy horses, predominantly Percherons, as the numbers and quality of horses in UK were inadequate. Officers were also sent to the USA, Canada and Egypt to buy mules; Colonel Bridge, for example, as Head of the Mule Purchasing Commission during 1914-1916, purchased 145,000 mules in America and was responsible for the expenditure of $29 million.

*   *   *

The Officer in Charge of ASC Records in Woolwich, Colonel F Horniblow, was instructed to bring units up to strength and to provide MT personnel for field force formations according to prepared plans. His staff still consisted of one Assistant Officer (Captain QM J Grapes, Retired Pay) and fourteen clerks. The pressure of numbers, however, caused the formation on 22 August of a separate branch (ASC Records 2) at Woolwich Dockyard to deal with new units being raised, which lasted for six months, when it was renamed 'ASC Records 1st New Army'. Colonel Horniblow served as OIC ASC Records until June 1918, a remarkable achievement, when he handed over to Colonel E I Ward.

It would be wrong not to mention the contribution made by Lieutenant Colonel F W Stringer, who dealt with the personnel administration side of the Corps throughout the early years of the war. The success of ASC mobilization plans reflected the competence of the man and his dedication to duty. He literally wore himself out at his desk and died at work in 1916. Clearly the efforts being made by everybody to support their comrades-in-arms in the Corps were those of total commitment during the first few months of the war, so much so that the following letter was sent to ASC units in the Aldershot Command at the direction of the GOC-in-C:

"Owing to the incessant work and the severe strain under which all ranks of our permanent staff have worked since mobilization, you are instructed to arrange that all officers and men have twenty-four hours continuous rest in each week. This is intended to relieve those on whom the greatest strain has fallen and is not to constitute a claim for others who are doing little more than an ordinary day's work. The most willing workers must be protected against themselves and I must insist on this order being carried out whether they like it or not. It is hoped that you will carry out this order in the spirit in which it is meant."

Much is read of young men under-age joining, but little is heard of the reverse. Certainly Major J C Woods ASC did his bit. Born in 1849, he joined the 8th Regiment of Foot in 1869 and served in Egypt 1882, Sudan 1885 and in the Boer War 1899-1902. He was serving in the Supply Reserve Depot, Deptford when he died on 13 May 1918, aged 69. Other tricks were played and it is said that one ASC subaltern at Rouen was aged 70, while an OC ASC at Hounslow District is alleged to have been aged 88, though this is difficult to believe.

*   *   *

The Wagoners Special Reserve received their orders to mobilize on 5 August 1914 and reported to the ASC Depot in Bradford. Military training was minimal as the need to send drivers overseas was paramount; and, as there was initially a shortage of larger size uniforms, the smaller men only were issued with service dress before they left, the first 200 being sent to join the 1st and 2nd Bridging Trains RE in Ireland, not the ASC as was originally intended. Soon after arriving in Bradford, the remaining Wagoners departed by rail, not to serve in one unit as they might perhaps have hoped, but distributed among the following ASC units:

5 Company in Portsmouth (6th Reserve Park)

9 Company in Aldershot (1st Reserve Park)

12 Company in Portsmouth (5th Reserve Park)

20 Company in Aldershot (4th Reserve Park)

30 Company in Devonport (2nd Reserve Park)

34 Company in Devonport (3rd Reserve Park)

A Reserve Park's task was to carry two days' reserve of Iron Rations (1 lb preserved meat, 1 lb biscuits, 5/8 oz tea, 2 oz sugar and 2 cubes meat extract 1 oz in a tin) with groceries for the men and two days' oats for a Division as well as a day (of groceries and oats) for a Cavalry Division and units forming Army Troops. Groceries included tea, sugar, tinned milk, bacon, jam and cheese. These Parks acted as mobile reserves in the event of a breakdown in the normal replenishment chain.

The majority of Wagoners, the first civilians to serve their country overseas in 1914, remained serving with the units they joined in August 1914, invariably declining promotion in order to look after the pair of horses in their charge; some were transferred to the Infantry as casualty replacements, giving excellent service in another field. Three of their number were commissioned during the war and four won Military Medals, Wagoners T Bulmer, R Davison, D Sheldrick and W Thompson. Wagoner 1030 William Thompson transferred to the Infantry and won his Military Medal as a stretcher bearer. He died in December 1992, the last of 'the Chums' (as the Wagoners called themselves), shortly before his hundredth birthday.

*　　*　　*

Shortly after mobilization was ordered, on 10 August, instructions were received from the War Office that it had been decided that no Motor Volunteer Corps was to be raised for Home Defence. The Royal Automobile Club, Automobile Association and Motor Union had undertaken, however, to provide the services of private gentlemen, members of their Associations, who were keen to place themselves and their cars at the disposal of the War Office for permanent duty in Commands; when this patriotic offer was accepted, arrangements were made for the supply of cars to meet requirements in the Commands up to the authorized establishments. The gentlemen received the following emoluments whilst employed on military service:

pay at 6 shillings a day

accommodation for themselves and their cars

free issue of petrol

running expenses

Priority in everything was given to sending the Expeditionary Force to France, with initial movements involving the concentration of five Divisions and the Cavalry Division in the neighbourhood of Le Cateau. This deployment to locations, pre-planned with the French in 1911, was completed by 20 August. The Sixth Division followed on 8-9 September. In addition, Army and Line of Communication troops were sent. The initial ASC units totalled some 15,000 men in thirty-four HT and nineteen MT Companies, three Remount depots and 60 supply units of various sizes, with a total of 1,200 MT vehicles of all types, of which only eighty were army owned. In detail these units were:

Horse Transport:
Headquarters Cavalry Divisional ASC
lst-6th Divisional Trains (see Annex R)
Army Troops Train (26 HT Company)
lst-6th Reserve Parks (9, 30, 34, 20, 12 and 5 HT Companies)
Advanced Horse Transport Depot (14 HT Company)
Base Horse Transport Depot (10 HT Company)

Mechanical Transport:
lst-6th Divisional Supply Columns (59, 61, 63, 65, 48, 50 MT Companies)
lst-6th Divisional Ammunition Parks (60, 62, 64, 47, 49, 51 MT Companies)
Cavalry Supply Column (57 and 58 MT Companies)
Cavalry Ammunition Park (45 MT Company)
5th Cavalry Brigade Supply Column (46 MT Company)
5th Cavalry Brigade Ammunition Park (56 MT Company)
Army Troops Supply Column (55 MT Company)
Advanced Mechanical Transport Depot (54 MT Company)
Base Mechanical Transport Depot (53 MT Company)

Supply:
lst-6th Field Bakeries
lst-6th Field Butcheries
lst-8th Railway Supply Detachments
1st- 8th Bakery Sections
lst-30th Depot Units of Supply
Central Requisition Office
Branch Requisition Office

Remounts:
Nos. 1 and 2 Advanced Remount Depots
Base Remount Depot

In addition to the above, the ASC provided all transport personnel for Field Ambulances and hospitals as well as for headquarters of formations, not forgetting the clerical members of staff headquarters.

*   *   *

The standard horse-drawn vehicle was the 30 cwt GS Mark X wagon (with or without brass hub caps), drawn by a pair of heavy draught-horses, sometimes by mules. Many of these GS wagons were built by the railway companies. There were also limbered GS wagons, ambulance wagons, Maltese carts, mess carts and water carts. A GS wagon could carry any of the following loads:

400 blankets	350 RE spades
300 felling axes	28 circular tents (single)
600 hand axes	20 circular tents (double)
780 bill hooks	4 hospital marquees
200 camp kettles	1,800 picketing ropes
600 picketing pegs	40-45 boxes small arms ammunition
240 large horse rings	600 ground sheets (in cases)
260 small horse rings	900 ground sheets (loose)
640 GS shovels	8 Soyer stoves

but any of the above needed to be reduced by one sixth for distances over 15 miles.

The Mark X GS wagon had been introduced in 1905 in an effort to get a serviceable vehicle at a cheaper cost than the Mark IX – it embodied all the principles of construction of previous marks but differed slightly in appearance. It cost £61, in contrast to the Mark IX which had cost £72 and the Marks VI to VIII which had cost £95. In comparison with the Mark IX, the Mark X was shorter, had stronger sides and a square front, and a locker with two lids. The seat was supported on the sides over the locker; no straps were provided for fixing the seat springs and the back board was secured by a chain fixed to the outside of the body. Its length was 23 feet (with pole) or 13 feet 6 inches (without pole); the height was 7 feet (with seat) or 4 feet 10 inches (without seat), width 6 feet 2½ inches, track 5 foot 2 inches, weight some 15 cwt and it had a turning circle of 34 feet.

*   *   *

The Expeditionary Force embarkation was delayed until 9 August, with the advance parties going on the 7th, including Major H O Knox, in command of the Supply Detachment for the first overseas base, who is credited with being the first Expeditionary Force member to land on the Continent, closely followed by Captain G E Terry (who had distinguished himself in 1902 by being the first ASC officer to be a Gold Medallist in the Royal United Service Institution prize essay competition). Embarkation for infantry units was largely achieved by train, with whole units completing a train load, via Southampton. Movement for ASC units was necessarily more complicated:

Avonmouth was used for MT and petrol

Newhaven for stores and supplies

Liverpool for frozen meat and MT, and

Southampton for HT units

Ports of disembarkation in France were Le Havre, Rouen and Boulogne, where Base Depots were opened in August 1914.

*   *   *

Some details of three Motor Ambulance Convoys (MACs) might well be of interest, illustrating as they do the sort of life and times of that type of unit, indeed of any unit mobilizing and moving to France. For the sake of continuity of interest, the accounts continue into 1915.

418 COMPANY (NO 1 MOTOR AMBULANCE CONVOY)

On 2 September 1914 the Wolseley Company had orders on hand for a number of 24-30 hp 6 cylinder ambulances. On twenty-four hours' notice, twenty-five of these were completed and fitted with their ambulance bodies. Their London manager undertook to supply the necessary drivers, men used to the Wolseley car and able to speak French. Volunteers were called for from the Hire Department of the Wolseley Company in London, from the Royal Automobile Club and the National Society of Chauffeurs. Over fifty men responded to the call.

These were gathered at the London depot of the firm on the morning of 3 September, then taken to the Central London Recruiting Office, medically examined and, with two exceptions, were enlisted into the ASC. They bore the classification 'SE' and were not given regimental numbers until some nine months later. These preliminaries were completed about two o'clock in the afternoon. The men were then marched to Paddington Station and entrained for Avonmouth, where they duly arrived the same evening.

At first the party was refused admission to the ASC Depot as no one seemed to quite know who or what they were, but eventually they were admitted, only later in the evening to be turned adrift. Through the good offices of a padre, they found lodgings in a Mission Church for the night. Next morning, the men again collected at the Depot where an officer had in the meantime arrived who knew about them. In the course of the morning a scanty amount of kit and equipment was issued.

On the afternoon of 4 September the ambulances began to arrive at Avonmouth by road from Birmingham, the journey down constituting the test run. As the cars came in, drivers were allotted to each one. The last of the twenty-five arrived late on the evening of the 5th. As quickly as possible, the ambulances were loaded on the SS *Lord Tredegar*. Sunday 6 September was spent by the men in altering their clothes so that they would fit. Twenty-two of the drivers were withdrawn from the convoy and allotted to various staff cars which were shipped that night, leaving thirty-two for the twenty-five ambulances. No officer accompanied the convoy and no NCOs had been appointed, so the men elected two of their party, Privates Edwards and Clunes, to fill the posts of responsibility, which they continued to do for quite a while.

Field Marshal Lord Roberts died in France during a visit on 14 November 1914 and his body was conveyed to Boulogne in one of 418 Company ambulances, WD No A658. From 15 October a number of ambulance cars, about thirty in all of various makes, were received by the company and the unit became officially known as No. 1 Motor Ambulance Convoy on that date.

Several other points recorded in the unit history may also be of interest.

- In April 1915 a number of barges were fitted up for ambulance work, conveying the more serious cases by canal to St Omer and Calais. No. 1 Motor Ambulance Convoy cleared and loaded these in addition to their ordinary hospital and ambulance train work.

- In June 1915 a floating stretcher was designed, made and fitted in the unit workshop, to carry a water bed (under authority of the DGMS) for the conveyance of a Royal Flying Corps Officer (Lieutenant W Marburg of Philadelphia) from the Officers' Hospital at St Omer to Boulogne. The stretcher was supported by a system of leather slings and tension springs to avoid any violent movement or vibration of the stretcher during the road journey.

419 COMPANY (NO 2 MOTOR AMBULANCE CONVOY)

This unit was formed in Paris in October 1914 by the Joint War Committee of the British Red Cross Society and the Order of St John of Jerusalem. A number of private cars had been secured by these organizations and ambulance bodies were substituted for the original ones. Drivers were in many cases their first owners; others were voluntary drivers, the remainder being men paid by the British Red Cross Society. A large number of these ambulances left Paris on 8 October 1914 for Abbeville, where they formed the 2nd and 4th Motor Ambulance Convoys.

The average daily distance run by the vehicles of the Convoy in March 1915 was 362 miles, a remarkable total considering the roads used and their worsening state. The original vehicles, of many types and makes, were eventually replaced by fifty Buick ambulances from the British Red Cross Society, to which organization they had been given by various donors, who varied from individuals to local authorities, from commercial firms to foreign places. A list of donated ambulances in 419 Company can be seen as part of Annex J. These ambulances, as with all vehicles donated or loaned for use in the field, were inspected before they were accepted – all vehicles had to be in good order.

As an example of public generosity in the provision of support to the army, the Du Cros family could perhaps be mentioned. Mr Arthur du Cros MP, a member of the Royal Automobile Club, suggested to the War Office soon after the outbreak of war that he and his friends should provide, equip and maintain an ambulance unit for the Expeditionary Force. The offer was immediately accepted and the column left England in mid-October 1914 with a total of 59 vehicles (41 ambulances, 2 workshop lorries, 3 stores lorries, 3 cars and 10 motor cycles), 5 officers (including Captain George du Cros and Lieutenant W du Cros, sons of the MP), 8 NCOs and 136 men, all of whom had been recruited by Mr du Cros and enlisted in the ASC. Until the arrival of this unit in France, all ambulances had been horse-drawn.

421 COMPANY (4 MOTOR AMBULANCE CONVOY)

During the Hill 60 offensive in 1915 the Distinguished Conduct Medal was won on 17 April by Driver Hook, whose ambulance was practically buried in a shell-hole from which it could not be moved. There were seven sitting cases on board. Six who were able to walk were escorted into Ypres and the seventh, unable to move, was carried by Driver Hook under shell-fire into the town.

On 24 April, when the Second Battle of Ypres was being fought, six of the ambulances were sent to Zonnebeke School, which had to be evacuated on account of the shelling, to convey stretcher bearers to Vlamertinghe. On the way back a high-explosive shell hit an ammunition wagon in front of the ambulances, killing all six horses and wounding all the occupants. Corporal Malone stopped his ambulance and dressed the wounded, whom he took to Vlamertinghe. For this he was awarded the Russian Cross of St George (Third Class).

The Third Battle of Ypres started on 31 July and, for the first seventy-two hours, the ambulances were running continuously from Sanctuary Wood and an Advanced Dressing Station about a hundred yards from German lines to the Asylum, and from there to the College in Poperinghe. On one of the nights thirty ambulances were taken up to Sanctuary Wood to evacuate over 1,000 cases lying in the wood, who could only be moved in the hours of darkness. The Germans started to advance up the slope on each side of the road and it became necessary for the ambulances to be hurriedly withdrawn. On starting up, the fifth ambulance in the column had a Sankey wheel destroyed by a shell and, so as not to hold up the others, the driver skilfully moved his ambulance on the brake drum to the Menin Road, where he fitted the spare wheel and carried on doing his duty.

*   *   *

The following MT and administrative support was provided at the front and at Bases by the ASC to British Red Cross Society ambulances, which worked directly under the orders of the Royal Army Medical Corps:

the supply of all spare parts and accessories

the supply of petrol, tyres and lubricants

the provision of rations and accommodation for chauffeurs

running repairs (except for ambulances at Boulogne, where repairs were undertaken by the British Red Cross Society)

garaging for vehicles (Boulogne only)

*   *   *

One of the lesser-known developments during the war concerned labour, a problem area which had always been unrecognized or evaded on peacetime manoeuvres. The move of the British Expeditionary Force through British and French ports and the resultant storage and movement of stocks on the Continent meant that separate military labour units were needed and these were formed by the employing Corps that initially needed them, the ASC. An Army Order of 4 August 1914 authorized ASC Labour Companies of 536 all ranks, consisting of five sections under a subaltern. A number of Foremen and Gangers were specially enlisted in August, September and October to be Sergeants (36) and

Corporals (60) in these new Labour Companies, and they were paid ordinary ASC rates of pay, with Corps pay if issuable. The first company arrived at Le Havre on 26 August. More followed in due course, along with labour units for the Royal Engineers, Army Ordnance Corps/Army Ordnance Department, railways and the Directorate of Works, mainly men from Africa and China. Infantry Labour Battalions were sent in 1915 to replace French Territorials and Belgian civilians who had been employed on road maintenance.

Naval transport officers at the base ports, who could brook no delay in ship turnaround, had a particular problem in guaranteeing the availability of labour for their purposes. To meet this difficulty, two ASC (Naval Labour) Companies were formed, with stevedores and men accustomed to the work of loading and unloading ships, but, as these two companies were under the control of local ASC officers, that alone did not solve the problem. It was, therefore, decided to transfer in February 1917 the OC concerned, Major J F Cable, to the Royal Marines along with his two labour companies, thus forming the Royal Marine Labour Corps.

Even the railway world had its own dedicated labour from January 1915. Captain A H Hartshorn reported to the ASC Depot in Aldershot on 6 January as the OC, and the first Railway Labour Company ASC, consisting of three officers and 210 Other Ranks, left for Le Havre on 9 January. One section of an NCO and twenty-five men remained in Le Havre and the remainder moved on to St Omer, with further sections of 1 + 25 being sent to Bailleul, Steenwerck, Caestre and Strazeele.

By August 1915 the unit had grown to a strength of four officers and 505 men; and still the work level increased, so two Railway Labour Companies were formed, No. 1 and No. 2, in October 1915. On 29 March 1916, however, the two companies came under command of the newly-promoted Major Hartshorn, renumbered as 33 and 34 Railway Labour Companies. (See Annex K for a list of ASC Labour Companies.)

*   *   *

From their initial contact with the German Army near Mons on 23 August the Expeditionary Force was hard pressed. In the face of a powerful and aggressive enemy, a withdrawal was effected so that British forces could stay in touch with their French allies and avoid an outflanking movement. The retreat from Mons continued over 250 miles to the gates of Paris, over roads congested with refugees, a nightmare for any supporting Service. The Base Supply Depots had to be hurriedly evacuated and reopened at St Nazaire and Nantes for a few weeks before the defeat of the Germans at the Battle of the Marne in September enabled a return to more northerly positions. New Supply Depots were opened at Calais, Cherbourg, Dieppe, St Valèry-sur-Somme and Marseilles. Bakeries, petrol depots, cold stores, mineral-water factories, storage depots and sheep and goat farms were also opened, which gradually developed into large installations.

During the retreat the Corps had been able to keep the army supplied, despite the difficulties. Many ASC units had a variety of strange adventures. They were frequently in close contact with the enemy, having to defend their own positions and glean news of the tactical situation from any source available, information which was usually conflicting. It was not uncommon for contact to be lost with units being supported, so ASC supply points issued food and ammunition at the road side on an opportunity basis to any grateful units which had lost contact with their own ASC support or their own formations. Convoys were attacked by Uhlan cavalry, not without loss, however. A number of casualties, including some sixty prisoners-of-war, were incurred and part of the 4th Divisional Ammunition Park were captured by German cavalry. This latter incident led to the creation of an ASC Prisoner of War Fund.

*　　*　　*

Private John Jackson (see also Chapter 1) had by now been promoted to Sergeant and found himself on the Western Front in August, just after the German Army made contact with the British Expeditionary Force at Mons.

"Well, I joined the Column, took over my section No. 3 and off we went as 4th Division Ammunition Column. We were about six miles from Mons when we met the troops falling back, or what was left of them, but it was orderly and they were knocking hell out of Jerry. We kept them supplied with ammo. It was all working out well till we got to Ermanville, about 20 miles from Paris. We stayed a night there and were ordered to evacuate the place as regiments of Uhlans had broken through near us.

"Off we went and had got about six miles from Ermanville when an Artillery Major came up and ordered our Captain to return as his guns were still in action. He persuaded our Captain to return and we did. The last lorry on No. 2 section, driven by Private White, was having engine trouble and there was a gap of about 100 ft between us and the rest of the column. As the head of the column entered Ermanville, firing broke out. During our absence, the Uhlans had occupied the place. Our officers in a car in front were shot or captured as were the motor-cycle despatch riders and drivers. There was a bend in the road which prevented the Uhlans from seeing us. I signalled my section to stop; Pte White kept on until he was fired on, then tried to reverse, got right across the road, then jumped into a ditch. The remainder of us turned and by the time we had started the Cavalry (Uhlans) were running with us poking at us with their lances. We were able to knock a tidy few out and they stopped and fired a few parting shots.

"We had gone about three miles, then we were stopped by an abandoned French train across the road. Sergt Major Rigby had taken charge of us and lined us up on the embankment whilst the carriages were uncoupled and pulled away. Suddenly down the road a vehicle came tearing. We opened fire until ordered to cease fire. It was Pte White. He had jumped into the ditch, crawled through the mud and slime and pursued by an Uhlan poking with his lance; finally got back to his lorry, found the engine still running and started after us, followed by a few parting shots, to be met by a warm welcome from us. When he left us his hair was a light brown; when he rejoined it was white, and ever after he was known as 'Snowy White'."

*　　*　　*

Sergeant E C H Rowland of the 5th Divisional Train, responsible with his section for delivering rations and ammunition, records in his dairy that he landed at Le

Havre on 13 August 1914. He was in the Mons area when German forces came upon the British and recorded the following:

"**23 August:** Left Dour (Belgique) at a minutes notices with all troops & HQ staff. . . . as the Germans were expected there any minute – people so kind to us here – we felt it very much to leave them to the mercy of the Germans – retreated many miles to Velandes . . . Artillery would not take food as they were off to take up position & to get into action – heard here we were surrounded by German cavalry & orders were given to set fire to the whole convoy & supply column consisting of about 50 motor lorries loaded with supplies – this was to prevent them getting into the hands of the Germans – however, we managed to get away safely – had a rotten fright though.

"**26 August:** Came through Le Cateau & served out rations to all units attached to the Train, giving them a good whack, & plenty over & tobacco. Settled down for the night two miles the other side of Le Cateau & went to bed at 10 pm, turned out again at 2 am and moved off at 2.30 am – reported Germans close at hand (wind up again) went like hell for miles, reaching St Quentin at 4 pm chased by German cavalry for miles who are very anxious to get hold of us & Train & supplies . . . Moved off from St Quentin . . . which we reached at 6 pm. As the convoy comes in a Sergeant of Infantry comes in absolutely exhausted and reports to the Colonel that a party of German cavalry or scouts are just behind us & that he has been chased for some miles by them. We. . . . line up in the village square, fall in with rifles and are told off to defend the town. We are determined to make a show if possible – we are about 500 strong & hope if possible to wipe this party of German cavalry right out or capture them, however, the night draws wearily on & they do not attack us. We are at our posts all night.

"**27 August:** We move off . . . at 7 pm & arrive at Ham at midday, resting for a couple of hours. We meet hundreds of stragglers all along the road who have been cut off from their Regiments & hear awful news of British disasters & casualties – Artillery cut up – guns taken – Infantry cut up . . . refugees leaving their homes – all villages & towns along the way neglected – sorrowing sight to witness – poor people & little children tramping away to God knows where in all weathers to escape the Germans who are approaching fast – women & children reported to have been massacred . . . The people do not know what to do – crying piteously everywhere. They expected much from us & we have done nothing for them . . . now we are forced to leave them at the mercy of the Germans – it's all horrible."

* * *

The 5th Division Supply Column (48 MT Company) had experiences which were probably typical of most units in the first few months of the war. The following extracts from their war diary give a taste of those times, particularly of the retreat from Mons:

"**24 August:** Le Cateau. Went round bivouacs at night. Started at 8 pm and had great difficulty in getting along owing to the crowd of troops and in finding the bivouacs, and lorries had to go down lanes which were scattered about. I issued to several units but had to stop at 4 am as troops were marching and wanted the roads clear . . . four lorries got into ditches but were pulled out. One Maudslay seized up and as there was no time to tow it away it was lost.

"**26 August:** Peronne. Loaded enough supplies to complete a full day's issue for the 5th Division and at 6 pm left for St Quentin and arrived there at 8 pm. It was very wet and the roads were in a bad condition. On arrival at St Quentin it was suggested that the Column should go north and dump supplies for units to pick up but it was eventually decided to park Column in the town . . . issues being made to any units that arrived. After a very wet night, Column was ordered to leave Beaumont at once as a general retreat had commenced . . . One lorry, an Albion from Sutton & Co, was lost on the road amongst the crowds of transport and three old lorries which could not be got along as the Column was loaded were also left and put out of action. Supplies were handed over to any troops as they were all badly in need of them.

"**27 August:** Left St Quentin at 7 am but was not allowed to unload outside the town as originally ordered as the Germans were pressing us. Went on to Olloyerre and transferred to Supply Sections on the road where the whole 2nd Army Corps passed during the day . . . One Maudslay lorry had carburettor trouble and was left behind for repair train to tow. Captain Haylor, passing it later on, ordered it to be destroyed owing to the approach of the Germans.

"**1 September:** Plessis-Belleville. German raiding party reported to be in the district and Column passed a lot of English cavalry and French troops and were delayed by barricades.

"**25 December:** Bailleul. Princess Mary's gifts were received at 7 am and sent out straight to refilling points and issued at once. All refilling was commenced at 7 am and so work was finished at 12 noon. Princess Mary's gifts were issued to the men, after this also cards from the King and Queen. In the evening there was a smoking concert for the Column, which was a great success. Heavy frost." Refilling work started as normal the next day.

*   *   *

Captain H N G Watson, Adjutant of the Cavalry Division Train, like many people, had a close shave or two in the retreat from Mons. He records in his diary on 25 August: "Next we pushed on through the village of Haussey. Shortly afterwards we (a horse transport column) were overtaken by one of the Divisional Staff in a staff car . . . I got into the seat beside the driver and off we set. We had not gone very far when I heard, above the noise of the engine, a sound which kept on repeating, but one that I could not place. I asked the driver what the sound was. He replied that it was stones we were throwing up against the mudguards. Still I was not satisfied and I told the driver to stop. As we slowed down I heard a peculiar sound overhead and on looking up I saw a German Taube (aircraft) above us with its pilot firing down at us with his rifle. I ordered the driver to drive on and to pull up under the cover of the first wall that we came across. We had an exciting run down a straight French road with the German firing down at us until we reached a protective wall. Here we stopped and the German went off. On examining the car I found that . . . . we had been hit three times, once in the running board, once in the dash and once through a wing. As far as I can ascertain this was the first occasion in the war of anyone being attacked from the air."

On 30 August he and his column stopped at Elincourt near Compiègne for watering and feeding. "After 'stables' had taken place, the men were allowed to swim in the local river, which provided the first opportunity for a week to take their uniforms off. Hardly had they begun to bathe when an excited staff officer arrived, forcibly expressing his surprise that the column was there; he issued orders that they were to be the other side of the river by 4 pm, as the bridge crossing was to be blown up at that time. It was then 3 o'clock, the men were naked in the river, the horses were grazing and the harnesses were all in pieces – and there was still an hour's march to the bridge. Somehow they achieved the impossible and the column crossed the bridge moments before the Sapper officer there blew it. Even as he did so German troops were crossing the bridge and were killed in the explosion."

* * *

Meanwhile, on the Western Front, units were making the best of the unsociable conditions and bad weather by arranging, when possible, Smoking Concerts. The following report on a smoking concert was published in an *ASC Journal* of the day:

"Notwithstanding the arduous duties imposed on the MT Section of the ASC, it is gratifying to learn that they are in no wise down-hearted, a fact that was evidenced very clearly on Saturday evening last, 9th October, at one of their advanced depots (1st and 2nd Advanced MT Depot) somewhere in France, when the Officers, Warrant Officers, NCOs and men of the 54th and 365th MT Companies gave a most successful concert in the Companies' Coliseum.

This is a real portable theatre, with elaborate decorations and scenic effects which are the result of the spare-time efforts of Corporal John and Private Marshall who is known amongst showmen as "Bob the Painter" and who for the past twelve months has held a retainer for Mr Jack Headley of Franco-British Exhibition fame. It is not too much to say that the artists acquitted themselves in a manner that would have done credit to the "paid" fraternity and Mechanical Sergeant Major Rennie who stage managed the concert is to be congratulated on the huge success he made of it. The programme consisted of fourteen items and it is difficult to pick out any one for special mention, but the most outstanding features in a specially strong programme were to be found in Private Nutter, a well-known manufacturer from Lancashire, who is a fine tenor vocalist and who gave a beautiful rendering of the "Toilers" and "By the Fountain." Lieutenant Marriott gave an exceedingly pleasing turn on the violin. Lance Corporal Carter, MFP, a baritone, received a great ovation. Sapper Broadhurst RE, who in private life is Mr Jack Hurst of "Black Cat" cigarette and pantomime fame, completely brought the house down with his antics as "The Eccentric Cat." Private Phillis, Saddler Walters and Company Sergeant Major Gale as comedians had in turn, the house rocking with laughter.

At the close of the entertainment, Sergeant Major Rennie put up for auction three programmes specially designed and painted by Private R Marshall and these after much spirited bidding realized the very respectable sum of 125 francs, which is being sent to the ASC Central Comforts Fund. After the "King" had been sung, all retired to their various abodes feeling that it is good to forget work and the horrors of war, if only for a short time."

It is of interest that the words of one of the most famous songs to come out of the 1914-18 war, 'Mademoiselle from Armentières', were written by an ASC man, 27-year-old Sergeant Edward ('Red') Rowland of Avenue Road, Belmont in Surrey. He was a larger than life character who involved himself with the stage before the war and extended this in France to helping entertain the men. A catchy song was needed for a troop concert in March 1915 and Sergeant Rowland scribbled the words on the back of an envelope in an Armentières café, the Café de la Paix in the rue de la Gare; the song was set to music by a Canadian friend, Lieutenant Gitz-Rice. Initially there were only four verses, but the song's popularity led to a demand for more and ultimately some 150 verses were written. The song was inspired by the 18-year-old Mme Marie Lecocq, already a widow, who slapped the face of an officer who was making improper advances in the café. She was in fact a very straight-laced person who would stand no nonsense from the troops. After the war Mr Rowland was well-known in Sutton, Surrey as the manager of the Gaumont County Cinema and a successful fund-raiser for charity. He is remembered today by a plaque erected by the local authorities on the site of the old cinema in the centre of Sutton. His song, too, is still remembered.

*   *   *

Early lessons were learnt in the field of mobility. The great majority of field ambulances were horse-drawn, motorized ambulances then being not widely available. The speed of the withdrawal from Mons affected the horses badly. They got little rest and inadequate food and shelter, which severely reduced their efficiency. Perhaps an influential factor in the subsequent use of motorized ambulances (with pneumatic tyres) was the comment received by the Quartermaster General's department that wounded officers suffered from the jolting of horse transport ambulances.

Many workshop trailers were towed by steam tractors, which were so slow that they proved unable to keep up with the retreating troops, so had to be left behind, immobilized by breaking radiators and cylinder blocks with sledge-hammers or picks. Eventually, they were recovered, repaired and taken back into use on the retreat of the German Army in September, the Germans having been unable to operate them.

*   *   *

When travelling in convoy, vehicles were divided into sections of six, with intervals of 25 yards between sections (platoons or troops nowadays). In order to indicate this clearly, every sixth vehicle had to carry an 18-inch diameter detachable red disc suspended from the left-hand side of the tailboard, also a 9-inch diameter red disc suspended from the radiator cap or other suitable part on the front of the vehicle. The rear vehicle of each convoy had to carry a double red disc suspended from the left-hand side of the tailboard. Traffic posts and military policemen had the duty to ensure that proper convoy intervals were maintained, easy enough in areas well to the rear but far from easy for vehicles at risk from shellfire or aerial attack. The distances between vehicles in convoy were laid down, varying with the type of vehicle:

light tractors:	5 yards
water tanks:	5 yards
travelling vans:	5 yards
lorries:	6 yards
4 ton trucks:	6 yards
5 ton platform trucks:	6 yards
light tractors with other vehicles:	16 yards

The Divisional Train of the 'Old Armies' was expected to take up 1,755 yards on the march, while, in the 'New Armies' 2,260 yards was the planning figure.
The speeds of vehicles were laid down by GHQ:

traction engines:	3 mph
light tractors:	4 mph
IC tractor:	5 mph
steam lorries:	5 mph
IC lorries:	7-10 mph
	but 6 mph in built-up areas
motor omnibus:	8-12 mph
trucks, water tanks and travelling vans:	15-20 mph
cars/ambulances:	20 mph

Empty vehicles had to give way to loaded convoys. After dusk all vehicles had to carry lighted lamps, with one light placed at the extreme left of the vehicle to indicate its position on right-hand drive roads. Motor cyclists were forbidden to carry passengers and MT drivers forbidden to use petrol for improper purposes (eg fires for cooking). Instructions were issued concerning road discipline:

All traffic must keep to the right of the road

Vehicles passing Infantry to do so at a slow pace to avoid covering the troops in dust or mud

If the road is narrow, vehicles to stop until Infantry have passed

Empty vehicles must give way to loaded convoys

When halted vehicles should pull into the side of the road

Rules may be rules but, alas, not everyone obeyed them. There was inevitably a three-way conflict between road users, foot soldiers, horse transport and motor transport, that caused irritation, a conflict that could never be regulated to everybody's satisfaction. Among the letters home of Captain A Gibbs MC, an Eton-educated Welsh Guardsman, in the Imperial War Museum is one dated 1 August 1916 in which he vents his fury at the ASC:

"The day before yesterday we marched along a main road, with lots of motor traffic. It was one of those long, straight roads with very chalky dust on it. . . . Several absolute beasts of ASC officers came tearing along in their motors and raising an enormous cloud of dust. I spent a lot of my time stopping them and cursing them like anything. I told them that we had already marched 16 miles, and had another 10 to do, and if they couldn't use a little more consideration, they were hardly fit to be called officers, and certainly not gentlemen. I really was angry. One hates the ASC at nearly all times, the more especially when one is slogging along a dusty road, and they pass in rather a nice Vauxhall or Sunbeam."

*   *   *

General Routine Orders laid down, for reasons of spares provision and work loading, which vehicles requiring repair not possible in the unit's own work-shop should go to one of the three ASC Repair Shops:

to the 1st Repair Shop in Paris:

(lorries) Commer, Halley, Hallford, Napier, Swiss Berna, Wolseley and all lorries of French make.

(cars and ambulances) Austin, Napier, Siddeley-Deasy, Talbot and all cars of French make.

to the 2nd Repair Shop in Rouen:

(lorries) AEC, Belsize, Daimler, Dennis, Karrier, LGOC, Maudslay, Straker Squire, steam lorries, steam tractors and other makes of lorry not allocated to Paris.

(cars and ambulances) Studebaker, Singer and all other makes of car not going to the 1st or 3rd Repair Shop.

to the 3rd Repair Shop in St Omer:

(lorries) Albion, Autocar, British Berna, Foster Daimler tractors, FWD, Garford, Holt caterpillars, Kelly, Leyland, motor buses, Locomobile, Packard, Pagefield, Peerless, Pierce-Arrow, Saurer, Seabrook, Thornycroft and White.

(cars and ambulances) Buick, Cadillac, Daimler, Ford, Rolls-Royce, Sunbeam, Vauxhall and Wolseley.

As ever, there were exceptions and variations: motor buses were sent to the 2nd Repair Shop in Rouen; Daimler cars were sent to Paris; motor cycles from the 3rd, 4th and 5th Armies, 4th and 5th Cavalry Divisions and Line of Communication units, as well as all Clyno sidecar combinations, were sent to Rouen; and motor cycles, including those with sidecars (except Clyno combinations) from the 1st and 2nd Armies, 1st, 2nd and 3rd Cavalry Divisions and GHQ Troops were sent to St Omer. Cars sent for repair to ASC Base repair workshops were considered as having been returned to store and were not necessarily re-issued to the unit concerned.

Because of the sense of ownership by some staff officers, GHQ had to order that cars were not to be transferred with an officer when he was posted to another staff appointment, without the previous sanction of the Quartermaster General.

In view of the wear and tear of vehicles on the Western Front, the attention of unit commanders was drawn to the care and working of their mechanical transport vehicles:

"Owing to the difficulties in procuring new vehicles from England for the replacement of casualties and in obtaining spare parts for the maintenance of such as are now in France, there is urgent necessity for the most careful supervision of the working of the mechanical transport.

It is essential that loads should be reduced on bad roads, and that the MT personnel should, wherever possible, be given time each day to clean and inspect their vehicles and to carry out any adjustments which may be found necessary.

The workshop personnel should not be employed on other duties to the detriment of their proper functions as the process of overhauling and adjusting the vehicles of a unit must be continuous in order to maintain the unit in a mobile and efficient condition.

'Spare' vehicles are included in war establishment in order that they may be available to relieve vehicles for periodical overhaul or workshop attention and thus allow the carrying capacity of a unit to be maintained at the authorized strength while some of the vehicles are being examined and repaired.

If 'spare' vehicles are employed to increase the carrying capacity of a unit, the object of their provision is frustrated and the breakdown of the unit will be the natural consequence."

Even the way vehicles were started by towing drew official comment:

"The number of breakages of rear axle driving shafts has recently been high, more especially in the case of Locomobile and Maudslay lorries. In a number of cases the cause has been traced to the fact that the breakage occurred whilst the lorry was being towed in order to start the engine during which the first or second speed had been engaged.

"The practice of starting engines by means of towing with either the first or second speed engaged must cease, as it causes undue and excessive strains on the transmission. When it is necessary to tow a lorry in order to start the engine, only the third or top speed in a four speed box, and the top speed only in a three speed box, should be engaged.

"Officers Commanding units will take the necessary steps at once to ensure that the foregoing order is communicated, and made clear to all ranks under their command, and will bring to notice any case of disobedience whether damage has been actually caused or not."

*   *   *

Although each ASC company had its own number within the Corps order of battle, OCs were instructed, through General Routine Orders of November 1914, not to use those 'peace designations' (although many were formed after war was declared) in official correspondence, indents or returns, as it "makes it difficult to trace companies when the war organization is not shown". For example, 7 Company ASC was No. 3 Company of the 1st Division, 166 Company was No. 19 Reserve Park for GHQ Troops and 355 Company was No. 9 Motor Ambulance Convoy. When every Divisional Train had four companies (ie initially with Brigade titles but subsequently numbered as No. 1

(HQ), 2, 3 and 4) and other companies elsewhere were allocated the same numbers one has to beware. Fortunately, the Divisional Train companies adopted the ASC-wide numbering system later in 1914, so this identification problem eased within Divisions, but it continues with many other units. A careful look at Annex Q will illustrate this point.

A typical routine day in a Divisional Train Horse Transport Company was:

5.00 am:	reveille
5.30 to 7.00 am:	water and feed horses
Thereafter:	refilling at Replenishment Parks, water and feed horses, men's dinner
	Noon at units
	HQ reloading at railhead
2.00 pm or as soon there-after as Train is in position:	to Replenishment Parks
4.30 to 6.00 pm:	dump supplies
5.00 to 6.30 pm:	back to wagon lines water , feed and groom horses men's tea (a hot evening meal with meat or bacon)
9.00 pm:	lights out

*   *   *

At a later stage in 1916 OCs of units which were in possession of American lorries were instructed to ensure that their "drivers did not keep their feet on the clutch more than is absolutely necessary for the operation of the clutch, such as in changing gear or in traffic checks", as was the custom with Subsidy and LGOC lorries which had strong clutch springs. American lorries were so designed that the weight of a foot on the clutch pedal would be sufficient to effect a gear change, but the clutch pedal's constant depression on British vehicles would burn out the clutch.

Clear instructions were issued for the marking of motor cars and lorries, all of which had to have their official registration number painted on the bonnet and also on the back of the vehicle. "This number is to be painted on both sides of the bonnet in white paint, and in a conspicuous position at the back where it is not likely to be obscured by the tyres, tarpaulins or other obstructions. The size of the figures in all cases is to be:

For motor cars:	4 inches high, 1/2 inch wide
For motor lorries:	6 inches high, 5/8 inch wide

A broad arrow is to be placed on top or on the side of the numbers, according to the shape of the bonnet, as may be found most convenient. No numbers or letters are to be painted on the bonnet or on the backs of the vehicles except the official registration number." When a vehicle was sent to a Heavy Repair Shop, the bonnet cover had to accompany it as part of its equipment.

The official registration number included the prefix 'M' in the case of motor cars, 'A' in the case of motor ambulances, and 'RA', 'RC', 'RL' in the case of British Red Cross Society motor ambulances, motor cars and motor lorries respectively, working under the direct orders of the Army.

Lorries were provided with carriers for petrol and oil tins, but many cases occurred when petrol was put into tins which had previously been used for oil and water, causing considerable waste and inconvenience. All tins that used oil, paraffin and water had to be painted black, with a white 'O', 'P' or 'W' marked on both sides. The letters had to be sufficiently large to enable the markings to be distinguished even in a bad light. Tins used for petrol had to be left their original colour. Care had to be taken that the petrol carrier was not unduly close to the exhaust pipe or silencer so as to prevent any possibility of fire breaking out through petrol leaking from the tins onto the silencer.

* * *

To bring order to a system that had developed in a slightly haphazard way and which tended to overload the Advanced MT Depots, instructions were later issued (in 1916) for the consignment to one of two Base MT Depots of stores and spare parts that had to be evacuated by units as surplus to requirement:

No. 1 Base MT Depot, Rouen:

Unused spare parts for all other makes not mentioned below

Unserviceable and part-worn stores and spare parts, irrespective of the make

No 2 Base MT Depot, Calais: all unused parts for the following vehicles:

American lorries
American tractors
American motor cars and motor ambulances
Foster-Daimler tractors
Albion lorries
Leyland lorries
Thornycroft lorries
Rolls-Royce motor cars
Vauxhall motor cars
Sunbeam motor cars

* * *

By the middle of September 1914 the BEF was 240,000 strong, with an additional 25,000 men from the Indian Army who needed logistic support from the British, not to mention some 100,000 animals, all of which needed support from the ASC. It is perhaps of interest, but no importance, that rations were also issued for pigeons, canaries and white mice.

The 'Christmas Truce' of 1914 is an affair to which considerable media attention has been paid; ironically the distribution of the brass Princess Mary boxes to every man in uniform, including prisoners-of-war, gets little attention. The work of distributing them in UK and on the Western Front certainly created problems for the ASC. Aware that soldiers and sailors away from home, as well as nurses, prisoners-of-war, internees and next-of-kin of the fallen, needed a little extra in the way of home comforts at the festive season, HRH Princess Mary, daughter of King George V and Queen Mary, had launched an appeal in October 1914, The Princess Mary's Sailors and Soldiers Fund, inspired perhaps by Queen Victoria's gift of a box of chocolates to her soldiers during the Boer War in South Africa in 1900. The appeal resulted in the magnificent total of £162,591 12s 5d being raised. The contents were variously 'Woodbine Willies' or Players' cigarettes, sweets (acid drops) or chocolates, and for Indian troops spices and sugar candy. Added to the boxes were pipes, tinder lighters, writing cases, bullet pencil cases and Christmas/New Year cards. It is said that the difficulty of issuing every man or woman with a box led to them being delivered right through the war, in one case as late as April 1919.

$$* \qquad * \qquad *$$

A new form of military transport appeared on the scene at the start of the war, the London omnibus. Within 48 hours of the outbreak of war in August 1914 London buses were commandeered for the movement of troops within the UK. Single deckers were also requisitioned for the Admiralty medical service and others were later employed on London defence duties and air-raid services. The London General Omnibus Company was asked by the Admiralty in early September to supply seventy-five omnibuses with drivers and complete tool kits for Antwerp by the next morning, quite a tall order, even if contingency planning had taken place. The response was overwhelming, with hundreds of men offering their services. Many did not leave work until midnight, but reported to the Embankment at 8 am as instructed. They were disappointed that only a small proportion of volunteers could then be accepted. The drivers, to their complete surprise, were enlisted as Royal Marines and left the next day with the Royal Naval Division, via Dunkirk, to help secure the area of Boulogne, Calais, Dunkirk and Ostend. They still wore busmen's uniforms and the Daimlers of the Tramways (MET) Omnibus Company were still in their blue livery, carrying commercial advertisements. One bus still advertised the play "One Damn Thing After Another", words which seemed so apposite at the time, providing many a good laugh for men at the front; another publicized the play "England Expects." Hardly had the buses arrived in France than they were employed with armoured cars and cyclists in patrolling around Douai, Lille, Tournai and Ypres to clear the area of marauding Germans.

The Royal Naval Division had been abroad for only a few weeks when the War Office also asked for buses: 300 were required to provide the army's only dedicated means of troop movement (other than railway and Shanks's pony), although Lord Kitchener initially preferred the use of charabancs rather than omnibuses for Infantry. Men who had previously volunteered when the Admiralty needed omnibuses were told to go to the LGOC Headquarters in Grosvenor Road; from there, via the ASC recruiting offices in Great Scotland Yard, they were sent to the recently requisitioned Grove Park Hospital in south-east London, the ASC MT Depot. Many of the NCOs in the new units were immediately appointed from ex-Servicemen the LGOC liked to employ. Perhaps the use of omnibuses and taxis by the French in the retreat towards

Paris helped to persuade the War Office that the British too could keep up with their continental cousins.

Private Edward Darby of Kensington recalled: "Soon after our arrival [in Grove Park] we were given a medical, and those who passed were kitted out, and then each man received his regimental number, also his pay book, which included one day's pay . . . The next morning after breakfast we filled up with petrol and also took aboard some large drums of grey paint . . . we were a motley crowd: there were bus drivers, lorry drivers, cabbies and car drivers; there was even a tram driver, who had a hazy idea of driving – I know, for he acted as my mate".

The 300 vehicles in red and white livery provided were AEC 'B' type buses, which had entered service in 1910, built in Walthamstow. Seventy-five buses were allocated to each of four units, 1, 2, 3 and 4 Auxiliary Omnibus Companies (functional names for what in fact were 90, 91, 92 and 93 Companies ASC), which were raised at Grove Park. Perhaps surprisingly, buses only came from London. Other cities in UK with omnibus fleets did not contribute.

No 1 Auxiliary Bus Company left Grove Park on 17 October for Marlborough, via Reading, arriving at Avonmouth on 18 October with seventy-five buses, four motor cars and two lorries, one of which was a workshop lorry. The OC, Major S W Morrison, and the other officers were MT trained officers of the ASC, but they had no special knowledge of buses. After landing at Rouen on 23 October the company moved to Blangy, attached to the Second Army. They carried out their first details on 25 October, carrying 600 men of the Seaforth Highlanders, Royal Warwicks and Royal Dublins from St Venant to Houplines during the First Battle of Ypres. On 30 October two buses were lost at St Eloi through heavy shell-fire.

Meanwhile, No. 2 Auxiliary Bus Company, under a Captain Coulston, left Grove Park on 22 October. They spent the night at Hampton Court, driving on to Avonmouth the next day. Unfortunately, one bus "sustained a severe collision with a lamp standard and was wrecked" in Bristol. The company arrived over the period 27-29 October in Rouen and drove to Bailleul, attached to the First Army. Work started immediately. On 3 November 1,000 French infantry were transported to Elverdinghe and on 12 November 1,800 men of the French Chasseurs Alpins were carried. Conditions were testing. The war diary for 12 November reports that the "wind and rain were very violent, rendering the vehicles keeping on the pavé very difficult. Delays through vehicles being ditched . . . Roads terribly bad and encumbered by Cavalry and Artillery . . . Windows of certain vehicles (including OC's car) shattered by concussion of firing." The unit knew it was at war.

Soon after arrival in France the red and white livery was painted over, army registration numbers were stencilled on bonnets and, as troops kept breaking the glass with their packs, windows were removed; planks were often nailed across the gaping holes. For the crews, the buses were home: they had no billets so slept on board, storing their belongings in old petrol cans. They had no cooks either so they fended for themselves initially.

The *Daily Mail* of 5 December 1914 shows that the drivers really joined in the spirit of the war: in a letter home, one driver wrote, "There is a Cricklewood omnibus out here today on ASC work . . . the driver . . . spotted a couple of stragglers in a wood at the side of the road. He pulled up with a jerk . . . and yelled, "Give me that blooming rifle, Bill", grabbed the only rifle they got, and hopped off across the field after the two Germans, leaving his astonished mates rubbing their eyes and staring through the omnibus window after him. The two struggling "Boches" evidently thought this must be a madman charging across the field at full gallop straight for them, and they "Hands-upped" pretty quickly, and so our hero proceeded to prod them in the ribs with his gun . . . He got them back to the omnibus, and the ASC . . . tied their hands behind them and shoved them inside. Our omnibus driver first vigorously interrogated them. "Speak English?" said he. A shake of the head in reply. "Parley-voo German?" Another shake. "Don't know their own blooming language," he said disgustingly . . . "What's the German for bread, Bill?" "Don't know", said Bill, "Show 'im some; that's the best way." "You should have seen 'em wolf it," said Bill afterwards, "they weren't half hungry and wet, and all covered in mud."

Nos. 3 and 4 Auxiliary Omnibus Companies suffered different fates. No. 3, raised at Grove Park on 26 October 1914 with LGOC drivers, was re-tasked as a GHQ Ammunition Park. No. 4, raised at Grove Park on 28 October with specially enlisted men (but not LGOC drivers), suffered the indignity of having their buses converted into lorries. The unit's Headquarters and workshop then took on a separate role as No. 1 Mobile Repair Unit.

*　　*　　*

In October 1914 the War Office directed that the Territorial units of the ASC should be incorporated into the Regular Order of Battle, and that the term, 'Transport & Supply Column' should be replaced by 'Train'. At the same time, a Divisional Supply Column MT (an MT company) was attached to each Train in an Infantry Division.

*　　*　　*

There were a few changes in GHQ senior staff appointments in the British Expeditionary Force at the turn of the year: Brigadier General C W King, Director of Supplies, returned to England and was replaced by Brigadier General E E Carter in January 1915; and Brigadier General Gilpin was replaced by Brigadier General Boyce in November 1914, both new men staying until the end of the war. At the same time the War Office was about to appoint Major General Clayton as Director Supplies & Transport in GHQ, but when he was selected and promoted for the new post of Inspector General Line of Communication in January 1915 the opportunity of a single Head of Service was missed. (As a result of a reorganization at the end of 1916 initiated by Sir Eric Geddes, a civilian railway expert hired by Mr Lloyd-George, this post was abolished and Lieutenant General Clayton returned to the United Kingdom, where he retired in 1917. Geddes became the Director General of Transportation with the Honorary rank of Major General.)

*　　*　　*

In December 1914 a Caterpillar Section of the ASC was formed and was attached to 52 Company at Aldershot. It soon became a separate unit and in February 1916 was given the title of 'Tractor Depot ASC', moving to Avonmouth three months later. This was the parent unit of all the tracked vehicles of the ASC in the war. The first overseas draft, consisting of fourteen Other Ranks and three caterpillars, went to France in February 1915 to join a siege battery of the Royal Garrison Artillery.

*   *   *

To give some indication of the success of the ASC in the first few months of the war, the following letter was sent from Brigadier General S S Long, then Director of Supplies at the War Office, to Major General F C Clayton:

War Office
London SW
8 December 1914

My dear General

Lord Kitchener, on his return from seeing the King yesterday afternoon, sent for the Quarter Master General and told him that the greater part of the King's conversation on his return from the Front was devoted to praise of the ASC and their wonderful work in the Supply and Transport of the Army. His Majesty kept on referring to it the whole time of the conversation with the Secretary of State. Lord Kitchener told the Quarter Master General to let me know, and to write privately across to the Director of Supplies and the Director of Transport and to suggest that they should send a private line to Officers Commanding Trains etc etc, to say how much His Majesty has appreciated the work of the Corps, so that the men might know. He did not wish an actual order to be published on the subject.

Yours Ever,
(Sgd) S S Long

CHAPTER 3

1915: Increasing Responsibilities

The year 1915 was one of stalemate and the opening of new theatres of war. The war was developing from a head-on confrontation between the European super-powers to a world-wide involvement to escape the stalemate imposed by trench warfare and no means yet of breaking through. In February Britain became involved in Mesopotamia to help the hard-pressed Indian Army, and later that year in Gallipoli and Salonika.

Turkey, as an ally of Germany, became involved when the Turks attacked Russia in December 1914, sparred with British detachments in February for control of the Suez Canal and opposed naval attempts to force the Bosphorus and allied landings on the Gallipoli peninsula. Italy declared war on Turkey and Germany in August 1915 and the Allies landed in Salonika in October to support the Serbian Army.

Meanwhile, in Europe, the British, with Indian support, chalked up small successes with the capture of the village of Neuve Chapelle in March and the town of Loos in September, but failed in their attacks in May on Aubers Ridge and Festubert; a defensive success was achieved, however, during the Second Battle of Ypres, when the German attack on Ypres failed, even though the Germans used gas for the first time. The British Army in France and Flanders, though, was becoming stronger by the week: in May the first of Kitchener's New Armies left for France.

From an ASC point of view units settled into their job of supporting the British Expeditionary Force but, as the army expanded and more functions were allocated to the Corps, new types of company were formed and the ASC staff in formation headquarters started to get to grips with problems created by the increase in mechanization and the employment of a large amount of MT away from the home base; and, whether it was with the employment of women or the development of Expeditionary Force Canteens and other periphery activities, the ASC was experiencing across the board increased responsibilities in the support of the army.

*   *   *

Territorial Divisions had been embodied in 1914 (91% of the Force had volunteered at once) and underwent six months' training before they were considered ready to take to the field. Units of the East Lancashire Division, the Middlesex Brigade and some of the lst London Division were the first ASC units to go abroad, but, instead of heading off to war as they had hoped, they replaced Regular ASC units in overseas garrisons. By the spring of 1915, however, the situation had changed and the casualty rate forced the War Office to deploy Territorial Divisions on the Western Front. The first to go was the 46th (North Midland) Division, closely followed by the 2nd London Division (47th).

On 1 April 1915 the pre-war designations of Territorial Force Divisions and Brigades changed and this affected the titles of ASC units at the same time with

ASC 'Columns' becoming 'Trains'. What had been, for example, the 1/1st Highland Division Transport & Supply Column ASC from 1908 now became the 51st (Highland) Divisional Train. In September 1916 the Territorial Force ASC was subsumed by the Regular Army, thus facilitating the posting and distribution of personnel in the Corps. The strength of a Train was also increased, from some 500 strong to almost 740, incorporating as it now did much of the 1st line transport and associated manpower of infantry battalions, leaving only a domestic minimum with the Infantry. When casualties were incurred early in the war there had been no problem in obtaining replacements from the appropriate area, but heavier casualties in 1915 and 1916 made this difficult if not impossible. In any event MT companies supporting Divisions rarely had soldiers from the Division's peacetime recruiting area.

*   *   *

MT Companies, the main 'brick' of the ASC, were 'commissioned' for their task by the Office of the Director of Supplies & Transport in the War Office; OIC Records made the necessary arrangements for posting personnel; arrangements were made with the Army Ordnance Corps, generally in Bulford, to issue Ordnance stores and equipment; other expendable stores were supplied on demand by the Home MT Depot in Short's Gardens, Drury Lane, in London; and field service stationery, army forms, books and other paperwork were issued by the Director of Transport in Bulford. In no time at all an efficient system was established and it took little time to form up a Company and send it abroad.

*   *   *

In December 1915 a number of Tyre Press Detachments (lettered A to N) were formed and attached to MT companies, their task being to change the solid tyres used by virtually all four-wheeled MT in the army. Each detachment consisted of an officer, two Sergeants, three Artificers (one Electrician and two Fitters) and fourteen rank & file (including one batman and one motor car driver), with one motor car. They were expected to change ten wheels a day by hand or twenty wheels a day using a power press. The life expectancy of a solid tyre was something over 10,000 miles, but the roads of France and Flanders took a heavy toll.

*   *   *

The ASC was the military arm responsible for military fire brigades. The major garrisons and ASC depots in the United Kingdom (Aldershot Command, Bulford, Colchester, Curragh and Shorncliffe) each had a military fire brigade, which was largely manned by local civilian firemen, but the ASC were responsible for their administration and the provision of drivers. This was also true of the army on the Western Front and in other theatres of war. The Base Depot in Le Havre and Calais, for instance, boasted of their own all-military fire brigade, as did Salonika and, subsequently, Constantinople (now Istanbul).

One of the duties of junior officers in the field was to censor the men's letters home, a time-consuming and sometimes embarrassing experience at the best of times.

The *Aldershot Gazette* of 2 February 1915 published the following article on the subject of censorship, which shows what imagination and a little initiative can achieve:

"Fickle Tommy! An officer, part of whose duty it is to censor the letters of his men, tells an amusing story of how he succeeded in reducing his labours in this direction. Incidentally he explains why anxious relatives – and those who aspire to that distinction – do not always receive as much news from the front as they would like. The officer is Lieutenant C Smallpiece, and this is his story.

For some time the section of the Army Service Corps of which I am in command was sent to rest at a base, and it became part of my duties to censor all the letters which the men wrote home. They had nothing else to do but to write letters, and the censoring became a very serious business for me, as I frequently had at night to wade carefully through 150 love-letters. So I decided to introduce a change, if possible, and one day I motored into Boulogne and bought a football, which I took back for my men to play with. The result was quite marvellous. The money I spent for the football proved the best investment I ever made. The men took to it so keenly that they played football all day, and had very little time left in which to write love-letters. After the introduction of the football I never had more than five love-letters to censor at night."

The main method of supply on the Continent was of no great complexity and had great flexibility in its simplicity, which was in the event often needed, with formations switching from one part of the front to another. Essentially, stores from the UK base were moved by train and ship to an entry port and then moved by rail through a Regulating Station, to which other stores were delivered and then to a Railhead. Motor transport then took the supplies to Refilling Points (RPs) where 2nd line horse transport (ie the Divisional Train) collected them to deliver forward to battalion or unit lines. Gun ammunition, re-supplied most of the way by rail, was initially carried by the Divisional Ammunition Column (an Artillery organization), but this was soon handed over as an ASC MT responsibility as horse transport was clearly inadequate for the task, especially when more and more guns were used and ammunition expenditure rates grossly exceeded pre-war planning figures; delivery was direct to dumps near the guns. Units along the Line of Communication collected their stores at appropriate locations. (See Annex L.)

It is easier to think of the Corps' work in transport terms since it is more visible; supplies, however, constituted a large part of the ASC's responsibilities and credit must be given to a large organization which worked with high efficiency and little recognition throughout the war.

Initially the feeding strength of the army in France was 12,000 men and 40,000 animals; by the end of the war the figures were 3,000,000 and 500,000 respectively. Advanced Supply Depots were established at Abbeville, Abancourt and Outreau, with a separate depot for Indian troops at Orleans. Field Supply Depots were opened at Barlin, Béthune, Doullens and Wardrecques. Bakeries were established at Boulogne, Calais, Dieppe, Etaples, Le Havre, Marseilles and Rouen.

No 5 Base Supply Depot was opened by the Indian Supply & Transport Corps in Marseilles, their port of entry in Europe, on 10 September 1914 to provide rationing support for Indian troops; from September 1916, however, it gradually became an ASC depot as the Supply & Transport Corps officers were recalled to India. Among the more usual components of the depot was a sizeable goat and sheep farm, which provided animals 'on the hoof' for the Indian troops – in 1917, for example, some 8,000 animals were held and a total of 95,246 goats and 175,158 sheep were 'issued' during the war.

Bread was cooked in the old 'Aldershot ovens' covered with clay, mud or turfs, 108 1¼ lb loaves in each oven, with a baking time of about 75 minutes, until May 1915 when the Perkins oven was introduced, although 'Aldershot ovens' continued to be used in various forms until 1939. Perkins ovens were set up on platforms built of railway sleepers, but later they were bricked in. In 1916 ovens of even greater capacity were required and Hunt's ovens were installed at each of the great bakeries in Boulogne, Le Havre, Rouen, Dieppe, Calais and Etaples. Members of the Queen Mary's Auxiliary Army Corps were employed as bakers to supplement ASC men, but they did not fully solve the problem due to the incessant need to transfer men to the fighting arms. The introduction of machinery for mixing, dividing, scaling and moulding bread helped make bakery less labour-intensive.

Small mineral-water factories were established at Boulogne, Le Havre, Rouen and Abbeville, mainly for personnel in hospitals, ambulance trains and Casualty Clearing Stations. The Etaples area was supplied from a local spring until May 1916, paid for with money from Expeditionary Force Canteens.

*   *   *

The famous plum-and-apple jam was a development of the pre-war plum-and-apricot jam. Unfortunately, apricots were not in easy supply during the war, so apples were used instead. Like plums they were cheap and grown in the UK. Less sugar, too, was needed in the jam-making process. Both before and during the war jam was packed in 11 lb tins, which could be bought by the pennyworth in canteens. Fourteen-pound stone, wide-mouthed jars were also used during the war. A soldier was entitled to an ounce of jam a day, and it was a favourite treat.

Mention should perhaps be made here of the Corps' best-known and longest-lasting nickname, 'Jam Stealers', which might or might not have some basis in truth. In the ration of the day there was a choice of jam or marmalade. Marmalade was essentially the accompaniment for toast, which was very much the preserve of officers. Soldiers did not eat toast so did not like marmalade, which seemed to appear with unfair regularity in the front lines. There was naturally the popular suspicion that the ASC had taken all the jam. Who knows?!

Three other well-known nicknames of the day were 'Commos' (from the

Commissariat & Transport days in the nineteenth century), 'Lampwicks' (from the double white stripes worn on the blue overalls and breeches) and 'Ally Sloper's Cavalry' (ASC) (inspired by a comic strip cartoon in Victorian times).

*   *   *

There is no record of the Corps Band's activities during the war, although it is known that they continued to entertain troops in the United Kingdom. It is not known if they went abroad, but it seems unlikely, if only because of the financial implications; in any event many units of the ASC formed their own bands during the war, which played on appropriate occasions, generally the more informal 'smoker' concerts given behind the lines.

*   *   *

The Official History of the Great War Volume III describes the work carried out by the Corps in the Ypres Salient in 1915:

"The dangers and hazards of getting ammunition and supplies into, and the wounded out of, the Salient each night were immense. The columns were brought to a certain rendezvous and then taken over by guides who knew how to avoid the areas most favoured by the German artillery. By careful observation of the areas and routes that the Germans shelled – of course on a methodical programme – it was possible after a little time for the RA, RASC and RAMC, and the regimental transport which had to go back across the canal, to the Refilling Points, to bring their columns through without heavy casualties; but shelled the enemy never so furiously, the transport moved slowly and deliberately, without lights, never pausing on its way except to avoid a shell hole or clear a lorry that had been hit. So ammunition and supplies were brought up and wounded got away. It was a marvellous display of cold-blooded courage and discipline which greatly impressed those who heard although they could seldom see the long procession of vehicles that went up night after night."

It is heart-warming to see that members of other Corps and regiments appreciated the efforts of the ASC, and it is certainly surprising that one officer, who evidently had benefited from ASC support during the Boer War, even wrote to a national newspaper to express his views. The following letter was published by *The Morning Post* on 10 May 1915:

"Sir, – May I draw your attention to the excellent work acknowledged by all ranks in the Expeditionary Force, and the admiration of our Allies, being done by the Horse Transport Companies of the Divisional Trains of the old Army Service Corps, whose duty it is to bring up supplies to the actual firing line? This work, which is carried out under constant shellfire, most gallantly and thoroughly, and the services of those responsible are seldom or never mentioned, even in Sir John French's despatches, an omission which is a great surprise to many old soldiers. We hear much of the Mechanical Transport work. It is good, no doubt, but not so dangerous, and the men are not the old ASC who did such excellent service in South Africa – and are now doing it, and have done since the

75

war began, in France. I hold no brief for the corps, being an infantryman, but I do like to see honour given where it is due. – Yours etc

8 May   Infantry Officer"

*   *   *

Whereas the pre-war work of the ASC involved only the provision of supplies and transport, the war saw a great widening of responsibilities. A co-operative, efficient organization became something of a 'maid of all work', notably in the fields of heavy vehicle repair, gun towing, ambulance operation, support for Engineer units, water, petrol and troop carrying, agricultural units, Expeditionary Force Canteens and, in the Middle East, armoured cars and armed motor-boats, in North Russia reindeer units, not to mention the transfer of men to other arms and contributing greatly to the formation of the Heavy Branch of the Machine Gun Corps. Some of the units with unusual roles were:

620 Company:	Army Postal Services, Regent's Park
650 Company:	Road Board, Wilton
728 Company:	Signal Service Training Centre, Hitchin
985 Company:	Light Railways and Crane Detachment, Deptford
1050 Company:	Artificer Instructional School, Aldershot
1053 Company:	Agricultural Work, France
1085 (Steam) Company:	Directorate of Forestry
1086 Company:	1 Tank Brigade MT Company

*   *   *

An ASC Comforts Fund had been started by Mrs F W B Landon, wife of Major General Landon, in September 1914 for the Horse Transport and Supply Branches of the Corps. A Ladies Committee collected funds to send parcels abroad. By mid-1915 9,247 parcels had been sent at a cost of £824 15s 9d.

One appreciative recipient send this letter to Mrs Landon on 29 June 1915:

Somewhere in France
29th June 1915

"Dear Madam

I have very much pleasure in writing to you, on behalf of No 2 Company ASC, Horse Transport, Meerut Divisional Train, and thanking you and your kind friends for the splendid parcels which you have so kindly sent out to us. They were received in perfect condition; not one had been tampered with; and what's more were received at a very appropriate moment, as we had been having it a bit rough for the past few days, in a deluge of rain, and the spirits of our lads were almost as gloomy as the weather.

But when the parcels were distributed, the change was remarkable; it put one in mind of a "school treat" or the after effects of a "Father Christmas." The boys (for really, some of them are not much more) were

76

highly delighted, and kept going from one to another, asking, "What have you got, Bill, in yours? I've got a khaki shirt, etc (proper swanky one too) in mine." "Oh! I've got a safety razor, and a blooming fine pocket book, etc in mine, it's just what I wanted." "I'm not cribbing." And so on.

It is indeed very kind of you, dear madam, and all the good people at home, to send us out these little comforts, which I can assure you are very highly appreciated by all of us; it keeps the spirits of the men up, and helps every one of us "to do our little bit" with a good heart.

Once more thanking you and your kind friends for thoughts of our welfare.

I remain,

Yours very gratefully,

C S Wilks CSM
No 2 Coy, ASC MD Train"

MT personnel, however, were not forgotten: *The Commercial Motor* (a weekly publication for commercial vehicle users world-wide) with a Ladies Committee headed by Mrs S S Long, wife of the Director of Supplies & Transport, formed a Comforts Fund for the ASC MT in October 1914, sending cases of 'comforts' on a regular basis to units abroad. By mid-1915 over £5,000 had been raised. The following list was published in the July 1915 *ASC Journal:*

Subscriptions (to end of July)	£5,053
Cases despatched	1,352
Individual gifts despatched	176,644
Total gifts in kind received	12,060
Total outward letters and circulars	20,955
Bachelors' buttons*	25,920
Boracic ointment tins*	10,080
Candles, lb*	1,200
Card Dominoes, packs purchased	5,000
Cigarettes (packets 20) despatched	18,594
Cigarette papers (packets) despatched	8,562
Cotton wool, packets*	7,000
Cricket bats (and 188 balls)	130
Dubbin, tins	5,000
Footballs*	5,000
Gloves, pairs despatched	10,283
Handkerchiefs*	20,000
Leather bootlaces, pairs despatched	2,000
Lint, packages*	2,000
Mouth organs*	952
Packets stationery*	16,628
Playing cards, packs purchased	4,000
Small bandages*	3,456
Soap, tablets*	19,480
Socks, pairs*	21,000
Sweets 8 oz tins*	21,469
Tooth brushes*	9,000
Tooth soap, tins*	10,000
Tobacco, 2 oz packets, despatched	8,500

Towels*	13,160
Undervests†	500
Want cards (in French)	24,000
Woollen comforts despatched ±	6,209

* Part despatched
† Special for Dardanelles
± No more "woollens" other than medium-weight socks, pants, vests
   and shirts required

At the same time a Prisoners-of-War Fund was opened for members of the ASC held in Germany (some eighty at that stage), this fund continuing the efforts of Lady Burghclere thus far. Donations came from Officers' Messes, Sergeants' Messes, canteens, units and individuals, with sums ranging from two shillings from Corporal Woolmer to a magnificent £95 from the ASC in Salisbury Plain Area. Up to 11 August the following articles had been despatched in weekly parcels:

400 Malt loaves	56 tins Corned beef
342 lbs Jam	32 packets Milk
172 lbs Granulated sugar	228 packets Soup
170 lbs Butter	286 packets Tea
114 lbs Chocolate	228 packets Peas
172 tins Milk	114 packets Muscatels
230 tins Cheese	92 packets Tobacco
56 tins Cocoa	548 packets Cigarettes
56 tins Herrings	56 packets Toilet paper
58 tins Golden syrup	56 packets Tooth powder
348 packets Lemon	59 pairs Shoes
58 packets Wheatmeal	129 pairs Socks
228 tablets Soap	114 Flannel shirts
404 Sausages	56 Tooth brushes
58 Galantines	56 khaki Handkerchiefs
114 Tinder Lighters	58 Towels
32 Pipes	73 Books
3 sets Dominoes	1 Cricket ball

Among others, the following card of appreciation was received by Mrs Landon:

"Madam
   I wish to tender you my deepest thanks for the splendid parcel received 17th inst. The contents were most welcome and much appreciated. I feel sure if you could see the pleasure with which any parcel is received, both yourself and other friends would be well repaid for their kindness. You will notice that I have been moved to a fresh camp and am very pleased to say it is a very healthy place. In conclusion, I again thank you & Remain Yours Obediently.

T30392 L/Cpl Alec Smith
AS Corps. Dulmen. Westphalia.
19 July 1915"

It was not long (in September 1915) before the hand of officialdom and the army's sense of rationalization took over and these three funds, the ASC

Prisoners-of-War Fund, Mrs Landon's Fund for Horse Transport and Supply Details, and the *Commercial Motor* Fund for Comforts for Men of the Mechanical Transport, were amalgamated under an ASC Central Comforts Fund, its committee at the War Office headed by three Major Generals, C E Heath CB, F W B Landon CB and S S Long CB. An appeal was made to officers to make a quarterly contribution by banker's order (Field Officers 15/-, Captain 10/- and Subalterns 7/6), with units and canteens instructed to subscribe. Just to ensure that generosity was rewarded, all contributors' names were published for all to see in the *Corps Journal*.

Later (in 1917) the fund applied to be an Authorised Association, since all provisions parcels to prisoners-of-war in enemy countries could only be sent by Authorised Associations. The London General Omnibus Company kindly placed premises at 8 Warner Road in Camberwell at the fund's disposal, to be used, rent free, as a store and packing depot. Setting up costs amounted to £25-8-8 and the Borough of Camberwell Council agreed to forego the payment of rates. The fund was allowed to send three parcels of provisions every two weeks for each prisoner-of-war, arrangements being made with the *Bureau de Secours aux Prisonniers de Guerre* in Berne. Bread seemed to get through in good condition, but this was not always the case with food parcels. The Corps had two prisoners-of-war in Turkey, but difficulties were experienced in sending them money and parcels, so the good offices of the Central Prisoners of War Committee were used.

* * *

When mechanical transport vehicles first arrived in France in the early days of August 1914, they had been required at short notice, and the transport staff in GHQ was too small to register them in any way. To regularize the situation, every effort was made to allot War Department numbers both to motor cars and lorries as they passed through the Headquarters of the Inspector General, Line of Communication up to June 1915, but the records were somewhat inaccurate and in some instances vehicles could not be traced. No one knew exactly what vehicles were where. Control was poor.

In June 1915, therefore, a Census Branch was organized at the Headquarters of the Transport Directorate in GHQ, affording an efficient check on the registration and numbering of every WD vehicle, excluding motor cycles, operating with the British Expeditionary Force. When the census was first struck in July, the total number of vehicles in the country was 9,845. By March 1919 this figure had risen to 59,840.

The practical use of the census was two-fold. On the one hand a complete history was maintained of the whereabouts of a vehicle from the time it entered the country for the use of the BEF up to the time of its official disposal, and this record was always comparatively up to date, providing a valuable check on the vehicle registers of Army Ordnance Corps units. On the other hand, any vehicle could be traced by referring its War Department number to the census. In the case of an accident, reference to the Census Branch established the name of the unit upon whose charge the vehicle was borne.

* * *

The repair of vehicles had been the responsibility of the Corps since the introduction of internal-combustion-engined vehicles in the army. The division of responsibility was that the ASC, as the sole operator of MT, would carry out unit repairs, and the Army Ordnance Corps would carry out the heavy work at a Base Depot. The circumstances of a war situation, coupled with the shortage of transport and spares, militated against this and January 1915 saw the return from the Army Ordnance Corps to the ASC of base repair. The AOC Base Depot in Rouen, for example, concentrated its skills on the repair of artillery equipment. Quite apart from the extensive base repair organization centred on Heavy Repair Shops (HRSs), the ASC recovered its own vehicles by means of Mobile Repair Units, each MT company having its own mobile workshop vehicle.

The repair of vehicles on the Western Front was substantially the same as in the United Kingdom: mobile workshops with field units carried out all running and light repairs, with the heavier work and complete overhauls left to the Base Heavy Repair Shops. The problem was that it was not until July 1916 that the first Heavy Repair Shop (660 MT Company) arrived in France, so units were obliged to carry out much more repair work themselves than had ever been intended.

* * *

It would appear that a number of units were having problems with vehicle lighting and, in 1915, the following tantalizing instructions were issued concerning the care of head-, side- and tail-lamps:

> "The number of motor vehicle lamps that are being sent down to the Base as unserviceable does not justify the demands that are being put forward on the Advanced MT Depot for new lamps etc.
>
> "Officers Commanding units are required to exercise the strictest supervision to ensure that all the lamps on vehicles under their command are properly looked after, are firmly secured to the vehicles, and are so placed as to be protected from injury as far as possible. It has been noticed in particular that an excessive number of containers for side and tail lamps have been lost from motor cars and motor lorries. Precautions should be taken to fit a suitable locking device on the lamps of motor vehicles so as to ensure that the containers do not fall off when travelling along the road. Owing to the number of different styles of lamps that are in use, it is not possible to lay down a universal method of fastening these containers. The oil containers are on no account to be removed from their lamps for such purpose as lighting billets, etc."

* * *

The high rate of pay for MT ASC drivers caused problems, even within the ASC, as it occasionally came to notice that drivers who enlisted for six shillings a day were employed as police, cooks or on sanitary duties. Instructions were issued that any such mis-employed men should be returned to Base in exchange for a similar number of drivers on the lower rates of pay. Regimental numbers of ASC Rank and File (officers did not have regimental numbers in these days) can be seen in Annex M.

A member of the ASC MT wrote in the *ASC Journal* of April 1915:

"Our company consists of 98 lorries, and this includes two store wagons, three first-aid lorries, breakdown cars, one office and two repair work-shops. The two travelling workshops are wonders, and are in duplicate. They are fitted with electric light, and have on board lathes, drilling and boring and slotting machines, electric riveters, forges, anvils and every-thing required in a workshop, even melting pots for running Babbitt's metal in the worn-out bearings before being turned up afresh. The machines are driven by a motor which is driven by a small motor engine. There are other wagons which carry heavy stuff such as portable forges, two or three grindstones, spare springs for cars, crowbars, jacks and heavy tools, and hundreds of other things."

Similarly an ASC officer wrote home:

"I don't think I have told you much about what sort of work we do. Of course, we carry ammunition, as you see by our address; but we carry other things besides, such as sandbags, bomb-making materials, consisting of gun cotton, detonators, primers etc. These we take as a rule direct to the Engineers, which gives us the chance of getting much nearer the front than when carrying ammunition, as the latter we fetch from railhead and deliver to the divisional ammunition column, which is generally a con-siderable distance behind the firing line."

And another wrote:

"Our Brigade has suffered heavily in the severe fighting, and some of the very best fellows, with whom we were dining on the previous night, have fallen on Hill 60. Never in my life do I wish to hear such a terrible shaking of the earth as we are experiencing now, and still less do I want to see such awful, unmentionable sights as I saw at Ypres three days ago. Thank God, I got my supply section out without casualty. I recommended two of our fellows for conspicuous coolness and courage. Our wagons were used for the conveyance of dead and wounded to the hospitals."

*　　*　　*

The following is an extract from a Despatch of the Field Marshal Commanding-in-Chief British Forces in the Field, Field Marshal Sir John French, dated 15 June 1915, published in a Supplement to the *London Gazette* of 10 July 1915:

Supplies and Transport

"In this dispatch I wish again to remark upon the exceptionally good work done throughout this campaign by the Army Service Corps . . . not only in the field, but also on the Line of Communication and at the Base ports.

"To foresee and meet the requirements in the matter of ammunition, stores, equipment, supplies and transport has entailed on the part of the officers, non-commissioned officers and men of these Services a sustained effort which has never been relaxed since the beginning of the war, and which has been rewarded by the most conspicuous success.

"The close co-operation of the Railway Transport Department, whose excellent work, in combination with the French Railway Staff, has ensured the regularity of the maintenance service, has greatly contributed to this success.

"The degree of efficiency to which these Services have been brought was well demonstrated in the course of the Second Battle of Ypres.

"The roads between Poperinghe and Ypres, over which transport, supply and ammunition columns had to pass, were continually searched by hostile heavy artillery during the day and night: whilst the passage of the canal through the town of Ypres, and along the roads east of that town, could only be effected under most difficult and dangerous conditions as regards hostile shellfire. Yet, throughout the whole five or six weeks during which these conditions prevailed the work was carried on with perfect order and efficiency."

* * *

As the army's sole transport operator, the ASC had a vital interest in the production of vehicles. One of the branches of the Director of Supplies & Transport managed the provision of vehicles for the army, a job which was considered vital to the interests of the ASC since it could not be left to the conflicting and vested interests of civilian organizations or politicians. At that time, the weekly production by major engineering firms was:

Leyland:	30	Commer :	12
Albion:	28	Maudslay :	8
AEC:	27	Hallford :	5
Thornycroft:	20	Pagefield:	2
Dennis:	12		

In May 1915, however, the Ministry of Munitions was established, with David Lloyd George as its head. The Minister sent Mr Eric Geddes to Whitehall to let the Army know that he intended to take control of all motor factories in the country and, to the fury of Major General Long, the supply of motor vehicles to the army. Lloyd George held the idiosyncratic view that war was too serious to matter to be left to Generals and that vehicle provision could be better organized by those involved in the trade (in all fairness, the military world often thinks that politics is too serious a matter to be left to politicians, but they rarely do anything about it). Major General Long told Geddes that he was opposed to this plan, as his military staff could do it better. Although logic and past performance supported his case, Major General Long was opposed by vested interests and political intrigue and the Ministry took over, which led to his resignation as Director of Supply & Transport in March 1916. The Quartermaster General seems to have been powerless in this matter, and it is a matter of regret that he did not even obtain a suitable decoration or knighthood for the man who had done so much to support him in his work. Perhaps he was too uncomfortable a subordinate. After all he had stood up to Kitchener in the Boer War when he disorganized transport in South Africa and won.

It was not long before the Ministry of Munitions took over a large hotel in London with 500 officials and an army of clerks, much of the work having been done by the ASC with 25 officers, led by Colonel C V Holbrook, and fewer than 100 clerks, all of whom were now incorporated into their new organization. There is, in fact, no statistical evidence that the changes imposed brought any improvements at all. Meanwhile Major General Long immediately joined Lever Brothers in Port Sunlight as the Director in charge of the company's transport operations, staying with the firm until 1931. It is a reflection of his status in the world of civilian transport management that he was elected President of the Commercial Users' Association.

* * *

During November 1915 a Forage Committee was formed for the supply of forage and other farm produce to troops overseas and at home. A representative of the Director of Supplies in the War Office was designated Administrative Member of the Forage Committee, which had its HQ at 64 Whitehall Court, London SW1. Other rank personnel were amalgamated with the ASC and were designated Forage Department ASC. Six Forage Department Companies were formed in England, one in Scotland and one in Ireland. The committee ceased to exist on 1 July 1920.

As trench warfare on the Western Front became a settled condition in 1915, local stocks of hay were speedily exhausted by purchase and supplies had to be sent from the UK. To meet this requirement, sixteen hay lorries were added to the establishment of Divisional Supply Columns in 1915.

Although we hear a lot about women driving ambulances and other transport, women drivers were preceded by a little-known department attached to the ASC, the Women's Forage Corps, founded in 1915. The Corps was administered from London and its members, ultimately some 6,000, worked throughout the UK, gathering forage for army horses. Their work involved baling, forking hay into machines, wiring and tying bales and weighing, as well as driving teams of horses and wagons from farms to railway stations. The Corps was administered by General H G Morgan CB CMG DSO at its Headquarters in Whitehall Court, with Mrs Athole Stewart as Superintendent of Women. In each area of the United Kingdom there was an Area Administrator and an Area Inspector of Women; areas were sub-divided into districts, each with its District Purchasing Officer of Supplies and Assistant Superintendent of Women.

There were five grades of worker:

Industrial members, in gangs of six, worked on hay baling, feeding the machine by forking hay from the stacks, wiring and tying the bales with wire and checking the weight of each bale when it left the machine

Horse Transport Drivers, who were in charge of teams of horses and wagons for taking bales of hay to the nearest railway station

Forwarding Supervisors (2nd grade officials), who worked at railway stations checking the weight of bales and supervised loading

Section Clerks (2nd grade officials), who dealt with all correspondence relating to the supply of forage

Quartermistresses, who drove Mechanical Supervisors on their rounds of inspection of hay baling machines and distributed rations

The work of the Women's Forage Corps was strenuous, involving great hardship and privation, but it was carried out cheerfully and bravely. The women wore uniforms of khaki and green, wore ASC badges and 'FC' shoulder titles. Only the Armistice in November 1918 stopped further development. It is ironic to think that, when the formation of the Corps was first suggested, the argument was advanced that the manual work of hay baling was too strenuous for women, but they proved without any doubt that they were up to the job.

*　　*　　*

The bus companies formed in 1914 had clearly proved to be valuable assets and in July 1915 another bus company was formed in Bulford, the 15th Auxiliary Omnibus Company (405 Company ASC), under the command of Captain J A Benn. On 18 September, it loaded at Avonmouth for St Omer, attached to the Third Army. On 31 August the original Royal Naval Division bus unit which had done such sterling work at Antwerp was transferred to army control at St Omer and was re-titled 16th Auxiliary Omnibus Company (563 Company ASC) and allocated in support of the Fifth Army. At that stage the company had a mix of forty-six buses, twelve lorries, three motor cars and two motor cycles, but additional buses and charabancs brought it up to a strength of seventy-five buses or charabancs in November.

This poem by an omnibus driver was published in the September-October 1915 *ASC Journal:*

From Rail'ead up to Rondyvoo
"I've never drove an 'orse 'bus though I used to drive a cart,
But 'orses ain't my fancy, they fairly break my 'eart.
When first the 'Vanguard' started I learned to sit and steer,
And after that a 'Road Car' – I could even change its gear.
Since then I joined the 'General', and till three months ago,
I took a number 24, as goes to Pimlico.
I tumbled to the 'points' and 'spots', knew all about the road,
Could drive to 'arf a minute, and always get a load.
I've done my share of pilin' up through 'Igh Street Camden Town,
But I've never passed a copper's 'and until he's put it down.
Most every week, long shift and short, and not too much 'relief',
I've drove a 'bus since 'nineteen-five, which ain't so very brief.
And 'ere I am as Private Brown, of ASC MT,
At rail'ead in some blooming town, in Northern France, DV,
For beer we're gettin' vinegar, the Frenchmen call it wine,
But there's rations from Maconochie which makes a stew that's fine.
We don't start now at Breakfast time, we're off at nine at night,
And 'make up time' till early morn, with belts pulled mighty tight
We're full inside of Tommies, and we're crowded on the top.
And when we're carryin' Indians we don't arf 'ave to 'op.
I tell yer this 'ere's better 'eaps than work from six to six,
We never go to bed at all – 'frustrate their knavish tricks',
But, lumme I just like the job, and so do all my mates,
We're soldiers now, and hours don't count in these 'ere 'tate-ar-tates'.

So lots of you who's still at home a-sittin' at the wheel,
Just chuck your job and come out here, make bully beef yer meal,
"Yer King and Country needs yer" to drive a load of shell,
Of fodder, kit and rations – from rail'ead up to 'ell."

*   *   *

The year 1915 saw a large increase in Royal Garrison Artillery Siege Batteries for the static warfare that had developed, and this had a considerable impact on the Transport Corps of the Army. The ASC Depot Company in Aldershot, 52 MT Company, had incorporated a caterpillar section in 1914 and it moved at the beginning of 1915 to Avonmouth to become the ASC Tractor Depot, providing caterpillar tractors and drivers for heavy-gun towing. The first Royal Garrison Artillery batteries sent to France in 1914 were 6 inch 30 cwt howitzers; these batteries were horse drawn, but 3 ton ASC lorries were attached for gun platforms and ammunition. Early in 1915 Brigades of two batteries were formed in England and sent to France – in these Brigades FWD tractors replaced horses for the 6 inch howitzers. In the case of 6 inch Mark VII guns and 8 inch and 9.2 inch howitzers, the early ones were drawn by steam tractors, but all batteries of these types which landed after April 1915 were drawn by Holt caterpillars imported from America.

   Some small alterations in the establishments of Brigade Columns took place during 1915, the chief being that one officer was added to each Column, while the number of ammunition lorries was reduced and the spare tractor was taken away. The establishment of 50% spare drivers was also reduced to fifteen per cent. No less than 293 ASC units, made up of 14,362 all ranks, worked in this heavy artillery role during the war.

*   *   *

The types of MT vehicles used in France contain some interesting names:

   Motor-Cycles: BSA, Clyno, Douglas, Enfield, Indian, Matchless, Rudge, Triumph and Zenith.
   Cars: Austin, Berliet, Chenard, Walcker, Clement Bayard, Clement Talbot, Crossley, Daimler, Darracq, De Dion Bouton, Delage, Delahaye, Delauney Belleville, Fiat, GWK, Hotchkiss, Lancia, Leon Bollee, Mercedes, Metallurgique, Napier, Panhard, Peugeot, Renault, Rolls-Royce, Sheffield Simplex, Siddeley Deasy, Singer, Sunbeam, Swift, Unic, Vulcan and Wolseley.
   Ambulances : Fiat, Ford, Napier, Sunbeam and Wolseley.
   Vans: Crossley, Fiat, Ford, Napier and Star.
   Lorries: AEC, Albion, Alldays Onions, Austin, British Berna, Buick, Cadillac, Commer, Daimler, Dennis, Foden (steam), FWD Garford, Hallford, Jeffrey Quadrant, Karrier, Kelly-Springfield, Lacre, Leyland, Locomobile, Maudslay, Packard, Pagefield, Peerless, Pierce-Arrow, Riker, Saurer, Seabrook, Straker-Squire, Studebaker, Vinot and White.
   Steam Tractors: Aveling & Porter, Burrell, Clayton, Foster, Fowler, McLaren & Tasker.
   Caterpillar Tractor: Holt.

*   *   *

From Peninsular War days through to the Crimea and beyond, the ASC and its predecessors were responsible for the transport of wounded men for the Medical Services. In addition, they now provided ambulance support for Field Ambulances – to carry wounded men from Regimental Aid Posts to Advanced Dressing Stations and from there to General Hospitals. If a 'Blighty' was involved (ie a wound which necessitated a return to UK) train to the UK base was the main method of transport. Transport to and from trains was an ASC task. Railways lacked, of course, the inherent flexibility of road transport and, either to replace or complement trains, a number of Motor Ambulance Convoys were formed, each one consisting of an ASC Transport Company, forty-eight in all. Many patriotic organizations and individuals at home and abroad raised money for motor ambulances for service in the field, led by Their Majesties the King and Queen. Ambulances had to be War Office approved, all with a 20 hp chassis and the smooth-running Daimler sleeve-valve engine, but it was not long before Model-T Fords joined their more prestigious companions. Those listed in Annex J are known to have donated ambulances to the war effort. The complete list might never be known, but this will do as a start.

*   *   *

The army decided late in 1915 to make all units operating in the war zone come under direct military orders and discipline and the British Red Cross Society drivers were given the choice of enlisting in the ASC or returning to their base at Boulogne. Out of the total of 108 British Red Cross Society personnel, sixty enlisted at six shillings a day and one Company Sergeant Major and seventy-eight new ASC drivers and NCOs to make up the difference were sent out from England, arriving on 2 December 1915.

*   *   *

As the war settled into its dreary routine in 1915, attention turned to welfare considerations. Many of the amenities of civilization back home were introduced for the men of the BEF: clubs, entertainment halls, laundries, baths and even soda-water factories, most of which the ASC had a major hand in.

The need for the provision of canteens for the army was acknowledged by the Army Council in February 1915. Major General Long was instructed to execute the Council's wishes. £27,000 from profits made by canteens in the Boer War were drawn upon and the Canteen and Mess Co-operative Society established a branch with the BEF. From this small beginning Expeditionary Force Canteens (EFCs), pioneered by Lieutenant Colonel E C Wright in France, increasingly supplied small comforts such as the troops were accustomed to buying in their own canteens in peacetime, for example writing-paper and envelopes, pencils, food and cups of tea, and ASC cap badges at 2d. a piece. The organization was amalgamated with the ASC on 7 July 1915 and designated 'Expeditionary Force Canteens Section ASC'.

By the end of the war there were 577 canteens in operation in France alone, let alone others in the Middle East, manned by some 5,000 members of the ASC

The ASC's first tracked vehicle, the 'Giant Caterpillar', a 13 ton Hornsby "travelling" (at approx 4 mph) in the Aldershot area, c. 1905 (B).

The ASC's second tracked vehicle, the 'Little Caterpillar', in the Tidworth area, c. 1910 (B).

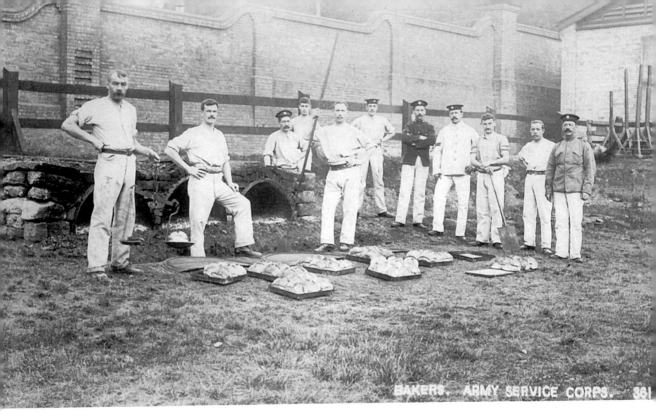

ASC Bakers in Woolwich, using 'Aldershot ovens' (B).

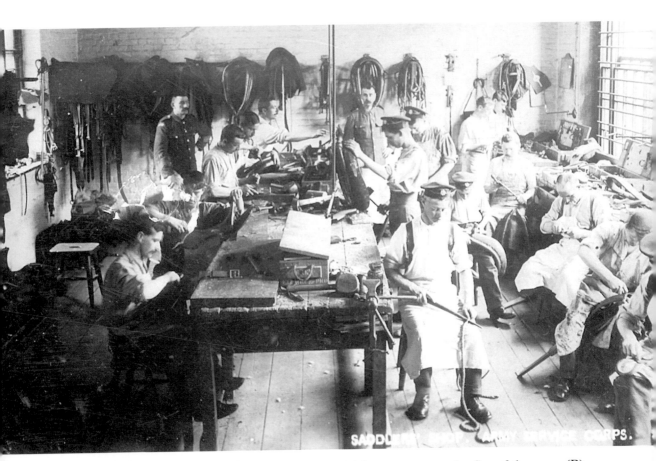

ASC Saddlers' Shop in Woolwich, c. 1905. Brodrick caps are worn by five of the men. (B).

A Snaffles cartoon of Lieutenant C G C Blunt, an early MT enthusiast, who attended a 1906 balloon course in Aldershot when Colonel Sam Cody was one of the instructors (A).

The ASC on parade, probably for church in Aldershot. Note typical barracks of the Victorian era, with stables on the ground floor (see pile of hay on the left) and the men's accommodation above, c. 1906 (B).

KINGS BIRTHDAY PARADE ARMY SERVICE CORPS.   Nº1.

The ASC drive past with covered GS wagons during the King's Birthday Parade on Laffan's Plain (later Farnborough aerodrome), c. 1906 (B).

'Preparing the downey couch'. Soldiers filling palliasses with straw, Portsmouth 1911 (B).

63 Company camping at Thornhill Camp, Stanhope Lines, Aldershot in July 1910. Note the old power station (B). This area is now covered by Travers Barracks and St Omer Barracks.

A beautifully decorated funeral hearse provided by 10 Company ASC, in Colchester (date unknown) (B).

WHEELERS' SHOP STAFF. ARMY SERVICE CORPS. 353

ASC Wheelers' Shop in Woolwich, c. 1905. Note the Brodrick caps (B).

The Army Fire Brigade Station on Queen's Avenue, Aldershot, with its horse-drawn and Merryweather engines on display, 1914 (B).

ASC and civilian crews pose proudly in front of their fire-fighting trailers (B).

A very impressive barrack room, where every effort has been made to make it look like home. Note the beds folded to make easy chairs (B).

Forty-eight ASC men, every one a volunteer, carrying wreaths in the funeral procession of Colonel Sam Cody along Lynchford Road, North Camp, Farnborough on 11 August 1913. 50,000 spectators lined the two-and-a-half-mile route from Ash Vale to the Aldershot Military Cemetery (B).

An artist's impression of an ASC lorry (still in Pickford's livery) being attacked by Uhlans on the retreat from Mons in 1914 (B).

A French interpreter and four ASC officers take tea during the retreat from Mons in September 1914. The British officer on the left is Captain L C Bearne, who was awarded the Albert Medal for gallantry in saving life while serving in Serbia in October 1916 (B).

THE SINEWS OF WAR.

'The Sinews of War', a well-known Punch cartoon, published in the
November/December 1914 ASC Journal (Courtesy of Punch Magazine) (A).

ASC supply column waggons in Albert in August 1914 (B).

Pay parade for men of 494 (MT) Company at Chipping Sodbury in September 1915. (Photographer: Murray Dowding.) The unit had formed on 11 August 1915 and saw service on the Western Front (41st Division) and in Italy (23rd Division) (B).

Three happy ASC men on Douglas motor cycles (B).

ASC company runners equipped with army bicycles. Note the Lee Enfield rifles and bayonets with which the ASC were equipped, acetylene lamps and message pouches (B).

The entrance to Grove Park Barracks, the main ASC location for driver training in south-east London (B).

An Auxiliary Omnibus Company forming at Grove Park in October 1914 (B).

A typical photograph of ASC trainee drivers with an LGOC driving instructor (wearing an ASC badge), based on Osterley Park, 1915 (B).

The Osterley Park Hairdressing and Shaving Saloon, 1915. Note the two brush orderlies (B).

A convoy of 244 (MT) Company stopped on the road at Holcombe, Devon on 26 February 1915, probably on a training drive, having formed only on 19 January. They were soon to be Salonika-bound (B).

A number of ASC companies trained in Wells, Somerset. 133 Company is seen here departing for service on the Western Front with the 10th and 14th Divisions (B).

Even the ASC got caught out by the flooding near Shrewton on Salisbury Plain in January 1915 (B).

The main road of the ASC Mobilisation Centre in Tidworth (B).

supplemented by 700 members of Queen Mary's Army Auxiliary Corps. The HQ of the EFC was in Eaton Square, London and depots were located in Gloucester, Newhaven, Deptford and London (Willow Walk). The EFC not only ran canteens, which by the end of the war brought in three-quarters of a million pounds profit, but also operated Officers' Rest Houses and Messes, Leave Billets, Mineral-Water Factories, Bakeries and a Cinema Department. It may be of interest that Lance Corporal E Seaman, who joined the ASC in December 1915 and was posted immediately to France, won a posthumous Victoria Cross on 29 September 1918 shortly after transferring from the EFC ASC to the Royal Inniskilling Fusiliers. He saw service around Passchendaele Ridge and other parts of the Ypres sector, being promoted Lance Corporal some fourteen days before he was killed. The citation to his Victoria Cross is included at the end of Annex S.

CHAPTER 4

1916: New Challenges

Any hope that the war would end quickly disappeared with the advent of 1916. In January the House of Commons passed the first of a number of Conscription Bills and, in April, the Turks captured Kut el Amara in Mesopotamia.

The German High Command took another gamble with the investment of Verdun, intending to knock out France in a battle of attrition, but their own losses eventually caused them to think again. While the battle for Verdun raged, the British and French opened a major campaign on the Somme in July, not only as part of a series of wearing-out operations but also to break through the German lines and start a war of movement which would unhinge the static lines of defence. Solid German defences, heavy losses and tactical failure put a stop to any further offensives this year.

On the Western Front the Corps was consolidating its position and, at the same time, looking critically at its own organization. At home the ASC Volunteer world was increasingly taking the strain, providing support when the serving army could not do so; thousands of men were transferred from the Corps to the fighting arms in exchange for unfit, wounded or older men; new vehicles for the transport of water in bulk were introduced and new MT companies were formed for Siege Batteries of the Royal Garrison Artillery, much needed fire-power to counter German superiority in this field. In a new role, ASC men were providing a major contribution to what was hopefully a means of breaking through the German lines – the tanks of the Heavy Branch of the Machine Gun Corps. New challenges were in the air.

*   *   *

The provision of water has never been a strong card in the army's hand, but this war saw a major turning point away from small horse-drawn water-carts with the introduction in 1916 of bulk water tankers. The first water tank company, 646 Company ASC, was formed on 27 January 1916, with the second, 718 Company ASC, forming on 20 June 1916 with the 1st and 2nd Armies, both at Grove Park in south-east London for use on the Western Front. They were followed by Nos. 3 and 4 Water Tank Companies in September and October 1917 for the 3rd Army and the Line of Communication respectively.

The companies were issued with twenty-four 1 ton Garfords, each carrying 150 gallons of water, and three lorries, which carried 500 gallons each. RAMC chemists were attached to operate the sterilizers and de-poisoners and later to analyse water in surrendered territory. By the end of August 1916 extra vehicles were issued to 646 and 718 Companies, bringing their total to 111 Garfords and thirty 3 tonners. Frequently the vehicles drove up to just behind the front line in order to refill the tins used for conveying water to the troops in the trenches, complementing the normal service provided routinely by smaller horse-drawn water carts.

In the extreme frosts of February 1917 the whole army water pipeline laid by the Royal Engineers froze up, which meant that these two water tank companies were the only means of supplying water to Casualty Clearing Stations, prisoner-of-war camps, Heavy Battery positions and other units located so far from other water supplies that it was impossible to do with horse-drawn carts.

The flexibility and value of the road tankers were illustrated during the attack on Messines Ridge in June 1917. All the water pipe lines laid by the Sappers were damaged by shellfire and the water tankers had to make return trips over several miles to satisfy needs. Even so the situation was critical, as four of the first five vehicles on the Ridge had their water tanks pierced by shrapnel.

* * *

In the early stages of the war the demand for skilled motor drivers was easily met owing to the high rates of pay offered to such men. This source eventually failed and it became necessary to train motor transport drivers for the army. It was soon found, however, that the usual reinforcement driver was an unreliable quantity. The high percentage of casualties to motor lorries and cars proceeding to the front in charge of these men, added to the constant complaints which were received from OCs of the inefficiency of drivers posted to them, showed that some system of selection and test at the Base was essential.

Small schools were established at the Base MT Depots in Rouen and Calais, but about the middle of 1916 it was decided that better results could be obtained in training officers and drivers by the formation of a properly established Central School of Instruction in the Caserne de Barre in St Omer. The School was designed to deal with 200 learner car and lorry drivers, fifty officers and six Caterpillar drivers at a time.

Lieutenant Colonel H A B Crawford was appointed as Commandant, with four other officers, a Company Sergeant Major, Company Quartermaster Sergeant, twelve Sergeant Instructors, a Technical Draughtsman, thirty-seven Driving Instructors, twenty-one general duties men, four clerks and 30 vehicles to help him. The total number of men trained in France up to March 1919 was 7,725 at the Base and 4,695 at the Central School.

* * *

In 1916 the transport and control of transport support for the heavy artillery of the Royal Garrison Artillery was reorganized, the scheme coming into force on 18 April. It had been found that the system of Brigade Columns was extravagant in officers, personnel and lorries and that a large saving could be made by grouping the whole of the Corps Heavy Artillery transport under an OC ASC attached to Headquarters Corps Heavy Artillery. This scheme had already been tried in the 1st Corps, where a Siege Park, formed in June 1915 and commanded by Major H N Pennington, had proved to be a success.

In active operations the control of ammunition and lorries was difficult as each Brigade in the Corps area handed in separate ammunition indents at the railhead, which led to one Brigade being starved while another was over-supplied, and the lorries of one Brigade being overworked while others were standing idle; it also frequently happened that the two batteries forming a Brigade were operating in different Corps areas. The new scheme did in general work well, but, with the massing of artillery for prolonged operations, was inclined to become unwieldy. This was partly met by the addition of a Captain to the HQ Company ASC and taking clerks out of Battery Ammunition Columns.

With the exception of the numbers of Workshop Officers attached, no other change took place.

When the scheme came into force in April 1916 one Workshop in addition to the HQ Workshop was added for each two tractor-drawn batteries and the number of Workshops was shortly afterwards limited to six and, for each battery in excess of twelve, a Fitters Outfit consisting of three Fitters, one Smith, and one Wheeler with tools and a 3 ton lorry was attached. Instead of one officer to each Workshop, a permanent establishment of four was made, who could be temporarily lent when required. This was found to be sufficient up to a certain point, but extra Workshops were added when the number of batteries or the condition of the transport required it. The original designation of HQ Company ASC attached Corps Heavy Artillery was altered to Corps Siege Park in 1917. The establishment of a Siege Park can be seen in Annex N (along with a number of other ASC units during the war). As part of the Workshop reorganization process, Field Ambulance Workshops were absorbed into Divisional Supply Columns in April 1916, ensuring a better maintenance and repair service for those units of the RAMC.

*　　*　　*

By the middle of 1916 the manpower situation was causing real anxiety at the War Office. The results of the recently introduced Conscription Act were yet to make themselves felt and heavy casualties were anticipated in the operations planned on the Somme. In May the Director of Supplies at the War Office initiated an exchange of 5,500 category 'A' men of the ASC for men of lower category in other regiments ('B' or 'C' men) and a wholesale examination of establishments at home and abroad was instituted.

The process was necessarily slow, as it was important not to cause serious dislocation in the Administrative Services by the sudden withdrawal of large numbers of trained men, also because no withdrawals could take place until 'B' and 'C' recruits to replace the 'A' men became available and had been trained; however, between November 1916 and the Armistice a total of 82,638 ASC Other Ranks has been transferred to the Artillery, Infantry, Machine Gun Corps and Royal Flying Corps.

Other steps were taken:

All Home Supply Depots had to employ not less than 50% women clerks

All increases of clerks at Command Headquarters and in ASC Administrative Offices were filled, whenever possible, by civilians or by women

In France 'A' men on the Line of Communication and, where possible, in field units were combed out; the arrival of eight Cape Boys Auxiliary Horse Companies from South Africa released approximately 2,300 men, and wherever possible at Bases, men were replaced by women

In Egypt all ASC HT establishments were organized on a basis of 50% native strength

In Salonika a considerable number of Macedonians, Cypriots and Maltese were employed in Divisional Trains and Field Ambulances

Large drafts of low category men were sent to France and Egypt during 1918 for substitution purposes (resulting in the release of 6,220 category 'A' men for fighting arms)

On the Western Front they were assembled at the ASC Base Depot at Le Havre and, after very brief training at Infantry Base Depots, were drafted to battalions and regiments.

Later, in 1917, some battalions of the 60th Rifles were badly mauled by the German Marines near Nieuport. These units had recently received large drafts of ASC men and the Adjutant of one of the battalions wrote to the OC of the ASC Depot asking whether it could be arranged that more men from the same source could be provided for the reconstitution of his unit, as those who had been previously incorporated had conducted themselves so splendidly in the face of the enemy. Less well-known is that over 100 officers were attached or transferred to the Royal Flying Corps.

*　　*　　*

Supply trades of the Corps too were not immune from transferring men to the Infantry. There was indeed one notable occasion when 1,000 men were required instantly for a certain regiment in the north of England. By chance there was a large surplus of Butchers in Aldershot at the time so all 1,000 men were transferred. An infantry battalion consisting only of Butchers must be quite unique in the history of the British Army. Records show that it did well, but, alas, it seems impossible to identify the unit today, probably advantageous for the unit concerned, which will have immediately developed its own infantry *esprit de corps*. The officers posted in would naturally never have been able to live it down had their 'provenance' become widely known.

*　　*　　*

With such a large Corps as the ASC, it will be understood than an analysis of its members is virtually impossible, but it is perhaps interesting to put a magnifying glass to the manpower of 82 Company ASC (MT), the only unit whose Company Register (AB 405a) is retained in the Corps archives. The register closed in 1916 when the unit was absorbed into 89 Company ASC (MT) in support of the 1st Indian Cavalry Division. Between its formation in Woolwich in November 1914 and its demise in October 1916 the following trades were listed for the 350 men of the company prior to enlistment:

175 Motor Drivers	22 Fitters	21 Labourers
16 Stevedores	7 Butchers	6 Clerks
6 Miners	4 Electricians	4 Engineers
3 Blacksmiths	3 Coach Builders	3 Warehousemen

and one or two of the following:

Angle Smith	Auctioneer	Book Binder
Bread Salesman	Brewer	Carman
Cellarman	Chauffeur	Coachman
Contractor	Cooper	Corn Porter

Cotton Weaver
Drayman
Fitter's Labourer
General Dealer
Grocer
Hay & Straw Merchant
Japanner
Mason
Millwright
Motor Dealer
Packer
Policeman
Printer
Sewerman
Storekeeper
Taxi Driver
Woollen Trade Rep

Cycle Dealer
Farm Labourer
Furniture Packer
Gramophone Repairer
GWR Police
House Decorator
Liftman
Mechanic
Motor Cycle Dealer
Motor Works Manager
Park Keeper
Porter
Schoolmaster
Stockbroker
Storekeeper
Table Blade Forger
(from Sheffield)
Vestryman

Dock Checker
Fishmonger
Garage Manager
Grinder/Printer
Hat Finisher
Ironmonger
Lighterman Manufacturer
Milkman
Motor Cycle Maker
Musician
Plumber/Boilermaker
Post Office
Seaman
Stockbroker's Clerk
Taxi Cab Owner
Vulcanizer

(eight were not annotated).

Home addresses were given in the following (very rough) areas:

London 148
South-East 26
Scotland 22
Canada 2

Home Counties 29
South-West 21
Wales 7
India 1

North of England 69
Midlands 13
Ireland 5
Rhodesia 1

(six were not annotated).

All except eleven (93%) were engaged for the duration of the war. There were twelve pre-war serving soldiers (1904, 1905, 1906, 1908, 1909, 1911, 1912 (x 3) and 1913 (x 3)) and 192 signed on in 1914, 134 in 1915 and twelve in 1916. There were still 123 men in the company (35%) in 1916 who had joined the unit on formation; of the remainder, seventy-seven (22%) came via the Base MT Depot in Rouen, sixty (17%) came via the Base HT Depot in Le Havre, the rest from a variety of units. There was a variety of regimental number prefixes: CMT, DM2, M, M1, M2, M5, S, S1, S4, S1SR, SS and T4.

*   *   *

A glance at another company might also not be out of place. 879 Company recorded that, in 1916, all Class 'A' men employed on horse transport work at Base had been replaced by 'B', 'PB' and 'PU' men, many of whom were drawn from infantry and artillery units. The unit employed Chinese, Egyptian and Cape Boys in the docks.

Class 'B' men were over 41 years of age or medically unfit for the front.

Class 'PB' men were those who worked permanently in the Base due to age or infirmity (wounds/injuries).

Class 'PU' men were those who, by virtue of severe wounds received in action, had become permanently unfit for service in the Armies.

92

Even horses supplied to the company were 'VB' (Veterinary Base) (ie recovering from wounds or debility), as Base work was supposedly lighter than that in the field. At Base such animals had a better chance of recovering condition. As they improved so they became useful for the front again and were drafted through Remount Depots and other unfit horses took their place.

*   *   *

The manpower shortage was, to a certain extent, improved by the employment of women, there having been none in the army in 1914. From April 1916 women were increasingly used in munitions factories and, in the army, the ASC led the way.

In 1916 Lady Londonderry, President of the Women's Legion, had been authorized to form a section of female motor drivers, with Miss Christobel Hills in charge. A contemporary report said: "It was reported in 1916 that, since August, about 2,000 have been successfully employed. The formation of a motor transport section of the Women's Legion in April of this year has now similarly successful results, and it is now officially recognized by the War Office as a civilian subordinate branch.

"The Commandant of this section of the Women's Legion has been in Serbia with the Red Cross and has driven motor transport for some weeks at the front. She hopes to obtain for the work women who may have to earn their own living after the war and who would find a congenial occupation in the driving of light vans. Already about 200 women have been placed, not all in War Office work, but some in munition areas, and some working for hospitals. All the expense of training both the camp cooks and the motor transport section are covered by a private fund subscribed by Lady Londonderry's personal friends. Training for the motor transport section is given free at certain garages and motor schools with which the Legion has made arrangements.

"The work done by the War Office so far has been in connection with the ASC. The women drive light cars only, and are drafted in to service units for home service. The Army Council were asked in April to try the women for a month; they agreed, and during the month's test the women were given cars which could not even be described as second-best. The women, however, accepted all difficulties as part of their test, and it was reported that their work was 'excellent' and that in many cases the cars were kept cleaner than they had been by the men."

606 Company ASC, largely composed of members of the Women's Legion, was attached to the Ministry of Munitions in London. As an experiment, this caused some anxiety at first but its success led to the wider use of women in the Services, until their strength reached some 4,000. The history of 606 Company relates of their women drivers: "They have been involved in driving cars and ambulances and have not been used for driving heavy lorries, owing to starting difficulties. Women washers have also been engaged – they are of a lower class than the women drivers, who are nearly all ladies."

At first female drivers were attached to 606 and other MT Companies in London, but after a year they were placed under the direct control of the War Office. A driving school started at Twickenham where a number of six-week courses for 150 females was run. They signed on for a year at a time and, after probation, received 38 shillings a month. They drove cars, ambulances, box vans, motor cycles and side cars at home. That they came from a wide range of backgrounds is evident in the following story: A well-known political peer and member of the Cabinet, having been delivered to his destination, told his driver to pick him up an hour later. "Very good," she replied. "Perhaps I should say", said the Minister, "that I am normally addressed as 'My Lord'." "Very good, my Lord", answered the chauffeuse, "but perhaps I ought to add that I am normally accustomed to be addressed as 'My Lady'." The subsequent exchange was sadly not recorded. A number of Women's Legion drivers replaced men in the Rhineland in 1919 to assist in demobilization.

Subsequent years' statistics show the increase in the employment of women in ASC units:

	March 1917	June 1918	January 1919
In Local Auxiliary MT Companies	121	1055	2158
QMAAC	285	707	
Civilians	194	310	

These figures might not appear too impressive, but most suitable women had already been employed by other government departments, a large number had gone overseas as clerks in the QMAAC, and pay and accommodation were hardly attractive.

Before leaving 'women at war' mention must be made of the First Aid Nursing Yeomanry (FANY), an organization which grew from the idea of a Sergeant Major Baker ASC in the Boer War of 1899-1902. Commissioned by the British Red Cross Society, they acted as ambulance drivers and mechanics, albeit in an unofficial capacity at first, in addition to their work of looking after the sick. True to form, the War Office had declared in 1914 that women would not be required to help in the war. They distinguished themselves early when two of their drivers were on duty during the first gas attack near Ypres in 1915. In all the confusion they still managed to drive their gassed casualties to safety. FANYs provided the first replacements for British soldiers during the war when they took up their duties at Calais in January 1916. From their early pre-war training days to practical help with fuel and maintenance in France, the FANYs had close links with the ASC, which continued long after the war.

*   *   *

There were, in addition to personnel changes, organizational changes instituted in 1916, which continued into 1917. These changes essentially involved the pooling of transport to provide greater efficiency and flexibility, especially in the face of a possible major breakdown in railway support. The previous Ammunition Sub Parks, as well as Army, Corps and Divisional Supply Columns were reorganized and the resultant MT companies were allocated on the basis of one to General Headquarters and one to each Army, Corps and Division. The men and vehicles saved were allocated partly as reinforcements but mainly as GHQ Reserve Companies. At the same time the commodity system, whereby one company carried one type of load only (eg ammunition or supplies), was changed and each company carried a mixed load or whatever type of load was necessary. Supply units, too, experienced their share of the upheaval. Records show that 279 units (mainly Supply) were disbanded or absorbed by other units in 1916, many of them to create Line of Communication Supply Companies, of which thirty-eight were formed.

*   *   *

Considering the fact that operating large road transport fleets was something entirely new to the army, the provision and supply of fuel never seems to have been a problem; the situation was helped of course by the only form of transport organic to a Division (ie the most forward) being horse-drawn. All ASC Trains were equipped only with GS wagons and horses; MT companies were only attached.

Until spring 1916 petrol issues were made from petrol depots in Calais, Le Havre and Rouen, as well as from a number of Detailed Issue Depots (DIDs). The decision was then made to centralize the issue of petrol in two large depots in July, No. 1 at Fontinettes near Calais for the Northern Line of Communication, and No. 2 at Grand Querilly near Rouen for the Southern Line of Communication, both set up by the Asiatic Petroleum Company. Fuel was received in bulk from petrol tankers at the port and pumped into tanks connected by pipeline to the refilling plants at the depots, where can-making and can-filling factories were opened.

The use of fuel tankers was then instituted in 1917 with the object of saving the two-gallon cans and cases, the normal means of refuelling vehicles. Eleven tankers were initially loaned from the French and Belgian Armies, but were later supplemented by 3,000-gallon tankers from England. As many as 150 of the latter were brought into service, filling from overhead tanks by means of 4-inch pipes.

The matter of petrol supply and the control of consumption later became such an important issue that Brigadier General Sir Charles King Kt CB CVO late ASC was appointed Inspector of Petrol Consumption on the staff of the Director of Supplies & Transport in the War Office. Several petrol experts were recruited into the Corps from industry, who had personal numbers with the prefix 'Petrol'.

*   *   *

Perhaps the most interesting and certainly the most successful of reorganizations was in the field of troop-carrying and a further increase was made to the four bus companies already at work. In February 1916 the 18th Auxiliary Omnibus Company (588 Company ASC) was formed by Captain H Leavis, in support of the Fourth Army. Like the other bus companies it worked independently under the 'Q' staff of the Army concerned, so, effectively, there was no co-ordination at the highest level. The company was issued with Locomobiles which had been sold by America to Germany but had been captured by the Royal Navy *en route*. It was felt by the men, in characteristic humorous fashion, that the Kaiser would like something done for them, so they were all given the Iron Cross (ie the unit sign was painted on them). See Annex P (unit signs).

All five companies on the Western Front had a heavy work load and, since the buses had never been designed for the roads on the Western Front, their condition became a cause of some concern, a situation exacerbated by the number of buses on permanent detachment from their parent units. By December 1916, however, it was accepted that vehicles of the 2nd and 16th Companies were practically incapable of further service and the 15th and 18th needed a complete overhaul. Ironically the drivers' natural pride in their vehicles often militated against regular workshop attention. They spoke of their buses in very personal terms, giving them all the credit due. Pte Gwynn, for example, recorded that " . . . the old bus . . . she has done good work . . . did her bit in our Somme offensive . . . she did some good work in rushing reinforcements up . . . " Another man wrote, "I have seen a few of our buses wounded here."

One of the additional tasks performed by omnibuses was that of mobile pigeon lofts. Operated by the Royal Engineers under the Director of Signals in GHQ, static and mobile pigeon lofts (loft superstructures were constructed in Ordnance workshops based on GS wagons) had been established in July 1915 throughout the area held by the British Armies. Each Army had ten pigeon stations, operated by a Sergeant and two Corporal despatch riders, with twenty NCOs or men from the Cavalry or Infantry; an ASC driver distributed birds to stations in a box motor car. At the end of 1916 six omnibuses were converted as pigeon lofts to complement the GS waggons already in use and a further six were ordered in 1917.

At the end of 1916, as part of the ASC reorganization in the field army, all five bus companies were centralized under an Auxiliary Omnibus Park, and it was decided that they would operate under G Ops at GHQ in strategic roles, solving previous administration problems. The Park was designed to be capable of transporting the dismounted portion of a Division, including the Pioneer Battalion, Machine Gun Corps and Field Ambulance. It was to be commanded by a Lieutenant Colonel, assisted by an Adjutant and a Mechanist Sergeant Major, supported by a clerk, cyclist, two batmen and a car driver. Once the scheme was authorized on 18 December 1916, companies were withdrawn from the Armies and concentrated at St Valèry-sur-Somme near Abbeville for reorganization and repair. Two GHQ Ammunition Parks (ie companies with lorries) were allocated to the Omnibus Park.

The Commanding Officer, Lieutenant Colonel G L H Howell, reported to GHQ on 18 December and received verbal orders from the Director of Transport, Major General W G E Boyce. Captain C B Cockburn reported as Adjutant on 23 January 1917 and Mechanist Sergeant Major F R Smith came as the Warrant Officer. 7 GHQ Ammunition Park (92 Company ASC) arrived at St Valèry on 19 December 1916 and 4 GHQ Ammunition Park (339 Company ASC) on 20 December, the former re-rolled as 51 Auxiliary Omnibus Company, the latter as 50 Auxiliary Omnibus Company, regaining its original task of October 1914.

Many changes were needed to convert Ammunition Parks to bus companies and to 'recondition' the existing bus companies. Sections of twenty-five lorries were withdrawn from 1, 3, 5, 6 and 8 Ammunition Parks and modified as charabancs. Twenty-five buses from each of the five Armies, along with eighty-two converted lorries, were assigned to 50 Company but remained with the Armies on detachment.

As a result of this reorganization, each company was made up to a strength of fifty buses and twenty-five lorries, except for 50 Company which operated seventy lorries (as well as the detached buses). Most vehicles transferred in needed a complete overhaul and all lorries needed fitting with seats. Including the detached vehicles and workshop personnel, the Omnibus Park now consisted of seven companies totalling 650 vehicles and 1,800 men with a carrying capacity of 13,300 men.

*　　*　　*

It is remarkable how most ASC units, not being issued with specialist equipment, were able to turn their hand to any role. A case in point was 44 MT Company, whose allocated role was as the Supply Column of the 7th Division. During preliminary preparations for the Somme offensive the company's vehicles were used to transport Engineer material up to the forward areas after they had carried out their routine resupply runs. This could only be achieved by working round the clock, with one of the two drivers resting while the other one drove. The junior officers worked practically night and day. For the first three days of the offensive in July their lorries were largely used in carrying wounded on the return from a resupply run, since the number of ambulances was totally inadequate for the number of casualties.

*　　*　　*

The demand for labour and the tactical situation created by the Somme offensive of 1916 focused attention on the organization of labour on the Western Front, increasing the necessity for ensuring flexibility in its distribution. Labour had originally been allocated by the ASC to other Services and Departments and none had been 'pooled', which caused some dissatisfaction to those units which did not get what they wanted. By the end of 1916 labour employed on the Line of Communication had risen to 42,000, with 45,000 employed elsewhere (by November 1918 the totals had risen to 249,000).

In December 1916 an Army Labour Corps was authorized by the War Office as a temporary measure and a Directorate of Labour was formed at GHQ, with appropriate staff at Army, Line of Communication, Corps and Base HQ levels. The Directorate dealt with non-technical labour (that is to say, labour used to supplement technical and specialist units when those units could not themselves do all the work required). Members were to receive the same pay as Infantry of the Line. The first Director of Labour was (Major, Brevet Colonel, Temporary) Brigadier General Evan Gibb late ASC, who was serving at the time in GHQ. He was subsequently appointed as Controller of Salvage in 1918 and was the last Commander British Troops in France and Flanders from 1 January to 30 June 1920. Brigadier General Gibb was followed by Colonel E Wace late RE as Director of Labour in February 1918.

*　　*　　*

590 MT Company was allocated as the 20th Auxiliary Petrol Company, but perhaps surprisingly not all of their work was involved with petroleum. They did general transport duties and forestry work too. In May 1916, for example nine charabancs were attached for the transportation of wounded arriving at the Rive Gauche Station in Rouen for transportation to local hospitals and to hospital ships.

When South African labourers were substituted in 1917 for British personnel in a number of ASC units, fifty of the Horse Transport men so released were sent to 590 Company for training in MT work, of which forty-nine were accepted.

They were fortunate in their accommodation as a result of working with the Forestry Commission in that they were able to use waste timber, the outside cuts from trees with bark, which allowed substantial buildings to be erected, with an overall artistic, rustic effect. Timber taken from forests by the Forestry Commission largely provided:

logs for sawmills

poles for buildings and defence purposes

pickets for wire entanglements

firewood for bakeries, trenches and camps

charcoal for front line trenches

By the time the Armistice was signed in 1918 their camp was as self-contained as any unit could be: an underground bulk petrol storage installation greatly reduced the risk of damage from fire or enemy aircraft, in addition to effecting economies in petrol, money and manpower; the unit was fed entirely on vegetables from its own plot; it mended its own boots, while a well-equipped tailor's shop and barber's saloon added to the personal comfort of the men; there was even a fat-extracting plant for dealing with the men's refuse, which not only provided money for company funds but also excellent fat for cooking purposes, which in turn helped maintain the company poultry farm, where could be seen the men's Christmas dinner in the shape of turkeys, geese, ducks and fowl.

*   *   *

Humour is never far away when men are in uniform and this poem shows how at least one member of the ASC, Frank Stayton, was able to laugh at his Corps:

If you're feeling rather hungry,
And you want your tea
Ask the ASC. (Chorus: Ask the ASC).
If you want a gentle joy-ride
By the silver sea,
Ask the ASC. (Chorus: Ask the ASC).
They are Whiteley, Selfridge, Harrod's; and they usually contrive
To furnish you with anything to keep yourself alive;
You simply press a button that is marked "B Fifty-five"
For the ASC. (Chorus: For the ASC).
O, the ASC!
Yes, the ASC!
They are never late for breakfast, but are rarely in to tea!
They provide you with your rations,
All the books – and latest fashions.
Ask for what you want – and get it

From the ASC.
If a steamer's lost its funnel,
And must go to sea,
Ask the ASC. (Chorus: Ask the ASC).
If your train sticks in a tunnel,
Ring up QMG
For the ASC. (Chorus: For the ASC).
They will send a four-ton lorry for your neatly packed valise,
Full of bully beef and biscuit, jam and sugar, tea and cheese;
It would move you to emotion, their anxiety to please,
Loyal ASC.
Willing ASC.
O, the ASC!
Yes, the ASC.
They will see you get your dinner though the shells disturb your tea.
It's a job that's not exciting,
And they haven't time for fighting,
Yet they do their bit! . . . So, hats off
To the ASC.

*　　*　　*

Much has been written about how much the Infantry suffered in the mud and trenches of the Great War. They were not alone. The following is an extract from the diary of the OC of an ASC Company in the 9th Divisional Train in the winter of 1916-17, showing the bad conditions in which the ASC Horse Transport had to work, day in day out: "Still in huts east of Bray. The men, wagons, harness and animals are in all a pretty bad state; the men are very dirty and their clothes in a very bad way; the animals are scarcely recognisable as such under the mud which almost hides them; the harness is a mass of mud and much of it bad and much deficient; the wagons are terrible, ten with broken perches, thirty-eight with broken tailboards, fourteen with one, two or three bad wheels, others with broken standards, bolsters, footboards, bottoms, brake bars, brake guides etc and over all one mass of mud."

And a month later: "All the men have colds and the greater number have temperatures, bronchitis or some loss of voice etc . . . . the road was much too narrow and in addition it was a sheet of glass, causing animals to fall repeatedly. To ride was quite impossible, all drivers had to dismount and walk. What with this difficulty and the intensely biting north wind, anything worse could not be imagined – every animal falling down, many of them three or four times. It took about four hours to cover this bare three miles."

Of the area between Béthune and Ypres, he wrote: "From here (Béthune) to the north round Ypres, a county of streams, dykes and morasses, and, in winter, waterlogged; the roads were mainly a type of pavé, practically without foundations, so that to see the stones of it sink and rise as a lorry passed along, had to be seen to be believed, in addition they were narrow, and on each side of the pavé one sank in mud – poor routes for intercommunication."

*　　*　　*

Damage to the roads occasionally rebounded on the ASC. On 31 August 1916 340 MT Company, the Supply Column of the 23rd Division, received an order from the Town Major of Baizieux to supply a fatigue party to mend Dundas Street (in Baizieux) as the "Corps Commander's car had slipped into a hole nearly throwing the Corps Commander out". And straightforward labouring was not done only by Labour units. On 26 December 1916 50% of 74 MT Company's vehicles were taken off the road and fifty drivers, under an officer, were sent to Meroc (near Loos) to clear out and repair the reserve trenches there, a change from the routine work of being the Supply Column of the 8th Division.

*   *   *

The ASC link with the formation of the Heavy Branch of the Machine Gun Corps (MGC) (later, on 28 July 1917, the Tank Corps) is known by few people, which is understandable since little has been published, certainly by the ASC or its successors. Tank Corps information has naturally tended to concentrate on their own cap badge, an exception being an excellent 1995 published book on the Battle of Flers-Courcelette on the Somme on 15 September 1916.*

The design, planning and production of the first tanks had taken place in 1915 and the first ASC involvement was in May or June 1916, when four officers visited Elveden, near Thetford, on Lord Iveagh's estate, recently acquired from Prince Duleep Singh. The Adjutant General had asked the Director of Supplies & Transport for drivers and others to undertake tank driver training and workshop support for the Heavy Branch of the MGC and he caused a trawl for suitability qualified personnel to take place in the Tractor Depot at Avonmouth, the port which handled the import of Holt Caterpillar tractors, and in MT Depots in London. Most of the men contacted were those earmarked for service overseas, who were invited to volunteer for a new employment of "a secret nature which might prove dangerous". Men also came from caterpillar companies in France.

A number of men responded to this challenge and a Mechanist Sergeant Major and twelve ASC men were the first to go to Elveden in early June, effectively the founders of a new unit, 711 MT Company ASC. Four officers too came at this early stage, including Major H Knothe as the Company Commander, 2nd Lieutenant H P G Steedman, responsible for the tank park, vehicles, inspection, maintenance and training of drivers, and 2nd Lieutenant St John, OC the workshop. Utmost secrecy was observed. The Home Defence Corps surrounded the camp with armed sentries and special passes were needed. The camp was even called the 'Elveden Explosives Area' to provide an element of deception.

After initial training in Bisley, the 711 Company men moved to Elveden at the end of May. The problem was that nothing in their past had prepared them for the shock of seeing the tanks and many were alarmed at the thought of driving these monsters. Those who were extremely unhappy were returned to Avonmouth, having been assessed by Major Knothe as incompetent, probably because they pretended to know nothing about internal combustion engines, which was obviously not true. There were some who believed their return to

* *The Tanks of Flers*, Trevor Pidgeon (Fairmile Books).

100

unit was unfair, since they were the best qualified people available. With good man management, fear of the tanks could probably have been overcome and they could have developed the same sort of pride in their work as did the others who remained. It was perhaps quite unnecessary for the OC of the Tractor Depot to be asked by the War Office for an explanation, but that was probably caused by the embarrassment felt by senior ASC staff involved.

The work level for officers and men was extremely heavy and the responsibility considerable. In addition to ordinary mechanical repairs, workshop personnel were responsible for unloading tanks from railway flats when they arrived at a local siding. The difficulty was that unloading had to take place at night for security reasons, as the siding was in full view of the main line. This was (and still is) a very dangerous operation. An additional reason for unloading not being carried out by day was the occasional visit by Zeppelins. On one occasion a bomb was dropped on the camp; on another, work was stopped when a Zeppelin flew overhead.

The establishment of 711 Company seemed to be in a state of constant flux in August 1916. At the end of the month the unit consisted of 303 all ranks, with nine cars, thirteen box vans, three charabancs, twenty-seven 3 ton lorries, fifteen 30 cwt lorries, seventeen motor cycles and three 105 hp Foster-Daimler tractors. Stores and spare parts were obtained from a variety of sources, mainly the Home MT Depot in London. The vehicles had come from numerous sources too and there was a certain amount of doubt about what was on whose charge.

The early days of any new project are always difficult, but when pressures to achieve wonders in a short time frame abounded (ie tanks were urgently needed for operations in France) there were many men who were somewhat unsettled. Leave was difficult to obtain and men who were promised leave for particular work done were refused it at the last moment. When extra exertions were demanded by further promises and they too were broken for no satisfactory reason, dissatisfaction spread, not helped by poor and insufficient food. In spite of all that, however, the men did their work well and two companies of tanks and an ASC workshop went via Avonmouth to France. An ASC road officer was attached to each MGC Company for movement purposes. The tanks travelled on railway flats, accompanied by some ASC personnel, which was lucky as one or two tanks' securing chains became loose during the journey and had to be properly secured. The workshop went by road. They were soon, too soon, involved in the Battle of Flers-Courcelette on 15 September, all the tanks being driven by ASC drivers (the list can be seen at Annex O).

Two weeks before the tanks left the UK the ASC Workshop Company consisted of seven officers, 150 artificers and fifty rank & file for general duties. Major Knothe took a much reduced team to France, with three officers, one Mechanist Sergeant Major and twenty-five men, along with two trailers fitted with lathes, drilling machines and emergency wheels; one trailer was fitted with a 60 ton hydraulic press. These two trailers were moved from Le Havre by two Holt caterpillar tractors to the Loop near Bray-sur-Somme. On arrival, all tank tracks had to be adjusted. This woeful lack of equipment was sorely felt in France, particularly when a Mechanist Sergeant Major and six men had to carry a complete tank track and its associated packing to help recover a tank at High Wood.

Bad reports, however, came back to the ASC men in Elveden, mainly to the effect that the tanks were largely unsuccessful, but other more human problems caused upset: officially only ASC men were allowed to drive, even though all crew members were given training in each others' tasks, but the tank commanders, all officers, failed to enforce this rule, which not only resulted in breakdowns, but also caused the ASC to be adversely and unfairly criticized; several tanks were lost because of incompetent driving, caused by MGC men being substituted for ASC drivers; engines seized up in the most strange way: oil was found to have been completely drained; reports came back that a certain tank was bogged in, but the ASC recovery party had no difficulty in moving it. Not all was bad news though: the ASC men in support of the tanks received particular praise and deserved a special mention. They worked day and night in trying conditions, constantly repairing and recovering damaged or abandoned tanks, in pouring rain, up to their knees in mud and under fire. At this early stage they had no tools other than what they could make or put together themselves. Almost all of these men had been supplied by the ASC Depot at Grove Park.

Meanwhile, back in Elveden, Captain B H Edkins arrived as OC but, when he followed Major Knothe to France, Steedman was promoted to Captain in command of 711 Company. After the September exodus to France twenty tanks were left behind, eight of which went to Egypt, where they fought in the Battle of Gaza, and twelve went to Bovington in Dorset. A number of 711 Company men went to Egypt with the tanks, forming the nucleus of 961 MT Company.

In late November 1916 a School of Instruction in Tank Driving was officially inaugurated on the western parade ground in Bovington Camp by the now promoted Lieutenant Colonel Knothe, the instructional staff consisting mainly of selected officers and men from 711 MT Company and several ASC officers who had been with the tanks in France. The tanks used were fifteen Mark Is obtained from the tankodrome in Barnham in Norfolk. They arrived in a dilapidated condition so were sent to Fosters in Lincoln for refurbishment. The first course, in January 1917, consisted of twenty-eight all ranks, a one-week 'refresher' course for those who had previous experience driving tanks. A total of four such courses were held in January.

In early December 1916 Major J G Brockbank Special Reserve ASC reported to Bermicourt, near Agincourt, in France as the OC of a new unit, the Central Repair Workshop & Stores, in support of the tanks, along with Lieutenant S H Foot and 2nd Lieutenant T G Leggott RE, ten other officers and 394 men. The first G1098 scale was designed for the workshop. After some experience it turned out to be quite inadequate so stores were requested direct from the Mechanical Warfare Supplies Depot in London (ie without going through 711 Company) for small tools, plant and machinery which the AOD would not issue as they were not on the original G1098 scale. The Stores Officer was Lieutenant Quartermaster Turner. A new workshop site was put in hand in early January 1917 and completed in June, just in time for a visit by HM Queen Mary on 7 July. To assist in labouring tasks within the Central Workshop, No. 51 Chinese Labour Company was attached with effect from 8 August 1917.

CHAPTER 5

1917: A Year of Contrasts

The year 1917 contained a mixed bag of success and failure. Kut el Amara was retaken in February; Baghdad and Jerusalem were captured. In April the bloody Battle of Arras won a gain of four-and-a-half miles but incurred heavy casualties, while the Canadians were successful on Vimy Ridge. The Third Battle of Ypres, often known as Passchendaele, the major British attack in Flanders, ground to a halt in late 1917, a failure, and the much-vaunted tank attack at Cambrai in November surprised the Germans but gained only small advantage.

Allies came and went. On the one hand Czar Nicholas II of Russia abdicated and a Provisional Government was formed, quickly leading to German armies in the east being reallocated to the Western Front; on the other the United States of America entered the fray, declaring war on the Central Powers on 17 April. Along with the contribution of 50,000 men of the Portuguese Expeditionary Force in February, the imminent arrival of fresh American manpower threatened to change the numerical balance in the battle of attrition in Europe, causing the German staff to reconsider their plans.

The ASC was heavily involved in creating reserves of stocks, not only for the attacks of 1917 but also for a major offensive in 1918, of which only a few had any idea at the time. An attack needed months of preparation by the staff and Logistic Services, as the work involved was in addition to routine replenishment. The beginning of the year saw the creation of a new Labour Corps, into which the ASC Labour Companies were transferred in mid-summer.

Most of the year was taken up with the greatest reorganization within the ASC during the whole war, the creation of units on a Corps basis, which provided necessary reserves; and in December, in keeping with the centralized control effected by that reorganization, the Auxiliary Omnibus Companies were withdrawn from the Armies in order to allow repair and refurbishment and the establishment of an Auxiliary Omnibus Park which was to play such a vital role some fifteen months later.

*   *   *

To continue with the Heavy Branch of the Machine Gun Corps, reorganization became the order of the day in early 1917. 711 MT Company ASC was transferred to the Heavy Branch of the MGC on 23 February 1917 with all its personnel (less Captain Steedham). Major F Strickland ASC was appointed Chief Instructor of Tank Training and the School in Bovington was reorganized to cope with increased numbers. With courses for twenty All Ranks extended to sixteen days, instruction was in two parts: on the tank park and in a Mechanical School. It was not long, however, before a further increase in demand led to the course being reduced to twelve days. A Minor Repairs School was also started in early 1917 to teach tank drivers, after their initial tank driver training, how to carry out repairs, thus reducing demands on the workshop. All training was carried out by ASC workshop personnel.

In December 1916 the four Tank Companies (A, B, C and D) had been expanded to battalion size and two Tank Brigades were formed in January 1917, each consisting of two Tank Battalions. (Three more Tank Brigades were formed: one in April 1917, one in December 1917 and one in March 1918.) Each of these battalions was initially served by its own workshop, but they were largely incorporated in the new Central Repair Workshop & Stores, whose establishment rose to 25 officers and 1,143 men. The establishment included five Advanced Workshops, an outstanding feature made possible by the better technical instruction now received and the cumulatively increasing tank crew knowledge of their machines. Each tank in fact became a self-contained unit. Each Advanced Workshop contained thirteen ASC men.

When 711 MT Company transferred to the Heavy Branch of the MGC, the problem of MT did not disappear. An MT section in support was still needed, however, and additional vehicles were required, but by this time everything had been transferred. It was therefore necessary to form a separate MT section, which was then commanded by Lieutenant H H Hicks, who had workshop and engineering experience. The War Office decided that the ASC should operate the MT, as well as maintain them, and a Board of Survey was held in April 1917, after which all vehicles (except for the three Foster Daimler tractors) were transferred to the OC of 831 Local Auxiliary MT Company ASC based in the Dorchester area who provided (with the assistance of ASC Records) the necessary personnel. The ex-ASC (by now MGC) men were therefore released to carry out other duties; most of them became instructors in driving and other training.

Initially transport was attached to tank battalions, each with a MT officer attached, but this proved unsatisfactory and transport was centralized under Brigade Headquarters which had an ASC Captain and three Subalterns attached. 711 Company was responsible for all MT vehicles in the Heavy Branch of the MGC.

It is amusing to see that officers driving were even a problem in the 1914-18 war. There is a note in PRO Kew from OC 711 Company in March 1917: "It would appear that MGC officers are in the habit of driving tanks contrary to War Office instructions in England. Have reported to OC MGC on several occasions. A great deal of minor troubles are the direct outcome of this practice, also the alterations of adjustments by inexperienced people".

Three members of 711 Company became well known after the war. Lieutenant J V Carden (later Sir John Carden) went on to become one of the great inter-war tank and transmission designers; with Lieutenant V H Lloyd he founded the firm of Carden-Lloyd, who introduced the idea of a 'tankette'. Eventually the firm was bought out by Vickers, the concept leading to the Bren gun carrier of the 1939-45 war.

Private P H Johnson, when travelling by train to Elveden in Suffolk to join 711 Company as one of the volunteer drivers, happened to meet on the train Colonel E D Swinton DSO late RE, one of the originators of the tank. This chance meeting resulted in a friendship that lasted through the war and well beyond. Johnson was soon commissioned in the ASC and was one of the tank commanders in the battle of Flers-Courcelette, helped set up the Central Repair Workshop at Bermicourt and was one of the technical advisers for the 'Hush' tank landing operations on the Belgian coast. At the end the war he was the officer in charge of the Department of Tank Design and Experiment working on Plan 1919, an imaginative concept using faster, lighter tanks to achieve a battlefield breakthrough. On retirement in 1920, as Lieutenant Colonel P H Johnson MBE DSO Legion of Honour, he founded the firm Roadless Traction, which specialized in off-road machines, initially for the Forces but later for agriculture.

*　　*　　*

Realizing that a railway breakdown was inevitable sooner or later, and appreciating the part MT could be made to play, as well as the need for economies in vehicles and manpower, the Quartermaster General approved on 17 January 1917 a reorganization of mechanical transport on a Corps basis. The winter of 1917-1918 saw this project put into effect, although some units were delayed in this. The policy adopted involved the principle that MT vehicles were for the common use and, except for a few cases (eg electric light lorries and signal lorries), should not be specialized for any particular task. Pooling was imposed on all units and formations. Considerable reductions in the number of vehicles were thus made and there was also a worthwhile saving in manpower, enabling a large number of vehicles to be put into a general reserve, part of which was used to provide replacement vehicles, the residue forming GHQ Reserve MT Companies.

All vehicles were reconditioned and then pooled. Divisional Supply Columns and Ammunition Sub Parks were consolidated into Divisional MT Companies; Corps Supply Columns and Corps Ammunition Parks were consolidated into Corps MT Columns, Army Troops Supply Columns each absorbed an Auxiliary MT Company, becoming Army Troops MT Companies, and Corps Troops Supply Columns were redesignated Corps Troops MT Companies. All this took some time and was aimed to be completed in March 1918. Some units were, unfortunately, caught in the middle of their reorganization at the time of the German offensive in March.

MT Companies were organized on a universal establishment of a headquarters and so many sections (platoons) of sixteen lorries each, fifteen to be working lorries, with one spare to allow for periodical overhaul. Divisional MT Companies consisted of five sections, Army Troop MT Companies of four sections and Corps Troops MT Companies of two sections each.

The following were laid down as the duties of the Senior MT Officer (usually referred to as 'SMTO', a Lieutenant Colonel ASC) in each Corps Headquarters:

"To exercise supervision from a technical transport point of view over the following units:

Corps Supply Columns (composed of the Corps Troops Supply Column and the three Divisional Supply Columns normally serving with a Corps)

Corps Ammunition Park (composed of three Ammunition Sub Parks)

Corps Siege Park (composed generally of a MT Company attached to the Corps Heavy Artillery)

Any other MT units which may from time to time be allotted as Corps Troops and to be responsible for bringing to notice of the Corps staff any cases in which MT vehicles are used in an improper or uneconomical manner. He will also be authorized to make such inspections and call for such returns as he considers necessary

He will assist the Corps staff in procuring and allotting all MT vehicles available in the above units for any extraneous services that may be required in the Corps area, without in any way dislocating the specific work for which the various MT units are allotted

He will be responsible for the general supervision of the working of all ASC Mobile Workshops and the even distribution of the spare parts and stores

He is not in any way to interfere with, or be responsible for, any matters connected with the distribution of, or accounting for, supplies or ammunition, nor will he be concerned with any technical question regarding the movement of guns

He will not be a channel of communication between the Corps staff and the Corps Ammunition Park or Supply Column Commanders, nor between the GOC Corps Heavy Artillery and the OC ASC Company attached to Corps Heavy Artillery except on technical MT subjects or employment on duties extraneous to their normal functions

He will deal with the Commanders of the MT units in all matters regarding the adjustment of surplus and deficient personnel and will therefore be, in this respect, the channel of communication between them and the office of the DAG 3rd Echelon

He will institute the necessary enquiries in the case of any accidents occurring to MT vehicles belonging to the Corps

Beyond the above limits, he will not be directly responsible for the interior economy of the units."

*   *   *

In January 1917 labour in the Expeditionary Force consisted of the following: ASC Labour Companies, RE Labour Battalions, Infantry Labour Battalions, Canadian Labour Battalions, Portuguese Labour Companies, 'Cape Men' of Infantry Labour Battalions, a Kaffir Labour Battalion, British West India Battalions, Bermuda Garrison Artillery, POW Companies, Non-Combatant Corps Battalions, Companies and French or Belgian civilians; later were added the South African Labour Corps, Egyptian Labour Corps, Indian Labour Corps, Chinese Labour Corps, a Fijian Labour Company, Middlesex (Alien) Infantry Labour Companies and Italian Labour. At GHQ the Labour Directorate consisted of a Controller (Director), two Deputy Controllers, two Assistant Deputy Controllers, ten clerks, four batmen and two ASC MT drivers.

*   *   *

During the early part of the war, it was not possible to spare many ASC officers for the fighting arms, but in May 1917 the Quartermaster General put forward a proposal to allow young ASC officers working in Horse Transport or Supply in France, and at home who were under thirty years of age, to be compulsorily attached to fighting arms for the period of the war. The proposal was approved and subsequently extended to the other fronts, and to some extent to the MT Branch. It resulted in 1,225 young officers being detached to the fighting arms. Also at this period it was decided to consider no candidates under the age of thirty-five years for a commission in the ASC, exceptions being made in the case of those certified as medically unfit for the fighting arms and those who possessed highly technical qualifications for MT duties.

*   *   *

By mid-March preparations in the Auxiliary Omnibus Park were complete. Previously bus companies had carried out a variety of tasks – carrying stores, course students, bathing parties, staff officers, refugees, wounded prisoners-of-war, reinforcements, reliefs, salvage and even French treasure hunters, but the new tasking system enabled the Park to respond to a GHQ master plan and, following the example of the French Army, speedily put into effect major operational moves. This was an entirely new concept for the British.

Such moves were practised in a concentration in March 1917 when all seven omnibus companies were located at intervals on the main roads running between Amiens, Doullens, St Pol and Ypres, a route that was to be of some significance a year later. GHQ sent orders direct to the Park Headquarters by telephone, confirmed by despatch rider, for the move of Divisions, based on a combined traffic, embussing and debussing map. Bus columns were ready to move within an hour of receiving their orders. Divisions seldom took more than half-an-hour to embus and debus. The record for a Brigade was four-and-a-half minutes. Clearly this was set up under ideal conditions but it showed what could be achieved with an imposed sense of discipline.

War diary entries of the various companies show a variety of taskings, including a number of operational moves on 18 November when 15 Company carried men of the Guards Division from the Liencourt area to Bus-les-Artois in thirty-five buses and thirty-two lorries in preparation for the Battle of Cambrai. On 20 November they sent forty-one buses and thirty-one lorries to various dressing stations to convey walking wounded. The administrative order of 21 Motor Ambulance Convoy for this battle shows that the buses, each catering for twenty-two wounded, supplemented the medical evacuation system provided by ambulances and the Decauville railway. The proposal by the medical authorities during the Hounslow-Shoeburyness move in 1908 had come to fruition. The companies moved location at Christmas 1917 and again in January-February 1918.

*   *   *

The life of an MT driver varied between dull and exciting. Few, though, had the excitement of one driver in 805 MT Company on 10 October 1917, when his 3 ton Commer collided with the Paris express at the Rouxmesnil level-crossing. The lorry was completely smashed and the railway engine overturned, telescoping two carriages. The driver, strangely enough, was found hanging onto the buffers of the engine, only slightly bruised, a lucky man.

It would appear, too, that the life of the fighting arms was often dull. 683 MT Company showed English films on a company cinematograph tour in the 12 Corps area in the period 11-28 June 1917, using a workshop lorry (even with the inconvenience involved). Films shown were *The Battle of the Ancre* and a selection of films from England. They also showed films in the 22nd Division area, being shelled *en route,* where up to 2,000 attended. Films were also shown at Headquarters 12 Corps for three nights, the audience including the Corps Commander and Headquarters 83rd Brigade, where 1,000 men attended. This tour led to a letter of thanks from the DA & QMG 12 Corps to the OC 683 Company thanking him for lending the 'cinematograph machine' to the Corps: "It is not perhaps realized by people at the Base how much men in the front line appreciate Entertainments of any sort that tend to relieve the monotony of routine. It does not often however fall to their lot to see a cinematograph performance every whit as good as those given at home, and it is thanks to your personal attention and that of Lieutenant Smith that the success of the tour has been largely due."

*   *   *

In 1917 a large number of drivers who had been evacuated from field units, either through hospitals or the Base MT Depot, were, after testing, found to be incapable of driving vehicles efficiently. These men were sent to the MT School of Instruction on the Lines of Communication, but, as the staff were there essentially to complete the training of drafts from UK, the School was completely overloaded. The only answer was to ensure that OCs gave their drivers, importantly the second or spare drivers, sufficient opportunity to practise their skills so that they did not deteriorate after a period away from the unit. Easier said than done as the normal MT driver was not necessarily a good instructor.

*   *   *

Early in March the German withdrawal to the Hindenburg Line started, a total surprise to the British, so no preparations for a forward move had been made. When the British move forward started supplies were drawn immediately by MT of the ASC, but it was not until the second or third day that real problems were felt by the Supply Columns. 352 MT Company (as the 32nd Division Supply Column), for instance, found that trees had been felled across the roads, there were mine craters at every crossroad and some villages were almost impassable as houses had been blown up to cover the roadways. With no means at their disposal other than self-help, one route through the debris was cleared, trees being dragged clear by lorries.

With the increased distance to travel from the railhead, something like sixty miles, the turn-round was about twelve hours, partly due to the state of the roads and the obstacles encountered. As ever, one has to admire the pluck and commitment of the drivers, who went straight back to load up at the railhead, missing their night's sleep in the process. What did not help was that trains carrying supplies were not always regular in their timings and the drivers' programmes were stretched beyond anyone's control.

When they arrived in Voyennes, which had been under German occupation during the war until then, 352 Company found that all the inhabitants from surrounding villages had been crowded into the town, which meant that six times the normal population were present. These civilians were mostly old folk and children, who were pathetically willing to do anything to be helpful to the troops, probably due to the oppression they had suffered under German hands and their relief at seeing allied soldiers in their midst. ASC vehicles took rations for these civilians for several days, as they had nothing, an activity that was otherwise routinely forbidden.

Once vehicles had passed through the initial devastation zone, drivers were amazed at the good condition of the roads. They had apparently been hardly used by German vehicles, the German Army preferring to use light railways to supply the front line; but of course all trackway and any other usable stores and equipment had been removed before the withdrawal. Sadly, the good state of the roads did not last long with the constant pounding they received from British transport, a situation not improved by heavy rainfall at the end of March.

* * *

806 Company, working as an Army Troops Mobile Repair Unit, recount in their war diaries that on 19 July 1917 nine lorries allocated to 171 Tunnelling Company RE, either ditched or too damaged to move, were temporarily abandoned in view of the enemy, thus drawing a fire so intense that the road between Zillebeke and Hell Fire Corner could not be used. It had been decided that it would be necessary to blow up these vehicles if they were not removed at once. The unit's first aid lorry, together with one belonging to 'B' Corps Ammunition Park, were deployed and, shortly after midnight on 19 July, the work of extracting them started. Seven were successfully moved; the remaining two, damaged beyond repair by shellfire, were pushed into a ditch, thus removing an easy target for enemy artillery. The work was done under continuous shellfire and, as a reward for this operation and other similar services, Second Lieutenant V W Ory was awarded the Military Cross and Lance Corporals Marshall and Reid the Military Medal.

This work was only one of many similar successful tasks performed by the unit in the Ypres district up to 8 October 1917. Altogether between 200-300 salvage operations were carried out, with 50 being successfully completed under shellfire. Fortunately the work was performed with the loss of only one man wounded. From January 1917 to the Armistice in November 1918 the company recovered 855 lorries and cars, of which fifty-three were damaged by shellfire and 101 recovered under shellfire. The units tyre presses replaced in the same period a total of 42,604 tyres, almost beyond imagination.

* * *

A feature of life on the Western Front in 1916, 1917 and 1918, let alone with the Occupation of the Rhineland in 1919, was the organization of Horse Shows. They could only take place away from the front when no great activity was expected, and they helped keep soldiers occupied. The ASC, as major users of horses, contributed much to the organization of these shows and made great efforts to do well in the prize lists; competition was stiff from the Cavalry and Gunners though. The programme of the day included close inspections of horses and wagons and also riding competitions. In August 1917 the 34th Division included a Camouflaged Vehicle Competition in their Horse Show, which was won by 231 HT Company ASC. Their winning entry consisted of a hayrick made up of a wooden frame, with wire netting interlaced with hay, concealing a limbered GS wagon, an ASC driver and two horses. The front was made to roll up like a blind so that the horses could pass in and out.

*   *   *

Until the Battle of the Somme prisoners-of-war were sent back to England, but, subsequently, under the Labour Directorate, POW companies were organized, each consisting of four platoons of about 100 men. In the early part of the war, there were several such companies at the ASC Heavy Repair Shops, but then the number of captured rose so that prisoners were sent to a main POW pen in Abbeville. From these numbers skilled units were formed for work in quarries and roads. Bavarians and foresters were drafted into POW Forestry Companies, while skilled units were formed for workshops of the ASC, Royal Engineers, Army Ordnance Department and locomotive shops.

Labour Groups were formed, commanded by Lieutenant Colonels, in charge of all Labour Companies in their allocated area, thus providing an elastic system of command, enabling companies to be moved from one Group to another in response to a changing situation. The OC was a Major or Captain, for whom a horse or bicycle was provided on establishment (but only when considered necessary by his General Officer Commanding). He was supported by four subalterns as platoon commanders, a Company Sergeant Major, Company Quartermaster Sergeant, eight Sergeants and eighteen Corporals, including Clerk and Cook Corporals.

Initially there were major problems: most Labour Corps officers sadly had little military experience, although some were transfers from the Infantry; the British soldiers were of a low physical category and it had not been possible to provide the transport laid down in the establishment. There was a weakness due to lack of command: Assistant Directors of Labour were only to "advise on Labour matters . . . with a view to its proper employment and economical working" and their deputies were overwhelmed with administrative work. Changes were soon effected, however, and the Labour Corps grew in strength and efficiency, but it was disbanded immediately after the war, to be resuscitated in 1939 as the Auxiliary Military Pioneer Corps, subsequently the Pioneer Corps.

The twenty-nine Labour Companies ASC were transferred *en bloc* to the Labour Corps in August 1917. This newly-formed Labour Corps, which also incorporated forty-seven prisoner-of-war labour companies, many of which worked well in ASC base installations, provided sterling service for the BEF.

*   *   *

604 Company ASC ('P' Corps Siege Park) recorded that it was sometimes forgotten by those who have no practical experience of actual work with Siege

Park lorries that it was the personnel who count. Without the right men, they opined, lorries and tractors are useless. The driver of a lorry was very limited in his choice of route up the line; indeed he invariably had to keep to up and down routes dictated by the staff. Roads and crossroads which were known to be shelled could not be avoided by making off across the fields. Roads could be seen from the air and made an easy target for enemy pilots. Not only did the men of the ASC MT know this but so too did the men of working parties who were transported into the forward areas to repair roads or dig new gun positions. Drivers were invariably asked to stop and allow the men to get out when wagons approached dangerous crossroads or junctions – "[They] would meet them further on the road." "Which way are you going, chum?" was often asked by an infantryman returning from the line with full kit. The driver would slow down and reply, but, hearing the answer, the infantryman preferred to take the route across the fields. "If you are going along that road, I will walk. Jerry's shelling."

Many of the roads in the forward area could not be repaired during the day, as they were under observation by the enemy and work had to finish soon after dawn. Lorries had to report at the dumps for working parties and material in the very early hours of the morning. Drivers of lorries had to be up and about at 2.00 am on frosty mornings to get their engines started, which was no easy task, and away in time to reach their destination at the required time. Even though lamps were placed under the bonnets, pumps sometimes froze, and the petrol was not always free from water. When under enemy observation, lamps were not allowed to be lighted. Roads were lined with traffic both ways, infantrymen coming and going to and from the trenches, GS wagons, guns and limbers, pack mules (sometimes obstinate and without guides), ambulances and lorries, and there were always the ditches, one on each side of the road which, if 'found', would not easily be got out of. Blocks in the traffic would invariably occur in the worst of places and lorry drivers would 'find' the ditch. The passage of two convoys on a road wide enough only for one was invariably decided by the seniority of the officer in command, even if it did not take into account the operational demands of the situation and the rules laid down by GHQ. As if all that were not bad enough, it was necessary to wear gas helmets when gas shells were falling. After completing one journey, a second and sometimes a third journey would have to be made. Life was not easy.

Caterpillars were always unpopular with officers on the staff and the Signals operators as their tracks regularly chewed up communication wires that had been laid across the road. The driver was not best pleased either, as he had to cut away a mass of tangled wire from his tracks when he could find time. Even when the wires were raised well off the ground to solve this problem, the caterpillar's canopy would catch them.

*   *   *

Siege Parks attached to Corps were designed for work with Heavy Artillery, but were administered by the ASC. They were answerable to the Heavy Artillery for the haulage of guns, supplying ammunition to batteries when in position, and the movement of batteries, and also to the MT Branch of the ASC for the upkeep of lorries and administration of personnel. Even the driver of the Battery Commander's car was only 'attached' to the battery. Battery Commanders did not have direct command over the separate columns attached to them, which had its disadvantages. The planning of parks for lorries and tractors was naturally dependent on the positions of guns and the situation of ammunition railheads, but the movement of lorries was a matter for the ASC. Members of the Corps who supported the heavy guns were often involved in activities which brought them in constant danger, largely due to enemy shelling, A good number became casualties and a number received decorations for bravery.

On 23 September 1917 Lance Corporal F Oxford of the 227th Siege Battery Ammunition Column (SBAC) was awarded the Military Medal for his work on the night of 1 September. He was in charge of six lorries loaded with RE stores to take to Nieuport. Immediately on arrival, the enemy started shelling heavily. The guides made a search for the unloading party but returned alone and asked that the lorries should be unloaded somewhere else to avoid the shelling. Lance Corporal Oxford took his convoy to the place required, but the enemy started to shell this location too. The unloading party not having been found, Lance Corporal Oxford and his drivers unloaded, but, whilst unloading, he and a driver were wounded. Immediately the first lorry was unloaded, he conveyed the wounded man to the nearest dressing station, giving orders that the remaining lorries should proceed after unloading and meet him on the road back. He met the five lorries on the Wulpen road, took charge and brought the convoy back to the Park. On his return he was immediately taken to hospital and the next day evacuated to the Base.

Another award of the Military Medal was made whilst the Siege Park was in this sector to Sergeant O D Bicknell of 122nd Siege Battery Ammunition Column for distinguished work when on ammunition duty. He was in charge of nine lorries which were detailed to remove ammunition from the old position of 32nd Siege Battery on the Ramscappelle/Pervyse road during the night of 7 September. When the lorries arrived at the battery it was shelled heavily. Seeing the conditions, Sergeant Bicknell decided to take three lorries at a time up to the old position to load, leaving the remainder on the main road. Of the first three to go forward, two lorries were hit and three men wounded but, in spite of this, Sergeant Bicknell, having seen to the wounded men and damaged lorries, returned and carried on with his duties. Hostile shellfire continued, but Sergeant Bicknell completed his duty and brought back the nine lorries to the park.

Several casualties, too, were caused whilst on the coast, chiefly by enemy aircraft – bombs were dropped day and night. The Forward Tractor Park suffered severely. On 26 September 2nd Lieutenant W H Bonfield was killed at the Tractor Park by a hostile shell. It was not always that the enemy made a raid specifically on the Siege Park and surrounding districts, but sometimes that occurred. The area was in such a position that it was overflown by enemy squadrons in the course of the day, with the set purpose of bombing French ports, England or shipping in the Channel. Often a stray machine would drop a bomb when making the journey to the coast or on the return. On 29 October the Tractor Park was bombed again; three men were killed and four severely wounded.

In autumn 1917 it was evident that preparations were being made by all branches of the Service to meet a German offensive in the spring of 1918. A defensive policy was being adopted: no large dumps of ammunition were made in the forward areas and no large amounts of ammunition were stored at battery locations, as had been the case when planning an offensive; only sufficient ammunition was delivered to batteries to just carry on; consequently few lorries were required for ammunition duty during this period and the greater number were engaged in the construction of the defensive system which was being prepared. Each day all available lorries were at work; some days it was necessary for all lorries to be detailed twice in order to carry out the duties required. The usual number were required for conveying rations and supplies to batteries and columns; the remainder were engaged each day by batteries in preparing reserve gun positions with the help of Royal Engineers companies and on road construction.

During this period a large amount of salvaging was done by Siege Parks themselves and by other units in the Corps who required transport from the Siege Parks for this purpose. Methods were adopted to save expenditure. A system of boot repairs was started in order to cope with the demand for boots and to save transport in receiving new pairs and returning old pairs to the Base. During February 284 pairs of boots were repaired and it was only necessary to issue fifty pairs of new boots. This compared with the previous month, when 280 pairs of new boots were issued before the boot repairing scheme was inaugurated, effecting a 70% reduction in the issue of new boots. As a result of all this indents to the Base were considerably reduced.

*   *   *

Sergeant Douglas Clark was in a Siege Battery near Passchendaele at the end of October 1917, in close support of the guns. His diary tells how lucky he was to escape with his life when he was on the road with 2nd Lieutenant Preed, his section commander.

"Mr Preed & I leave park at 12.45 pm. FWD takes us to Pocklington Dump to collect 8 lorries . . . and take to our Battery. It is now quite dark and wind favourable for Fritz gas. All guns this side of Bavaria House in action. We enquire of Military Police how Fritz was behaving & he said he was shelling worse where we were now standing than over the ridge so we decided to take all vehicles over ridge keeping 200 yds distance between each lorrie. Mr Preed and I rode on first vehicle. We had not gone far until we found the gas very bad, so we pulled up to warn drivers, Mr Preed going back to following lorries while I took ours forward to unload, finding great difficulty in finding position. When we eventually did find it the place was deserted so first and second drivers and myself started unloading.

"I pulled off my [gas] helmet 3 times . . . I was almost overcome at this point. One of ours or Fritzes green lights flared up & then the place was turned into hell. I doubt if ever Fritz has sent over so many shells on such a small stretch as he did round us, even putting the shelling of the previous days in the shade. I received a nasty wound in the left arm . . . I thought it certain all would be killed. I ordered [the] boys to go back and take cover near other lorries. Here I found Mr P and reported I was wounded. He wanted to take me to hospital but I refused to leave lorries.

Shells were falling in front behind and all sides so we decided to get lorries out of this but the road is so narrow in places this was bound to be a difficult job. This done I soon proceeded to try & get No 1 lorrie but Dvr turned back. I had got lorrie turned and . . . [a] shell burst hitting me in abdomen and chest and throwing me some distance. I was bleeding very heavy from stomach and having lost my gas helmet I thought the end must be near. It's then a man starts to think of the dear ones & home and I prayed I might just be able to see them to say goodbye when another shell threw me back onto the road where I was picked up & taken to Ypres Dressing Station (the Prison) & my wounds dressed. The journey left me very weak from loss of blood. It was simply murder. I was taken to the 10 CCS outside of Poperinge & there operated upon, my abdomen coming in for special attention." (Sergeant Clark was subsequently awarded the Military Medal for his part in this action.)

*   *   *

The following poem was written by Private George Curtis, a caterpillar driver during the war:

The Song of the Silkworm
(Cats)

Clang, clatter and rattle,
Wheeze, splutter and bang,
This is the song the engine sings
To the boys of the silkworm gang!
We're a smart-looking lot when cleaning down
And scraping the mud off the tracks,
Right up to our elbows in grease and fat
In filthy shirts and slacks.
We wear the badge of the ASC
And draw their blooming pay,
But the boys who can tell you we're really there
Are the boys of the RGA.
It looks easy enough in the daylight time,
Some think that's all we do.
Just drawing our Cats with a gun behind -
Well, that could be easier too.
But it's when we get the blinking call
'Cats of 221: proceed to gun positions' – Oh my!
And that's there you see the fun.
It's easy enough until you leave the road
Though the only light you get is the flash
From the guns or the star shells' glare:
A joy ride – yes, you bet;
The shells may burn and gas may come,
And it may prove more than fun -
But our Old Cat bumps and rattles along,
Till she gets hitched on to her gun.

Then in and out through shell-holes go,
With mud right up to the plates.
But whether we are hit by shell or bomb,
Well, that's in the hand of fate.
So clang and clatter and rattle along,
And behind when we are out on the road again,
It's only a gun-shift done.
What do you know of us there at home?
To you we are hardly a name,
And the work we do isn't known to you,
But we are not out for laurels or fame.
We wear the badge of the ASC,
And proud to wear it too!
Just mention Cats to the RGA,
And they are certain to give us our due.

*   *   *

One of the characteristics of individuals and units in the British Army has always been that they like to be different from others. This is reflected in different uniforms, badges and customs. The ASC was not immune to this and in fact led the way in the use of unit signs on vehicles. The year 1915 saw companies designing and using their own signs but they were not officially recognized and were always banned in routine orders. In the winter of 1916-1917, however, signs that had been used only by Divisional Trains were placed on all vehicles of the Division and registered officially as Divisional signs by order of GHQ. Other units in the Field Army and in Line of Communication units followed suit, abroad too. These signs had the advantage of enabling a unit's identity to be established from a distance and contributed to morale. (A number of ASC unit signs can be seen at Annex P.)

Some elaborate signs appeared, but the majority were simple, often resulting from an interest of the OC concerned, the function of the unit in the field or its background at home. Lieutenant Colonel A M Cockshott was an enthusiastic student of heraldry and it was he who in 1917 designed the sign of XVIII Corps, an 'M' above two crossed axes (for Lieutenant General Sir Ivor Maxse, the Corps Commander); and it was Captain F Dunbar Wilson, nephew of Sir Henry Wilson (later Chief of the Imperial General Staff) who is credited with the design of the 'HD' motif of the Highland Division. Initially the 'blade' of the 'D' pointed downwards, but that made the initials less obvious. One of the better known signs, and certainly a popular one, was the reverse of the penny coin, showing a seated Britannia for the 16th Auxiliary Omnibus Company (563 Company ASC), with their motto 'Penny All The Way'.

*   *   *

One of the 'finds' of the war was mules, which proved invaluable. In the wet and cold of the winter on the Somme mules were able to endure conditions which proved fatal to horses, and they became liked for their sterling qualities and independent personalities. They were not, of course, admirable all of the time. The following appealing story entitled "Evil-minded Army Mules" was published in the *Daily Mail* on 14 November 1917, written by a dry-humoured Gunner officer identified only with the initials 'JD':

"Returning from the OP on a misty and muddy morning, I met two mules taking four ASC men for a walk. When I arrived the party had halted before a plank bridge thrown across one of the evil-looking, nasty-smelling ditches to be found only in Flanders during the wet season. The mules were looking at the bridge and the men were looking at the mules. They had been engaged in this occupation, I learned, for three-and-a-half hours.

"Can I be of any assistance?" I enquired, prompted more by curiosity than sympathy.

"You can," replied one of the clay bipeds fervently. "You can take these unmentionable mules and have them shot, drowned or gassed, or you can keep 'em and take 'em home to play with the children."

"It's no use, Herbert," whined another clay man. "He's no use; it would take a blooming army corps to move these mules. We're here for the duration, we are."

"Can't you push them over?" I suggested.

The first speaker looked at me pityingly. "Push 'em over!" he echoed bitterly.

"Let him try, Herbert," said the other. "Another little push won't do them any harm."

Nettled by the tone rather than by the words, I placed my shoulder against the near-side mule and shoved. The wretched animal did not resist and merely sat down, and I pitched forward full-length in the mud. The other animal never took its eyes from the plank bridge.

The men did not laugh as they helped me to my feet. By the bored expression on their faces I gathered that the performance was more monotonous than amusing.

Then the four men individually and in chorus gave me the black record of that pair of mules. They were actually the cleverest and hardiest mules in the service, but so burdened with original sin that their virtues were lost in the shadow of their crimes. Both had carried ammunition through a barrage without blinking or faltering; both had gone farther with heavier burdens than any other pair of mules in the corps; and neither was to be trusted to do a straight-forward job in a straight-forward way.

"It's not as if they were frightened of the bridge," explained one of the weary escort. "They would cross a mountain torrent on a tight-rope if they were in the mood. It's just their mulishness. My opinion is that the blighters have made a bet with each other as to which shall be the first to move, and nothing short of a land-mine will shift 'em.

Cordite (the one you shoved) was the only survivor of a score of mules that got in the way of a shell the other day. He dropped, and we thought he had gone. But when the fragments stopped dropping Cordite raised his head cautiously, looked round deliberately for any more shells, then scrambled to his feet without so much as a scratch. Lyddite (his partner in crime) has been knocked down by a 'caterpillar,' and it was the 'caterpillar' that needed attention".

I walked in front of the mules and regarded them with deepened interest. Their eyes were fixed on the plank bridge in a stare as uncompromising as truth, as immutable as fate, and I drew away in awe from the vision of stark finality.

When I left the four ASC men, the mud was slowly drying on their clothes, and their faces were the faces of men for whom hope is dead."

*   *   *

CHAPTER 6

1918: Ebb and Flow

In January President Woodrow Wilson of the United States of America announced fourteen points in a peace programme for Europe, which inexorably led to the end of the war, acting as the basis for negotiation at Versailles a year later; in January too the first full American Division entered the front line in the south and they were followed, week after week, by more reinforcements. This was the spectre that filled the German High Command with dread, as they were running out of reserves of manpower just as the United States was beginning to play a major role in Europe. The German offensive of March-April was intended to destroy allied resistance before the full force of the American Army could be deployed. When they failed, Germany began to realize that the war would not bring an outright victory.

The allied counter-offensive starting in July pushed the Germans back as far as Ghent in the north and the line of the German border in the south. Even with Austria-Hungary suing for peace in early November, the German Army could have gone on fighting. After all, it would arguably have been even more dangerous on its own soil, – but a disillusioned and hungry population had had its fill of war, suffering as it was from political unrest, hunger and incipient revolt. The Kaiser abdicated on 9 November and the Armistice was signed on 11 November.

The early months of 1918 saw the ASC completing its reorganization of 1917 and providing support for the Expeditionary Force, not only in surviving the German offensive in March, but also the build-up of stocks for the counter-offensive. Like the rest of the army, its men and horses were exhausted and the vehicles were in a bad state, but they too summoned reserves of strength, determined not to let down the fighting arms.

* * *

At the start of the war, there had been no special organization to deal with salvage. Such work was regarded as part of the duties of the Armies and various departments of ASC Supplies. Within twelve months, however, it was realized that the war would be a long one and that the national resources of material would be strained to the utmost. Initial steps, therefore, were taken to save wastage.

In 1915 Divisional Salvage Companies had been formed, but they were under local arrangements, not working as independent units. Their duty was to search abandoned billets and the zone behind the trenches for derelict material of all descriptions, and to form a salvage dump where material could be sorted for re-issue or for despatch either to the Corps main dump or direct to the Base. At the same time the troops were told that it was their duty to prevent material becoming derelict and to collect salvage material from the trench zone into convenient collecting stations from where it could be removed either by the Salvage Company or by transport returning empty after the delivery of rations or ammunition.

TRAINING ARMY SERVICE CORPS RECRUITS TO PASS SUPPLIES ACROSS A RIVER.

Recruits at the ASC Training Establishment in Aldershot training to pass supplies over a river (actually the Basingstoke Canal) (B).

"NOW THEN, BRING THEM OVER HERE"
"I DON'T KNOW ABOUT BRINGIN' 'EM SIR—BUT I'LL ASK 'UM IF 'UM'LL COME."

No wise man ever orders a mule to do anything (B).

Men and horses undergoing gas training (A).

Loading horses into a barge at the ASC Training Establishment in Aldershot, February 1918 (A).

Lieutenant General Sir Frederick Clayton KCB KCMG (A).

Major General S S Long CB (A).

Major General A R Crofton Atkins KCB CMG (A).

Brigadier E Gibb CB CMG DSO (A).

ASC officer in No 1 Dress Ceremonial (B).

A smart soldier about to catch the girl's eye (B).

Equipped and ready for war (B).

A studio photo with wife and daughter (B).

A cottage industry blossomed in northern France producing silks for all regiments and Corps. They were invariably sent back home with instructions that they should be kept (B).

The A. S. C.

-:::-

IF you're short of Ammunition,
Or of Grub you're wanting more,
The Boys you're looking out for
Are the ARMY SERVICE CORPS.

30.   THE ARMY SERVICE CORPS.

This well-known and indispensable department of the Army has for its motto "Nil sine labore"—"Nothing without labour," and it is ever bearing witness to the fact that great victories cannot be achieved by the fighting regiments alone and unaided. The Army Service Corps has rendered incalculable aid to all our Armies since about the middle of the 18th century, and although it has been known under different names, such as "The Corps of Royal Waggoners," "Commissariat Dept.," and "The Royal Military Train," it has never failed in its duty. The gigantic task of feeding, clothing, and transporting five million men in the great European War will add a page of glory and romance to the history of the Corps which cannot be surpassed.

BRAVO
"THE COMMOS."

ITS A LONG LONG WAY TO THE FIGHTING LINE
WHERE'ER THAT MAY BE.
BUT DONT DESPAIR WE'LL SOON BE THERE
HELPED ON BY THE A.S.C.
THEY'RE A JOLLY FINE LOT OF WORKERS
AS THE LADS AT THE FRONT CAN SEE.
SO RAISE A CHEER FOR THOSE IN THE REAR
FOR THE GOOD OLD A.S.C.

From One of the
ARMY
SERVICE CORPS.

Serving His
King and
Country.

I clasp your hand
in fancy
But all the while I feel
My hand is fairly
itching for
The grip that's truly real

FORGET-ME-NOT
You are always in
my Thoughts
and Prayers.

Patriotic cards were popular with the soldiers (B).

TOMMY.
on Transport Work.

The British always have the capacity for gentle humour (B).

ARMY SERVICE CORPS.

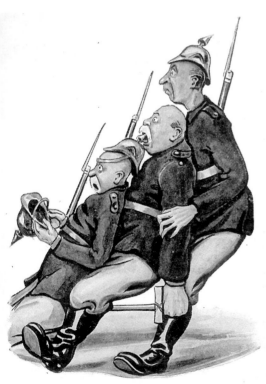

For gootness sake go back here kom
der A.S.C.

Goot gracious me ! Here kom
der ARMY SERVICE CORPS

A Berna lorry used by ASC Butchers (photo by Ricardo Studios, St Albans) (B).

The cheese store in a Base Depot - the round containers hold New Zealand cheeses (A).

Unit GS wagons pick up supplies at a roadside dump at Acheux (A).

A typical railhead at Ecurie in France in 1915. Note the wooden 'standings' and
how busy the railhead was, which must have required a good level of control (A).

Supplies being unloaded from a refrigerated ship in Boulogne. Note the LGOC
truck, after its conversion from a B-type London bus superstructure, and an over-
type Foden steam engine (A).

Electricians at work in 978 Company ASC in Claydon near Ipswich (B).

Foster and Fowler steam traction engines in No 2 ASC Repair Shop, Rouen (B).

A Foden steam lorry carrying hay for No 3 Veterinary Field Section of the Army Veterinary Corps (B).

An ASC 75 hp Fowler Lion traction engine, 'The Great Bear', probably in Melksham, where the ASC had its traction engines overhauled (B).

A 105 hp Foster-Daimler tractor nicknamed 'Absolutely It' (B).

Women of the Forage Corps ASC and men of the ASC loading bales of hay (A).

A Daimler lorry earmarked for 'walking wounded' in France (B).

Two Daimler lorries provided by the ASC to carry mail for the Royal Engineers (B).

Two Vauxhall staff cars belonging to the Bulford Garrison staff (B).

A typical mobile workshop in France, its crew lined up for the visit of British and French Officers. The second man from the left is Private P N S Mills, whose son, Major T E B Mills, presented the photograph to the RCT in 1991 (A).

Wheels and bodies being repaired in the Woodwork Shop of an ASC workshop on the Western Front (A).

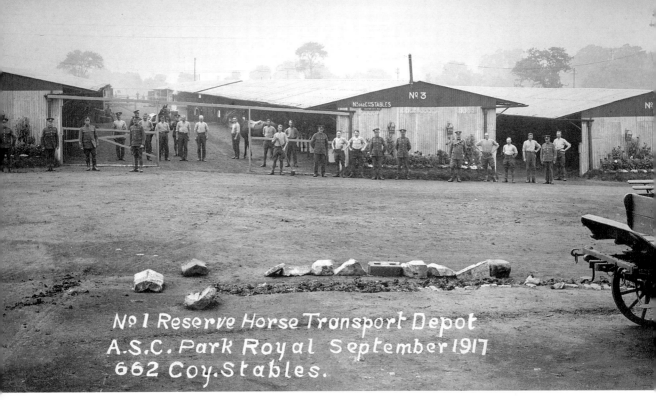

No 1 Reserve HT Depot (662 HT Company) at Park Royal, London, September 1917 (A).

A Garrett tractor in northern France, 1918 (B).

In 1917 the formation of Employment Companies gave salvage personnel a more definite status, although still without creating independent salvage units. One officer and fifty men of a Divisional Employment Company formed the authorized quota for salvage work, and one officer and forty-four Other Ranks from an Area Employment Company were allotted to each Corps Headquarters for similar duties.

The ASC dealt with all salvage coming under the headings of Supplies and Transport. The largest item under the former heading was the recovery and return of empty containers of all natures, including boxes, crates, sacks, collapsible jam cases, wrappers, jars, kegs and drums, all of which were required for refilling; even solder from empty meat tins was recovered. Under the heading of Transport came the collection and repair of all derelict or damaged mechanical transport vehicles and accessories, work which necessitated the maintenance of large depots and repair shops. Other supply items for salvage might not be apparent to most readers: flour sweepings, sheep, goat and rabbit skins, and empty bottles. An example of the latter is that a GHQ General Routine Order was published in September 1918 to the effect that all empty pickle jars which could be collected were urgently required for bottling the pickle output of Egypt. Salvage economies were also effected by the construction of labour-saving devices (eg old lorries converted into coal elevators). Other Corps were responsible for salvage within their functional areas of responsibility.

An important step was taken in the formation of the department of the Controller of Salvage. The organized recovery of expended material represented a financial saving of considerable significance, but, during the later stages of the war, material came to have a military worth not to be measured only in pounds. The world's supply of war material was running low and the nation's factories were working at the highest pressure, absorbing manpower at the expense of the fighting line. Every economy, however small, was worth the effort. Much of the recovered material was made serviceable for re-use by the development of repair shops, which obviated the need for its return to the UK. The Department of Salvage was instrumental in saving significant amounts of money which were then available to spend on more essential items. By September 1918 £4 million had been saved.

As the Controller of Salvage in the BEF in 1918, Brigadier General Gibb was occasionally subject to a great deal of leg-pulling by his friends as being 'GOC Swill'. He once even received a proposal that the round discs of paper which fall out of paper punches (for filing) should be collected in all Army areas, to be used as confetti at the weddings of WAACs. Humour apart, there is no denying that, with the economies involved and the hundreds of thousands of tons of ammunition collected from the battlefields, this was an important function.

*　　*　　*

The establishment of the Directorate of Agriculture Production was another effective move in the direction of organized economy. In the first place, the strain upon home supplies of vegetables and upon shipping was relieved. In the second, a great reduction in the quantities of fresh vegetables purchased in France was made. In addition, the Directorate was able to give invaluable help to the French in harvesting the crops sown in territory captured by the enemy and later regained by the allies. The result of the year's working of the Directorate, apart altogether from the material benefits to the troops, was considerable profit after all expenses had been paid.

*　　*　　*

The operations of the Directorate of Forestry, which worked in conjunction with the Canadian Forestry Corps, covered a considerable portion of France, including the Army and Line of Communication Areas, and the districts of the Jura and Vosges Mountains, as well as the Departments of the Landes and the Gironde. More than 2,000,000 tons of fascines, hurdles and pickets were made for the formations in Belgium and northern France. The Canadian Forestry Corps alone felled 2,000,000 cubic metres of standing timber, representing some 2,000,000 tons. In all, the Directorate produced for the use of the Armies about 3,500,000 tons of timber.

*　　*　　*

With transport and supply taking place round the clock, feeding was often a problem, especially for MT drivers who led such a peripatetic life, invariably working at the beck and call of other units. The quality and quantity of food may have varied but the war diaries of 74 MT Company ASC, the Supply Column for the 8th Division, record an appreciation in January 1918 to one lucky (and obviously hard-working) man: "At Ficheux, the Corporals and men of the Column presented the Sergeant Cook with a gold watch subscribed for by them, costing £25. This was a spontaneous tribute paid to the care and consideration given in the preparation of the meals, and to the fact that, at no matter what hour of the day or night drivers returned to the park, hot food was always ready for them." It would be reassuring to think that everyone was in receipt of such good nourishment.

*　　*　　*

Even in 1918 new transport companies were being formed, albeit for service in the Middle East. One of these companies had a short and frustrating life: 1057 Company ASC, an Auxiliary Petrol Company, was formed in Bulford on 1 March 1918 under the command of a Captain D H Harris. The shortfall of 100 MT drivers was to be made up in Egypt. After moving to Larkhill on 5 March, the unit left for Portsmouth on 12 March for Rouen *en route* to Marseilles and Egypt. On arrival in Marseilles on 31 March orders were received to return to Bernay, north-west of Abbeville in France, but when it arrived in Rouen on 17 April the Company carried out local duties for the Assistant Director of Transport for a week before handing in vehicles and equipment, disbanding on 27 April. About eight weeks' hard work for nothing. And no explanation was ever given.

*　　*　　*

By the time the German offensive opened on 21 March the new MT organization initiated in 1917 was ready, fifty-seven MT Companies having been absorbed by other units to bring them up to strength in March alone, and was immediately put to the test as the development of the German attack rapidly disorganized the railway system on which so much resupply was dependent. The system could not cope with heavy shelling, which was followed by the Germans over-running light and broad gauge railways. The progressive loss of communication lines, such as Amiens-Achiet-Arras line, additionally made it increasingly difficult to provide return routes for empty rolling-stock. Main routes became congested and constant delays in the movement of troops and reinforcements, as well as the delivery of ammunition and supplies, were the inevitable result. Army Commanders were anxious to save as much material as possible from falling into enemy hands and to ensure the evacuation of hospitals and other medical units; the demands for Engineer material to construct rear lines of defence became urgent and much work was necessary to evacuate French civilians and material, as well as to supply French, American and Portuguese troops, let alone co-ordinate replacement British lines of supply with the new French lines. All this put enormous pressure on the officers and men of the ASC.

Railway disorganization reached its worst point when the great lateral line (St Just-Amiens-St Pol-Hazebrouck) came under intense shellfire and had to be abandoned as a railway route. Only one lateral route, Eu-Abbeville-Etaples, remained open and that was seriously threatened by air raids on the Canche Bridge at Etaples. The railway system for many miles behind the front line was hopelessly overtasked and the maintenance of the Armies as an effective fighting machine was in serious peril. Railheads were now far back and the needs of the Armies had to be provided by long-distance road work, which was carried out entirely by MT.

GHQ Reserve MT Companies were kept untasked until the last possible moment and, when allotted to meet a specific task, were withdrawn into reserve as soon as the situation permitted. As a result, the fullest and most economic use was made of MT companies within Divisions, Corps and Armies. Meanwhile, the formation of additional GHQ Reserve MT Companies had been continued and, by the time the railway situation had reached its worst stage, there were fortunately sufficient companies to ensure the maintenance of the Armies. One of the lessons learned during this crisis was that it had been beneficial to bring all transport under central control.

Rebuilding and repairing the railways was a slow process and the advance of railheads could not keep pace, so the troops had to be supplied by MT over long hauls. There is no doubt that mechanical transport of the ASC saved the Armies, from the time when the Amiens-Arras railway line was rendered useless until it was regained in July 1918.

Great difficulty was experienced on congested roads during the retreat in March and April. Ammunition was delivered direct to the guns for several days, until the German guns were brought forward and it became too dangerous to continue. The ammunition was then dumped and delivered by the Divisional Ammunition Column.

*　　*　　*

It is perhaps of interest to look at several units during this last great German attack, to illustrate the work of the ASC at the time.

Siege Park plans had been arranged, in view of any enemy attack, for the rapid movement of troops in reserve, or from one sector of the line to another by motor transport. When the Germans first attacked on 21 March, these plans were put into operation. On 27 March a convoy of fifty lorries from a Siege Park proceeded to the Marshalling Area of the Canadian Corps at Mont St Eloi and conveyed troops from that sector to the Somme. Not knowing how the battle would go, an extra lorry accompanied the convoy with a supply of petrol, oil and spare parts, and three days' rations were taken by the drivers to meet emergencies which might occur.

During these operations their Tractor Park was worked extremely hard under dangerous conditions. On 9 April, at Sailly, occasional shells fell into the village from about 6.30 pm, but the usual routine work was done. At 10.30 pm shelling became somewhat heavy and various details for caterpillars and tractors received during the morning were complied with immediately. At about noon on the 10th, since numerous shells were falling in the neighbourhood of the Park, arrangements were made to move, but during a conversation on the telephone between the Tractor Park Officer and the Siege Park the line was cut. Half an hour later tractors and caterpillars remaining in the Park moved out for Doulieu, getting away just as the road was being badly ploughed up. A despatch rider was sent to Headquarters with information of the move from Sailly and the new position to which the tractors were proceeding.

At 1.10 pm Private Hill, riding the motor cycle of Lieutenant Taylor who had gone out in charge of four tractors to haul the guns of 298th Siege Battery, reported, while the Tractor Park was on the move, that they had come under enemy machine-gun and rifle fire, which put the convoy out of action. He had been sent back to report to Lieutenant Taylor when that officer was seriously wounded. Private Hill himself had a wound in the leg from a machine-gun bullet and was immediately sent to hospital. At 6.00 pm two caterpillars, which had been out on duty with Lieutenant Ware to haul guns of 62nd Siege Battery, returned to the Park, the Sergeant reporting that Lieutenant Ware had been dangerously wounded.

During the night of the 9th a further retirement of the Tractor Park was made under instructions from Siege Park Headquarters, a motor cyclist being left behind to direct all caterpillars and tractors returning from gun shifts to the new Park. At 1.30 am on 11 April Staff Sergeant Clark arrived, having abandoned his steam tractor as impossible to extricate; he had pulled out a gun of 208th Siege Battery instead and hauled it to Vieux Berquin.

During withdrawal and regrouping following the German attack lorries were working continuously on ammunition duty. It was necessary to work two lorry drivers in shifts so that maximum work could be done. When lorries were not delivering ammunition from the railheads and dumps to the batteries or removing battery stores they were engaged in salvaging ammunition. Even when batteries had fallen back, large amounts of ammunition were brought back from the old positions.

From 13 April the enemy continued to advance until towards the end of the month, but not so rapidly. His main push had been contained. Guns were hauled back to reserve positions in good order. New guns were supplied and put into action as quickly as possible.

After the enemy's first great blow arrangements were made to have tractors and a number of lorries parked near batteries for immediate use, should it again be necessary to fall back. Each battery with 6 inch howitzers had one FWD and one lorry for every two guns; each battery with caterpillar-drawn guns had one caterpillar and two lorries for every two guns. Without the ASC caterpillars and lorries the guns were lost.

✳   ✳   ✳

Up to March 1917 610 Company, the Supply Company for the New Zealand Division, had done little work outside the ordinary supply details; their life changed, however, when they moved to Bath Camp on the Nieppe-Bailleul road on 4 March. From then on most of their work was done on Royal Engineers duty, transporting road materials into the Ploegsteert-Wulverghem area. Then, in June, with the attack on the Messines Ridge, thirty lorries were employed as a medical bus service, when the vehicles ran day and night every five minutes, carrying walking wounded, a total of 5,000 cases in all.

On 25 March 1918, several days after the start of the great German offensive, 610 Company received orders which entailed an enormous amount of dis-organization and work as part of the amalgamation of Divisional MT units. In fact this had been timed to take place well before the German offensive: they had to exchange fifty-one Peerless lorries for a similar number of Dennis lorries from the Australian Corps. There was not a unit in the entire army that would have wished to carry out this exchange at that particular time. The condition of the replacement vehicles was deplorable: most were without even a reasonable tool kit. Only an extraordinarily fine performance on the part of the lorry drivers enabled the unit to complete a move the following day from Westoutre to Ribecourt.

On 27 March a small arms ammunition section of eleven lorries was formed in 610 Company and detached until May under the direct orders of the Division in order to keep the front line supplied with ammunition, grenades and trench mortars, something of a change from the routine method of resupply. One driver had an interesting detail on 28 March when his lorry was sent into Albert, then virtually in No Man's Land, to collect abandoned machine guns. Another driver had a tale to tell much later, on 9 October, when a vehicle was detailed by the Division to assist the Cavalry in an attack on the canal at Marcoing. Its task was to carry machine-gunners and proceed with them over the canal bridge until stopped by enemy action, an extraordinary task for a soft-skinned vehicle. The driver reached a point within a few hundred yards of the canal and stopped there for two hours under severe shellfire, after which the tasking was abandoned due to the non-arrival of the Cavalry. It's a pity his views were never recorded for posterity.

✳   ✳   ✳

On 15 January the Auxiliary Omnibus Park Headquarters moved from Wormhoudt in Belgium to Frevent, and companies moved variously to Frevent, Nunq, Herlin-le-Sec, St Pol, Pernes and Lillers, in depth in a line, like a net, to be able to respond to the expected German offensive. On 22 January 8 GHQ Reserve MT Company (341 Company ASC) under Major A H Lees was attached to the Omnibus Park, located at Caulers, adding extra carrying capacity. The company attached three lorries to each of the seven Omnibus Companies to carry reserve supplies of petrol for the buses; forty-five lorries, too, were to be used by the Park for the carriage of blankets and baggage for the Divisions to be moved. The remaining lorries provided a Park reserve.

On 21 March, the day on which the massive German attack started, a telegram was received from GHQ ordering all bus companies to be prepared to move troops at four hours' notice. A further wire gave details of the move of the 31st Division the following day. The Commanding Officer went to Headquarters 31st Division to arrange for the move, sending details direct to the bus companies concerned. The Division embussed from 9 am onwards and moved via St Pol, Frevent and Doullens; meanwhile Lieutenant Colonel Howell arranged details of the move of the 42nd Division on the 23rd, from the Busnes area to the Gommecourt area, again via St Pol, Frevent and Doullens. The 42nd Division history tells of their men being "packed into many hundreds of motor-buses and lorries . . . straggling groups of refugees, women, children and old men, hastening with the more portable of their possessions out of reach of Hun savagery and rapacity."

On the 24th the Commanding Officer went to Headquarters 17 Corps to meet representatives of the 12th Division to arrange their move the next day. The AA & QMG was unable to give Brigade strengths but promised to telephone by 4 pm. Orders were then received from G Ops GHQ that the 12th Division was to embus at 9 pm for Baizieux. In the absence of details from the AA & QMG all available transport was sent to the agreed embussing points. To provide against all eventualities, forty-five lorries of 4 GHQ Reserve MT Company were also sent, but their efforts were wasted as they proved to be unnecessary. It had been impossible to raise the Division Headquarters by telephone due to congested lines, so the move went ahead and the buses drove through the night delivering the leading Brigade to its debussing point on the Albert-Doullens road at 6.30 am on the 25th.

Subsequent days saw the move of all or parts of the 2nd, 3rd, 4th, 14th, 20th, 21st, 29th, 35th, 37th, 41st, 50th and 62nd British Divisions, as well as the 2nd, 3rd and 5th Australian Divisions, 1st Canadian Division and the 31st and 32nd French Infantry Divisions, a total of 211,213 men over 855,638 miles, an almost unimaginable performance. At one stage drivers were at the wheel for sixty hours continuously, with no sleep. It is clear that the Park made a major contribution to the war, a contribution which, like most logistic effort, is rarely mentioned. The movement of these Divisions, coupled with similar French moves, enabled the allies to contain the German offensive. No railway system, even one not under heavy artillery bombardment, could ever have provided the quick reaction and flexibility of a fleet of buses and charabancs in the hands of inspired and courageous ASC bus drivers.

On 26 April information was received that twenty-one Military Medals had been awarded to men of the Omnibus Park, and subsequently the Commanding Officer and Adjutant were awarded the CMG and DSO respectively. The following letter was sent to the Commanding Officer by the Quartermaster General, Lieutenant General Travers Clarke, on 26 April:

"It affords me the greatest pleasure to inform you that under authority granted by His Majesty the King, the Field Marshal, Commanding-in-Chief, has approved the award of the Military Medal to the undermentioned 21 NCOs and men serving under your command, whose names will be published in the London Gazette in due course:

1st Auxiliary Bus Company	M1/6387	Pte Benjamin Leverton
1st Auxiliary Bus Company	M1/6250	Pte Frank Montgomery
1st Auxiliary Bus Company	M/32252	CSM Albert William Wellbelove
2nd Auxiliary Bus Company	M1/6826	Pte Arthur Andrew Morris
2nd Auxiliary Bus Company	M1/09171	Pte John Parkinson Blackie
2nd Auxiliary Bus Company	C/3003	Sgt Frederick Herbert Keene
15th Auxiliary Bus Company	M2/115456	Pte Frederick Earle Palmer
15th Auxiliary Bus Company	M2/115811	Pte John Notton Camp
15th Auxiliary Bus Company	M2/104393	Cpl Frederick Charles Jackson
16th Auxiliary Bus Company	M2/046487	Pte Leonard Richardson
16th Auxiliary Bus Company	M2/119422	Sgt Charles Percy Fox
16th Auxiliary Bus Company	M2/050671	Cpl Samuel Plevey
18th Auxiliary Bus Company	M2/121922	Pte David Jones
18th Auxiliary Bus Company	M2/115464	Sgt Percival Bridge
18th Auxiliary Bus Company	M/32539	Cpl Reginald George Carpenter
50th Auxiliary Bus Company	M/321094	Pte Donald Hesketh
50th Auxiliary Bus Company	MS/4279	Cpl Bertie Edwin Major
50th Auxiliary Bus Company	M2/033755	Cpl Gilbert Calder
51st Auxiliary Bus Company	M2/136330	Pte Robert Ferguson
51st Auxiliary Bus Company	M2/113196	Sgt George Staynes
51st Auxiliary Bus Company	M2/106457	Sgt Ernest Stratford Campling

The work performed by the Auxiliary Omnibus Park has, under trying circumstances during the battle which is still in progress, been excellent, and the recognition of their services will I feel sure stimulate all ranks under your command to even greater efforts should occasion demand."

On 6 May 1918 Field Marshal Sir Douglas Haig, Commander-in-Chief of the British Armies in France, sent the following letter to the Commanding Officer:

"Please convey to all ranks of the Auxiliary Omnibus Park my great appreciation of the services rendered by them since the 2 March. The details of the work they have accomplished, in circumstances of peculiar hardship and difficulty, have been brought to my notice and constitute a record of which every officer and man may well be proud. They may rest assured that in meeting the heavy demands recently made upon them, through long hours of continual duty both on the road and in the workshops, they have greatly assisted the operations of our troops and have contributed in no small degree to the frustration of the enemy's plans. I thank them for the work they have done, and count with confidence upon the same loyal service and devotion in the future."

The end of 1918 saw the Park still hard at work, moving American units in October-November and repatriating British prisoners-of-war in November; and in early January 1919 thousands of German prisoners-of-war were moved from Abbeville to the Hesdin area.

For the occupation of the Rhineland in 1919 1 and 51 Companies moved to Cologne, but orders came to disband in February. MT stores were returned to the Base, all indents were cancelled and personnel and vehicles moved to Wissant, near Calais, one of the twenty-odd MT Reception Parks, for demobilization and disposal. Over 100 buses were selected for repatriation to England out of a total of 1,319 B type buses and chassis which had served on the Western Front, but they did not last long on the streets of London, even though they were largely rebuilt – they were worn out.

On 10 May 1919 the last war diary entry, signed by Lieutenant Colonel Howells, reported: "Handed in papers, records etc and the Auxiliary Park BEF ceased to exist." There was no fanfare, no ceremony, but their efforts deserve to be remembered. They, too, helped shape history.

Amazingly, a staff officer in Headquarters Fourth Army had written on 4 May to the Quartermaster General complaining pedantically of road damage and poor convoy discipline of the buses during the German offensive: " . . . insufficient officers with the convoys . . . . absence of discs (on) the last lorry of each section . . . inadequate . . . . periodic halts." The Commanding Officer's comprehensive explanation hopefully persuaded Fourth Army that battles are not won by blind obedience to regulations.

A representative of those buses, No. B43, so-called 'Ole Bill', is currently on display in the Imperial War Museum, reconditioned and gleaming in its original livery. HM King George V inspected a number of ex-Great War ASC bus drivers at Buckingham Palace in 1920 and actually climbed onto the running board of B43, the first monarch ever to take such a proletarian step. It continued to run after the war, proudly displaying a large RASC badge on the front of the bus (it really should have been an ASC badge) as well as its 'honours', the battles at which it had provided support. If the class-conscious British Army was not going to award the Corps battle honours, the bus drivers were going to create their own.

*   *   *

It was during this last major German offensive that two members of the Corps were awarded the Victoria Cross. Lieutenant Alfred Herring, who was attached to the 16th Battalion, The Northamptonshire Regiment, held up the German attack on 23 March at Montagne Bridge at Jussy, thus enabling the rest of the battalion to withdraw. He was captured and was imprisoned at Graudenz (now in Poland); it was while he was being moved away from the fighting area, at St Quentin, that he was introduced to and shook hands with the Kaiser. His VC medal ribbon was presented to him at a special parade in Graudenz, where even his German guards were keen to congratulate him.

Private George Masters was an ambulance driver in April 1918 attached to the 141st Field Ambulance at Béthune, the only Corps VC winner to receive this award for performing purely Corps duties. Private Masters was a great character, older than one would expect for such heroic work. Aged 41, a pre-war chauffeur and with a wife and three children in Southport, he had been one of the country's leading cyclists in 1898-1900, establishing world tandem records with a Mr W Birtwhistle at quarter-mile and mile distances. He had even raced motor cycles too. The citation for these awards can be seen in Annex S.

Not everyone who was recommended for the Victoria Cross, of course, was honoured with the award: this disappointment had in fact been suffered by Assistant Commissary Walter Dunne of the Commissariat & Transport Department at the battle of Rorke's Drift in 1879; his case was rejected by the Commander-in-Chief of the Army, HRH The Duke of Cambridge. It would appear that 1st Class Staff Sergeant Major White of the ASC was another such example. At Le Cateau in 1914, according to a French postcard in the author's collection, he was wounded in both legs but, under heavy fire, saved the life of Lieutenant Frederick Roberts, son of Lord Roberts. Since Lord Roberts' son, however, had been killed in the Boer War of 1899-1902, this was clearly not true and the card could conveniently have been distributed as clumsy propaganda, had it not been for an account of his life in the 1914-18 war by Private James Cross, an ASC soldier from Liverpool serving in a Field Ambulance. He deposited 'Star Without Clasp', his story of the Great War, in the RCT archives, which contains a tantalising account of a meeting in 1917 with an old friend, the ex-Staff-Sergeant Major White:

> "Another great surprise I had was meeting with ex-Staff Sergeant Major White MC. He had been resting at our camp on his way to report to HQ. It was actually arranged that I should be detained on the parade ground to meet him, where we were left alone to have a good talk. I told him that I knew that he was recommended for the VC in the very early days of the war. He said there was a fuss and to-do over awarding the first VC to a member of the Army Service Corps, and he was given the MC instead. His present rank was that of Corporal, and I asked him how he had come to lose the rank of WO 1st Class.
>
> "You see, I was stripped to driver because of a 'drunk while on active service'. The findings of the Court Martial could not have been otherwise," he said. But he hoped to attain to his former rank some day. I wished him the best of luck, as we shook hands and said goodbye. I never did hear how he fared. His name of White belied his looks, for he was of a rather dark complexion. I must mention that he wore the ribbon of the MC on his serge, and it was the only time I ever saw the ribbon of the MC worn by a Corporal."

*   *   *

In the spring of 1915 a second Base MT Depot had been found necessary and was eventually established at Calais. The two Base Depots supplied the necessary spares for a large number of makes and types of cars. Each unit in the field could demand on the Advanced Mechanical Transport Depot regardless of make, and the Advanced Mechanical Transport Depot would demand upon either Base according to the make required.

The depot in Calais was designed to provide and maintain an adequate stock of spare parts for all types of American vehicles with the British Expeditionary Force in France, as well as for a number of particular British makes. In 1916 the Portuguese MT Section had been added to that at Calais and, up to the departure of the Portuguese Expeditionary Force from France in May 1919, all spare parts, accessories and tyres were obtained on demand by the OIC of this Portuguese Section. Similarly all cars, lorries and cycles, both for new services and in replacement of casualties in the Portuguese Expeditionary Force, were issued by this depot.

In August 1918 His Majesty the King visited the Calais Depot. At that time it was responsible for the upkeep, maintenance and provision of the spare parts for all five Armies, the Cavalry Corps, GHQ Troops and other units. Unfortunately, on 11 August 1918 three-quarters of the depot was destroyed as the result of a German air-raid and spare parts of some 19,000 cars and lorries were lost. To replace them, orders were sent to all units in the field as well as on the Line of Communication for the return of all surplus spare parts in their possession. The War Office authorized that the Calais depot's demands on the UK base took priority, such was the critical situation. The loss of these stores was kept under wraps as far as possible, but it had an effect on planning in England (see the Home Front chapter and information on the Slough Depot).

*　　*　　*

The following article, which gives a good idea of a horse transport column under fire, was published in the *Daily Mail* of 14 September 1918. Its somewhat heroic tone cannot disguise the constant risk of routine resupply on the roads of France.

THE FOOD MUST GET THERE

"There was a wagon fifty, perhaps a hundred yards ahead, plodding down the scorching white road. The subaltern who had been to the rear of his little convoy of four wagons to see that all was well with them, shook his mare into a trot to take the lead again, when there was a crescendo squeal – a spitting, vicious crash, and the white road was clear in front. Clear, except for the debris of a wagon, some heaps that had once been a driver's cherished 'pair', and a gaping hole bitten out of the hard pavé.

"Just the chance of war, but the subaltern, galloping forward, swallowed a lump in his throat as he held his quivering horse long enough beside the wreck to be sadly sure that the lad driving that wagon had finished with all war's chances now. Then he gently placed the limp figure in the flower-edged ditch and signalled to the other three wagons he had halted in rear to 'carry on'. For that is war – to 'carry on' until the job is finished.

"A day's food for 3,000 men had been in that convoy, and though some of it had been smashed irretrievably, the rest should get there – somehow. He set his lips grimly as he pondered on the fate that had taken him back from the convoy's head for those few minutes. The shells were coming over now at steady intervals of four minutes – he timed them; it kept his thoughts off the poor young driver a bit – but the three wagons plodded steadily on down the white dusty road.

"Another horse was wounded, then a driver slightly, but both could 'carry on' and an hour later the little convoy came back down the white road – empty. Those men would have their food tomorrow – if a bit short. There was no shelling now; it seemed curiously quiet in the splendour of the evening sunset as they halted to lift the still form into the leading wagon for the last ride.

"The next day five wagons went plodding along the white road – the shortage in the battalion's food stores had to be made good – and five came back empty.

"Some days are unlucky, on others the convoy gets through without trouble, but always it gets through – it is a proud claim of the Army Service Corps which all will support who have 'fought and fed' in France and Flanders mud, the deserts of the East, or the veldt of Africa.

"There is none of the stimulant of speed, no dashing forward, no heart-stirring plunge through the barrage – just the steady plod-plod of the slow, strong old horses and the rock and bump of wagons on the rutted, broken roads. Even if the shelling be such that working parties and infantry make temporarily for shelter, the ASC driver must still stick to his box seat. Horses and wagons cannot be run into dug-outs, and 'Driver's Orders' say, "A driver will under no circumstances leave his horses and wagons unattended." But the regulation was not needed to ensure that."

*   *   *

The last few months of the war, although rarely highlighted in general histories, were in fact times of great difficulty for the ASC. The Corps had poured new blood into the fighting arms to replace the losses of 1916; it had been partially reorganized in the winter of 1917-18 and had survived the German onslaught of March-April 1918. From the late summer onwards there was an unbroken record of British victory; the Hindenburg Line was smashed at the end of September; the German right wing in Flanders was driven in and the coast of Belgium cleared in early October. Hundreds of thousands of men and thousands of guns swept forward in the face of obstinate German resistance. The work level of the ASC as it moved a massive weight of material over devastated countryside —neither railways nor roads could cross shell-pitted areas quickly enough to keep pace with a rapid advance – exceeded everything that had ever been achieved before, an unsung epic of the war. In October 1918 a remarkable decision was made by the Army Council which can only be taken as a recognition of the efficiency and performance of senior Army Service Corps officers: they were made eligible for the command of fighting units and formations, in line with officers of the Royal Engineers. It is not known, however, whether any officers were selected for such appointments. It was too late in the war for all practical purposes.

There was inevitably a price to pay, however, for the success achieved by the Corps: personnel and horses were exhausted and the vehicles were in a poor state of repair. The speed with which the German Army had been driven back left railways used by the British Army behind and supplies and ammunition had to be carried over execrable roads in foul weather. Bridges everywhere had been destroyed; routes were strewn with enemy dead and the wreckage of war. At times supply trains could not reach their railheads in the rear and supplies constantly had to be issued at night.

The extent that logistic support of the army could have been guaranteed in a continuing winter campaign of 1918-19 was undoubtedly a major factor in the recognition by the allied High Command in early October that an advance in the spring of 1919 was the only option open. Fortunately the Armistice of 11 November 1918 stopped further debate.

The German Army withdrew behind the Rhine in November/December and the allies occupied areas of the Rhineland, the British concentrating in the Cologne-Bonn area, later in Wiesbaden. Demobilization was put in hand, miners being given the highest priority for repatriation; meanwhile the ASC was heavily involved in clearing the battlefield of salvage and other junk. Among the myriad tasks was the move of thousands of British prisoners who had been in German hands; many of them, haggard, starving, footsore and in rags, were making their way westwards as best they could, without money or food, their treatment in captivity a stain on the reputation of their captors.

The Second Army, less the Guards Division, was made responsible to the War Office for the occupation of the Rhineland, and was renamed the British Army of the Rhine (abbreviated as BAR, but sometimes as BAOR). Rhine Garrison Troops included an RASC Train of three HT companies and an MT company; there were in addition a number of Corps units for HQ Troops. The Director of Supplies & Transport from November 1918 to November 1919 was Brigadier General F M Wilson.

Under the terms of the Armistice, the RASC (the Corps had been honoured by the grant of the prefix 'Royal' in November) took over 1,260 German Army vehicles in December 1918, some of which were sent back to Aldershot for trials. Those retained for Army use in Germany had the letters 'CV' (captured vehicle?) painted on the bonnet as part of the registration number.

CHAPTER 7

The Home Front: Springboard for Success

Literature on the Great War tends naturally to concentrate on theatres of war overseas, and it is not generally appreciated the extent to which the UK base was the heart of a great and dynamic war machine. Out of a total strength of 3.8 million men just under half were in the UK; of these some 73,000 were ASC, five per cent of the whole. 48,000 of these ASC men were under training or were otherwise non-effective, 12,000 were in units awaiting embarkation and 13,000 were unfit for service overseas. The numbers of unfit men may seem high but it will be remembered that there were regular trawls during the war to find men suitable for the fighting arms and some 82,000 men, irrespective of trade or value to the ASC, were exchanged for others of lower medical category.

*   *   *

The affairs of the Corps were controlled by two Directorates under the Quartermaster General in the War Office in Whitehall, through the Headquarters of the major UK Commands: Northern, Southern, Eastern, Western, Scottish, Irish and Aldershot, each of which had appropriate ASC staffs. Subordinate to them was a network of Districts and Garrisons in which were located almost eighty Transport units and some forty Remount units. The great Corps depots (for Mechanical Transport, Horse Transport and Supply) and other Corps functions came under the QMG's Directorates for technical control but under local Commands for administration.

*   *   *

The first real appearance of army motor transport in London was on mobilization, when a number of cars and drivers were requisitioned and located in Kensington Barracks, mainly for use by members of the War Cabinet and senior officers in the War Office. These cars were eventually taken over by 882 MT Company when it was formed in December 1916.

In London OC ASC was authorized to settle traffic accident claims up to £10 (instead of the more usual £5), which eased the accident situation. It was found that many of the accidents were due to collisions with vehicles owned by the London General Omnibus Company, which agreed to waive the usual inspection if the damage was estimated to be less than £10.

Rolls-Royce cars were requisitioned by the War Office for Army Commanders overseas. They were sent when the occasion demanded it. Some seventy types and makes of cars were requisitioned, of which thirty-six were Rolls-Royces. A staff of ASC Fitters and Turners were specially trained for these vehicles.

*   *   *

Not all Rolls-Royces were requisitioned, however, and the national motoring organisations did their bit, although some Rolls were clearly not going to be used for senior officers. There were many gentlemen in the country who enjoyed a life style of considerable comfort, unaffected by the developments on the Western Front – being over age for military service, they were only too willing to contribute. The problem was, what would they contribute?

'Somewhere in England' there was a chauffeur called Jack, who drove a Rolls-Royce for his master, enjoying the comfort and security of personal service. His duties were to keep the Rolls clean until it sparkled, to drive His Lordship to and from town and to take the ladies out in the country, so life was great. His Lordship was a member of the Royal Automobile Club and one day, when Jack picked him up from Pall Mall at about 5 o'clock in the evening, His Lordship was reading the *RAC Journal* and muttering to himself as he sat in the back. He was not in his normally good mood. Jack did not take much notice of this and dropped His Lordship at the front door of his home, before taking the car round to the garage to clean it.

Next morning, Jack took His Lordship back to town, dropped him off at the bank and picked him up at Pall Mall again in the evening. His Lordship was reading the *RAC Journal* in the back and muttering to himself again; when they reached home, he came round to the garage and watched Jack clean the car. As he had never done this before, Jack was worried, especially when His Lordship took out a ruler and began to measure the back of the car, consulted the *RAC Journal* and said, "Yes, it will fit."

Jack was almost out of his mind with worry about what was going on and why the car was being measured. He was sure that Rolls-Royce would not like what His Lordship was doing. The next day His Lordship left the *Journal* on the back seat of the car and this is what Jack saw:

RAC
To All Motorists
Your country may want you.
It is important to be prepared.
The **ROYAL AUTOMOBILE CLUB** is organising **THE BRITISH MOTOR SERVICE VOLUNTEER CORPS,** and invites you to send in your name and all particulars of your car.

Come and register, or wire or write to the Royal Automobile Club, Pall Mall, London.

GOD SAVE THE KING

He thought that His Lordship was going to give the car to the army and buy a new car for Jack to drive. That would be nice. Two days later Jack was called into the house and told by His Lordship that he had to take the car to the RAC Depot to be examined to see if it was suitable for conversion into an ambulance. Jack's jaw dropped – his beautiful Rolls turned into an ambulance! At least it would mean a new Rolls-Royce, he thought, but he had a further shock when His Lordship told him that he would be staying with the converted Rolls. Apparently it was not only the car that was being given to the army, but His Lordship was also donating his chauffeur, so Jack was sent to the army at a wage of six shillings a day! The ASC gained a superb vehicle and driver and His Lordship had done his bit for the war effort.

* * *

From the early days of the war, manpower was always a matter of concern and a careful eye was kept on the misuse of soldiers. In November 1914 the Army Council issued an instruction that no soldiers fit for service should be retained at Depots in employments which could be performed by others. To carry out the necessary regimental employments a proportion of old soldiers over forty-five years of age or suitable civilians not fit for ordinary enlistment were specially enlisted as batmen and cooks. In the case of the ASC Depot in Aldershot, the numbers were thirty-five, and twenty for locations in Woolwich, Bradford and Richmond. They were enlisted for the duration of the war and were not required to leave the depot.

* * *

The Supply Reserve Depot at Deptford, the major source of supplies for the British Army world-wide, was taken over by the War Department a few weeks after the outbreak of war (having moved from Woolwich), being held on lease from the City of London Corporation until it was purchased in 1926. The site itself had an interesting history going back to the times of Henry VIII and had 'hosted' Peter the Great of Russia when he went to Deptford to work as a ship-wright, learning the trade of naval shipbuilding. The 38-acre site abutting the River Thames had its own jetty, cold storage plant, transit sheds, a broad-gauge access railway line and almost six miles of light railway track within the depot; cranes, locomotives, trucks and hay presses (to compress the war reserve of hay) contributed to the depot's ability to hold thirty days of war reserves of foodstuffs, forage, lubricating oils and disinfectants for the Expeditionary Force. To give an idea of the importance of this establishment, it was commanded by a Brigadier General.

The Supply side of the Corps was based on Supply Companies in Aldershot and the Supply Reserve Depot in Deptford, as well as a host of Base, Main or Field Supply Depots in the various theatres of war. Troops in the home base were fed by local contractors. The essential Supply trades were Butcher, Baker, Clerk and Issuer; a little later in the war men who were rejected for various reasons as MT Drivers were employed as Packers and Loaders, working on general duties in the Packers and Loaders Branch of the Corps.

Since pre-war days 'A' Supply Company in Aldershot had provided the depot functions of reception and training, while 'C' Supply Company (also in Aldershot) trained men and provided drafts for units. In fact 'C' Supply Company was totally used up in providing men for the BEF in August 1914, so, after 'A' Company 'held the fort' until December, 'K' Supply Company was formed to fill the gap. By the end of 1914 the two companies had handled almost 300 men, and 10,000 during the first half of 1915. An additional task thrown on the Supply Companies was the recruitment and training of men as Skilled Labourers, Stevedores, and Packers and Loaders for the Labour Companies ASC, 21,000 having joined up for this purpose by the end of 1915. In mid-1917, in order to concentrate Supply resources and skills, a Reserve

Supply Personnel Depot (RSPD) was formed in Aldershot, initially under the command of Lieutenant Colonel E G Evans OBE and subsequently, from January 1918, under Lieutenant Colonel G B Dartnell.

*　　*　　*

The reception, testing and training of the thousands who flocked through Army Recruiting Offices for the MT ASC needed a new organization, as the pre-war depot companies in Aldershot and Woolwich could not cope. A large workhouse in Grove Park, south-east London, was taken over in September 1914 and became No. 1 MT Reserve Depot ASC; in due course it was the nucleus of the later Lee Reception & Training Area and, when this proved inadequate, Osterley Park and a number of other locations in Camberwell, Catford, Eltham, Hounslow, Isleworth, Lee, Sydenham and Twickenham were taken over. Tents and huts were erected on playing fields and other green areas, vehicles were parked on local roads and repairs even took place on the roads under the eyes of local inhabitants going about their daily business. No. 2 Reserve MT Depot was formed at Bulford on 1 April 1915 to help with units mobilizing, supplementing the previously established Mobilization and Embarkation Area.

Eight hundred recruits arrived at Grove Park on the first day in September 1914 and it was not unusual for 400 men to report in a day; many who could already drive departed within twelve hours for Avonmouth, the port of embarkation, often with a minimal uniform issue and no regimental number. Those men who required instruction in driving spent several weeks in training, night and day, on routes which included Marble Arch, Hyde Park Corner, Oxford Circus and Pall Mall. Each man had to drive four types of vehicle, not exceeding 8 mph. In the years 1915-17 some 100 drivers of the London General Omnibus Company were used extensively for training ASC drivers. The highest day's intake was recorded in November 1915: 819; the greatest number tested in one day, in May 1916, was 876, and the highest strength attained during the war, in December 1916, was 24,135. These figures give an idea of the training and organizational problems faced by the ASC.

*　　*　　*

Sergeant Douglas Clark (see Chapter 5) was serving at Grove Park in 1915-1916, where he played in the depot rugby football team. His papers in the Imperial War Museum in London contain a booklet which recounts two stories involving HM King George V. He appears to have been out on the training convoys. On the first occasion, "while on convoy duty, a halt was made near Windsor and a gentleman came up and, seeing one of the men trying to open a bully beef tin at the wrong end, said: "Don't you think, sonny, you'd do better if you opened the other end?" He took a great interest in the proceedings and made a number of enquiries. Eventually Clark said: "Look, sir, we're busy." The gentleman smiled and walked away, and you can imagine how Clark felt when he was informed that the gentleman was the King."

On another occasion "one of the lorries killed a cow and the Grove Park CO issued orders that more care must be taken when passing cattle. The following day Clark's convoy was held up on the road and the lorries became so mixed up that all traffic was stopped. When matters were at their worst, a car drove up and, of course, could not get through the confusion. In the car were the King and Mr Lloyd George. Clark was sent forward to ascertain the cause of the congestion. When he reached the leading lorry he saw the officer in charge and a Corporal doing all they could to drive a cow into a cottage garden, but as fast as they drove it in the old woman who lived in the cottage drove it out with a fire-shovel, much to the quiet amusement of the onlookers. The news of the King's presence speeded things up, and eventually the cow was cornered and the traffic was resumed."

Sergeant Clark became a well-known rugby player and wrestler after the war. He played for Brookland Rovers, Huddersfield, Cumberland and England; he was also the British Empire heavyweight all-in wrestling champion. When he died of coronary thrombosis at the age of 59, it was said that, in his day, he was "the finest (rugby) forward in the world" and "the world's strongest man". He had clearly been a great contributor to the ASC and was a major loss to the world of rugby and all-in wrestling.

*   *   *

Grove Park and Osterley Park sent their trained men to the Bulford Mobilization and Embarkation Area ('The Camp'), which opened in September 1914 under the command of Major F L Lindsay Lloyd. Its functions were the issue of vehicles and the mobilization of MT units, the repair of vehicles and the despatch of units and individuals overseas. This was achieved by its four organic companies and two embarkation depots, the former using camps, billets and tents for the large numbers of men who passed through. The Workshop and Stores Department, commanded by a Lieutenant Colonel, dealt with up to 100 vehicles at a time which came in from civilian factories or firms or from units overseas. At any one time 700 vehicles were held in covered accommodation for issue to units being formed. Bulford and Salisbury photographers did a roaring trade by photographing all new companies – the elongated pictures are still to be seen today.

Subordinate to Bulford were the embarkation depots of Avonmouth and Portsmouth, the latter being opened in January 1917 when the former could not handle the necessary throughput. To give an idea of the size of their task, 30,000 men and 22,000 vehicles passed through Avonmouth during 1917 and 13,200 men and 7,840 vehicles through Portsmouth during the first five months of 1917 alone. Bulford also controlled the ASC Tractor Depot in Avonmouth (where caterpillar tractors were issued to units, not in Bulford as with lorries), which saw nineteen officers, 532 men, 1,500 caterpillar tractors and 200 lorries pass through its hands on their way to support, mainly, the heavy-gun batteries of the Royal Garrison Artillery.

The following Embarkation Ports were nominated:

No 1:	Southampton
No 2:	Newhaven
No 3:	Avonmouth
No 4:	Liverpool
No 5:	Belfast

| No 6: | Dublin |
| No 7: | Queenstown (Cork) |

The demands in MT matters were considerable, but the expansion in horse transport too led to new units being formed: No. 1 Reserve HT Depot was formed initially at Deptford, moving to Park Royal in London on 28 February (in due course consisting of 661, 662, 663 and 664 HT Companies), and No. 2 Reserve HT Depot at Blackheath on 24 February 1915 (in due course consisting of 665, 666, 667 and 668 HT Companies).

Blackheath was selected because of its proximity to the extensive railway system centred on London, a gravel sub-soil facilitating horse transport training without undue expenditure on road building, an elevated and healthy location, along with the potential for expansion. Early in January 1915 'The Ranger's House' was acquired by the War Department for use as the Depot Headquarters, offices and stores, together with 'Macartney House' nearby. These two buildings, with a triangular portion of the heath bordered by the Dover and Greenwich roads immediately to the west, were fenced in and the construction of wooden huts for the men and corrugated-iron stables for the horses started. Preparations were also made to take over suitable rented houses in the immediate vicinity for troop accommodation and for the construction of a veterinary hospital on the south side of the Dover road.

Initially the establishment of the depot allowed for only one company, but a second company was added a year later, eventually a third and a fourth. A Lieutenant Colonel was in command (Lieutenant Colonel J C M Canny OBE), supported by a Second-in-Command, Adjutant, Assistant Adjutant, OIC Stores, a Regimental Quartermaster, Riding Master and Veterinary Officer. To achieve this eleven Subalterns and 160 NCOs and men were initially appointed as training staff. More came as the work level increased. The depot came under GOC-in-C Eastern Command for discipline and interior economy, but otherwise direct control was exercised by the Director of Supplies & Transport; Remount matters were referred to the Director of Remounts in the War Office and matters concerning mobilization stores to the Deputy Director Ordnance Services in Woolwich Arsenal.

The depot's task was to 'turn out' complete horse transport units ready for service anywhere, complete with officers, NCOs and men, animals, vehicles (wagons) and stores. Ironically, two lorries were obtained in order to speed up depot administration.

Only a few days after the depot formed, orders were received to form three special HT Companies for the RN Division and four Reserve Parks. So successful was the training that they left four weeks later. One unit then followed another so that, between March 1915 and March 1917, forty complete units as well as a host of individuals were equipped, trained and despatched, the throughput in personnel for training in the period April 1915 to October 1917 being almost 1,100 officers and over 28,000 men. Training was not limited to ASC personnel only. Infantry Regimental Transport Officers courses were run and infantrymen from the Machine Gun Corps at Grantham were trained in mounted duties.

A Zeppelin attack over Blackheath during the night of 24-25 August 1916, which wounded nineteen ASC men and a horse, and killed a mule (as well as completely wrecking the YMCA hut), was a nuisance, but real problems arose in the first six months of 1916 when 4,315 category 'A' men were transferred from the Blackheath Depot alone to the Infantry and Machine Gun Corps, with category 'B' and 'C' men posted in place of them.

*　　*　　*

Towards the end of the war all unwanted or unroadworthy army vehicles were returned to an MT Vehicle Depot established in the western outskirts of London, at Kempton Park Racecourse, where the race track and central area soon became completely covered with vehicles; however, Prime Minister Lloyd George, who understood the gambling needs of the public in the immediate post-war days, had the Vehicle Depot moved to Slough in early 1919. This latter depot had begun life in 1917, when Major General A R Crofton-Atkins was convinced that the difficult situation regarding the supply of vehicles from vehicle manufacturers, especially with an increasing emphasis being placed on the production of armaments, tanks and aero engines, would be improved if the life of vehicles already in service could be extended by a major repair and maintenance programme. With an eye to the future, too, he realized that the army would be left with a huge and unusable fleet of vehicles at the end of the war, vehicles which would either have to be reconditioned if they were to be attractive to a civilian market starved of vehicles during the war or scrapped.

There were several spare-parts stores in London, based on Short's Gardens, and various small MT workshops were distributed around the country with the Home MT organization, but there was nothing to deal with the massive influx he forecast. The ASC Heavy Repair Workshops on the Western Front were hard-pressed to do their business and had no spare capacity to deal with a UK base problem, even if it were politically possible to reduce working units in a theatre of operations.

In October Major General Crofton-Atkins' staff started looking for a location suitable for a central repair depot where repair activities and spare-parts storage could be centralized; at the same time Mr Andrew Weir, recently appointed as Surveyor-General of Supplies at the War Office, was invited to examine the vehicle and location situation. With 2,540 lorries, 1,486 cars and 1,800 motor cycles then awaiting repair in UK and on the Western Front, something had to be done. As for the location, somewhere within 40 miles of London was sought, close to a rail link and preferably west of the capital in order to be less vulnerable to Zeppelin attacks. Possible sites at Aylesbury, Basingstoke, Dunstable, Sunningdale, Wembley, Hayes, Perivale and Harrow Weald were examined, but no site was as ideal as the one at Cippenham near Slough, once the site of a palace for Saxon and Norman kings. Whereas Lord Derby, Secretary of State for War, agreed speedily with the proposed plans, the War Office became bogged down in bureaucracy, the Food Production Department, Board of Agriculture and local worthies naturally opposing the scheme.

It was not until April 1918 that the Treasury approved plans involving the expenditure of £2 million and in May the War Cabinet agreed. What helped them in their deliberations was the recent German offensive in France, the loss of repair depots at Bergues and St Omer, not to mention the loss by fire of most of the spare parts in the Base MT Depot at Calais and secret contingency plans to repatriate repair work to England. Known only to a few at the time were considerations of a major offensive in spring or summer 1919, which would have to be "based almost entirely on mechanical effort" because it was considered that horse transport had neither the radius of operations nor the operational stamina to make an effective and far reaching breakthrough.

After delays for the rest of 1918, the scheme at Slough was almost the victim of media attacks and criticism by those with vested interests. Difficulties of all sorts bedevilled plans and it was only in early 1919 that building started, variously with Royal Engineers and Austrian or German prisoners-of-war. Meanwhile there was an outcry over the situation at Kempton Park, where 16,000 vehicles were standing axle-deep in mud, rotting gently. Among row after row of battle-weary vehicles with broken axles, crankshafts, connecting rods, disembodied engines and other dismembered MT paraphernalia, Holt caterpillar tractors made their way to dump the latest harvest of transport surplus. In addition to the Kempton Park lorry junk pile, a number of unwanted cars were awaiting garage attention in Cumberland Market, just near Regent's Park: almost new Lancias, Clement-Talbots and Wolseleys, some costing as much as £800 when new, were corroding fast, vulnerable to any child who wanted a different sort of playground.

With the war now over, newspapers carried reports almost every day of mountains of military equipment defacing the countryside in France and Belgium. It was estimated that £50 million worth of surplus stock was involved. Perhaps this was inevitable towards the end of a war when the production of supplies and vehicles could not be harmonized with negotiations to end the war. Critics would naturally have screamed the roof down had the war gone on and there had not been sufficient to meet immediate demands. Ultimately, in 1919, the Slough depot was finished, albeit in modified form, and the vehicles at Kempton Park could be moved, at a rate of 600 vehicles a day, so that repair work could be carried out. It was not long before vehicles were being auctioned off at irresistible prices and Kempton Park was available for horse racing again, enabling racing enthusiasts in the south of England to enjoy at least one of the less expensive pleasures of peacetime conditions. At the same time the auctions were providing cheap road transport for a market that not only now had a wealth of qualified drivers but was also becoming increasingly dependent on the internal combustion engine.

*   *   *

Mechanical transport needs constant repair and the timely provision of spares, stores and equipments. Before 1914 this had been handled by twelve men in the Aldershot-based Inspection Branch Mechanical Transport (IBMT) for the relatively small fleet of ASC vehicles. When war was declared the work load increased considerably and October 1914 saw the staff increase to seventy-five, and ultimately (in December 1918) to 2,431 military and civilian staff. In addition to serving the British Army, they provided vehicle spares for the Admiralty, Royal Air Force, Dominion , American, Belgian, Greek, Italian, Portuguese and Serbian Armies as well as a host of government organizations in UK (eg Foreign Office, YMCA and the British Red Cross Society).

During the end of 1914 and January 1915 the growth of MT was so rapid and the demand for spare parts increased to such a degree that it was necessary to move the Inspector of MT with his organization for provision, receipt and despatch of spare parts from Aldershot to some other central and suitable accommodation. The IBMT moved to Short's Gardens in London on 6 March 1915 and in 1916 became known as the Home MT Depot.

It was augmented by a number of sub-depots in various parts of the City, Camden Town, Carlow Street, Gray's Inn Road and Cressy Road, and in Liverpool. The variety of vehicles and operating conditions around the world presented enormous problems in forward planning and storage, as can be inferred from the fact that the MT stores issued during the war were valued at approximately £60 million. In 1916, when Lieutenant Colonel M C Brander took command, the unit's name was changed to the Home Repair Depot ASC.

What did not help was that units of Kitchener's New Armies were formed with such rapidity that it was only possible for the CIMT to attend to the provision of spare parts, with the result that inspections were sadly neglected; with Regular MT companies departed on mobilization, too, local transport became chaotic, especially due to the rapid growth to meet the demands of numerous training centres and camps. The staff of CIMT was therefore augmented by resident inspectors called Deputy Inspectors MT at the Headquarters of various Commands. These officers worked under the control of the Command HQ but dealt with the CIMT on all technical matters. They were responsible for:

scrutinizing demands for spare parts and expendable stores before they were sent to Short's Gardens

the systematic inspection of all transport in their Command area

placing vehicles out with civilian contractors for repair up to a limit of £25. Civilian repairs exceeding £25 were referred to CIMT for approval.

During February 1915 an extract from Supplies, Transport & Barracks Regulations was issued, which led to considerable confusion, poor methods of accounting and was wasteful in personnel. It laid down that "MT vehicles, including motor cycles, issued as part of the authorized equipment of units other than ASC, will be held on charge by the units concerned". Thus, non-technical units such as Cyclists and Yeomanry Regiments, Anti-Aircraft Batteries, Labour Companies and Hospitals had to hold on their charge vehicles which required considerable technical knowledge for their satisfactory maintenance. As perhaps was only to be expected, when no control was exercised, they were used for joy-riding and were neglected and left in fields, out-houses and local garages to rust and ruin. A considerable number of vehicles in use by these units were not even recorded as on their charge.

Unfortunately, the Deputy Inspectors were never able to carry out their primary duties of inspection. Their difficulties and the chaotic condition of the transport, however, were soon appreciated and a number of Local Auxiliary MT Companies (LAMTs) were formed. These companies, with defined transport areas covering the whole country, took on charge and were responsible for the repair of vehicles of the Home Service ASC, also for the repair of vehicles on the strength of units other than ASC. This was a matter of considerable relief to the units which owned vehicles and had no idea what to do with them; the result, though, was the creation of a large network of static units which did essential but unsung work.

As the number of LAMT Companies increased, the Deputy Inspectors of MT were again under pressure and, in June 1916, an officer was appointed

Travelling Inspector of MT by the War Office, based at Kensington Barracks in London. His duty was to visit each Command and inspect the LAMT Companies and report his recommendations direct to the War Office. At this stage there were seventeen companies in existence. After six months he submitted a critical report.

The Travelling Inspector recommended on 25 November 1916 that:

the appointment of DIMT be abolished

a Department with a staff of Travelling Inspectors be created

an officer with technical MT knowledge was to be left at the HQ of each Command to give technical advice (MT TA)

These recommendations were agreed in January 1917.

At this stage there were twenty-one LAMT Companies allotted to Commands in the United Kingdom. In February 1917 the War Office ordered that all transport not on charge to LAMT Companies (less RFC) and those allotted to units awaiting mobilization or mobilization for service overseas and not attached to an ASC Depot should be taken on charge by a LAMT Company.

In November 1918 a further increase in establishment was granted to the Department of the SIMT in order to cope with the still increasing amount of MT, and also to form a branch for the inspection of personnel and for statistics.

The Inspection Branch of the SIMT's Department undertook:

general inspection of LAMT Companies (less personnel)

inspection of vehicles overhauled in the Heavy Repair Shops

attending Boards of Officers to give technical advice

Since the formation of SIMT in January 1917 it was found that the inspection of LAMT Companies, vehicles and workshops was inseparable from the inspection of personnel and on 17 April 1918 the War Office authorized the inclusion in SIMT's duties, additionally to those held already:

to give technical advice in all matters concerned with the employment of personnel in MT units and Depots at home

technical inspection of MT personnel in LAMT Companies

At last, but somewhat late in the war, the control of MT on a vast scale was being tackled.

*　　*　　*

February 1916 saw the introduction of a little-known auxiliary organization, the Motor Volunteer Corps (MVC), not to be confused with the Motor Volunteer Corps of 1903-1906. They were, nevertheless, part of the Volunteer Force, from which they obtained great support. They had started life in a typically British sort of way, when interested individuals wanted to provide transport support for the Volunteer Infantry Brigades throughout the country in the event of mobilization. Initially they were Transport Sections for the Volunteer battalions, as regimental transport in 1915 and 1916. Most of these units formed part of an organization which had been known until then as National Motor Volunteers.

With a groundswell of enthusiasm, the Army Council authorized the formation of Motor Volunteer Corps by counties as part of the Volunteer Training Corps in early 1917 and Lords Lieutenant and other interested parties applied themselves to the task. Motorists who were desirous of forming themselves into squadrons were invited to contact Lords Lieutenant. They received an initial grant of £2. In September 1917 MVC officers were made eligible for the issue of a uniform allowance. At this stage the War Office could not provide uniforms or equipment because drills were not compulsory, but, undeterred, most men bore the cost of obtaining uniforms and running their own vehicles, sometimes with the help of generous benefactors, although petrol was supplied at public expense (on a voucher system) when it was necessary for units to be exercised in manning their emergency stations. In fact in April 1917 Territorial Force Associations were authorized to submit demands for serge uniforms to the Royal Army Clothing Department, although a note was added that the cloth was in restricted supply. Badges of rank, chevrons and buttons were those as used by the Regular Army, with the Royal Arms as a cap badge and 'V' as a collar badge for officers. In October 1917 officers and men of the MVC were authorized to wear a white embroidered 'Motor' on the upper part of the sleeve of their jackets and greatcoats. In August 1918 the War Office authorized, on an optional basis, members of the MVC to wear ASC badges; additionally officers were authorized to wear the ASC silver collar-badge with the 'V' below it, and soldiers could wear the same shoulder titles as their ASC Territorial Force brothers-in-arms, with the 'V' above, the titles to be embroidered in white on khaki drab cloth. Perhaps surprisingly, the relevant Army Council Instruction insisted that, when the ASC badge was adopted, the new shoulder titles also had to be worn.

As the War Office was unable to provide vehicles, local efforts were made to obtain them, with mixed results, as most lorries were earmarked 'for emergency service' and therefore not available for other uses, however praiseworthy. The East Yorkshire unit had so many problems in trying to obtain MT that they soon abandoned the idea and formed, in 1917, a horse transport company entitled the 'East Yorkshire Volunteer Brigade Transport & Supply Company', the only non-MT unit in the Motor Volunteer Corps. Initially they wore grey-green uniforms, but, when the War Office declined to provide khaki uniforms as they did to the MT Volunteers, the East Yorkshire men bought their own. At this stage various Volunteer units were attached to Regular units for training, which was undoubtedly a great boost to the part-timers. The East Yorkshire Company, for instance, was attached to 532 HT Company ASC based in Grimsby. Initially every recruit for the MVC had to undergo training in infantry drill, map reading and attend lectures on march discipline, the organization of various arms of the service and running repairs, twelve drills (each of an hour's length) a month until he was passed by an officer. No petrol was authorized, however, for this training. In March 1918 this requirement was changed, not only to reduce the monthly drill requirement to four but also to ensure that an MVC Volunteer on enrolment was required either to produce a driving certificate or pass a test to show that he was a competent driver, possessed some knowledge of running repairs and was conversant with the rule of the road, a much more practical approach.

Other counties progressed in their own way, approaching local vehicle owners for the loan of their cars or lorries when needed. At first Light Squadrons were raised, consisting of cars and motor cycles. Cars were provided, for instance, to Commanding Officers of Volunteer battalions to enable them to carry out weekly inspections of their units; and officers attached to garrison staffs and Territorial Associations were transported, a useful pool of convenient transport. In May 1918 a form of agreement for the enrolment of motor vehicles in the County MVCs was produced and a record was kept by OCs of each county force, with the originals being sent to the OIC Volunteer Force Records on the Victoria Embankment in London.

In the nation's capital the General Officer Commanding London District, Lieutenant General Sir Francis Lloyd, approved the formation of the MVC as early as February 1916 so that free transport could be provided for members of His Majesty's Forces arriving in London after midnight when all other forms of transport had ceased to provide a service. This was initially achieved by the hire of buses, but the growing size of our armies and the consequent increase in the number of men on leave meant that costs rose to an unacceptable level.

An appeal was made in London for the enrolment of private motorists with their vehicles as well as to commercial firms, but, even though a patriotic response brought relief, it was realized twelve months later that the Corps needed to acquire its own vehicles in order to maintain the service. A further appeal was made, both in UK and in the USA, under the auspices of Lady Lister Kaye, wife of the Commanding Officer, Major Sir John Kaye, and many vehicles were donated; fortunately the army provided the petrol. Thus men who had no knowledge of the nation's capital were given assistance, even financial when there was a genuine need, and transported from the major railway and bus stations to their destinations in London.

There is no record of the number of vehicles owned, indeed even the strength of these Volunteers in London, but their usefulness can be judged by statistics published in early 1919 for the City of London unit: on some nights as many as 5,000 or 6,000 men were transported, weekly averages varied between 20,000 and 35,000 men, and in the three years of its existence 1.35 million had been helped. Even after the war had ended, funds and 200 more volunteers were still being sought. To this end a concert was held in the London Coliseum on 15 February 1919 with such leading entertainers of the day as Wilkie Bard, Cicely Courtneidge, Nelson Keys, George Robey (himself a Lieutenant in the MTV) and Bransby Williams.

At the end of May 1918, however, the War Office ordered a reorganization of the Motor Volunteer Corps, which they wanted to consist primarily of heavy vehicles in what were known as Heavy Sections, although Ambulance Sections also were authorized. They wanted something more functional and useful. This meant that units once again had to canvass vehicle owners. This time, perhaps because one last contribution was needed, they were more successful and the offers of loans were more generous than before.

In July 1918 the title of the Corps changed from Motor Volunteer Corps to ASC Mechanical Transport (Volunteers) and members wore the ASC badge that arguably should have been worn from the start (although it is known that at least one unit wore it much earlier). The October 1918 Volunteer Force List shows one Horse Transport unit and sixty-four MT units, totalling sixty-three Light Sections, 484 Heavy Sections, thirty-four Ambulance Sections, four Special

Sections, one Composite Section, one Signal Company and thirty-four Sections with no specific description.

*   *   *

In January 1917 the Adjutant General chaired a conference on the organization of women employed by the army. He said there appeared to be no problem in obtaining women of the right class. Other than the excellent nurses, he was considering three general classes of employment: clerical, housekeeping and motor drivers. He believed that women should be treated in the same way as men, but a small body was needed to advise the Army Council on women's questions. For the ASC, Major General Crofton-Atkins explained that the Corps employed a limited number of female chauffeurs and that their service had to be extended; there was considerable opposition from staff officers in Commands, as they did not like women driving them at night. There was currently no intention of sending women chauffeurs to France. On the other hand it was understood that women were anxious to be under every sort of army discipline and to take the place of male soldiers.

*   *   *

It is worth spending a little time looking at several of the static transport companies, since otherwise one might get the impression that they were a bed of inactivity. 606 Company was formed at Beckenham, Kent in December 1915 and shortly afterwards moved to London District. The company was responsible for the supply of transport required for the sole use of the Ministry of Munitions. The work and size of this unit increased correspondingly with the general augmentation in the supply of munitions. This increase was gradual but was particularly marked during the last year of the war.

The company's work extended over the whole of England and Wales, south of a line drawn across the northern boundaries of Lincolnshire, Nottinghamshire, Derbyshire, Staffordshire, Shropshire and Montgomeryshire. It had about 100 detachments and, in order to decentralize the work as far as possible, officers were stationed at Birmingham, Cardiff, Porton and Woolwich so as to be on the spot and deal with the munition transport services in these immediate vicinities. The Officer Commanding dealt directly with the Ministry of Munitions for taskings, many of which were carried out at short notice.

606 Company, in the guise of No 23 Local Auxiliary MT Company, was organized as follows:

Company Headquarters was at Shepherd's Bush. Transport was provided for London District and Eastern Area

The Southern Area, which included Hampshire, Wiltshire, Devonshire and Somersetshire, came under an officer at Porton on Salisbury Plain

The Western Area included Gloucestershire, Herefordshire and South Wales, with its Headquarters in Cardiff

The Eastern Area included Essex, Kent, Sussex and Surrey

The Midland Area had Headquarters offices with the Ministry of Munitions in Birmingham.

The work carried out involved:

Conveyance of Ministry of Munitions officials on inspection duty and conferences

Transport of munitions of war at various factories, including a large detachment at the Woolwich Arsenal

Transport for the Aircraft Inspection Department

Transport of clothing for the Royal Army Clothing Department

Ambulances stationed at various factories

Tractors employed at Shoeburyness Proof Ranges

Vehicles supplied to the Royal Engineers Experimental Stations at Porton and Imbercourt

Vans used for conveying Canteen Stores at factories

Steamers employed hauling wood.

Its yearly mileage of roughly 3,000,000 shows the level of work. At one time there were 1,151 vehicles of all kinds on strength, roughly made up as shown:

3 ton lorries	273
30 cwt lorries	23
Mobile workshop lorries	2
Gun lorry (Leyland)	1
Box body vans	108
Light cars	230
Covered light cars	33
WD ambulances	21
Motor cycle and sidecar combinations	192
Motor cycles solo	124
John Warwicks	3
Steamers and wagons	15
Petrol tankers	3
Petrol tractors	6
Trailers	57
Charabancs	12
Chassis (all kinds)	32
Wagonnettes	2

Personnel totalled 1,658 all ranks, comprising twenty officers, 1,274 Warrant Officers, NCOs and men, 217 Women Legion drivers and 147 QMAAC, a size-able unit by army standards, all under the command of a Major.

To give an idea of the spares problem, the following makes of vehicles were dealt with: AEC (LGOC), Austin, Berna, Buick, Clydesdale, Clayton, Crossley, Daimler, Dennis, Fiat, Foden, Ford, Foster-Daimler, Garrett, Holt, Kelly, Lancia, Marshall, Maxwell, Mercedes, Metallurgique, Napier, Overland, Packard, Pagefield, Peerless, Sandusky, Singer, Studebaker, Sunbeam, Talbot, Thornycroft, Vulcan, Wolseley, Willys, Wallis & Stevens and Vauxhall; and the following motor cycles: BSA, Clyno, Douglas, Phelon & Moore, Royal Enfield, Scott, Triumph, Zenith and Warwick.

The greatest difficulty was the non-standardization of vehicles, there being no fewer than sixty-seven different makes in the company and any number of different types. In addition, working hours were long and all transport was heavily overworked. It was suggested at one time that each vehicle should have one full day off the road a fortnight, but, due to the lack of transport, this was found to be impossible. In July 1918 the Ministry of Munitions decided that the company should take over the transport of the Aircraft Department. This meant an increase of 170 vehicles. The Headquarters offices were in 176-178 Holland Park Avenue, Shepherd's Bush, London and the Workshops and Stores were at the London General Omnibus Company's Garage in Goldhawk Road, Shepherd's Bush.

Members of the Women's Legion were employed to drive all light cars and vans, both in London and in the provinces. They proved themselves very useful and capable of taking the place of male drivers. In London, men helped with running repairs and changing tyres but, when left to their own devices on detachment, women proved quite able to carry on without help.

Some 250 members of the Queen Mary's Auxiliary Army Corps were accommodated in hostels in Holland Park under a capable Superintendent. All of them were on the strength of 606 Company, although only about 100 were actually employed by the company as clerks, cooks, waitresses and orderlies.

In February 1919 it was decided by the War Office to disband the company and all roadworthy vehicles were gradually handed over to the Ministry of Munitions. In London they were handed over to an accredited official of the Ministry; in the provinces, direct to the Factory Managers or Local Representatives.

*　　*　　*

Another London-based company, 620 MT Company, is worthy of mention. It was formed in 1915 to transport both civil and military mail to and from sorting offices and railway stations in London, as well as parcels for troops overseas to and from the Royal Engineers Postal Depot in Regent's Park and Mount Pleasant. On 1 December 1915 a detachment of 300 NCOs and men arrived from Grove Park, under the command of a Lieutenant Newton. Captain D M Turner arrived a week later to assume command of the company.

The initial seventeen lorries drawn from Kempton Park in December were on duty carrying mail at 5.00 pm the day they arrived. Other vehicles were taken over in quick order and the unit was immediately caught up in the Christmas rush. Unit records state wryly that "the heavy duties . . . were performed with more expedience than method." It was soon evident that vehicles were required to work day and night, but fifteen men for each section of ten lorries were quite inadequate for this task and a case was made for a more generous manning ratio. It took, however, until July 1917 before two men per vehicle were authorized. As it was, for a period of six weeks each year, from the beginning of December, a hundred extra vehicles with appropriate drivers were temporarily attached for the Christmas period. Interestingly, as a reflection of the pressures on the men, the War Office unusually agreed to additional working pay, in response to a request from a deputation of NCOs and men, a remarkable occurrence.

It will not surprise anyone to learn that the strain of driving in London traffic by day and in the badly-lit streets at night, even in those early days when much of the 'opposition' was horse-drawn, was difficult for the majority of army-trained drivers. At first the capital's roads were in fairly good condition, except for the long roads to the docks in the East End, but they suffered gradual deterioration, which made driving difficult and caused unexpected wear and tear on vehicles.

The work level naturally also affected members of the workshop, whose equipment consisted only of a mobile Thornycroft workshop lorry and an Albion stores lorry. Repairs were made on the public roads in the Park (eg Chester Road and the Inner Circle in Regent's Park were routinely used for parking vehicles as no space was available in Albany Street (now Regent's Park Barracks)). Twenty additional fitters were posted in for Christmas 1916 and ten were permanently retained, subsequently helped by batches of fifty and a 100 learner fitters immediately after their training.

If parking space was in short supply for the task vehicles and workshop, living accommodation was also at a premium. Men were billeted in private houses in Camden Town, with subsistence allowance; this, however, ceased in June 1917 when empty houses in Park Crescent (numbers 5, 6, 22 and 27 (later 35) and 36 Chester Terrace) were taken over. This in turn necessitated an increase in administrative staff with the introduction of cooks, butchers and mess orderlies, so the savings may well have been minimal.

Although the transport of mail was the main task of 620 Company, it carried out a number of others that may be of interest: ferrying prisoners-of-war at the request of London District; the movement each Sunday in summer of Volunteer Companies from north London to the eastern defences in Essex for trench-digging work and other training, usually a dozen lorries each time; the transportation of timber from the Canadian Forestry Depot at Esher to Caterham; carrying first aid and rescue parties to the scenes of air-raid damage; carrying coal from central coal depots to various hospitals and government offices (fortunately with fifty lorries provided on top of the company establishment); and, in October 1917, the provision of three vehicles (a Renault car, a Daimler 3 ton lorry and a Thornycroft 3 ton lorry) for trials to substitute coal gas for petrol, which soon proved unsuccessful.

It is difficult sometimes to escape the impression that the ASC was considered a maid of all work. If the staff could think of no obvious unit, the job was given to the ASC. So it was in June 1915 with 'night soil' and Meldrum Destructors. Fortunately, this undesirable task was taken over by the Royal Engineers, who subsequently (and wisely) handed it over to the RAMC.

*   *   *

614 Company, based in Edinburgh, worked mainly for the Canadian Forestry Corps. As part of its duties in 1917, it sent a number of vehicles to gather sphagnum moss, which was used for hospital dressings (nowadays better known for hanging flower-baskets). 100 vehicles from the company were later sent (in February 1918) to Glasgow because of the strike there, their work including the transportation of infantry battalions which carried out policing duties in the Glasgow area.

*   *   *

882 Company recorded in September 1917 that thirteen cars and drivers were sent to Scotland for the use of HM King George V and his suite who were making a tour of inspection. Their records also show that a fleet of four Rolls-Royces was earmarked for numerous allied missions and special fast cars were held in readiness night and day for the Secret Service and journeys of a particularly urgent nature, the rough average per day being almost 250 miles.

*   *   *

Horse transport training in the Corps was provided by three HT Depots, in Aldershot, Bradford and Woolwich, whose training included Saddlers, Wheelers and Farriers. These depots dealt with some 7,000 reservists on mobilization before they turned their attention to recruit training. Bradford and Woolwich each dealt with 25,000 recruits during the war, while the depot in Aldershot formed no less than thirty-one Divisional Trains, thirty Reserve Parks and five Trains for Army Troops by the end of 1915.

At the instigation of Brigadier General S S Long, complete equipments were issued through one of the HT Depots. The Army Ordnance Department, which issued wagons, saddlery, harness and other transport equipment, and the Remount Department, which provided animals, normally issued items separately to units. This change greatly benefited infantry battalions and TA units which generally had neither Saddlers nor men accustomed to putting together and fitting saddlery or harness.

A number of Remount Depots were formed in 1915 at: Ormskirk (12 January), Swaythling (12 January), Shirehampton (12 January), Romsey (12 January), Kettering (9 June), Redhill (6 May) (51st Squadron), Market Harborough (6 May) (52nd Squadron), Leicester (6 May) (53rd Squadron), Arborfield Cross (15 May) (54th Squadron), Newcastle-on-Tyne (24 May) (55th Squadron), York (29 May) (56th Squadron) and Croft Spa (later, but exact date not known) (964th Squadron) (see Annex H).

ASC Company Sergeant Majors and Company Quartermaster Sergeants in the Remount Service became Squadron Sergeant Majors and Squadron Quartermaster Sergeants respectively on 17 July 1917.

*   *   *

At the end of 1915 a transport training school was formed at Grantham as part of the Machine Gun Training Centre. Five HT ASC Companies (Numbers 872, 873, 874, 875 and 876) were formed, equipped and ready to start training by 27 December 1915. Each company was to have 264 men under training, with a target of fifty-five fully-trained 'ride and drive' Drivers a week, a total of 275, sufficient for twelve machine-gun companies.

*   *   *

The ASC Discharge Depot, which consisted of 1 Company, 621 Company and 'A' Company, moved on 10 April 1916 from Aldershot to Scotton Camp, Catterick, changing its name to ASC Depot, Catterick on 28 June. Commanded by Major J S Iredell, its strength at any one time varied between 1,500 and 3,000 men. The Catterick location was, however, unsuitable and the climate poor, so it moved to Southport in Western Command on 1 December 1916. The role of the Depot was to receive all ASC men returning from the BEF, not to train recruits or prepare reinforcements or drafts for overseas, although the last two tasks appear to have been performed. Men who were invalided from overseas were, after a medical board, either sent for retraining or discharged. Men who were fit for 'Home Only' service were reported to OIC ASC Records for posting, while men found fit for general service were transferred to one of the Reserve Depots.

*   *   *

On 30 June 1917 a MT Depot was formed at Lee (in London) with sub-depots at:

>   Eltham (disbanded 7 April 1920)
>   Kelsey Manor (disbanded 7 April 1920)
>   Shortlands (disbanded 6 August 1919)
>   Norwood (disbanded 22 February 1919)
>   Sydenham (disbanded 15 March 1919)

The MT Depot itself disbanded on 17 November 1921.

*   *   *

The Comforts Fund mentioned in the 1915 chapter was not the only fund-raising effort in the ASC. There were many other worthy causes, tanks for the newly-formed Heavy Branch of the Machine Gun Corps being one of the best known. A notable event was held at the MT Depot in Osterley Park in Middlesex on 10 August 1918, when an aeroplane was commissioned for the Royal Air Force. The leading personalities in attendance were HRH The Duke of Connaught; Princess Patricia of Connaught; Lieutenant General Sir C Woollcombe KCB, Commander-in-Chief Eastern Command; Major General A R Crofton-Atkins, Director Supplies & Transport; Colonel T J Kearns, Commander ASC Osterley Park; and Bishop Taylor Smith, the Chaplain General.

In mid-1917 an ASC branch of the National War Savings Association had been opened at Osterley Park, which resulted in a total sum of £12,982 being invested. This entitled the Depot to have two aeroplanes named after it, 'Osterley No 1' being christened with champagne on 10 August. After the ceremony the pilot, Lieutenant I C Sanderson of 210 Squadron RAF, gave a flying display, eventually speeding away amidst rousing cheers.

The Sopwith F1 Camel was not the only attraction on the day, which had started with two guards of honour, one from ASC men of the Depot, the other by members of the QMAAC and Women's Legion. There were 'physical displays' by the women cooks, athletics races, a conjuring display and other amusements. Taking advantage of the large numbers of spectators present, a mock tank collected more War Savings donations and the Depot donkey mascot, 'Neddy', was employed collecting money for St Dunstan's, £159 11s 0d and £11 14s 6d being donated respectively. Clearly a good day was had by all. It is not known whether 'Osterley No 2' was ever commissioned.

*   *   *

On 1 November 1918 'S' (Statistical) Branch was formed, eventually located at 11-12 Pall Mall. Its task was to supply the War Office with information on all Home Service vehicles, the movement of vehicles and the cost of maintenance and repair. They were also able to trace gift and loan vehicles, supply information to the Police, assist disposal boards, assist Inspectorate of MT inspectors, provide data on the interchangeability of spare parts and ascertain the most suitable form of transport and the most economical use of different kinds of transport.

*   *   *

The signing of the Armistice on 11 November 1918 brought great relief all round. The problem was, it did not mean that everyone could pack up and go home, as so many thought: there was still much work to be done in clearing battlefields, in occupying the Rhineland, in closing-down formations even. The heaviest load in closing down in fact focused on troops in UK, the army's base, where expectations of an early return to life in plain clothes were highest; however, as demobilization took place, too slowly as ever for the soldiers involved, a good deal of unrest took place among units in England. There was, for instance, a short-lived strike of the ASC at the Remount Depot in Kettering during the war; and there was considerable unrest, particularly in the RASC at the various depots around London, as a result of which the Quartermaster General arranged for Regular officers to be brought in to help keep the men in hand.

*   *   *

The Western Front may well be the theatre of war which attracts the most attention today but there were several other areas which involved the British Army and the ASC: Italy, Egypt/Palestine, Mesopotamia, the Balkans, the Dardanelles, East Africa and Russia. The Corps was everywhere, more than most others deserving the motto 'Ubique'. Each campaign has its points of interest, in sum far greater than in mainland Europe. It seems, however, regrettable though it may be, that the greater the distance from the cliffs of Dover the less that is recorded, which means that those chapters dealing with the overseas campaigns are rather shorter and less informative than one would wish. The following pages concentrate on the main ASC involvement and points of interest elsewhere in the world, with a number of annexes at the end providing much information of archival interest.

CHAPTER 8

Italy

Italy was one of the Western allies in the fight against Germany and Austria and contingency plans were drawn up in 1917 for the involvement of British and French troops. The major defeat of the Italian Army by the Austrian Army at Caporetto on 24 October 1917, which involved the loss of 180 guns and over 270,000 prisoners, led to 200,000 British and French troops being moved speedily to reinforce Italy and keep her in the war.

The British formations involved were the 7th, 23rd and 48th Divisions, their units moving by rail on the coastal road via Modane. ASC MT units drove the 1,100 miles in November via Amiens, Meaux, Dijon, Lyons, Avignon, Nice, Savona or Genoa to Cremona and Camposampiero, averaging seventy miles a day, practically without the loss of a vehicle. This remarkable achievement, with Albions and Thornycrofts well-worn from operations in France and Belgium, says much for the skill and determination of the personnel involved. They joined a number of Siege Battery Ammunition Columns, each one an ASC unit with caterpillar tractors, supporting batteries which were fulfilling the dual role of reinforcing the somewhat inadequate Italian heavy artillery and 'showing the flag' to our Allies.

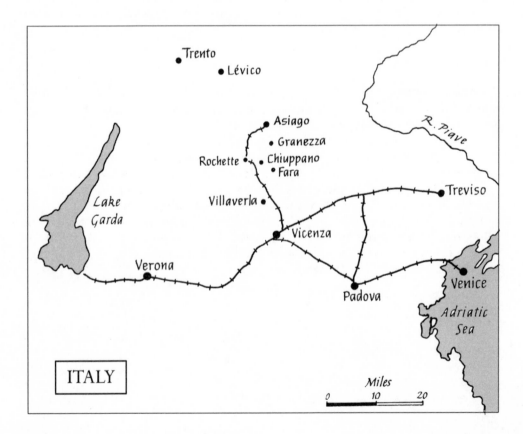

Rolls-Royce on the Western Front, January 1917. This car was used later by Their Majesties The King and Queen on a visit to the Western Front (B).

First Aid Nursing Yeomanry in rabbit skin coats, Calais, January 1917. Their Commandant, Miss Franklin, is on the left (A).

An 8-inch howitzer drawn by a Holt caterpillar travelling alongside GS wagons on the road from Mametz to Bazentin-le-Grand, September 1916 (A).

Horse lines near Amiens in sunken pits, one way of protecting them during German bombing raids, May 1918 (A).

Albion petrol tankers, date and location unknown. Note that each vehicle carries a warning sign, 'Danger. No Smoking/Lights within 15 yds' (B).

Manhandling a wheel at an ASC tyre-pressing depot in Hesdin, April 1918 (A).

A Foden Thresh Disinfector, used to de-louse uniforms and blankets (B).

ASC drivers of armoured cars training in England (B).

The Mobile Repair Workshop of 8 Scottish Motor Ambulance Convoy (326 MT Company) at Lewarde, October 1918. Note 'Scotia's Iron Queen' and 'Coatbridge' on the front of the vehicles (A).

RAMC personnel of No 2 Water Tank Company ASC (718 (MT) Company) testing water at the roadside in France, July 1918 (A).

Two Model T Fords presented by Queenswood School, Clapham Park, London
SW (See Annex J) (B).

Would-be drivers having fun in Cambrai, October 1918 (A).

A young ASC officer explains the workings of a gearbox to members of the WAAC (B).

'Amusements Unlimited': the cinema team of 92 MT Company (note the elephant sign), sometime in 1919 (B).

Daimler lorries lined up at the Kempton Park ASC depot. The race course buildings can be seen in the background. (A).

A supply column on the Merville Road, 12 April 1918, with an over-tired Corporal (A).

1037 Company in barracks in Italy. The company was commanded by Major E R
Loder, a well-known pre-war Brooklands racing driver (A).

Screens to hinder enemy artillery observation in Italy (B).

A wire road near Gaza, suitable for cars and vans but not lorries or camels, May 1917 (Palestine) (A).

A T-type Ford car and a convoy of Packards near Birkandi in 1919 (Mesopotamia) (A).

An ASC fire engine in Baghdad (Mesopotamia) (A).

A Holt tractor towing a 6-inch howitzer, with members of the Siege Battery hitching a ride (Mesopotamia) (A).

A Fiat car after repainting in an ASC workshop, Constantinople, 1919 (A).

A variety of vehicles in the ASC workshop at a gas works, Constantinople, 1919 (A).

A camouflaged mule-drawn ambulance passes ammunition limbers on the Seres road in the Struma Valley, September-October 1916 (Balkans) (A).

Efforts being made to recover an ASC caterpillar tractor which has somehow embedded itself in a ditch, March 1917 (Balkans) (A).

Mule-drawn transport and supplies on 'W' beach, 10 May 1915 (Gallipoli) (A).

A Holt tractor breaks up a derelict barge on 'K' beach (Gallipoli) (A).

An Overland car on a Sapper-built bridge near the Dhikukwe Swamps, 1918
(East Africa) (A).

One of the gunboats being transported overland *en route* to Lake Tanganyika
(East Africa) (A).

Reindeer sleigh, with a reindeer tied behind to act as a brake (North Russia) (A).

ASC pony-drawn limbers entered for a horse show, 1919 (North Russia) (A).

Within two months Brigadier General W S Swabey, who had been sent to Italy as the Director of Supplies, was appointed the Director of Supplies & Transport. The Base Supply Depot at Arquata, north of Genoa, was commanded by Lieutenant Colonel C Rowe ASC; opened in November 1917, it was part of a Base complex commanded by Brigadier General E V Riddell DSO, late ASC. Heavy Repair Shop duties were carried out by 1081 Company and the Base MT Depot by 1034 Company ASC. Part of the contingency planning which was implemented immediately was the loan of 500 1 ton Fiat lorries and drivers. The base at Arquata closed in April 1919.

Initially operations went well and ASC work presented no problems. The rail-head was well forward, with field bakeries established near the railheads to provide fresh bread for the troops, and Divisions drew direct from their Train companies without MT being interposed. On the Line of Communication transport work was carried out by auxiliary HT companies assisted by small detachments of MT. A little known unit on the Line of Communication was the Stationery & Printing Depot in Genoa, which was manned largely by ASC personnel. There seemed, however, to be a problem in the supply of typewriters: by the end of 1917 none had arrived from UK, so four were hired from the Remington Company to enable the paper war to progress. Eventually Sergeant Typewriter Mechanic A Crump went on a tour of typewriters in theatre in November 1918.

In March 1918, however, the British troops were moved to the Asiago plateau in the north, to counter a likely Austrian spring offensive, where they were to be involved in mountain warfare. The ASC inevitably needed to adapt its organization for its first ever involvement in Alpine terrain. Two sectors were established, each quite different: the left sector entailed the use of a rack and pinion railway and the right sector enabled only road transport to be used.

The railhead town of Chiuppano for the left sector had its exciting moments as it was in full view of the Austrians in the mountains and was occasionally shelled; the staging point of Rochette near Chiuppano was even under enemy searchlight observation and was therefore frequently shelled. Limbered wagons and mule transport carried supplies forward from the railhead. As had happened at Hellfire Corner east of Ypres on the Western Front, hessian netting was erected at critical points on the road in order to limit observation by the Austrians and this undoubtedly reduced casualties by shelling. For the right sector the railhead was at Villaverla, from which Divisional Trains initially moved supplies the six miles to Fara, where first line units took over for onward movement to Granezza. Mountainous roads and the twenty miles involved were too much, however, and No 2 Auxiliary HT Company, under Major J B Wheater MC, converted into a pack mule company and, supplemented by first line transport, operated a double echelon system to solve the problem, using limbered wagons where possible.

In the event the Austrians opened their attack in June but were forced to accept an Armistice on 4 November 1918, not before the right sector formation (the 48th Division) needed to capture Austrian forage to ease its supply problems. In addition the Division had to use fifty light Fiat lorries with Italian drivers during its advance to Trent and Levico in lieu of the Divisional Train heavy draught horses, which could not be used on the steep mountain roads. Adaptability and good allies saved the day for the ASC.

Before leaving the Italian front several other points should be mentioned. A driving school was established by the ASC to train drivers in mountain driving techniques; nearly a thousand men passed through between April and November 1918. Then there was an exchange of vehicles between the ASC and their Italian counterparts: six Pavesi tractors for nine British four-wheel drive lorries to enable guns to be moved on difficult roads, a good bargain under the circumstances. Finally the ASC Corps Pontoon Park's four-wheel drive lorries moved sixty-six 18 pounder guns and twenty-four 4.5 inch howitzers in March from the plains to the Asiago plateau, all by night and without lights on difficult roads. Each lorry carried one gun and towed another.

In April the same unit fitted its vehicles with 300 gallon water tankers for supplying troops on the plateau, while later, for the crossing of the Piave, they carried footbridges, fascines and boats to the bridgehead, day and night under enemy shellfire.

1150 MT Company was formed in March 1919 in Milan as No 1 Evacuation Depot, disbanding on 3 February 1920 at the end of its task.

The maximum strength of the ASC in Italy was 275 officers, 4,180 MT Other Ranks, 2,120 HT Other Ranks, 900 Supply personnel and 1,534 vehicles. The Corps obtained useful experience in operating MT in mountainous country and worked well in supporting a successful small campaign.

The somewhat brief extract from a despatch from General The Earl of Cavan KP, Commanding-in-Chief British Forces in Italy, published in a supplement to the London Gazette of 4 December 1918, hardly does credit to the efforts of the Corps in this campaign: "The rapid advance during the operations entailed great strain on the Supply and Transport Services. My thanks are due to Brigadier General W S Swabey CB CMG and all ranks of those services who maintained the supply of both ammunition and rations in spite of bad roads, hastily constructed bridges and long distances from railheads."

CHAPTER 9

Egypt and Palestine

There were in fact two campaigns in the Near East: a minor campaign in 1914-16 to defend the Suez Canal by defeating the Senussi in the Western Desert and a major campaign in 1916-18, advancing from Egypt through the Sinai, Palestine and Syria, ending with the defeat of the Turkish Army near Aleppo. In the former campaign, using Alexandria as the base, British forces 8,000 strong progressed westwards along the coast by rail, road or camel, eventually to Sollum, 350 miles away. The ASC provided over 2,000 gallons of petrol in Sollum for a raid westwards for 120 miles by armoured cars to rescue the survivors of two British ships, *Tara* and *Moorina*, who were held prisoner; and also used light MT lorries to assist in the capture of the Siwa Oasis, 180 miles south-west of Mersa Matruh.

The main campaign in 1916-18 involved 250,000 men, the senior ASC officer being Brigadier General G F Davies (later to be the Director of Supplies & Transport in the War Office), brilliantly supported by Colonel W Elliott, a Reserve officer with pre-war service in Egypt and the Middle East and war experience in Gallipoli. The initial aim was to safeguard the Suez Canal from the Turks, whose main force was at El Arish on the eastern edge of the Sinai Desert, 100 miles from Qantara on the Suez Canal.

With the Sinai an effective barrier to movement, transportation took on an special significance. To solve the problem the Royal Engineers built a standard gauge railway from Qantara to Wadi Ghuzze near Gaza. Qantara soon developed into the main base, with a Base Supply Depot being established for a feeding strength of nearly 500,000 men and 160,000 animals. At the same time a new form of transportation was introduced, the pipeline, essential for the supply of water, another Engineer responsibility. Until the pipeline was ready, however, water was moved in bulk on the new railway and then distributed to the forward troops by the ASC on animal transport, camel. A Camel Transport Corps, organized in companies of 2,000 animals each, was formed under Colonel C W Whittingham, an ASC Reserve officer, and was employed as first line transport and as special columns. The ASC provided supervisory personnel (111 officers and 208 NCOs) for the Egyptian drivers. Each camel carried twenty-five gallons, twelve-and-a-half gallons being carried in each of two small tanks, *fanatis*. The Camel Corps gradually developed to a strength of 35,000 animals. Later, reservoirs and wells were established forward, but the capture of the wells at Beersheba eased the water supply situation.

After fighting against the Turks in the Romani area, which opened the way to El Arish, Rafa on the Palestine border was occupied in January 1917. It must be mentioned at this stage that a rail line and a water pipeline from the base in Egypt into Palestine did not obviate the need for a road and more normal form of transport ; accordingly a track along the coast was laid, with wire netting laid on the sand and pegged down. Mounted troops were forbidden to use this track as horses' hooves would have cut the wire.

General Sir Edmund Allenby replaced General Sir Archibald Murray as Force Commander in June 1917. He moved GHQ from Cairo forward to Rafa and

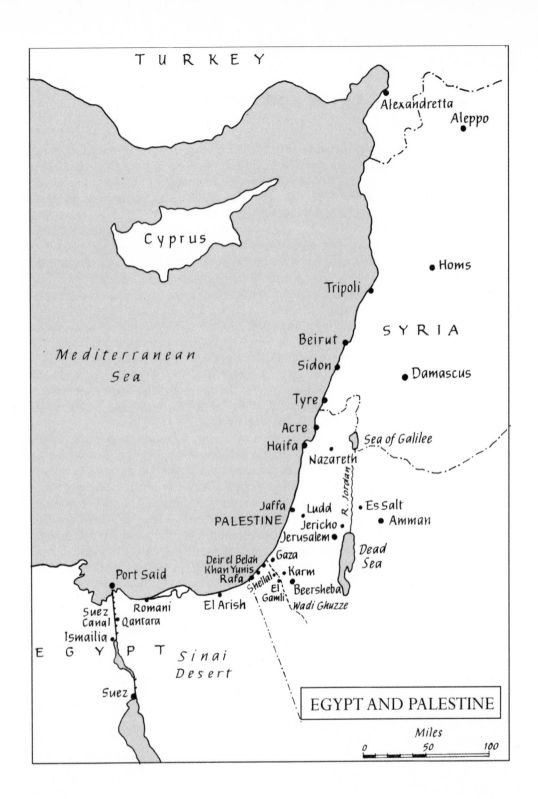

EGYPT AND PALESTINE

reorganized and revitalized the army for its next offensive against the Turks. As part of this reorganization the ASC Trains of the 52nd, 53rd and 54th Divisions as well as the Train of the Anzac Mounted Division exchanged their limbered waggons for standard GS waggons, each with a team of four mules. As operations proceeded Trains from other newly-arrived Divisions were broken up and reorganized to meet the particular needs of the new formations, until there were ultimately fourteen Trains and four auxiliary mule transport companies on the Line of Communication with a total strength of nearly 17,000 men, of whom just over half were Egyptian. Two donkey companies were also formed, another new form of locomotion in the ASC; each company had 2,000 donkeys and was conceived for employment in the difficult goings of the Judean Hills. They accomplished a variety of tasks, carrying ammunition, water, entrenching tools and stones for road making. Reserve and advanced depots were also created in a wide area occupied by British troops, notably at El Arish, Rafa, Khan Unis, Deir El Belah, Shellal, El Gamli and finally at Karm, the last named having to be set up in full view of the Turkish positions and subject to attack by artillery.

General Allenby, reinforced by two additional divisions, mounted a surprise attack on the Turks and took Beersheba, which forced a Turkish withdrawal from the Gaza area to a precarious line between Jerusalem and Jaffa. At this stage, excluding Line of Communication units, General Allenby's army had thirteen MT companies available to him, made up of one Ford van company and twelve caterpillar tractor companies, eleven of which towed the heavy guns of the Royal Artillery. On the eve of the attack, however, three companies of lorries were brought up from Qantara to provide additional lift capacity. MT came into its own again as desert and sand were left behind, replaced by rough country with occasional roads and tracks, which provided good goings until the rains came and the surface broke up, low-lying areas becoming impassable swamps.

The subsequent pursuit lengthened the distances over which the ASC worked, but great flexibility and the co-ordination of all forms of transport available, rail, MT and all forms of animal transport, carried the day, complemented by the use of water transport along the coast to resupply over the beaches. Jerusalem fell in December and Jericho in February 1918. Camels working in three echelons along the coastal sand dunes overcame the problems caused by lengthy period of rains, saving the operational situation, but in some places camels sank up to their girths in mud and had to be abandoned. By the end of December 1917 fresh supply depots had been formed along the entire front, from Jerusalem to Jaffa, and other depots were opened at Ludd, Jericho, Es Salt, Amman, Haifa, Tyre, Beirut, Damascus, Tripoli, Homs and Aleppo in response to the British advance. Fortunately the ASC were sometimes able to use metalled roads which had been built by the Turks.

After something of a delay in operations in early 1918, due to two of the five British Divisions being moved to the Western Front and replaced by the inexperienced 3rd and 7th Indian Divisions, the offensive continued in September. Within thirty-six hours the Turkish 7th and 8th Armies were broken and forced to retire, which forced their 4th Army east of Jordan to conform. Thereafter the fighting developed into a general pursuit and harassment of a fleeing enemy. In this welter of constantly developing operational scenarios the ASC with its forty companies was at full stretch in close support of the fighting troops. Maintenance of the force was assisted by coastal landings at Haifa, Tyre, Sidon,

Beirut and Tripoli, with the Camel Transport Corps co-operating until the MT could take up the work on the repaired coastal road north of Beirut and on the Haifa-Nazareth-Galilee road to Damascus. East of the River Jordan the Cavalry Division in pursuit of the 4th Turkish Army was supported by MT from Jericho and by mule transport.

It can be imagined that this campaign, sweeping up from east of the Sinai through Jerusalem, Damascus and on to Aleppo, was a memorable achieve-ment in which logistic support necessarily matched the determined brilliance of the forward troops. The brunt of the work was borne by the MT companies, whose drivers worked day and night through much of this period, to the point that men were so exhausted and ill that it was sometimes difficult to provide one driver for each lorry; but the support provided by camel and mule units should not be underestimated as they too played an essential part in a successful team.

*   *   *

This campaign had an additional point of interest, the involvement of Colonel T E Lawrence, famous then and now as 'Lawrence of Arabia'. He led Emir Feisal's Arab irregulars in harassing operations against the Turks, much of it directed at the Hejaz Railway. Units of the Machine Gun Corps with Rolls-Royce armoured cars were used in this role, manned by ASC drivers. Colonel Lawrence's driver was an ASC man, though sadly his name seems not to be recorded.

*   *   *

On their way to act as the 54th Auxiliary Petrol Company, 905 (MT) Company was less fortunate than its fellow companies *en route* to Alexandria: on 4 May 1917 its ship, D32, was torpedoed. The OC, Captain R O Nelson, two of his subalterns and eighteen men were lost. The ship's despatch said: "The gallantry of nurses, officers and men were remarkable, even the second torpedo failed to break the ranks, although several were blown up by the explosion. Many magnificent examples of gallantry and devotion to duty have been reported, but . . . more than half the troops on board must be specially mentioned".

Later in 1917 the company was highly complimented by various staff officers for the work done, in particular for taking ammunition etc into very difficult positions right up to the guns, at times under heavy fire and action from enemy aircraft. During this period drivers were working day and night over very rough and heavy roads, often only camel tracks, and frequently those tracks had to be built up by the drivers where they cross waddies and broken bridges before a crossing could be attempted. Only one accident occurred and that was when a lorry fell into a well on the route during a sandstorm at night.

*   *   *

Following support given by tanks in the Battle of the Somme it was decided to send a small number of tanks to Egypt to provide support for the Infantry in the Sinai. It was originally intended that twelve should be sent but in the event only eight went, unfortunately all Mark 1s. In December 1916 the tanks, support vehicles and men embarked at Devonport and Avonmouth, arriving in Egypt in January 1917; they were located at Gilban, ten miles north of Qantara on the Suez Canal, where demonstrations were laid on for the Commander-in-Chief and his staff.

Major W Midwinter was OC of 961 Company, the ASC Company providing support to the tanks in the Middle East. He recorded that the eight tanks had arrived in a disgraceful state; tracks and running gear were clogged with mud and rusted solid, secondary gears were not visible as the housings were full of mud, engines and all bright work were coated with rust and there was not a trace of oil or grease anywhere except in the engine base cylinder.

In no time at all, in February, instructions came to send the tanks to the fighting zone. They were loaded onto railway flats and unloaded at the frontier town of Rafa, from where they moved on to Khan Yunis, fifteen miles south-west of Gaza. The tanks' contribution to this Second Battle of Gaza in April was a total surprise to the Turks but it was not decisive, partly due to the lack of understanding on infantry/tank co-operation and partly due to the lack of preparation.

In any event there were enough problems in maintaining the tanks in desert conditions. Sand caused considerable wear on road chain sprockets and pinions, and tracks had to be slackened off at night due to the big drop in temperature and tightened up again in the morning, but otherwise the engines ran as well as they did in England, other than the cooling system. The real problem, however, was the supply of stores through the Army Ordnance Department Base in Alexandria; understandably tanks had never operated under these conditions before so assessing the scale of spares was difficult if not impossible. On 27 June 1917 the Director of Artillery in Cockspur Street, London SW1 wrote to the Director of Ordnance Services in Egypt: "It is not possible to meet in full the large demands for shafts. Twenty-four are being sent at present. The scale on which these are demanded is greatly in excess of what experience in this country and France has found necessary, and it is important to know if the conditions under which tanks are used in Egypt cause any excessive wear to this part."

The Third Battle of Gaza in November 1917 was more successful and the tanks, involving later Marks this time, played an important role. One tank was completely destroyed and there were a number of casualties and damaged tanks, which were recovered from the battlefield and repaired, but they were not used again. The November battle saw the last use of tanks with the army in Palestine. 961 Company ASC, in line with developments in England and on the Western Front, was absorbed into the Tank Corps on 9 October 1917.

*　　*　　*

As with other MT companies 906 (MT) Company had their problems with mobility. Their record recounts that, "All the land looked alike and there were very few landmarks. A few dead animals left about at first were found quite useful . . . The country, however, being full of wadies there was difficulty in getting through these when the rainy season sets in. After a time culverts were built but before then planks had to be carried to make a wheel case for the tyres to pass. The same difficulties arose as soon as the tracks were wet, the soil then turned into a ploughed field and the wheels often sank to the axles.

The means used to get along were skid chains but these soon caked up and in the worst patches it was only possible to get along by getting one lorry through and linking up the remainder. It has always been found possible to get a convoy along if one lorry got through."

* * *

In support of a force (in September 1918) of 466,750 men and 159,900 animals, the ASC operated a total of 1,601 lorries, 1,467 cars and vans, 530 ambulances, 1,487 motor cycles and 288 tractors, with 1,094 officers and 17,817 Other Ranks, complemented by 2,725 Indians and 32,744 Egyptians. The best traditions of the Corps had been upheld, their efforts described by the Commander-in-Chief as "a triumph of organization and perseverance". This striking tribute was equalled after the war by the Turkish General Refet Pasha's offer to General Allenby to fight the Palestine campaign over again with an equal commissariat.

CHAPTER 10

Mesopotamia (Iraq)

Moving more to the east, Mesopotamia offers another little-known campaign, in which the most intense demands were placed on vehicles and men of the Corps, indeed many contend that conditions were often worse than on the Western Front.

In 1914 the Indian government landed a force at Basra to protect the Royal Navy's oil supplies from the Turks. The scope of the operations was expanded, with the aim of capturing Baghdad, but, after some initial success, the British and Indian forces under General Townshend were forced back to Kut el Amara and, after a siege lasting 143 days, surrendered in April 1916 after a gallant defence. At this stage the Indian Army Supply & Transport Corps was involved in support of the Western forces, with under-strength animal transport only. Seven British Other Ranks serving with Indian MT were captured by the Turks at Kut el Amara.

It is generally recognized that the first airdrop of supplies took place in March 1916 during the siege of Kut el Amara, where some 12,000 British troops were besieged by the Turks. Late in December 1915 a large store of grain was discovered by the British, but they had no way of grinding it into flour. The Turks

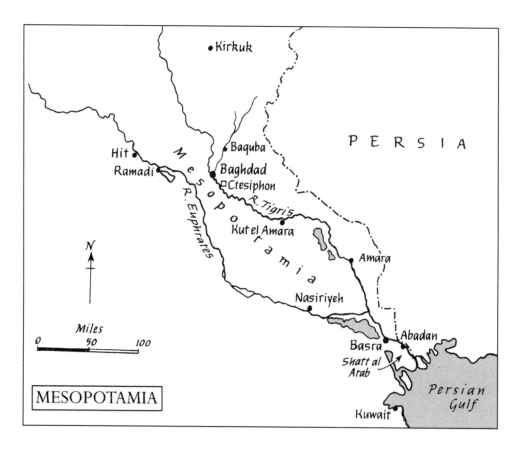

had shrewdly removed all millstones from the only flour mill in town. Following a wireless request a 70 lb millstone was dropped by a Royal Naval Air Service BE2C biplane on 27 March; subsequently fourteen aircraft, variously BE2Cs, a Voisin, a Farman and Short seaplanes, flew 140 sorties and dropped a total of 16,000 lbs of flour, fishing nets (Kut was located on the River Tigris), sugar, cigarettes, salt, mail, chocolate, wireless equipment and medical stores. Sadly it was not enough, but the practicality of air supply had been proved; however, in spite of its minor use during the Battle of Arras on the Western Front in 1917, all thought of further development in air supply was abandoned.

In early 1916, with British prestige at stake, the War Office was directed to recover the situation and assumed responsibility for the maintenance of the forces in Mesopotamia. Problems abounded, however: roads were non-existent and the only railway ran north of Baghdad; no maritime transport had been employed in an area of rivers and waterways; in the rainy season the country was almost impassable and in summer dust and the lack of water supply made movement highly uncomfortable; furthermore, the Indian logistic system was totally inadequate.

The appointment of General Maude in August 1916 set in train a range of improvements; on the S & T side Brigadier General P J C Scott was appointed Director of Supplies & Transport, at the head of 659 officers and 12,200 Other Ranks of the ASC who eventually served in the campaign. The first ASC unit to arrive (from Egypt) was 596 Company, some 400 strong, equipped with 110 Peerless lorries, followed by a Motor Ambulance Convoy (656 Company) and a Base MT Depot (695 Company); a Base Supply Depot was established in Basra; the port was reorganized; a frozen meat ship was obtained from England; the troops' rations were improved out of all recognition; canteens and bakeries were established; petrol was bought from the Anglo-Persian Company in Abadan; even grass farms were started. The administrative base to support a successful campaign was being built up.

Lieutenant Colonel F W Leland was soon appointed as Assistant Director of MT and the War Office was requested to send a number of MT companies. By the end of December two Ford van companies, two Holt caterpillar tractor companies (for howitzer towing) and another Motor Ambulance Convoy had arrived; ultimately there were forty-two ASC MT companies. Additionally infantry battalions were provided for the first time with their own first line MT lorries. The whole administrative situation was changing; the end of 1916 marked the end of failure.

General Maude was now able to go on the offensive. 1917 and 1918 were a story of uninterrupted success based on good administrative support and operational mobility, both provided by the ASC. Kut was recaptured in February and Baghdad taken in March; the line of communication was thereby extended to some 500 miles from the base in Basra and the army reached a total strength of 300,000 men and 66,000 animals.

In September 1917 the 3,000-strong Turkish garrison at Ramadi was attacked and for this operation the ASC, commanded by Major E Snepp, concentrated 350 Ford vans and ten Fiats as a column for troop-carrying duties, the first time the ASC had performed this task outside Europe. In a subsequent aborted attack on Hit 100 cars carrying Infantry and Lewis guns moved at night, without lights, over unknown and difficult country, a remarkable operation. The success of these concentrations was immediately reinforced and four Columns were organized, three of them under the command of Lieutenant Colonels. Commanding Officers were:

No 1 MT Column:	Lieutenant Colonel E Snepp DSO
No 2 MT Column:	Lieutenant Colonel E G Pelly DSO MC
No 3 MT Column:	Lieutenant Colonel H Dickinson
No 4 MT Column:	Major P Weir
(formed 10 March 1918)	

The Headquarters of each Column consisted of:

A Commanding Officer	with one Ford car
Adjutant (Captain)	with two Ford vans
Company Sergeant Major	with one motor cycle
Corporal Clerk	
1 Despatch Rider	
2 Batmen	

The composition and strength of these Columns varied according to the operational requirements, but the largest number of vans reached 1,200 for one specific operation, the control of which must have been challenging to even the most professional of transport officers. In March 1918, however, the Columns consisted of the following:

No 1:	971, 1013, 1014 and 1016 MT Companies
No 2:	784, 815, 918 and 954 MT Companies
No 3:	729, 730, 783 and 1023 MT Companies
No 4:	Detachment from 596, 976 and 953 MT Companies

(No 5 Column came into existence in December 1918 for the Persian Line of Communication, consisting of 596, 954, 976, 1015, 1016, 1018 and 1020 MT Companies)

The extensive demands for vehicles in this theatre could not, however, be met from the UK base. Model-T Fords from America provided the answer and some 3,300 were eventually used; their lightness and ease of maintenance made them ideal for the desert and rough goings in Mesopotamia. Henry Ford's pacifist views, which had originally only entertained the provision of ambulances, had changed, to the enormous benefit of the ASC and the British Army. Many Fords were driven by Indian and Burmese drivers, armed mostly with DP (display purpose) rifles. Another American vehicle, later well-known in its limousine form, the Packard 3 tonner , provided the heavy lift in two transport companies. Ultimately there were forty-two MT companies, of which twenty-two were Ford van companies, the total number of vehicles in theatre amounting to 6,930. Vehicles used all available tracks or old camel caravan routes.

An interesting additional task carried out by the ASC was the provision of men, vehicles, spares and repairs for six light armoured motor batteries, six anti-aircraft sections and a railway armoured motor battery; not to be forgotten either was the use of a large river barge, converted by an ASC officer into a double-decker floating mobile MT workshop, as no suitable building was available ashore. Even the Expeditionary Force Canteen took over a barge, the SS *Masoodi,* on the Tigris.

A 172 ft long Floating Workshop, fitted out by the MT Depot staff, was completed in mid-December 1916. Initially it was towed upstream to Aziziyeh, where support was provided to a MT company and an armoured car; it then moved to Baghdad, where it acted as the Advanced MT Depot and Advanced MT Stores until the Heavy Workshop arrived in June from Amara. It eventually ceased operating in March 1919.

Expeditionary Force Canteens started operations in Mesopotamia in July 1916, with canteens in all main locations. Horse transport occupied an unusually subordinate position compared with MT.

The high casualties were due to ASC tasks which allowed no break in the work, whatever the season. The men were out in the sun when personnel of other arms rested under shelter. During July 1917, for example, there were ninety-two deaths and 307 men were invalided home, the majority due to heat stroke or heat exhaustion. There were, however, in spite of the abysmal conditions, no desertions.

1018 Company, which has been formed in Bulford in the autumn of 1917, recorded in their war diary a number of experiences on the bad roads. These were typical of all the MT units in the theatre. Only a small example is given: "*En route* from Ezrah's Tomb to Amara, on a road which was in a shocking state, waterlogged and with 18 inch ruts, forty Ford vans were ditched and four vehicles were totally stranded in the rain. Fortunately all were recovered later."

Two companies, formed in Bulford in the autumn of 1917 for service in Mesopotamia, had a frustrating time, 1023 and 1024 Companies MT. They were conceived as Ford van units, to be brought fully up to establishment after they had disembarked from the SS *Lydia*. The only problem was that the War Office had totally forgotten it had already selected the numbers 1023 and 1024 for two Burmese MT Companies, one of which was already in theatre. When the OCs, Captain C N Draper and Captain R G Swanston, reported, the second Burmese company (1024) had not yet arrived. 1023 Company was initially renumbered 1024 Company as a temporary measure and employed as Base transport. It was then absorbed into the Base MT Depot as a detachment under Captain Draper, so he was not too unhappy. 1024 Company was disbanded in mid-March 1918 and its men sent to 1020 Company as reinforcements, not such a happy solution for the company's command element.

Occasionally the most extraordinary things are recorded in a unit's war diary which, like all others, can be looked at in the Public Record Office Kew. 1024 Company's shows that the army exchanged vehicles for petrol: "On the Persian Line of Communication many things were in short supply, including petrol. The Russians had petrol but would not sell it for money. In July 1918 the Resht detachment was ordered to prepare ten fully equipped Ford vans to exchange for petrol with the Russians on the basis of 300 pods of petrol for each van. All went well and soon after a convoy of seventy-three vans left Resht for Kasvin with 1,500 gallons of Russian petrol."

The shortage of men on the Western Front in mid-1918 even caused the ASC to look elsewhere for MT drivers: twenty-six men of the Mauritius Labour Corps were attached to 1056 Company ASC for driver training, one of a series of experiments with men of other races, Armenians and Arabs being tried too. Any source was welcome, as few if any reinforcements could be expected from England.

There were no ASC Remount personnel with the Middle East Forces, Remount Services being entirely in the hands of the Indian Army.

*   *   *

The following is an extract from the Despatch to the Chief of the General Staff India from Lieutenant General W R Marshall KCB KCSI, Commanding-in-Chief Mesopotamian Expeditionary Force, dated 1 October 1918:

"Supplies have been satisfactorily maintained and delivered to the troops with a regularity which is worthy of all praise, when it is remembered that not a single metallic road exists throughout the length and breadth of Mesopotamia.

"The work of the transport, particularly the Mechanical Transport, has been extremely arduous. Immense wear and tear to vehicles has been caused on the Persian roads, and it reflects great credit on all concerned to have kept so many vehicles in working order. It is safe to say that a line of communication of such a length has never previously been kept up. The strain thrown on the personnel of the Mechanical Transport Branch has been very considerable, but the demands on them have been met with unfailing regularity and willingness." (Supplement to the *London Gazette* 20 February 1919.)

When the Armistice was signed in 1918 the ASC in Mesopotamia had reached a strength of 12,660, of which 3,000 were Indian or Burmese and 800 Arabs. Just under 400 ASC died or were killed. You will find their graves but you will look in vain for mention of the ASC in the index of the Official History of this campaign.

*   *   *

Chapter 11

The Balkans (Salonika)

The Balkans were something of a messy campaign, the highlights of which, for the ASC, were the unique award of the French Croix de Guerre, the use of armed motor boats and the performance of two fire engines. The British High Command, in its own way, distinguished itself by the decision to send formations without their own transport, both at first and second line. From this chaotic start things could at least only get better, and inevitably much improvisation and hard work on the part of the ASC saved the day.

The deployment of British and French troops (150,000 were promised) was designed solely to save the Serbian Army and persuade Greece to honour her treaty obligations to side with the Western allies against the Austro-Bulgarian Army. Both aims failed.

* * *

The advanced party which landed at Salonika in September 1915 included Lieutenant Colonel O Striedinger, Assistant Director of Supply & Transport, the sole 'Q' representative . The 10th Division followed in a disorganized manner, not helped by the torpedoing of the *Marquette* carrying the Ammunition Column, which left ASC units short in transport and supply numbers. Energetic action, however, and the co-operation of the French recovered the situation, and a Base Supply Depot was quickly established just outside Salonika. The ASC borrowed shamelessly from the French, who were very kind. The wet and stormy weather did not help with the baking of bread, as the grass sods were constantly washed off the 'Aldershot ovens', leading to the request for the more modern Perkins ovens. Initial movement was based on animal transport, but then MT vehicles started arriving and a Base MT Depot (598 Company ASC) was established in the town of Kalamaria, Salonika.

In spite of unhelpful Greek authorities, who requisitioned all available horses and mules to delay the allies, which meant that the MT had to work twenty-four hours a day, seven days a week, on appalling roads, the British moved to the Doiran area in November to assist the French with their two Divisions. By December the mountainous forward areas were badly affected by heavy snow and rain and the few roads and tracks became morasses, thus making resupply difficult. Instead of six mules to a wagon ten or twelve were often necessary, which had a knock-on delaying effect. Blizzard conditions and the deteriorating operational situation in December forced a withdrawal by both the French and the British to a new defensive line north of Salonika, and the 29th Divisional Supply Column (244 Company ASC) had to make the difficult conversion to a pack transport role, the only way to operate in the mountains.

* * *

An idea of the difficulties experienced in setting up support for the army is provided by part of a letter of 11 November 1915 from Colonel Striedinger to Major General Long in the War Office:

"It has been extraordinarily difficult to make arrangements and to "look forward" at all, as we have been kept in almost complete ignorance of what to expect in the way of troops, and ships have been "blown in" without any warning. The system of sending troops without their transport animals has been a little difficult . . . We cannot get the stuff away as quickly as the Navy lands it. The quays are very narrow and vehicles are difficult to manoeuvre thereon; and until the siding which is being made to the Main Supply Depot is completed, the railway can be made very little use of. Before the lorries arrived we had to use local carts. I have bought hay and wood, but the Greeks may – and <u>do</u> – requisition it at any moment. The Greeks have just requisitioned all the French hay and I have lent him 500 tons in exchange for wood which the Greeks have taken from me. The Greeks treat us (British and French) both equally badly. This moment the ADRT has come in to tell me that the Greek Government have sent him a notice that they have raised all passenger goods fares on the railways by 7½ per cent. (They certainly intend to make all they can out of us.)"

*   *   *

This campaign, perhaps more than in any other theatre of war, had elements of farce which would have been suitable for any comic opera. There was for example the incident of the Nehamas barn in Salonika: several hundred tons

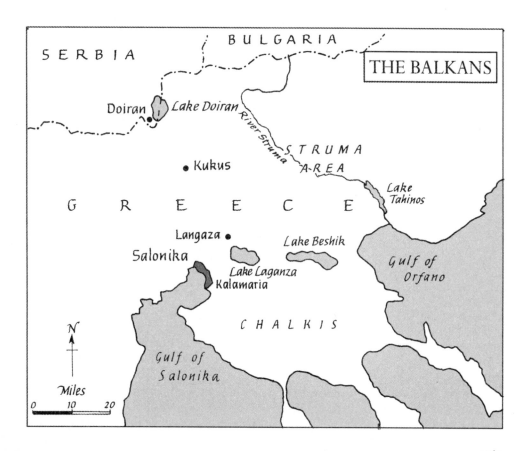

165

of hay had been bought locally by the British and it was under army guard; meanwhile the ever unhelpful Greeks forbade its removal and added a sentry of their own to reinforce their orders. The wily local vendor, an entrepreneur to his back teeth, then sold the hay to the unknowing French, who posted their own sentry. The three guards happily watched each other for several days.

The UK base was not immune to well-meaning advice, of course, and a cable arrived from home proposing the use of olive trees for fire wood, in spite of their importance to the local community, each mature tree being then valued at £80. The Greeks also prohibited the sale of petrol and placed a guard on the Standard Oil Company premises, but fortunately the ASC depot was next door and the Greeks never noticed that fuel stocks were passed over the wall.

*   *   *

By December 1915 the British force was 90,000 strong, with 25,000 animals. Colonel P C J Scott arrived in November as the Director of Supplies & Transport and Brigadier General A Long took over from him in January 1916, with Major General F W G Koe as the Inspector-General Line of Communication. The army was expanding rapidly, with four more Divisions (22nd, 26th, 27th and 28th), each with its own Train, so that by February the force being supported was 120,000 men and 50,000 animals strong, later to increase even more. Additional ASC supply units and motor transport arrived, some seventy lorries, which allowed resupply to be carried out by a combination of rail, MT and animal transport. Each Division had 4,000 mules and a mix of wagons, in addition to the large number of army and Line of Communication units.

In January 1916 Colonel Scott wrote to Major General Long from Salonika:

"I arrived here on 23 November, after having been delayed ten days at Alexandria owing to shipping difficulties.

With bad main roads, hopeless tracks, lack of transport etc keeping the troops supplied daily is a very difficult proposition. Divisions have been arriving in front of their transport, and even when this arrives it is incomplete. Many stray units say "They took away our transport in France". We are now using two MT Companies, a Reserve Park, and such odds and ends of Formation transport that have arrived.

We have Advanced Supply Depots at Atvatli and Lairia and are in the process of forming others at Akbunar, Hortiacn and Langavuk.

We have got together a pack mule company, run by the Base HT Depot, consisting of 200 mules; the drivers were luckily some odd lots from the 13th Division that somehow found their way here. I am setting up a Serbian mule or donkey pack transport company to fill up gaps. On petrol we are living from hand to mouth . There are 80,000 gallons here in the Standard Oil Company, but the Greeks will not allow us to touch it, nor will they let us have anything but a small quantity on loan.

The 27th Division has arrived complete . . . but not a stitch of first line or Train transport. They have not even got a Divisional staff here yet. This is an example of one sort of difficulty. My only wish now is that I may be able to kill a Greek before I die!"

In May 1916 the allies began preparing for a move north from the Salonika area, towards Struma, moving over the mountains north of Lakes Beshik and Langaza. This greatly influenced the transport and supply situation and

Divisional Trains needed to be doubled in size (to eight companies each Train) for mountain warfare. The war situation with the BEF in Europe meant that the extra men could only be obtained locally and some 4,700 Muleteers were recruited from Cyprus, who complemented the 2,100 Muleteers already recruited in Greece (the Macedonian Mule Corps) .

In addition to extra manpower and mules for the British Army six MT companies (706, 707, 708, 709 (Fords), and 688 and 689 (Albions)) arrived in October 1916, their sole purpose being to support the Serbian Army. Under extremely difficult circumstances, in vile weather and with sickness rife (sandfly fever and dysentery), Lieutenant Colonel L C Bearne's command performed magnificently and 688 Company, which had operated over primitive roads in South Croatia constantly exposed to enemy gun fire and aircraft attack, had the honour of being awarded the French *Croix de Guerre,* along with eleven other units of the British Army. 688 Company, however, was the only unit to receive the cross 'with Bronze Star' *('avec Palme').* (Lieutenant Colonel Bearne was himself awarded the Albert Medal on 22 October 1916 when he helped extinguish a fire on a lorry loaded with 3,000 lbs of aeroplane bombs.)

* * *

As in every other theatre of war the ASC found itself involved in duties outside its normal role. In January 1916 33 ASC Motor Boat Section, under the command of Lieutenant G Swann ASC, was established, initially with one boat which had arrived from Mudros on 30 November. Then there were two boats, Motor Boat 5 and Motor Boat 13, which were transported on GS wagons to Lake Beshik and Lake Langaza, the latter boat being 'launched' by Lieutenant P Knox-Gore. Thirty feet long and armed with machine guns, these patrol boats kept all native boats off the lake at night and prevented any landings on the northern shores. They were also used very effectively on the River Struma with support from the Sussex Yeomanry. On 5 June 1916, when the Royal Navy took over, they moved to Lake Tahinos, where the boats carried out 4-6 hour patrols nightly, hiding up in the reeds on the side of the lake by day to escape shellfire. The section certainly led a much more exciting life on Lake Tahinos, with exchanges of fire with the Bulgarian Army, until they were withdrawn in June 1918. Eventually, in December 1916, a War Office letter arrived, authorizing the formation of the Motor Boat Section, the establishment being for eleven boats and thirty-three personnel. Until then unit administration had been carried out through the Base MT Depot.

After the war, in February 1919, 33 Motor Boat Section moved from Salonika to Constantinople, under the command of Lieutenant C J Stewart. There it took on charge a German boat, *Rita,* and other launches and motor boats (including *Sylvia, Badger, Hawk, Swift, Sapper, Lahore, Magda, Barbara, Lily, Lola, Sparrow, Prince Ardur and Yildirun).* The *Hawk* and *Sparrow* were taken over from the British Serbian Mission.

* * *

18 August 1917 provided an interesting event when a fire broke out in Salonika which destroyed a square mile of the town. Two ASC fire engines from the Base MT Depot at Kalamaria and the docks provided assistance – one engine

for ten days, the other for seventeen. One driver remained at his post without sleep for almost sixty hours. Innumerable ASC lorries and vans transported refugees out of danger. The fire may have been unimportant from a campaign point of view, but it achieved wonders for the reputation of the British Army.

*   *   *

One of the more unusual units spawned by the war in Salonika was an Agricultural Park ASC, which operated between October 1918 and June 1919, under the command of Captain R C Gaymer. This was unlike many units on the Western Front which cultivated their own vegetables locally when the opportunity arose. In Salonika, clearly, a major effort was made to provide hay for the army's horses which could not be provided on the local market, as well as vegetables for consumption by the units. The unit operated a considerable amount of mechanical equipment, including hay balers, ploughs, potato diggers and a variety of steam tractors, and was able to use Bulgarian and Turkish prisoners in purely manual tasks.

*   *   *

Due to the shortage of MT and its limited performance in bad weather, 'A' Provisional HT Company was formed on 15 January 1918 at Akbunar, with locations at Adjvasil and Langavuk, commanded by Captain A R G Hoffman. Its task, with two officers, 106 British Other Ranks, 144 Muleteers, 425 mules and 64 GS wagons, was to support 267 Railway Company RE in moving railway material, but this task did not last long and it disbanded on 10 April without even having the distinction of being allocated a company number.

The OC of 777 Company, Captain C B Waterlow, had good grounds for dissatisfaction, too. When he formed the company in August 1916 in Bulford, he was told that his vehicles and equipment were already overseas. On arrival in Salonika he was somewhat taken aback when he reported to his Director Supplies & Transport, Brigadier General A Long, who told him that his company had not been expected. In fact the unit's disembarkation from England should have been cancelled, but somehow this message clearly never got through; furthermore, with the severe shortage of vehicles and Ordnance stores in Salonika, there were none to issue to 777 Company's personnel. A cable was sent to England suggesting that the next MT Company's vehicles and equipment should be sent to Salonika without the personnel (a good try) but this was rejected and the now totally confused manpower was used to make up deficiencies in other units.

*   *   *

Towards the end of 1918 the concentrated effort of the Anglo-Greek and Franco-Serbian Armies in the areas east and west of Doiran led to the defeat of the Bulgarian Army and an Armistice was signed on 29 September. At the end of the campaign the ASC was supporting a ration strength of 385,000 men and 120,000 animals, with 19,959 ASC officers and men and 6,800 Cypriot and Greek Muleteers. The Corps suffered just under 700 dead.

This extract from a Despatch dated 1 December 1918 from General Sir George

F Milne KCB DSO, Commanding-in-Chief, British Salonika Force, was published in a Supplement to the *London Gazette* of 22 January 1919:

"The work of all branches of the Royal Army Service Corps deserves special praise. Their responsibilities include not only supplying the British Army requirements but those of the whole Greek Army and a very large proportion of the Supplies for the other Armies in Macedonia. That in spite of the difficulties by sea and by land, the Supply and Transport services of forces extending from the Black Sea to the Adriatic has never failed for one day is a great tribute to the work of all ranks serving both with the British and with the Serbian Army, and reflects great credit on the organising ability of Brigadier General A Long CB CMG DSO, Director of Supplies and Transport and his staff. Large areas of country have also been brought under cultivation in order to supply the troops from local resources, under the management of the Royal Army Service Corps."

*　　*　　*

When the campaign was over, allied forces occupied Constantinople, among them a combined 766 and 877 MT Company, commanded by Lieutenant Colonel J E Davies, carrying out duties as the Local MT Company. Their war diary contains the following interesting account: "The company occupied premises of the *Société Anonyme Ottomane de Gare de Constantinople* which had been taken over by the German MT attached to the Turkish Army during the war. The large workshop was well equipped and contained twenty semi-serviceable lorries with iron tyres driven by Turkish soldiers, who were only too keen in the circumstances to work for the British, since they were then fed and paid. Most of the compound, however, was occupied by decrepit vehicles of all kinds, including thirty old, quite unserviceable lorries and a number of scrap cars, car bodies, wheels, rims, chassis frames and a vast amount of miscellaneous rubbish, together with several hundred unpaid, unfed and unclothed Turkish soldiers with their equally undesirable personal effects.

"Concerning vehicles, Article 20 of the Armistice provided that the enemy should hand over the whole transport of that part of their army required to be demobilized and under this authority the Turkish War Office handed over with the garage the vehicles which had been previously mentioned and also twenty which were capable of being made serviceable and were put on the road and are running. These included serviceable Benz, Knight Mercedes, Grafa and Stifts and miscellaneous vehicles. It was further found that, as openly confessed by Captain Hecker, German Liaison Officer with the Turkish War Office, the Germans had sold to private Turkish individuals a number of government motor cars with a view to avoiding being requisitioned and many of these, having been traced, were taken from the individuals who were in unlawful possession of them and used for the needs of the British Army.

"While the work of repairing and equipping these for the road proved a serious tax on the garage resources, especially in the matter of tyres, they have been of the greatest value. Several of them proved to have been originally British vehicles. One, a Napier Ambulance captured on Gallipoli, and one almost historical car, a Rolls-Royce taken from General Townshend at Kut and seized by us at Mahmoud Pasha's House at Makrikeuy, were overhauled and fitted with a new body and are now placed at the service of the General Officer Commanding-in-Chief.

"The need for motor transport being great, a rather amusing rivalry arose between the Allies as to who should first obtain possession of cars which had been the late property of the Central Powers, while the difficulty of ascertaining legal ownership promises considerable entertainment for the authority which finally disposes of these claims.

"A typical difficult case is worth recording:

"A Wolseley car, the property of an Englishman who fled on the declaration of war, was left in the custody of the American Ambassador. He in turn was forced to flee and effected a forced sale for half the value of the car, such money being duly handed to the original owner. The history then becomes obscure but it is alleged that the car passed into the service of the Turkish Government, worked in the interior, was returned to Constantinople, sold as scrap to a Greek and Armenian who renovated the vehicle and sold it to a Turkish Pasha who did not pay the full price, this sale taking place sometime before the Armistice. The car is subsequently retrieved by us and put into commission at considerable expense. The question of ownership of this car remains undetermined. Many such instances could be enumerated showing that the work of this unit has not been altogether that of a normal MT Company."

CHAPTER 12

The Dardanelles (Gallipoli)

If the Balkans campaign was messy that of the Dardanelles was a disaster, an embarrassing operation that has been the source of controversy and acrimony ever since.

After the unsuccessful naval attack to force a passage through the Bosphorus in March 1915 the army sent the 29th Division, the last of the Regular Divisions, to gain the Gallipoli Peninsula, along with the Royal Naval Division, the Australian and New Zealand Army Corps (ANZAC) and an Indian brigade, a total of 60,000 men and 13,000 animals. The French were also to contribute 17,000.

The force assembled at Alexandria under the command of General Sir Ian Hamilton. The designated Advanced Base was on the Aegean islands of Lemnos and Imbros, sixty and fifteen miles respectively distant from the landing area. A Supply Depot and Horse Transport Depot were established at Mudros on the island of Lemnos and an Advanced Supply Depot and Horse Transport Depot on Imbros; a coldstore ship was also chartered and used as a floating cold store at Mudros and 10,000 tons of hay were obtained from India. Brigadier General F W G Koe, located at Mudros, was the Director of Supplies & Transport and he dealt personally with Cape Helles, while his staff at Imbros dealt with Suvla Bay, a strange division of duties. Brigadier General R Ford was Director of Supplies & Transport in Egypt.

Unfortunately the Intelligence Branch of the War Office was unable to advise on roads and Lord Kitchener, who had proved his lack of knowledge on transport matters in the Boer War, directed that no transport of any sort was to be taken. He was persuaded to change his mind by Major General Long, Director of Supplies & Transport in the War Office. A Field Bakery, Field Butchery, Reserve Parks, Ammunition Parks and Supply Column were also considered essential by Major General Long, but he was overruled. Instead of standard 3 ton lorries, the 29th Divisional Train was re-equipped with 30 cwt vehicles, and this in spite of Lord Kitchener being informed by General Hamilton that pack transport was necessary. In the event these vehicles were moved as far as Mudros, but were then returned to be used in the Alexandria base, and only 29th Divisional Train Supply personnel, under the command of Lieutenant Colonel Longfellow-Cooper, were used in Gallipoli.

Landings took place over the period 25 April-1 May at a considerable cost, in the face of determined Turkish opposition, at Cape Helles by the British, French and Indians, and at Anzac Cove by the Australians and New Zealanders. In the south the allies fought their way two miles inland, in the north some 1,500 yards. All areas were under constant observed shelling and rifle fire from the Turks.

Under these circumstances normal transport and supply arrangements could not operate and, after initial difficulties in getting the animals ashore, animal transport was used as far as possible, although several Holt caterpillar tractors were later used at Cape Helles, and twenty 30 cwt lorries and a few Ford cars and ambulances were used at Suvla Bay.

Field Supply Depots were established at Helles, Anzac Cove and later at Suvla, with, in the event, a Field Bakery at Helles. Because of the limited size of the bridgehead these were located on the narrow beaches and duties were carried out under enemy observation and shellfire. Extremes of climate were a problem: the weather varied from torrid heat to icy cold weather, with a blizzard raging for days on one occasion which caused a number of deaths from exposure.

To add to these problems, all surplus animals had been left in Egypt and officers' kits and men's blankets were left behind; but at least troops were provided with 200 rounds of ammunition and three days' food, and each sea transport put ashore a reserve of 300 rounds and seven days' food. Although in the event a supply of wells was discovered ashore, water was supplied by means of a chartered water tank steamer, and a variety of skins, tanks, oil tins and other receptacles were used for the purpose of storing water on the beaches or sending it forward. Carriage forward was by pack transport or fatigue parties of men who were already exhausted from their duties in the trenches.

* * *

Captain C A Cooke was a company commander in the Train of the 29th Division. Entries in his diaries held in the Imperial War Museum show what life was like in Gallipoli, particularly when sending supplies forward.

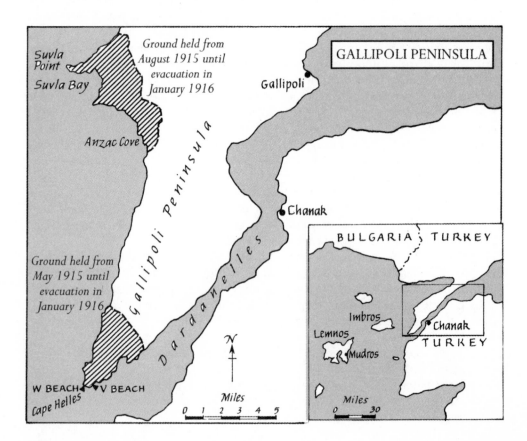

"3 & 4 May 1915. Started off with supplies on pack mules at 7 pm. At present it is impossible to ride as the country which I have to go through is like the landslip at Seaton for the first three miles and then we go up a ravine for about 1½ miles walking all the way in a shallow stream which was the only way up. Then we unloaded and started to return. At one point we had to lie down for quite 15 minutes as three snipers hidden in holes on the hillside opened fire on us, however, they fired about thirty shots and hit no one, the bullets going over our heads . . . Well, to resume, we worked until . . . and then resumed our return journey under cover of the mules, getting in 12.15 am just before the moon rose, which was very lucky. The mules have packs, as waggons at present are impossible, but shortly we hope to have better arrangements . . . We have no tents, of course, but have spread our waterproof sheets over a stick.

"16 May 1915. Tonight have rather a long convoy job as our lot have gone back to the trenches again. High explosive shells have a most remarkable way of varying. I have seen them drop into a bunch of mules, where one would think you couldn't drop a stone without hitting something, explode and do no damage. Another time they will drop in an open space and kill people standing a hundred yards apart.

"27 May 1915. The scene as I write this is most interesting. The camp [is] bounded on three sides by the sea and running about 2 miles long and about ¼ mile broad, dotted with dugouts, horse lines, mule lines, vehicles, sea supplies, naval parties, road makers, Engineers, Veterinary Hospitals, Red Cross, Ordnance Depots, great stores of hay, biscuits, bully beef etc. Waggons moving about all over the place. The aeroplanes rising from close to you, in fact one hardly looks up at them now. The harbour with the ships and transports, men and war. White men, Black men, Brown men. Every nationality in the British Empire. Men marching to the beaches, others marching from them. Despatch riders on motor cycles etc. All part of the great machine and beyond us the French camp (more picturesque but not so workmanlike).

"5 June 1915. Only a small convoy as the battalions in our brigade (87th) are all over the place and impossible to reach with one convoy. There is a lot to interest one in convoy work. Starting as soon as possible after dusk and keeping away from the skyline as much as possible you ride on with a man from the battalion as guide. When you are near the firing line you have to make up your mind where you will dump. You must go as far as you can for the sake of the battalion (who have to come down and manhandle the supplies from where you dump them to the trenches) and you also have to think of the safety of your own men and animals. If it is fairly quiet you go as far as you can and then try for a sheltered spot to unload in. Unloading must be done very quickly. A case of biscuits or bully beef falling on the ground is quite enough to start the whole line firing. Having unloaded (no lights of course) you turn back to camp. Every now and then one is bound to come up on the skyline and it always seems as though the enemy put up their star lights (which light up a very big radius) for the purpose of spotting you. You also feel about 20 ft tall and all the waggons enormous. However it is mostly fancy and after perhaps losing your way once or twice you return to camp, glad to turn in and dream of:

A night in a decent bed with sheets and pillows

A hot bath, 30 minutes at least

A d-d good dinner

A speedy return to England and my family

"7 June 1915. Apart from the fighting there is always a tremendous amount of interesting work going on. Ships coming in, unloading, and their supplies going to various depots. Ammunition carts and limbers constantly going up to the guns and trenches. Signal companies running telephones to the various points. Engineers making roads and sinking wells. The Post Office trying to cope with mails inward and outward which amount to many hundreds of bags every day. Fresh troops being landed or sick and wounded being sent off to the Hospital ships. The Field Ambulances (which have done wonderful work), the Army Veterinary Corps ditto; the Ordnance Depot, where you can get any equipment from a boot to a splinter bar for a waggon. The Signal station whence official messages are sent to all parts of the field, fleet or home. Numberless fatigues doing 1001 odd jobs which one doesn't think of in connection with an Army. Hundreds of waggons with sweating drivers urging on the stubborn but hard working mule. The Field Bakery turning out about 30,000 lbs bread daily, and many other things. Picture this going on day and night, and you get some idea of what war is like, and add the fact that all this has had to be carried on under more or less continuous shellfire ever since the troops landed. It really is a triumph of organization and energy."

*   *   *

At the end of May the transport situation eased when a remarkable organization known as the Zion Mule Corps disembarked, the first transport unit to come ashore. This unit of 750 pack mules, formed in Egypt from Russian Jews who had fled from Palestine, was commanded by Lieutenant Colonel J H Patterson, an ASC Reserve officer; he was supported by Lieutenants Carver and McLean, an Egyptian officer, and eight Jewish officers selected from among the 500 refugees. One of the 300 men, Private Groushkonsky, distinguished himself when his ammunition convoy was shelled and he was awarded the Distinguished Conduct Medal. Unfortunately most of the men were not up to the work required so were sent to the ships *Surada* and *Goslar,* where they looked after the horses remaining on board, while the New Zealand ASC took over the mules and donkeys. An Indian mule cart Train of some 700 carts and 1,500 animals from France was also employed in the wheeled or pack role supporting formations at Cape Helles and Anzac Bay.

In May the 42nd East Lancashire Division and a French Division arrived as reinforcements, followed by the 52nd (Lowland) Division in June. An extract from *Citizen Soldiers* illustrates well the involvement of the 52nd Division ASC:

"The Lancashire Fusilier Brigade with the 2nd ASC Company (re-numbered 429 Company) landed over "W," and "V" beaches at Gallipoli and were attached to the 29th Division. Wagons and mules were slung over the side and brought to the beach in lighters. The mules were all new, having been drawn from the Reserve Park at Alexandria only a few hours before embarkation, and none of the drivers knew them. The task of bringing them ashore and over the beaches must have been formidable. Due to congestion on the beaches the 1st (428), 3rd (430) and 4th (431) ASC Companies were ordered back to Egypt, leaving the 2nd (429) Company to cope with the work on the beaches and to run a Divisional Supply dump on the cliff-top above "W" Beach.

"Everything needed for the Gallipoli force had to be brought from the base at Mudros on the island of Lemnos. Mules, rations, ammunition and even water were brought ashore from lighters, usually under Turkish fire, and the ASC men acted as stevedores, shore labour, Port detachment, mule handlers, porters, issuers; in fact, everything connected with the maintenance of the Force, they did. Rations, more often than not, had to be taken up at night, when the Turk was at his best after his afternoon siesta, and casualties were high among the men of the ASC. The mules were vastly more difficult to handle than the pack horses. The horse did not mind his pack being unbalanced, but the mule utterly refused to carry a pack unless the balance was perfect, and when the pack consisted of tins of bully beef, tins of biscuits, jars of rum, sacks of loaves and sugar, whole cheeses, sides of bacon, tins of jam, bags of letters and parcels, the men had to learn the knacks of packaging pretty quickly.

"A somewhat left-handed compliment was paid to the 2nd Brigade Company in Gallipoli, to the effect that the Company was so efficient that, despite the fact that they lost 41 animals killed, when they left they had one more than the original number landed."

Further developments arrived in July and August, bringing the strength of the force up to twelve Divisions, all of which enabled a three-pronged attack to be made on the Turkish positions in August. Sadly, for a variety of reasons, these attacks were unsuccessful, although some ground was gained.

*   *   *

Lieutenant Frank Howitt (later promoted to Brigadier after his transfer to the RAMC as a doctor) worked with supplies at Suvla Bay. He had left school when war broke out and had just gone up to Trinity College to study medicine. Along with many other young men he volunteered for service and was commissioned into the ASC, for which he had no particular qualifications. As he knew nothing about fodder or horses his father bought him an old Lagonda car and engaged an equally old farmer to go with him and educate him in the selection of fodder. When the pair visited farms to buy for the army, the old farmer used to look at the hay or straw being offered at too high a price and say to his young master, "We couldn't buy at that price, could we, sir? It's full of giant fescues." "Oh, no, not possibly," said the young officer, in due course being complimented by his superiors on his skill and perspicacity in buying fodder at lower prices than anyone else. His papers in the Imperial War Museum contain much of great interest and illustrate well what life was like in the ASC in close support of the Infantry in Gallipoli.

When he was on the island of Imbros in July he comments amusingly on the constant battle with flies: "The pestilential flies seem to be the cause of it [illness], and every piece of bread, every scrap of meal, every tin of jam is literally and absolutely plastered with them. For the benefit of those who have not had the opportunity of playing it, I will set down briefly the rules of the game.

Each player takes his slab of bread and jam tin and spreads his jam in the ordinary way. Both jam and bread are now invisible for flies. Now take a deep breath (being careful not to do this with the mouth) and blow with all possible energy upon both jam and bread, at the same time deftly transferring the whole to the mouth. The winner is he who swallows the least flies."

On 1 October he recorded: "Now we come to the water question, the nightmare of our lives, and even now a cold shudder runs down my spine as I think of it. The provision made for us for carrying up the water to the trenches was the masterpiece, the very 'crème de la crème' of the gross and numberless blunders committed by the General Staff at Suvla. The water used to come to us in boats, designed for the purpose, the most famous of which was the *Blossom* . . . It was then pumped ashore into tanks capable of holding one day's supply, and as the water depot was the subject of particular attention on the part of the enemy, we were seldom able even to draw our gallon per man.

"The trenches . . . were some three miles away, the roads exceedingly bumpy with great cavities and rocks on the surface, the transport the lightest possible. The receptacles given us to take up this water were chiefly 4 gallon oil tins with holes in the top, also a motley collection of old cans such as disused petrol tins, camel tanks and what not! And so, night after night, and week after week, if we were lucky enough to get over the initial difficulty of supply from the sea, over a thousand of these had to be filled, the holes and leakages stopped up as best we could. They then had to be loaded (each Brigade required about sixty or seventy carts) and then, as there were insufficient mules, we used to have to take it in turn to do a double journey! During the march, a mule would very often shy at a bullet or a can falling off the cart ahead, and cart, driver and all go hurtling down the side of the cliff; and the sequel to this and to the leaking state of the battered cans was one continuous complaint from the units that they did not get their full return of water. It was heartbreaking.

"Nor let it be thought that with water finished and distributed our work was done. All the rations had to be carried up in bulk, off-loaded in the dark (because the glimmer of a light or candle would have brought retribution on our heads) and then given over to the clamouring representatives of the various regiments. The different commodities were piled up together on the ground, so that when the last cart had gone, we were ready to give them out, each Supply man having his particular vocation in life.

"In the dusk over there is Corporal Ince, his axe glistening in the moonlight as he swirls it round and round to descend upon the carcase of frozen ox. With the lifelong experience of a Wigan butchery he delivers the exact amount to each zealous quartermaster as he comes along, although all his calculations must be by guesswork, the scales being useless to him.

"Beyond him is England with the bully and biscuits, which are simple, as the boxes all contain the same number. Here is Griffiths with his great casks of tea, dealing it out with his scoop, which is safe or moderately so in the darkness. Hutchings has the charitable job; he gives out the changeable luxuries such as rum, lime-juice, cigarettes and tobacco. Hutchings is a teetotaller and non-smoker, and impervious to the overtures of quartermasters of the most persuasive character, which is a worthier trait than either. There are numerous other articles of food and comfort, and over the whole, Sergeant Claret, in the guise of general overseer, keeps his kindly eye. His is the duty of calculating the total for each unit, thus: 6th Border Regt, strength 978. Ration of tea 5/8 of an ounce per man per day. Total amount . . . (ask Claret). But I have seen even this great mathematician in difficulties in issuing the exact amount of rum to, say, the 68th Field Company Engineers numbering 138, when the rum ration is 1/30 gallon per man, and the receptacles containing it are 2 gallon sealed jars!

"Everything had to be finished and the rations carried away by daylight, for the Turks had our range completely, and they had a sniper with a machine-gun trained on the dump and path to it, so that the place was quite impossible by day."

*　　*　　*

The Corps operated a Motor Boat Company in the Middle East theatre in 1915. It was at Helles during the operations. Of the thirty-three boats listed at the beginning of 1916, five were in Egypt, nine were on their way back from Mudros to Egypt, ten were at Mudros, four of which were earmarked for Salonika, three were in Salonika and six had been lost. When Gallipoli was evacuated the company moved from Lemnos to Ismailia. Consisting of 140 all ranks, the unit was used for port, escort and patrol work as well as providing detachments on the Dead Sea and at Haifa and Tripoli.

A number of troopers and hospital ships were used in the campaign, the latter to handle the flood of casualties, 250,000 alone from the British, ANZAC and Indian contingents. Enteric fever and dysentery were major contributors to the high casualty rate. One incident involving the ASC should be recorded: HM Transport *Royal Edward* was torpedoed by a German submarine on 13 August in the Gulf of Kos. Among the 1,400 troops on board were 300 men of the ASC, the majority of whom were elderly and not fit for service in the Infantry. Most perished, but reports of survivors place the calmness and magnificent discipline of those who died on a level equal to the heroic story of the loss of the *Birkenhead* in 1852.

The split staff mentioned earlier and lack of logistic influence by ASC commanders on the operational situation led Brigadier General Koe, somewhat later, to write personally to the Director Supplies & Transport in London. Subsequently Major General Long sent his letter to the Quartermaster General remonstrating on the hazardous state of affairs:

"QMG

"In the interests of the State I feel reluctantly compelled to make use of an unofficial letter in calling attention to the gravity of the position at the Dardanelles. The letter [not published] practically explains itself. It amounts to this: that the Commander-in-Chief there has decided to depart from all the experience that has been gained in every campaign and relegated to the Line of Communication one of the most important officers on the technical staff of his QMG, viz: the Director of Transport.

"If Sir Ian Hamilton is dissatisfied with General Koe he should say so and we will take steps to send another officer to replace him, but if he is merely carrying out some of his theories on administration, of which, with all respect, he has no expert knowledge, then I wish to say that from the information in our possession it is quite clear that this is not the time for theorising.

"If the Commander-in-Chief and his QMG cannot understand the necessity of the Director of Transport's presence at GHQ then they are gravely imperilling the safety of the Force, and, therefore, I must plainly and unequivocally draw your attention to this danger which if not checked the responsibility for failure must inevitably rest upon your shoulders as well as on those of Sir Ian Hamilton.

"I would therefore suggest that you bring the matter in front of the Council with a view to peremptory instructions being given to the Commander-in-Chief Med Force as to how the Administrative Service must be conducted.

QMG5
11 October 1915   Director of Supplies & Transport"

Some of Brigadier Koe's other concerns can be seen in the following letter, one of a series of regular reports to his Head of Service:

Mudros
21 October 1915

"My dear Long

I think you will see from my semi-official that I have done everything a man could do to make the troops take fresh meat and bread. I could not say it except between ourselves, but the fact is that if you have a Commander-in-Chief who ignores the administrative side entirely, GOCs of Corps, Divisions etc take their cue from him, and when this is the case the staffs do not worry. I could never get any backing in my attempts to impress on people the necessity of taking fresh meat. The extraordinary thing is that I have never heard a word of complaint about the food except from the Commission who came out. I cannot help thinking that they took for gospel anything that every irresponsible grouser said, but they never made any proper investigations. On the other hand dozens of officers coming from the Peninsula have said to me how very well they have been fed and that the rations did not require supplementing in any way. I am certain that once the canteen gets going all this talk will subside, but the canteen will sell large quantities of tinned food which the troops will eat and thrive on in spite of the medical contention that they have had too much preserved stuff.

"About Salonika. You will have had my notes on this. Forage is the only trouble, but I can give them a good start with a couple of months, but I should like to know definitely, as soon as possible, for how long I am to be responsible for feeding them. In the meantime I will keep them up to a reserve of not less than 42 days, so do not worry about them.

"Very curious this. When I was there I asked how the troops enjoyed being camped at Salonika instead of Suvla, and was told that they liked it very much, especially the change of rations. Now they were getting exactly the same rations as at Suvla except that they were getting locally killed beef and mutton of a quality vastly inferior to the frozen meat. These things are hard to account for.

178

"I'm very sorry for having these sort of worries which are caused not by any fault of yours or mine or the ASC but simply by want of proper care on the part of staffs and regimental officers. However, I suppose we are here to be shot at and must grin and bear it.

Yours ever
(Signed) Fred Koe"

On 16 October General Sir Charles Monro succeeded General Sir Ian Hamilton, and he immediately recommended evacuation, a view confirmed by Lord Kitchener when he visited Mudros. Suvla and ANZAC were evacuated in December, and only such guns, animals and stores which were needed until the last were abandoned. Helles was evacuated in early January 1916 but in this case a considerable amount of supplies and material had to be left behind.

The Expeditionary Force Canteen suffered too in the evacuation: their stores had arrived at Helles just before the order to evacuate was given. The poor canteen manager had the operational situation explained to him, but he was unable to remove stores as the canteen was under heavy shell fire at the time, indeed some of the canteen employees had already been wounded. It was heart-breaking for everyone concerned that much wine and liquor had to be destroyed, under the supervision of the canteen manager and an officer; but at least the manager did his best under the circumstances by distributing 'dry' goods to anyone who came along, far preferable to letting them fall into the hands of the Turks. The value of the stores written off was £1,609-3-1. All was not totally lost, however, as 1,800 gallons of rum and 2,000 cases of champagne, wine and spirits were taken to 'W' Beach and shipped by the Royal Navy on the evening of 30 December. The Turks could celebrate our departure, but not with our wine cellar.

Both evacuations were carried out in great secrecy at night and were described by a German writer as a "hitherto quite unattainable masterpiece". 118,000 men, 5,000 animals and 300 guns were withdrawn and redistributed to Egypt, France and Salonika, but 508 mules were shot and 1,590 vehicles were abandoned. Thus ended the intended spear thrust into the heart of the Turkish empire, a tragic, ill-judged and badly planned and executed campaign, the only opposed amphibious operation of the war, one, however, in which thirty Victoria Crosses were awarded.

CHAPTER 13

East Africa

The Colony of German East Africa lay between the British Colony of Kenya in the north and Northern Rhodesia and Nyasaland over 600 miles to the south. Reaching to the Indian Ocean to the east of Nyasaland lay Portuguese Mozambique allied to Britain. In 1914 the Germans invaded Kenya. Widely dispersed and confused fighting continued until 1916 in which mainly Indian and South African troops were used against the invaders, but as time went on British troops were increasingly employed and the Germans were eventually driven back into their own Colony. They consisted of a force of some 5,000 strong, of which only the Command and Supervisory element were German. The enemy native troops, Askaris, and porters, lived off the country they knew well, moving on foot, carrying portable boats for river crossing but otherwise unhindered by pack or mechanical transport. Using the difficult climate and terrain to their advantage the German forces ranged far and wide over a vast territory, evading capture or destruction until an Armistice was signed in late November 1918 at Abercorn in Northern Rhodesia.

The British field force in 1916, when the ASC was first employed, consisted of the 1st and 2nd East African Divisions. After service in France Brigadier General P O Hazleton took on the post of Director of Supplies & Transport in January, working hard to regularize the situation. Transport support until then had been provided by a volunteer East African MT Corps raised in Nairobi and the South African ASC. From now on animals provided the main means of transport, but the wastage of horses, mules, oxen and donkeys was extremely high, largely due to the ravages of the tsetse fly, some 28,000 dying in one operation alone. The ASC and mechanical transport were imported. 30 cwt lorries with solid tyres for the Divisional Supply and Ammunition Columns arrived in June, but they proved unsuitable, in that in dry weather they quickly ground the surface into dust, and in the rains they sank axle deep. The main movement was along the line of the railway wherever possible, which eased the ASC task, ameliorated in turn by the arrival of ox transport formations from South Africa, some of whose animals were converted into supplies as difficulties in maintaining the army at the end of a long line of communication developed.

During August 1916 MT reinforcements began to arrive from England and South Africa, 300 Ford vans forming the majority of the vehicles. The 3 tonners were relegated to the bases and Line of Communication. Spare parts remained a critical problem throughout the campaign, which placed great demands on the imagination and adaptability of the fitters. European drivers, however, quickly contracted malaria and operations had to be postponed owing to sickness and casualties in the Supply and Ammunition Columns. Some 1,000 Swahili, Ugandan, Indian and Nigerian drivers were engaged to make up the deficiencies, a driving school being set up for them in East Africa, while Chinese were recruited as artificers.

In April 1916 a Base MT Depot of 201 all ranks arrived in Mombasa and set up initially in Nairobi, moving in September to Dar-es-Salaam; Advanced MT Depots were opened at Mbuyuni, Mombo and Handeni as the advance progressed that summer. During 1916 and 1917 some 3,000 vehicles were bought in South Africa and two Motor Ambulance Convoys, a light armoured motor battery and two MT companies used as special long-distance supply columns were also added. A certain element of frustration and poor organiz-ation can perhaps be seen, if only based on two comments in May and June 1916 in 570 Company's war diaries: "Am unable to trace more than half of the Company's lorries" and "Practically all the vehicles and personnel attached to different units, making it impossible to keep any record of their doings".

Motor boats manned by the ASC were also used in East Africa, commanded by Lieutenant Chatfield, rendering considerable assistance in the campaign against the Germans. These boats were fitted up by the workshops of several MT companies, using variously Daimler, Ford and Studebaker engines. Several paddle boats were also made as shallow-draft punts, fitted with Ford engines, for operating in the swamps of the Ruaha in February 1917. Unfortunately they were not a success as the speed of the current was too strong for the under-powered boats.

Another ASC involvement with boats in East Africa concerned the British naval expedition in 1915 to Lake Tanganyika, when the German gunboat *Kingani* was forced to surrender and the *Hedwig von Wissman* was sunk. The expedition, consisting of twenty-seven officers and men under the command of Commander Geoffrey Spicer-Simson RN, sailed from Tilbury on 12 June 1915, taking with them two Thornycroft 40 ft, 56 bhp motorboats, *Mimi* and *Toutou*. Each had a 6 pounder gun in the bow and a 3 pounder gun in the stern.

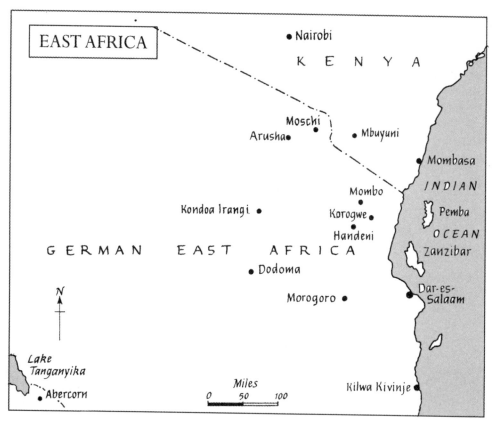

After landing in Cape Town, a wide variety of transport was used, with an ASC detachment being responsible for the land transport of the boats, initially 2,488 miles by train via Kimberley, Mafeking, Bulawayo, Victoria Falls and Elizabethville to Kamborie. An ASC lorry was used to carry provisions and camp equipment, with native porters and ox wagons carrying ammunition and other stores, while two ASC Lion class traction engines pulled trailers carrying the gunboats. The supply of water and good routes were essential, not only for drinking purposes but also for the traction engines. Delays of several days were regrettably caused by the traction engines sinking into unmetalled roads and by the inadequacy of bridges, not to mention the buckling of the trailers; on one occasion, when it became impossible for the traction engines to reach water because of the density of the bush, 150 native women were rounded up from local villages to carry water in pots and gourds from a water hole a distance of 8 miles to the engines. Early in September a 6,000 ft plateau was reached and some forty-two oxen were needed to supplement the pulling power of the traction engines. Having surmounted the difficulties of ascent and descent, the expedition trekked a further 146 miles to Sankosia, after which rail, river and steamer were used to cover the remaining distance to Lake Tanganyika, which was reached in late October. This was the smallest expeditionary force which was sent against the enemy during the war; no previous expedition travelled so far and no expedition had taken its boats overland intact or used so many methods of transport on the approach march. It was a masterpiece of daring, initiative, perseverance and transport skills, and extraordinary success created out of chaos.

The war in this theatre is notable for the largely unknown employment of a unit of four heavy armoured cars of 322 Company ASC, named 1 (Willoughby's) Armoured Motor Battery, raised and trained in February 1915 in England by Sir John Willoughby. The armoured cars (actually converted Leyland lorries) were wholly manned by the ASC, a remarkable enterprise at a time when armoured vehicles were in their infancy. They arrived in East Africa in 1917 but were disbanded in July that year.

At the time of the Armistice the strength of the army was 111,731. At its strongest the ASC numbered just over 4,000 all ranks, of whom 270 died.

CHAPTER 14

Russia

The revolution in Russia caused her to withdraw from the war and make a separate peace with Germany. In June 1918 the British committed a Brigade strength force in North Russia, part of which was landed at Murmansk to prevent the Germans using the Kola Inlet as a submarine base, the other part in Archangel to assist the anti-Bolshevik forces, thereby ensuring that the Germans could not withdraw entirely from the Russian front. The British were involved in a few minor skirmishes, but in the event achieved nothing and withdrew in September 1919.

* * *

The ASC was commanded by Lieutenant Colonel T C R Moore as Assistant Director Supplies & Transport in Murmansk. Major H N G Watson was located in Archangel. It is of interest that Major W J English, who had won his VC in the Boer War on 3 July 1901 with the Scottish Horse and was commissioned into the ASC in October 1906, served with the force in North Russia.

With units located up to 400 miles from base, poor communications and extremes of climate, resupply was not easy. Transport was mixed. Initially horse transport units were used with limbered GS wagons but these proved unsuitable and the ASC turned its hand to manufacturing a local type of cart, which was successful; a shortage of saddlery and harness also involved local manufacture under ASC control. As no Veterinary Service personnel were in the force the ASC also became responsible for this as well as for Remount duties. In summer pony carts and pack transport were used to supplement the ASC ration boats and barges on the rivers, but in winter sleighs were drawn by ponies, Canadian huskies and reindeer, often using frozen rivers as 'roads'. Mechanical transport was tried, but was not successful due to the bad weather and absence of proper roads. Ford cars, ambulances and vans were used in Archangel, as well as 3 ton and 30 cwt lorries, a section being attached to 1152 Company in 1919.

In 1919 a Reindeer Transport Corps was formed under Captain E M Squarey, with Laplanders as drivers, each sleigh carrying 600-800 lbs, three reindeer pulling, with one at the back to act as a brake. Some 2,000 reindeer, 500 sleighs and 1,000 Laplanders were employed in this example of local innovation. Sleighs were demanded from England, but, pending their arrival, a small sleigh factory was established locally, which was so successful that it provided sufficient sleighs within several months.

An officer with the Murmansk Force wrote home:

Kandalasha, 20 January 1919

"This place is not so bad as one or two other places in the line. I believe it has been more than 30 degrees below zero during the past day or two, but I lose

interest in the thermometer when it gets below -15. However, it is fairly decent weather, calm and sometimes even sunny about midday.

"I live with a collection of other lost souls in a place colloquially known as the 'slum'. It is a sort of shed in which Serbs have died of typhus and Russians have lived in squalor, and is now inhabited by mice and bugs. Water freezes 3 ft from a red-hot stove. My bed is 18 inches from the stove which keeps me just comfortable when it is glowing; I hang my sheepskin coat on the head of the bed, and then button it so that it makes a cone over my head and saves my nose from frost-bite.

"This expedition has added another word to the Tommy's vocabulary, 'skolko', which means 'how much?' It is used to express the art of barter with a native; thus you 'skolko' furs for tobacco, etc. The Russians are now opening their mouths so wide that they are themselves putting an end to the trade. A common red fox skin costs at least 4 lb of tobacco and three bottles of whisky. When the first troops came out cigarettes sold at a rouble apiece, and ½ lb of tobacco would acquire a fox skin.

"We go about here in any old clothes, and no-one looks like a soldier. Our meals are dreams, fresh or salted salmon, ptarmigan, capercailzie, or black game, reindeer venison (we have discovered that reindeer heart is quite one of the best dishes imaginable). Of course, the vegetable courses are rather meagre, the only fresh vegetables we get being watery potatoes, locally grown, which are not improved by being frozen.

"There is no 'spit and polish' here, no parades, no reveilles, no lights-out, no padres, no CB, and no pubs. We have breakfast at 10.00 am; at 10.30 I drive off to my office with Archibald (my reindeer), lunch at HQ (a mixed mess of officers, NCOs, Swedes and Finns), then walk back to the 'slum' at 6.00 pm and to bed about 9.30. Last night we had in the local orchestra, who are our sworn friends, and had a typical 'evening'. They came at 9.00 pm and stayed till 2.00 am. After they had played some pieces, two young RAMC doctors came in and we started dancing Mazurkas, Vengerkas, and Gopacks, or imitations thereof, all in a space 9 ft square. Then to vary the proceedings we tried clog dancing on skis.

"This locality has a partiality for fires, not to be wondered at when the mercury has dropped out of sight. We have had two fire blazes within a week. Of course, when a log and shingle house gets going nothing can stop it. The efforts of the brigade with a hand pump fed by water brought to the spot in 20 gallon barrels on a sledge are priceless.

"I have got two reindeer which constitute our ASC transport, and are very kind creatures. They are quite easy to drive; you lead them to the road, turn their heads in the right direction, smack them on the rump and take a flying leap into the sledge. When you come to cross-roads you jerk the one rein, and if they do not grasp your wishes they stop and you have to get out, turn them into the right track, and start again. They pull by a single trace which passes between their legs; there are no shafts, and of course the sledge swings very erratically behind.

"One of the sights is my daily 'market'. My office is in a big log building by the railway where we 'skolko' flour, sugar, etc for fresh meat, fish and game, which the natives bring in from 100 miles around on sledges. Sometimes a convoy of twenty or more sledges turn up. Some of the natives speak Finnish, some Lapp, and most have a smattering of Russian. They wear fine furs and beaded hats. The goods are weighed in, and the men get chits numbered 1, 2, 3, and so on. Then they come into the office and sit on a bench. I call out 'No 1'. He comes forward and I say, "You have brought 200 lb of reindeer meat and 150 fish, you are entitled to so much flour. Will you have it all in flour, or half in flour and the rest in other commodities?" and I explain that 5 lb flour = 1 lb sugar, and 8 lb flour = 1 lb tea or coffee and so forth. Then he scratches his head, and tries to work out how much of each thing he can have. Finally, after much thinking and questioning, he makes up his mind, and I give him a chit on the storekeeper, and so on with the next. They bring frozen milk sometimes and butter, and once I had a quarter of elk; I am still waiting for bear meat.

"Besides our own people, I feed the French and local Russian troops as well as a few Russian civilians."

Another ASC officer wrote home in 1919, his letter being published in the *Corps Journal* of the day:

"When we arrived at Archangel with the rest of the Brigade we were given a tremendous reception by the civilians and the poor devils who had done the winter out here. The town was decorated, bands played continuously, and everyone seemed very glad we had at last arrived. Colonel Crawley, DDST, was very good to us, and we settled down with 1122 Company, commanded by one Major Williams, who had a business in Moscow before the war. The Supply Depot and MT people all messed together and we had a very jolly mess – about thirty of us altogether.

"Do you know Archangel at all? It is a large town, lots of wharves and quays, about six really fine wooden buildings, tramways, and about the worst roads I have ever seen in my life; there are practically no metal roads, all mud. Local transport is rather humorous but the only possible contrivance to carry anything for a long distance. It is a pair of wheels, and stuck on the top are two logs of wood with cross-bars to hold them together, sometimes a plank is put between them to prevent the cargo falling through the middle.

"After ten days at Archangel I went with Major H N G Watson DAD of S & T, Forward Area, up river by motor-boat, Sears taking the Company up by road – and a hellish time he must have had going through the forests. Insects are appalling, enormous horse flies and mosquitoes being the chief irritators. The forests are enormously dense and long, and start about 300 yards from the river on each side and there appears to be no limit to their length; granted there are a few clearings now and again, and in these clearings one finds villages. The forests have just one track through them and frequently on each side of the track is swampy ground which is very dangerous. Horse Transport is exceedingly difficult; in most parts and as far as possible everything has been done by river but now with the river so low, as we have had so little rain and so much heat, it is a question as to whether river transport will be much good soon as tugs and food barges are constantly running aground. Until recently I have been away from the Company and have done all my work with the Russian Troops and local transport, the majority of drivers being girls and women who do most of the work out here. They are really splendid and exceptionally brave, taking stores, etc right up to the outpost line without the slightest fear or hesitation. The scheme of supplies during winter was shore depots, being supplied from the Base by sleighs and Units drawing with local transport from those Depots. In the middle of June, Supply Depot barges came up the river and were to all purposes taking the place of the Divisional Supply Column in France. The officer on board representing SCSO. I sent him a 3316 and he produced the goods which were sent ashore on a small light barge and this stuff was dished out to the Units. The theory of course is excellent but practically it is a very difficult method as we had to feed about 8,000 troops, 6,000 on one bank and 2,000 on the other bank of the river and with so many difficulties which arose between the Russians and ourselves and the river transport things did not work out as easily as anticipated. Now however, the thing goes fairly easily as on receiving indents I get the figures made out, write a chit to barge depot and the Unit draws direct from the barge as we got a pier built out to it and a couple of planks form a slide for goods to be shoved down from the deck to the pier where it is then manhandled on to the droskies on the beach ready to cart off to the Units' QM Stores. But of course, having just got the thing working fairly well the Brigade gets shifted from the river front downstream to the Pineya Front.

"I think that there is very little more of interest which I can say, as the Censor regulations are assuming greater proportions than before. Everybody out here is in a great hurry to get back, but I suppose we shall remain here for another year or more. The novelty has certainly worn itself to shreds, and the houses, which are built on the Canadian system, are very hot in this weather.

"The villages consist of rows of log houses on either side of the sleigh track, and for every commune of about six villages is a wonderful-looking church rather like the Greek Moslems. The six villages generally are about a quarter of a mile away from each other and the church is invariably at one end of the commune and never in the middle."

Other citations appear in Annex S.

In addition to units listed in Annex R, the following ASC units were employed:

> 1122 Company
> 1153 Company ⎫ with mules
> 1160 Auxiliary HT Company ⎭
> Base Supply Depot (in Bakharitza, Murmansk)
> Advanced Base Supply Depot (in Archangel, Kem)
> An HT/MT School of Instruction (to train Russians)
> An Agricultural Company
> Remount Depot.

Before leaving Russia, mention must be made of a Military Mission under Major General H C Holman CB CMG DSO, which assisted the anti-Bolshevik forces in South Russia in 1918-1919, based mainly at Odessa. A number of ASC officers, clerks and car drivers were attached to this Mission, including Brevet Lieutenant Colonel H G Reid CMG DSO as AA & QMG, Major G W C Hickie as the DADST, Major G Simpson OBE as the Camp Commandant, Major J Ward as the Supply Company Commander and Captain G Girdlestone-Edwards as the MT Company Commander; Lieutenant Colonel A W Chichester was the Crimea Base Commandant. Their work was mainly advisory or connected with the distribution of supplies and war material, including 25 workshop lorries, 374 lorries, 174 ambulances, 55 cars, 215 motor cycles and 378 cycles, made over by the allies to General Denikin, the South Russian leader. These people, albeit under different circumstances, had as difficult and adventurous a time as their compatriots in the north: Private H Nixon and Private C E Morgan died of typhus in January 1920 and Corporal G O'Neill was shot by the Green Guards in September 1919 while road testing a motor car.

The campaign in Russia is poorly documented and only limited material exists on the work of the ASC. This tantalizing fragment was published, sadly in an unknown newspaper on an unknown date:

"Military Honours. An interesting function took place at Berwick-on-Tweed on Tuesday 29 June, when Mr James Douglas, chauffeur to Capt Paton Harwood, was invested with the DCM and Meritorious Medal for conspicuous gallantry in action in April 1918 in the Tartar country south of Erivan, when, with a Ford car, he proceeded to the rescue of the Allied Consuls who had been held-up on the top of Kasbek Mountain. He came under heavy fire on the Georgian Road, and the guide accompanying him was killed. The medals were pinned on by the CO in front of a full parade of the KOSB. In connection with the same act of gallantry, Pte Douglas was presented by the Czar of Russia with the Russian Medal for Gallantry."

Epilogue

The end of the Great War saw the strength of the ASC world-wide rise to 10,547 officers and 315,334 men. It operated in total 56,659 lorries, 23,133 cars and vans, 7,045 ambulances, 5,400 tractors, 1,285 steam wagons and 34,865 motor-cycles, variously in 715 Horse Transport units, 648 Mechanical Transport units and 346 Supply units. Casualties were 280 officers and 8,187 men killed, with almost the same number wounded. Twenty-two officers and ninety-nine men were taken prisoner-of-war. In addition to the two Victoria Crosses in France and 688 Company's *Croix de Guerre avec Palme* in Serbia there was a host of national and international awards and decorations, including 277 DSOs, 518 OBEs, 512 MCs, 1,761 MMs, 10 Albert Medals and 335 DCMs (See Annex S for more information.)

The Corps' performance during the war could not be kept under wraps in 1918 as Kitchener had done with the King's admiration of the ASC in 1914. A Royal Warrant was published on 27 November 1918 in which HM King George V noted with great satisfaction the splendid work performed by the ASC during the Great War and commanded that the Corps should in future enjoy the distinction of 'Royal'. Officers and men alike were fiercely proud of this honour, which gave a considerable boost to their self-confidence.

The success of the ASC can be attributed to a combination of reasons: a vital task which was clearly understood by every member of the Corps, after all, if they failed in their support of the fighting arms, the front line could not survive for more than a day or two; the support given by the Quartermaster General, both in the War Office, in France and elsewhere; the dynamic synergy of the skills and sheer hard work of the soldiers throughout the Corps, but perhaps above all because of the high quality of senior officers who had developed their professionalism from experience as junior or middle-ranking officers in small wars of the Victorian army and in South Africa and who were of the right age and seniority when it mattered most. The army was lucky to have key ASC officers with such depth of experience in the field of logistics.

The officers who retired before the Great War had contributed too, in that they had helped to raise the standards of the ASC from its uncertain beginnings in 1888 to the confident and authoritative performance as a major player during the war, when it towered above all others on the logistic stage. Brigadier General Bridge had been highly influential in the world of Remounts; Major General Bunbury, the first Corps officer of two star rank, had led the way in the early years of the century; and Colonel Sir Edward Ward, retiring early in 1901, was a major influence at the very top of the army as Permanent Under Secretary of State at the War Office after the Boer War, always a good friend of the Corps.

The needs of the war years found a host of men ready for responsibility, with two outstanding men at the top: Major General Long, a forceful, completely independent man, who, after establishing a strong supplies situation which saw the army well set up at the start of the war, took over the appointment of Director Supplies & Transport in the War Office, an appointment people said

189

was too much for any one man; and Major General Crofton Atkins, catapulted from being Deputy Director Supplies & Transport as a Temporary Brigadier General (Brevet Colonel) to Director in place of Major General Long on his unexpected resignation, was a brilliant, no-nonsense administrator who wore himself out in the post.

Supplies on the Western Front were always in good hands: Major General Clayton was Director in 1914 before his promotion to Inspector General Line of Communication in 1915, the first logistician to reach 3-star rank, handing over as Director to Brigadier General Carter in 1915, who held the post of Director of Supplies until 1919, partnered magnificently by Brigadier General Boyce as Director of Transport from 1914 to 1919. Brigadier Generals Ford and Koe were solid as Director of Supplies & Transport in the Mediterranean Expeditionary Force and for Gallipoli respectively, before the former became Deputy Quartermaster General on the Western Front from 1916 to 1919 and the latter became Inspector General Line of Communication in Salonika from 1916 to 1917.

It would be wrong not to mention one ASC officer of more junior rank who does not, in all conscience, really justify listing here, even though he was probably typical of many worthy officers who served in the Corps during the war. Major I L Hore-Belisha, a Reserve officer, served with 48 Company in the 5th Divisional Train on the Western Front and also in Salonika and Cyprus, gaining a Mention-in-Despatches in the process. He became Minister of War in the late 1930s until he clashed with devious politicians and arrogant, old-school Generals. Before he resigned he did good work in helping to improve the state of the British Army after the neglect of the 1920s and 1930s. In spite of his political duties he was an enthusiastic Honorary Colonel of 43rd (Wessex) Column RASC (TA) before the Second World War and is well remembered by the Corps.

There are many others who could be mentioned as important contributors (See Annex C for a number of senior officers during the period 1902-1918) but it is perhaps appropriate to finish with a genial all-rounder, Brigadier General Gibb, who was pulled out of relative obscurity as an Assistant Quartermaster General in GHQ on the Western Front in 1916 to be the first Director of Labour, forming not only a new Directorate but also a new Corps, the Army Labour Corps; as if that was not enough, he became the first Director of Salvage in 1918, a fierce task towards the end of the war, which probably no one envied him, as well as the last General Officer Commanding British Troops in France and Flanders, which can only be taken as something of a compliment to the ASC as a whole.

Were there flaws? How can one say 'no'? And yet it is impossible to provide a list of negative comment to give some sort of balanced judgement. The facts are simply not available. The Corps went into the war better prepared than most others, having made tremendous strides since the end of the Boer War, but it took a year or two to realize that higher level co-ordination and control were really needed in a large continental army, the like of which, in all fairness, the British had never previously possessed. Major General Clayton was about to be appointed as Director Supplies & Transport on the Western Front, but thoughts of the post came to nothing as he was promoted to be Inspector General Line of Communication. Who knows what he would have achieved had he been responsible for both Supplies and Transport? Or what would have happened if one of the other contenders, Brigadier Generals Boyce or Carter, had become overall Director?

Some say that mechanization did not progress fast enough during the war. It is difficult to know how much faster would have answered this comment, especially bearing in mind the heavy costs of mechanical transport in comparison with horse-drawn transport, as well as the availability of vehicles from trade and trained MT drivers. First line (ie fighting arms) and second line transport (ie the Divisional Train) remained horse-drawn for the duration of the war, essentially because horse transport could traverse poor roads and difficult countryside which would have been inaccessible to vehicles of the day. An MT company, however, was attached to each Division in quick order, which gave it the best of both worlds. Certainly, by the end of the war, 51% of all ASC soldiers were in the MT trade, something like a 20% increase on the pre-war situation. That mechanization was desirable is arguably beyond debate, since it swept through the army in the 1920s and 1930s so that, when the BEF went to France in 1939-40, even First Line and Divisional Second Line Columns, including the Territorial Army, were mechanized, in contrast to the French and German Armies of that time. On balance the 1914-18 war was too early for extensive or even complete mechanization.

Although nothing too dramatic happened to the ASC in operational terms, life in the Corps, certainly for the higher echelons, was never less than dynamic, as they had to respond quickly to the needs of the army in the different theatres of war. At the lower level a hard grind was the order of the day, every day, and at night too. Re-supply at night became a routine for the ASC to escape German observation and the resultant shelling, something that had not happened in previous wars but was subsequently to became the accepted norm. The soldiers of the ASC were probably no better or worse than the fighting arms in disciplinary terms, but they were generally more independent in the performance of their work, were more loosely administered and probably responded better to the framework of responsibility that was evident to them. The number of court-martial cases is not known, nor other disciplinary cases, but there were at least no ASC deserters.

A glance at Annex T will show the inexorable growth of MT, horse transport and other types of unit. A total of 631 MT units, 563 horse transport units and 1,109 other types of units (mainly MT and Supply) was formed between July 1914 and December 1918, a massive undertaking which must have required inhuman patience, determination and a first-class organization. The total of 2,302 should in all fairness be abated by the 588 units that were absorbed into other units or disbanded in the same period (147 MT units, 51 horse transport units and 390+ other units). The work level in amalgamating or disbanding in itself was considerable. Annex U, showing some Supply statistics, is equally impressive.

The war of 1914-1918 confirmed the place of the Territorial in the Field Army. Whereas individual Volunteers had performed well in the Boer War, Territorial units earned their place abroad in 1914 and 1915 before they were subsumed into the Army's Regular order of battle, although not before reinforcements became something of a problem. In a war as lengthy as this and with the drain on manpower so relentless, the Territorial became essential, even if volunteers flocked to the Colours at the first opportunity. Territorials were at least part-trained whereas individual volunteers needed training from scratch. Women too made great inroads in a world which had always been the preserve of men. Nursing, clerical and domestic work may have been acceptable before the war, but driving lorries had been unthinkable.

Although the growth of MT and horse transport was roughly balanced during the war, the development and wider use of MT was one of the war's greatest success stories. The only real horse transport advance was the increased use of mules (and perhaps camels in Palestine), but otherwise the situation remained more or less stagnant; in contrast, under the guiding hand of Brigadier General Boyce, motor transport became the real workhorse for the army, largely because of the weight of re-supply needed, especially ammunition for the heavy guns and mortars.

Petrol and water tankers were introduced, mobile workshop and recovery vehicles became essential, motorized ambulances became standard, troop-carrying in buses or lorries became commonplace, even the carriage of Lewis guns and 'Archie' anti-aircraft guns too. Field artillery might retain their horses for a while yet, but powerful vehicles were needed to pull the heavy guns — horses simply could not do it; that said, steam traction vehicles and tracked caterpillars may also have done the job during the war, but their slow speed was a severe disadvantage in a really mobile situation, which led to their replacement soon after the war. The day of the horse had passed and the internal combustion engine won the day; steam vehicles were finished, as were those with tracks, other than for the great new weapon of war, the tank.

In spite of the large numbers of MT units there was, however, never enough transport. Mobility, too, was a constant problem on the roads, not only on the Western Front but also in the mountains of Italy, the deserts of Mesopotamia, the scrub hills of Palestine, the dust of East Africa and the mud of Salonika. Post-war developments were to concentrate on improved reliability and mobility, leading to the 6-wheeler and 4-wheel drive. Hand-in-hand with the increase in MT was the increase in drivers, men and women who would never otherwise have had the opportunity of obtaining a driving licence before the war; these drivers were to provide the human means throughout the United Kingdom for the explosion in the use of lorries in the commercial world of the 1920s and 1930s.

When Major General Sir A R Crofton Atkins KCB CMG vacated the appointment of Director of Supplies & Transport at the War Office on 20 January 1919, he published the following Special Corps Order:

"On vacating his appointment at the Headquarters of the Army, Major General Crofton Atkins wishes to place on record his high appreciation of the work accomplished by all ranks of the Royal Army Service Corps, including the civilian subordinate establishments and the women who have undertaken military obligations.

"The important results achieved are not due to the efforts of any particular individuals, but to the collective determination of the whole Corps to secure at all costs the welfare of their comrades in fighting formations. In this spirit only has it been possible to maintain the troops in all theatres of war in food and transport, and to contribute so materially to the victorious success of the military operations."

It may, however, be more appropriate to finish with Brigadier General Gibb's Special Order of the Day, published when he vacated his appointment at the end of June 1920, as the Great War presence of the British Army on the Western Front effectively came to an end. The Special Order was not aimed at the ASC, even though many of those involved since the Armistice would undoubtedly have been members of the Corps, but it could well be applicable to the efforts of the ASC world-wide throughout the war as well as those who remained in Europe after the great majority had left.

"Special Order of the Day
by
Brigadier General Evan Gibb
CMG CBE DSO

General Officer Commanding British Troops
in France and Flanders

On relinquishing the Command of the British Troops in France and Flanders, I wish to take the opportunity of expressing to all ranks my very grateful thanks for their hard work, unfailing support, and loyal determination to overcome difficulties and see the task through.

"The work of the past six months has been very strenuous and the obstacles encountered have been many.

"The fact that we have collected from the battlefields many hundred thousand tons of ammunition is testimony to this. The removal of this ammunition from districts which before the war were rich and prosperous, and are now ruined and devastated, has assisted materially the unfortunate inhabitants to make their first efforts in rehabilitation. This work has been greatly appreciated by our Allies in France and Belgium.

"The variety, scope and extent of the many problems which have confronted the Force out here preclude mention in detail. The assistance the Army has rendered to the Ministry of Munitions and the Disposals Board should, however, not be lost sight of. Energy and application have been brought to bear, and real, rapid and solid progress has been made in clearing up and in bringing to a satisfactory conclusion the many and varied problems which are the inevitable legacy of a great war.

"The task of closing down this vast organisation has been a heavy one, but the speed with which all the work has been accomplished is a striking tribute to the way in which all have worked for the object in view. Service of undoubted value to the State has been accomplished by those out here, and I regard it as a great privilege to have been able to assist and co-operate in that work.

"The administration and maintenance of the personnel engaged in the arduous and solemn duties connected with the re-burial of those who lost their lives during the war have been admirably carried out. This work has been rendered particularly complex by reason of the immensity of the territory to be covered and the necessity of scattering the personnel employed in small detachments over this vast area — an area, it should be remembered, which extends from the Mediterranean to the English

Channel, and from the devastated regions of France and Belgium right up to the boundaries of our Rhine Army of Occupation.

"I owe a special debt of gratitude to my Staff and Representatives of the Services at my Headquarters, and to my District Commandants, who, with depleted and ever diminishing personnel have carried out their duties with admirable efficiency and industry. They have, indeed, worked almost at war pressure throughout.

"The members of the various women's organisations, likewise, have largely contributed to the successful results achieved by their work and exemplary conduct.

"I wish you all Good Luck.

Evan Gibb
General Officer Commanding
British Troops in France and Flanders"

General Headquarters
30 June 1920

As a postscript, the Corps war memorial to all ranks who fell in the war was unveiled in Stanhope Lines, Aldershot on Sunday 29 May 1928 in the presence of a large gathering of serving and retired officers from all parts of the country. Lieutenant General Sir Frederick Clayton unveiled the memorial of Portland stone, which was dedicated by the Reverend F I Anderson CMG, Assistant Chaplain General, Chaplain to the King. Detachments and wreaths were sent from the major stations of the Corps, Bulford, Colchester, Feltham, London, Portsmouth, Woolwich and York, as well as Southern Command and the Corps Old Comrades Association. A guard of honour was furnished by No 1 Corps Depot RASC under the command of Captain J W Witt MC, with the parade commanded by Major/Brevet Lieutenant Colonel A C Robinson DSO, Lieutenant J A Middleton acting as Adjutant. The memorial is still in the same barracks, albeit since renamed and rebuilt, and reference to the fallen in subsequent wars had been added. Military memory is long and steadfast and wreaths are laid every year by the Association of the Royal Army Service Corps and Royal Corps of Transport. Time might pass and the army might change but the memory of our predecessors' achievements remains a sacred duty.

ASC Company Locations 1902–1914

(As at 31 March each year unless otherwise indicated.
Horse transport unless indicated*. Date annotated is move of location)

Key:

A: Aldershot	DP: Devonport	OR: Orange River Colony
AV: Avonmouth	DV: Dover	P: Portsmouth
AT: Athlone	E: Edinburgh	PD: Perham Down
B: Bradford	EG: Egypt	PS: Preston
BD: Bordon	F: Fermoy	PT: Pretoria
BF: Bulford	G: Gibraltar	S: Shorncliffe
BL: Belfast	GO: Gosport	SA: South Africa
BM: Bloemfontein	L: London	SN: Southampton
C: Chatham	LF: Longford	SO: Somaliland
CC: Cape Colony	LM: Longmoor	ST: Stobs
CL: Colchester	LU: Lusk	T: Tidworth
CO: Cork	M: Manchester	TR: Transvaal
CT: Cape Town	MA: Malta	W: Woolwich
CU: Curragh	N: Natal	WK: Woking
CY: Cape Colony	NR: Norwich	Y: York
D: Dublin	OF: Orange Free State	

* MT Units

(Footnotes - see pages 201–3)

Co	1902	1903	1904	1905	1906	1907	1908	1909	1910	1911	1912	1913	1914
1	A	A	A	A	A	A	A	A	A	A	A	A	A
2	W	W	W	W	W	W	W	W	W	W	W	W	W
3	SA	AT/LF 18 Sep	LF	LF	LF	LF	LF	LF	LF	LF	LF	-	B(47)
4	SA	A	A	A	A	A(22)	M	M	M	M	M	M	D(47)
5	SA	W/L 21 Oct	L	L	W	W	W	W	W	W	W	W	W
6	SA/C	C	C	C	C	C	C	C	C	C	C	C	CU (46) (47)
7	SA	TR	TR	TR	TR	TR	TR	TR	TR	A(27)	A	A	A
8	SA/W 8 Nov	W/ST	ST	ST	ST	ST	ST	ST	ST	ST	ST	E	E
9	SA	CT	CT	CT	CT	CT	CT	CT	A	A(23)	A	A	A

Co	1902	1903	1904	1905	1906	1907	1908	1909	1910	1911	1912	1913	1914
10	SA/CL	CL	CL	CL	CL	CL	CL	CL	CL	CL	CL	CL	A (46) (47)
11	SA/W	W/L	A	A	L	L	L	L	L	L (26) (27)	L	L	L
12	SA	OR	OR	OR	OR	OR	OR	P 1Mar	P	P	P (42) (43)	P	P
13	SA	A	LM	A	A	A	BD	BD	BD	BD	BD	BD	BD
14	SA	N	N/W (14)	W	W	W	W	W	W	W	W	W	W
15	SA	SO	SO/A	BF	BF	BF	BF	BF	BF	BF	BF	BF	BF
16	SA	A	A	A	A	A	A	A	A	A	A	A	A
17	SA/CO	CO	CO	CO	CO	CO	CO	CO	CO	CO(35)	CO(36)	CO	CO
18	A	A	W	W	L	L	L	L	L	L	L	L	L
19	SA	CY	CY	CY	CY	CY	CY	CY	OR	OF	D(36)	D	D
20	SA	A	A	A	A	A	A	A	A	A	A	A	A
21	SA	A/CY	BD	BD	BD	BD	BD	BD	BD	DP (26) (27)	DP	DP	DP
22	SA	SO	SO/A	BF	BF	BF	BF	BF	BF	BF	BF	BF	BF
23	SA	A/CU 29 Oct	CU	CU	CU	CU	CU	CU	CU	CU	CU	CU	CU
24	SA	TR	PT	PT	PT	PT	PT	PT	PT	Y(27)	Y	Y	Y
25	SA/W 3 Nov	W	W	W	W	W	W	W	W	W	W	W	W
26	SA	A	A	A	A	A	A	A	A	A	A	A	A
27	SA	A	A	A	A	A	A	A	A	A	A	A	A
28	SA	OR	OR/W/ A	BF	BF	BF	BF	BF	BF	A (30) (31)	A	A	A
29	SA/P	P	P	P	P	P	P	P	P	P	P	P	P
30	SA	TR	TR	TR	TR	TR	TR	TR/DP 1 Mar	DP	DP	DP	DP	DP
31	SA	TR	TR	TR	TR	TR(21)	BF	BF	BF	A (26) (27)	A	A	A

Co	1902	1903	1904	1905	1906	1907	1908	1909	1910	1911	1912	1913	1914
32	SA	A/S 29 Oct	S	S	S	S	S	S	S	S(35)	S(36)	S	S
33	SA	OR	OR	OR	OR	OR	OR	OR	OR	BL(27)	BL	BL	BL
34	SA/DP	DP	DP	DP	DP	DP	DP	DP	DP	DP(27)	DP	DP	DP
35	SA/A	A/WK	WK	WK	WK	WK	WK	WK	WK	A (26) (27)	A	A	A
36	SA	A	A	A	A	A	A	A	A	A	A	A	A
37	SA	OR/A	BD	BD	BD	BD	BD	BD	BD	BD	CO (42) (43)	CU	CU
38	W	W	W	W	W	W	W	W	W	W	W	W	DV (46) (47)
39	M	M	M	M	M	M(22)	A	A	A	A	A	A	G (46) (47)
40	SA/A	A	A	A	A	A	A	A	A	A(24)	A	A	MA (47) (48)
41	SA	SA/W 15 Jun	W	W	W	W	W	W	W	W	W (42) (43)	DV	CR (47)
42	SA/CU	CU	CU	CU	CU	CU	CU	CU	CU	CU	CU	CU	PS(47)
43	SA	SA 28 Jun	D	D	D	D	D	D	D	D	D	D	BM(47)
44	TR	TR/W 14 Nov	W	W	W	W	W	W	W	W	W	W	BF* (1) (46)
45	W	W	W	W	W	W	W	W	W	W	W (42) (43)	G	DP* (47) (48)
46	DV	DV	DV	DV	DV	DV	S 19 Feb	S	DV 21 Feb	DV	DV(43)	MA	W* (47) (48)
47	SN/NR 12 Jun	CU	CU	CU	CU	CU	CU	CU	CU	CU	CU(43)	CR	W* (47) (49)
48	A	A/L 28 Sep	L	L	L	C	C	C	C	BM (27) (28)	BM	BM/A (45)	D*(49)
49	W	W/Y	Y	Y	Y	Y	Y	Y	Y	PS(27)	PS	PS	CU* (47) (49)

Co	1902	1903	1904	1905	1906	1907	1908	1909	1910	1911	1912	1913	1914
50	CO	CO	CO	CO	CO	CO	CO	CO	CO	CO	OF(36)	BM/A (45) 10 Mar	F*(49)
51	A	A	A	A	A	A	A	A	A	OF(27)	OF	-	CU* (47) (49)
52	A	A	A	A	A	A	A	A	A	A* (27) (29)	A*	A*	A*
53	DP	DP	DP	DP	DP	DP	DP	DP	DP	A* (27) (28)	A*	A*	A*
54	P	P	P	P	P	P	P	P	P	P(34)	A*(44)	A*	A*
55	A	A	A	A	A	A	A	A	A	BF* (31) (33)	BF*	BF*	BF*
56	S	S	S	S	S	S	DV 19 Feb	DV	S 21 Feb	S	BF* (36) (41)	BF*	BF*
57	CU	CU	CU	CU	CU	CU	CU	CU	CU	CU	A*(37)	A*	A*
58	A	A	A	A	A	A	A	A	A	A*(27) (28) (35)	A*	A*	A*
59	W/L 15 May	L/A 16 May	LM	LM	BD	BD	A	A	A	A* (23) (25)	A*	A*	A*
60	W	W	W/LF (18) 12 Oct	A	A	A	A	A	A	A* (24) (25)	A*	A*	A*
61	D	D	D	D	D	D	D	D	D	D	D (42) (43)	A*	A*
62	W 16 Aug	W/BL 1 Oct	BL	BL	BL	BL	BL	BL	BL	A* (27) (29)	A*P* (37) (40) (41)	P*	P*
63	-	C 12 Jan	C	C	L	L	L	L	L	BF* (27) (28)	BF*(38)	BF*	BF*
64	D	D	D	D	D	D	D	D	D	D	BF* (36) (38)	BF*	BF*
65	C	C	C	C	C	C	C	C	C	C	C*(39)	C*	C*
66	D	D	D	D	D	D	D	D	D	D	D(42) W*(44)	W*	BF* (2) (49)

Co	1902	1903	1904	1905	1906	1907	1908	1909	1910	1911	1912	1913	1914
67	-	**DP** 12 Jan	DP	DP	DP	DP	DP	DP	DP	DP(30)	**DP/D*** (44) 1 Oct	**D***	**AV*** (3) (49)
68	-	**P** 2 Feb	P	P	P	P	P	P	P	P	P(43)	**CU***	**AV*** (4) (49)
69	-	G	G	G	G	G	G	G	G	G	**G**(44) **CO***(43)	C? F*	**A*** (5) (49)
70	-	MA	MA	MA	MA	MA	MA	MA	MA	MA	MA(43)	**CU***	**A*** (6) (49)
71	-	EG	EG	EG	EG	EG	EG	EG	EG	EG	EG(43)	-	**P***(7)
72	-	A/BF	BF	BF	BF	BF(21)	**A*** 1 Apr	**A***	**A***	**A***(29)	-	-	**P***(8)
73	-	A/BF	BF(15)	-	-	-	**CU*** 1 Apr	**CU***	**CU***	**CU***	**CU***(43)	**CU***	**W***(9)
74	-	A/BF	BF(16)	-	-	-	-	**A*** 1 Apr	**A***	**A***(25)	-	-	**BF***(10)
75	-	A/BF	BF(17)	-	-	-	-	-	**CU*** 27 Jun	**CU***	**CU***(43)	-	**BF***(11)
76	-	W/ST	**ST** temp (13)	-	-	-	-	**C*** 1 Sep	**C***	**C***	**C*** (37) (39)	-	**W***(12)
77	-	C	**W/C*** 16 Feb	**C***	**C***	C*/BF 17 Dec	**BF***	**BF***	**BF***	**BF***(33)	(38)	-	-
78	-	-	**A*** 1 May	**A***	**A***	**A***	**A***	**A***	**A***	**A***(29)	-	-	-

Remount Companies	1902	1903	1904	1905	1906	1907	1908	1909	1910	1911	1912	1913	1914
A	W	W	W	W	W	W	W	W	W	(32) W			
B	D	D	D	D	D	D	D	D	D	(32) D			GO
C			LU (19)	LU	LU	LU	LU	LU	LU	(32) LU			
D			D(20)	D	D	D	D	D	D	(32) D			CU
AA	-	-	-	-	-	-	-	-	-	(32)	W	W	W
BB	-	-	-	-	-	-	-	-	-	(32)	D	D	D
CC	-	-	-	-	-	-	-	-	-	(32)	LU	LU	LU
DD	-	-	-	-	-	-	-	-	-	(32)	D	D	D

*The word 'Remount' was omitted wef 30 November 1911.

Supply Companies	1902	1903	1904	1905	1906	1907	1908	1909	1910	1911	1912	1913	1914
A	A	A	A	A	A	A	A	A	A	A	A	A	A
B	SA	SA	SA	SA	SA	SA	-	-	G	G	G	G	G
C	A	A	A	A	A	A	A	A	A	A	A	A	A
D	D	D	D	D	D	D	D/CU 7 Sep	CU	CU	CU	CU	CU	CU
E	W	W	W	W	W	W	W	W	W	W	W	W	W
F	-	P	T	T	T	T/G 23 Nov	G	G	G	(32)			
K	-	-	-	-	-	-	-	-	-	-	-	-	A
AA													
BB													
CC	-	-	-	-	-	-	-	-	-	(32)			
DD	-	-	-	-	-	-	-	-	-	(32)			

(1) Absorbed 20 March 1914. Reformed as 44 (MT) Company in Bulford on 1 September 1914.

(2) Renumbered as 47 (MT) Company 20 March 1914. New 66 (MT) Company formed in Bulford 1 September 1914.

(3) Renumbered as 48 (MT) Company 20 March 1914. New 67 (MT) Company formed in Avonmouth 28 August 1914.

(4) Renumbered as 49 (MT) Company 20 March 1914. New 68 (MT) Company formed in Avonmouth 28 August 1914.

(5) Renumbered as 50 (MT) Company 20 March 1914. New 69 (MT) Company formed in Aldershot 28 September 1914.

(6) Renumbered as 51 (MT) Company 20 March 1914. New 70 (MT) Company formed in Aldershot 7 September 1914.

(7) New 71 (MT) Company formed in Portsmouth on 19 September 1914.

(8) New 72 (MT) Company formed in Portsmouth on 19 September 1914.

(9) New 73 (MT) Company formed in Woolwich on 4 September 1914.

(10) New 74 (MT) Company formed in Bulford on 14 September 1914.

(11) New 75 (MT) Company formed in Bulford on 14 September 1914.

(12) New 76 (MT) Company formed in Woolwich on 4 September 1914.

(13) Absorbed by 8 Company in order to raise to the Higher Establishment on 1 November 1904.

(14) On Lower Establishment wef 1 November 1904 to act as Station Staff Woolwich.

(15) Absorbed by 15 Company wef 1 November 1904.

(16) Absorbed by 22 Company wef 1 November 1904.

(17) Absorbed by 28 Company wef 1 November 1904.

(18) On move to Aldershot employed as Station Staff Aldershot, absorbing Station Staff already there.

(19) Formed 1 November 1904.

(20) Formed 1 November 1904.

(21) On its return from South Africa on 14 March 1907 31 Company was disbanded. 72 Company was renumbered as 31 Company.

(22) The designation of 39 Depot Company was changed on 3 June 1907 to 4 Depot Company. 4 Company became 39 Company on the same date.

(23) 9 Company was absorbed from 15 June 1911. The existing 59 Company became 9 Company.

(24) 40 Company was absorbed from 15 June 1911. The existing 60 Company became 40 Company.

(25) In order to increase the number of MT Companies, 74 (MT) Company was reduced from the Higher Establishment and the manpower was used to establish 59 (MT) and 60 (MT) Companies.

(26) 11, 21, 31, 35 and 48 Companies were absorbed from 21 October 1911.

(27) Wef 21 October 1911 the following companies were renumbered:
     7 Company was renumbered 51 Company
     24 Company was renumbered 49 Company
     35 Company was renumbered 48 Company
     49 Company was renumbered 34 Company
     51 Company was renumbered 7 Company
     52 Company was renumbered 35 Company
     53 Company was renumbered 21 Company
     58 Company was renumbered 31 Company
     62 Company was renumbered 33 Company
     63 Company was renumbered 11 Company

(28) In order to increase the number of MT Companies 53 (MT) and 58 (MT) Companies were formed wef 21 October 1911, 53 (MT) Company to be part of the ASC Training Establishment in Aldershot. An additional 63 (MT) Company was formed in Bulford wef 21 October 1911.

(29) Wef 21 October 1911:

    72 (MT) Company was renumbered 52 (MT) Company

    78 (MT) Company was renumbered 62 (MT) Company

(30) Wef 15 November 1911, 28 and 67 HT Companies were absorbed.

(31) Wef 15 November 1911, 55 HT Company was renumbered 28 HT Company.

(32) Wef 1 December 1911 the following designation changes to Supply and Remount Companies were made:

    'F' (Supply) Company became 'B' Company

    A Remount Company became 'AA' Company (as a predominantly civilianized company)

    B Remount Company became 'BB' Company (as a predominantly civilianized company)

    C Remount Company became 'CC' Company (as a predominantly civilianized company)

    D Remount Company became 'DD' Company (as a predominantly civilianized company)

(33) In order to increase the number of MT Companies, 77 (MT) Company was reduced in establishment and an additional unit, 55 (MT) Company, was formed in Bulford, wef 15 December 1911.

(34) 54 HT Company was absorbed from 15 December 1911.

(35) Wef 1 January 1912, 17, 32 and 57 HT Companies were absorbed.

(36) Wef 1 January 1912:

    19 Company was renumbered 50 Company

    50 Company was renumbered 17 Company

    56 Company was renumbered 32 Company

    64 Company was renumbered 19 Company

(37) Wef 1 January 1912, 62 and 76 (MT) Companies were reduced in establishment in order to form 57 (MT) Company in Aldershot.

(38) Wef 1 January 1912:

    77 (MT) Company was renumbered 63 (MT) Company

    63 (MT) Company was renumbered 64 (MT) Company

(39) 65 HT Company was absorbed from 8 February 1912 and 76 (MT) Company was renumbered 65 (MT) Company wef 8 February 1912.

(40) The designation of 62 (MT) Company was altered from 1 March 1912 until 1 October 1912 to 61A (MT) Company.

(41) Wef 1 March 1912, 56 (MT) Company was formed at Bulford and 62 (MT) Company was formed at Portsmouth.

(42) From 1 October 1912, 12, 37, 41, 45, 61 and 66 HT Companies were absorbed.

(43) The following companies were renumbered wef 1 October 1912:

    46 HT Company was renumbered 41 HT Company

    47 HT Company was renumbered 37 HT Company

    68 HT Company was renumbered 12 HT Company

    69 HT Company was renumbered 45 HT Company

    70 HT Company was renumbered 46 HT Company

    71 HT Company was renumbered 47 HT Company

    61A (MT) Company was renumbered 61 (MT) Company

    73 (MT) Company was renumbered 68 (MT) Company

    75 (MT) Company weas renumbered 70 (MT) Company

(44) Four new MT Companies were formed wef 10 October 1912:

    54 (MT) Company in Aldershot.

66 (MT) Company in Woolwich
67 (MT) Company in Dublin
69 (MT) Company in Cork

(45) 48 and 50 HT Companies were absorbed from 19 March 1913.

(46) 6,10, 38,39 and 44 HT Companies were absorbed from 20 March 1914.

(47) Wef 20 March 1914, the following HT companies were renumbered:
4 (Depot) Company to 3 (Depot) Company
43 Company to 4 Company
42 Company to 6 Company
40 Company to 10 Company
41 Company to 38 Company
45 Company to 39 Company
46 Company to 40 Company
47 Company to 41 Company
49 Company to 42 Company
51 Company to 43 Company

(48) 45 and 46 (MT) Companies were formed wef 1 April 1914.

(49) Wef 20 March 1914 the following MT Companies were renumbered:
66 (MT) Company to 47 (MT) Company
67 (MT) Company to 48 (MT) Company
68 (MT) Company to 49 (MT) Company
69 (MT) Company to 50 (MT) Company
70 (MT) Company to 51 (MT) Company

Establishment of ASC
Horse Transport Company

(Corps Order 188 of 13 September 1902)

Men/Horses	Higher Establishment	Lower Establishment
Officers	3	2
HT Men		
Warrant Officer	1	1
Company Sergeant Major	1	1
Company Quartermaster Sergeant	1	1
Sergeants	3	2
Corporals	3	2
2nd Corporal	1	1
Trumpeter	1	1
Lance Corporals	2	2
Drivers	43	15
Artificers		
Wheeler Staff Sergeant or Corporal	1	1
Saddler Staff Sergeant or Corporal	1	1
Farrier Staff Sergeant or Corporal	1	1
Farrier Shoeing & Carriage Smith	1	-
TOTAL	**3 + 60**	**2 + 29**
Horses		
Officers	3	2
Riding	5	3
Draught	26	12
TOTAL	**34**	**17**

Key ASC Officers 1902-1918

Major General Sir William George Bertram BOYCE KCMG CB DSO

Born 27 May 1868; commissioned Royal Berkshire Regiment 1887; transferred to ASC 1898; on Staff Cork District 1899; Commandant ASC Training Establishment 1909; DAAG 2 Division South Africa 1899-1900, DSO; AD S & T Eastern Command 1913; Director of Transport British Armies in France November 1914-June 1919; created CB and CMG 1917; promoted Major General 1917; promoted KCMG 1919; retired 1920; Secretary Soldiers' & Sailors' Help Society and Comptroller Lord Roberts' Memorial Workshop; appointed to the Board of Directors of Rolls-Royce 1933; Order of St Stanislaus 2nd Class with Swords, Order of Legion of Honour; died 18 July 1937.

Brigadier General Sir Charles Henry BRIDGE KCMG CB

Born 16 June 1852; entered the Control Department from Cambridge University 1872; service in the West Indies, Woolwich and Dublin; active service with the Commissariat & Transport Staff Egyptian Campaign 1882; Adjutant, Aldershot 1885; DAQMG Army Headquarters 1886-1888; worked with General Buller for the formation of the ASC; Lieutenant Colonel in ASC 1889; commanded ASC, Aldershot 1891-1896; service South Africa; Matabeleland Campaign 1896; created CB; Brevet Colonel 1898; Director of Transport, South Africa Field Force 1899-1901; created CMG; AAG Aldershot 1901-1902; Director of Transport 1902; retired 1903; re-employed as Assistant Inspector of Remounts; organized Remount Depot at Arborfield Cross; Inspector Remount Depots from 1906; promoted Brigadier General 1914; head of Mule Purchasing Commission in America 1914-1916; promoted KCMG 1916; retired 1916; died 18 July 1926.

Major General Sir Herbert Napier BUNBURY KCB

Born 15 February 1851; commissioned Royal Artillery 1871; transferred to ASC 1889; (the first officer to join the Corps from the Regimental List); Deputy Assistant Commissary General Commissariat & Transport Staff 1880-1888; DAAG Headquarters ASC 1888-1890; DAAG Eastern District 1890-1891; DAQMG Army Headquarters 1891-1896 (while in this appointment he signed the order authorizing the ASC badge in 1894); service in South African War, AAG for Supplies 1899; Assistant Director of Transport 1899-1900; Director of Transport (Colonel) 1900-1901; AAG Cork District 1901-1902; Director of Transport 3rd Army Corps 1902-1903; Director of Supplies & Transport 3rd Army Corps 1903-1905; AD Supply & Transport Irish Command 1905; Brigadier General IC Administration Gibraltar 1906; KCB 1906; Major General IC Administration Irish Command 1907-1908 (the first Major General in the Corps); retired 1913; retired Officer employed in Ministry of Munitions 1913-1919; President RASC Club 1919-1922; Commissioner Royal Hospital Chelsea 1915-1919; died 18 January 1922.

Major General Sir Evan Eyre CARTER KCMG CB MVO

Born 11 August 1866; commissioned The Leicestershire Regiment 1889; transferred to ASC 1890; Staff College 1895-1896, one of the Corps' first psc officers; DAAG Belfast District and South Africa 1897; South Africa War, staff of Line of Communication and Army Headquarters; CMG 1900; DAQMG War Office 1902, MVO; Chief Instructor ASC Training Establishment 1905-1908; AD S & T London District 1913; Colonel IC ASC Records 1914; AQMG Line of Communication, France 1914; Director of Supplies British Armies in France 1915-1919; promoted Major General 1918; Director of Supplies & Transport; War Office March 1919 to August 1921; retired 1921; Colonel Commandant RASC 1921-1933; Honorary Colonel 54th (East Anglia) Divisional Train RASC (TA); Colonel-in-Chief First Aid Nursing Yeomanry; Chairman of RASC Regimental Association until 1933; Commander Legion of Honour, Order of St Stanislaus 2nd Class; *Commandeur Ordre de la Couronne* St Anne of Russia (2nd Class), Honorary Associate St John of Jerusalem, Belgian Croix de Guerre, US Distinguished Service Medal; died 2 February 1933.

Lieutenant General Sir Frederick Thomas CLAYTON KCB KCMG

Born 7 October 1855; commissioned Royal Warwickshire Regiment 29 November 1876; joined the Commissariat & Transport Staff 1882; appointed Deputy Assistant Commissary General (Captain) 1883; service in Bechuanaland and China 1883-1886; transferred to the Permanent List of the ASC 1 April 1889; OC ASC Ashanti Expedition 1895; promoted Brevet Lieutenant Colonel 25 March 1886; Chief Instructor ASC Training Establishment 1896-1899; service in South Africa 1899-1900; recalled to command ASC, Aldershot 1900; appointed AQMG for ASC, War Office (virtual head of the Corps) 1902; Assistant Director of Transport 1904-1905; Director of Supplies, War Office (Brigadier General) 1906-1909; promoted Major General 2 April 1909; Major General IC Administration South Africa Command 1911; Director of Supplies BEF and Inspector of QMG Services in France 1914; Inspector General of Communications (Temporary Lieutenant General) 1915-1917; retired with the honorary rank of Lieutenant General 7 October 1917; Colonel Commandant RASC September 1921-October 1925; President RASC Club November 1928-December 1933; Vice-Patron Regimental Association 1927. Decorations: CB 1901, KCMG 1917, Commander Order of Leopold (Belgium), Grand Officer, Legion of Honour (France), Grand Cordon of the Order of the Sacred Treasure (Japan), Croix de Guerre (Belgium); died 4 December 1933.

Major General Sir Alban Randall CROFTON ATKINS KCB CMG

Born 29 January 1870; commissioned Royal Marine Light Infantry 1889; transferred to ASC 1894; Curragh 1894; Adjutant 1895; service in Ashanti 1895-1896 and Sierra Leone 1899; service in South African war 1899-1900; Brevet Major; Adjutant ASC Aldershot 1901-1902; Barbados 1902-1904; Staff Captain and Deputy Assistant Director of Supplies, Army Headquarters 1904-1908; Chief Instructor ASC Training Establishment 1908-1911; DAD T War Office 1911-1914; Brevet Lieutenant Colonel 1913; AD S & T London District 1914; AD T British Expeditionary Force 1914; DD S & T (Temporary Brigadier General) War Office 1915; Brevet Colonel; succeeded Major General S S Long as Director of Supplies & Transport 11 March 1916; promoted Major General June 1918; vacated appointment of D S & T January 1919; retired 13 April 1920; CB 1917, KCB 1918, Order of White Eagle 3rd Class (Serbia); died 29 April 1926.

Major General George Freshfield DAVIES CB CMG CBE

Born 18 January 1872; commissioned Lincolnshire Regiment 1892; transferred to ASC 1895; service in Egypt 1898; South Africa War 1899; present at Relief of Ladysmith; Adjutant, West Lancashire Division Transport & Supply Column (TF), Liverpool 1908; DAD S & T South Africa 1909; DAA & QMG South Midland Division (TF) 1914; DD S & T Egyptian Expeditionary Force 1916-1919 (Temporary Brigadier General), CB 1918, CBE 1919; DD of T War Office June 1920-1923; Inspector RASC April 1923; Director of Supplies & Transport War Office 9 August 1925-1929; retired August 1929; Honorary Colonel 43rd (Wessex) Divisional Train TA 1933; Orders of El Nahda and the Nile; died 20 October 1936.

Major General Sir Reginald FORD KCMG CB DSO

Born 7 December 1868; commissioned Royal Marines Light Infantry 1889; transferred to ASC 1893; commanded 6 Company ASC, Aldershot 1893-1896; Assistant Instructor ASC Training Establishment, Aldershot 1899; service in South Africa, AAG, DSO; ASC Training Establishment 1901; AD S & T lst Army Corps Aldershot 1903-1905; OC ASC Singapore 1906-1908; OC ASC Straits Settlements 1909; OC Service Companies, Aldershot 1911-1914; AD of Supplies, France 1914; DAA & QMG XI Corps 1915; DST Mediterranean Expeditionary Force 1915-1916; DQMG British Forces in France and Flanders 1916-November 1919; promoted Major General June 1918; CB 1918, KCMG 1919; retired 1920; emigrated to Rhodesia February 1920. On staff of Dunlops; Colonel Commandant RASC 1930-1938; Chief Traffic Commissioner, Southern Area 1931; Chief Divisional Officer for London and the Home Counties for organizing food control in the event of war; died 28 April 1951.

Major General Sir Evan GIBB CB CMG DSO

Born 12 March 1877; commissioned West India Regiment 1898; transferred to ASC 1899; active Service on West Coast, Sierra Leone 1898; service in South Africa 1899-1902, DSO; Relief of Ladysmith, Transvaal and Orange Free State; Adjutant ASC, Aldershot 1905; Staff Captain (1907) and Deputy Assistant Director (1910) QMG Branch, War Office; Instructor ASC Training Establishment, Aldershot January 1911; DAQMG, BEF France 1914; AD of T November 1914; AQMG GHQ France 1915; Director of Labour BEF (Brigadier General) 1916; Controller of Salvage BEF 1918; Brigadier General (DA & QMG) GHQ, British Troops in France and Flanders 1919; General Officer Commanding the Forces in France and Flanders 1920; AD of S & T; Brevet Colonel 1923; AD of S & T, Aldershot (Temporary Colonel on the Staff) August 1924; promoted Major General 15 June 1927; military member NAAFI Board of Management 1923-1929; Director of Supplies & Transport 1929-1933; retired 1933; Honorary Colonel 47th (2nd London) Division RASC (TA) 1929-1934; Honorary Colonel First Aid Nursing Yeomanry; Colonel Commandant RASC 1933-1947; joined firm of Sir Alexander Gibb & Partners (Consulting Engineers) 1934; Director Herring Industry Board 1939-1940; Director of Salvage 1940; President London Chamber of Commerce 1943-1945; Commander of the Crown

(Belgium), Croix de Guerre (France), Croix de Boyaca (Columbia); died 13 July 1947.

Major General Charles Arthur HADFIELD

Born 27 March 1852; joined 2nd Derby Militia (Chatsworth Rifles) 1871; commissioned North Staffordshire Regiment 1874; Commissariat & Transport Staff as Deputy Assistant Commissary General 1881-1889; transferred to ASC 1889; DAAG Portsmouth 1889-1892; OC ASC Curragh 1892-1895; DAAG HQ Ireland 1895-1897; OC ASC Dublin District 1898; Director of Transport (Colonel) HQ 2nd Army Corps 1902-1903; Director of Supplies & Transport HQ 2nd Army Corps 1903-1905; AD of Supply & Transport Southern Command 1905; AD of Supply & Transport Eastern Command 1906-1907; Inspector of the ASC (Colonel) 1907-1909; promoted Major General 1908 (third officer to be promoted Major General in the Corps); Major General IC Administration South Africa Command 1909-1910; Major General IC Administration Ireland 1911-1912; retired April 1913; Vice-President RASC Club 1912 and 1932; died 2 October 1938.

Major General Sir Charles Ernest HEATH KCB CVO

Born 20 September 1854; commissioned 32nd Cornwall Light Infantry 1873; Adjutant 1877-1881; Deputy Assistant Commissary General in Commissariat & Transport Corps 1881; transferred to ASC 1888. DAAG Malta December 1888-1892; DAAG Southern District Headquarters 1892-1894; OC ASC Dublin District 1894-1897; Staff South Eastern District 1898-1901; AQMG ASC Army Headquarters (War Office) 1901-1905; Brigadier General IC Administration Aldershot 1905-1907; Major General IC Administration Aldershot 1907 (second Corps officer to be promoted to Major General); awarded CVO by HM the King after Royal Review 12 June 1907; Director of Transport & Remounts War Office 1907-1911; CB 1911; Director of Quartering War Office 1914-1916, KCB 1916; Deputy Quartermaster General War Office 1916-1917; retired 1917; Vice-President RASC Club 1920; died 23 October 1936.

Major General Percy Eyre Francis HOBBS CB CMG

Born 18 February 1865; commissioned Royal Marine Light Infantry 1883; transferred to ASC 1889 (first officer to be so transferred); DAAG 1899; service in South Africa 1899-1900, CMG 1900; Assistant Instructor and Chief Instructor ASC Training Establishment 1901-1905; Editor of *ASC Journal* for four years; Brevet Colonel 1908; Assistant Director of Supplies & Transport Irish Command and Eastern Command 1909-1913; half-pay 1913; DA & QMG (Temporary Brigadier General) Headquarters 1st Army 1914; promoted Major General 1915; CB 1915; retired 1917; Colonel Commandant RASC 1915-1935; first PMC of HQ ASC Officers' Mess in Stanhope Lines Aldershot (later Buller Barracks) on its formation in 1895; *Croix de Commandeur Légion d'Honneur* (France); died 26 October 1939.

Major General Frederick Francis JOHNSON CB OBE DL

Born 1 May 1852; commissioned 69th Foot 1874; 50th Regiment 1875; attached Commissariat & Transport Staff 1881-1889; Deputy Assistant Commissary General Egyptian Campaign (Tel-el-Kebir) 1882; DAAG and Chief Staff Officer Jamaica 1887-1890; transferred to ASC 1889; DAAG Belfast District 1891-1894;

OC ASC Woolwich 1899; Assistant Director of Supplies South Africa 1899-1900; AAG North Eastern District 1900-1903; ADST and AQMS Eastern Command 1903-1907; retired 1907; AQMG Southern Command August 1914; Major General IC Administration Southern Command 1915-1916; Honorary Major General June 1917; Secretary Essex Territorial Forces Association 1917-1922; died 6 September 1931.

Major General Frederick William Brooke KOE CB CMG

Born 6 January 1862; commissioned Royal Marine Light Infantry 1881; transferred to ASC 1889; service on west coast of Africa 1893-1894 (Sofa Expedition); OC ASC and ADST Pretoria 1907-1911, CB 1909; half-pay 1911; AQMG Western Command 1912-1914; Assistant Director of Transport 1914; Director of Supplies & Transport Mediterranean Expeditionary Force, Gallipoli; Brigadier General 1915-1916; promoted Major General 1916; Inspector General of Communications, Salonika, August 1916-March 1917, CMG 1917; retired 1917; Commissioner of Salvage East Africa 1918-1919; retired 1920; Vice-President RASC Club 1920; died 6 February 1935.

Major General Sir Frederick William Bainbridge LANDON KCM GCB

Born 27 February 1860; commissioned West Riding Regiment 1879; transferred to ASC 1889; DAAG Jamaica 1890-1895; Second-in-Command and Supply & Transport Officer Benin Expedition (Niger Coast) 1897; Brevet Lieutenant Colonel South Africa, DAAG Natal 1899; Assistant Director and Director of Supplies 1900-1902; Brevet Colonel 1900; OC ASC Aldershot 1902; CB 1904; OIC Records (Colonel) and Depot Commander Woolwich Dockyard 1905; Assistant Director of Supplies & Transport Aldershot Command 1908-1909; Inspector ASC (Brigadier General) Headquarters of the Army 1909-1912; Director of Transport & Movements War Office (Major General) 1913-1914; Inspector of the ASC and QMG Services 1914; Chief Inspector of QMG Services 1918; retired 1 October 1919; KCMG 1919; Colonel Commandant RASC 1921-1930; Honorary Colonel East Anglia Transport & Supply Column (TF) 1914-1922; Honorary Colonel 44 (Home Counties) Division RASC (TA) 1925-1930; President RASC Club December 1933; died 26 October 1937.

Major General Sidney Seldon LONG CB

Born 31 March 1863; son of Commissary General J Long JP; commissioned Durham Light Infantry from Militia 1884; transferred to ASC 1889; DAAG South China 1896-1899; South Africa 1899-1902; DAAG for Transport, later AAG; Brevet Lieutenant Colonel; first Commandant ASC Training Establishment Aldershot 1908-1909; OC Supply Reserve Depot Woolwich 1909; Assistant Director of Supplies 1909-1912; Director of Supplies & Quartering (Brigadier General) 1913-1914, CB 1914; Director of Supplies & Transport War Office 1914-1916; retired 11 March 1919; Director of Lever Bros Ltd, Port Sunlight (later Unilever) 1916-1931; President Commercial Users' Association; President RASC Club November 1937; died 31 January 1940.

Major General Harry Neptune SARGEANT CB CBE DSO

Born 6 April 1866; commissioned Devon Regiment from Militia 1886; transferred to ASC 1890; Adjutant 1895-1897; Nile Expedition 1898; South Africa 1899-1902,

DAAG; present at Relief of Ladysmith, DSO 1902; Lieutenant Colonel 1906; Colonel 1909; OIC ASC Records 1912; AD of S & T 1913; AQMG 1st Army Corps 1914; DA & QMG (Brigadier General) 1st Army Corps 1914-1916; CB 1915; DA & QMG Reserve and Fifth Army 1916-1917; Chief of British Mission, HQ Services of Supply, American Expeditionary Force, 1918 to July 1919; retired with the honorary rank of Major General 16 October 1919; Commander US Legion of Honour, US Distinguished Service Medal; died 6 February 1946.

Major General William Knapp TARVER CB CMG
Born 2 November 1872; commissioned Cheshire Regiment 1892; transferred to ASC 1896; service in Jamaica and Ireland; Instructor ASC Training Establishment, Aldershot; Deputy Assistant Director of Supplies, War Office November 1911; Assistant Director of Supplies QMG 6 War Office 1914; service in Macedonia, Serbia, Bulgaria and Dardanelles; Deputy Director of Supplies, War Office 1917; Brevet Colonel 1917; Deputy Director of Supplies & Transport (Brigadier General) 1918; CB 1918; temporary appointment as Director of Supplies & Transport, War Office 20 January 1919 to 13 March 1919 (Temporary Major General); CMG 1919; DD of S & T 1919; Assistant Director of Supplies & Transport, Western Command 1920; Colonel August 1920; ADST QMG 6 War Office 1923-1925; Inspector RASC 1925-1929; Major General June 1925; Chairman RASC Regimental Association 1934; Colonel Commandant RASC 1935-1942; *Croix de Chevalier,* Legion of Honour, France, Order of the White Eagle 3rd Class; died 8 April 1952.

Colonel Sir Edward Willis Duncan WARD Bt GBE KCB KCVO
Born 17 December 1853; Sub-Assistant Commissary in the Control Department 1874; Assistant Commissary in the Commissariat & Transport Department 1876; Adjutant Woolwich 1882-1885; Sudan Expedition 1885; promoted Major in the ASC (Supernumerary List from the Commissariat & Transport Staff) 1889; Lieutenant Colonel 1890; DAAG HQ Ireland 1892; AAG Ashanti Expedition 1895-1896; DAAG Home District 1895-1899; Honorary Secretary of the Royal Military Tournament 1895-1899; Brevet Colonel 1898; AAG South Africa 1899-1900; at Relief of Ladysmith, KCB; Director of Supplies South Africa Field Force 1900; appointed by Lord Roberts to take over all Supply arrangements at Army Headquarters as AQMG 1901; retired 1901; Permanent Under-Secretary of State at the War Office 1901-1914; Secretary of the War Office (the first Secretary of the Army Council) 1904; Honorary Colonel the Canadian Army Service Corps 15 April 1904; Honorary Colonel 2nd London Divisional Transport & Supply Column ASC (TF) 1908; Chairman of the County of London Territorial Force Association 1908; retired January 1914 (Baronetcy); Commanding and Chief Staff Officer of the Metropolitan Special Constabulary 1914 to November 1918; Director General of Voluntary Organizations; Representative of the Secretary of State for War on all question relating to the welfare and comfort of Colonial Troops; Chairman RASC Club 1919-1928; President Union Jack Club; Officer of the Legion of Honour, Knight of Grace of St John; died 11 September 1928.

Major General Frederick Maurice WILSON CB CMG
Born 19 November 1868; joined Royal Lancaster Regiment 1890; Ashanti Expedition 1895-1896; transferred to ASC 1898; Commandant ASC Training Establishment 1913-1914; Assistant Director of Supplies, Deputy Director of

Supplies, Deputy Director of Supplies & Transport Western Front 1914-1918 (Temporary Brigadier General 1917); CMG 1915; Director of Supplies & Transport, Rhine Army November 1918-November 1919; CB 1918; Assistant Director of Supplies & Transport Eastern Command 1920; Director of Supplies & Transport India 17 August 1921-1925; retired 15 September 1925; Colonel Commandant Indian ASC 1930; died 16 August 1956.

Territorial Force Transport & Supply Columns
April 1908

ASC Units	Location	Personnel		Remarks
		Offrs	Men	
1/1st Highland Division Transport & Supply Column (1)				No 1 District.
Highland Division HQ Company	Perth	4	206	Includes 6 additional 2nd Line Drivers for Mountain Artillery Brigade, less 1 Driver for Field Company in No 2 District.
Black Watch Brigade Company	City of Dundee	4	97	
Gordon Brigade Company	City of Aberdeen	4	97	
Seaforth & Cameron Brigade Company	Perth	4	127	Includes 30 2nd Line Drivers for 5 Infantry Battalions (Army Troops) in Renfrew (2), Stirling, Argyll and Dumbarton.
Highland Mounted Brigade Company	Inverness	4	119	Includes 7 2nd Line Drivers for Yeomanry Regiment, Inverness, for No 5 District, West Riding Division.
1/1st Lowland Division Transport & Supply Column (2)				No 2 District.
Lowland Division HQ Company	Glasgow	8	205	Includes 3 2nd Line Drivers for 1 Cable, 1 Airline and 1 Wireless Telegraph Company and 1 other. Field Company for Highland Division, No 1 District.
Highland Light Infantry Brigade Company	Glasgow	4	127	Includes 30 2nd Line Drivers for 5 Infantry Battalions (Army Troops), Ayr (2), Dumfries, Roxburgh and Lanark.
Scottish Rifles Brigade Company	Lanark	4	97	Includes 12 2nd Line Drivers for 2 Infantry Battalions (Army Troops), Peebles and Midlothian.
Lothian Brigade Company	Edinburgh	4	109	
Lowland Mounted Brigade Company	Ayr	4	112	
1/1ˢᵗ East Lancashire Division Transport & Supply Column (3)				No 3 District.
East Lancashire Division HQ Company	Lancashire	8	208	Includes 7 2nd Line Drivers for 1 Yeomanry Regiment, Cumberland, for Welsh Division, No 4 District.
East Lancashire Brigade Company	Lancashire	4	97	
Lancashire Fusiliers Brigade Company	Lancashire	4	97	
Manchester Brigade Company	Lancashire	4	97	

ASC Units	Location	Personnel		Remarks
		Offrs	Men	
1/1st West Lancashire Division Transport & Supply Column (3a)				No 3 District.
West Lancashire Division HQ Company	Lancashire	8	201	
Liverpool Brigade Company	Lancashire	4	97	
South Lancashire Brigade Company	Lancashire	4	97	
North Lancashire Brigade Company	Lancashire	4	112	Includes 12 2nd Line Drivers for 2 Infantry Battalions (Army Troops) in Cumberland and 3 Drivers for 1 Cable, 1 Airline and 1 Wireless Telegraph Company.
1/1st Welsh Division Transport & Supply Column (4)				No 4 District.
Welsh Division HQ Company	Hereford	8	194	Less 7 Drivers for Yeomanry Regiment Cumberland, provided by East Lancashire Division HQ Company, No 3 District.
South Wales Brigade Company	Glamorgan	4	127	Includes 30 2nd Line Drivers for 5 Infantry Battalions (Army Troops) in Shropshire, Hereford, Carmarthen, Brecknock and Monmouthshire.
Cheshire Brigade Company	Cheshire	4	97	
North Wales Brigade Company	Denbigh	4	97	
Welsh Border Mounted Brigade Company	Cheshire	4	112	
South Wales Mounted Brigade Company	Glamorgan	4	112	
1/1st Northumbrian Division Transport & Supply Column (5)				No 5 District.
Northumbrian Division HQ Company	Durham	8	204	Includes 3 2nd Line Drivers for 1 Airline, 1 Cable and 1 Wireless Telegraph Company.
Durham Brigade Company	Durham	4	97	
Northumberland Brigade Company	Northumberland	4	97	
York & Durham Brigade Company	East Riding of Yorkshire	4	97	
Yorkshire Mounted Brigade Company	West Riding of Yorkshire	4	112	

ASC Units	Location	Personnel		Remarks
		Offrs	Men	
1/1st West Riding Division Transport & Supply Column (5a)				No 5 District.
West Riding Division HQ Company	West Riding of Yorkshire	8	194	Less 7 2nd Line Drivers for Yeomanry Regiment, Inverness provided by Highland Division HQ Company, No 1 District.
1st West Riding Brigade Company	West Riding of Yorkshire	4	97	
2nd West Riding Brigade Company	West Riding of Yorkshire	4	97	
3rd West Riding Brigade Company	West Riding of Yorkshire	4	97	
1/1st North Midland Division Tranport & Supply Column (6)				No 6 District.
North Midland Division HQ Company	Stafford	8	194	Less 7 2nd Line Drivers for Yeomanry Regiment, Northampton provided by East Anglian Division, HQ Company, No 9 District.
Stafford Brigade Company	Stafford	4	97	
Lincoln & Leicester Brigade Company	Lincoln	4	97	
Notts & Derby Brigade Company	Nottingham	4	97	
North Midland Mounted Brigade Company	Leicester	4	112	
Notts & Derby Mounted Brigade Company	Derby	4	112	
1/1st South Midland Division Transport & Supply Column (7)				No 7 District.
South Midland Division HQ Company	Warwick	8	197	Includes 3 2nd Line Drivers for 1 Airline, 1 Cable and 1 Wireless Telegraph Company; less 7 Drivers for Yeomanry Regiment, Hertfordshire provided by East Anglian Division, No 9 District.
Warwick Brigade Company	Warwick	4	97	
Gloucester & Worcester Brigade Company	Gloucester	4	97	
South Midland Brigade Company	Buckinghamshire	4	97	
1st South Midland Mounted Brigade Company	Berkshire	4	112	
2nd South Midland Mounted Brigade Company	Worcester	4	112	

ASC Units	Location	Personnel		Remarks
		Offrs	Men	
1/1st Wessex Division Transport & Supply Column (8)				No 8 District.
Wessex Division HQ Company	Hampshire	8	201	
Hampshire Brigade Company	Hampshire	4	103	Includes 6 2nd Line Drivers for 1 Infantry Battalion in Hampshire (Army Troops).
South Western Brigade Company	Somerset	4	97	
Devon & Cornwall Brigade Company	Devon	4	103	Includes 6 2nd Line Drivers for 1 Infantry Battalion in Devon (Army Troops).
1st South Western Mounted Brigade Company	Wiltshire	4	112	
2nd South Western Mounted Brigade Company	Somerset	4	112	
1/1st East Anglian Division Transport & Supply Column (9)				No 9 District.
East Anglian Division HQ Company	Essex	8	215	Includes 14 2nd Line Drivers for 1 Yeomanry Regiment, Hertfordshire for South Midland Division, No 7 District and 1 Yeomanry Regiment, Northampton for North Midland Division, No 6 District.
Essex Brigade Company	Essex	4	97	
East Midland Brigade Company	Northampton	4	97	
Norfolk & Suffolk Brigade Company	Norfolk	4	97	
Eastern Mounted Brigade Company	Essex	4	112	
1/1st Home Counties Division Transport & Supply Column (10)				No 10 District.
Homes Counties Division HQ Company	Sussex	8	201	
Surrey Brigade Company	Surrey	4	97	
Middlesex Brigade Company	Middlesex	4	97	
Kent Brigade Company	Kent	4	109	Includes 12 2nd Line Drivers for 2 Infantry Battalions (Army Troops) in Sussex.
South East Mounted Brigade Company	Surrey	4	105	Less 7 2nd Line for Horse Artillery Battery provided by London Mounted Brigade ASC Company.

ASC Units	Location	Personnel		Remarks
		Offrs	Men	
1/1st London Division Transport & Supply Column (11)				London District.
1st London Division HQ Company	London	8	205	Includes 4 2nd Line Drivers for 1 Balloon, 1 Cable, 1 Airline and 1 Wireless Telegraph Company.
1st London Brigade Company	London	4	97	
City of London Brigade Company	London	4	97	
City of London Brigade Company	London	4	97	Includes 7 2nd Line Drivers for Horse Artillery Battery for South East Mounted Brigade, No 10 District and 3 for 1/2 Infantry Battalion.
London Mounted Brigade Company	City of London	4	122	
1/2nd London Division Transport & Supply Column (12)				
2nd London Division HQ Company	London	8	201	
2nd London Brigade Company	London	4	97	
3rd London Brigade Company	London	4	97	
4th London Brigade Company	London	4	97	
	TOTAL	336	8619	

NOTE:

Attached details from other Arms: 4 officers and 4 men should be added to each Division HQ Company. 1 officer and 2 men should be added to each Mounted Brigade Company.

(1) Subsequently 51st (Highland) Division Column/Train

(2) Subsequently 52nd (Lowland) Division Column/Train

(3) Subsequently 42nd (East Lancashire) Division Column/Train

(3a) Subsequently 55th (West Lancashire) Division Column/Train

(4) Subsequently 53rd (Welsh) Divison Column/Train

(5) Subsequently 50th (Northumbrian) Division Column/Train

(5a) Subsequently 49th (West Riding) Division Column/Train

(6) Subsequently 46th (North Midland) Division Column/Train

(7) Subsequently 61st (South Midland) Division Column/Train

(8) Subsequently 43rd (Wessex) Division Column/Train

(9) Subsequently 54th (East Anglian) Division Column/Train

(10) Subsequently 67th (Home Counties) Division Column/Train

(11) Subsequently 56th (London) Division Column/Train

(12) Subsequently 47th (London) Division Column/Train

Wagon Mounting & Dismounting Competition

Rules for
Dismounting and Packing GS Wagons and
Army Service Corps Harness for Shipment
(Royal Naval & Military Tournament 1908)
and Results 1903-1913

Dress: Review Order. Vests, belts and service pantaloons to be worn; dismounted men to wear blue putties and carry rifles.

1st Whistle. Dismounted men ground arms in rear, take off helmets and tunics and place them with arms neatly on the ground. They then assist the sergeant, drivers and spare men to unhook and take the horses to their places on the piquet lines, getting out and putting down the picketing gear and sacks for harness. The whole party then fall in, the wagon detachment in rear of wagon, and the remainder in rear of horses. Picket lines to be put down in line with lead horses. Helmets of drivers and spare men to be placed in line in front of horse lines.

NB: No straps or buckets are to be undone, and the neck collars are not to be turned round before the second whistle is blown. No time is taken, but 20 marks are given for quickness, smartness and style.

2nd Whistle. Sergeants, drivers and spare men unharness and pack harness and saddlery into sacks; wagon detachment dismount and pack wagon, then assist to put harness away. The whole fall in in their places as above, and stand at ease by order of the non-commissioned officer, when the time will be taken. One spare man to be on sentry on horse lines. Standard time, 1 minute. Full marks, 60.

Harnessing and Mounting Wagon

1st Whistle. Harness up, mount wagon, hook in, pack up picketing gear; the wagon detachment, as soon as they have finished mounting wagons, going to assist drivers.

Sergeant, drivers and spare men mount, and wagon detachment falls in, but do not put on helmets and tunics or take up arms.

Time will be taken directly last man has fallen in, or is mounted and ready to move off. No omission, etc can afterwards be rectified.

Standard time, 2 minutes.

2nd Whistle. Wagon detachment fall out, dress and take up arms, then fall in again in same place.

No marks given specially for this.

Notes

Sacks not to exceed 3 feet wide.
No shoe cases.
Quick release for pole chains allowed.
No carbines or buckets to be carried on horses.
ASC harness to be used.
No surcingles to be worn.
No breast harness to be worn.
Centre board of wagon not to be used.
GS Mark IV. Wagons to be used, with new Mark IV cover.
Head ropes to be fastened round horses necks.
No side reins to be used.

A certificate giving the weight of each wagon used (not including weight of wagon cover) will be handed to the judges on the first day of the competition.

RULES FOR MARKING

Deductions

Dismounting and Packing. 3 marks per second beyond standard time.

Pins, bolts, washers, etc left on ground, or found in men's possession	2 each
Wheels not properly packed dish down	5 each
Harness not completely packed in sack	5 each

Mounting and Hooking in. 3 marks per second beyond standard times.	
Linch pins, pole pins, or dragwashers not replaced	6 each
Hoop or rave stay ends not replaced	2 each
Keys not replaced	3 each
Parts broken and not able to be replaced	3 each
Any part of harness wrong	3 each

Additions

2 marks per second below standard time.

Results 1903-1913

1903:	Aldershot
1904:	Woolwich
1905:	Aldershot
1906:	Woolwich
1907:	Woolwich
1908:	Woolwich (No 2 (Depot) and 38 Companies)
1909:	Woolwich (No 2 (Depot) and 38 Companies)
1910:	Woolwich
1911:	Woolwich
1912:	Woolwich
1913:	Aldershot (1 and 36 Companies)

ASC Vehicles in 1910

Wagons

ASC Number	Make	Load (tons)	Year of Make	Cost (£)
1-50 (less 17)	Fowler	4	1903	74.00
17	Aveling & Porter	4		
51-54	Fowler	6	1901	79.00
55	Tasker	8	1903	181.00
57-58	Fowler	8	1901	75.00
59-60	Gloucester	8	1902	149.00
61-62	Tasker	8	1903	181.00
63	Fowler	3½	1904	74.00
64	Clayton & Shuttleworth	4		70.00
65-68	Fowler	6	1904	79.00
69-80	Fowler	3½	1904	74.00
81	Ruston Proctor	6		
82-87	Fowler	3½	1904	74.00
88	Gloucester	8	1902	149.00
89-99	Fowler	3½	1904	74.00
102-106	Fowler	6	1901	75.00
107-108	Fowler	8	1901	75.00
110-111	Fowler	6	1901	75.00
112-131	Wantage Co	3½	1906	57.00
132	Fowler	3½		57.00
133	Fowler	6	1901	75.00
134-151	Wantage	3½	1907	57.00
152-162	Fowler Armoured Trucks			
163	Aveling & Porter	4		
167-169	Marshall & Son	6		
170	Aveling & Porter	6		

ASC Number	Make	Load (tons)	Year of Make	Cost (£)
171	Marshall & Son	6		
172-198	Fowler	5	1909	56.00
199-201	Tasker	6		
202	Fowler	3		
203-204	Ruston Proctor	4		

Motor Traction Engines

ASC Number	ASC Company	Maker	Year of Make	Cost (£)
1	72	Fowler 'Lion'	1900	840.00
2	77	Fowler 'Lion'	1903	1714.00
4	72	Burrell 'Large'	1899	590.00
5	72	McLaren 'Crane'	1900	1152.00
7	Cambridge	Fowler 'Lion'	1903	1426.00
10-17	77 (3) 75 (4)	Fowler 'Lion'	1903	1426.00
18-19	74	Fowler 'Ursula'	1904	994.00
20-21	78	Fowler 'Doll'	1904	994.00
22-23	72	Wallis & Stevens 'Small'	1904	381.00
24-25	78	Tasker 'Little Giant'	1904	510.00
26	72	Hornsby I C Tractor		
28-29	Malta	Fowler 'Florence'	1903	1400.00
30	Malta	Fowler 'Lion'	1903	
31	Woolwich	Fowler 'Baby'	1905	925.00
32	74	Thornycroft I C Tractor	1905	850.00
34-35	74	Fowler 'Baby'	1905-06	870.00
37	72	Wolsely 30 hp Vertical	1908	950.00
38-43	78 (1) 73 (2) 76 (3)	Foster 'Small'	1906	477.00
44-47	76 (2) Malta (2)	Aveling & Porter 'Small'	1906	450.00
49	72	Aveling & Porter 'Large' (obsolete)	1906	

ASC Number	ASC Company	Maker	Year of Make	Cost (£)
50-55	73 (3) Cork 78 74	Foster 'Light'	1908	492.00
56-57	77	Burrell 'Small'	1908	549.00
58	72	Clayton & Shuttleworth 'Portable'	1908	
60-62	74 (2) 78 (Somaliland)	Fowler 'Light'	1909	490.00
63	74	Fowler 'Baby'	1909	490.00
64-65	76	Fowler 'Commercial'	1909	425.00
66-67	76	Aveling & Porter 'Commercial'	1909	463.00
68	74	Thornycroft I C 40 hp Vertical	1909	975.00
69	78	Fowler 'Doll'	1900	633.00
70-72	78 (2) 74	Thornycroft I C Tractor	1910	950.00
73-75	74 78 (2)	Hornsby I C Tractor	1910	850.00
76-80	73, 74, 76, 77, 78	Burrell 'Steam Jib'	1910	550.00
81-82	74, 76	Burrell 'Commercial'	1910	446.00
83-84	78	Fowler 'Commercial'	1910	425.00
85	74	Burrell 'Steam Jib'	1910	550.00
86	72	Hornsby 'Small Chain'	1910	1250.00

Motor Lorries

ASC Number	Maker	Year of Make	Cost (£)
1	IC Stirling	1903	
2-9	Steam Thornycroft	1903	600.00
13	Milnes Daimler 'Marienfeldt'	1904	645.00
15-16	Milnes Daimler 'Neustadt'	1904	810.00
19	Thornycroft 'Paraffin'	1907	500.00
20	Maudslay 'Petrol'	1908	835.00
21	Thornycroft 'Steam'		

ASC Number	Maker	Year of Make	Cost (£)
22	Thornycroft 'Steam'	1902	680.00
23-26	Straker-Squire		
27-28	Milnes Daimler I C	1910	640.00
29-30	Thornycroft I C	1910	618.00

Motor Ambulances

ASC Number	ASC Company	Maker	Year of Make	Cost (£)
1	78	Straker-Squire	1906	860.00
2	78	Siddeley	1908	649.00
3	77 (Portsmouth)	Siddeley	1908	649.00
4	77 (Tidworth)	Siddeley	1908	649.00
5	76 (Millbank)	Straker-Squire		620.00
6	Edinburgh	Straker-Squire		620.00
7	(Shorncliffe)	Straker-Squire		620.00
8	73	Straker-Squire		620.00
9	(Malta)	Leyland		

Motor Cars

ASC Number	ASC Company	Maker	Registered Number	Year of Make	Cost (£)
2	72	Wolseley	A 1551	1902	500.00
4	73	Wolseley	A 1553	1902	450.00
9	78	Wolseley	A 4321	1904	418.00
10	Cork	Wolseley	A 4322	1904	418.00
12	72	Wolseley	A 4324	1904	418.00
13	72	Wolseley	A 4325	1904	418.00
17	York	Wolseley	LC 837	1905	365.00
18	72	Wolseley	LC 838	1905	365.00
19	77	Wolseley	LC 839	1905	365.00
20	77	Siddeley	LC 4648	1906	

ASC Number	ASC Company	Maker	Registered Number	Year of Make	Cost (£)
21	London	Siddeley	LC 4649	1906	
22	Cork	Albion	LN 1520	1907	460.00
23	77	Siddeley	LN 1519	1907	317.00
24	Pretoria	Siddeley		1908	
25	London	Siddeley	LB 3014	1908	
26	73	Shamrock	AA 1876	1908	
27	77	Shamrock	AA 1877	1908	
28	78	Siddeley	AA 2506	1908	
29	Chester	Thornycroft	AA 2516	1908	
30	78	Star	AA 2566	1909	200.00
31	77	Vulcan	AA 2825	1909	422.00
32	Dublin	Vulcan	AA 2826	1909	422.00
33	London	Daimler	LD 2848	1909	
34	73	Swift	AA 2985	1910	274.00
35	76	Swift	AA 2986	1910	274.00
36	74	Swift	AA 2987	1910	274.00
37	Edinburgh	Arrol Johnston	AA 2988	1910	400.00
38	York	Arrol Johnston	AA 2990	1910	400.00
39	78	Arrol Johnston	AA 2989	1910	400.00

Sleeping Vans (Office Trucks)

ASC Number	ASC Company	Maker	Year of Make	Cost (£)
1-2	78	Gloucester		
3	78	Stagg & Robson	1902	
4	73	Wantage	1903	68.00
5	77	Wantage	1903	87.00
6-7	Malta	Stagg & Robson	1902	87.00 151.00
8	74	Stagg & Robson		151.00
9	72	Stagg & Robson		

224

Water Carts

ASC Number	ASC Company	Capacity	Year of Make
1	74	480 gallons	
2-4	78	350 gallons	
5	76	350 gallons	1905
6-7	Malta	450 gallons	
8	76	350 gallons	1905
9	77 (Bulford)	350 gallons	1905
10	Cork	350 gallons	1905
11-13	73	350 gallons	1905-06
14	76	350 gallons	1906
15-16	Bulford	350 gallons	1906
17	Somaliland	350 gallons	1906
18	73	350 gallons	1906
19-20	74	350 gallons	1907
21	72	350 gallons	1907

Expeditionary Force Tables November 1912
ASC Companies Allocated to Formations/Tasks

Formation	No 1 (HQ) Company	No 2 Company	No 3 Company	No 4 Company	No 5 Company
Cavalry Division Troops:	27	20	18	23	6
1 Division:	36	16	7	13	
2 Division:	39	11	28	31	
3 Division:	22	15	21	29	
4 Division:	25	32	10	41	
5 Division:	42	43	37	19	
6 Division:	17	33	8	24	
Army Troops:	26				

Lines of Communication

Cavalry Ammunition Park:	58 Company	)
No 1 Division Ammunition Park:	60 Company	)
No 2 Division Ammunition Park:	62 Company	)
No 3 Division Ammunition Park:	64 Company	) Plus Artillery personnel for the
No 4 Division Ammunition Park:	66 Company	) care of ammunition
No 5 Division Ammunition Park:	68 Company	)
No 6 Division Ammunition Park:	70 Company	)
Army Troops Ammunition Park:	56 Company	
Cavalry Supply Column:	57 Company	
1 Division Supply Column:	59 Company	
2 Division Supply Column:	61 Company	
3 Division Supply Column:	63 Company	
4 Division Supply Column	65 Company	
5 Division Supply Column	67 Company	
6 Division Supply Column;	69 Company	
Army Troops Supply Column:	55 Company	
Base MT Depot:	53 Company	
Advanced MT Depot:	54 Company	
Base HT Depot:	40 Company	
Advanced HT Depot:	14 Company	
No 1 Reserve Park:	9 Company	
No 2 Reserve Park:	30 Company	
No 3 Reserve Park:	34 Company	
No 4 Reserve Park:	38 Company	
No 5 Reserve Park:	44 Company	
No 6 Reserve Park:	5 Company	

Remounts

Establishment of ASC Remount Companies 1 November 1904

	A Company Woolwich	B Company Dublin	C Company Lusk	D Company Dublin	Totals
Warrant Officers	2	1	-	-	3
Company Sergeant Majors	1	1	1	1	4
Company Quartermaster Sergeants	1	1	1	1	4
Sergeants	8	2	2	2	14
Corporals	6	2	2	2	12
2nd Corporals	4	-	-	-	4
Privates	85 (1)	12 (2)	16 (2)	10	123
Farriers Quartermaster Sergeants	1	1	-	-	2
Staff Sergeants	1	1	1	1	4
Corporals	1	1	1	1	4
Shoeing Smiths	6	2	2	2	12
Totals	116	24	26	20	186

(1)   Includes 4 Lance Corporals
(2)   Includes 1 Lance Corporal

Remount Depots in UK 1915

Shrivenham
Romsey (March 1915)
Swaythling (Southampton)   (Board of Agriculture)
Liverpool
Avonmouth

Leicester   )
Melton Mowbray   )
York   )   Northern Command
Ripon   )
Croft   )

Rugby   )
Worcester   )
Strensham   )
Gloucester   )
Templecombe   )
Sherbourne   )   Southern Command
Hursley   )
Bulford   )
Rugeley Park   )
Purton   )
Gosport (17 August 1914)   )

Chester   )
Hardwick   )
Leighton   )   Western Command
Shrewsbury   )
Monmouth   )
Carmarthen   )

Pluckley (4 August 1914)   )
Brentwood (5 August 1914)   )
Luton (22 October 1917)   )   Eastern Command
Market Harborough (6 August 1914))
Kettering (30 June 1915)   )
Redhill (4 August 1914)   )

Aldershot (Eelmoor Bridge)   )   Aldershot Command
Arborfield Cross (pre-war)   )

Belfast   )
Bullsbridge, Dublin   )
Island Bridge   )   Irish Command
Lusk   )
The Curragh   )

Ayr   )   Scottish Command
St Boswells   )

228

No	Formed	Located At	Disposal
34	13 November 1917	BEF	Post November 1917
35	19 November 1917	Not known For Service with BEF	Not known
48	3 October 1916	Ormskirk	Not known
51	6 May 1915	Redhill	Disbanded June 1921
52	6 May 1915	Market Harborough	Disbanded
53	6 May 1915	Leicester	Disbanded 10 November 1919
54	15 May 1915	Arborfield Cross	March 1920 (replaced by a Remount Depot with civilian personnel)
55	24 May 1915	Newcastle-on-Tyne	Disbanded 1920
56	24 May 1915	York (moved to Romsey 16 January 1918)	Disbanded 1920
62	21 February 1917	York	Disbanded 20 September 1919
63	2 March 1917	Swaythling	Absorbed into the Remount Depot Luton on 30 October 1917
64	26 March 1917	Croft Spa	Disbanded 7 November 1919
65	6 October 1917	Woolwich	Not known
66	18 October 1917	Luton	Not known
67	5 January 1918	BEF	Not known
96	5 January 1918	Western Front (location not known)	For service with the BEF

MT Vehicles in the Army in August 1914

Vehicle	Northern Command	Southern Command	Eastern Command	Western Command	Aldershot Command	Irish Command	Scottish Command	Malta Command	South Africa	Egypt	Totals
Lorries	-	38	18	-	46	22	-	-	-	-	124
Cars	1	11	8	1	13	8	-	1	2	-	45
Ambulances	1	2	2	1	3	3	1	1	-	1	15
Motor cycles	-	6	4	-	9	4	-	1	-	-	24
Petrol tractors	-	-	1	-	6	-	-	-	-	-	7
Steam tractors	-	13	6	-	22	9	-	7	-	-	57
Wheeled trucks	-	40	18	-	81	31	-	18	-	-	188
Workshop trucks	-	5	2	-	6	5	-	-	-	-	18
Miscellaneous	-	8	2	-	12	3	-	4	-	-	29
Totals	2	123	61	2	198	85	1	32	2	1	507

Ambulance Donors 1914–1918

HM The King
HM The Queen
The Dowager Empress of Russia

Aberdeenshire
Australian Red Cross
Association of Saint Peters Collegians, South Australia
Ayrshire, Bonnie Jean
Bilbao Shipowners
The Boilermakers' and Shipbuilders' Society
Boot and Shoe Operatives
Bonnybridge
Bothwell
British Bowlers
British Esperantists
British Farmers Red Cross Fund (Cambridge County Branch)
British Farmers Red Cross Fund (Devonshire County Branch) Cullompton
    District Farmers
British Medical Men of Shanghai
British Red Cross Society/St John Ambulance Association
British Red Cross Society, Scottish Branch
British Sportsmen's Fund
Burnley Young Kitcheners
Bus, Cab and Tram Workers of London
Canadian Red Cross
Canadian Women (27 Field Ambulance)
Chemists' Assistants
Chiefs of Barwanldhar, Alirajpur and Jhabua Kathiawar States
The Children of Nova Scotia
City of Aberdeen
City of Calcutta (50 ambulances)
Clovelly
Clydeside
Coatbridge
Commercial Travellers of the United Kingdom
County of Fife
County of Fife Numbers 1-3
Cunard Line
Mr & Mrs Debenham, Melbourne (RA 629)
Director, Officers and Employees of the Glasgow and South Western Railway
Domestic Servants of England Fund
Drumsheugh
Dunblane
Duncavel (Duke & Duchess of Hamilton)

Dundee Numbers 1-6
Durham Miners Association
Edinburgh and Midlothian VAD
Elrick Adler. Presented by Friends in America
Enara
Employees Vickers Limited, River Don Works, Sheffield
Fair Maid of Perth
Federation of Master Cotton Spinners Association Ltd, Heywood & District
    Association
Fettesian-Lorettonian
Francis-Maud
Freemasons of North London
Freemasons of West Lancashire
Galashiels Number 2
Geo. M Inglis of Murlindon Memorial
Glasgow Corporation
Glasgow and District Bakers
For Grimsby Men, from Grimsby Folk
Grand Orange Lodge of Ireland
Hamilton L Hamilton
Hopeful
Heah Swee Lee
Hellenic Committees of London and Liverpool
James Dick's Trustees
James Hill Esq, Australia
J P Raynar Esq
Kilmacolm
Kirkcaldy
Lady Nairn
The Lady Sempill
The Lancashire, Cheshire and Isle of Man Province
Lancashire and Cheshire Miners Association
The Lau Island (Fiji)
Lochbrae
London Cartage Contractors
"Maindiff"
McCowan
Member and Friends of the Amalgamated Society of Watermen, Lightermen and
    Bargemen
Members of the Belvoir Hunt
Members of the British Medical Association in Australia
Members of Mr Fernie's Hunt
Members of Pytchley Hunt
Members of Tarporley Hunt
The Morgan Crucible Company Limited, Battersea SW
Morgan Grenfell Co Ltd, Battersea Works
Natal Farmers
New Club
Newmarket District Farmers
Oldham and District Trades and Labour Council

People of Barbados
People of Bahamas
People of Fiji
People of Jamaica
People of Hong Kong and Shanghai
People of West Indies
W B Perry & Compton, New South Wales, Australia
Primrose League
Proprietors of 'Punch' (Soup Kitchen)
Queenswood School, Clapham Park SW
Rag, Scrap, Metal and Waste Trades
Roxburghshire

Royal Antediluvian Order of the Buffaloes, Grand Lodge of England

> No 1
> No 2: The Nottingham Car
> No 8: The Nottingham Car
> No 9: The District of Gloucestershire

Royal York Lodge of Freemasons
Salvation Army
Schools of Barrow-in-Furness
Scotia's Iron Queen Numbers 1-2
Scottish Lassie Numbers 1-2
The Silver Thimble (No 2 + No 3 attached to London District)
Sir Walter Scott, Edinburgh Numbers 1-2
The Spiritualists of Great Britain (5 ambulances)
Stirling Centre Free Gift Sale (Scotland)
Stirlingshire
Sunday School Association
Thanet
Toungoo District, Burma
Union of Wrapping Paper Makers
United Provinces of India
Vanduara
Walneuk
Watermen, Lightermen and Bargemen (in connection with the Dennis Bayley
     Fund
West of Scotland Football Clubs
William Cullen
Wine and Spirit Trades
Wire Rope Makers
Women of Bermondsey
The Women's Liberal Federation
The Woolwich War Workers
Worshipful Company of Fishmongers
Worshipful Company of Haberdashers
Worshipful Company of Mercers
Various Districts in New Zealand

Woolwich War Workers Organisation
Workers of the National Fillers Factory, Hayes, Middlesex
Zara

Ambulances donated in 1915 to 419 Company ASC. Letters and numbers in brackets were the WD registration numbers.

Bensons, Bayley Fund, Warwickshire Coalfields, Owners & Men (RA 788)
Bensons, Bayley Fund, Warwickshire Coalfields, Owners & Men (RA 790)
Bensons, Bayley Fund, Warwickshire Coalfields, Owners & Men (RA 793)
The Blanche Ambulance (RA 728)
Borough of Halifax (RA 625)
Borough of Keighley (RA 613)
Borough of Merthyr Tydfil (RA 714)
Borough of Pool (RA 617)
Borough of Rotherham (RA 616)
Borough of Shoreditch (RA 643)
Borough of Southport (RA 631)
Borough of Warrington (RA 636)
Britons & Uruguyans of Uruguay (RA 702)
Charlotte, Charles, Caroline, Jessie Ambulance (RA 756)
Children of Rhodesia (RA 704)
Children of Rhodesia (RA 665)
City of Birmingham (RA 615)
City of Kington-on-Hull (RA 632)
City of London (RA 612)
City of Sheffield Magness Fleet (RA 633)
Constance, Dorothy, Nellie, Eleanor, Audrey Ambulance (RA 738)
County of Huntingdon (RA 614)
E B Creasy & Co, Colombo, Ceylon (RA 739)
The Croydon Ambulance (RA 635)
In memory of Captain the Honorable G H Douglas-Pennant (RA 618)
Earl of Harwood & Viscount Boyne (RA 630)
Elementary Schools of Sheffield (RA 703)
Employees of Messrs Vickers Limited, Crayford (RA 791)
Farmers & Landowners of the area of Clitheroe & Bowland (RA 666)
The Harrogate Ambulance (RA 619)
The Hellenes of Liverpool (RA 792)
Isobel, Lilian, Grace, Geraldine, Frances, Vera Ambulance (RA 489)
Jean, Jane, John, Sydney, Leila, Sophie Ambulance (RA 689)
Kings Norton Metal Co, Birmingham Metal, Ammunition & Eley Bros Limited
    (RA 718)
Kynocks Limited (RA 626)
Lloyd Jones family (RA 715)
Members of Ceylon Chamber of Commerce (RA 620)
Mildred, Effie Ambulance (RA 490)
Miss Dow of Montreal (RA 713)
Mrs Alfred H Heath (RA 789)
Mrs Urban H Broughton (RA 623)
North Caucasian Oilfields (RA 721)

(Not known) (RA 624)

The Augusta Ambulance (RA 491)

The Leather Trade Federation & Worshipful Company of Leather Sellers (RA 622)

Reginald C Cory Esq (RA 720)

Residents of Milford-on-Sea (RA 621)

The Three Penny Stamps Car (RA 672)

United Provinces War Fund (RA 1205)

Winifred and Alice (RA 488)

Labour Companies ASC

No	Formed On	Disposal	Served In
1	24 August 1914	Absorbed into Labour Corps June 1917	BEF (Le Havre/St Valery)
2	25 August 1914	Absorbed into Labour Corps June 1917	BEF (Rouen)
3	14 September 1914	Absorbed into Labour Corps June 1917	BEF (Abancourt)
4	4 October 1914	Absorbed into Labour Corps 25 March 1917	BEF (Boulogne)
5	6 October 1914	Absorbed into Labour Corps June 1917	BEF (Le Havre, Marseilles, Dunkirk)
6	30 December 1914	For service with AOD in France. Absorbed into Labour Corps June 1917	BEF (Le Havre)
7	8 February 1915	Not known	BEF (Dieppe, Abbeville)
8	25 April 1915	Absorbed into Labour Corps June 1917	BEF (Rouen, Abbeville, Dunkirk, Abancon)
9	1 April 1915	Absorbed into Labour Corps June 1917	BEF (Calais)
10	2 May 1915	Absorbed into Labour Corps June 1917	BEF (Boulogne, Audruicq)
11	11 May 1915	Absorbed into Labour Corps June 1917	BEF (Boulogne)
12	15 May 1915	Absorbed into Labour Corps June 1917	BEF (Calais)
13	27 May 1915	Absorbed into Labour Corps June 1917	BEF (Calais)
14	3 June 1915	Absorbed into Labour Corps June 1917	BEF (Le Havre)
15	4 July 1915	Absorbed into Labour Corps June 1917	BEF (Le Havre)
16	12 July 1915	Absorbed into Labour Corps June 1917	BEF (Rouen)
17	15 August 1915	Disbanded 25 March 1917	BEF (Dunkirk, Calais, Abancon)
18	17 July 1915	Absorbed into Labour Corps June 1917	BEF (Calais, Dunkirk, Gallipoli))
19	29 August 1915	Absorbed into Labour Corps June 1917	BEF (Calais, Dunkirk)
20	7 September 1915	Absorbed into Labour Corps June 1917	BEF (Rouen, Abancourt, Dieppe)
21	19 December 1915	Disbanded 25 March 1917	BEF (Boulogne, Abancourt, Calais, Dieppe, Etaples)
22	25 October 1915	Absorbed into Labour Corps 1 April 1917	BEF (Boulogne, Dunkirk, Calais, Audruicq, Marseilles)
23	1 November 1915	Disbanded 25 March 1917	BEF (Rouen)
24	5 October 1915	Absorbed into Labour Corps June 1917	BEF (Boulogne, Calais, Dieppe)
25	9 October 1915	Absorbed into Labour Corps June 1917	MEF (Salonika)
26	5 November 1915	Disbanded 25 March 1917	BEF (Boulogne, Calais)
27	14 October 1915	Absorbed into Labour Corps June 1917	BEF (Abancourt, Dieppe)
28	12 November 1915	Absorbed into Labour Corps June 1917	MEF (Salonika)
29	12 November 1915	Absorbed into Labour Corps 8 April 1917	MEF (Salonika)
30	26 November 1915	Disbanded 8 April 1917. Personnel transferred to Royal Marines	BEF (Le Havre, St Valery, Calais, Dunkirk)
31	17 January 1916	Absorbed into Labour Corps June 1917	BEF (Calais, Dunkirk)
32	31 January 191	Absorbed into Labour Corps June 1917	BEF (Audruicq)

No	Formed On	Disposal	Served In
33	8 December 1914	Disbanded 15 June 1917	BEF (Railways)
34	18 October 1915	Absorbed into Labour Corps June 1917	BEF (Railways)
35	17 December 1914	Disbanded 14 January 1915. Personnel transferred to Royal Marines	BEF (Naval)
36	Not Known	No details known	BEF (Naval)
37	25 February 1916	Absorbed into Labour Corps 1 February 1917. Personnel transferred to the Royal Marines	BEF
38	23 March 1916	Formed from Supply personnel in 395, 396, 397, 398, 441 and 442 Companies ASC. Disbanded 20 July 1917	Stationed in London for local duty

Resupply Chain

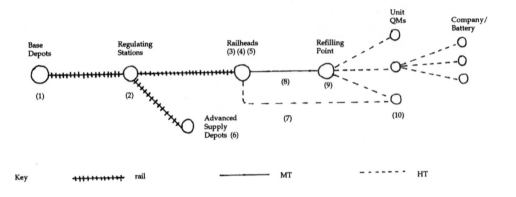

Key   +++++++++++   rail   —————————   MT   - - - - - - -   HT

Notes:

(1) Calais and Boulogne were the Base Depots for the Northern Line of Communication, and Dieppe, Le Havre and Rouen were the Base Depots for the Southern Line of Communication. The Northern ports received all kinds of commodities, whereas the Southern ports each dealt exclusively with one commodity only (petrol, forage or preserved supplies).

(2) Abbeville and Romescamps were the Regulating Stations for the Southern Line of Communication. A Regulating Station provided an essential control point for the onward movement of supplies by reorganizing loads on a Divisional basis under the direction of a Railhead Supply Officer, usually a subaltern.

(3) Issues from the Railhead were made by the Railhead Supply Officer. Supplies were collected by the Supply Officers of Brigade/Divisional Troops using MT vehicles of the Divisional Supply Column.

(4) Corps Troops units' supplies were drawn at the Railhead using MT vehicles of the Corps Troops Supply Column, then delivered to Corps Dumps where bulk items were broken down and delivered direct to units.

(5) When the Railhead was located in a forward area the Refilling Point would be located if possible in the station yard, so, instead of using Reserve Park MT vehicles, supplies were loaded directly onto HT wagons of the Divisional Train, which then delivered direct to unit QMs, obviating the need for off-loading at the Refilling Point.

(6) The Advanced Depot for the Northern Line of Communication was at Outreau and for the Southern Line of Communication at Abancourt.

(7) Later in the war, when Reserve Park Companies were reorganized, HT wagons of the Divisional Train took supplies from the Railhead to unit QMs via the Refilling Point, thus making MT vehicles available for other tasks.

(8) Movement between the Railhead and Refilling Point was by MT vehicles of the Divisional Supply Column or Reserve Park Company.

(9) Supplies were normally broken down into four dumps at the Refilling Point, one for each of the three Brigades and one for Divisional Troops.

(10) If forward operations were envisaged troops drew 'Fortress' or 'Barrage' rations, which were dumped in the rear of the unit or behind the trenches so as to cover the possibility of an interruption to routine resupply.

Regimental Prefixes and Numbers

Prefix	Branch	
Prefix	**Branch**	
M/	Mechanical Transport	
R/	Remounts	
S/	Supply	
T/	Horse Transport	
A (HT)	Horse Transport (Special Reserve)	
B (HT)	Horse Transport (Special Reserve) (TF)	
C (MT)	Mechanical Transport (Special Reserve)	
C (MT)	Mechanical Transport (Special Reserve)	
T1 & 2/(SR)	Horse Transport	) Enlisted Special
M1 & 2/(SR)	Mechanical Transport	) Reserve for New
	S1 & 2/(SR) Supply	) Armies
MS	Mechanical Specials	)
SS	Supply Specials and Labour	) Special Enlistments
TS	Transport Specials	)
RS and R/TS	Remount Specials	
T1, 2, 3 and 4	Horse Transport	)
S1, 2, 3 and 4	Supply (S4 Labour)	) 1st, 2nd, 3rd and 4th
R4, RX4	Remounts	) New Armies
M1 and 2	Mechanical Transport	)
DM/2	Mechanical Transport Learners	
F	Forage (not paid from Army Funds)	
E	Forage (ordinary rates of Army Pay for Army Service Corps)	
PET	Petroleum Department	
Canteen Section	Categories A and E were first allotted, and represent: (A) Accountants (Clerks); (E) Employees (Workmen). Later, Categories A and B were allotted, and represent: (A) Employees (Workmen); (B) Accountants (Clerks)	
SA and Africa	Colonial Enlistments, ASC (HT)	

EM	Mechanical Transport	) After War — Army
ER	Remounts	) Re-enlistments under
ES	Supply	) AO 4/19
ET	Horse Transport	)

Retain former category prefix	Armies of Occupation, Volunteers for one year's further service

Notes
Discontinuance of Branch Category Prefixes

With a view to simplifying the question of Regimental Numbers and Prefixes in the ASC, it was decided from 20 November 1916, inclusive, to discontinue the use of the /2/ and the /4/ as denoting the New Army numbers, and simply to use the T, S, M or R as the case might be.

The allotment of 'DM/2/' regimental numbers was also discontinued in November 1916.

Regimental Numbers ASC

An ever present difficulty in dealing with ASC accounts is the repetition of the same regimental number in different categories. Sometimes men of the same name have been allotted similar numbers, the difference being one of category only; therefore, before taking action in regard to any correspondence or voucher, it is essential that the category prefix, as well as the regimental number, as shown thereon, be carefully compared with the record on the soldier's pay sheet.

In a few cases men had been given two numbers, or were associated with even three or four, belonging to other men of the same name, the whole of their pay transaction being mixed on perhaps a couple of pay sheets.

Alterations in Prefix and Regimental Numbers
Inter-Branch Transfers

Prior to December 1917, the usual procedure in such cases was to allocate an entirely new prefix letter and regimental number, providing the transfer placed the soldier in a different category for pay; otherwise the category prefix letter only was altered, the soldier retaining the same regimental number. There were, however, a few exceptions to this rule, as in the case of T4 Labourers.

Prior to the institution of category R4 specially enlisted personnel for the Remount Branch were allotted regimental numbers in the TS series, but such men were afterwards allotted the additional prefix letter R, to distinguish them from Transport Special Enlistments.

From December 1917 regimental numbers of transfers within the Corps are dealt with as follows:

- Men serving on normal engagements retain their regimental numbers, but the category letter is altered according to the branch (HT, Supply, MT or R) to which transferred.

- Specially enlisted men of categories SS, TS, R/TS, MS and Expeditionary Force Canteens, if transferred to a New Army branch, receive a fresh New Army number.

- Men of the New Armies (Duration of War), categories T or S, receive a fresh New Army number on transfer to the MT branch, and men of the MT branch transferred to other New Army branches are similarly dealt with. Transfers from Transport to Supply (New Army), or *vice versa*, retain their numbers and change the prefix letter only.

- Soldiers of the Remount branch, other than in the first paragraph above, transferred to any other branch of the ASC, or *vice versa*, receive fresh regimental numbers.

- Men serving on Duration of War engagements on re-transfer from other Arms of the Service to a branch of the Corps other than that from which originally transferred, receive fresh New Army numbers (eg a soldier belonging to the Horse Transport branch of the ASC transferred to the Infantry and re-transferred to the MT branch of the ASC). If re-transferred to the same branch they resume the regimental number held prior to transfer.

Territorial Force Postings to Regular Establishments
July and September 1916

New regimental numbers were given within the New Army series to all Territorial Force personnel so transferred under ACI 1677 of 1916 etc. They did not receive any distinguishing prefix letter, except that of the particular branch of the ASC to which posted.

Local Numbers

In the early part of the war local identity numbers were given to certain ASC personnel owing to their being drafted, or detached for duty, before regimental numbers were allotted.

These temporary numbers were associated with categories as follows and may still be found quoted on certain documents. In a few instances the soldiers' kit numbers were used.

Prefix	Category
GP	*'Grove Park'* MT personnel (Recruits) — correct prefix 'M2' etc. Used on AFD 418, etc, and copied on to W 3085 in certain cases
SL	*'Special Supply'* Labour Category — correct prefix 'SS'
STA	*'Special Transport Aldershot'* (Posted to 1 Company HT ASC) Category: Horse Transport — correct prefix 'TS'. (Enlisted under the conditions of Army Order 283/14)
LDT	*'Lahore Divisional Train'* HT Drivers ASC, posted to IEF early in 1914 — correct prefix 'T1'-'T2'
IB	*'Indian Base Details'* Category 'S'/.Loaders detailed for Supply Columns, subsequently stationed at Indian Base, Marseilles (No 2 Labour Camp)

Annex N

Unit Establishments

Divisional Train
Four Horse Transport Companies ASC

War Establishment

April 1912

(1) Personnel and Horses

Detail	Personnel							Horses			
	Offrs	WOs	SSgts & Sgts	Arti-ficers	Trump-eters	R & F	Total	Riding	Draught	Pack	Total
Headquarters (including attached)	5	-	2	-	-	9	16	6	5	1	12
Headquarters Company:											
Transport details	4	1	7	25	1	200	238	16	280	-	296
Supply details	2	-	3	-	-	17	22	1	-	-	1
Transport details (detached)	-	-	-	-	-	*3*	*3*	-	-	-	-
Other Companies:											
1. Transport details	3	1	4	14	1	82	105	12	104	-	116
Supply details	2	-	3	-	-	17	22	1	-	-	1
Transport details - (detached)	-	-	*3*	-	-	*60*	*63*	-	-	-	-
2. Transport details	3	1	4	14	1	82	105	12	104	-	116
Supply details	2	-	3	-	-	17	22	1	-	-	1
Transport details - (detached)	-	-	*3*	-	-	*60*	*63*	-	-	-	-
3. Transport details	3	1	4	14	1	82	105	12	104	-	116
Supply details	2	-	3	-	-	17	22	1	-	-	1
Transport details - (detached)	-	-	*3*	-	-	*60*	*63*	-	-	-	-
										-	
Total Divisional Train (including attached but excluding detached personnel)	26	4	42	67	4	523	657	62	597	1	660

Details Left at the Base
(Not included in the above totals)

Drivers (storemen)	-	-	-	-	-	4	)				
First reinforcement:							)				
							) 87				
Transport	1	-	2	-	-	73	)	-	-	-	-
Supply	-	-	-	-	-	7	)				

(2) Transport

Detail	Headquarters and Headquarters Company			Three Companies			Total		
		Horses			Horses			Horses	
	Vehicles	Draught	Pack	Vehicles	Draught	Pack	Vehicles	Draught	Park
Bicycles:									
For inter-communication	2	-	-	-	-	-	2	-	-
For requisitioning duties and inter-communication	7	-	-	21	-	-	28	-	-
Pack animals for veterinary equipment	-	-	1	-	-	-	-	-	1
Cart, Maltese, for medical equipment	1	1	-	-	-	-	1	1	-
Wagons GS for postal service	1	4	-	-	-	-	1	4	-
Carts:									
Forage, for technical equipment	1	2	-	3	6	-	4	8	-
Water			-	3	6	-	4	8	-
Wagons GS:	1	2							
For baggage, stores, material for repairs and forges etc	2	8	-	6	21	-	8	32	-
Cooks	2	8	-	6	24	-	8	32	-
Spare draught horses	-	26	-	-	30	-	-	56	-
Motor-car for supply and requisitioning duties	1	-	-	3	-	-	4	-	-
Total on mobilization	18	51	1	42	90	-	60	141	-
Baggage Section									
Cart, forage, for headquarters and divisional engineers	1	2	-	-	-	-	1	2	-
Wagons GS:									
For headquarters of division	2	8	-	-	-	-	2	8	-
For headquarters of divisional artillery	1	4	-	-	-	-	1	4	-
For 3 field artillery brigades	15	60	-	-	-	-	15	60	-
For field artillery howitzer brigade	5	20	-	-	-	-	5	20	-
For heavy artillery battery & ammunition column	1	4	-	-	-	-	1	4	-
For divisional ammunition column	5	20	-	-	-	-	5	20	-
For 2 mounted infantry companies	2	8	-	-	-	-	2	8	-
For headquarters of 3 infantry brigades	-	-	-	3	12	-	3	12	-
For 12 infantry battalions	-	-	-	24	96	-	24	96	-
Supply Section									
Carts:									
For headquarters of division	1	2	-	-	-	-	1	2	-
For headquarters of divisional artillery	1	2	-	-	-	-	1	2	-
For headquarters of divisional engineers	1	2	-	-	-	-	1	2	-
For signal company with division	1	2	-	-	-	-	1	2	-
For headquarters of 3 infantry brigades	-	-	-	3	6	-	3	6	-

Detail	Headquarters and Headquarters Company			Three Companies			Total		
	Vehicles	Horses		Vehicles	Horses		Vehicles	Horses	
		Draught	Pack		Draught	Pack		Draught	Park
Wagons GS:									
For 3 field artillery brigades	12	48	-	-	-	-	12	48	-
For field artillery howitzer brigade	4	16	-	-	-	-	4	16	-
For heavy artillery battery & ammunition column	1	4	-	-	-	-	1	4	-
For divisional ammunition column	4	16	-	-	-	-	4	16	-
For 2 mounted infantry companies	2	8	-	-	-	-	2	8	-
For 2 field companies	2	8	-	-	-	-	2	8	-
For 12 infantry battalions	-	-	-	24	96	-	24	96	-
For 3 field ambulances	-	-	-	3	12	-	3	12	-
Total transport of divisional train after concentration	79	285	1	99	312	-	178	597	1

An Auxiliary (Petrol) Company ASC
((L of C)
(Headquarters and 3 Sections, each of 15 Petrol Lorries)

War Establishment

November 1916

Detail	Offrs	WOs	SSgts & Sgts	Arti-ficers	R & F	Total	Motor Cars	Motor Cycles	Lorries, 3 ton Steam	Lorries, Work-shop	Lorries, Store
Headquarters	2	2	2	12	16	34	1	1	1	1	1
1st Section	1	-	1	-	36	38	-	1	15	-	-
2nd Section	1	-	1	-	36	38	-	1	15	-	-
3rd Section	1	-	1	-	36	38	-	1	15	-	-
Total	5	2	5	12	124	148	1	4	46	1	1
Headquarters											
Captain	1	-	-	-	-	1	-	-	-	-	-
Subaltern	1	-	-	-	-	1	-	-	-	-	-
Warrant Officer (Class 1)	-	1	-	-	-	1	-	-	-	-	-
Company serjeant-major	-	1	-	-	-	1	-	-	-	-	-
Company quartermaster-serjeant	-	-	1	-	-	1	-	-	-	-	-
Serjeant	-	-	1	-	-	1	-	-	-	-	-
Foreman (staff-serjeant)	-	-	-	1	-	1	-	-	-	-	-
Fitters and turners	-	-	-	6	-	6)	-	-	-	-	-
Blacksmiths	-	-	-	2	-	2)	-	-	-	-	-
Wheelers	-	-	-	2	-	2) (a)	-	-	-	-	-
Electrician	-	-	-	1	-	1)	-	-	-	-	-
Driver, MT:											
For motor car	-	-	-	-	1)	1	1	-	-	-	-
For motor cycle	-	-	-	-	1)	1	-	1	-	-	-
For workshop lorry	-	-	-	-	2) (b)	2	-	-	-	1	-
For store lorry	-	-	-	-	2)	2	-	-	-	-	1
For headquarters lorry	-	-	-	-	2)	2	-	-	1	-	-
Spare	-	-	-	-	6)	6	-	-	-	-	-
Batmen	-	-	-	-	2	2	-	-	-	-	-
Total Headquarters	2	2	2	12	16	34	1	1	1	1	1

(a) Includes 2 serjeants and 2 corporals

(b) Includes 1 corporal and 1 lance corporal

An Auxiliary (Steam) Company ASC
(Headquarters and 3 Sections (each of 15 Steam Lorries))

War Establishment

November 1916

	Offrs	WOs	SSgts & Sgts	Arti- ficers	R & F	Total	Motor Cars	Motor Cycles	Lorries, 3 ton Steam	Lorries, Work- shop	Lorries, Store
Headquarters	2	2	2	15	16	37	1	1	1	1	1
1st Section	1	-	1	-	36	38	-	-	15	-	-
2nd Section	1	-	1	-	36	38	-	-	15	-	-
3rd Section	1	-	1	-	36	38	-	-	15	-	-
Total	5	2	5	15	124	151	1	1	46	1	1
Headquarters											
Captain	1	-	-	-	-	1	-	-	-	-	-
Subaltern	1	-	-	-	-	1	-	-	-	-	-
Warrant Officer (Class 1)	-	1	-	-	-	1	-	-	-	-	-
Company serjeant-major	-	1	-	-	-	1	-	-	-	-	-
Company quartermaster-serjeant	-	-	1	-	-	1	-	-	-	-	-
Serjeant	-	-	1	-	-	1	-	-	-	-	-
Foreman (staff-serjeant)	-	-	-	1	-	1	-	-	-	-	-
Fitters and turners	-	-	-	7)	-	7	-	-	-	-	-
Blacksmiths	-	-	-	2)	-	2	-	-	-	-	-
Wheeler	-	-	-	1) (a)	-	1	-	-	-	-	-
Coppersmith	-	-	-	1)	-	1	-	-	-	-	-
Boilermakers	-	-	-	2)	-	2	-	-	-	-	-
Electrician	-	-	-	1)	-	1	-	-	-	-	-
Driver, MT:											
For motor car	-	-	-	-	1	1	1	-	-	-	-
For motor cycle	-	-	-	-	1	1	-	1	-	-	-
For workshop lorry	-	-	-	-	2	2	-	-	-	1	-
For store lorry	-	-	-	-	2	2	-	-	-	-	1
For headquarters lorry	-	-	-	-	2	2	-	-	1	-	-
Spare	-	-	-	-	6	6	-	-	-	-	-
Batmen	-	-	-	-	2	2	-	-	-	-	-
Total Headquarters	2	2	2	15	16	37	1	1	1	1	1

(a)   Includes 2 serjeants and 2 corporals

II - For each Section of 15 Steam Lorries

	Offrs	WOs	SSgts & Sgts	Arti- ficers	R & F	Total	Motor Cars	Motor Cycles	Lorries, 3 ton Steam	Lorries, Work- shop	Lorries, Store
Subaltern	1	-	-	-	-	1	-	-	-	-	-
Serjeant	-	-	1	-	-	1	-	-	-	-	-
Corporal	-	-	-	-	1	1	-	-	-	-	-
Drivers, MT:											
For lorries	-	-	-	-	30	30	-	-	15	-	-
Spare	-	-	-	-	4	4	-	-	-	-	-
Batman	-	-	-	-	1	1	-	-	-	-	-
Total for each Section	1	-	1	-	36	38	-	-	15	-	-

Notes:

1.   Additional Sections, each of 15 steam lorries, can be added as required.

2.   Add, for the fourth and subsequent section which may be allotted, artificers as under:

   Fitters   2   Blacksmith   1   Wheeler   1

Army Troops Supply Column

War Establishment

November 1916

Detail	Personnel					Vehicles						
	Offrs	SSgts & Sgts	Arti-ficers	R & F	Total	Motor Cars	Motor Cycles	Mobile Laboratory 5 ton	Lorries 3 ton	Lorries 30 cwt	Lorries Work-shop	Lorries Store
Transport details	2	1	12	38	53	1	1	-	-	6	1	1
Transport details (detached)	-	*1*	-	*60*	*61*	*19 (a)*	-	*1*	*8*	*10*	-	-
	1	-	-	7	8	-	-	-	-	-	-	-
Supply details	1	2	-	3	6	-	-	-	-	-	-	-
Attached (ordnance services)												
Total supply column (including attached)	4	3	12	48	67	1	1	-	-	6	1	1

(a) 1 with box body

Corps Troops Supply Column
One Mechanical Transport Company ASC

War Establishment

October 1916

Detail	Personnel						Vehicles					
	Offrs	WOs	SSgts & Sgts	Arti-ficers	R & F	Total	Motor Cars	Motor Cycles	Lorries 3 ton	Lorries, 30 cwt	Lorries, Work-shop	Lorries, Store
Transport details	3	-	2	12	45	62	2	2	7	4	1	1
Supply details	1	-	-	-	12	13	-	-	-	-	-	-
Attached	1	1	1	-	3	6	-	-	-	-	-	-
Total supply column (including attached)	5	1	3	12	60	81	2	2	7	4	1	1

Divisional Supply Column
One Mechanical Transport Company ASC

War Establishment

August 1915

(1) Personnel

Detail	Personnel						Remarks
	Offrs	WOs	SSgts & Sgts	Arti-ficers	R & F	Total	
Transport and workshop detail	4	2	5	24	234	269	
Transport details detached	-	-	3	-	63	66	
Supply details	1	-	1	-	67	69	
Attached:							
Interpreter	-	-	-	-	1 (a)	1	(a)
Army postal service	-	-	-	-	3	3	Provided by French authorities after disembarkation.
Total supply column (including attached)	5	2	6	24	305	342	

(2) Transport

Detail	Motor Cars	Motor Cycles	3 ton Lorries	30 cwt Lorries	Workshop Lorries	Store Lorries	Drivers
For postal service	-	-	-	2	-	-	4
For supplies	-	-	30	-	-	-	60
For hay and oats	-	-	-	14	-	-	28
For ordnance stores	-	-	4	-	-	-	8
For first aid repairs	-	-	3	-	-	-	6
25 per cent for reliefs	-	-	8	-	-	-	16
For personnel	2	7	-	-	-	-	2
For workshop	-	-	-	-	2	2	8
Total	2	7	45	16	2	2	132

Mechanical Transport for a Siege Artillery Battery
(12 inch Mark II Howitzers)
(Western Front)

War Establishment

August 1915

(1) Personnel

Detail	Offrs	WOs	SSgts & Sgts	Artificers	R & F	Total	Remarks
Captain	1	-	-	-	-	-	
Subalterns (a)	3	-	-	-	-	-	(a)
Mechanist serjeant-major	-	1	-	-	-	-	Includes 2 for workshops
Company serjeant-major	-	1	-	-	-	-	
Company quartermaster-serjeant	-	-	1	-	-	-	
Artificers:							
Foremen	-	-	-	2	-	2	
Fitters and turners	-	-	-	12	-	12	)
Blacksmiths	-	-	-	4	-	4	) Includes 4 sergeants
Wheelers	-	-	-	4	-	4	) and 4 corporals
Electricians	-	-	-	2	-	2	)
) Serjeants	-	-	2	-	-	2	
) for tractors	-	-	-	-	39	39	
Drivers) for lorries	-	-	-	-	52	52	) Includes 8 corporals and
) for motor cars	-	-	-	-	4	4	) 8 lance-corporals
) spare	-	-	-	-	47	47	)
Batmen	-	-	-	-	4	4	
Total	4	2	3	24	146	179	

(2) Transport

Details	Vehicles					Remarks
	Motor Cars	Motor Cycles	3 ton Lorries	30 cwt Lorries	Caterpillar Tractors	
For howitzers and equipment	-	-	-	-	12	
For ammunition	-	-	8	-	-	
For baggage and stores	-	-	10	-	-	
For personnel	2 (b)	5 (c)	-	-	-	(b) One for Royal Artillery
For workshops	-	-	2	-	-	(c) Three for RA
For workshop stores	-	-	2	-	-	(1 with side car)
For workshop personnel	2	4	-	2	-	
Spare lorries and tractors	-	-	2	-	1	
Total	4	9	24	2	13	

Mechanical Transport for a Siege Artillery Battery
(Egypt and Mesopotamia)

War Establishment
1917

Personnel

Detail	Offrs	WOs	SSgts & Sgts	Artfers	R & F	Total	Motor cars	Motor cycles
Headquarters & Workshop								
Captain	1	-	-	-	-	1	1	-
Subaltern (1)	1		-	-	-	1	-	1
Mechanist Sergeant Major	-	1	-	-	-	1	-	1
Company Sergeant Major	-	1	-	-	-	1	-	-
Company Quartermaster Sergeant	-	1	1	-	-	1	-	-
Workshop								
Foreman (MSM)	-	-	-	2	-	2	-	-
Fitters & Turners	-	-	-	12)	-	12	-	-
Blacksmiths	-	-	-	4) (2)	-	4	-	2
Wheelers	-	-	-	4)	-	4	-	-
Electricians	-	-	-	2)	-	2	-	-
Spare Drivers								
For lorries	-	-	-	-	12)	12	-	-
For motor cars	-	-	-	-	1) (3)	1	-	-
For tractors	-	-	-	-	8)	8	-	-
Batmen	-	-	-	-	2	2	-	-
Cooks	-	-	-	-	2	2	-	-
Total Headquarters & Workshop	2	2	1	24	25	54	1	4
Each of the four sections								
Subaltern	1	-	-	-	-	1	1	-
Sergeants	-	-	2	-	-	2	-	1
Drivers								
For tractors	-	-	-	-	18)	18	-	-
For motor cars	-	-	-	-	1) (3)	1	-	-
Batmen	-	-	-	-	1	1	-	-
Total	1	-	2	-	20	23	1	1
Total four sections	4	-	8	-	80	92	4	4
Total Company	6	2	9	24	105	146	5	8

Notes:

(1)   Workshop officer
(2)   Includes 4 Sergeants and 4 Corporals
(3)   Includes 1 Corporal and 1 Lance Corporal

Transport

Detail	For haulage of Guns	For Baggage & Stores	For Workshop	For Workshop Stores	For Personnel	Total
Headquarters						
Motor cars	-	-	-	-	1	1
Motor cycles	-	-	-	-	4	4
Heavy lorries	-	1	-	-	-	1
Workshop	-	-	2	-	-	2
Workshop stores	-	-	-	2	-	2
Drivers	-	2	4	4	1	11
For each of Nos 1-4 Sections						
Motor cars	-	-	-	-	1	1
Motor cycles	-	-	-	-	1	1
Trailers	12	-	-	-	-	12
Tractors	6	-	-	-	-	6
Drivers	18	-	-	-	1	19
Totals						
Motor cars	-	-	-	-	-	5
Motor cycles	-	-	-	-	-	8
Heavy lorries	-	-	-	-	-	1
Workshop	-	-	-	-	-	2
Workshop stores	-	-	-	-	-	2
Tractors	-	-	-	-	-	24
Trailers	-	-	-	-	-	48
Drivers	-	-	-	-	-	87

Divisional Ammunition Park
(Territorial Division)

One Mechanical Transport Company ASC

War Establishment

August 1915

(1) Personnel

Detail	Personnel					
	Offrs	WOs	SSgts & Sgts	Artificers	R & F	Total
Headquarters	2	1	2	36	79	120
Headquarters attached	1	-	-	-	2	3
No 1 Section	1	-	2	-	64	67
No 1 Section attached	-	-	1	-	22	23
No 2 Section	1	-	2	-	43	46
No 2 Section attached	-	-	1	-	14	15
No 3 Section	1	-	2	-	55	58
No 3 Section attached	-	-	1	-	18	19
Total (excluding attached)	5	1	8	36	241	291
Total (including attached)	6	1	11	36	297	351

(2) Transport

Detail	Headquarters and Workshop		No 1 Section		No 2 Section		No 3 Section		Total	
	Vehicles	Drivers MT	Vehicles	Drivers MT	Vehicles	Drivers MT	Vehicles	Drivers MT	Vehicles	Drivers MT
Motor cars	1	1	1	1	1	1	1	1	4	4
Motor cycles	9	-	-	-	-	-	-	-	9	-
Workshop lorries	3	6	-	-	-	-	-	-	3	6
Store lorries	3	6	-	-	-	-	-	-	3	6
Lorries - 3 ton:										
For stores, spares etc	3	6	-	-	-	-	-	-	3	6
For first aid repairs	3	6	-	-	-	-	-	-	3	6
Spare	9	18	-	-	-	-	-	-	9	18
For 15 pr ammunition	-	-	20	40	-	-	-	-	20	40
For 5 inch howitzer ammunition	-	-	-	-	13	26	-	-	13	26
For SAA	-	-	-	-	-	-	17	34	17	34
Total	31	43	21	41	14	27	18	35	84	146

252

Ammunition Park
(Territorial Force)

War Establishment

April 1915

(1) Personnel

Detail	Personnel						Remarks
	Offrs	WOs	SSgts & Sgts	Arti-ficers	R & F	Total	
Army Service Corps details	-	-	-	-	12	12	
Attached:							
For care of ammunition (a)	-	-	-	-	4	4	(a) Provided by the Royal Artillery
Total (including attached)	-	-	-	-	16	16	

(2) Transport

Detail	Lorries	Drivers	Remarks
3 ton lorries for 4.7 inch ammunition	4	8 (b)	(b) Provided by the Army Service Corps

Ammunition Sub-Park for Divisions

(Carrying 280 rounds 13 pr, 3,600 rounds 18 pr. Gun Ammunition 480 rounds 4.5 inch Howitzer and 840,000 rounds SA Ammunition)

One Mechanical Transport Company ASC

War Establishment

August 1915

(1) Personnel

Detail	Offrs	WOs	SSgts & Sgts	Artificers	R & F	Total
Headquarters	2	2	1	12	73	90
Headquarters attached	-	-	-	-	1	1
No 1 Section	1	-	2	-	38	41
No 1 Section attached	-	-	1	-	18	19
No 2 Section	1	-	2	-	34	37
No 2 Section attached	-	-	1	-	16	17
Total (excluding attached)	4	2	5	12	145	168
Total (including attached)	4	2	7	12	180	205

(2) Transport

Detail	Headquarters		No 1 Section		No 2 Section		Total	
	Vehicles	Drivers MT	Vehicles	Drivers MT	Vehicles	Drivers MT	Vehicles	Drivers MT
Motor cars	1	1	1	1	1	1	3	3
Motor cycles	6 (a)	-	-	-	-	-	6	-
Workshop lorries	1	2	-	-	-	-	1	2
Store lorries	1	2	-	-	-	-	1	2
Lorries 3 ton								
For first aid	2	4	-	-	-	-	2	4
Royal Artillery and Royal Engineer stores	3	6	-	-	-	-	3	6
Spare for reliefs	5	10	-	-	-	-	5	10
For 13 pr ammunition	-	-	1	2	-	-	1	2
For 18 pr ammunition	-	-	16	32	-	-	16	32
For 4.5 inch ammunition	-	-	-	-	4	8	4	8
For small arm ammunition	-	-	-	-	11 (b)	22	11	22
Total	19	25	18	35	16	31	53	91

(a) Includes 2 with side cars   (b)   Includes 1 30 cwt lorry

Note 1:   For Division on Part I, War Establishments, add to No 2 Section for the carriage of SAA one 3 ton lorry, 3 drivers (including 1 spare and 1 gunner for the care of ammunition).

Note 2:   The following table gives the carrying capacity of a 3 ton lorry. Should there be any variation in the number of rounds to be carried in the sub-park, the number of vehicles and drivers will be correspondingly increased or decreased.

Number of Rounds per 3 ton Lorry					
13 pr	15 pr	18 pr	4.5 inch Howitzer	5 inch Howitzer	SAA
280	280	225	120	100	80,000

Field Ambulance (3 Sections)
(Accommodating 150 Patients)
(7 Motor Ambulance Cars and 3 Horsed Ambulance Wagons)

War Establishment

October 1916

(1) Personnel and Horses

Detail	Personnel						Horses				Motor Cycles
	Offrs	WOs	SSgts & Sgts	R & F	ASC	Total	Riding	Draught	Heavy Draught	Total	
Section A (including attached)	4	1	3	58	21	87	6	7	6	19	2
Section B (including attached)	3	-	5	55	14	77	4	5	7	16	-
Section C (including attached)	3	-	5	55	14	77	4	5	7	16	-
Drivers ASC (Train transport)	-	-	-	-	1	1	-	-	2	2	-
Total field ambulance (including attached)	10	1	13 (a)	168	49	241	14	17	20	51	2

(a)   Includes in TF units 1 quartermaster-serjeant and 2 staff-serjeants

(2) Transport

Detail	Vehicles	Drivers ASC	Draught Horses	Heavy Draught Horses
Sections A, B and C				
Motor cycles	2	-	-	-
Bicycle, for intercommunication	1	-	-	-
Carts (water (1 per section)	3	3	6	-
(Maltese for stores, material for repair, (forge etc	1	(a)	1	-
Wagons, limbered GS (for cooks	1	1	2	-
(for medical stores (1 per section)	3	3	6	-
Wagons (ambulance (1 per section)	3	3	-	6
(GS for medical stores and baggage (2 per (section)	6	6	-	12
Cars, motor ambulance (3 for Section A, 2 each for Sections B and C)	7	11 (b)	-	-
Drivers (for spare draught horses	-	2	2	2
(spare	-	3	-	-
Train				
Wagons, GS for supplies	1	1	-	2
Total	27	32	17	20

(a) Driven by one of the farriers attached to Section A

(b) 1 per ambulance and 50 per cent spare

Workshop ASC for Anti-Aircraft Batteries
of an Army (France)

December 1916

(1) Personnel

Detail	Offrs	WOs	Artificers	R & F	Total	Remarks
Captain	1	-	-	-	1	
Subalterns	2	-	-	-	2	
Mechanist serjeant major	-	1	-	-	1	
Artificers:						
Foremen	-	-	3		3	(a) Includes 6
Fitters and turners	-	-	18)		18	serjeants and
Blacksmiths	-	-	6)	(a)	6	6 corporals
Wheelers	-	-	6)		6	
Electricians	-	-	3)		3	(b) Includes 3
						corporals
Drivers	-	-	-	20 (b)	20	
						(c) Provided from
Batmen (c)	-	-	-	3	3	"Permanent
						Base" details
Attached:						
Armament artificer, AOC	-	-	-	-	1	
Total	3	1	37	23	64	

(2) Transport

Detail	Vehicles	Drivers	Remarks
Motor cars	2	2	
Motor cycles	5	-	
Workshop lorries	3	6	
Store lorries	3	6	
Lorries 3 ton	3	6	
Total	16	20	

Divisional Ambulance Workshop ASC
for the Motor Ambulance Cars of a Division

(To be attached to one of the Field Ambulances of the Division)

War Establishment

August 1915

(1) Personnel

Detail	Offrs	SSgts & Sgts	Artificers	R & F	Total	Remarks
Subaltern	1	-	-	-	1	
Foreman	-	-	1	)		
Fitters and turners	-	-	6	)		
Blacksmiths	-	-	2	) -	12 (a)	(a) Includes 1 serjeant and 2 corporals
Wheelers	-	-	2	)		
Electrician	-	-	1	)		
Drivers	-	-	-	7	7	
Batman	-	-	-	1	1	
Total	1	-	12	8	21	

(2) Transport

Detail	Vehicles	Drivers	Remarks
Lorries (3 ton) for workshop and stores	2	4	
Lorries (30 cwt) for stores and personnel	1	2	
Motor car, for personnel	1	1	
Total	4	7	

Mobile Repair Unit
One Mechanical Transport Company ASC

War Establishment

August 1915

Detail	Personnel					Vehicles					
	Offrs	SSgts & Sgts	Arti-ficers	R & F	Total	Box Body Motor Cars	Motor Cycles	Lorries 5 ton	Lorries 30 cwt	Lorries, Workshop	Lorries, Store
Transport details	3	3	12	36	54	2	3	2	1	1	1
Detached (a), tyre detachment	1	2	3	14	20	1	-	-	-	-	-

(a) For each tyre press detachment for dealing with 10 wheels per diem by hand press or 20 wheels per diem by power press.

258

ASC TANK DRIVERS WITH THE
MACHINE GUN CORPS HEAVY SECTION
DURING THE BATTLE OF FLERS-COURCELETTE

15 September 1916

C Company

No 1 Section

C1 721:	M2/105514	Pte H Brotherwood	Killed
C2 522:	M2/188970	Pte H Ledger	
C3 701:	M2/0339691	Pte A Boult	
C4 503:	M2/188881	Pte D D Cronin	
C5 721:	M2/102696	Sgt G B Shepherd	
C6 504:	T4/141180	Pte J Barton	

No 2 Section (no details known)

No 3 Section

C14 509:		Pte S L Heath
? 508:		Pte Stewart

No 4 Section (no ASC details known)

DM2/151356 Pte W J Nightingale and M2/074533 Pte J A Tetlow were members of C Company, but their tasks are not known.

D Company

Company HQ:	M2/191290	Pte S Precious
	MS/3547	Pte V T Gale

No 1 Section

D1 763:	M2/188383	Pte A S Wateredge	
D2 539:	M2/136283	Cpl T A Keats	
D3 728:	M2/182923	Pte G A Simpson	
D4 516:	M2/191254	Pte W J Shortland	
D5 540:	M2/191493	Pte G H Thomas	Wounded
D6 747:	MS/4771	Sgt H L Thacker	Shock

No 2 Section

D7 742:	M2/191857	Pte S G Barnes	
D8 720:	M2/191650	Pte B J Young	
D9 546:	M2/104198	LCpl G A Sanders	Wounded
D10 535:	M2/192431	LCpl E Phillips	Wounded
D11 547:	M2/194988	Pte F Still	
D12 719:	M2/191040	Cpl R R Murray	

No 3 Section

D14 534:	M2/178194	LCpl L W Upton	Died of wounds
D15 537:	MS/241	Pte A Rowe	Shock
D16 538:	M2/147741	Pte S Workman	
D17 759:	M2/149737	Pte C A Wescomb	
D18 743:	M2/191132	Pte F Burrows	
D19 753:	M2/077826	Pte T Hinds	

No 4 Section

D20 744:	M2/191886	Pte A J Bowerman	Shock
D21 512:	DM2/163936	Pte H E Wilson	
D22 745:	M2/152282	Pte E C Howes	
D23 528:	M2/192019	Pte P W Rossiter	
D24 751:	M2/138915	Pte F G Wood	Wounded
D25 511:	DM2/170078	Pte J Maude	

Company Reserve (Park)

D13 548:	M2/104154	LCpl A P Blomfield

Unit Signs

ASC Company	Unit Sign
44	Black circle on a plain background
45	White Invicta horse rampant on red shield on black background
47	White ram's head on black background (same as 4th Divisional sign)
48	Charles Chaplin figure. Also figure V on four-pointed gold star superimposed on black four-pointed star on a plain background
51	5 & 1 domino in a white square
55	Bulldog (as on cover of *John Bull* newspaper)
59	White spot on blue triangle flag with white edges, on black mast
60	Yellow letter A inside two vertical white lines within blue circle on black background
62	White ace of spades on black background
63	Letters ATN over a clover leaf. Also yellow X on broken circle inside ring on black background
64	White crown over seven-pointed star with figure 3 in centre, on black background
65	White ram's head on black background (same as 4th Divisional sign)
67	Red dragon on a plain background (same as Division)
68	Red triangle on white circular background on black square
71	Broken spur
74	Red square on plain background (8th Division sign)
76	White heraldic lion facing left holding gold ASC badge in front paws on black background
77	White Tower of London. Wef 1918 a serpent (asp) was added to the Tower on a shield in ASC colours of blue, gold and white
79	Red letters YX on white square framed in white on black background
80	Three red sevens joined in the centre on a black background (same as 21st Division)
82	A red bull's eye on a white square background with a St Andrew's Cross in blue
89	Blue St George's Cross on red circle on white background
90	Black winged eight spoked wheel on white background
91	Black arrow pointing left on white background
92	Black elephant facing left inside red circle on black background
131	Green thistle with purple petals on plain background
132	Green thistle with red petals on plain background
133	Two white crossed lines on emerald oblong on a black background (same design as Division)

ASC Company	Unit Sign
134	Black and white penguin on a yellow oblong on a black background
136	Red ball on a plain background
175	Black ace of spades inside black ring on a plain background
177	Red triangle inside black circle on plain background
178	Black circle on diagonally striped black and white background
179	3rd Corps - letters ATN, red on black background, later 34-square chequerboard, black and white 10th Corps - Two white diamonds on black background
180	Red shell on blue triangle on a black background
244	Three blue fish intertwined on black background
257	Two white crescent moons, horizontal, on a black background
260	White hand with fingers closed across the palm and the thumb raised prominently
261	White nut with split pin on a black background (wef March 1918, Lord Derby's coat of arms)
262	White hand grenade on a black background
263	Black cat
264	White fish with red eye and tongue on a black background yellow line edges
265	Red joined letters HD on a white background
266	Green joined letters HD on a white background with the blade of D facing downwards
267	Red spot on centre of a black cross inside a white circle on a black background (same as 20th Division)
271	White framed oblong divided diagonally (top left to bottom right) red and blue on black background
273	Three red sevens joined in the centre on a black background (same as 21st Division)
277	Eight-pointed star on a black circle within a blue square (wef 1915)
278	Red seven-pointed star on a plain background
290	Three legs (Isle of Man)
302	White Roman letters LXI closed up, on a black background
304	Seven-sided plan of fortress in red on plain background
305	Blue circle with seven semi-circles on the circumference, on a plain background, with red letters ASP inside the circle
306	Eye on red/blue shield, on black background (same as Guards Division sign)
315	White letters ET (for Etaples) on black background
316	Black five-pointed star in red circle on black square
317	White dove on black background
318	White initials LB inside yellow lozenge on black background
321	Eleven-pointed star
323	Female face diagonally on plain background
324	Black bird hanging from hook on white background

ASC Company	Unit Sign
326	White Roman numerals VIII on black background
328	Black words `Dickens Column' on a plain background
339	Red/white circle on black background
341	Yellow eight-pointed star in red circle on black background
342	Circle and square in centre of white pointed star on a red background (same as 24th Division)
343	Red lion on a red crown on a black background
344	Four red squares at corners of a red oblong on a white background, all on a black background (same as Division)
349	White Rose of Yorkshire on a black background (same as Division)
350	White Rose of Yorkshire on a black background (same as Division)
352	Four white figures eight superimposed so as to form five circles on a black background
353	White winged shell on a black background
354	Fifteen-squared black/white chequerboard (same as 34 Division)
356	Black, white and gold flag on plain background
359	Red X inside laurel wreath on six-pointed star on black background
360	Red Indian on blue background, framed inside white circle on black background
368	Bull dog
370	White Japanese bridge (Torii) on black background
371	Blue horse shoe on white background (after 591 Co)
374	Three vertical blue stripes on a white background (same as Division)
379	White Tower of London or Red Hand of Ulster
380	Two yellow arms holding blue scimitars on a plain background
382	Seven stars in the constellation of the Great Bear combined with arctic snow
386	Red diamond on white background
388	Spark plug
399	Yellow horizontal oval on black background
405	Black sitting bulldog in white circle on a black background
407	Red diagonal bar on white shield on black background
408	Side view of white sitting rabbit inside yellow box on black background
410	White bow and arrow pointing vertically on black background
411	Two red triangles at either end of a white bar on black background
418	White numeral 1 on a black background
419	Fleur de Lys
420	White snail facing right on a black background

ASC Company	Unit Sign
428	Non-supply wagons - 10" x 8" oblong with 3" circle on both sides; supply wagons carried 3-leaf clover with 3" circle
429	Non-supply wagons - 10" x 8" oblong with two 3" circles on both sides; supply wagons carried twelve 3-leaf clover with two 3" circles
430	Non-supply wagons - 10" x 8" oblong with three 3" circles on both sides; supply wagons carried twelve 3-leaf clover with three 3" circles
431	Non-supply wagons - 10" x 8" oblong with four 3" circles on both sides; supply wagons carried twelve 3-leaf clover with four 3" circles
495	White triangle inside orange circle on black background
496	Flat red triangle on black background (same as Division)
497	Red tear shape inside a white circle on black background
498	Black and white dot/dash (same as 17th Division)
560	Keyhole outline on white background (35 SBAC)
561	White cross within black background (50 SBAC)
562	An Egyptian moon with three swallows
563	Britannia side of penny piece with motto in scroll `Penny all the way' (white on black)
566	Black Chinese swastika on black background
567	Black/white striped snake and intermingled red Roman numeral XIV on white eight- pointed lozenge on black background
568	Musical clefs in white circle on black background
569	Side view of swimming black tortoise on white background
587	White hand on black background
588	White Saxon cross on black background
589	White lozenge inside another white lozenge on black background
590	White sitting rabbit on black background
591	Blue horse shoe on a white background
596	Pioneer
601	Black circle inside rim of white circle on black background
604	Open right hand within oval on black background (65 SBAC)
607	White Maltese cross inside a white broken circle on black background
608	Red dagger on a white triangle on a plain background
609	White cross on small white circle surrounded by eight letters Y inside a white broken circle on black background
616	Triangle on black background (58 SBAC)
617	Black lines on white (60 SBAC)
624	Gold ASC badge on black background
625	Black cat on fawn square background
627	Figure of running Mercury; also white fire bellows on black background

ASC Company	Unit Sign
628	Four white lines showing full face of the moon on black background
629	Three yellow balls dangling from red bars on black background
637	Three spots in horizontal line on dark background
638	Red A on white oblong, framed in red frame on black background
640	Sphinx head (later a baby sphinx was added)
641	White crossed line inside ring on black background (57 SBAC)
642	Eternal life ball on black background (61 SBAC)
643	Anchor within Norman arch on black background (62 SBAC)
644	Bulldog head within ring on black background
645	Golden owl on perch, inside white circle on black background
646	Blue swordfish pointing right on black background
647	Yellow six-sided shape (of bolt head) inside red circle framed in yellow on black background
649	Two six-spot dominoes, one above the other (66 SBAC)
651	Shooting star (top right to bottom left) (67 SBAC)
652	Dutch clog inside circle (68 SBAC)
654	Prehistoric figure within oval on black background
656	Blue star in white circle on black square
681	Three white pear shapes pointing inwards on black background; or white cross inside oval on black background
682	White life belt superimposed on the white crossed oars on black background
687	Fox
692	Micrometer screw gauge
695	Magneto
700	Fish outlined in black on white background
701	Peach and green leaf attached to horizontal stem, with black anchor bottom right
702	Narrow white flag on mast showing two black crosses, on black background
703	Star of David on white keyhole on black background
704	Yellow circle on black background
705	Black and white face of a bulldog on black background
714	Six-pointed star with Egyptian Key of Life
715	Six-pointed star with Egyptian Key of Life
718	Blue spanner crossed with glass retort (red liquid in bottom) on black background
720	White Maltese cross inside white circle on a black background
729	Golliwog

ASC Company	Unit Sign
730	Harp
732	Letter D on its side on black background. The bar is white and the curved part of the letter is white (same as the Division)
733	Black figure of Charlie Chaplin with stick on white background (with 5 Division). ASC flag of gold, blue and white horizontal stripes on a mast with a black background (with 58 Division)
734	Coiled, raised yellow and green snake on black background
735	No entry sign (white circle and bar on red background)
736	Crossed white axes on black background
773	Tortoise (seen from above) in circle, with motto "Festina Lente" in scroll
774	White horse shoe with five-pointed star between the ends on black background
775	Egyptian head with cobra headband on blur round background against black background
783	Bulldog
784	Squirrel and nut
788	Rabbit
789	Black cat. Flag (four horizontal stripes) on mast within white oblong (157 SBAC)
804	White diamond inside white oblong on black background
812	White anchor on black background
815	Figure eight with line down middle
818	Black cat
883	Three query marks on a red square
888	Two white hands on black background
892	Cross of Offa (onetime King of Mercia 800 AD)
893	White comma inside red ball on a black square
897	Sixteen-pointed white star on black background, a blue letter R in the centre of the star
901	Triangle with circle in centre
902	Black butterfly
903	Black shield, forked lightning
904	Ace of Spades card on black background (8 MAC)
905	Dark triangle inside circle
911	Five legs in a circle. Elephant on white background (199 SBAC)
912	Red letter F on black background in white frame
915	Circle (top half blue, bottom half yellow) on black background
916	Sitting white cat on black background
918	Horned goddess inside white oval on black background
932	Blue/white world globe on stand on black background

ASC Company	Unit Sign
933	Blue triangle on red square within white frame on black background
934	Boiling kettle over winged wheel on white background
935	White crossed pickaxe and shovel on orange background
936	Top view of white tortoise, facing left on black background
937	Red sphinx facing left on black background
938	Black glass chemical bottle on white background
939	Blue club inside blue lined red diamond on black background
940	White duck, orange beak and legs on black background
946	Terrier dog head within circle (317 SBAC)
951	Triangle ? (189 SBAC)
952	Topiary tree in shape of ace of spades on a thick base, black on white
953	Four Ds
954	Rising sun
958	Red letter W on white background
959	Yellow intertwined Star of David inside 5-sided lozenge on black background
960	Orange letters LXV inside broken circle on black background
968	Red/white
969	Red/white
970	Domino - the four blank
971	Dog
976	Red triangle with white circle
978	An Arabian Chortal in white, inside a red circle, on black background
987	H_2O
1012	Harp
1013	Ace of Spades
1014	Dragon
1015	Squirrel
1016	14lb weight
1017	Ace of Hearts
1018	Butterfly
1019	Lion rampant
1020	Ring broken in three places
1023	Skull and cross-bones

ASC Company	Unit Sign
1024	Peacock
1028	Two spanners crossed
1054	Ace of Diamonds
1055	Snake
1056	Question mark
1060	Black Lawrence of Arabia (?) silhouette on red background
1076	An arm encased in armour holding a battle axe
1091	Switch key
1093	Four black/white check squares
1094	Noughts and crosses board, with X O X from bottom left to top right
1095	Red lion couchant
1096	Six diamonds
1097	Touchwood charm
1098	Green on white square
1099	Yellow on black
1100	Bird in blue in yellow circle in red circle on yellow square
1110	black/white
1111	Acorn in black circle with white outer ring
1114	White cock on black background
1115	Yellow man-faced dog on drum
1132	Dragon

ASC Company Information 1914–1918

ASC Co	(a) Formed (b) Disbanded	Theatre/Order of Battle	Role in First World War	WO 95
1	(a) 1870 (b) *	Aldershot, Catterick, Bradford	HT Depot. Discharge Depot ASC. ASC Depot	-
2	(a) 1870 (b) *	Woolwich	HT Depot No 3 Reserve HT Depot	-
3	(a) 1870 (b) *	Bradford	HT Depot No 4 Reserve HT Depot	-
4	(a) 1870 (b) *	Western Front, Italy, 5th Division	Train, No 2 Company (HT)	1542-47 4215
5	(a) 1870 (b) *	Western Front, GHQ Troops	6 Reserve Park (HT) 12 Auxiliary (HT) Company	132, 139
6	(a) 1870 (b) *	Western Front, Italy, 5th Division	Train, No 1 (HQ) Company (HT)	1542-47 4215
7	(a) 1870 (b) *	Western Front, 1st Division	Train, No 3 Company (HT)	1260
8	(a) 1870 (b) *	19 Infantry Brigade Western Front, 2nd Division Western Front, 33rd Division	Train (HT) Train, No 2 Company (HT) Train (Exchanged for 172 Company (33 Division Train) on 25 November 1915)	-
9	(a) 1870 (b) *	Western Front, GHQ Troops	1 Reserve Park (HT) 1 Cavalry Reserve Park (HT)	137 138
10	(a) 1870 (b) *	Western Front, Havre, L of C Troops	1st Base (HT) Depot 1 ASC Base Depot (HT and Supply)	4188
11	(a) 1871 (b) *	Western Front, 2nd Division Guards Division	Train, No 3 Company (HT) Transferred with 4 Guards Brigade (2nd Division) to Guards Division and became 1st Guards Brigade on 19 August 1915	1209
12	(a) 1871 (b) *	Western Front, GHQ Troops	5 Reserve Park (HT) 11 Army Auxiliary (Horse) Company	139 132
13	(a) 1878 (b) *	Western Front, 1st Division	Train, No 4 Company (HT)	1260
14	(a) 1878 (b) *	Western Front, L of C Troops, Rouen	1st Advanced (HT) Depot	-
15	(a) 1878 (b) *	Western Front, 3rd Division	Train, No 2 Company (HT)	1409 -12
16	(a) 1878 (b) *	Western Front, 1st Division	Train, No 2 Company (HT)	1260
17	(a) 1878 (b) *	Western Front, 6th Division	Train, No 1 (HQ) Company (HT)	1604

ASC Co	(a) Formed (b) Disbanded	Theatre/Order of Battle	Role in First World War	WO 95
18	(a) 1878 (b) *	Western Front, 4th Division	Train, No 3 Company (HT)	1476
19	(a) 1885 (b) *	Western Front, 6th Division	Train, No 2 Company (HT)	1604
20	(a) 1885 (b) *	Western Front, GHQ Troops	4 Reserve Park (HT) 10 Army Auxiliary (Horse) Company	132 138
21	(a) 1885 (b) *	Western Front, 3rd Division	Train, No 3 Company (HT)	1409 -12
22	(a) 1887 (b) *	Western Front, 3rd Division	Train, No 1 (HQ) Company (HT)	1409 -12
23	(a) 1887 (b) *	Western Front, 6th Division	Train, No 3 Company (HT)	1604
24	(a) 1887 (b) *	Western Front, 6th Division	Train, No 4 Company (HT)	1604
25	(a) 1887 (b) *	Western Front, 4th Division	Train, No 1 (HQ) Company (HT)	1476
26	(a) 1887 (b) *	Western Front, GHQ Troops	Army Troops Train (HT) GHQ Troops Train (HT)	144
27	(a) 1887 (b) *	Western Front, 1 Cavalry Division	No 1 (HQ) Company (HT)	-
28	(a) 1887 (b) *	Western Front, 2nd Division	Train, No 3 Company (HT)	1340
29	(a) 1887 (b) *	Western Front, 3rd Division	Train, No 4 Company (HT)	1409 -12
30	(a) 1887 (b) *	Western Front, GHQ Troops	2 Reserve Park (HT) 7 Army Auxiliary (HT) Company	138 132
31	(a) 1887 (b) *	Western Front, 2nd Division	Train, No 4 Company (HT)	1340
32	(a) 1887 (b) *	Western Front, 4th Division	Train, No 2 Company (HT)	1476 4533
33	(a) 1887 (b) *	Western Front, Italy, France, 5th Division	Train, No 4 Company (HT)	1542-47 4215 4533
34	(a) 1887 (b) *	Western Front, GHQ Troops	3 Reserve Park (HT) 2 Cavalry Reserve Park (HT)	137,138 4533
35	(a) 1887 (b) *	Western Front, 2nd Division	Train, No 1 (HQ) Company (HT)	1340
36	(a) 1887 (b) *	Western Front, 1st Division	Train, No 1 (HQ) Company (HT)	1260
37	(a) 1887 (b) *	Western Front, Italy, France, 5th Division	Train, No 3 Company (HT)	1542 -47 4215
38	(a) 1892 (b) *	Western Front, 4th Division	Train, No 4 Company (HT)	1476

ASC Co	(a) Formed (b) Disbanded	Theatre/Order of Battle	Role in First World War	WO 95
39	(a) 1899 (Ex Gibraltar) (b) 27 May 1919	Western Front, Italy, 7th Division,	Train, No 1 (HQ) Company (HT)	1649 4222
40	(a) 1899 (Ex Malta) (b) 27 May 1919	Western Front, Italy, 7th Division,	Train, No 2 Company (HT)	1649 4222
41	(a) 1906 (Ex Egypt) (b) 28 June 1919	Western Front, 8th Division	Train, No 2 Company (HT)	1705
42	(a) 1900 (Ex South Africa) (b) 27 May 1919	Western Front, Italy, 7th Division	Train, No 4 Company (HT)	1649 4222
43	(a) 1900 (Ex South Africa) (b) 27 May 1919	Western Front, GHQ Troops	7 Reserve Park (HT)	139
44	(a) 1900 (b) 17 November 1919	Western Front, 7th Division Western Front, 3rd Division	Division Supply Column (MT) Division Supply Column (with 63 Company) Division (MT) Company	800 799
45	(a) 1900 (b) 1921	Western Front, 1st Cavalry Division, GHQ Troops	Division Ammunition Park (MT) 12 Reserve (MT) Company	135 1107
46	(a) 1900 (b) Absorbed into 44 Co 13 March 1918	Western Front, 2nd Cavalry Division	Supply Column (MT) No 1 Section MT Company (See also 413 Company)	1129
47	(a) 1901 (b) March 1918	17th Corps, 4th Division	4 Ammunition Sub Park (MT) 4 Ammunition Column (MT)	950
48	(a) 1901 (b) May 1919	Western Front, 4th Corps Western Front, 5th Division	5th Division Supply Column (MT) (with 733 Company), 5th Division MT Company 17 Division Supply Column (with 498 Company)(MT)	739 762
49	(a) 1901 (b) November 1919	Western Front, 5th Division Western Front, 6th Division	Division Ammunition Park (MT) 6 Ammunition Sub Park (MT)	893
50	(a) 1901 (b) June 1919	Western Front, 9th Corps	6th Division Supply Column (MT) 6th Division (MT) Company	848
51	(a) 1901 (b) November 1919	Western Front, 6th Division Western Front, GHQ Troops	6th Division Ammunition Park (MT) 3 GHQ Ammunition Park (MT) 3 GHQ Reserve MT Company	130 134
52	(a) 1901 (b) *	Aldershot Catterick, Southport	Home Depot MT Aldershot Discharge Depot ASC	-
53	(a) 1901 (b) March 1919	Western Front, L of C Troops	1st Base (MT) Depot	4188
54	(a) 1901 (b) November 1919	Western Front, Rouen, Abbeville, L of C Troops	1st Advanced (MT) Depot	4179 -4183
55	(a) 1901 (b) June 1918	Western Front, GHQ Troops	GHQ Troops Supply Company (MT)	144
56	(a) 1901 (b) March 1919	Western Front, 2 Cavalry Division Western Front, GHQ Troops	Ammunition Park (MT) No 2 Reserve (MT) Company	1128 134
57	(a) 1901 (b) September 1919	Western Front, 1 Cavalry Division	Supply Column (MT) No 1 Section Cavalry Division MT Company	1107

ASC Co	(a) Formed (b) Disbanded	Theatre/Order of Battle	Role in First World War	WO 95
58	(a) 1901 (b) Absorbed into 57 MT Co 9 October 1916	Western Front, 1 Cavalry Division	Supply Column (MT) No 2 Section Division MT Company	–
59	(a) 1901 (b) July 1919	Western Front, 9th Corps	1st Division Supply Column (MT) 1st Division (MT) Company	847
60	(a) 1901 (b) March 1918	Western Front, 19th Corps	1st Ammunition Sub Park (MT)	973
61	(a) 1902 (b) June 1919	Western Front, 6th Corps	2nd Division Supply Column (MT) 2nd Division (MT) Company	795 796
62	(a) 1902 (b) 5 July 1919	Western Front, GHQ Troops Fourth Army, Western Front	2nd GHQ then 2 GHQ Ammunition Park (MT) 44th Auxiliary (Steam) Company (Two workshop tractors and lorries were captured by Germans in the retreat from Mons)	130 513
63	(a) 1902 (b) April 1919	Western Front, 3rd Corps Western Front, 6th Corps	3rd Division Supply Column (MT) (with 44 Company) 18th Division Supply Column (MT) (with 179 Company)	704 799
64	(a) 1902 (b) February 1918	Western Front, 1st Corps	3 Ammunition Sub Park (MT)	628
65	(a) 1902 (b) May 1919	Western Front, 17 Corps Western Front, 22 Corps Western Front, GHQ Troops	4th Division Supply Column (MT) 4th Division (MT) Company 18 Auxiliary HT Company	949 979 133
66	(a) 1902 (b) March 1918	Western Front, 7th Corps	7 Ammunition Sub Park (MT)	802
67	(a) 1903 (b) 26 May 1919	Western Front, Indian (Meerut) Division Western Front, 5 Corps GHQ Troops, Western Front	Division Supply Column (MT) Division Supply Column (MT) 38th Division (MT) Company 20 Auxiliary (HT) Company	1095 763 133
68	(a) 1903 (b) 1 September 1919	Western Front, Indian (Lahore) Division Western Front, 1st Division GHQ Troops, Western Front	Division Ammunition Park (MT) 1 GHQ Ammunition Park (MT) GHQ Reserve MT Company	130 134 1094
69	(a) 1903 (b) 17 May 1919	Western Front, Indian (Lahore) Division Western Front, 16th Division	Division Supply Column (MT) Division Supply Column (MT) Division (MT) Company	1095 626
70	(a) 1903 (b) Absorbed into 67 Co 13 March 1918	Western Front, Indian (Meerut) Division Western Front, 38th Division	Division Ammunition Sub Park (MT) 38 Ammunition Sub Park MT Division Supply Column (MT)	893 1094
71	(a) 1903 (b) 17 May 1919	Western Front, 2nd (Indian) Cavalry Division Western Front, 5 Cavalry Division Western Front, 74th Division	Division Supply Column (MT) (No 1 Section) with 83 Company) Division Supply Column (MT) Division Supply Column (MT) Division (MT) Company	1184 1163 892

ASC Co	(a) Formed (b) Disbanded	Theatre/Order of Battle	Role in First World War	WO 95
72	(a) 1903 (b) 14 April 1920	Western Front, 2nd (Indian) Cavalry Division Western Front, 5 Cavalry Division Western Front, GHQ Troops	Division Ammunition Park (MT) Division Ammunition Park (MT) No 4 GHQ Reserve MT Company	1184 1163 134
73	(a) 1903 (b) 27 June 1919	Western Front, 3rd Cavalry Division	Division Supply Column (MT) Division (MT) Company, No 1 Section (see 414 Company)	1150
74	(a) 1903 (b) 14 August 1919	Western Front, 8th Division	Division Supply Column (MT) Division (MT) Company	830
75	(a) 1903 (b) Absorbed into 1 Army Arty Park 16 March 1916	Western Front, 8th Division Western Front, 1st Army	Division Ammunition Park (MT) 1st Army Artillery Park (late 8 Ammunition Park) (MT)	265
76	(a) 1903 (b) 23 April 1919	Western Front, 3rd Cavalry Division, Western Front, GHQ Troops	Division Ammunition Park (MT) 7 GHQ Reserve MT Company	1151 135
77	(a) 1903 (b) 15 May 1919	Western Front, 27th Division Western Front, 55th Division Western Front, 58th Division	Division Supply Column (MT) Division Supply Column (MT) (with 354 Company) Division Supply Column (MT) (with 733 Company) Division (MT) Company	704 627 830
78	(a) 1904 (b) Absorbed into 2 Army Arty Park 16 March 1916	27th Division Western Front, Second Army	Division Ammunition Park (MT) Army Artillery Ammunition Park (MT)	353
79	(a) 15 October 1914 (b) Absorbed into 45 MT Co 13 May 1920	Western Front, 1st Indian Cavalry Division Western Front, 4 Cavalry Division GHQ Troops, Western Front	Division Ammunition Park (MT) Division Ammunition Park (MT) 9 GHQ Reserve MT Company	1172 1158 135
80	(a) 28 October 1914 (b) Absorbed into 273 MT Co 13 March 1918	Home, 2nd Mounted Division Western Front, 4th Corps	Ammunition Park (MT) 21 Ammunition Sub Park (MT)	741
81	(a) 14 September 1914 (b) 10 June 1919	Western Front, 3rd Cavalry Division	HQ Division ASC (HT)	1150
82	(a) 10 October 1914 (b) Absorbed into 89 MT 9 October 1916	Western Front, 1st Indian Cavalry Division	Division Supply Column, No 2 Section (MT)	-
83	(a) 27 November 1914 (b) Absorbed into 71 MT 9 October 1916	Western Front, 2nd Indian Cavalry Division	Division Supply Column, No 2 Section (MT) (with 71 MT Company)	1184
84	(a) 7 October 1914 (b) 28 June 1919	Western Front, 8th Division	Train, No 1 (HQ) Company (HT)	1705
85	(a) 7 October 1914 (b) 28 June 1919	Western Front, 8th Division	Train, No 3 Company (HT)	1705
86	(a) 24 September 1914 (b) 27 May 1919	Western Front, 7th Division Italy, 7th Division	Train, No 3 Company (HT)	1649 4222
87	(a) 7 October 1914 (b) 28 June 1919	Western Front, 8th Division	Train, No 4 Company (HT)	1705

ASC Co	(a) Formed (b) Disbanded	Theatre/Order of Battle	Role in First World War	WO 95
88	(a) 7 October 1914 (b) 26 January 1920	Western Front, GHQ Troops	8 Reserve Park (HT) 8 Army Auxiliary (HT) Company	140 132
89	(a) 15 October 1914 (b) 18 April 1919	Western Front, 1st Indian Cavalry Division Western Front, 4 Cavalry Division Western Front, 52nd Division	Division Supply Column, No 1 Section (MT) Division Supply Column (MT) Division Supply Column (MT) Division (MT) Company	1173 1158 949
90	(a) 17 October 1914 (b) 31 October 1919	Western Front, 2nd Army Western Front, GHQ Troops	1st Auxiliary (Omnibus) Company (MT)	148
91	(a) 22 October 1914 (b) 14 May 1919	Western Front, 1st Army Western Front, GHQ Troops	2nd Auxiliary (Omnibus) Company (MT)	148
92	(a) 26 October 1914 (b) 14 May 1919	Home, Grove Park Western Front, 3rd Army Western Front, GHQ Troops	3rd Auxiliary (Omnibus) Company (MT) 4 GHQ Ammunition Park (MT) 50th Auxiliary (Omnibus) Company (MT)	130
93	(a) 28 October 1914 (b) 3 June 1919	Home, Grove Park Western Front, 2nd Army, GHQ Tps Italy, GHQ Troops	4th Auxiliary (Omnibus) Company (MT) 1 MT Mobile Repair Unit	356 4210
94	(a) 28 october 1914 (b) Absorbed into 55 MT Co 11 October 1915	Western Front, Artillery Brigade, 22 Siege Battery RGA	Brigade Pack Ammunition Park (MT)	353
95	(a) 28 November 1914 (b) 14 July 1919	Western Front, 27th Division Western Front, 55th Division	Train No 1 (HQ) Company (HT) Train, No 1 (HQ) Company	2259 2919
96	(a) 28 November 1914 (b) 14 July 1919	Western Front, 27th Division Western Front, 55th Division	Train, No 2 Company (HT) Train, No 2 Company (HT)	2259 2919
97	(a) 28 November 1914 (b) 14 July 1919	Western Front, 27th Division Western Front, 55th Division	Train, No 3 Company (HT) Train, No 3 Company (HT)	2259 2919
98	(a) 28 November 1914 (b) 14 July 1919	Western Front, 27th Division Western Front, 55th Division	Train, No 4 Company (HT) Train, No 4 Company (HT)	2259 2919
99	(a) 21 November 1914 (b) 15 October 1919	Western Front, GHQ Troops	27th Reserve Park (HT) 13 Army Auxiliary (Horse) Company OC 1916-18 Major J W English VC	142 132
100	(a) 28 August 1914 (b) 21 June 1919	Western Front, 14th Division	Train, No 1 (HQ) Company (HT)	1893
101	(a) 28 August 1914 (b) 21 June 1919	Western Front, 14th Division	Train, No 2 Company (HT)	1893
102	(a) 28 August 1914 (b) 21 June 1919	Western Front, 14th Division	Train, No 3 Company (HT)	1893
103	(a) 28 August 1914 (b) 21 June 1919	Western Front, 14th Division	Train, No 4 Company (HT)	1893
104	(a) 21 August 1914 (b) November 1919	Western Front, 9th Division	Train, No 1 (HQ) Company (HT)	1761
105	(a) 21 August 1914 (b) November 1919	Western Front, 9th Division	Train, No 2 Company (HT)	1761
106	(a) 21 August 1914 (b) November 1919	Western Front, 9th Division	Train, No 3 Company (HT)	1761

274

ASC Co	(a) Formed (b) Disbanded	Theatre/Order of Battle	Role in First World War	WO 95
107	(a) 21 August 1914 (b) November 1919	Western Front, 9th Division	Train, No 4 Company (HT)	1761
108	(a) 29 August 1914 (b) 4 March 1919	Western Front, 10th Division Salonika, 22nd Division	Train, No 1 (HQ) Company (HT) Train (Wheeled Echelon) (HT)	4849
109	(a) 29 August 1914 (b) 4 March 1919	Western Front, 10th Division Salonika, 22nd Division	Train, No 2 Company (HT) Train, (Wheeled Echelon) (HT)	4849
110	(a) 29 August 1914 (b) 4 March 1919	Western Front, 10th Division Salonika, 22nd Division	Train, No 3 Company (HT) Train, (Wheeled Echelon) (HT)	4849
111	(a) 29 August 1914 (b) 4 March 1919	Western Front, 10th Division Salonika, 22nd Division	Train, No 4 Company (HT) Train, (Wheeled Echelon) (HT)	4849
112	(a) 28 August 1914 (b) May 1919	Western Front, 11th Division Salonika, 26th Division Bulgaria	Train, No 1 (HQ) Company (HT) Train, (Wheeled Echelon) (HT) "Norseman" torpedoed on 22 January 1916 in Gulf of Salonika. All Train personnel and 500 out of 1,000 mules were saved.	4868
113	(a) 28 August 1914 (b) May 1919	Home, 11th Division Salonika, 26th Division Bulgaria	Train, No 2 Company (HT) Train, (Wheeled Echelon) (HT)	4868
114	(a) 28 August 1914 (b) 18 July 1919	Home, 11th Division Salonika, 26th Division Bulgaria	Train, No 3 Company (HT) Train, (Wheeled Echelon) (HT)	4868
115	(a) 28 August 1914 (b) May 1919	Home, 11th Division Salonika, 26th Division	Train, No 4 Company (HT) Train, (Wheeled Echelon) (HT)	4868
116	(a) 31 August 1914 (b) May 1919	Western Front, 12th Division	Train, No 1 (HQ) Company (HT)	1845
117	(a) 31 August 1914 (b) May 1919	Western Front, 12th Division	Train, No 2 Company (HT)	1845
118	(a) 31 August 1914 (b) May 1919	Western Front, 12th Division	Train, No 3 Company (HT)	1845
119	(a) 31 August 1914 (b) May 1919	Western Front, 12th Division	Train, No 4 Company (HT)	1845
120	(a) 28 August 1914 (b) April 1919	Home, 13th Division Egypt, Salonika, 28th Division	Train, No 1 (HQ) Company (HT) Train, Pack and Wheeled Echelon	-
121	(a) 28 August 1914 (b) April 1919	Home, 13th Division Egypt, Salonika, 28th Division	Train, No 2 Company (HT) Train, Pack and Wheeled Echelon	-
122	(a) 28 August 1914 (b) April 1919	Home, 13th Division Egypt, Salonika, 28th Division	Train, No 3 Company (HT) Train, Pack and Wheeled Echelon	-
123	(a) 28 August 1914 (b) April 1919	Home, 13th Division Egypt, Salonika, 28th Division	Train, No 4 Company (HT) Train, Pack and Wheeled Echelon	-
124	(a) 28 August 1914 (b) 27 April 1919	Home Western Front, Guards Division	Army Troops Train (HT) Train No 2 Company (HT)	1209
125	(a) 28 September 1914 (b) 15 November 1919	Western Front, GHQ Troops	9 Reserve Park (HT) 9 Army Auxiliary (Horse) Company	140 132
126	(a) 21 September 1914 (b) Absorbed into 5 Cavalry Reserve Park 24 June 1917	Western Front, GHQ Troops	10th Reserve Park (HT)	140

ASC Co	(a) Formed (b) Disbanded	Theatre/Order of Battle	Role in First World War	WO 95
127	(a)e 7 October 1914 (b) 7 June 1916	Home, Western Front	11th Reserve Park (HT)	-
128	(a) 26 September 1914 (b) 5 July 1917	Home, 4th New Army Perham Down L of C Troops, Salonika	12th Reserve Park (HT) HT Company, local duties 19th Auxiliary (HT) Company	4942
129	(a) 3 October 1914 (b) 21 June 1919	Fovant Western Front, GHQ Troops	HT Company, local duties 5 Auxiliary (HT) Company 5 Army Auxiliary (HT) Company	570 132
130	(a) 28 September 1914 (b) 23 March 1920	Western Front, GHQ Troops	14 Reserve Park (HT) 14 Army Auxiliary (HT) Company	140 132
131	(a) 11 January 1915 (b) 15 November 1919	Western Front, 9th Division	Division Supply Column (MT) Division (MT) Company	666
132	(a) 10 January 1915 (b) Absorbed by 131 MT Co 13 March 1918	Western Front, 7th Corps	9 Ammunition Sub Park (MT)	819
133	(a) 11 January 1915 (b) 14 May 1919	Western Front, 10th Division 14th Division	Division Supply Column (MT) Division Supply Column (MT) Division (MT) Company	932
134	(a) 12 January 1915 (b) Absorbed into 133 MT Co 13 March 1918	Western Front, 10th Division	Division Ammunition Sub Park (MT) 14 Ammunition Sub Park (MT)	958
135	(a) 12 January 1915 (b) 11 June 1919	Western Front, 11th Division 37th Division	Division Supply Column (MT) Division Supply Column (MT) Division (MT) Company	740
136	(a) 12 January 1915 (b) Absorbed into 135 MT Co 13 March 1918	Western Front, 11th Division	Division Ammunition Park (MT) 37 Ammunition Sub Park (MT)	849
137	(a) 20 February 1915 (b) 28 March 1920	Egypt, Ismailia District Kantara, Alexandria	2nd Base HT Depot (HT)	4414
138	(a) 14 October 1914 (b) 17 July 1919	Western Front, 15th (Scottish) Division	Train, No 1 (HQ) Company (HT)	1933
139	(a) 14 October 1914 (b) 17 July 1919	Western Front, 15th (Scottish) Division	Train, No 2 Company (HT)	1933
140	(a) 14 October 1914 (b) 17 July 1919	Western Front, 15th (Scottish) Division	Train, No 3 Company (HT)	1933
141	(a) 14 October 1914 (b) 17 July 1919	Western Front, 15th (Scottish) Division	Train, No 4 Company (HT)	1933
142	(a) 15 October 1914 (b) 26 June 1919	Western Front, 16th (Irish) Division	Train, No 1 (HQ) Company (HT)	1968
143	(a) 15 October 1914 (b) 26 June 1919	Western Front, 16th (Irish) Division	Train, No 2 Company (HT)	1968
144	(a) 15 October 1914 (b) 26 June 1919	Western Front, 16th (Irish) Division	Train, No 3 Company (HT)	1968
145	(a) 15 October 1914 (b) 26 June 1919	Western Front, 16th (Irish) Division	Train, No 4 Company (HT)	1968

ASC Co	(a) Formed (b) Disbanded	Theatre/Order of Battle	Role in First World War	WO 95
146	(a) 14 October 1914 (b) April-May 1919	Western Front, 17th (Northern) Division	Train, No 1 (HQ) Company (HT)	1997
147	(a) 14 October 1914 (b) April-May 1919	Western Front, 17th (Northern) Division	Train, No 2 Company (HT)	1997
148	(a) 14 October 1914 (b) April-May 1919	Western Front, 17th (Northern) Division	Train, No 3 Company (HT)	1997
149	(a) 14 October 1914 (b) April-May 1919	Western Front, 17th (Northern) Division	Train, No 4 Company (HT)	1997
150	(a) 12 October 1914 (b) May-June 1919	Western Front, 18th (Eastern) Division	Train, No 1 (HQ) Company (HT)	2032
151	(a) 12 October 1914 (b) May-June 1919	Western Front, 18th (Eastern) Division	Train, No 2 Company (HT)	2032
152	(a) 12 October 1914 (b) May-June 1919	Western Front, 18th (Eastern) Division	Train, No 3 Company (HT)	2032
153	(a) 12 October 1914 (b) May-June 1919	Western Front, 18th (Eastern) Division	Train, No 4 Company (HT)	2032
154	(a) 12 October 1914 (b) 11 June 1919	Western Front, 19th (Western) Division	Train, No 1 (HQ) Company (HT)	2074
155	(a) 12 October 1914 (b) 11 June 1919	Western Front, 19th (Western) Division	Train, No 2 Company (HT)	2074
156	(a) 12 October 1914 (b) 11 June 1919	Western Front, 19th (Western) Division	Train, No 3 Company (HT)	2074
157	(a) 12 October 1914 (b) 11 June 1919	Western Front, 19th (Western) Division	Train, No 4 Company (HT)	2074
158	(a) 15 October 1914 (b) 21-24 June 1919	Western Front, 20th (Light) Division	Train, No 1 (HQ) Company (HT)	2110
159	(a) 15 October 1914 (b) 21-24 June 1919	Western Front, 20th (Light) Division	Train, No 2 Company (HT)	2110
160	(a) 15 October 1914 (b) 21-24 June 1919	Western Front, 20th (Light) Division	Train, No 3 Company (HT)	2110
161	(a) 15 October 1914 (b) 21-24 June 1919	Western Front, 20th (Light) Division	Train, No 4 Company (HT)	2110
162	(a) 13 November 1914 (b) 24 November 1919	Western Front, GHQ, Troops	15th Reserve Park (HT) 15 Army Auxiliary (HT) Company	141 133
163	(a) 3 November 1914 (b) 5 May 1916	Home, Farnham Army Troops, Salonika	16th Reserve Park (HT) local duties 18th Auxiliary (HT) Company	4809
164	(a) 12 November 1914 (b) 7 June 1916	Western Front	17th Reserve Park (HT)	-
165	(a) 21 November 1914 (b) 30 April 1921	Western Front, GHQ Troops	18th Reserve Park (HT) 18 Army Auxiliary (Horse) Company	141 133
166	(a) 4 November 1914 (b) 18 December 1919	Western Front, GHQ Troops	19th Reserve Park (HT) 19th Auxiliary (HT) Company	141 133
167	(a) 11 November 1914 (b) 8 November 1919	Western Front, GHQ Troops	20th Reserve Park (HT) 20 Army Auxiliary (Horse) Company	141 133

ASC Co	(a) Formed (b) Disbanded	Theatre/Order of Battle	Role in First World War	WO 95
168	(a) 17 October 1914 (b) 27 April 1919	Army Troops Western Front, Guards Division	Army Troops Train (HT) Train, No 4 Company (HT)	1209
169	(a) 27 November 1914 (b) Absorbed into 181 MT Co 13 March 1918	Western Front, 8th Corps	28 Ammunition Sub Park (MT) 33 Ammunition Sub Park (MT)	834
170	(a) 14 December 1914 (b) 29 August 1919	Winchester, 1st London Division Western Front, Salonika, 28th Division Western Front, 33rd Division	Train, No 1 (HQ) Company (HT)	2272 2419
171	(a) 14 December 1914 (b) 29 August 1919	Winchester, 1st London Division Western Front, Salonika, 28th Division Western Front, 33rd Division	Train, No 2 Company (HT)	2272 2419
172	(a) 14 December 1914 (b) 9 November 1919	Winchester, 1st London Division Western Front, Salonika, 28th Division Western Front, 33rd Division	Train, No 3 Company (HT) Train, No 2 Company, 2nd Division Train (HT) (in exchange for 8 Company)	2272 2419
173	(a) 14 December 1914 (b) 29 August 1919	Winchester, 1st London Division Western Front, Salonika, 28th Division Western Front, 33rd Division	Train, No 4 Company (HT)	2272 2419
174	(a) 19 December 1914 (b) 16 June 1919	Western Front, GHQ Troops	28th Reserve Park (HT) 3 Cavalry Reserve Park (HT) OC 1915-16 Maj J W B Landon, later Major General	142 137
175	(a) 21 January 1915 (b) 2 May 1919	Western Front, 12th Division	Division Supply Column (MT) Division (MT) Company	704
176	(a) 21 January 1915 (b) Absorbed into 175 MT Co 13 March 1918	Western Front, 12th Division	12 Ammunition Sub Park (MT)	933
177	(a) 19 January 1915 (b) 25 July 1919	Home, 13th Division Western Front, 15th Division	Division Supply Column (MT) Division Supply Column (MT)	626
178	(a) 19 January 1915 (b) Absorbed into 177 MT Co 13 March 1918	Home, Western Front, 13th Division	15 Ammunition Sub Park (MT)	950
179	(a) 19 January 1915 (b) 3 November 1919	Home, 14th Division Home, 10th Division Western Front, 18th Division Western Front, 34th Division	18 Division Supply Column (MT) (with 63 Company) 34 Division Supply Column (with 354 Company) 34th Division (MT) Company	704 878
180	(a) 19 January 1915 (b) Absorbed into 179 MT Co 13 March 1918	Home, 14th Division Home, 10th Division Western Front, 6 Corps	Division Ammunition Sub Park (MT) 18 Ammunition Sub Park	803
181	(a) 27 December 1914 (b) Absorbed into 303 MT Co 20 November 1919	Western Front, 5th Corps	28th Division Supply Column (MT) 33rd Division Supply Column (MT) 33rd Division MT Company	763
182	(a) 26 November 1914 (b) April-June 1919	Western Front, 21st Division	Train, No 1 (HQ) Company (HT)	2149 2150

ASC Co	(a) Formed (b) Disbanded	Theatre/Order of Battle	Role in First World War	WO 95
183	(a) 26 November 1914 (b) April-June 1919	Western Front, 21st Division	Train, No 2 Company (HT)	2149 2150
184	(a) 26 November 1914 (b) April-June 1919	Western Front, 21st Division	Train, No 3 Company (HT)	2149 2150
185	(a) 26 November 1914 (b) April-June 1919	Western Front, 21st Division	Train, No 4 Company (HT)	2149 2150
186	(a) 23 November 1914 (b) 27 June 1919	Western Front, 22nd Division Salonika, 30th Division	Train, No 1 (HQ) Company (HT)	2166 2326
187	(a) 23 November 1914 (b) 30 July 1919	Western Front, 22nd Division Salonika, 30th Division,	Train, No 2 Company (HT)	2166 2326
188	(a) 23 November 1914 (b) 24 January 1920	Western Front, 22nd Division Salonika, 30th Division,	Train, No 3 Company (HT)	2166 2326
189	(a) 23 November 1914 (b) 7 August 1919	Western Front, 22nd Division Salonika, 30th Division,	Train, No 4 Company (HT)	2166 2326
190	(a) 28 November 1914 (b) April 1919	Western Front, Italy, 23rd Division	Train, No 1 (HQ) Company (HT)	2180 4234
191	(a) 28 November 1914 (b) April 1919	Western Front, Italy, 23rd Division	Train, No 2 Company (HT)	2180 4234
192	(a) 28 November 1914 (b) April 1919	Western Front, Italy, 23rd Division	Train, No 3 Company (HT)	2180 4234
193	(a) 28 November 1914 (b) April 1919	Western Front, Italy, 23rd Division	Train, No 4 Company (HT)	2180 4234
194	(a) 28 November 1914 (b) 25 June 1919	Western Front, 24th Division	Train, No 1 (HQ) Company (HT) Pte T Moore ASC was shot by firing squad on 26 February 1917 for the murder (by shooting) of Farrier SSgt James Pick. Moore's name is on the Menin Gate in Ypres. Pick is buried in Poperinge New Cemetery.	2203
195	(a) 28 November 1914 (b) 25 June 1919	Western Front, 24th Division	Train, No 2 Company (HT)	2203
196	(a) 28 November 1914 (b) 25 June 1919	Western Front, 24th Division	Train, No 3 Company (HT)	2203
197	(a) 28 November 1914 (b) 25 June 1919	Western Front, 24th Division	Train, No 4 Company (HT)	2203
198	(a) 23 November 1914 (b) June-July 1919	Western Front, 25th Division	Train, No 1 (HQ) Company (HT)	2240
199	(a) 23 November 1914 (b) June-July 1919	Western Front, 25th Division	Train, No 2 Company (HT)	2240
200	(a) 23 November 1914 (b) June-July 1919	Western Front, 25th Division	Train, No 3 Company (HT)	2240
201	(a) 23 November 1914 (b) June-July 1919	Western Front, 25th Division	Train, No 4 Company (HT)	2240
202	(a) 1 December 1914 (b) 25 October - 7 November 1919	Western Front, 26th Division Western Front, 32nd Division	Train, No 1 (HQ) Company (HT) Train, No 1 (HQ) Company (HT)	2252 2387

ASC Co	(a) Formed (b) Disbanded	Theatre/Order of Battle	Role in First World War	WO 95
203	(a) 1 December 1914 (b) 25 October - 7 November 1919	Western Front, 26th Division Western Front, 32nd Division	Train, No 2 Company (HT) Train, No 2 Company (HT)	2252 2387
204	(a) 1 December 1914 (b) 25 October - 7 November 1919	Western Front, 26th Division Western Front, 32nd Division	Train, No 3 Company (HT) Train, No 3 Company (HT)	2252 2387
205	(a) 1 December 1914 (b) 25 October- 7 November 1919	Western Front, 26th Division Western Front, 32nd Division	Train, No 4 Company (HT) Train, No 4 Company (HT)	2252 2387
206	(a) 9 December 1914 (b) Amalgamated with 12 HT Co 31 March 1921	Home, 3rd Army Troops Home Forces, Troops, London, Bisley, Newbury, Londonderry, Portsmouth	Army Troops Train (HT) HT Company, local duties 54 Reserve Park (HT) 48 Reserve Park (HT)	5460
207	(a) 17 December 1914 (b) Absorbed 14 April 1918	Western Front, GHQ	21st Reserve Park (HT)	141
208	(a) 14 December 1914 (b) 9 April 1919	Home, Salonika, Army Troops	22nd Reserve Park (HT) 12th Auxiliary (HT) Company	4808
209	(a) 19 December 1914 (b) 5 June 1919	Home, Salonika, Army Troops	23rd Reserve Park (HT) 13th Auxiliary (HT) Company	4808
210	(a) 18 December 1914 (b) 3 August 1917	Home, Heytesbury, Third New Army Salonika, Macedonia, Turkey, Black Sea, Caucasus 7th Mounted Brigade	24th Reserve Park (HT) local duties Brigade Supply Column (HT)	4793
211	(a) 16 December 1914 (b) 7 June 1916	Western Front	25th Reserve Park (HT)	-
212	(a) 20 December 1914 (b) 8 October 1919	Clipstone Camp, Notts, Scarborough Fifth New Army	26th Reserve Park (HT) Local duties	-
213	(a) 13 January 1915 (b) May-June 1919	Home, 30th Division Western Front, 56th Division	Train, No 1 (HQ) Company (HT)	2945
214	(a) 13 January 1915 (b) May-June 1919	Home, 30th Division Western Front, 56th Division	Train, No 2 Company (HT)	2945
215	(a) 13 January 1915 (b) May-June 1919	Home, 30th Division Western Front, 56th Division	Train, No 3 Company (HT)	2945
216	(a) 13 January 1915 (b) May-June 1919	Home, 30th Division Western Front, 56th Division	Train, No 4 Company (HT)	2945
217	(a) 14 January 1915 (b) 22 June 1919	Egypt, 31st Division, Dardanelles, Western Front, 52nd Division North Persia Force, 13 (Western) Division	Train No 1 (HQ) Company (HT) Division Troops Company (HT)	5154 4589 2895 4605 4606
218	(a) 14 January 1915 (b) 22 June 1919	Egypt, 31st Division, Dardanelles, Western Front, 52nd Division North Persia Force, 13 (Western) Division	Train, No 2 Company (HT) Division Troops Company (HT)	5154 4589 2895 4605 4606

ASC Co	(a) Formed (b) Disbanded	Theatre/Order of Battle	Role in First World War	WO 95
219	(a) 14 January 1915 (b) 22 June 1919	Egypt, 31st Division, Dardanelles, Western Front, 52nd Division North Persia Force, 13 (Western) Division	Train, No 3 Company (HT) Train, Division Troops Company (HT)	5154 4589 2895 4605 4606
220	(a) 14 January 1915 (b) 22 June 1919	Egypt, 31st Division, Dardanelles, Western Front, 52nd Division North Persia Force, 13 (Western) Division	Train, No 4 Company (HT) Division Troops Company (HT)	4589 2895 4605 4606
221	(a) 11 January 1915 (b) 3 June 1919	Western Front, 32nd Division Western Front, 11th Division Egypt, 31st Division	Train, No 1 (HQ) Company (HT)	2355
222	(a) 11 January 1915 (b) 3 June 1919	Western Front, 32nd Division Western Front, 11th Division Egypt, 31st Division	Train, No 2 Company (HT)	2355
223	(a) 11 January 1915 (b) 3 June 1919	Western Front, 32nd Division Western Front, 11th Division Egypt, 31st Division	Train, No 3 Company (HT)	2355
224	(a) 11 January 1915 (b) 31 October 1919	Western Front, 32nd Division Western Front, 11th Division Egypt, 31st Division	Train, No 4 Company (HT)	2355
225	(a) 13 January 1915 (b) 14-29 February 1920	Home, 40th Division Home, 33rd Division Home, 52nd Division Western Front, 29th Division	Train, No 1 (HQ) Company (HT)	152 2297
226	(a) 13 January 1915 (b) 14-29 February 1920	Home, 40th Division Home, 33rd Division Home, 52nd Division Western Front, 29th Division	Train, No 2 Company (HT)	152 2297
227	(a) 13 January 1915 (b) 14-29 February 1920	Home, 40th Division Home, 33rd Division Home, 52nd Division Western Front, 29th Division	Train, No 3 Company (HT)	152 2297
228	(a) 13 January 1915 (b) 14-29 February 1920	Home, 40th Division Home, 33rd Division Home, 52nd Division Western Front, 29th Division	Train, No 4 Company (HT)	152 2297
229	(a) 12 January 1915 (b) 7 November 1919	Home, 41st Division Western Front, 34th Division	Train, No 1 (HQ) Company (HT)	2454
230	(a) 12 January 1915 (b) 7 November 1919	Home, 41st Division Western Front, 34th Division	Train, No 2 Company (HT)	2454
231	(a) 12 January 1915 (b) 7 November 1919	Home, 41st Division Western Front, 34th Division	Train, No 3 Company (HT)	2454
232	(a) 12 January 1915 (b) 7 November 1919	Home, 41st Division Western Front, 34th Division	Train, No 4 Company (HT)	2454
233	(a) 15 January 1915 (b) 31 May 1919	Western Front, 35th Division	Train, No 1 (HQ) Company (HT)	2480 2481
234	(a) 15 January 1915 (b) 31 May 1919	Western Front, 35th Division	Train, No 2 Company (HT)	2480 2481

ASC Co	(a) Formed (b) Disbanded	Theatre/Order of Battle	Role in First World War	WO 95
235	(a) 15 January 1915 (b) 31 May 1919	Western Front, 35th Division	Train, No 3 Company (HT)	2480 2481
236	(a) 15 January 1915 (b) 31 May 1919	Western Front, 35th Division	Train, No 4 Company (HT)	2480 2481
237	(a) 2 April 1915 (b) NK	Home, Prees Heath, Eighth New Army	44 Reserve Park (HT) Local duties	-
238	(a) 11 February 1915 (b) 21 May 1919	Home Salonika, Army Troops	37 Reserve Park (HT) 14th Auxiliary (Horse) Company	4808
239	(a) 6 February 1915 (b) 12 May 1920	Seaford, Bedford	38 Reserve Park (HT) (formed for MEF)	-
240	(a) 11 February 1915 (b) 27 March 1920	Lichfield, Brocton, Cannock Chase	39 Reserve Park (HT) (formed for MEF) Local duties	-
241	(a) 10 February 1915 (b) 27 March 1920	Home, Scotton Camp, Catterick, Seventh New Army	40 Reserve Park (HT) Local duties	-
242	(a) 10 February 1915 (b) 31 March 1920	Home, Leith, Edinburgh, Seventh New Army	41 Reserve Park (HT) Local duties	-
243	(a) 12 February 1915 (b) 27 March 1920	Home, Ripon, Seventh New Army	42 Reserve Park (HT) Local duties	-
244	(a) 19 January 1915 (b) March 1919	Salonika, 29th Division 10th Division, Army Troops	Division Supply Column (MT) 89th Auxiliary (MT) Company	4810
245	(a) 19 January 1915 (b) 22 April 1920	Salonika, 29th Division 10th Division	Division Ammunition Park (MT) 90th Auxiliary (MT) Company	4811
246	(a) 23 January 1915 (b) 1 July 1919	Egypt, Gallipoli, 29th Division Egypt, Gallipoli, 53rd (Welsh) Division	Train, No 1 (HQ) Company (HT)	4309 4624
247	(a) 23 January 1915 (b) 1 July 1919	Egypt, Gallipoli, 29th Division Egypt, Gallipoli, 53rd (Welsh) Division	Train, No 2 Company (HT)	4309 4624
248	(a) 23 January 1915 (b) 1 July 1919	Egypt, Gallipoli, 29th Division Egypt, Gallipoli, 53rd (Welsh) Division	Train, No 3 Company (HT)	4309 4624
249	(a) 23 January 1915 (b) 1 July 1919	Egypt, Gallipoli, 29th Division Egypt, Gallipoli, 53rd (Welsh) Division	Train, No 4 Company (HT)	4309 4624
250	(a) 8 February 1915 (b) Absorbed 25 April 1915	Western Front, 7th Brigade, RGA	Brigade Ammunition Column (MT)	-
251	(a) 16 November 1914 (b) 14 June 1919	Western Front, 36th (Ulster) Division	Train, No 1 (HQ) Company (HT)	2501
252	(a) 3 December 1914 (b) 14 June 1919	Western Front, 36th (Ulster) Division	Train, No 2 Company (HT)	2501
253	(a) 12 December 1914 (b) 14 June 1919	Western Front, 36th (Ulster) Division	Train, No 3 Company (HT)	2501
254	(a) 8 December 1914 (b) 14 June 1919	Western Front, 36th (Ulster) Division	Train, No 4 Company (HT)	2501

ASC Co	(a) Formed (b) Disbanded	Theatre/Order of Battle	Role in First World War	WO 95
255	(a) 15 May 1915 (b) 24 January 1920	Home, Fifth New Army Larkhill Western Front, L of C Troops	30 Reserve Park (HT) Local duties 8th Auxiliary (HT) Company	4163
256	(a) 8 February 1915 (b) 31 May 1919	1st Brigade RGA Western Front, 1st Army	Brigade Ammunition Column (MT) Army Siege Park (MT)	265
257	(a) 17 February 1915 (b) 16 June 1919	Western Front, 17th Division	Division Supply Column (MT) Division (MT) Company	892
258	(a) 17 February 1915 (b) Absorbed into 257 MT Co 13 March 1918	Western Front, 17th Division	Division Ammunition Park (MT) 19 Ammunition Sub Park (MT)	764
259	(a) 20 February 1915 (b) 8 July 1919	Western Front, 15th Division Western Front, 32nd Division Western Front, 31st Division	Division Supply Column (MT) Division Supply Column (MT) Division (MT) Company	932
260	(a) 20 February 1915 (b) Absorbed into 259 MT Co 13 March 1918	Western Front, 16th Division	Division Ammunition Park (MT) 32 Ammunition Sub Park (MT) 31 Ammunition Sub Park (MT)	909
261	(a) 25 February 1915 (b) 29 May 1920	Western Front, 17th Division Western Front, 22nd Division Western Front, 30th Division	Division Supply Column (MT) Division Supply Column (MT) Division (MT) Company	894 878
262	(a) 25 February 1915 (b) Absorbed into 261 MT Co 13 March 1918	Western Front, 17th Division Western Front, 22nd Division Western Front, 30th Division	Division Ammunition Park (MT) 22 Ammunition Sub Park (MT) 30 Ammunition Sub Park (MT) 30 Division Supply Column (MT)	878 849
263	(a) 4 March 1915 (b) 1 August 1919	Home, 18th Division Home, 33rd Division Western Front, 56th Division	Division Supply Column (MT) 56th Division (MT) Company	908 979
264	(a) 4 March 1915 (b) Absorbed into 263 MT Co 13 March 1918	Home, 18th Division Home, 33rd Division Western Front, 56th Division	56 Ammunition Sub Park MT Division Supply Column (MT) Division (MT) Company	909
265	(a) 27 February 1915 (b) 12 May 1919	Home, 19th Division Home, 15th Division Western Front, 51st (Highland) Division	Division Supply Column (MT) Division Supply Column (MT) Division (MT) Company	740 979
266	(a) 27 February 1915 (b) Absorbed into 265 MT Co 13 March 1918	Home, 19th Division Home, 15th Division Western Front, 4th Corps	Division Ammunition Park (MT) 51st Ammunition Sub Park (MT)	742
267	(a) 4 March 1915 (b) 9 May 1915	Western Front, 20th Division	Division Supply Column (MT) Division (MT) Company	831 832
268	(a) 5 March 1915 (b) Absorbed into 267 MT Co 13 March 1918	Western Front, 14th Corps	20 Ammunition Sub Park (MT)	920
269	(a) 15 February 1915 (b) Absorbed into 344 MT Co 13 March 1918	Western Front, 46th (North Midland) Division	Division Ammunition Park (MT) 46 Ammunition Sub Park (MT)	819
270	(a) 20 February 1915 (b) March 1920	Home Salonika, Army Troops	SA Ammunition Park for RN Division (HT) 29 Reserve Park (HT)	4809
271	(a) 16 February 1915 (b) 6 August 1919	Western Front, 46th (North Midland) Division	Division Supply Column (MT) Division (MT) Company	848

ASC Co	(a) Formed (b) Disbanded	Theatre/Order of Battle	Role in First World War	WO 95
272	(a) 1 March 1915 (b) 27 June 1919	5th Brigade RGA HQ Canadian Corps Heavy Artillery HQ 1st Australian & New Zealand Corps Australian Corps Heavy Artillery	Ammunition Column (MT) 12 Siege Battery Attached Corps Heavy Artillery Attached Corps Heavy Artillery	-
273	(a) 9 November 1914 (b) 28 May 1919	Home, 2nd Mounted Division Italy, 21st Division	Division Supply Column (HT) Division Supply Column (MT) Division (MT) Company	762
274	(a) 11 March 1915 (b) 20 November 1919	42nd Division Plumstead, Home Forces	Division Supply Column (MT) 13th Local Auxiliary (MT) Company Driver Training Centre	5460
275	(a) 2 March 1915 (b) 18 March 1916	Egypt, Gallipoli, Royal Naval Division	Division Supply Column (HT) Small Arms Ammunition Column (HT)	-
276	(a) 2 March 1915 (b) 16 February 1916	Egypt, Gallipoli, Royal Naval Division	Division Supply Column (HT) Small Arms Ammunition Column (HT)	-
277	(a) 6 March 1915 (b) 14 May 1919	Western Front, 47th (London) Division	Division Supply Column (MT) Division (MT) Company	892
278	(a) 8 March 1915 (b) Absorbed into 277 MT Co 13 March 1918	Western Front, 47th (London) Division	Division Ammunition Park (MT) 47 Ammunition Sub Park (MT)	765
279	(a) 3 March 1915 (b) 3 June 1919	Western Front, 11th Division Western Front, 31st Division	Division Supply Column (HT) Train, No 4 Company (HT)	-
280	(a) 9 March 1915 (b) 5 November 1919	Western Front, Rouen	1st Auxiliary HT Company	-
281	(a) 9 March 1915 (b) 5 July 1919	Western Front, Havre	2nd Auxiliary HT Company	-
282	(a) 4 March 1915 (b) 28 June 1919	Home, Western Front, 15th Brigade RGA Western Front, 1st Corps, Heavy Artillery	Brigade Ammunition Column (MT) Corps Siege Park (MT)	628
283	(a) 4 March 1915 (b) 1 September 1919	Home, Western Front, 19th Brigade, RGA Western Front, 7th Corps, Heavy Artillery	Ammunition Column (MT) 'G' Corps Siege Park (MT)	817
284	(a) 6 March 1915 (b) 29 January 1919	Western Front, 39th Division	Train, No 1 (HQ) Company (HT)	2580
285	(a) 6 March 1915 (b) 29 January 1919	Western Front, 39th Division	Train, No 2 Company (HT)	2580
286	(a) 6 March 1915 (b) 29 January 1919	Western Front, 39th Division	Train, No 3 Company (HT)	2580
287	(a) 6 March 1915 (b) 25 April 1919	Western Front, 39th Division Western Front, Fifth Army	Train, No 4 Company (HT) Army HT Vehicle Reception Park	2580 570
288	(a) 6 March 1915 (b) 4-20 April 1919	Western Front, 37th Division	Train, No 1 (HQ) Company (HT)	2526
289	(a) 6 March 1915 (b) 4-20 April 1919	Western Front, 37th Division	Train, No 2 Company (HT)	2526

ASC Co	(a) Formed (b) Disbanded	Theatre/Order of Battle	Role in First World War	WO 95
290	(a) 6 March 1915 (b) 4-20 April 1919	Western Front, 37th Division	Train, No 3 Company (HT)	2526
291	(a) 6 March 1915 (b) 4-20 April 1919	Western Front, 37th Division	Train, No 4 Company (HT)	2526
292	(a) 6 March 1915 (b) 16 June 1919	Western Front, 40th Division	Train, No 1 (HQ) Company (HT)	2603
293	(a) 6 March 1915 (b) 16 June 1919	Western Front, 40th Division	Train, No 2 Company (HT)	2603
294	(a) 6 March 1915 (b) 16 June 1919	Western Front, 40th Division	Train, No 3 Company (HT)	2603
295	(a) 6 March 1915 (b) 16 June 1919	Western Front, 40th Division	Train, No 4 Company (HT)	2603
296	(a) 6 March 1915 (b) Re-roled as 4 HT Co on 1 June 1923	Western Front, Italy, 41st Division	Train, No 1 (HQ) Company (HT)	4242 2631
297	(a) 6 March 1915 (b) Re-roled as 5 HT Co on 1 June 1923	Western Front, Italy, 41st Division	Train, No 2 Company (HT)	4242 2631
298	(a) 6 March 1915 (b) 1 April 1923	Western Front, Italy, 41st Division	Train, No 3 Company (HT)	4242 2631
299	(a) 6 March 1915 (b) 28 October 1919	Western Front, Italy, 41st Division	Train, No 4 Company (HT)	4242 2631
300	(a) 11 June 1915 (b) Re-roled as 1 Australian MT Co 17 August 1918	Formed as 17th Division Supply Column Western Front, 1 Australia & New Zealand Corps	1st Australian Division Supply Column (MT) 1st Australian Division MT Company	1021
301	(a) 11 June 1915 (b) Absorbed into 300 MT Co 13 March 1918	Formed as 17th Division Ammunition Park Western Front, 1 Australia & New Zealand Corps	1 Ammunition Sub Park (MT)	1028
302	(a) 14 June 1915 (b) 23 January 1920	Western Front, 17th Corps	61st Division Supply Column (MT) 61st Division (MT) Company	949
303	(a) 14 June 1915 (b) 28 February 1921	Egypt, Alexandria, L of C	35th Division Ammunition Park (MT) 35 Ammunition Sub Park (MT)	4467 4721
304	(a) 14 June 1915 (b) 4 June 1919	Western Front, 19th Corps	35th Division Supply Column (MT) 35th Division (MT) Company	972
305	(a) 14 June 1915 (b) Absorbed into 304 MT Co 13 March 1918	Western Front, 2nd Corps	35 Ammunition Sub Park (MT)	667
306	(a) 16 June 1915 (b) 24 April 1919	Western Front, 6th Corps	Guards Division Supply Column (MT) Guards Division (MT) Company	797 798
307	(a) 16 June 1915 (b) Absorbed into 306 MT Co 13 March 1918	Western Front, 17th Corps	Guards Ammunition Sub Park (MT)	950
308	(a) 2 April 1915 (b) 1 December 1921	Wendover, Crowborough Camp, Sussex, Eighth New Army	45 Reserve Park (HT) Local duties	-

ASC Co	(a) Formed (b) Disbanded	Theatre/Order of Battle	Role in First World War	WO 95
309	(a) 2 April 1915 (b) Re-roled as No 1 HT Co 30 July 1920	Portslade, St Albans, Aldershot, Eighth New Army	35 Reserve Park (HT) Local duties	-
310	(a) 4 April 1915 (b) 27 March 1920	Western Front, GHQ Troops	33 Reserve Park (HT) 17 Auxiliary (Horse) Company	142 133
311	(a) 3 April 1915 (b) May 1917	Winchester, Eighth New Army Home Forces	36 Reserve Park (HT) Local duties	5460
312	(a) 4 January 1915 (b) 17 April 1916	Oswestry, Seventh New Army	43 Reserve Park (HT) Local duties	-
313	(a) 2 April 1915 (b) July 1921	Egypt, Cairo District Troops	6th Auxiliary HT Company	4469 4457
314	(a) 21 April 1915 (b) 10 June 1919	Western Front	2nd Advanced HT Depot	-
315	(a) 9 March 1915 (b) 2 February 1920	Western Front, Havre, Etaples, L of C Troops	3rd Auxiliary (Petrol) Company (MT)	4164
316	(a) 9 March 1915 (b) 6 September 1919	Western Front, L of C Troops	4th Auxiliary (Petrol) Company (MT) Local transport Rouen and forestry work (Clayton steam tractors)	4164
317	(a) 9 March 1915 (b) 25 September 1919	Western Front, L of C Troops	5th Auxiliary (Petrol) Company Detachment of Advanced MT Depot	4164
318	(a) 9 March 1915 (b) 31 March 1920	Western Front, L of C Troops Boulogne	6th Auxiliary (Petrol) Company Local transport	4164
319	(a) 9 March 1915 (b) 4 May 1919	Western Front, Paris, L of C Troops	1st Heavy Repair Shop (MT)	4166
320	(a) 9 March 1915 (b) 22 July 1919	Western Front, Rouen, L of C Troops	2nd Heavy Repair Shop (MT)	4167
321	(a) 26 August 1914 (b) 2 August 1919	19 Infantry Brigade Western Front, Italy, 11th Corps	Brigade Supply Column (MT) Corps Troops Supply Column (MT) Corps Troops (MT) Company	891 4211
322	(a) 18 March 1915 (b) 22 October 1919	Mesopotamia, Ramadie East Africa	1 (Willoughby's) Armoured Motor Battery Workshop 15 Light Armoured Battery	-
323	(a) 9 March 1915 (b) 22 October 1919	Western Front, Second Army	5 Motor Ambulance Company (MT)	340
324	(a) 9 March 1915 (b) 2 July 1919	Western Front, Third Army	6 Motor Ambulance Convoy (MT)	410
325	(a) 9 March 1915 (b) 19 November 1919	Western Front, First Army Salonika, Army Troops	7 Motor Ambulance Convoy (MT)	248 4804
326	(a) 9 March 1915 (b) 11 August 1920	Western Front, First Army	8 Motor Ambulance Convoy (MT)	248
327	(a) 8 March 1915 (b) 9 December 1919	Home Western Front, GHQ Troops	44 Reserve Park (HT) 32 Reserve Park (HT) 16 Auxiliary (HT) Company	142 133
328	(a) 13 March 1915 (b) 29 March 1919	Western Front, 48th (South Midland) Division Italy, GHQ Troops	Division Supply Column (MT) Division (MT) Company	958 4210

ASC Co	(a) Formed (b) Disbanded	Theatre/Order of Battle	Role in First World War	WO 95
329	(a) 13 March 1915 (b) Absorbed into 719 MT Co 13 March 1918	Western Front, 48th South Midland)	Division Supply Column (MT) 48 Ammunition Sub Park (MT)	909
330	(a) 29 April 1915 (b) 16 June 1919	Western Front, 38th (Welsh) Division	Train, No 1 (HQ) Company (HT)	2550
331	(a) 29 April 1915 (b) 16 June 1919	Western Front, 38th (Welsh) Division	Train, No 2 Company (HT)	2550
332	(a) 29 April 1915 (b) 16 June 1919	Western Front, 38th (Welsh) Division	Train, No 3 Company (HT)	2550
333	(a) 29 April 1915 (b) 16 June 1919	Western Front, 38th (Welsh) Division	Train, No 4 Company (HT)	2550
334	(a) 29 April 1915 (b) 15 November 1919	Home, Porthcawl Western Front, GHQ Troops Western Front, Fourth Army	31st Reserve Park (HT) 4 Auxiliary (HT) Company Army Auxiliary (HT) Company	132 512
335	(a) 16 March 1915 (b) 10 August 1919	14th Brigade RGA 13th Corps, Heavy Artillery	Brigade Ammunition Column (MT) Corps Siege Park (MT)	907
336	(a) 1 April 1915 (b) 6 March 1919	Western Front, 50th (Northumbrian) Division, Italy, GHQ Troops Italy, 7th Division	Division Supply Column (MT) Division (MT) Company	878 4210 4213
337	(a) 1 April 1919 (b) Absorbed into 336 MT Co 18 February 1918	Western Front, 2 Australia & New Zealand Corps Italy, 14th Corps	50 Ammunition Sub Park (MT)	1044 4213
338	(a) 25 April 1915 (b) April 1919	Home, 22nd Division Home, 31st Division Egypt, 10th Division Salonika, Army Troops	Division Supply Column (MT) 91st Auxiliary (MT) Company	4466 4811
339	(a) 25 April 1915 (b) August 1919	Home, 22nd Division Home, 31st Division Western Front, GHQ Troops	Division Ammunition Park (MT) 7 GHQ Ammunition Park (MT) 51 Auxiliary (Omnibus) Company	149 131
340	(a) 12 May 1915 (b) 24 May 1919	Western Front, 23rd Division Western Front, 50th Division	Division Supply Column (MT) Division (MT) Company	830 908
341	(a) 12 May 1915 (b) Absorbed into No 1 MT Depot 14 October 1919	Home, 23rd Division Western Front, GHQ Troops	Division Supply Column (MT) 8 GHQ Ammunition Park (MT) 8 GHQ Reserve (MT) Company	131 135
342	(a) 12 May 1915 (b) 18 July 1919	Western Front, 24th Division	Division Supply Column (MT) Division (MT) Company	626
343	(a) 12 May 1915 (b) Absorbed into 342 MT Co 13 March 1918	Western Front, 2nd Corps	24 Ammunition Sub Park (MT)	667
344	(a) 20 May 1915 (b) 17 July 1919	Western Front, 25th Division	Division Supply Column (MT) Division (MT) Company	908
345	(a) 20 May 1915 (b) Absorbed into 733 MT Co 19 February 1918	Home Western Front, 2 Australia & New Zealand Corps, 25 Division Italy, 11 Corps	25 Ammunition Sub Park (MT) 25 Division Supply Column (MT)	1043 4211

ASC Co	(a) Formed (b) Disbanded	Theatre/Order of Battle	Role in First World War	WO 95
346	(a) 17 June 1915 (b) 26 April 1919	Western Front, 34th Division Salonika, Army Troops Salonika, 28th Division	Division Supply Column (MT) 92nd Auxiliary (MT) Company	4811
347	(a) 17 June 1915 (b) 30 September 1919	Home Egypt, L of C Egypt, Ismailia District Palestine, L of C Troops	34 Ammunition Sub Park (MT) 347 MT Company	4721 4413 4737
348	(a) 29 March 1915 (b) Re-roled as Nos 10 & 11 Companies 1 August 1922	Home Forces, 42nd Division Larkhill, Wilton	Division Ammunition Park (MT) 14th Auxiliary MT Company	5460
349	(a) 1 April 1915 (b) 19 May 1919	Western Front, 2 Australia & New Zealand Corps Western Front 49th (West Riding) Division (22 Corps)	Division Supply Column (MT) Division (MT) Company	1042 979
350	(a) 1 April 1915 (b) Absorbed into 349 MT Co 13 March 1918	49th (West Riding) Division Western Front, 2 Australia & New Zealand Corps	Division Ammunition Park (MT) 49 Ammunition Sub Park (MT)	1044 979
351	(a) 28 March 1915 (b) 30 November 1921	Bulford, Southern Command Home Forces	3rd Auxiliary (HT) Company	5460
352	(a) 25 April 1915 (b) 31 October 1919	Home, 15th Division Home, Western Front, 26th Division Western Front, 32nd Division	Division Supply Column (MT) Division (MT) Company	848
353	(a) 25 April 1915 (b) Absorbed into 352 MT Co 13 March 1918	Home, 15th Division Home, Western Front, 26th Division	Division Ammunition Park (MT) 32nd Ammunition Sub Park (MT)	667
354	(a) 28 April 1915 (b) 14 May 1919	Western Front, 52nd (Lowland) Division Western Front, 30th Division Western Front, 34th Division Western Front, 55th Division	Division Supply Column (MT) Division Supply Column (MT) (with 77 Company) Division Supply Column (MT) (with 179 Company), Division (MT) Company	627 878
355	(a) 14 April 1915 (b) March 1920	Western Front, Second Army Salonika, Army Troops	9 Motor Ambulance Convoy	340 4804
356	(a) 20 April 1915 (b) Absorbed into 45 MT Co 1 February 1920	Western Front, L of C Troops	7th Auxiliary (Steam) Company (MT)	4165
357	(a) 23 April 1915 (b) Absorbed into 354 MT Co 13 March 1918	Home, 52nd (Lowland) Division Western Front, 1st Corps	Division Ammunition Park (MT) 30 Ammunition Sub Park (MT) 34 Ammunition Sub Park (MT)	628
358	(a) 3 May 1915 (b) 5 July 1919	Western Front, L of C Troops	3rd ASC Repair Shop (MT) 3rd Heavy Repair Shop (MT) 26 MT Vehicle Reception Park	4167
359	(a) 10 May 1915 (b) 28 October 1919	Western Front, Fourth Army, Army Troops	10 Motor Ambulance Convoy (MT)	496
360	(a) 4 May 1915 (b) 18 January 1919	Western Front, Fourth Army, Army Troops, GHQ Troops Italy, GHQ Troops	4 Bridging Train (MT) 4 Pontoon Park (MT)	514 4210

ASC Co	(a) Formed (b) Disbanded	Theatre/Order of Battle	Role in First World War	WO 95
361	(a) 6 May 1915 (b) 11 March 1920	Western Front, Marseilles	4th Auxiliary (HT) Company	-
362	(a) 7 May 1915 (b) 18 February 1919	Home Salonika, Army Troops	34 Reserve Park (HT) 21st Auxiliary (HT) Company	4809
363	(a) 7 May 1915 (b) 18 February 1919	Home, 18th Brigade RGA 5th Corps Heavy Artillery	Brigade Ammunition Column (MT) Corps Siege Park (MT)	764
364	(a) 10 May 1915 (b) 14 August 1920	Western Front, Calais, L of C Troops	2nd Base MT Depot	4188
365	(a) 18 May 1915 (b) 9 April 1921	Western Front, L of C Troops, Northern L of C	2nd Advanced MT Depot	4184
366	(a) 24 May 1915 (b) 30 September 1919	Western Front, L of C Troops	8th Auxiliary (Steam) Company (MT)	-
367	(a) 21 May 1915 (b) 11 June 1919	Western Front, Hazebrouck, Second Army Troops	9th Auxiliary (Steam) Company (MT)	353
368	(a) 26 May 1915 (b) 17 November 1919	Western Front, 6th Corps	Corps Troops Supply Column (MT) Corps Troops (MT) Company	795
369	(a) 27 May 1915 (b) Designated 12 MT Co 1 August 1922	Home Forces, Fulham	10th Auxiliary (MT) Company	5460
370	(a) 1 June 1915 (b) 30 June 1919	Western Front, Third Army Army Troops	6 Bridging Train (MT) 6 Pontoon Park (MT)	427
371	(a) 13 July 1915 (b) 31 October 1919	Western Front, Third Army Army Troops	Supply Column (MT) MT Company	428
372	(a) 9 June 1915 (b) Absorbed into 22 L of C Supply Co (date unknown)	Western Front, Boulogne, L of C Troops	5th Auxiliary (HT) Company	4163
373	(a) 23 June 1915 (b) 30 June 1920	Colchester, Bedford, Hitchin	11th Auxiliary (MT) Company	-
374	(a) 28 June 1915 (b) 21 September 1919	Home, 38th Division Western Front, 39th Division	Division Supply Column (MT) Division (MT) Company	818
375	(a) 28 June 1915 (b) Absorbed into 374 MT Co 13 March 1918	Home, 38th Division Western Front, 39th Division	38 Ammunition Sub Park (MT) 39 Ammunition Sub Park (MT)	667
376	(a) 29 June 1915 (b) 26 March 1919	Home, 24th Brigade RGA Salonika, Army Troops	Brigade Ammunition Column (MT) 43rd Siege Park (MT), MT Company	4812
377	(a) 3 July 1915 (b) 5 June 1919	Home, 23rd Brigade RGA Western Front, Third Army, Heavy Artillery	Brigade Ammunition Column (MT) Army Siege Park (MT)	427
378	(a) 7 July 1915 (b) 14 January 1921	Western Front, Fourth Army	11 Motor Ambulance Convoy	496
379	(a) 12 July 1915 (b) 5 August 1919	Western Front, 36th Division	Division Supply Column (MT) Division (MT) Company	666
380	(a) 12 July 1915 (b) Absorbed into 379 MT Co 13 March 1918	Western Front, 36th Division	36 Ammunition Sub Park (MT)	705

ASC Co	(a) Formed (b) Disbanded	Theatre/Order of Battle	Role in First World War	WO 95
381	(a) 12 July 1915 (b) Reformed as 13 and 14 MT Companies 1 August 1922	Home Forces Southampton, Portsmouth	12th Local Auxiliary (MT) Company	5460
382	(a) 13 July 1915 (b) 30 November 1919	Western Front, 7th Corps	Corps Troops Supply Column (MT) Corps Troops (MT) Company (Peace Conference MT Company in Paris)	817
383	(a) 13 July 1915 (b) 21 November 1919	Western Front, 10th Corps	Corps Troops Supply Column (MT) Corps Troops (MT) Company	877
384	(a) 1 January 1915 (b) 27 October 1919	Western Front, First Army	Army Troops (MT) Company Army Troops Supply Column (MT)	265
385	(a) 2 January 1915 (b) 4 November 1919	Western Front, Second Army Italy, GHQ Troops Western Front, Fifth Army	Army Troops Supply Column (MT) GHQ Troops Supply Column (MT) Army Troops Supply Column (with 393 Company) (MT)	354 4209 570
386	(a) 19 August 1914 (b) 13 August 1919	Western Front, 1st Corps	Corps Troops Supply Column (MT) Corps Troops (MT) Company	625
387	(a) 18 August 1914 (b) 4 November 1919	Western Front, 2nd Corps	Corps Troops Supply Column (MT) Corps Troops (MT) Company	665
388	(a) 2 September 1914 (b) 21 June 1919	Western Front, 3rd Corps	Corps Troops Supply Column (MT) Corps Troops (MT) Company	703
389	(a) 2 October 1914 (b) 12 October 1919	Western Front, 4th Corps	Corps Troops Supply Column (MT) Corps Troops (MT) Company	738
390	(a) 16 January 1919 (b) 18 July 1919	Western Front, 5th Corps	Corps Troops Supply Column (MT) Corps Troops (MT) Company	762
391	(a) 1 November 1914 (b) 1 March 1919	Western Front, Indian Corps Western Front, 14 Corps Italy, GHQ Troops	Corps Troops Supply Column (MT) Corps Troops Supply Column (MT) "J" Corps Troops MT Company Corps Troops (MT) Company	920 4209
392	(a) 10 October 1914 (b) 19 May 1919	Western Front, Cavalry Corps	Corps Troops Supply Column (MT) Corps Troops (MT) Company	584
393	(a) 15 December 1914 (b) 18 September 1919	Western Front, Indian Cavalry Corps Troops Western Front, 5th Army Troops	Army Troops Supply Column (MT) (with 385 Company) Army Troops Supply Column (with 585 Company)	514 570
394	(a) 9 January 1915 (b) Absorbed (date unknown)	Gallipoli, MEF	3rd Advanced HT Depot	-
395	(a) 7 July 1915 (b) Absorbed into Labour Corps June 1917	Home, 10th Division	Division Supply Column (MT) (Supply details)	-
396	(a) 7 July 1915 (b) Absorbed into Labour Corps June 1917	Home, 11th Division	Division Supply Column (MT) (Supply details)	-
397	(a) 7 July 1915 (b) Absorbed into Labour Corps June 1917	Home, 13th Division	Division Supply Column (MT) (Supply details)	-

ASC Co	(a) Formed (b) Disbanded	Theatre/Order of Battle	Role in First World War	WO 95
398	(a) 7 July 1915 (b) Absorbed into Labour Corps June 1917	Home, 53rd Division	Division Supply Column (MT) (Supply details)	-
399	(a) 19 July 1915 (b) Absorbed into 1 MT Depot Grove Park 14 October 1919	Western Front, GHQ Troops	6 GHQ Ammunition Park (MT) 6th GHQ Reserve MT Company	131 134
400	(a) 19 July 1915 (b) 2 October 1919	Western Front, GHQ Troops	5 GHQ Ammunition Park (MT) 5th GHQ Reserve MT Company	131 134
401	(a) 13 July 1915 (b) Absorbed into 8 Corps Troops Supply Column March 1916	Western Front, Third Army Western Front, 4th Corps, HQ Heavy Artillery	Army Troops Ammunition Park (MT) Corps Heavy Artillery (MT)	427
402	(a) 16 July 1915 (b) 26 June 1919	Home, 25th Brigade RGA Western Front, 4th Corps HQ Heavy Artillery Western Front, Canadian Corps Heavy Artillery	Brigade Ammunition Column (MT) 'D' Corps Siege Park (MT) Corps Siege Park (MT)	1080
403	(a) 19 July 1915 (b) 18 July 1919	Home, 26th Brigade RGA Western Front 2 Australia & New Zealand Corps Western Front, 22nd Corps	Ammunition Column (MT) 'Y' Corps Siege Park (MT) Attached Corps Heavy Artillery	1041 978
404	(a) 24 July 1915 (b) 5 June 1919	Western Front, Third Army St Omer, Albert, Terramesnil	Army Historical Records. 2nd Mobile Repair Unit (MT)	428
405	(a) 24 July 1915 (b) 14 May 1919	Western Front, GHQ Troops	15th Auxiliary (Omnibus) Company	149
406	(a) 29 July 1915 (b) 11 October 1919	Home, 27th Brigade RGA HQ 10th Corps Heavy Artillery HQ 2nd Corps attached 4th Corps	Brigade Ammunition Column (MT) Corps Siege Park (MT) Attached Heavy Artillery	665
407	(a) 18 July 1915 (b) Absorbed into 63 MT Co 13 March 1918	Western Front, 19th Corps	2 Ammunition Sub Park (MT)	973
408	(a) 4 July 1915 (b) Absorbed into 48 MT Co 13 March 1918	Western Front, 3rd Corps	5 Ammunition Sub Park (MT)	705
409	(a) 8 July 1915 (b) Absorbed into 74 MT Co 13 March 1918	Western Front, 8th Corps	8 Ammunition Sub Park (MT)	833
410	(a) 18 July 1915 (b) Absorbed into 61 MT Co 13 March 1918	Western Front, 6th Corps	27 Ammunition Sub Park (MT) 55 Ammunition Sub Park (MT)	803
411	(a) 18 July 1915 (b) Absorbed into 69 MT Co 13 March 1918	Western Front, 7th Corps,	Lahore Ammunition Sub Park (MT) 16 Ammunition Sub Park (MT)	819
412	(a) 22 September 1914 (b) Absorbed into 415 MT Co 13 March 1918	Western Front, Canadian Corps	1 Canadian Ammunition Sub Park (MT) (Canadian ASC)	1082
413	(a) 16 September 1914 (b) Absorbed into 46 MT Co 9 October 1916	Western Front, 2nd Cavalry Division	Division Supply Column (MT) (No 2 Section)	-

ASC Co	(a) Formed (b) Disbanded	Theatre/Order of Battle	Role in First World War	WO 95
414	(a) 16 September 1914 (b) Absorbed into 73 MT Co 10 October 1916	Western Front, 3rd Cavalry Division	Division Supply Column (MT) (No 2 Section) (with 73 MT Company)	-
415	(a) 22 September 1914 (b) March 1919	Western Front, Canadian Corps	1 Canadian Division Supply Column (MT) (Canadian ASC) 1st Canadian Division (MT) Company	1081
416	(a) 30 March 1915 (b) 25 April 1916	Home, Western Front, 6th Brigade RGA	Brigade Ammunition Column (MT)	-
417	(a) 30 March 1915 (b) 25 April 1916	Home, 12th Brigade RGA Western Front Second Army	Brigade Ammunition Column (MT) Army Troops (MT Company)	355
418	(a) 5 October 1914 (b) 17 June 1919	Western Front, GHQ Troops,	1 Motor Ambulance Convoy	129
419	(a) 8 October 1914 (b) 10 May 1919	Western Front, Second Army	2 Motor Ambulance Convoy	339
420	(a) 12 October 1914 (b) 12 January 1921	Western Front, Fourth Army	3 Motor Ambulance Convoy	496
421	(a) 4 August 1915 (b) 17 May 1919	Western Front, Fifth Army	4 Motor Ambulance Convoy	
422	(a) 2 January 1915 (b) 25 May 1919	Western Front	No 1 Workshop for Anti-Aircraft Batteries (MT)	-
423	(a) 24 June 1915 (b) 6 November 1919	Western Front, Italy, Second Army	No 2 Workshop for Anti-Aircraft Batteries (MT)	-
424	(a) 10 October 1914 (b) 5 July 1919	Western Front, 2nd Cavalry Division	Train, HQ Company (HT)	1128 1129
425	(a) 18 September 1915 (b) 12 July 1919	Western Front, First Army Western Front, GHQ Troops	1st Army Auxiliary (HT) Company	265 132
426	(a) 13 December 1914 (b) January 1918	Western Front, 1st Indian Cavalry Division Western Front, 4th Cavalry Division	HQ Company (HT) (Indian Supply & Transport Corps) Division No 1 (HQ) Company (HT)	1172 1158
427	(a) 13 December 1914 (b) December 1917	Western Front, 2nd Indian Cavalry Division Western Front, 5th Cavalry Division	HQ Company (HT) (Indian Supply & Transport Corps) HQ Company Division Train (HT)	1184 1163
428	(a) 8 January 1915 (b) 3-17 April 1919	Western Front, Lahore Division Egypt, 54th (East Anglian) Division Western Front, 42nd Division	Train, No 1 (HQ) Company (HT)	2653
429	(a) 8 January 1915 (b) 3-17 April 1919	Western Front, Lahore Division Egypt, 54th (East Anglian) Division Western Front, 42nd Division	Train, No 2 Company (HT)	2653
430	(a) 8 January 1915 (b) 3-17 April 1919	Western Front, Lahore Division Egypt, 54th (East Anglian) Division Western Front, 42nd Division	Train, No 3 Company (HT)	2653
431	(a) 8 January 1915 (b) 3-17 April 1919	Western Front, Lahore Division Egypt, 54th (East Anglian) Division Western Front, 42nd Division	Train, No 4 Company (HT)	2653

ASC Co	(a) Formed (b) Disbanded	Theatre/Order of Battle	Role in First World War	WO 95
432	(a) 8 January 1915 (b) 10 March 1922	Western Front, Meerut Division Home Forces, 13th Division Bulford, Perham Down	No 1 HQ Company (Indian Supply & Transport Corps) Train (HT) Local duties/remount training	5460
433	(a) 8 January 1915 (b) 23 April 1918	Western Front, Meerut Division Home Forces, 13th Division Aldershot	No 2 HQ Company (Indian Supply & Transport Corps) Train (HT) Local duties	5460
434	(a) 8 January 1915 (b) 23 April 1918	Western Front, Meerut Division Home Forces, 13th Division Bordon	No 3 HQ Company (Indian Supply & Transport Corps) Train (HT) Local duties	5460
435	(a) 8 January 1915 (b) 16 December 1921	Western Front, Meerut Division Home Forces, 13th Division Chatham (with dets throughout Kent)	No 4 HQ Company (Indian Supply & Transport Corps) Train (HT) Local duties	5460
436	(a) 28 July 1915 (b) 27 April 1919	Western Front, Guards Division	Train, No 1 (HQ) Company (HT)	1209
437	(a) February 1915 (b) March 1919	Western Front, 1 Canadian Division	Train, No 1 (HQ) Company (HT) (Canadian ASC)	3757
438	(a) February 1915 (b) March 1919	Western Front, 1 Canadian Division	Train, No 2 (HQ) Company (HT) (Canadian ASC)	3757
439	(a) February 1915 (b) March 1919	Western Front, 1 Canadian Division	Train, No 3 (HQ) Company (HT) (Canadian ASC)	3757
440	(a) February 1915 (b) March 1919	Western Front, 1 Canadian Division	Train, No 4 (HQ) Company (HT) (Canadian ASC)	3757
441	(a) 27 July 1915 (b) Absorbed into 38 Labour Co 23 March 1916	Home, 52nd Division	Division Supply Column (MT) (Supply details)	-
442	(a) 22 July 1915 (b) Absorbed into 38 Labour Co 23 March 1916	Home, 54th Division	Division Supply Column (MT) (Supply details)	-
443	(a) 19 September 1915 (b) 13 April 1919	Western Front, Second Army Italy, GHQ Troops	2 Army Auxiliary (HT) Company 2 Auxiliary Pack Train (HT)	353 4209
444	(a) 1 October 1914 (b) 22 December 1919	Western Front, GHQ Troops	Lahore Reserve Park (HT) 47 Reserve Park (HT) 22nd Auxiliary (Horse) Company	142 133
445	(a) 10 October 1914 (b) 10 November 1919	Western Front, GHQ Troops	Meerut Reserve Park (HT) 46 Reserve Park (HT) 21 Army Auxiliary (Horse) Company	142 133
446	(a) 22 September 1914 (b) March 1919	Western Front, GHQ Troops	1 Canadian Reserve Park (HT) (Canadian ASC) 1 Canadian Auxiliary (Horse) Company	143 133
447	(a) Ex East Lancs Division Column (TF) (b) 30 June 1919	Egypt, Palestine 42nd (East Lancashire) Division 53 (Welsh) Division Egypt, Palestine, 74th (Yeomanry) Division	Train, No 1 (HQ) Company (HT)	4593 4676 3151
448	(a) Ex East Lancs Division Column (TF) (b) 30 June 1919	Egypt, Palestine 42nd (East Lancashire) Division 53 (Welsh) Division Egypt, Palestine, 74th (Yeomanry) Division	Train, No 2 Company (HT)	4593 4676 3151

ASC Co	(a) Formed (b) Disbanded	Theatre/Order of Battle	Role in First World War	WO 95
449	(a) Ex East Lancs Division Column (TF) (b) 30 June 1919	Egypt, Palestine 42nd (East Lancashire) Division 53 (Welsh) Division Egypt, Palestine, 74th (Yeomanry) Division	Train, No 3 Company (HT)	4593 4676 3151
450	(a) Ex East Lancs Division Column (TF) (b) 30 June 1919	Egypt, Palestine 42nd (East Lancashire) Division 53 (Welsh) Division Egypt, Palestine, 74th (Yeomanry) Division	Train, No 4 Company (HT)	4593 4676 3151
451	(a) Ex North Midland Division Column (TF) (b) 12 August 1919	Western Front, 46th (North Midland) Division	Train, No 1 (HQ) Company (HT)	2682
452	(a) Ex North Midland Division Column (TF) (b) 12 August 1919	Western Front, 46th (North Midland) Division	Train, No 2 Company (HT)	2682
453	(a) Ex North Midland Division Column (TF) (b) 12 August 1919	Western Front, 46th (North Midland) Division	Train, No 3 Company (HT)	2682
454	(a) Ex North Midland Division Column (TF) (b) 12 August 1919	Western Front, 46th (North Midland) Division	Train, No 4 Company (HT)	2682
455	(a) Ex 2nd London Division Column (TF) (b) 23 April - 19 May 1919	Western Front, 47th (2nd London) Division	Train, No 1 (HQ) Company (HT)	2726
456	(a) Ex 2nd London Division Column (TF) (b) 23 April - 19 May 1919	Western Front, 47th (2nd London) Division	Train, No 2 Company (HT)	2726
457	(a) Ex 2nd London Division Column (TF) (b) 23 April - 19 May 1919	Western Front, 47th (2nd London) Division	Train, No 3 Company (HT)	2726
458	(a) Ex 2nd London Division Column (TF) (b) 23 April - 19 May 1919	Western Front, 47th (2nd London) Division	Train, No 4 Company (HT)	2726
459	(a) Ex 1st South Midland Division Column (TF) (b) March 1919	Western Front, Italy 48th (South Midland) Division	Train, No 1 (HQ) Company (HT)	2753 4247
460	(a) Ex 1st South Midland Division Column (TF) (b) March 1919	Western Front, Italy 48th (South Midland) Division	Train, No 2 Company (HT)	2753 4247
461	(a) Ex 1st South Midland Division Column (TF) (b) March 1919	Western Front, Italy 48th (South Midland) Division	Train, No 3 Company (HT)	2753 4247
462	(a) Ex 1st South Midland Division Column (TF) (b) March 1919	Western Front, Italy 48th (South Midland) Division	Train, No 4 Company (HT)	2754 4247
463	(a) Ex West Riding Division Column (TF) (b) 17 June 1919	Western Front, 49th (West Riding) Division	Train, No 1 (HQ) Company (HT)	2791

ASC Co	(a) Formed (b) Disbanded	Theatre/Order of Battle	Role in First World War	WO 95
464	(a) Ex West Riding Division Column (TF) (b) 17 June 1919	Western Front, 49th (West Riding) Division	Train, No 2 Company (HT)	2791
465	(a) Ex West Riding Division Column (TF) (b) 17 June 1919	Western Front, 49th (West Riding) Division	Train, No 3 Company(HT)	2791
466	(a) Ex West Riding Division Column (TF) (b) 17 June 1919	Western Front, 49th (West Riding) Division	Train, No 4 Company (HT)	2791
467	(a) Ex Northumberland Division Column (TF) (b) 8 July 1919	Western Front, 50th (Northumbrian) Division	Train, No 1 (HQ) Company (HT)	2825
468	(a) Ex Northumberland Division Column (TF) (b) 8 July 1919	Western Front, 50th (Northumbrian) Division	Train, No 2 Company (HT)	2825
469	(a) Ex Northumberland Division Column (TF) (b) 8 July 1919	Western Front, 50th (Northumbrian) Division	Train, No 3 Company (HT)	2825
470	(a) Ex Northumberland Division Column (TF) (b) 8 July 1919	Western Front, 50th (Northumbrian) Division	Train, No 4 Company (HT)	2825
471	(a) Ex Highland Division Column (TF) (b) 19-25 April 1919	Western Front, 51st (Highland) Division	Train, No 1 (HQ) Company (HT)	2860
472	(a) Ex Highland Division Column (TF) (b) 19-25 April 1919	Western Front, 51st (Highland) Division	Train, No 2 Company (HT)	2860
473	(a) Ex Highland Division Column (TF) (b) 19-25 April 1919	Western Front, 51st (Highland) Division	Train, No 3 Company (HT)	2860
474	(a) Ex Highland Division Column (TF) (b) 19-25 April 1919	Western Front, 51st (Highland) Division	Train, No 4 Company (HT)	2860
475	(a) Ex Lowland Division Column (TF) (b) 7 July 1919	MEF, 52nd (Lowland) Division Egypt, 10th (Irish) Division Dardanelles, Salonika	Train, No 1 (HQ) Company (HT)	4833 4577 4319
476	(a) Ex Lowland Division Column (TF) (b) 7 July 1919	MEF, 52nd (Lowland) Division Egypt, 10th (Irish) Division Dardanelles, Salonika	Train, No 2 Company (HT)	4833 4577 4319
477	(a) Ex Lowland Division Column (TF) (b) 7 July 1919	MEF, 52nd (Lowland) Division Egypt, 10th (Irish) Division Dardanelles, Salonika	Train, No 3 Company (HT)	4833 4577 4319
478	(a) Ex Lowland Division Column (TF) (b) 7 July 1919	MEF, 52nd (Lowland) Division Egypt, 10th (Irish) Division Dardanelles, Salonika	Train, No 4 Company (HT)	4833 4577 4319
479	(a) Ex Welsh Division Column (TF) (b) 1-4 July 1919	Western Front, 11th (Northern) Division (ex 53rd (Welsh) Division left behind in England) Dardanelles, Egypt	Train, No 1 (HQ) Company (HT)	1804

ASC Co	(a) Formed (b) Disbanded	Theatre/Order of Battle	Role in First World War	WO 95
480	(a) Ex Welsh Division Column (TF) (b) 1-4 July 1919	Western Front, 11th (Northern) Division (ex 53rd (Welsh) Division left behind in England) Dardanelles, Egypt	Train, No 2 Company (HT)	1804
481	(a) Ex Welsh Division Column (TF) (b) 1-4 July 1919	Western Front, 11th (Northern) Division (ex 53rd (Welsh) Division left behind in England) Dardanelles, Egypt	Train, No 3 Company (HT)	1804
482	(a) Ex Welsh Division Column (TF) (b) 1-4 July 1919	Western Front, 11th (Northern) Division (ex 53rd (Welsh) Division left behind in England) Dardanelles, Egypt	Train, No 4 Company (HT)	1804
483	(a) Ex East Anglian Division Column (TF) (b) 11 October 1919	54th (East Anglian) Division (Train left behind in England) 27th Division, Salonika	Train, No 1 (HQ) Company (HT)	-
484	(a) Ex East Anglian Division Column (TF) (b) 11 October 1919	54th (East Anglian) Division (Train left behind in England) 27th Division, Salonika	Train, No 2 Company (HT)	-
485	(a) Ex East Anglian Division Column (TF) (b) 11 October 1919	54th (East Anglian) Division (Train left behind in England) 27th Division, Salonika	Train, No 3 Company (HT)	-
486	(a) Ex East Anglian Division Column (TF) (b) 11 October 1919	54th (East Anglian) Division (Train left behind in England) 27th Division, Salonika	Train, No 4 Company (HT)	-
487	(a) 1 January 1916 (b) 21 January 1922	Home Devonport	50 Reserve Park (HT) HT Company, local duties	-
488	(a) 1 January 1916 (b) 5 May 1920	Home Northampton, Colchester	51 Reserve Park (HT) HT Company, local duties	-
489	(a) 1 January 1916 (b) 31 March 1922	Home Cambridge, Shorncliffe, Dover	52 Reserve Park (HT) HT Company, local duties	-
490	(a) 1 January 1916 (b) 18 October 1919	Home Kinmel Park, Rhyl	53 Reserve Park (HT) HT Company, local duties	-
491	(a) 1 August 1915 (b) 26 June 1919	Western Front, 28th Brigade RGA Western Front, Italy, 11th Corps Heavy Artillery	Ammunition Column (MT) 'L' Corps Siege Park (MT)	891 4211
492	(a) 17 August 1915 (b) Absorbed into 600 MT Co 13 March 1918	Western Front 2nd Australia Division	2 Ammunition Sub Park (MT) 2 Australian Sub Park (MT) (Australian ASC)	1209
493	(a) 17 August 1915 (b) 31 March 1922	Home Egypt, Ismailia District Egypt, Southern Canal Section Palestine, L of C Troops Egypt, Kantara District	31 Ammunition Sub Park (MT) MT Company	4413 4737 4435 4470
494	(a) 11 August 1915 (b) 8 April 1919	Home, 39th Division Western Front, 41st Division Italy, 23rd Division	39th Division Supply Column (MT) 41st Division Supply Column (MT) 23rd Division (MT) Company	972 4210
495	(a) 11 August 1915 (b) Absorbed into 585 MT Co 12 March 1918	Western Front, Fourth Army	39 Ammunition Sub Park (MT) 30 Auxiliary Petrol Company (MT)	512

ASC Co	(a) Formed (b) Disbanded	Theatre/Order of Battle	Role in First World War	WO 95
496	(a) 11 August 1915 (b) 19 March 1920	Home, 40th Division Western Front, 29th Division	Division Ammunition Supply Column (MT) Division Supply Column (MT) Division (MT) Company	666
497	(a) 11 August 1915 (b) Absorbed into 302 MT Co 13 March 1918	Home Western Front, 5th Corps	40 Ammunition Sub Park (MT) 61 Ammunition Sub Park (MT)	766
498	(a) 11 August 1915 (b) 31 May 1921	Home, 41st Division Western Front, 2nd Australian Division Western Front, Italy, 17th Division Italy, Western Front, 41st Division	Division Supply Column (MT) Division Supply Column (MT) Division Supply Column (MT) Division MT Company	972 4213 762
499	(a) 11 August 1915 (b) Absorbed into 340 MT Co 13 March 1918	Home Forces, Western Front, 8th Corps	41 Ammunition Sub Park (MT)	834
500	(a) 3 September 1915 (b) April 1919	Egypt, Alexandria	3rd Base MT Depot	-
501	(a) 27 March 1916 (b) 7 December 1920	Home Forces, 45th Division Western Front, L of C Troops	Train, No 1 (HQ) Company (HT) 11 Auxiliary (Horse) Company	4163
502	(a) 27 March 1916 (b) Absorbed 22 February 1918	Home Forces, 45th Division Codford	Train, No 2 Company (HT) HT Company, local duties	-
503	(a) 27 March 1916 (b) 31 March 1920	Home Forces, 45th Division Winchester, Warminster	Train, No 3 Company (HT) HT Company, local duties	-
504	(a) 27 March 1916 (b) 31 March 1920	Home Forces, 45th Division Bovington	Train, No 4 Company (HT) HT Company, local duties	5460
505	(a) 1 September 1915 (b) June 1919	Home Forces, 55 (West Lancashire) Division Western Front, 57th (West Lancashire) Division	Train, No 1 (HQ) Company (HT)	2975
506	(a) 1 September 1915 (b) June 1919	Home Forces, 55 (West Lancashire) Division Western Front, 57th (West Lancashire) Division	Train, No 2 Company (HT)	2975
507	(a) 1 September 1915 (b) June 1919	Home Forces, 55 (West Lancashire) Division Western Front, 57th (West Lancashire) Division	Train, No 3 Company (HT)	2975
508	(a) 1 September 1915 (b) June 1919	Home Forces, 55 (West Lancashire) Division Western Front, 57th (West Lancashire) Division	Train, No 4 Company (HT)	2975
509	(a) 1 September 1915 (b) 21 June 1919	Western Front, 58th (London) Division	Train, No 1 (HQ) Company (HT) Was 2nd/1st (London) Division Column (TF)	2998
510	(a) 1 September 1915 (b) 21 June 1919	Western Front, 58th (London) Division	Train, No 2 Company (HT) Was 2nd/1st (London) Division Column (TF)	2998
511	(a) 1 September 1915 (b) 21 June 1919	Western Front, 58th (London) Division	Train, No 3 Company (HT) Was 2nd/1st (London) Division Column (TF)	2998
512	(a) 1 September 1915 (b) 21 June 1919	Western Front, 58th (London) Division	Train, No 4 Company (HT) Was 2nd/1st (London) Division Column (TF)	2998

ASC Co	(a) Formed (b) Disbanded	Theatre/Order of Battle	Role in First World War	WO 95
513	(a) 10 September 1915 (b) 15 August 1919	Western Front, 59th (North Midland) Division	Train, No 1 (HQ) Company (HT) Was 2nd/1st (North Midland) Division Column (TF)	3019
514	(a) 10 September 1915 (b) 15 August 1919	Western Front, 59th (North Midland) Division	Train, No 2 Company (HT) Was 2nd/1st (North Midland) Division Column (TF)	3019
515	(a) 10 September 1915 (b) 15 August 1919	Western Front, 59th (North Midland) Division	Train, No 3 Company (HT) Was 2nd/1st (North Midland) Division Column (TF)	3019
516	(a) 10 September 1915 (b) 15 August 1919	Western Front, 59th (North Midland) Division	Train, No 4 Company (HT) Was 2nd/1st (North Midland) Division Column (TF)	3019
517	(a) 14 September 1914 (b) 28 May 1919	Western Front, Salonika, Palestine, 60th (London) Division	Train, No 1 (HQ) Company (HT) Was 2nd/2nd (London) Division Column (TF)	3029 4666
518	(a) 14 September 1914 (b) 28 May 1919	Western Front, Salonika, Palestine, 60th (London) Division	Train, No 2 Company (HT) Was 2nd/2nd (London) Division Column (TF)	3029 4666
519	(a) 14 September 1914 (b) 28 May 1919	Western Front, Salonika, Palestine, 60th (London) Division	Train, No 3 Company (HT) Was 2nd/2nd (London) Division Column (TF)	3029 4666
520	(a) 14 September 1914 (b) 28 May 1919	Western Front, Salonika, Palestine, 60th (London) Division	Train, No 4 Company (HT) Was 2nd/2nd (London) Division Column (TF)	3029 4666
521	(a) September/October 1914 (b) June - August 1919	Western Front, 61st (South Midland) Division	Train, No 1 (HQ) Company (HT) Was 2nd/1st (South Midland) Division Column (TF)	3052
522	(a) September/October 1914 (b) June - August 1919	Western Front, 61st (South Midland) Division	Train, No 2 Company (HT) Was 2nd/1st (South Midland) Division Column (TF)	3052
523	(a) September/October 1914 (b) June - August 1919	Western Front, 61st (South Midland) Division	Train, No 3 Company (HT) Was 2nd/1st (South Midland) Division Column (TF)	3052
524	(a) September/October 1914 (b) June - August 1919	Western Front, 61st (South Midland) Division	Train, No 4 Company (HT) Was 2nd/1st (South Midland) Division Column (TF)	3052
525	(a) 7 September 1915 (b) 17 December 1919	Western Front, 62nd (West Riding) Division	Train, No 1 (HQ) Company (HT) Was 2nd/1st (West Riding) Division Column (TF)	3078
526	(a) 7 September 1915 (b) 17 December 1919	Western Front, 62nd (West Riding) Division	Train, No 2 Company (HT) Was 2nd/1st (West Riding) Division Column (TF)	3078
527	(a) 7 September 1915 (b) 17 December 1919	Western Front, 62nd (West Riding) Division	Train, No 3 Company (HT) Was 2nd/1st (West Riding) Division Column (TF)	3078
528	(a) 7 September 1915 (b) 17 December 1919	Western Front, 62nd (West Riding) Division	Train, No 4 Company (HT) Was 2nd/1st (West Riding) Division Column (TF)	3078
529	(a) 7 September 1915 (b) 26 July 1916	Home, 63rd (Northumbrian) Division Belton Park, Grantham	Train, No 1 (HQ) Company (HT) Was 2nd/1st (Northumbrian) Division Column (TF) HT Company, local duties	-

ASC Co	(a) Formed (b) Disbanded	Theatre/Order of Battle	Role in First World War	WO 95
530	(a) 7 September 1915 (b) 30 September 1919	Home, 63rd (Northumbrian) Division Newcastle-upon-Tyne	Train, No 2 Company (HT) Was 2nd/1st (Northumbrian) Division Column (TF) HT Company, local duties	-
531	(a) 7 September 1915 (b) 18 February 1922	Home, 63rd (Northumbrian) Division York	Train, No 3 Company (HT) Was 2nd/1st (Northumbrian) Division Column (TF) HT Company, local duties	-
532	(a) 7 September 1915 (b) 17 September 1916	Home, 63rd (Northumbrian) Division Grimsby	Train, No 4 Company (HT) Was 2nd/1st (Northumbrian) Division Column (TF) HT Company, local duties	-
533	(a) 8 September 1915 (b) 14 January 1919	Home, 64th (Highland) Division Norwich	Train, No 1 (HQ) Company (HT) Was 2nd/1st (Highland) Division Column (TF)	-
534	(a) 8 September 1915 (b) 11 March 1922	Home, 64th (Highland) Division Cork, Taversham	Train, No 2 Company (HT) Was 2nd/1st (Highland) Division Column (TF)	-
535	(a) 8 September 1915 (b) 11 March 1922	Home, 64th (Highland) Division Fermoy, Cromer	Train, No 3 Company (HT) Was 2nd/1st (Highland) Division Column (TF)	-
536	(a) 8 September 1915 (b) 14 April 1919	Home, 64th (Highland) Division Thetford	Train, No 4 Company (HT) Was 2nd/1st (Highland) Division Column (TF)	-
537	(a) 8 September 1915 (b) 11 March 1922	Home, 65th (Lowland) Division Fermoy	Train, No 1 (HQ) Company (HT) Was 2nd/1st (Lowland) Division Column (TF)	-
538	(a) 8 September 1915 (b) 18 March 1919	Home, 65th (Lowland) Division Curragh	Train, No 2 Company (HT) Was 2nd/1st (Lowland) Division Column (TF)	-
539	(a) 8 September 1915 (b) 31 March 1922	Home, 65th (Lowland) Division Curragh	Train, No 3 Company (HT) Was 2nd/1st (Lowland) Division Column (TF)	-
540	(a) 8 September 1915 (b) 27 January 1919	Home, 65th (Lowland) Division Dublin	Train, No 4 Company (HT) Was 2nd/1st (Lowland) Division Column (TF)	-
541	(a) 8 November 1915 (b) 25 May 1919	Home, 66th (East Lancs) Division Western Front	Train, No 1 (HQ) Company (HT) Was 2nd/1st (East Lancs) Division Column (TF)	3133
542	(a) 8 November 1915 (b) 25 May 1919	Home, 66th (East Lancs) Division Western Front	Train, No 2 Company (HT) Was 2nd/1st (East Lancs) Division Column (TF)	3133
543	(a) 8 November 1915 (b) 25 May 1919	Home, 66th (East Lancs) Division Western Front	Train, No 3 Company (HT) Was 2nd/1st (East Lancs) Division Column (TF)	3133
544	(a) 8 November 1915 (b) 2 July 1919	Home, 66th (East Lancs) Division Western Front	Train, No 4 Company (HT) Was 2nd/1st (East Lancs) Division Column (TF)	3133
545	(a) 8 November 1915 (b) 14 April 1919	Home, 67th (Home Counties) Division Colchester	Train, No 1 (HQ) Company (HT) Was 2nd/1st (Home Counties) Division Column (TF)	5463
546	(a) 8 November 1915 (b) 14 April 1919	Home, 67th (Home Counties) Division Colchester	Train, No 2 Company (HT) Was 2nd/1st (Home Counties) Division Column (TF)	5463

ASC Co	(a) Formed (b) Disbanded	Theatre/Order of Battle	Role in First World War	WO 95
547	(a) 8 November 1915 (b) 28 March 1920	Home, 67th (Home Counties) Division Ipswich	Train, No 3 Company (HT) Was 2nd/1st (Home Counties) Division Column (TF)	5463
548	(a) 8 November 1915 (b) Renumbered 2 HT Co 30 July 1920	Home, 67th (Home Counties) Division Colchester	Train, No 4 Company (HT) Was 2nd/1st (Home Counties) Division Column (TF)	5463
549	(a) 8 November 1915 (b) 14 April 1919	Home, 68th (Welsh) Division Bungay	Train, No 1 (HQ) Company (HT) Was 2nd/1st (Welsh) Division Column (TF)	-
550	(a) 8 November 1915 (b) Renumbered 23 HT Co 30 July 1920	Home, 68th (Welsh) Division Yarmouth	Train, No 2 Company (HT) Was 2nd/1st (Welsh) Division Column (TF)	-
551	(a) 8 November 1915 (b) 14 April 1919	Home, 68th (Welsh) Division Bury St Edmunds	Train, No 3 Company (HT) Was 2nd/1st (Welsh) Division Column (TF)	-
552	(a) 8 November 1915 (b) Renumbered 9 HT Co 30 July 1920	Home, 68th (Welsh) Division Lowestoft	Train, No 4 Company (HT) Was 2nd/1st (Welsh) Division Column (TF)	-
553	(a) 8 November 1915 (b) 14 April 1919	Home, 69th (East Anglian) Division Retford, Doncaster	Train, No 1 (HQ) Company (HT) Was 2nd/1st (East Anglian) Division Column (TF)	-
554	(a) 8 November 1915 (b) Renumbered 6 HT Co 30 July 1920	Home, 69th (East Anglian) Division Retford, Darlington, Aldershot	Train, No 2 Company (HT) Was 2nd/1st (East Anglian) Division Column (TF)	-
555	(a) 8 November 1915 (b) 30 March 1920	Home, 69th (East Anglian) Division Retford, Chipstone, Aldershot	Train, No 3 Company (HT) Was 2nd/1st (East Anglian) Division Column (TF)	-
556	(a) 8 November 1915 (b) 31 March 1920	Home, 69th (East Anglian) Division Retford, Ripon, Aldershot	Train, No 4 Company (HT) Was 2nd/1st (East Anglian) Division Column (TF)	-
557	(a) 26 November 1915 (b) Absorbed 25 April 1916	Home (for Near East) Home Home Western Front, GHQ Troops	Special Base MT Depot Ammunition Column (MT) for 69 Siege Battery RGA Ammunition Column (MT) for 68 Siege Battery RGA 4 Cavalry Division Auxiliary (HT) Company	144
558	(a) 26 November 1915 (b) Absorbed 25 April 1916	Home (for Near East) Home, Western Front, 12th Brigade RGA	Special Base Repair Unit (MT) Ammunition Column (MT) for 70 Siege Battery RGA	-
559	(a) 26 November 1915 (b) 7 November 1919	Western Front, Fifth Army	12 Motor Ambulance Convoy	561
560	(a) 27 November 1915 (b) Absorbed overseas 25 April 1916	Western Front	Ammunition Column (MT) for 35 Siege Battery RGA	-
561	(a) October 1915 (b) March 1916	Brigade RGA Western Front, Third Army	50 Siege Battery RGA (Caterpillars) Army Troops Company (MT) Ammunition Column (MT)	427
562	(a) 29 August 1915 (b) 29 September 1919	Western Front, 30th Brigade RGA HQ 1st ANZAC Corps Western Front, Heavy Artillery HQ 4th Corps Heavy Artillery	Ammunition Column (MT) Corps Siege Park (MT) Corps Siege Park (MT) Corps Siege Park (MT)	355 741

ASC Co	(a) Formed (b) Disbanded	Theatre/Order of Battle	Role in First World War	WO 95
563	(a) 29 August 1915 (b) 14 May 1919	Western Front, GHT Troops	16th Auxiliary (Omnibus) Company (ex Royal Naval Division)	149
564	(a) 30 August 1915 (b) 31 July 1919	Home, Western Front, 12th Corps Western Front, 13th Corps	Corps Troops Supply Column (MT) Corps Troops (MT) Company	907
565	(a) 30 August 1915 (b) 13 November 1919	31st Brigade RGA Western Front, 6th Corps	Brigade Ammunition Column (MT) Corps Siege Park (MT)	794
566	(a) 12 September 1915 (b) 14 May 1920	Western Front, First Army	13 Motor Ambulance Company	248
567	(a) 12 September 1915 (b) 21 September 1919	Western Front, Second Army	14 Motor Ambulance Company	341
568	(a) 12 September 1915 (b) 12 January 1921	Western Front, First Army	15 Motor Ambulance Company	249
569	(a) 12 September 1915 (b) 2 July 1919	Western Front, Third Army	16 Motor Ambulance Company	410
570	(a) 17 September 1915 (b) Absorbed into 648 MT Co 21 June 1917	East Africa, Mbuyuni, L of C Troops	Brigade Supply Column (MT)	5377
571	(a) 16 September 1915 (b) 30 June 1919	Western Front, Third Army Western Front, GHQ Troops	Auxiliary (HT) Company 3 Army Auxiliary (Horse) Company	427 132
572	(a) 4 October 1915 (b) 31 March 1922	Aldershot, ASC Training Establishment	Station Staff Company (HT)	-
573	(a) 8 October 1915 (b) 3 October 1919	Salonika, L of C Troops	3rd Base HT Depot	4947
574	(a) 23 September 1915 (b) 20 September 1919	Western Front, 1st Cavalry Division	Auxiliary (Horse) Company	1107
575	(a) 25 September 1915 (b) 3 July 1919	Western Front, 2nd Cavalry Division	Auxiliary (Horse) Company	1128
576	(a) 23 September 1915 (b) 29 May 1919	Western Front, 3rd Cavalry Division	Auxiliary (Horse) Company	1151
577	(a) 28 September 1915 (b) 21 February 1919	Western Front, 1st Indian Cavalry Division Western Front, 4th Cavalry Division	Division Auxiliary HT Company	131 144 1158
578	(a) 28 September 1915 (b) 13 March 1919	Western Front, 2nd Indian cavalry Division Western Front, 5th Cavalry Division	Division Auxiliary (Horse) Company	1163 1172
579	(a) 19 October 1915 (b) 1 May 1919	Salonika, L of C Troops	4th Advanced HT Depot	4947
580	(a) 1 December 1916 (b) Renumbered 8 HT Co 30 July 1921	Aldershot	7 Auxiliary Horse Company	-
581	(a) 15 September 1915 (b) 18 June 1916	Cameroons, HQ Troops	MT Company	5388
582	(a) 15 September 1915 (b) 21 July 1919	Western Front, 17th Corps	Corps Troops Supply Column (MT)	948

ASC Co	(a) Formed (b) Disbanded	Theatre/Order of Battle	Role in First World War	WO 95
583	(a) 19 September 1915 (b) 8 November 1919	22nd Siege Battery RGA 2nd Army Heavy Artillery GHQ Troops	GHQ Ammunition Column (MT) 11 GHQ Reserve (MT) Company	135
584	(a) 18 September 1915 (b) 11 October 1919	Western Front, Second Army	3 Mobile Repair Unit (MT0	356
585	(a) 18 September 1915 (b) Renumbered 28 MT Co 1 June 1923	Western Front, Fourth Army Second Army	Army Troops Supply Column (with 393 Company) (MT) Fourth Army Troops (MT) Company Second Army Troops (MT) Company	355 514
586	(a) 19 September 1915 (b) Absorbed into 610 Co 13 March 1918	Home Western Front, 22 Corps 2 Australia & New Zealand Corps	Artillery Ammunition Park (MT) 1 New Zealand Ammunition Sub Park (MT)	1044 979
587	(a) 18 September 1915 (b) 1 September 1919	Western Front, Second Army Western Front, GHQ Troops	17 Auxiliary (Petrol) Company (MT) 10 GHQ Reserve MT Company	135 353
588	(a) 23 September 1915 (b) 14 May 1919	Western Front, GHQ Troops	18 Auxiliary (Omnibus) Company	149
589	(a) 20 September 1915 (b) Absorbed into 384 MT Co 12 March 1918	Western Front, First Army	19 Auxiliary (Petrol) Company	266
590	(a) 20 September 1915 (b) 5 September 1919	France, Rouen, L of C Troops	20th Auxiliary (Petrol) Company Local transport work and forestry	4164
591	(a) 20 September 1915 (b) Absorbed into 371 MT Co 12 March 1918	Western Front, Third Army	21 Auxiliary (Petrol) Company Third Army Auxiliary MT Company	426
592	(a) 28 September 1915 (b) 5 September 1919	Home, 32nd Brigade RGA Western Front, 8th Corps	Brigade Ammunition Column (MT) Corps Troops Supply Column (with 885 Comapny), 8 Corps Troops MT Company 123rd Auxiliary (Petrol) Company	829 4165
593	(a) 1 October 1915 (b) 12 July 1918	Home, 33rd Brigade RGA Western Front, 14th Corps Western Front, 8th Corps	Brigade Ammunition Column (MT) Corps Siege Park (with 886 Company) 'H' Corps Siege Park	829
594	(a) 4 October 1915 (b) 31 October 1919	Home, 34th Brigade RGA Western Front, 2nd Corps Heavy Artillery Western Front, 10th Corps Heavy Artillery	Brigade Ammunition Column (MT) 'B' Corps Siege Park (MT) 'X' Corps Siege Park (MT)	877
595	(a) 8 October 1915 (b) 6 March 1919	Salonika, Army Troops	17 Motor Ambulance Convoy	4804
596	(a) 11 October 1915 (b) 31 October 1921	Egypt, GHQ Mesopotamia, Army Troops Bushire Force	GHQ Ammunition Company (MT) (Took part in relief of Kit el Almara) Division Supply Column (MT) Detachment with Bushire Force in the Persian Gulf	5276 5005 5010
597	(a) 11 October 1915 (b) 19 April 1919	Home, GHQ Salonika, Army Troops	Ammunition Park (MT) 29th Ammunition Sub Park (MT) 26th Division Supply Column (MT) 93rd Auxiliary MT) Company	4811
598	(a) 29 October 1915 (b) 31 July 1920	Salonika, L of C Troops Kalamaria	4th Base MT Depot	4948

ASC Co	(a) Formed (b) Disbanded	Theatre/Order of Battle	Role in First World War	WO 95
599	(a) 20 October 1915 (b) 20 August 1919	Home, East Africa, L of C Troops	Advanced MT Depot Based MT Depot and Repair Unit	5378
600	(a) 29 October 1915 (b) Designated 2 Australian MT Co 17 August 1918	Home (for Egypt) Western Front, 2nd Australian Division	Auxiliary Petrol Company (MT) Division Supply Column (MT) Australian ASC vice ASC in July 1917 Division MT Company	1022
601	(a) 29 October 1915 (b) Absorbed into 496 MT Co 13 March 1915	Home, 4th Corps Western Front, 29 Division	Corps Troops Supply Column (MT) 29 Ammunition Sub park (MT)	920
602	(a) 30 October 1915 (b) Absorbed 7 June 1916	Home, 36th Brigade RGA Western Front, 48 Siege Battery RGA	Ammunition Column (MT)	-
603	(a) 5 November 1915 (b) Renumbered 32 MT Co 1 June 1923	Malta	22nd Local Auxiliary (MT) Company	-
604	(a) 15 November 1915 (b) 21 June 1919	Home, 65th Siege Battery Western Front, 15th Corps Heavy Artillery	Ammunition Column (MT) Corps Siege Park (MT)	931
605	(a) 26 November 1915 (b) 6 March 1921	Home (for Near East) Salonika, Army Troops, Black Sea Troops	No 1 Special Service Column (MT) 38 Auxiliary (MT) Company (Light Vans)	4957 4810
606	(a) 22 November 1915 (b) 21 February 1919	London, Shepherds Bush (with detachments in other Commands)	23rd Local Auxiliary (MT) Company (Munitions Services)	5460
607	(a) 26 November 1915 (b) Absorbed into 498 MT Co 18 February 1918	Home (for Near East) Western Front, 10th Corps Italy, 14th Corps	Special Service Column (MT) 2 Australian Ammunition Sub Park (MT) 23 Ammunition Sub Park (MT)	4213 879
608	(a) 26 November 1915 (b) 14 June 1919	Home (for Near East) Western Front, 15th Corps	Special Service Column (MT) 40th Division Supply Column (MT) 40th Division (MT) Company	932
609	(a) 26 November 1915 (b) Absorbed into 494 MT Co 18 February 1918	Home (for Near East) Western Front, 10th Corps Italy, 14th Corps	Special Service Column (MT) 17 Ammunition Sub Park (MT)	879 4213
610	(a) 26 November 1915 (b) 14 May 1919	Home (for Near East) Western Front, 4th Corps Western Front, 1st New Zealand Division	Special Service Column (MT) Division (MT) Company Division Supply Column (MT)	1042 740
611	(a) January 1917 (b) July 1919	Western Front, 17th Corps Heavy Artillery	Corps Siege Park (MT)	948
612	(a) 6 January 1916 (b) Renumbered 15 MT Co 1 August 1922	York, Northern Command	24 Local Auxiliary (MT) Company	-
613	(a) 6 January 1916 (b) Renumbered 16 MT Co 1 August 1922	Liverpool, Western Command	25 Local Auxiliary (MT) Company	-
614	(a) 6 January 1916 (b) Renumbered 17 MT Co 1 August 1922	Edinburgh, Scottish Command	26 Local Auxiliary (MT) Company	-
615	(a) 6 January 1916 (b) 31 March 1923	Dublin, Irish Command	27 Local Auxiliary (MT) Company	-

ASC Co	(a) Formed (b) Disbanded	Theatre/Order of Battle	Role in First World War	WO 95
616	(a) 25 December 1915 (b) Absorbed 25 April 1916	Home, Western Front, 58 Siege Battery RGA	Ammunition Column (MT)	-
617	(a) 25 December 1915 (b) Absorbed 25 April 1916	Home, Western Front, 60 Siege Battery RGA	Ammunition Column (MT)	-
618	(a) January 1916 (b) June 1918	East Africa, L of C Troops	18 Motor Ambulance Convoy	5371
619	(a) 28 December 1915 (b) 8 November 1919	Home, Egypt, 29th Division Egypt, Salonika, 22nd Division, Army Troops	Divisional Supply Column (MT) Division Supply Column (MT) 94th Auxiliary (MT) Company	4811 4413
620	(a) 28 December 1915 (b) 7 April 1919	Regents Park and Kensington Barracks, London	28 Local Auxiliary (MT) Company (Army Postal Services)	-
621	(a) 21 January 1916 (b) 17 November 1917	Aldershot, Catterick, Southport	MT Reception & Discharge Depot	-
622	(a) 30 December 1915 (b) Absorbed into 648 MT Co 21 June 1917	Home (for East Africa) East Africa	Naval Kite Balloon Section (MT)	-
623	(a) 2 January 1916 (b) 31 March 1919	Home (for Mediterranean) London	3 Kite Balloon Section (MT) 31 Local Auxiliary (MT) Company (Railway Assistance)	-
624	(a) 15 January 1916 (b) 13 June 1919	Western Front, Fourth Army 1st ANZAC Corps	8 Pontoon Park (MT)	514
625	(a) 5 January 1916 (b) 30 April 1920	Home Home, 40th Brigade RGA Western Front, 13 Corps Heavy Artillery, Fourth Army Heavy Artillery Western Front, Second Army Heavy Artillery	Ammunition Column (MT) for 49th Siege Battery RGA Siege Park (MT) Second Army Siege Park (MT)	353 514
626	(a) 5 January 1916 (b) December 1918	Egypt, East Africa, L of C Troops	19 Motor Ambulance Convoy	5371
627	(a) 5 January 1916 (b) 24 February 1920	Home Western Front, Fifth Army	20 Motor Ambulance Convoy 25 Motor Ambulance Convoy	561
628	(a) 5 January 1916 (b) 14 April 1920	Home Western Front, Fouth Army	21 Motor Ambulance Convoy 26 Motor Ambulance Convoy	497
629	(a) 5 January 1916 (b) 12 May 1919	Home Western Front, Third Army	22 Motor Ambulance Convoy 27 Motor Ambulance Convoy	411
630	(a) 5 January 1916 (b) Renumbered 26 (Indian) MT Co 6 May 1921	Home India Bangalore, Rawalpindi and East Persia - Corps Troops	23 Motor Ambulance Convoy 28 Motor Ambulance Convoy North West Frontier operations	5390
631	(a) 12 January 1916 (b) 19 July 1919	Home, 38 Brigade RGA East Africa, L of C Troops	MT Company (Artillery Support)	5378
632	(a) 12 January 1916 (b) Absorbed into 648 MT Co 21 June 1917	Royal Marine Artillery Brigade East Africa	Ammunition Column (MT) Artillery Support in East Africa	
633	(a) 12 January 1916 (b) Absorbed into 648 MT Co 21 June 1917	East Africa	Ammunition Column (MT) for 134th (Cornwall) Heavy Battery RGA MT Company	-

ASC Co	(a) Formed (b) Disbanded	Theatre/Order of Battle	Role in First World War	WO 95
634	(a) 13 January 1916 (b) Absorbed into 648 MT Co 21 June 1917	East Africa	Division Ammunition Column (MT)	-
635	(a) 13 January 1916 (b) 19 July 1919	East Africa, Kilwa L of C Troops	Brigade Supply Column (MT) L of C Column (MT), MT Company	5377 5378
636	(a) 15 January 1916 (b) 25 April 1916	Western Front, Third Army	Ammunition Column (MT) attached to 56 Siege Battery RGA	427
637	(a) 16 January 1916 (b) 7 June 1916	Western Front	Siege Park (MT) for 80th Siege Battery RGA	-
638	(a) 22 January 1916 (b) Renumbered 29 MT Co 1 June 1923	Home Western Front, Second Army	25 Motor Ambulance Convoy 20 Motor Ambulance Convoy	341
639	(a) 22 January 1916 (b) 26 November 1919	Home Western Front, Third Army	26 Motor Ambulance Convoy 21 Motor Ambulance Convoy	411
640	(a) 22 January 1916 (b) Absorbed into 45 MT Co 1 January 1921	Home Western Front, Fifth Army	27 Motor Ambulance Convoy 22 Motor Ambulance Convoy	561
641	(a) 27 January 1916 (b) 28 June 1919	Home Western Front, 3rd Corps	Siege Park (MT) for 57th Siege Battery RGA Corps Siege Park (MT)	703
642	(a) 24 January 1916 (b) Absorbed 25 April 1916	Western Front	Siege Park (MT) for 61st Siege Battery RGA	-
643	(a) 25 January 1916 (b) Absorbed 25 April 1916	Western Front, Third Army	Attached 62 Siege Battery RGA (MT)	427
644	(a) 24 January 1916 (b) Redesignated Palestine MT Unit 1 June 1922	Home Alexandria District, Ismailia District Egypt	Heavy Repair Workshop (MT) for 51st Siege Battery RGA	4467 4413
645	(a) 26 January 1916 (b) 10 May 1919	Western Front, Fourth Army	24 Motor Ambulance Convoy	497
646	(a) 27 January 1916 (b) 30 June 1919	Home Western Fron, Fourth Army	Army Corps Water Company (MT) 1 Water Tank Company (MT)	513
647	(a) 6 February 1916 (b) 9 June 1919	Home Western Front, First Army	10 Bridging Train (MT) 10 Pontoon Park (MT)	265
648	(a) 9 February 1916 (b) 19 July 1919	Home East Africa	Water Tank Company (MT) 4th Auxiliary (MT) Company (for maintenance services) Artillery Support	-
649	(a) 11 February 1916 (b) Absorbed 25 April 1916	Home, Western Front	Ammunition Column (MT) for 66th Siege Battery RGA	-
650	(a) 11 February 1916 (b) 15 March 1919	Home Forces, Wilton	32nd Local Auxiliary (MT) Company (Road Board)	5460
651	(a) 15 February 1916 (b) Absorbed 25 April 1916	Western Front	Ammunition Coloumn (MT) for 67th Siege Battery RGA	-
652	(a) 19 February 1916 (b) Absorbed 25 April 1916	Western Front	Ammunition Column (MT) for 68th and 69th Siege Batteries, RGA	-

ASC Co	(a) Formed (b) Disbanded	Theatre/Order of Battle	Role in First World War	WO 95
653	(a) 3 March 1915 (b) Absorbed 25 April 1916	Western Front	Ammunition Column (MT) for 76th Siege Battery RGA	-
654	(a) 4 March 1916 (b) 8 April 1919	Western Front Western Front, 8th Corps Western Front, Italy, 14th Corps	Ammunition Column (MT) for 77th Siege Battery Corps Siege Park (MT) 'J' Corps Siege Park (MT)	4210 920
655	(a) March 1916 (b) Absorbed 7 June 1916	Western Front	Ammunition Column (MT) for 44th Brigade RGA	-
656	(a) 9 March 1916 (b) Renumbered 27 Indian MT Co 6 May 1921	Mesopotamia, Baghdad L of C Troops India & East Persia, Corps Troops	23 Motor Ambulance Convoy MT Company	5248 5390
657	(a) 9 March 1916 (b) 5 June 1919	Western Front, First Army	4 Mobile Repair Unit (MT)	266
658	(a) 13 March 1916 (b) Absorbed 7 June 1916	Western Front	Ammunition Column (MT) for 48th Brigade RGA	-
659	(a) 28 March 1918 (b) Reallocated 6 Australian MT Co 17 August 1918	Western Front, 1st Australian & New Zealand Corps Western Front, Australian Corps	Corps Troops Supply Column (MT) (Australian ASC) Corps Troops (MT) Company 6th Australian (MT) Company	1019 1020
660	(a) 29 March 1916 (b) 29 May 1919	Salonika, L of C Troops	Heavy Repair Shop (MT)	4942
661	(a) 1 April 1916 (b) 17 May 1919	Home, Park Royal	1 Reserve (HT) Depot	-
662	(a) 1 April 1916 (b) 7 April 1919	Home, Park Royal	1 Reserve (HT) Depot	-
663	(a) 20 April 1916 (b) Absorbed 1 April 1917	Home, Park Royal	1 Reserve (HT) Depot	-
664	(a) 20 June 1916 (b) Absorbed 1 April 1917	Home, Park Royal	1 Reserve (HT) Depot	-
665	(a) 1 April 1916 (b) 31 December 1919	Home, Blackheath	2 Reserve (HT) Depot (with 667/668 Companies)	-
666	(a) 1 April 1916 (b) 7 April 1919	Home, Blackheath, Park Royal, Willesden, London	2 Reserve (HT) Depot (Later 1 Reserve (HT) Depot)	-
667	(a) 16 June 1916 (b) 31 December 1919	Home, Blackheath	2 Reserve (HT) Depot (with 668 and 665 Companies)	-
668	(a) 30 June 1916 (b) 31 December 1919	Home, Blackheath	2 Reserve (HT) Depot (with 665 and 667 Companies)	-
669	(a) 18 May 1916 (b) 21 March 1919	Western Front, GHQ Troops	1st Indian Cavalry Reserve Park (HT) 4 Cavalry Reserve Park (HT)	137
670	(a) 18 May 1916 (b) 31 March 1919	Western Front, GHQ Troops	2nd Indian Cavalry Reserve Park (HT) 5 Cavalry Reserve Park (HT)	-
671	(a) 30 June 1916 (b) 31 July 1921	Egypt, District Troops Ismailia District	9 Auxiliary (Horse) Company	4411 4466
672	(a) 20 June 1916 (b) February 1919	Western Front, 2nd Canadian Division	Train, No 1 (HQ) Company (HT) (Canadian ASC)	3810

ASC Co	(a) Formed (b) Disbanded	Theatre/Order of Battle	Role in First World War	WO 95
673	(a) 20 June 1916 (b) February 1919	Western Front, 2nd Canadian Division	Train, No 2 Company (HT) (Canadian ASC)	3810
674	(a) 20 June 1916 (b) February 1919	Western Front, 2nd Canadian Division	Train, No 3 Company (HT) (Canadian ASC)	3810
675	(a) 20 June 1916 (b) February 1919	Western Front, 2nd Canadian Division	Train, No 4 Company (HT) (Canadian ASC)	3810
676	(a) 20 June 1916 (b) March 1916	Western Front, 3rd Canadian Division	Train, No 1 (HQ) (HT) Company (Canadian ASC)	3863
677	(a) 20 June 1916 (b) March 1919	Western Front, 3rd Canadian Division	Train, No 2 Company (HT) (Canadian ASC)	3863
678	(a) 20 June 1916 (b) March 1919	Western Front, 3rd Canadian Division	Train, No 3 Company (HT) (Canadian ASC)	3863
679	(a) 20 June 1916 (b) March 1919	Western Front, 3rd Canadian Division	Train, No 4 Company (HT) (Canadian ASC)	3863
680	(a) 20 June 1916 (b) March 1919	Western Front, GHQ Troops	2 Canadian Reserve Park (HT) 2 Canadian Auxiliary (Horse) Company (Canadian ASC)	143 133
681	(a) 30 March 1916 (b) Absorbed into 393 MT Co 12 March 1918	Western Front, Fifth Army	33 Auxiliary (Petrol) Company (MT)	570
682	(a) 1 April 1916 (b) 11 June 1919	Home, Western Front, Fifth Army	12 Bridging Train (MT) 12 Pontoon Park (MT)	570
683	(a) 31 March 1916 (b) 22 April 1919	Western Front, 60th Division Salonika, Army Troops	Division Supply Column (MT) 95th Auxiliary (MT) Company	949 4811
684	(a) 31 March 1916 (b) Absorbed into 608 MT Co 13 March 1918	Western Front, 6th Corps	40 Ammunition Sub Park (MT)	803
685	(a) 31 March 1916 (b) Absorbed into 778, 810 MT Companies and Base MT Depot 25 November 1917	Western Front, 17th Corps Salonika, 12th Corps	60 Ammunition Sub Park (MT)	950 4822
686	(a) 6 May 1916 (b) Designated 4 Australian DSC 13 March 1918	Western Front, 4 Australian Division	Division Supply Column (MT) 4 Australian (MT) Company (Australian ASC personnel wef November 1917)	1024 1025
687	(a) 1 April 1916 (b) 8 August 1919	Western Front, 2 Australian and New Zealand Corps Western Front, 22 Corps	Corps Troops Supply Column (MT) Corps Troops Supply Column (MT) Corps Troops (MT) Company	1040 978
688	(a) 1 April 1916 (b) 19 July 1919	Salonika, Army Troops	MT Supply Column with Serbian Army (Awarded Croix de Guerre Avec Palme)	4814
689	(a) 1 April 1916 (b) 22 June 1919	Salonika, Army Troops	MT Supply Column with Serbian Army	4814
690	(a) 6 May 1916 (b) Absorbed into 686 MT Co 13 March 1918	Western Front, 1 Australian and New Zealand Corps	4th Australian Ammunition Sub Park (MT) (Australian ASC)	1030
691	(a) 4 April 1916 (b) Absorbed 7 June 1916	Western Front, 50 Brigade RGA	Ammunition Column (MT)	-

ASC Co	(a) Formed (b) Disbanded	Theatre/Order of Battle	Role in First World War	WO 95
692	(a) 7 April 1916 (b) Renumbered 16 (Indian) MT Co 6 May 1921	India (Bangalore), Peshawar Mesopotamia	Base MT Workshop Heavy Repair Shop	5390
693	(a) 7 April 1916 (b) Renumbered 21 (Indian) MT Co 6 May 1921	India (Bangalore), Nowshera, Rawalpindi and East Persia - Corps Troops, Northern L of C	MT Supply Column MT Company	5390 5393
694	(a) 7 April 1916 (b) Renumbered 22 (Indian) MT Co 6 May 1921	India (Bangalore) Rawalpindi and East Persia - Corps Troops	MT Supply Column	5390
695	(a) 12 April 1916 (b) 31 March 1920	Mesopotamia, Makina, L of C	Base (MT) Depot/Base MT Stores/Advanced MT Stores Section	5284
696	(a) 16 April 1916 (b) 19 June 1919	Western Front, 15th Corps	Corps Troops Supply Column (MT) Corps Troops (MT) Company	931
697	(a) 22 April 1916 (b) Absorbed 23 December 1916	Western Front	No 5 Workshop for Anti-Aircraft Guns	-
698	(a) 22 April 1916 (b) 13 July 1919	Western Front, Fifth Army - Army Troops	No 4 Anti-Aircraft Battery Workshop Unit No 5 Workshop for Anti-Aircraft Guns No 6 Workshop for Anti-Aircraft Guns	570
699	(a) 17 April 1916 (b) 21 February 1919	East Africa, L of C Troops	29 Motor Ambulance Convoy	5371
700	(a) 24 April 1916 (b) 21 July 1919	Manchester, Southport	34 Local Auxiliary (MT) Company (Ministry of Munitions)	-
701	(a) 5 May 1916 (b) 14 May 1919	Western Front, 63rd (Royal Naval) Division	Division Supply Column (MT) Division (MT) Company	949
702	(a) 5 May 1916 (b) Absorbed into 701 MT Co 13 March 1918	Western Front, 63rd (Royal Naval) Division	Royal Naval Ammunition Park (MT) 63 Ammunition Sub Park (MT)	766
703	(a) 30 May 1916 (b) 26 July 1919	Western Front	34 Auxiliary (Petrol) Company 35 Auxiliary (Petrol) Company	-
704	(a) 3 June 1916 (b) 17 May 1920	Western Front, Third Army	30 Motor Ambulance Convoy	411
705	(a) 3 June 1916 (b) 10 May 1919	Western Front, First Army	31 Motor Ambulance Convoy	249
706	(a) 5 June 1916 (b) 23 November 1919	Salonika, Army Troops Black Sea Troops	MT Supply Column with Serbian Army MT Company	4814 4954
707	(a) 5 June 1916 (b) 27 June 1919	Salonika, Army Troops	MT Supply Column with Serbian Army	4814
708	(a) 5 June 1916 (b) 26 May 1919	Salonika, Army Troops	MT Supply Column with Serbian Army	4814
709	(a) 5 June 1916 (b) 18 July 1919	Salonika, Army Troops	MT Supply Column with Serbian Army	4814
710	(a) 9 June 1916 (b) 3 December 1918	Newton Street, London	36 Local Auxiliary (MT) Company Home MT Depot ASC	-

ASC Co	(a) Formed (b) Disbanded	Theatre/Order of Battle	Role in First World War	WO 95
711	(a) 13 June 1916 (b) 23 February 1917 to Machine Gun Corps Heavy Branch	Home, Heavy Branch Machine Gun Corps Western Front, Tank Corps Egypt, Eastern Force Troops	MT Company/Workshop/Instr School (see WO 158/800-805) 1 Brigade ASC Workshop (MT)	116 4454
712	(a) 18 June 1916 (b) Designated 5 Australian Div MT Co 13 March 1918	Western Front, 5th Australian Division	Division Supply Column (MT) Australian (MT) Company	1026
713	(a) 18 June 1916 (b) Absorbed into 712 Co 13 March 1918	1 Australian and New Zealand Corps Troops	5 Australian Ammunition Sub Park (MT)	1031
714	(a) 18 June 1916 (b) 26 July 1919	Western Front, 11th Division	Division Supply Column (MT) Division (MT) Company	626
715	(a) 18 June 1916 (b) Absorbed 714 MT Co 13 March 1918	Western Front, 18th Corps	11 Ammunition Sub Park (MT)	958
716	(a) 16 June 1916 (b) 2 October 1919	Western Front, 9th Corps	Corps Troops Supply Column (MT) Corps Troops (MT) Company	847
717	(a) 16 June 1916 (b) 1 January 1920	Western Front, 9th Corps	'E' Corps Siege Park (MT)	846
718	(a) 20 June 1916 (b) 10 December 1919	Western Front, Second Army	2 Water Tank (MT) Company	353
719	(a) 23 June 1916 (b) 20 November 1919	Home Western Front, 62nd (West Riding) Division	48 Ammunition Supply Park (MT) 62 Division Supply Column (MT) 62nd Division (MT) Company	800
720	(a) 23 June 1916 (b) Absorbed into 328 MT Co 18 February 1918	Western Front, 18th Corps Italy, 11th Corps	62 Ammunition Sub Park (MT)	958 4211
721	(a) September 1915 (b) May 1919	Western Front, Canadian Corps	Corps Troops Supply Column (MT) Corps Troops (MT) Company (Canadian ASC)	1080
722	(a) September 1915 (b) 24 April 1919	Western Front, Canadian Corps	2 Canadian Division Supply Column (MT) 2nd Canadian Division (MT) Company (Canadian ASC)	1081
723	(a) September 1915 (b) Absorbed into 722 MT Co 13 March 1918	Western Front, Canadian Corps	2nd Canadian Ammunition Sub Park (MT) (Canadian ASC)	1082
724	(a) February 1916 (b) January 1919	Western Front, Canadian Corps	3 Canadian Division Supply Column (MT) 3rd Canadian Division (MT) Company (Canadian ASC)	1081
725	(a0 April 1916 (b) Absorbed into 724 MT Co 13 March 1918	Western Front, Canadian Corps	3 Canadian Ammunition Sub Park (MT) (Canadian ASC)	1082
726	(a) 20 June 1916 (b) 12 May 1919	Western Front	No 3 Workshop for Anti-Aircraft Guns/Batteries	-
727	(a) 12 May 1916 (b) 12 May 1919	Western Front	No 4 Workshop for Anti-Aircraft Guns/Batteries No 5 Workshop for Anti-Aircraft Guns/Batteries	-

ASC Co	(a) Formed (b) Disbanded	Theatre/Order of Battle	Role in First World War	WO 95
728	(a) 28 June 1916 (b) 31 March 1919	Hitchin, Herts	37th Local Auxiliary Company (Signal Service Training Centre)	-
729	(a) 1 July 1916 (b) 31 January 1922	Mesopotamia, Army Troops Persian L of C	MT Supply Column	5005
730	(a) 1 July 1916 (b) 27 February 1919	Mesopotamia, Army Troops Persian L of C	MT Company Suported General Dunsterville's Mission	5005
731	(a) 30 June 1916 (b) 21 July 1919	Western Front, 17th Corps	57th Division Supply Column (MT) Division (MT) Company	949
732	(a) 30 June 1916 (b) Absorbed into 731 MT Co 13 March 1918	Western Front, 57th Division	57 Ammunition Sub Park (MT)	933
733	(a) 30 June 1916 (b) 25 April 1919	Home, Western Front, Italy, 58th Division Italy, Western Front, 5th Division	Division Supply Column (MT) (with 77 Company) Division Supply Column (MT) Division (MT) Company	4211 830 739
734	(a) 30 June 1916 (b) Absorbed into 77 MT Co 13 March 1918	Western Front, 2nd Corps	58 Ammunition Sub park (MT)	667
735	(a) 8 July 1916 (b) 15 July 1919	Western Front, L of C Troops	39 Auxiliary (Petrol) Company (Forestry duties)	4164
736	(a) 8 July 1916 (b) 21 June 1919	Western Front, L of C Troops	40 Auxiliary (Petrol) Company	4164
737	(a) 8 July 1916 (b) 10 October 1916	Home	Auxiliary (Petrol) Company Reformed on 20 October 1916 as an Auxiliary Omnibus Company but disbanded 10 December 1916	-
738	(a) 13 July 1916 (b) 7 March 1920	27th Division Salonika, Army Troops, Black Sea Troops	Division Supply Column (MT) 96 Auxiliary (MT) Company MT Company	4811 4954
739	(a) 8 July 1916 (b) 24 May 1919	Salonika, Army Troops 127th Siege Battery RGA	MT Company Ammunition Column (MT)	4812
740	(a) 8 July 1916 (b) 21 October 1919	Salonika, Army Troops 130th Siege Battery RGA	MT Company Ammunition Column (MT)	4812
741	(a) 23 June 1916 (b) October 1918	Western Front, 1st Australian Division	Train, No 1 (HQ) Company (HT) Australian ASC) Renumbered 1 Company AASC in 1918	3208
742	(a) 23 June 1916 (b) October 1918	Egypt, Western Front, 1st Australian Division	Train, No 2 Company (HT) (Australian ASC) Renumbered 2 Company AASC in 1918	3208
743	(a) 23 June 1916 (b) October 1918	Egypt, Western Front, 1st Australian Division	Train, No 3 Company (HT) (Australian ASC) Renumbered 3 Company AASC in 1918	3208
744	(a) 23 June 1916 (b) October 1918	Egypt, Western Front, 1st Australian Division	Train, No 4 Company (HT) (Australian ASC) Renumbered 4 Company AASC in 1918	3208
745	(a) 23 June 1916 (b) October 1918	Western Front, 2nd Australian Division	Train, No 1 (HQ) Company (HT) (Australian ASC) Renumbered 20 Company AASC in 1918	3305 3306

ASC Co	(a) Formed (b) Disbanded	Theatre/Order of Battle	Role in First World War	WO 95
746	(a) 23 June 1916 (b) October 1918	Western Front, 2nd Australian Division	Train, No 2 Company (HT) (Australian ASC) Renumbered 15 Company AASC in 1918	3305 3306
747	(a) 23 June 1916 (b) October 1918	Western Front, 2nd Australian Division	Train, No 3 Company (HT) (Australian ASC) Renumbered 16 Company AASC in 1918	3305 3306
748	(a) 23 June 1916 (b) October 1918	Western Front, 2nd Australian Division	Train, No 4 Company (HT) (Australian ASC) Renumbered 17 Company AASC in 1918	3305 3306
749	(a) 23 June 1916 (b) January 1919	Egypt, Western Front, New Zealand Division	Train, No 1 (HQ) Company (HT) (New Zealand ASC)	3684
750	(a) 23 June 1916 (b) January 1919	Egypt, Western Front, New Zealand Division	Train, No 2 Company (HT) (New Zealand ASC)	3684
751	(a) 23 June 1916 (b) January 1919	Egypt, Western Front, New Zealand Division	Train, No 3 Company (HT) (New Zealand ASC)	3684
752	(a) 23 June 1916 (b) January 1919	Egypt, Western Front, New Zealand Division	Train, No 4 Company (HT) (New Zealand ASC)	3684
753	(a) 23 June 1916 (b) October 1918	Western Front, 4th Australian Division	Train, No 1 (HQ) Company (HT) (Australian ASC) Renumbered 14 Company in 1918	3486
754	(a) 23 June 1916 (b) October 1918	Western Front, 4th Australian Division	Train, No 2 Company (HT) (Australian ASC) Renumbered 7 Company AASC in 1918	3486
755	(a) 23 June 1916 (b) October 1918	Western Front, 4th Australian Division	Train, No 3 Company (HT) (Australian ASC) Renumbered 26 Company AASC in 1918	3486
756	(a) 23 June 1916 (b) October 1918	Western Front, 4th Australian Division	Train, No 4 Company (HT) (Australian ASC) Renumbered 27 Company AASC in 1918	3486
757	(a) 23 June 1916 (b) October 1918	Western Front, 5th Australian Division	Train, No 1 (HQ) Company (HT) (Australian ASC) Renumbered 10 Company AASC in 1918	3610
758	(a) 23 June 1916 (b) October 1918	Western Front, 5th Australian Division	Train, No 2 Company (HT) (Australian ASC) Renumbered 18 Company AASC in 1918	3610
759	(a) 23 June 1916 (b) October 1918	Western Front, 5th Australian Division	Train, No 3 Company (HT) (Australian ASC) Renumbered 28 Company AASC in 1918	3610
760	(a) 23 June 1916 (b) October 1918	Western Front, 5th Australian Division	Train, No 4 Company (HT) (Australian ASC) Renumbered 29 Company AASC in 1918	3610
761	(a) July 1916 (b) April 1919	Gallipoli, Western Front, 63rd (Royal Naval) Division	Train, No 1 (HQ) Company (HT)	3107
762	(a) 23 June 1916 (b) 24 May 1919	Gallipoli, Western Front, 63rd (Royal Naval) Division	Train, No 2 Company (HT)	3107
763	(a) 23 June 1916 (b) 24 May 1919	Gallipoli, Western Front, 63rd (Royal Naval) Division	Train, No 3 Company (HT)	3107
764	(a) 23 June 1916 (b) 24 May 1919	Gallipoli, Western Front, 63rd (Royal Naval) Division	Train, No 4 Company (HT)	3107
765	(a) 13 July 1916 (b) 30 November 1919	132nd Siege Battery RGA Salonika, Army Troops Black Sea Troops	Siege Park (MT) MT Company	4954 4813

ASC Co	(a) Formed (b) Disbanded	Theatre/Order of Battle	Role in First World War	WO 95
766	(a) 13 July 1916 (b) Absorbed into 887 MT Co early 1919	134th Siege Battery RGA Salonika, Army Troops Black Sea Troops Constantinople	Siege Park (MT) GHQ Troops Supply Column (MT) MT Company Local MT (combined with 887 MT Company)	4813 4954
767	(a) 13 July 1916 (b) 17 September 1919	138th Siege Battery RGA Salonika, Army Troops Black Sea Troops	Siege Park (MT) MT Company	4954 4813
768	(a) 14 July 1916 (b) Absorbed 23 December 1916	Western Front	No 7 Workshop for Anti-Aircraft Gun Detachments (MT)	-
769	(a) 14 July 1916 (b) Absorbed 23 December 1916	Western Front	No 8 Workshop for Anti-Aircraft Gun Detachments (MT)	-
770	(a) 15 July 1916 (b) 5 June 1919	Western Front, Fifth Army Western Front, Fourth Army	Army Siege Park (with 1113 Company) Siege Park (MT)	570 514
771	(a) 27 July 1916 (b) 18 September 1919	Salonika, Army Troops	32 Motor Ambulance Convoy	4805
772	(a) 10 August 1916 (b) 20 August 1919	Egypt, L of C	Field Ambulance Workshop Unit (MT) 15(E) Mobile Repair Unit	4720
773	(a) 4 August 1916 (b) 24 April 1919	Mesopotamia, Army Troops	33 Motor Ambulance Convoy	5003
774	(a) 10 August 1916 (b) 25 November 1919	Western Front, Army Troops, Second Army	9 Pontoon Park (MT)	357
775	(a) 10 August 1916 (b) 31 May 1919	Western Front, Army Troops, Fourth Army	11 Pontoon Park, Army Troops (MT)	514
776	(a) 12 August 1916 (b) Renumbered 18 MT Co 1 August 1922	Chatham, Tonbridge	45 Local Auxiliary (MT) Company	-
777	(a) 21 August 1916 (b) 31 October 1916	Salonika, Army Troops	Supply Column (MT) (attached to 738 Company)	4813
778	(a) 21 August 1916 (b) 31 March 1919	Egypt, 28th Division Salonika, Army Troops	Division Ammunition Park (MT) 97 Auxiliary (MT) Company	4812
779	(a) 21 August 1916 (b) 31 March 1919	Egypt, Salonika, Army Troops	22 Ammunition Park (MT) 98 Auxiliary (MT) Company	4812
780	(a) 21 August 1916 (b) 31 March 1919	Egypt, Salonika, Army Troops Black Sea Troops, Constantinople	10 Ammunition Park (MT) 99 Auxiliary (MT) Company	4954 4812
781	(a) 21 August 1916 (b) 12 April 1919	Egypt, Salonika, Army Troops	27 Ammunition Park (MT) 100 Auxiliary (MT) Company	4812
782	(a) 21 August 1916 (b) Absorbed into 781/388 MT Companies 25 November 1917	Egypt, Salonika, 12 Corps Troops	26 Ammunition Park (MT)	4822
783	(a) 20 August 1916 (b) 28 February 1920	Mesopotamia, Army Troops Persian L of C 1918	Special Supply Column (MT) Remained with Army of Occupation	5005
784	(a) 20 August 1916 (b) Absorbed into 3 Burma MT Co 6 March 1919	Mesopotamia, Army Troops Persian L of C 1918	Special Supply Column (MT)	5005 3894

ASC Co	(a) Formed (b) Disbanded	Theatre/Order of Battle	Role in First World War	WO 95
785	(a) 24 July 1916 (b) 12 May 1919	Western Front, Canadian Corps	4 Canadian Division Supply Column (MT) (Canadian ASC) 4th Canadian Division (MT) Company	1081
786	(a) 24 July 1916 (b) Absorbed into 785 MT Co 13 March 1918	Western Front, Canadian Corps	4 Canadian Ammunition Sub Park (Canadian ASC)	1082
787	(a) 12 September 1916 (b) 6 March 1921	Salonika, Army Troops	34 Motor Ambulance Convoy	4805
788	(a) 12 September 1916 (b) 15 November 1919	Mesopotamia, Army Troops Persian L of C 1918	159th Siege Battery RGA Ammunition Column, MT Company Remained with Army of Occupation	5005
789	(a) 16 September 1916 (b) Renumbered 33 (Indian) MT Co 6 May 1921	Mesopotamia, Army Troops Persian L of C 1918	157th Heavy Battery RGA Ammunition Column, MT Company	5005
790	(a) 2 October 1916 (b) Absorbed into 907 MT Co 1 May 1921	Egypt, Delta and Western Force	MT Company Embarked for India 27 March 1919	4444 4457
791	(a) 21 August 1915 (b) NK	Royal Naval Division, Blandford, Farnham. Home Forces Troops	Division Reinforcement Company (HT) (RN Personnel)	5460
792	(a) 21 August 1915 (b) NK	Royal Naval Division, Blandford, Farnham. Home Forces Troops	Local Transport Company (HT) (RN Personnel)	5460
793	(a) 28 August 1916 (b) 9 November 1921	London, Kensington Palace Barracks	HT Company, local duties Renumbered 7 HT Company 30 July 1920	-
794	(a) 24 July 1916 (b) March 1919	Western Front, 4th Canadian Division	Train No 1 (HQ) Company (HT) (Canadian ASC)	3894
795	(a) 24 July 1916 (b) March 1919	Western Front, 4th Canadian Division	Train, No 2 Company (HT) (Canadian ASC)	3894
796	(a) 24 July 1916 (b) March 1919	Western Front, 4th Canadian Division	Train, No 3 Company (HT) (Canadian ASC)	3894
797	(a) 24 July 1916 (b) March 1919	Western Front, 4th Canadian Division	Train, No 4 Company (HT) (Canadian ASC)	3894
798	(a) 10 January 1917 (b) 9 May 1919	Salonika, Army Troops	15 Auxiliary (HT) Company	4808
799	(a) 9 December 1916 (b) 13 March 1919	Salonika - Army Troops	16 Auxiliary (HT) Company	4808
800	(a) 20 December 1916 (b) 30 October 1919	Salonika - Army Troops Black Sea Troops	17 Auxiliary (HT) Company	4808 4954
801	(a) 20 September 1916 (b) 26 May 1919	Salonika, 16 Corps Troops	Corps Troops Supply Column (MT)	4827
802	(a) 20 September 1916 (b) Absorbed into 684 MT Co 25 November 1917	Salonika, 7 Mounted Brigade	Brigade Supply Column (MT)	4793
803	(a) 20 September 1916 (b) Absorbed into 738/780 MT Cos 25 November 1917	Salonika, 7 Mounted Brigade	Brigade Ammunition Park (MT)	4793

ASC Co	(a) Formed (b) Disbanded	Theatre/Order of Battle	Role in First World War	WO 95
804	(a) 14 September 1916 (b) Renumbered 19 MT Co 1 August 1922	Darlington, Catterick, with detachments in Newcastle and Filey	42 Local Auxiliary (MT) Company Coast Defences Northern Command, also assistance to Canadian Forestry Corps	-
805	(a) 10 October 1916 (b) 20 August 1919	Western Front, L of C Troops Rouen, Dieppe	2 GHQ Ammunition Park (MT) 43 Auxiliary (Petrol) Company (MT)	4164
806	(a) 18 October 1916 (b) Absorbed into 393 MT Co 24 April 1919	Western Front, Fourth Army, Beauval, Poperinge	5 Mobile Repair Unit	513
807	(a) 19 October 1916 (b) Designated 3 Australian Division MT Co 13 March 1918	Western Front, 3rd Australian Division Corps Troops	Division Supply Column (MT) (ex-Australia) Divison (MT) Company (Australian ASC)	1023
808	(a) 19 October 1916 (b) Absorbed into 807 MT Co 13 March 1918	Western Front, 3rd Australian Division	3 Ammunition Sub Park (MT) (Australian ASC)	1029
809	(a) 16 October 1916 (b) 25 September 1917	Salonika, Army Troops	205 Siege Battery RGA Ammunition Column (MT), MT Company	4813
810	(a) 16 October 1916 (b) 31 March 1919	Egypt, 21 Corps Salonika, Army Troops	209th Siege Battery RGA (MT) MT Company attached 424 Siege Battery RGA	4502 4813
811	(a) 1 November 1916 (b) 28 February 1919	Eastern Force Troops, Egypt 21 Corps, Egypt 20 Corps, Egypt	199th then 201st Siege Battery RGA (MT) MT Company	4502 4454 4488
812	(a) 5 November 1916 (b) 25 September 1919	Western Front, L of C Troops Rouen	41 Auxiliary (Ambulance Car) Company (MT)	4165
813	(a) 5 November 1916 (b) 25 September 1919	Western Front, L of C Troops Abbeville	47 Auxiliary (Ambulance Car) Company (MT)	4165
814	(a) 5 November 1916 (b) 2 June 1920	Western Front, L of C Troops St Omer	48 Auxiliary (Ambulance Car) Company (MT)	4165
815	(a) 2 December 1916 (b) 27 February 1919	Mesopotamia, Army Troops Persian L of C 1918	Supply Column (MT)	5005
816	(a) 2 December 1916 (b) Absorbed into 648 MT Co 1 July 1918	Home. Formed for Mesopotamia East Africa	Supply Column (MT) (long distance moves)	-
817	(a) 2 December 1916 (b) Absorbed into 648 MT Co 1 July 1918	Home. Formed for Mesopotamia East Africa	Supply Column (MT) (long distance moves)	-
818	(a) 2 December 1916 (b) 21 May 1921	Mesopotamia, Army Troops	Supply Column (MT). Matthews Column Only Ford van company manned solely by British personnel (Norperforce)	5006
819	(a) 2 December 1916 (b) 14 April 1919	Salonika, Army Troops	Supply Column (MT) with Serbian Army	4814
820	(a) 2 December 1916 (b) 14 July 1919	Salonika, Army Troops	Supply Column (MT) with Serbian Army	4814
821	(a) 26 October 1916 (b) 2 March 1918	71st Division, Home Defence Saxmundham, Basingstoke, Colchester	Train No 1 (HQ) Company (HT)	-

ASC Co	(a) Formed (b) Disbanded	Theatre/Order of Battle	Role in First World War	WO 95
822	(a) 25 November 1916 (b) 2 March 1918	71st Division, Home Defence Guildford, Colchester	No 2 Company (HT)	-
823	(a) 10 December 1916 (b) Absorbed 13 February 1918	71st Division, Home Defence Whitchurch, Colchester	No 3 Company (HT)	-
824	(a) 30 December 1916 (b) Absorbed 11 February 1918	71st Division, Home Defence Hungry Hill (Woking), Colchester	No 4 Company (HT)	-
825	(a) 26 October 1916 (b) 15 April 1918	72nd Division, Home Defence Northampton, Ipswich	Train No 1 (HQ) Company (HT)	-
826	(a) 26 October 1916 (b) 15 April 1918	72nd Division, Home Defence Bradford, Ipswich	Train No 2 Company (HT)	-
827	(a) 26 October 1916 (b) 15 April 1918	72nd Division, Home Defence Bedford, Ipswich	Train No 3 Company (HT)	-
828	(a) 26 October 1916 (b) 15 April 1918	72nd Division, Home Defence Wellingborough, Ipswich	Train No 4 Company (HT)	-
829	(a) 26 October 1916 (b) 26 February 1918	73rd Division Home Defence Blackheath, Chelmsford	Train No 1 (HQ) Company (HT)	-
830	(a) 26 October 1916 (b) 26 February 1918	73rd Division, Home Defence Braintree, Witham	Train No 2 Company (HT)	-
831	(a) 26 October 1916 (b) 26 February 1918	73rd Division Home Defence Malden, Chelmsford	Train No 3 Company (HT)	-
832	(a) 26 October 1916 (b) 27 March 1918	73rd Division, Home Defence Blackpool, Chelmsford	Train No 4 Company (HT)	-
833	(a) 12 January 1917 (b) 14 April 1919	221st Infantry Brigade Deal	Brigade Train (HT)	-
834	(a) 12 January 1917 (b) 14 April 1919	222nd Infantry Brigade Margate	Brigade Train (HT)	-
835	(a) 12 January 1917 (b) 14 April 1919	64th Division 223rd Infantry Brigade Holt, Norfolk	Brigade Train (HT)	-
836	(a) 12 January 1917 (b) 14 April 1919	64th Division, 224th Infantry Brigade North Walsham, Norfolk	Brigade Train (HT)	-
837	(a) 12 January 1917 (b) 31 March 1920	68th Division, 225th Infantry Brigade Gorleston-on-Sea, Catterick, Aldershot	Brigade Train (HT)	-
838	(a) 12 January 1917 (b) 14 April 1919	67th Division, 226th Infantry Brigade Thorpe-le-Soken	Brigade Train (HT)	-
839	(a) 12 January 1917 (b) 14 April 1919	67th Division, 227th Infantry Brigade Saxmundham, Suffolk	Brigade Train (HT)	5458
840	(a) 25 October 1916 (b) 3 October 1917	10th Division, Salonika	Train Pack Echelon (HT)	-
841	(a) 25 October 1916 (b) 3 October 1917	10th Division, Salonika	Train Pack Echelon (HT)	-

ASC Co	(a) Formed (b) Disbanded	Theatre/Order of Battle	Role in First World War	WO 95
842	(a) 25 October 1916 (b) 3 October 1917	10th Division, Salonika	Train Pack Echelon (HT)	-
843	(a) 25 October 1916 (b) 3 October 1917	10th Division, Salonika	Train Pack Echelon (HT)	-
844	(a) 25 October 1916 (b) 4 March 1919	22nd Division, Salonika	Train Pack Echelon (HT)	-
845	(a) 25 October 1916 (b) 3 October 1917	22nd Division, Salonika	Train Pack Echelon (HT)	-
846	(a) 25 October 1916 (b) 3 October 1917	22nd Division, Salonika	Train Pack Echelon (HT)	-
847	(a) 25 October 1916 (b) 3 October 1917	22nd Division, Salonika	Train Pack Echelon (HT)	-
848	(a) 25 October 1916 (b) 5 September 1919	26th Division, Salonika	Train Pack Echelon (HT)	-
849	(a) 25 October 1916 (b) 3 October 1917	26th Division, Salonika	Train Pack Echelon (HT)	-
850	(a) 25 October 1916 (b) 3 October 1917	26th Division, Salonika	Train Pack Echelon (HT)	-
851	(a) 25 October 1916 (b) 3 October 1917	26th Division, Salonika	Train Pack Echelon (HT)	-
852	(a) 25 October 1916 (b) 19 June 1919	27th Division Salonika, Army Troops	Train Pack Echelon (HT)	4886
853	(a) 25 October 1916 (b) 3 October 1917	27th Division Salonika, Army Troops	Train Pack Echelon (HT)	4886
854	(a) 25 October 1916 (b) 28 February 1919	27th Division Salonika, Army Troops	Train Pack Echelon (HT), Auxiliary Pack Co Decauville (HT) Company railway work	4886 4809
855	(a) 25 October 1916 (b) 28 February 1919	27th Division Salonika, Army Trops	Train Pack Echelon (HT) Auxiliary Pack Company (HT)	4886 4809
856	(a) 25 October 1916 (b) 18 February 1919	28th Division Salonika	Train Pack Echelon (HT) Struma Decauville railway	4912
857	(a) 25 October 1916 (b) 21 June 1919	28th Division, Western Front Salonika	Train Pack Echelon (HT) Auxiliary Pack Company (HT)	4912 4809
858	(a) 25 October 1916 (b) 7 February 1919	28th Division, Western Front Salonika	Train Pack Echelon (HT) Auxiliary Pack Company (HT)	4912 4809
859	(a) 25 October 1916 (b) 3 October 1917	28th Division, Western Front Salonika	Train Pack Echelon (HT) Auxiliary Pack Company (HT)	4912
860	(a) 29 October 1916 (b) 3 August 1917	Salonika, 8 Mounted Brigade	Brigade Supply Column (HT)	4793
861	(a) 27 October 1916 (b) Absorbed June 1917	Western Front, Salonika 60th (London) Division	No 1 (HQ) Company (HT) Train (Pack Echelon) (HT)	4927
862	(a) 27 October 1916 (b) Absorbed June 1917	Western Front, Salonika 60th (London) Division	No 2 Company (HT) Train (Pack Echelon) (HT)	4927

ASC Co	(a) Formed (b) Disbanded	Theatre/Order of Battle	Role in First World War	WO 95
863	(a) 27 October 1916 (b) Absorbed June 1917	Western Front, Salonika 60th (London) Division	No 3 Company (HT) Train (Pack Echelon) (HT)	4927
864	(a) 27 October 1916 (b) Absorbed June 1917	Western Front, Salonika 60th (London) Division	No 4 Company (HT) Train (Pack Echelon) (HT)	4927
865	(a) 18 October 1916 (b) Renumbered 24 HT Co 30 July 1920	Londonderry, Belfast	HT Company, local duties	-
866	(a) 18 October 1916 (b) Renumbered 22 HT Co 30 July 1920	Dublin	HT Company, local duties	-
867	(a) 23 November 1916 (b) October 1918	Western Front 3rd Australian Division	Train, 22 Company AASC (HT)	3394
868	(a) 23 November 1916 (b) October 1918	Western Front 3rd Australian Division	Train, 23 Company AASC (HT)	3394
869	(a) 23 November 1916 (b) October 1918	Western Front 3rd Australian Division	Train, 24 Company AASC (HT)	3394
870	(a) 23 November 1916 (b) October 1918	Western Front 3rd Australia Division	3rd Australian Division Train 25 Company AASC (HT)	3394
871	(a) 28 November 1916 (b) Absorbed into S & T Personnel Depot, Umballa 1 July 1921	India (Bangalore) and East Persia Corps, Corps Troops	ASC Personnel Depot Company (MT), (HT) Supply Mobilization Companies	5390
872	(a) 4 December 1916 (b) 26 April 1919	Grantham Machine Gun Training Centre	HT Training School	-
873	(a) 4 December 1916 (b) 31 May 1919	Grantham Machine Gun Training Centre	HT Training School	-
874	(a) 4 December 1916 (b) 26 April 1919	Grantham Machine Gun Training Centre	HT Training School	-
875	(a) 4 December 1916 (b) Absorbed 22 January 1918	Grantham Machine Gun Training Centre	HT Training School	-
876	(a) 4 December 1916 (b) Renumbered 4 HT Co 30 July 1920	Grantham, Bordon Machine Gun Training Centre	HT Training School	-
877			No record of this company's formation	
878	(a) 1 February 1917 (b) 31 March 1920	42nd Division Larkhill	Train for Home Service personnel HT Company, local duties	-
879	(a) 1 April 1917 (b) 16 January 1920	Western Front, L of C Troops Calais, Dunkirk	22 Auxiliary (HT) Company Dock loading/unloading	4163
880	(a) 2 December 1916 (b) 16 May 1919	Salonika, Army Troops	Supply Column (MT) with Serbian Army	4814
881	(a) 2 December 1916 (b) 16 May 1919	Formed for Mesopotamia Salonika, Army Troops	Supply Column (MT) with Serbian Army	4814

ASC Co	(a) Formed (b) Disbanded	Theatre/Order of Battle	Role in First World War	WO 95
882	(a) 10 December 1916 (b) Renumbered 20 MT Co 1 August 1922	Belgrave Square, London Home Forces - Troops	49 Auxiliary (MT) Company Ceremonial/Allied duties	5460
883	(a) 11 December 1916 (b) 21 June 1919	Western Front, 18th Corps Western Front, 19th Corps	Corps Troops Supply Column (MT) Corps Troops (MT) Company	971
884	(a) 11 December 1916 (b) 26 June 1919	Western Front 18th Corps, Heavy Artillery 19th Corps - Corps Troops	"T" Corps Siege Park (MT) Corps Siege Park (MT)	971
885	(a) 12 December 1916 (b) 6 August 1919	Western Front, 19th Corps Western Front, 18th Corps Western Front, 8th Corps	Corps Troops Supply Column (MT) Corps Troops Supply Column (MT) Corps Troops (MT) Company Corps Troops (MT) company	829 957
886	(a) 12 December 1916 (b) 31 July 1919	Western Front, 19th Corps Western Front, 18th Corps Western Front, 8th Corps	Corps Troops Supply Column (MT) "S" Corps Siege Park (MT) "H" Corps Siege Park (MT)	829 957
887	(a) 12 December 1916 (b) Absorbed into 605 MT Co 7 May 1919	Western Front, Salonika 12th Corps, Corps Troops Black Sea Troops, Constantinople	Corps Troops Supply Column (MT) MT Company combined with 766 MT Company	894 4822 4954
888	(a) 8 January 1917 (b) 16 June 1919	Western Front, 66th Division,	Division Supply Column (MT) Division (MT) Company	908
889	(a) 8 January 1917 (b) Absorbed into 888 MT Co 13 March 1918	Western Front, 66th Division 2 Australian & New Zealand Corps, Corps Troops Western Front, 22 Corps	66 Ammunition Sub Park (MT)	1044 979
890	(a) 8 January 1917 (b) 25 June 1917	Thame 67th Division	Division Supply Column (MT)	-
891	(a) 8 January 1917 (b) 25 June 1917	Petersfield 67th Division	67 Ammunition Sub Park (MT)	-
892	(a) 19 January 1917 (b) 21 November 1919	Western Front, 59th Division	Division Supply Column (MT) Division (MT) Company	892
893	(a) 19 January 1917 (b) Absorbed into 892 MT Co 13 March 1918	Western Front, 59th Division 3rd Corps Troops,	59 Ammunition Sub Park (MT)	705
894	(a) 22 January 1917 (b) Absorbed into 907 MT Co 1 May 1921	Egypt, Zahle, L of C	35 Motor Ambulance Convoy	4720
895	(a) 24 January 1917 (b) April 1919	Egypt, Ismailia District, Kantara, Ramleh	1st MT (Tractor) Company	4412
896	(a) 26 January 1917 (b) 13 May 1919	42nd Division, Western Front	Division Supply Column (MT) Division (MT) Company	740
897	(a) 26 January 1917 (b) Absorbed into 896 MT Co 13 March 1918	42nd Division, Western Front	42 Ammunition Sub Park (MT)	628
898	(a) 29 January 1917 (b) March 1918	Liverpool	83 Local Auxiliary (MT) Company Depot for reception of agricultural motor tractors from USA	-

ASC Co	(a) Formed (b) Disbanded	Theatre/Order of Battle	Role in First World War	WO 95
899	(a) 12 January 1917 (b) 30 November 1919	France, L of C Troops Rouen	4th ASC Repair Shop (German POWs) 4th Heavy Repair Shop (MT) ASC	4167
900	(a) 3 May 1917 (b) 19 April 1919	Egypt, Ramleh Southern Canal Section Palestine L of C	23 Auxiliary (HT) Company	4435 4737
901	(a) 5 February 1917 (b) 1 November 1919	Mesopotamia, Army Troops Persian L of C 1918	Ammunition Column (MT) for 246th Siege Battery RGA	5006
902	(a) 5 February 1917 (b) 1 November 1919	Mesopotamia, Army Troops Persian L of C 1918	Ammunition Column (MT) for 257th Siege Battery RGA	5006
903	(a) 5 February 1917 (b) 25 June 1919	Mesopotamia, Army Troops Persian L of C 1918	Ammunition Column (MT) for 269th Siege Battery RGA	5006
904	(a) 7 February 1917 (b) 11 February 1919	Egypt, Tul Keram, 21 Corps,	Ammunition Column (MT) for 10th and 195th Heavy Batteries RGA	4502
905	(a) 20 February 1917 (b) 25 February 1920	Egypt, Ismailia District, Corps Troops, Desert Mounted Corps, North Force	54 Auxiliary (Petrol) Company	4411 4478 4460
906	(a) 20 February 1917 (b) 30 June 1922	Egypt, Ismailia District, Corps Troops, Desert Mounted Corps, North Force	52 Auxiliary (Petrol) Company	4411 4478 4460
907	(a) 20 February 1917 (b) Reformed as 30/31 MT Cos 1 June 1923	Egypt, Ramleh, Cairo District, District Troops Ismailia District	53 Auxiliary (Petrol) Company	4469 4411
908	(a) 21 February 1917 (b) 5 September 1919	Western Front, Third Army Italy	36 Motor Ambulance Convoy	411
909	(a) 21 February 1917 (b) 16 May 1919	Western Front, Fourth Army Army Troops	37 Motor Ambulance Convoy	497
910	(a) 20 February 1917 (b) 27 May 1919	Salonika, L of C Troops	Heavy Repair Workshop (MT)	4943
911	(a) 18 May 1917 (b) 31 May 1921	Mesopotamia, Army Troops Persian L of C 1918	39 Motor Ambulance Convoy Remained Army of Occupation 1919	5003 5288
912	(a) 28 February 1917 (b) 14 May 1919	Salonika	55 Auxiliary (Petrol) Company	-
913	(a) 28 February 1917 (b) 31 May 1919	Salonika, Army Troops	56 Auxiliary (Petrol) Company	4810
914	(a) 28 February 1917 (b) 9 July 1919	Western Front, L of C Troops Facture	57 Auxiliary (Petrol) Company	4164
915	(a) 4 March 1917 (b) 19 June 1919	Western Front, L of C Troops Rouen	58 Auxiliary (Petrol) Company	4164
916	(a) 4 March 1917 (b) 25 June 1919	Western Front	59 Auxiliary (Petrol) Company	-
917	(a) 14 March 1917 (b) Absorbed 13 September 1917	Salonika	Ammunition Column (MT) for 292nd Siege Battery RGA	-
918	(a) 19 March 1917 (b) 29 July 1919	GHQ Troops (for Salonika)	Troops Supply Column (MT) 77 Auxiliary (Petrol) Company	-

ASC Co	(a) Formed (b) Disbanded	Theatre/Order of Battle	Role in First World War	WO 95
919	(a) 22 March 1917 (b) 31 May 1919	Salonika, Army Troops	Workshop for Anti-Aircraft Batteries	4813
920	(a) 22 March 1917 (b) 18 September 1919	Salonika, Army Troops	38 Motor Ambulance Convoy	4805
921	(a) 13 January 1917 (b) 24 August 1919	54th (East Anglian) Division Egypt	Train No 1 (HQ) Company (HT)	4648
922	(a) 13 January 1917 (b) 24 August 1919	54th (East Anglian) Division Egypt	Train No 2 Company (HT)	4648
923	(a) 13 January 1917 (b) 24 August 1919	54th (East Anglian) Division Egypt	Train No 3 Company (HT)	4648
924	(a) 13 January 1917 (b) 24 August 1919	54th (East Anglian) Division Egypt	Train No 4 Company (HT)	4648
925	(a) 2 April 1917 (b) 10 October 1919	75th Division Egypt, Palestine	Train No 1 (HQ) Company (HT)	4687
926	(a) 2 April 1917 (b) 4 October 1919	75th Division Egypt, Palestine	Train No 2 Company (HT)	4687
927	(a) 2 April 1917 (b) 6 October 1919	75th Division Egypt, Palestine	Train No 3 Company (HT) (Formed in Alexandria)	4687
928	(a) 2 April 1917 (b) 8 October 1919	75th Division Egypt, Palestine	Train No 4 Company (HT) (Formed in Alexandria)	4687
929	(a) 6 July 1917 (b) 5 June 1919	Western Front	25 Auxiliary (HT) Company	-
930	(a) 1 May 1917 (b) 31 March 1922	Egypt, Alexandria, District Troops	24 Auxiliary (HT) Company	4466
931	(a) 7 April 1917 (b) 30 November 1919	Western Front, Third Army, Army Troops	60 Auxiliary (Steam) Company	427
932	(a) 7 April 1917 (b) 21 August 1919	Western Front	61 Auxiliary (Steam) Company	-
933	(a) 10 May 1917 (b) 17 May 1919	Western Front, L of C Troops	66 Auxiliary (Petrol) Company	426 4165
934	(a) 10 May 1917 (b) 23 July 1919	Western Front, Second Army	67 Auxiliary (Steam) Company Worked for Assistant Director Roads	353
935	(a) 13 July 1917 (b) 20 August 1919	Western Front, Third Army	68 Auxiliary (Petrol) Company	426
936	(a) 13 July 1917 (b) 11 November 1919	Western Front, First Army	69 Auxiliary (Steam) Company (MT)	266
937	(a) 13 July 1917 (b) 30 May 1919	Western Front, Fourth Army - Army Troops	70 Auxiliary (Petrol) Company (MT)	513
938	(a) 13 July 1917 (b) 23 July 1920	France, L of C Troops	71 Auxiliary (Steam) Company Road Repairs	4165

ASC Co	(a) Formed (b) Disbanded	Theatre/Order of Battle	Role in First World War	WO 95
939	(a) 20 August 1917 (b) 22 July 1919	Western Front, Fourth Army, Army Troops	75 Auxiliary (Petrol) Company	513
940	(a) 20 July 1917 (b) 1 June 1920	Western Front, L of C Troops	76 Auxiliary (Steam) Company	4165
941	(a) 6 April 1917 (b) Absorbed 1 May 1917	Home Italy, GHQ Troops	Ammunition Column (MT) for 307th Siege Battery RGA	-
942	(a) 6 April 1917 (b) Absorbed 1 May 1917	Home Italy, GHQ Troops	Ammunition Column (MT) for 302nd Siege Battery RGA MT Company	4210
943	(a) 6 April 1917 (b) Absorbed 1 May 1917	Home	For 314th Siege Battery RGA	-
944	(a) 6 April 1917 (b) Absorbed 1 May 1917	Home	For 315th Siege Battery RG,	-
945	(a) 6 April 1917 (b) Absorbed 1 May 1917	Home	For 316th Siege Battery RGA	-
946	(a) 6 April 1917 (b) Absorbed 1 May 1917	Home	For 317th Siege Battery RGA	-
947	(a) 6 April 1917 (b) Absorbed 1 May 1917	Home	For 334th Siege Battery RGA	-
948	(a) 6 April 1917 (b) Absorbed 1 May 1917	Home	For 320th Siege Battery RGA	-
949	(a) 6 April 1917 (b) Absorbed 1 May 1917	Home	For 304th Siege Battery RGA	-
950	(a) 6 April 1917 (b) Absorbed 1 May 1917	Home	For 322nd Siege Battery RGA	-
951	(a) 11 April 1917 (b) 30 April 1919	Egypt, Kantara Eastern Force Troops, 21 Corps, Corps Troops	Ammunition Column (MT) for 189th Heavy Battery RGA MT Company	4454 4502
952	(a) 11 April 1917 (b) 11 February 1919	Egypt, Kantara 21 Corps, Corps Troops	Ammunition Column (MT) for 202nd Heavy Battery RGA	4502
953	(a) 17 April 1917 (b) 22 February 1919	Mesopotamia, Army Troops L of C, Baghdad	Special Supply Column (MT) (Ford vans) All drivers were Arabs or Armenians	5006
954	(a) 17 April 1917 (b) 21 March 1919	Mesopotamia, Army Troops Persian L of C 1918	MT Company (Ford vans)	5006
955	(a) 17 April 1917 (b) 11 February 1919	Egypt, Kantara 21 Corps, Corps Troops	Ammunition Column (MT) for 300th Siege Battery RGA MT Company	4502
956	(a) 20 May 1917 (b) 24 July 1919	Egypt, Sarafand Ismailia District	82 Auxiliary (MT) Company 82 Auxiliary (Petrol) Company	4412
957	(a) 12 February 1917 (b) Absorbed into 960 MT Co 20 April 1918	Western Front, First Army,	62 Auxiliary (MT) Company	266
958	(a) 12 February 1917 (b) Absorbed into 960 MT Co 28 April 1918	Western Front, Fourth Army, Army Troops	63 Auxiliary (Petrol) Company	512

ASC Co	(a) Formed (b) Disbanded	Theatre/Order of Battle	Role in First World War	WO 95
959	(a) 9 February 1917 (b) 19 December 1919	Western Front, GHQ Troops Fourth Army, Army Troops	64 Auxiliary (Petrol) Company 13 GHQ Reserve (MT) Company	136 512
960	(a) 1 March 1917 (b) 1 December 1919	Western Front, Fourth Army, Army Troops Western Front, GHQ Troops	65 Auxiliary (Petrol) Company 14 GHQ Reserve (MT) Company	136 512
961	(a) 23 February 1917 (b) Absorbed into the Tank Corps 9 October 1917	Egypt, Eastern Force Troops	MT Company. Nucleus formed by men ex 711 MT Company (attached Tank Corps)	4454
962	(a) 1 July 1917 (b) 16 May 1920	Mesopotamia, Basra	Heavy Repair Shop (MT) for Base MT	-
963	(a) 21 June 1917 (b) 3 March 1919	Egypt, 20 Corps L of C Troops, Palestine, Tul Keram	Ammunition Column (MT) for 378th Siege Battery RGA	4488 4737
964	(a) 21 June 1917 (b) April 1919	Egypt, 21 Corps 20 Corps, Tul Keram	Ammunition Column (MT) for 379th Siege Battery RGA	4503 4488
965	(a) 21 June 1917 (b) 6 May 1919	Egypt, Kantara, 21 Corps	Ammunition Column (MT) for 380th Siege Battery, RGA	4503
966	(a) 21 June 1917 (b) 11 February 1919	Egypt, Jerusalem 20 Corps	Ammunition Column (MT) for 383rd Siege Battery RGA	4488
967	(a) 14 June 1917 (b) 30 April 1919	Egypt, Tul Keram 21 Corps	Ammunition Column (MT) for 387th Battery RGA	4503
968	(a) 14 June 1917 (b) 21 April 1919	Mesopotamia, Army Troops	Ammunition Column (MT) for 384th Battery RGA	5006
969	(a) 14 June 1917 (b) March 1919	Mesopotamia, Army Troops	Ammunition Column (MT) for 177th Heavy Battery RGA	5006
970	(a) 16 June 1917 (b) 1 November 1921	Mesopotamia, Army Troops	40 Motor Ambulance Convoy Remained Army of Occupation 1919	5004
971	(a) 15 June 1917 (b) 22 March 1919	Mesopotamia, Army Troops	Supply Column (MT)	5006
972	(a) 22 June 1917 (b) 17 November 1921	Egypt, Ramleh, Palestine L of C Troops, Ismailia District, North Force	2nd MT (Tractor) Company	4460 4412 4737
973	(a) 26 April 1917 (b) 3 June 1919	Egypt, Ludd Ismailia District	5th Advanced (HT) Depot	4414
974	(a) 2 July 1917 (b) 19 November 1919	Western Front, Dunkirk/Rouen L of C Troops	5th Heavy Repair Shop (MT) ASC	4167
975	(a) 2 July 1917 (b) 11 August 1920	Western Front, GHQ Troops	ASC Workshop for MT with Director General of Transportation	144
976	(a) 14 July 1917 (b) 22 February 1919	Mesopotamia, Army Troops Persian L of C 1918	72 Auxiliary (Petrol) Company	5006
977	(a) 30 September 1917 (b) 3 February 1920	Norwich	73 Local Auxiliary (MT) Company (Personel ex-373 Company)	-

ASC Co	(a) Formed (b) Disbanded	Theatre/Order of Battle	Role in First World War	WO 95
978	(a) 30 September 1917 (b) Renumbered 21 MT Co 1 August 1922	Home Forces Troops Claydon, Suffolk	74 Local Auxiliary (MT) Company	5460
979	(a) 25 August 1917 (b) 7 July 1919	Western Front, L of C Troops Alencon	78 Auxiliary (Petrol) Company	4165
980	(a) 11 August 1917 (b) 11 February 1919	Egypt, Alexandria, Jerusalem District Troops, 20 Corps	Ammunition Column (MT) for 423rd Siege Battery RGA, MT Company	4466 4488
981	(a) 11 August 1917 (b) 3 April 1919	Egypt	Ammunition Column (MT) for 424th Siege Battery RGA	-
982	(a) 7 August 1917 (b) 11 February 1919	Egypt, Kantara 21 Corps Troops, Egypt	Ammunition Column (MT) for 420th Siege Battery RGA	4503
983	(a) 7 August 1917 (b) 30 March 1919	Egypt, Tul Keram 21 Corps, Corps Troops 20 Corps	Ammunition Column (MT) for 421st Siege Battery RGA	4503 4488
984	(a) 7 August 1917 (b) 11 February 1919	Egypt, Kantara 21 Corps, Corps Troops	Ammunition Column (MT) for 422nd Siege Battery RGA	4503
985	(a) 31 August 1917 (b) 31 March 1919	Supply Reserve Depot Deptford	Light Railway and Crane Detachment (MT)	5460
986	(a) 16 September 1917 (b) 25 August 1919	Western Front Third Army Troops	3 (Water Tank) Company (MT)	427
987	(a) 29 October 1917 (b) 25 July 1919	Western Front, First Army L of C	4 (Water Tank) Company (MT)	266
988	(a) 29 August 1917 (b) 19 July 1919	Egypt, Ismailia 21 Corps Troops Palestine, L of C Troops	Ammunition Column (MT) attached to 134th Siege Battery RGA MT Company	4503 4738
989	(a) 29 August 1917 (b) 11 February 1919	Egypt, Kantara 21 Corps, Corps Troops	Caterpillar Tractor Company attached to 205th Siege Battery RGA MT Company	4503
990	(a) 4 September 1917 (b) 11 February 1919	Egypt, Jerusalem 21 Corps, 20 Corps Palestine L of C Troops	Caterpillar Tractor Company attached to 43rd Siege Battery RGA MT Company	4503 4488 4738
991	(a) 21 August 1917 (b) March 1919	Egypt, Australian and New Zealand Mounted Division	Division Train (AASC)	4533
992	(a) 21 August 1917 (b) March 1919	Egypt, Australian and New Zealand Mounted Division	Division Train (AASC)	4533
993	(a) 21 August 1917 (b) March 1919	Egypt, Australian and New Zealand Mounted Division	Division Train (AASC)	4533
994	(a) 21 August 1917 (b) March 1919	Egypt, Australian and New Zealand Mounted Division	Division Train (New Zealand Company) (HT)	4533
995	(a) 21 August 1917 (b) NK	Egypt, Australian Division	Train No 1 (HQ) Company (HT)	-
996	(a) 21 August 1917 (b) NK	Egypt, Australian Division	Train No 2 Company (HT)	-
997	(a) 21 August 1917 (b) NK	Egypt, Australian Division	Train No 3 Company (HT)	-

ASC Co	(a) Formed (b) Disbanded	Theatre/Order of Battle	Role in First World War	WO 95
998	(a) 21 August 1917 (b) NK	Egypt, Australian Division	Train No 4 Company (HT)	-
999	(a) 21 August 1917 (b) 15 March 1923	Egypt, Yeomanry Mounted Division Egypt, 1st Mounted Division Egypt, Palestine, 4th Cavalry Division	Train No 1 (HQ) Company (HT)	4505 4508 4512
1000	(a) 21 August 1917 (b) 15 January 1922	Egypt, Yeomanry Mounted Division Egypt, 1st Mounted Division Egypt, Palestine, 4th Cavalry Division	Train No 2 Company (HT)	4505 4508 4512
1001	(a) 21 August 1917 (b) 30 April 1922	Egypt, Yeomanry Mounted Division Egypt,1st Mounted Division Egypt, Palestine, 4th Cavalry Division	Train No 3 Company (HT)	4505 4508 4512
1002	(a) 21 August 1917 (b) 30 September 1920	Egypt, Yeomanry Mounted Division Egypt 1st Mounted Division Egypt, Palestine, 4th Cavalry Division	Train No 4 Company (HT)	4505 4508 4512
1003	(a) 19 July 1917 (b) 13 December 1918	Ballykinler Randalstown (Ireland), Catterick	Command Depot (for HT & Supply Personnel)	-
1004	(a) 19 July 1917 (b) 13 December 1918	Ballykinler Randalstown (Ireland), Shoreham, Ripon	Command Depot (for MT Personnel)	-
1005	(a) 19 August 1917 (b) 15 October 1920	Malta	HT Company, garrison duties	-
1006	(a) 10 September 1917 (b) 25 June 1919	Egypt, Ismailia District Palestine, L of C Troops 20 Corps	Ammunition Column (MT) for 440th Siege Battery RGA MT Company	4413 4489 4738
1007	(a) 10 September 1917 (b) 27 February 1919	Egypt, Kantara 20 Corps	Ammunition Column (MT) for 445th Siege Battery RGA	4489
1008	(a) 10 September 1917 (b) 11 February 1919	Egypt, Jerusalem, Ismailia District, 20 Corps	Ammunition Column (MT) for 443rd Siege Battery RGA	4413 4489
1009	(a) 12 September 1917 (b) 14 June 1919	Egypt, Tripoli, Ismailia District. Desert Mounted Corps	79 Auxiliary (Petrol) Company (MT)	4411
1010	(a) 12 September 1917 (b) 26 June 1919	Egypt, Alexandria, Ismailia District	80 Auxiliary (Petrol) Company (MT)	4412 4466
1011	(a) 12 September 1917 (b) 17 June 1919	Egypt, Tripoli, Ismailia District	81 Auxiliary (Petrol) Company (MT)	4412
1012	(a) 30 September 1917 (b) 15 June 1920	For Egypt L of C Western Front	MT Company 102 Auxiliary (Petrol) Company (MT)	-
1013	(a) 11 October 1917 (b) 3 November 1919	Mesopotamia, Army Troops Persian L of C 1918	Supply Column (Ford vans) Transferred to Britforce 1 January 1919	5006
1014	(a) 11 October 1917 (b) Post March 1919	Mesopotamia, Army Troops Persian L of C 1918	Supply Column (Light vans) Field Repair Unit in Army of Occupation	5006

ASC Co	(a) Formed (b) Disbanded	Theatre/Order of Battle	Role in First World War	WO 95
1015	(a) 11 October 1917 (b) 21 May 1919	Mesopotamia, Army Troops Persioan L of C 1918	Supply Column (Ford vans) Remained Army of Occupation	5007
1016	(a) 11 October 1917 (b) 16 May 1921	Mesopotamia, Army Troops	Supply Column (Ford vans) Remained Army of Occupation	5007
1017	(a) 11 October 1917 (b) April 1919	Mesopotamia, Army Troops	Supply Column (Ford vans)	5007
1018	(a) 11 October 1917 (b) March 1918	Mesopotamia, Army Troops Persia	Supply Column (Light vans) Mauritian drivers	5007
1019	(a) 11 October 1917 (b) 1 June 1920	Mesopotamia, Army Troops Persia	Supply Column (Light vans) Attached to Political Dept (Army of Occupation)	5007
1020	(a) 11 October 1917 (b) 22 February 1919	Mesopotamia, Army Troops Persia	Supply Column (Light vans)	5007
1021	(a) 6 October 1917 (b) 31 March 1922	Stirling, Bridge of Allan	HT Company, local duties	-
1022	(a) 6 October 1917 (b) 24 April 1918	Aberdeen	Local Auxiliary HT Company, local duties	-
1023	(a) 11 October 1917 (b) November 1919	Mesopotamia, Army Troops Persia	Supply Column (Light vans) No 1 Burmese MT Company	5007
1023A	(a) Autumn 1917 (b) Absorbed into Base MT Depot January (?) 1918	For service in Mesopotamia	Ford van company	
1024	(a) 11 October 1917 (b) November 1919	Mesopotamia, Army Troops Persia	Supply Column (Light vans) No 2 Burmese MT Company	5008
1024A	(a) Autumn 1917 (b) 16 March 1918	For service in Mesopotamia	Ford van company	-
1025	(a) 11 October 1917 (b) 23 December 1917	Formed/disbanded in Bulford for duty in Mesopotamia	Supply Column (Light vans)	-
1026	(a) 11 October 1917 (b) 23 December 1917	Formed/disbanded in Bulford for duty in Mesopotamia	Supply Column (Light vans)	-
1027	(a) 11 October 1917 (b) 23 December 1917	Formed/disbanded in Bulford for duty in Mesopotamia	Supply Column (Light vans)	-
1028	(a) 13 October 1917 (b) July 1919	Mesopotamia, Army Troops India	Ammunition Column (MT) for 392nd, 394th, 395th, 396th Siege Batteries RGA Renumbered 34 (Indian) MT Company 6 May 1921	5008 5390
1029	(a) 13 October 1917 (b) 2 September 1918	Special Brigade Location not known	Auxiliary MT Company	-
1030	(a) 17 October 1917 (b) 24 May 1919	Egypt, Alexandria, 20 Corps	MT Company for 6 in Howitzer Siege Battery RGA	4489
1031	(a) 17 October 1917 (b) 26 March 1919	Egypt, Alexandria District Salonika, Army Troops	MT Company for 6 in Howitzer Siege Battery RGA, MT Company	4466 4813
1032	(a) 17 October 1917 (b) 24 November 1919	Egypt, Alexandria District Salonika	MT Company for 6 in Howitzer Siege Battery RGA, MT Company	4466 4813

ASC Co	(a) Formed (b) Disbanded	Theatre/Order of Battle	Role in First World War	WO 95
1033	(a) 1 November 1917 (b) 8 April 1919	Italy	41 Motor Ambulance Convoy	-
1034	(a) 6 November 1917 (b) 10 March 1920	Italy, L of C Troops Serravalle (Arquata)	Base MT Depot	4262
1035	(a) 3 November 1917 (b) Absorbed 18 February 1918	Italy	82 Auxiliary (Petrol) Company	-
1036	(a) 8 November 1917 (b) Absorbed 11 March 1918	Italy, GHQ Troops	83 Auxiliary (Petrol) Company	4209
1037	(a) 10 November 1917 (b) 31 May 1919	Italy, GHQ Troops	MT Company for Corps Heavy Artillery GHQ Reserve MT Company	4209
1038	(a) December 1917 (b) November 1919	Egypt, Tripoli, Ismailia District Desert Mounted Corps, Corps Troops, North Force	87 Auxiliary (Petrol) Company	4460 4412 4478
1039	(a) 16 November 1917 (b) 31 March 1923	Egypt, Homs, Ismailia District Desert Mounted Corps, Corps Troops, North Force	88 Auxiliary (Petrol) Company	4460 4412 4478
1040	(a) 23 November 1917 (b) 18 September 1919	Egypt, Cairo District, Ismailia District	101 Auxiliary (Petrol) Company (MT)	4469 4412 4457
1041	(a) 17 October 1917 (b) 18 June 1918	Home Forces, Blackheath	Att No 2 Reserve HT Depot	-
1042	(a) 14 November 1917 (b) 10 April 1919	Egypt, 20 Corps	Corps Troops Train (HT)	4489
1043	(a) 14 November 1917 (b) 22 April 1919	Egypt, 21 Corps, Corps Troops, North Force	Corps Troops Train (HT)	4460 4503
1044	(a) 14 November 1917 (b) 27 February 1920	Egypt, 7th Mounted Brigade Egypt, 2nd Mounted Division Syria, 5th Cavalry Division	Brigade Train (HT) Division Train (HT) Division Train (HT)	4405 4517
1045	(a) 14 November 1917 (b) 17 April 1918	Western Front Italy, L of C Troops, Arquata, Cremona	6 Advanced HT Depot	4262
1046	(a) 1 November 1917 (b) 15 April 1920	Western Front Italy, L of C Troops, Arquata	2nd ASC Base Depot (HT & Supplies)	4262
1047	(a) 26 November 1917 (b) 4 April 1919	Italy, GHQ Troops	6th Army Auxiliary (Horse) Company	4209
1048	(a) 22 December 1917 (b) NK	Western Front, New Zealand Division	Train 4th Brigade Company (HT)	-
1049	(a) 29 December (b) 20 June 1919	Italy	42 Motor Ambulance Convoy	249
1050	(a) 27 December 1917 (b) Re-allocated as 'P' MT Depot Co 25 February 1921	Aldershot	ASC MT Instruction School	-
1051	(a) 26 January 1918 (b) 5 April 1919	Western Front	103 Auxiliary (Petrol) Company (Agricultural work)	-

ASC Co	(a) Formed (b) Disbanded	Theatre/Order of Battle	Role in First World War	WO 95
1052	(a) 10 January 1918 (b) 8 May 1918	Western Front	104 Auxiliary (Petrol) Company (Agricultural work)	-
1053	(a) 28 April 1918 (b) 6 April 1919	Western Front	105 Auxiliary (Petrol) Company (Agricultural work)	-
1054	(a) 4 March 1918 (b) 31 May 1921	Mesopotamia, Army Troops Persia	Special Supply Column (Ford vans) Included 74 Indian drivers	5008
1055	(a) 4 March 1918 (b) 31 May 1921	Mesopotamia, Army Troops Persian L of C 1918	Special Supply Column (Ford vans) Included 75 Indian drivers	5008
1056	(a) 4 March 1918 (b) 17 November 1920	Mesopotamia, L of C Troops Basrah	Special Supply Column (Ford vans) Employed Mauritian, Arab, Armenian and Negro drivers	5276
1057	(a) 2 March 1917 (b) May 1918	Western Front, Rouen (for Egypt)	Formed as Auxiliary (Petrol) Company. Diverted to France for disbandment.	4165
1058	(a) 2 March 1917 (b) Post March 1918	Western Front (for Egypt)	Formed as Auxiliary (Petrol) Company. Diverted to France for disbandment.	-
1059	(a) 16 March 1918 (b) 24 June 1918	Birkenhead	Artificer Training College	-
1060	(a) 16 March 1918 (b) March 1920	Western Front, Fifth Army	43 Motor Ambulance Convoy	561
1061	(a) 16 January 1918 (b) 6 January 1919	Salonika, 228 Infantry Brigade	Brigade Train (HT)	-
1062	(a) 27 January 1918 (b) NK	Randalstown (Ireland), Catterick	Command HT Depot	-
1063	(a) 18 March 1918 (b) 3 April 1918	Home (for Egypt)	108 Auxiliary (Petrol) Company	-
1064	(a) 18 March 1918 (b) 3 April 1918	Home (for Egypt)	109 Auxiliary (Petrol) Company	-
1065	(a) 18 March 1918 (b) 3 April 1918	Home (for Egypt)	110 Auxiliary (Petrol) Company	-
1066	(a) 18 March 1918 (b) 3 April 1918	Home (for Egypt)	111 Auxiliary (Petrol Company	-
1067	(a) 18 March 1918 (b) 3 April 1918	Home (for Egypt)	112 Auxiliary (Petrol) Company	-
1068	(a) 18 March 1918 (b) 3 April 1918	Home (for Egypt)	113 Auxiliary (Petrol) Company	-
1069	(a) 18 March 1918 (b) 3 April 1918	Home (for Egypt)	114 Auxiliary (Petrol) Company	-
1070	(a) 18 March 1918 (b) 3 April 1918	Home (for Egypt)	115 Auxiliary (Petrol) Company	-
1071	(a) 4 April 1918 (b) 3 April 1919	Mesopotamia, Baghdad Salonika, Army Troops	Ammunition Column (MT) for 396th Siege Battery RGA, MT Company	4813
1072	(a) 4 April 1918 (b) 11 February 1919	Mesopotamia Egypt, 20 Corps	Ammunition Column (MT) for 392nd Siege Battery RGA	4489

ASC Co	(a) Formed (b) Disbanded	Theatre/Order of Battle	Role in First World War	WO 95
1073	(a) 28 March 1918 (b) 19 July 1919	Mesopotamia, Egypt, L of C Palestine, Haifa L of C Troops	Ammunition Column (MT) for 394th Siege Battery RGA MT Company	4721 4738
1074	(a) 21 June 1918 (b) 15 April 1920	Italy, L of C Troops Tortona, Cremona	116 Auxiliary (Petrol) Company	4262
1075	(a) 2 April 1918 (b) 30 September 1919	Western Front, Fourth Army	44 Motor Ambulance Convoy	497
1076	(a) 3 April 1918 (b) 16 August 1919	Home, 52nd Division Western Front, GHQ Troops	MT Company 15 GHQ Reserve MT Company	136
1077	(a) 3 April 1918 (b) 6 February 1920	Home, 74th Division Western Front, GHQ Troops	MT Company 16 GHQ Reserve MT Company	-
1078	(a) June 1918 (b) April 1919	Egypt, Alexandria, District Troops	No 1 (Alexandria) Motor Ambulance Transport Company	4466
1079	(a) April 1918 ? (b) April 1919 ?	Egypt, Cairo	No 2 (Cairo) Motor Ambulance Transport Company	-
1080	(a) April 1918 ? (b) April 1919 ?	Egypt, Kantara	No 3 (Kantara) Motor Ambulance Transport Company	-
1081	(a) 19 April 1918 (b) 31 May 1919	Italy, L of C Troops Pavia	Heavy Repair Shop (MT)	4262
1082	(a) 16 April 1918 (b) 3 October 1919	Western Front, L of C Troops	7 Workshop for Anti-Aircraft Batteries (MT)	4813
1083	(a) 19 April 1918 (b) 26 March 1919	Salonika, Army Troops	Ammunition Column (MT) for 320th Siege Battery RGA, MT Company	4813
1084	(a) 1 May 1918 (b) 20 May 1919	London, Chelsea	75 Local Auxiliary MT Company, Anti-Aircraft Defence	-
1085	(a) 15 May 1918 (b) 29 May 1919	Western Front	117 Auxiliary (Steam) Company (with Forestry Directorate)	-
1086	(a) 20 June 1918 (b) 29 March 1919	Western Front, 1 Tank Brigade	1st Brigade (Tank Corps) MT Company	100
1087	(a) 20 June 1918 (b) 7 December 1919	Western Front, 2 Tank Brigade	2nd Brigade (Tank Corps) MT Company	103
1088	(a) 20 June 1918 (b) 23 July 1919	Western Front, 3 Tank Brigade	3rd Brigade (Tank Corps) MT Company	107
1089	(a) 20 June 1918 (b) 29 March 1919	Western Front, 4 Tank Brigade	4th Brigade (Tank Corps) MT Company	111
1090	(a) 20 June 1918 (b) Absorbed into 1087 MT Co 11 October 1919	Western Front, 5 Tank Brigade	5th Brigade (Tank Corps) MT Company	115
1091	(a) 12 June 1918 (b) Renumbered 28 (Indian) MT Co 6 May 1921	Mesopotamia, Baghdad Euphrates Defence, Communications Advanced Base	45 Motor Ambulance Convoy (Ford vans) (Indian Army personnel)	5036
1092	(a) 14 June 1918 (b) 14 May 1919	Western Front, L of C Troops	118th Auxiliary (Petrol) Company (with Forestry Directorate)	4165
1093	(a) 10 July 1918 (b) 15 Jnauary 1919	Mesopotamia, L of C Troops	Supply Company (Light vans)	5276

ASC Co	(a) Formed (b) Disbanded	Theatre/Order of Battle	Role in First World War	WO 95
1094	(a) 10 July 1918 (b) 15 January 1919	Mesopotamia, Army Troops	Supply Column (Ford vans)	5008
1095	(a) 10 July 1918 (b) 15 January 1919	Mesopotamia, Army Troops	Supply Column (MT)	5008
1096	(a) 10 July 1918 (b) 15 January 1919	Mesopotamia, Army Troops	Supply Column (MT)	5008
1097	(a) 10 July 1918 (b) 15 January 1919	Mesopotamia, Army Troops	Supply Column (MT)	5008
1098	(a) 10 July 1918 (b) 15 January 1919	Mesopotamia, Army Troops	Supply Column (MT)	5276
1099	(a) 10 July 1918 (b) 15 January 1919	Mesopotamia, Army Troops	Supply Column (Light vans)	5008
1100	(a) 10 July 1918 (b) 15 January 1919	Mesopotamia, Army Troops	Supply Column (Light vans)	5008
1101			No record of this company's formation	-
1102			No record of this company's formation	-
1103	(a) 30 May 1918 (b) 27 February 1920	Egypt, 2nd Mounted Division, Syria, 5th Cavalry Division	No 1 (HQ) Company (HT)	4517
1104	(a) 30 May 1918 (b) 27 February 1920	Egypt, 2nd Mounted Division Syria, 5th Cavalary Division	No 2 Company (HT)	4517
1105	(a) 30 May 1918 (b) 27 February 1920	Egypt, 2nd Mounted Division Syria, 5th Cavalry Division	No 3 Company (HT)	4517
1106	(a) 8 May 1918 (b) 10 April 1919	Egypt, 20th (Garhwal) Indian Infantry Brigade	Brigade Train (HT)	-
1107	(a) 6 July 1918 (b) 9 August 1918	West Lancs Reserve Brigade TF, Blackheath	Local Auxiliary (HT) Company	-
1108	(a) 6 July 1918 (b) 14 April 1919	Welsh Reserve Brigade TF Herne Bay	Local Auxiliary (HT) Company	-
1109	(a) 6 July 1918 (b) 14 April 1919	Attached 2nd London Reserve Brigade TF, Bungay, Kings Lynn, Aldershot	Local Auxiliary (HT) Company	-
1110	(a) 10 July 1918 (b) 15 January 1919	Mesopotamia, Army Troops	Local Auxiliary (HT) Company	5008
1111	(a) 10 July 1919 (b) 15 January 1919	Mesopotamia, Army Troops	Supply Column (Light vans)	5008
1112	(a) 5 July 1918 (b) 5 June 1919	Western Front, Fifth Army, Army Troops	6 Mobile Repair Unit (MT)	570
1113	(a) 3 June 1918 (b) April 1920	Western Front, Fifth Army, Army Troops	5th Siege Park (MT) (with 770 (MT) Company) 25 Vehicle Reception Park	570
1114	(a) 21 August 1918 (b) 15 March 1921	Mesopotamia, Army Troops	Auxiliary (Petrol) company GHQ Reserve MT Company	136 5008
1115	(a) 21 August 1918 (b) 28 July 1919	Mesopotamia, Army Troops	Auxiliary (Petrol) Company GHQ Rerserve MT Company	5008

ASC Co	(a) Formed (b) Disbanded	Theatre/Order of Battle	Role in First World War	WO 95
1116	(a) 21 August 1918 (b) 3 October 1918	Mesopotamia, Army Troops	Auxiliary (Petrol) Company GHQ Reserve MT Company	-
1117	(a) 21 August 1918 (b) 28 July 1919	Mesopotamia, Army Troops	Auxiliary (Petrol) Company 19 GHQ Reserve MT Company	136
1118	(a) 21 August 1918 (b) Absorbed into 1 MT Depot 14 October 1919	Mesopotamia, Army Troops	Auxiliary (Petrol) Company 20 GHQ Reserve MT Company	-
1119	(a) 15 October 1918 (b) 14 May 1919	Western Front Canadian Corps, Corps Troops	Canadian Motor Machine Gun MT Company (Canadian ASC)	1080
1120	(a) 15 October 1918 (b) 14 May 1919	Western Front Canadian Corps, Corps Troops	Canadian Engineers MT Company (Canadian ASC)	1080
1121	(a) 10 July 1918 (b) 14 April 1919	West Riding Reserve Brigade TF, Woodbridge (Suffolk), Southend	Local Auxiliary (HT) Company	-
1122	(a) 19 November 1918 (b) 14 September 1919	North Russia	HT Depot (mules)	-
1123	(a) 8 September 1918 (b) 2 October 1919	North Russia/Siberia, L of C Troops	HT Company	5432
1124	(a) 8 November 1918 (b) Renumbered 22 MT Co 1 August 1922	Home Forces, Troops Canterbury	119th Local Auxiliary MT Company for Kent Force/transport in Eastern Area	5460
1125			No record of this company's formation	-
1126	(a) 11 September 1918 (b) 25 November 1918	Home (for service in Salonika)	46 Motor Ambulance Convoy	-
1127	(a) 1 November 1918 (b) 13 April 1919	Western Front, 6 Tank Brigade	Brigade MT Company	116
1128	(a) 30 September 1918 (b) Absorbed into 1 MT Depot 14 October 1919	Western Front, Army Troops	21 GHQ Reserve Company (MT)	-
1129	(a) 7 October 1918 (b) 31 October 1919	Western Front, Second Army	47 Motor Ambulance Convoy	341
1130	(a) 7 October 1918 (b) 9 October 1919	Western Front	48 Motor Ambulance Convoy	-
1131	(a) 17 October 1918 (b) 14 April 1920	Western Front, GHQ Army Troops	17 GHQ Reserve MT Company	135
1132	(a) 17 October 1918 (b) 15 December 1919	Western Front, GHQ Troops	18 GHQ Reserve MT Company	135
1133			No record of this company's formation	-
1134			No record of this company's formation	-
1135			No record of this company's formation	-
1136			No record of this company's formation	-
1137			No record of this company's formation	-

ASC Co	(a) Formed (b) Disbanded	Theatre/Order of Battle	Role in First World War	WO 95
1138	(a) 8 October 1918 (b) 21 January 1919	Home (for service in Mesopotamia)	Heavy Repair Shop	-
1139	(a) 17 October 1918 (b) 18 November 1918	Western Front	121st Auxiliary (Petrol) Company	-
1140	(a) 17 October 1918 (b) 18 November 1918	Western Front	122nd Auxiliary (Petrol) Company	-
1141	(a) 21 October 1918 (b) 16 November 1918	Home (for service in Salonika)	Special Supply Column (Light vans)	-
1142	(a) 21 October 1918 (b) 16 November 1918	Home (for service in Salonika)	Special Supply Column (Light vans)	-
1143		Western Front, Army Troops	22 GHQ Reserve MT Company	-
1144		Western Front, Army Troops	23 GHQ Reserve MT Company	-
1145			No record of this company's formation	-
1146	(a) 2 December 1918 (b) 3 January 1919	Home (for service in North Russia)	124th Auxiliary (Petrol) Company	-
1147	(a) 3 December 1918 (b) 20 January 1919	Home (for service in Salonika)	MT Company	-
1148	(a) February 1919 (b) June 1919	Egypt	MT Company	-
1149	(a) March 1919 (b) 4th June 1919	Egypt	HT Company	-
1150	(a) March 1919 (b) 3 February 1920	Italy, Milan	No 1 MT Evacuation Depot	-
1151	(a) March 1919 (b) 31 March 1920	Deptford	HT Company for Supply Reserve Depot Deptford	5422
1152	(a) March 1919 (b) 13 May 1919	North Russia/Siberia	HT Company for Special Brigade (mules)	5422
1153	(a) May 1919 (b) 27 September 1919	North Russia	HT Company (mules)	-
1154	(a) NK (b) NK	Belfast	125 Local Auxiliary MT Company	-
1155	(a) NK (b) NK	Cork	126 Local Auxiliary MT Company	-
1156	(a) July 1919 (b) NK	Devonport	127 Local Auxiliary MT Company	-
1157	(a) NK (b) NK	Dublin	MT Company	-
1158	(a) July 1919 (b) 23 April 1921	Constantinople	MT Company	-
1159	(a) December 1919 (b) 31 July 1921	Constantinople	MT Company	-
1160	(a) July 1919 (b) 31 July 1921	North Russia, Murmansk	Local Auxiliary HT Company	-

ASC Co	(a) Formed (b) Disbanded	Theatre/Order of Battle	Role in First World War	WO 95
1161	(a) NK (b) NK	Deptford	HT Company	-
1162	(a) NK (b) NK	Deptford	HT Company	-
1163	(a) NK (b) NK	Woolwich	HT Company	-
1164	(a) February 1919 (b) 31 March 1921	Mesopotamia	MT Company	-
1165	(a) NK (b) NK	Curragh	MT Company	-
1166	(a) NK (b) NK	Limerick	MT Company	-
1167			No record of this company's formation	-
1168	(a) NK (b) NK	Londonderry		-
'A' Provisional	(a) 15 January 1918 (b) 10 April 1919	Salonika, Army Troops	Movement of railway material in support 267 Railway Company RE	4809
A	(a) NK (b) NK	ASC Depot, Aldershot	Supply Details Company	-
B	(a) NK (b) NK	ASC Training Establishment, Aldershot	Supply Details Company	-
AA	(a) NK (b) NK	Aldershot Woolwich	New Army	-
BB	(a) NK (b) NK	Dublin		-
CC	(a) NK (b) NK	Lusk		-
DD	(a) NK (b) NK	Dublin		-
'D' (Station Staff) Supply	(a) 28 March 1918 (b) 31 December 1919	Formed in Egypt		
'E' Supply	(a) 28 March 1918 (b) 30 June 1919	Formed in Salonika		
'F' Supply	(a) 7 December 1918 (b) NK	Woolwich		
'G' Supply	(a) 7 December 1918 (b) 31 February 1920	Chester		
'H' Supply	(a) 7 December 1918 (b) NK	York		
'I' Supply	(a) 7 December 1918 (b) Relettered as 'G' on 30 July 1920	Dublin		
'J' Supply	(a) 7 December 1918 (b) 27 March 1920	Edinburgh		

ASC Co	(a) Formed (b) Disbanded	Theatre/Order of Battle	Role in First World War	WO 95
'L' Supply	(a) 7 December 1918 (b) Relettered as 'G' on 30 July 1920	Salisbury		
'M' Supply	(a) NK (b) NK	North Russia	Subsumed 393, 394 and 395 Depot Units of Supply on 16 July 1919	
Forage Co	(a) 15 November 1915 (b) 1 July 1920?	England		
Forage Co	(a) 15 November 1915 (b) 1 July 1920?	England		
Forage Co	(a) 15 November 1915 (b) 1 July 1920?	England		
Forage Co	(a) 15 November 1915 (b) 1 July 1920?	England		
Forage Co	(a) 15 November 1915 (b) 1 July 1920?	England		
Forage Co	(a) 15 November 1915 (b) 1 July 1920?	England		
Forage Co	(a) 15 November 1915 (b) 1 July 1920?	Scotland		
Forage Co	(a) 15 November 1915 (b) 1 July 1920?	Ireland		
1-38 Line of Communication Supply Co	Variously 1917 to 1919	Western Front	Details not known	
1 Donkey	a. 8 October 1917 b. December 1918	Egypt, GHQ Troops, Palestine	762 donkeys	4413
2 Donkey	a. October 1917 b. December 1918	Egypt, Palestine	Attached 10th Division	4413
3 Donkey	a. 21 December 1917 b. November 1918	Egypt, Palestine		4413
Auxiliary Water Co	a. 3 February 1917 b. NK	Fifth Army, Western Front Albert	Garford lorries with 500 gallon tanks (No Company number allocated)	570
Agricultural Park ASC	a. October 1918 b. June 1919	Salonika	Agricultural work. Employed Bulgarian and Turkish POW.	4943

*Did not disband at the end of the war. Many companies annotated with an asterisk continue to this day in The Royal Logistic Corps, a successor Corps to the Army Service Corps, but might not necessarily have had continuous service since the First World War.

Note

1   The disbandment dates cannot always be listed accurately. The dates provided sometimes reflect the closing of war diaries (as can be seen in the Public Record Office Kew) or information available in the Royal Corps of Transport archives.

2   When 'absorbed' is annotated individuals in the company were absorbed (posted) into other (unrecorded) units.

3   Dates of war diaries available in the Public Record Office Kew are sometimes different from the formation and disbandment dates listed in this annex.

4   War diaries were not kept by Home units on local duties.

Units in Formations/Theatres of War

FRANCE AND BELGIUM

Division	ASC Companies	PRO Kew WO 95/	Division	ASC Companies	PRO Kew WO 95/
1 Cavalry	45, 57, 574	1107	24	194, 195, 196, 197	2203
2 Cavalry	46, 56, 575	1128-29	25	198, 199, 200, 201	2240
3 Cavalry	73, 76, 81, 576	1150-51	26	202, 203, 204, 205	2252
4 Cavalry	79, 89, 426, 577	1158	27	95, 96, 97, 98	2259
5 Cavalry	71, 72, 427, 578	1163	28	170, 171, 172, 173	2272
1 Indian Cavalry	79, 89, 426, 577	1172-73	29	225, 226, 227, 228	2297
2 Indian Cavalry	71, 72, 83, 427	1184	30	186, 187, 188, 189	2326
Guards	11, 124, 168, 436	1209	31	221, 222, 223, 224	2355
1	7, 13, 16, 36	1260	32	202, 203, 204, 205	2387
2	28, 31, 35, 172	1340	33	170, 171, 172, 173	2419
3	15, 21, 22, 29	1409-12	34	229, 230, 231, 232	2454
4	18, 25, 32, 38	1476	35	233, 234, 235, 236	2480-81
5	4, 6, 33, 37	1542-47	36	251, 252, 253, 254	2501
6	17, 19, 23, 24	1604	37	288, 289, 290, 291	2526
7	39, 40, 42, 86	1649	38	330, 331, 332, 333	2550
8	41, 84, 85, 87	1705-06	39	284, 285, 286, 287	2580
9	104, 105, 106, 107	1761	40	292, 293, 294, 295	2603
10	Served in Gallipoli, Macedonia, Palestine		41	296, 297, 298, 299	2631
11	479, 480, 481, 482	1804	42	428, 429, 430, 431	2653
12	116, 117, 118, 119	1845	43	Served in India	
14	100, 101, 102, 103	1893	44	Served in India	
15	138, 139, 140, 141	1933	45	501 Home only	
16	142, 143, 144, 145	1968	46	451, 452, 453, 454	2682
17	146, 147, 148, 149	1997	47	455, 456, 457, 458	2726
18	150, 151, 152, 153	2032	48	459, 460, 461, 462	2753
19	154, 155, 156, 157	2074	49	463, 464, 465, 466	2791
20	158, 159, 160, 161	2110	50	467, 468, 469, 470	2825
21	182, 183, 184, 185	2149-50	51	471, 472, 473, 474	2860
22	186, 187, 188, 189	2166	52	217, 218, 219, 220	2895
23	190, 191, 192, 193	2180	53	Served in Gallipoli, Egypt and Palestine	

Division	ASC Companies	PRO Kew WO 95/
54	Served in Gallipoli, Egypt, Palestine	
55	95, 96, 97, 98	2919
56	213, 214, 215, 216	2945
57	505, 506, 507, 508	2975
58	509, 510, 511, 512	2998
59	513, 514, 515, 516	3019
60	517, 518, 519, 520	3029
61	521, 522, 523, 524	3052
62	525, 526, 527, 528	3078
63 (RN)	761, 762, 763, 764	3107
64	Served in UK only	
65	Served in UK only	
66	541, 542, 543, 544	3133
67	Served in UK only	
68	Served in UK only	
69	Served in UK only	
70	Was not formed	

Division	ASC Companies	PRO Kew WO 95/
71	Served in UK only	
72	Served in UK only	
73	829, 830, 831, 832	Home only
74 Yeomanry	447, 448, 449, 450	3151
1 Australian	741, 742, 743, 744	3208
2 Australian	745, 746, 747, 748	3305-06
3 Australian	867, 868, 869, 870	3394
4 Australian	753, 754, 755, 756	3486
5 Australian	757, 758, 759, 760	3610
New Zealand	749, 750, 751, 752	3684
1 Canadian	437, 438, 439, 440	3757
2 Canadian	672, 673, 674, 675	3810
3 Canadian	676, 677, 678, 679	3863
4 Canadian	794, 795, 796, 797	3894
5 Canadian	Divisional Train Detachment	3910
3 Indian (Lahore)	Divisional Train and Indian Mule Corps	3921
7 Indian (Meerut)	Divisional Train and Mule Transport	3939

Lines of Communication Units

Unit title/function/Company	ASC Company	PRO Kew WO 95/
5 Auxiliary Horse Transport	372	4163
8 Auxiliary Horse Transport	255	4163
11 Auxiliary Horse Transport	501	4163
22 Auxiliary Horse Transport	879	4163
3 Auxiliary Petrol	315	4164
4 Auxiliary Petrol	316	4164
5 Auxiliary Petrol	317	4164
6 Auxiliary Petrol	318	4164
20 Auxiliary Petrol	590	4164
39 Auxiliary Petrol	735	4164
40 Auxiliary Petrol	736	4164
43 Auxiliary Petrol	805	4164
57 Auxiliary Petrol	914	4164
58 Auxiliary Petrol	915	4164
66 Auxiliary Petrol	933	4165
78 Auxiliary Petrol	979	4165
118 Auxiliary Petrol	1092	4165
123 Auxiliary Petrol	592	4165
7 Auxiliary Steam	356	4165
71 Auxiliary Steam	938	4165
76 Auxiliary Steam	940	4165
41 Auxiliary Ambulance Car	812	4165
47 Auxiliary Ambulance Car	813	4165
48 Auxiliary Ambulance Car	814	4165
Formed as Auxiliary Petrol Company	1057	4165
1 Heavy Repair Shop (HRS)	319	4166
2 Heavy Repair Shop (HRS)	320	4167
3 Heavy Repair Shop (HRS)	358	4167
4 Heavy Repair Shop (HRS)	899	4167
5 Heavy Repair Shop (HRS)	974	4167
MT School of Instruction	-	4172
7 MT Reception Park	-	4172
8 MT Reception Park	-	4172

Unit title/function/Company	ASC Company	PRO Kew WO 95/
10 MT Reception Park	-	4172
24 MT Reception Park	-	4172
33 Labour Company (Railways)	-	4174
34 Labour Company (Railways)	-	4174
Advanced Horse Transport Depot	-	4177
No 1 Advanced MT Depot	54	4179-4183
No 2 Advanced MT Depot	365	4184
No 1 HT Base Depot	10	4188
No 1MT Base Depot	53	4188
No 2 MT Base Depot	364	4188
No 4 Base Supply Depot	-	4189
No 5 Base Supply Depot	-	4189
No 7 Base Supply Depot	-	4189
British Military Base Depot (Indian contingent)	-	4192
2 Advanced Base Supply Depot (Indian contingent)	-	4193
Indian Transport Base Depot	-	4193
Indian Mule Transport Base Depot	-	4193

Corps ASC Units

1 Corps

Unit title/function/Company	ASC Company	PRO Kew WO 95/
Cavalry Corps Troops Column MT	392	584
Corps Troops Supply Column MT	386	625
11 Division Supply Column MT	714	626
15 Division Supply Column MT	177	626
16 Division Supply Column MT	69	626
24 Division Supply Column MT	342	626
55 Division Supply Column MT	77, 354	627
Corps Siege Park	282	628
Corps Ammunition Park	-	628
3 Ammunition Sub Park MT	64	628
34 Ammunition Sub Park MT	357	628
42 Ammunition Sub Park MT	897	628

2 Corps

Corps Troops Supply Column MT	387	665
9 Division Supply Column MT	131	666
29 Division Supply Column MT	496	666
36 Division Supply Column MT	379	666
Corps Siege Park MT	406	665
Corps Ammunition Park	-	667
24 Ammunition Sub Park MT	343	667
32 Ammunition Sub Park MT	353	667
35 Ammunition Sub Park MT	305	667
39 Ammunition Sub Park MT	375	667
58 Ammunition Sub Park MT	734	667

338

3 Corps

Unit title/function/Company	ASC Company	PRO Kew WO 95/
Corps Troops Supply Column MT	388	703
12 Division Supply Column MT	175	704
18 Division Supply Column MT	179, 63	704
27 Division Supply Column MT	77	704
Corps Siege Park MT	641	703
Corps Ammunition Park	-	705
5 Ammunition Sub Park MT	408	705
36 Ammunition Sub Park MT	380	705
39 Ammunition Sub Park MT	893	705

4 Corps

Corps Troops Supply Column MT	389	738
5 Division Supply Column MT	48, 733	739
37 Division Supply Column MT	135	740
42 Division Supply Column MT	896	740
51 Division Supply Column MT	265	740
New Zealand Division Supply Column MT	610	740
Corps Siege Park MT	562	741
Corps Ammunition Park	-	741
21 Ammunition Sub Park MT	80	741
51 Ammunition Sub Park MT	266	742

5 Corps

Unit title/function/Company	ASC Company	PRO Kew WO 95/
Corps Troops Supply Column MT	390	762
17 Division Supply Column MT	498, 48	762
21 Division Supply Column MT	273	762
28 Division Supply Column MT	181	763
33 Division Supply Column MT	181	763
38 Division Supply Column MT	67	763
Corps Siege Park MT	363	764
Corps Ammunition Park	-	764
19 Ammunition Sub Park MT	258	764
47 Ammunition Sub Park MT	278	765
61 Ammunition Sub Park MT	497	766
63 Ammunition Sub Park MT	702	766

6 Corps

Unit title/function/Company	ASC Company	PRO Kew WO 95/
Corps Troops Supply Column MT	368	795
2 Division Supply Column MT	61	796
Guards Division Supply Column MT	306	797-798
3 Division Supply Column MT	44, 63	799
7 Division Supply Column MT	44	800
62 Division Supply Column MT	719	800
Corps Siege Park MT	565	794
Corps Ammunition Park	-	801
7 Ammunition Sub Park MT	66	802
18 Ammunition Sub Park MT	180	803
40 Ammunition Sub Park MT	684	803
55 Ammunition Sub Park MT	410	803

7 Corps

Unit title/function/Company	ASC Company	PRO Kew WO 95/
Corps Troops Supply Column MT	382	817
39 Division Supply Column MT	374	818
Corps Siege Park MT	283	817
Corps Ammunition Park	-	819
9 Ammunition Sub Park MT	132	819
16 Ammunition Sub Park MT	411	819
46 Ammunition Sub Park MT	269	819

8 Corps

Corps Troops Supply Column MT	592, 885	829
8 Division Supply Column MT	74	830
23 Division Supply Column MT	340	830
58 Division Supply Column MT	733, 77	830
20 Division Supply Column MT	267	831-832
Corps Siege Park MT	593, 886	829
Corps Ammunition Park	-	833
8 Ammunition Sub Park MT	409	833
33 Ammunition Sub Park MT	169	834
41 Ammunition Sub Park MT	499	834

9 Corps

Corps Troops Supply Column MT	716	847
1 Division Supply Column MT	59	847
6 Division Supply Column MT	50	848
32 Division Supply Column MT	352	848
46 Division Supply Column MT	271	848
Corps Siege Park MT	717	846
Corps Ammunition Park	-	849
30 Ammunition Sub Park MT	262	849
37 Ammunition Sub Park MT	136	849

10 Corps

Unit title/function/Company	ASC Company	PRO Kew WO 95/
Corps Troops Supply Column MT	383	877
30 Division Supply Column MT	261	878, 894?
34 Division Supply Column MT	354. 179	878
50 Division Supply Column MT	336	878
Corps Siege Park MT	594	877
Corps Ammunition Park	-	879
17 Ammunition Sub Park MT	609	879
23 Ammunition Sub Park MT	607	879

11 Corps

Corps Troops Supply Column MT	321	891
19 Division Supply Column MT	257	892
47 Division Supply Column MT	277	892
59 Division Supply Column MT	892	892
74 Division Supply Column MT	71	892
Corps Siege Park MT	491	891
Corps Ammunition Park	-	893
6 Ammunition Sub Park MT	49	893
38 Ammunition Sub Park MT	70	893

12 Corps

Corps Troops Supply Column MT	887	894
22 Division Supply Column MT	261	894

13 Corps

Unit title/function/Company	ASC Company	PRO Kew WO 95/
Corps Troops Supply Column MT	564	907
25 Division Supply Column MT	344	908
50 Division Supply Column MT	340	908
56 Division Supply Column MT	263	908
66 Division Supply Column MT	888	908
Corps Siege Park MT	335	907
Corps Ammunition Park MT	-	909
31 Ammunition Sub Park MT	260	909
48 Ammunition Sub Park MT	329	909
56 Ammunition Sub Park MT	264	909

14 Corps

Corps Troops Supply Column MT	391	920
Corps Siege Park MT	654	920
Corps Ammunition Park MT	-	920
20 Ammunition Sub Park MT	268	920
29 Ammunition Sub Park MT	601	920

15 Corps

Corps Troops Supply Column MT	696	931
14 Division Supply Column MT	133	932
31 Division Supply Column MT	259	932
40 Division Supply Column MT	608	932
Corps Siege Park MT	604	931
Corps Ammunition Park MT	-	931
12 Ammunition Sub Park MT	176	933
57 Ammunition Sub Park MT	732	933

17 Corps

Unit title/function/Company	ASC Company	PRO Kew WO 95/
Corps Troops Supply Column MT	582	948
4 Division Supply Column MT	65	949
52 Division Supply Column MT	89	949
57 Division Supply Column MT	731	949
60 Division Supply Column MT	683	949
61 Division Supply Column MT	302	949
63 Division Supply Column MT	701	949
Corps Siege Park MT	611	948
Corps Ammunition Park MT	-	950
Guards Ammunition Sub Park MT	307	950
4 Ammunition Sub Park MT	47	950
15 Ammunition Sub Park MT	178	950
60 Ammunition Sub Park MT	685	950

18 Corps

Corps Troops Supply Column MT	885	957
48 Division Supply Column MT	328	958
Corps Ammunition Park MT	-	958
11 Ammunition Sub Park MT	715	958
14 Ammunition Sub Park MT	134	958
62 Ammunition Sub Park MT	720	958

19 Corps

Corps Troops Supply Column MT	883	971
35 Division Supply Column MT	304	972
41 Division Supply Column MT	494	972
Corps Siege Park MT	884	971
Corps Ammunition Park MT	-	973
1 Ammunition Sub Park MT	60	973
2 Ammunition Sub Park MT	407	973

22 Corps

Unit title/function/Company	ASC Company	PRO Kew WO 95/
Corps Troops Supply Column MT	687	978
4 Division Supply Column MT	65	979
49 Division Supply Column MT	349	979
51 Division Supply Column MT	265	979
56 Division Supply Column MT	263	979
Corps Siege Park MT	403	978
49 Ammunition Sub Park MT	350	979
66 Ammunition Sub Park MT	889	979
1 New Zealand Ammunition Sub Park MT	586	979

1 Australia and New Zealand Corps

Corps Troops Supply Column MT	659	1019-1020
1 Division Supply Column MT	300	1021
2 Division Supply Column MT	600	1022
3 Division Supply Column MT	807	1023
4 Division Supply Column MT	686	1024-1025
5 Division Supply Column MT	712	1026
Corps Ammunition Park	-	1027
1 Ammunition Sub Park	301	1028
2 Ammunition Sub Park	492	1029
3 Ammunition Sub Park	808	1029
4 Ammunition Sub Park	690	1030
5 Ammunition Sub Park	713	1031
No 4 MT Company	-	1017
No 6 MT Company	-	1017

2 Australia and New Zealand Corps

Unit title/function/Company	ASC Company	PRO Kew WO 95/
Corps Troops Supply Column MT	687	1040
49 Division Supply Column MT	349	1042
New Zealand Division Supply Column MT	610	1042
25 Division Supply Column MT	345	1043
Corps Siege Park MT	403	1041
49 Ammunition Sub Park MT	350	1044
50 Ammunition Sub Park MT	337	1044
66 Ammunition Sub Park MT	889	1044
1 New Zealand Ammunition Sub Park MT	586	1044

Canadian Corps

Corps Troops Supply Column	721	1080
1 Division Supply Column MT	415	1081
2 Division Supply Column MT	722	1081
3 Division Supply Column MT	724	1081
4 Division Supply Column MT	785	1081
Corps Siege Park MT	402	1080
Corps Ammunition Park MT	-	1082
1 Ammunition Sub Park MT	412	1082
2 Ammunition Sub Park MT	723	1082
3 Ammunition Sub Park MT	725	1082
4 Ammunition Sub Park MT	786	1082
Motor Machine Gun MT Company	1119	1080
Canadian Engineers MT Company	1120	1080

Indian Corps (until December 1915)

Corps Ammunition Park MT	-	1094
2 Indian Ammunition Park MT	-	1094
Lahore Ammunition Sub Park MT	68	1094
Meerut Ammunition Sub Park MT	70	1094
Lahore Division Supply Column MT	69	1095
Meerut Division Supply Column MT	67	1095

ITALY

GHQ Troops

Unit title/function/Company	ASC Company	PRO Kew WO 95/
Troops Supply Column MT	385	4209
14 Corps Troops Supply Column MT	391	4209
14 Corps Siege Park MT	654	4210
7 Division MT Company	336	4210
23 Division MT Company	494	4210
48 Division MT Company	328	4210
942 MT Company	942	4210
Reserve MT Company	1037	4209
83 Auxiliary Petrol Company	1036	4209
4 Pontoon Park	360	4210
1 Mobile Repair Unit	93	4210
6 Army Auxiliary Horse Company	1047	4209
2 Auxiliary Pack Train	443	4209

11 Corps Troops

Troops Supply Column MT	321	4211
11 Corps Siege Park MT	491	4211
Corps Ammunition Park	-	4211
58 Division Supply Column MT	733	4211
5 Division MT Company	733	4211
25 Ammunition Siege Park MT	345	4211
62 Ammunition Sub Park MT	720	4211

14 Corps Troops

Corps Ammunition Park	-	4213
17 Division Supply Column MT	498	4213
17 Ammunition Sub Park MT	609	4213
23 Ammunition Sub Park MT	607	4213
50 Ammunition Sub Park MT	337	4213

Divisions

Unit title/function/Company	ASC Company	PRO Kew WO 95/
5 Division Train	4, 6, 33, 37	4215
7 Division Train	39, 40, 42, 86	4222
23 Division Train	190, 191, 192, 193	4234
41 Division Train	296, 297, 298, 299	4242
48 Division Train	459, 460, 461, 462	4247

Lines of Communication

Base MT Depot	1034	4262
2 HT Base Depot	1046	4262
6 Advanced HT Depot	1045	4262
116 Auxiliary Petrol Company	1074	4262
Heavy Repair Workshop	1081	4262

GALLIPOLI/DARDANELLES

Advanced HT Depot (L of C)	-	4358
29 Division Train	246, 247, 248, 249	4309
42 Division Train Detachment		4314
52 Division Train	-	4319
53 Division Ammunition Column and Park		4322

EGYPT/PALESTINE/SYRIA

Ismailia District

Unit title/function/Company	ASC Company	PRO Kew WO 95/
7 Mounted Brigade	1044	4405
Advanced HT Depot	973	4414
Base HT Depot	137	4414
Motor Boat Company ASC	-	4414
347 MT Company	347	4413
493 MT Company	493	4413
619 MT Company	619	4413
1006 MT Company	1006	4413
1008 MT Company	1008	4413
52 Auxiliary Petrol Company	906	4411
53 Auxiliary Petrol Company	907	4411
54 Auxiliary Petrol Company	905	4411
79 Auxiliary Petrol Company	1009	4411
80 Auxiliary Petrol Company	1010	4412
81 Auxiliary Petrol Company	1011	4412
82 Auxiliary Petrol Company	956	4412
87 Auxiliary Petrol Company	1038	4412
88 Auxiliary Petrol Company	1039	4412
101 Auxiliary Petrol Company	1040	4412
1 MT Tractor Company	895	4412
2 MT Tractor Company	972	4412
Heavy Repair Workshop	644	4413
9 Auxiliary HT Company	671	4411
1 Donkey Transport Company	-	4413
2 Donkey Transport Company	-	4413
3 Donkey Transport Company	-	4413
18 (L of C) Supply Company	-	4413
20 (L of C) Supply Company	-	4413
18 Field Bakery	-	4414

Southern Canal Section

Unit title/function/Company	ASC Company	PRO Kew WO 95/
493 MT Company	493	4435
23 Auxiliary HT Company	900	4435

Delta Western Force

OC Supplies Column	-	4442
790 MT Company	790	4444

Eastern Force Troops

711 MT Company	711	4454
811 MT Company	811	4454
951 MT Company	951	4454
961 MT Company	961	4454

Force in Egypt

790 MT Company	790	4457
6 Auxiliary HT Company	313	4457
101 Auxiliary Petrol Company	1040	4457
23 (L of C) Supply Company	-	4457
26 Field Bakery	-	4457

North Force

21 Corps Troops Train	1043	4460
2 MT Tractor Company	972	4460
52 Auxiliary Petrol Company	906	4460
54 Auxiliary Petrol Company	905	4460
87 Auxiliary Petrol Company	1038	4460
88 Auxiliary Petrol Company	1039	4460
34 (L of C) Supply Company	-	4460
35 (L of C) Supply Company	-	4460
19 Field Bakery	-	4460
27 Field Bakery	-	4460

Alexandria District Troops

Unit title/function/Company	ASC Company	PRO Kew WO 95/
980 MT Company	980	4466
1031 MT Company	1031	4466
1032 MT Company	1032	4466
10 Division Supply Column MT	338	4466
35 Division Ammunition Park	303	4467
1 Motor Ambulance Transport Company	1078	4466
80 Auxiliary Petrol Company	1010	4466
Heavy Repair Workshop	644	4467
Base MT Depot	-	4467
1 Motor Ambulance Transport Company	1078	4466
9 Auxiliary HT Company	671	4466
24 (L of C) Supply Company	-	4467
25 (L of C) Supply Company	-	4467

Cairo District Troops

53 Auxiliary Petrol Company	907	4469
101 Auxiliary Petrol Company	1040	4469
6 Auxiliary HT Company	313	4469
26 Field Bakery	-	4469

Kantara District Troops

493 MT Company	493	4470

Desert Mounted Corps Troops

52 Auxiliary Petrol Company	906	4478
54 Auxiliary Petrol Company	905	4478
87 Auxiliary Petrol Company	1038	4478
88 Auxiliary Petrol Company	1039	4478

20 Corps

Unit title/function/Company	ASC Company	PRO Kew WO 95/
Corps Troops Train	1042	4489
811 MT Company	811	4488
963 MT Company	963	4488
964 MT Company	964	4488
966 MT Company	966	4488
980 MT Company	980	4488
983 MT Company	983	4488
990 MT Company	990	4488
1006 MT Company	1006	4489
1007 MT Company	1007	4489
1008 MT Company	1008	4489
1030 MT Company	1030	4489
1072 MT Company	1072	4489

21 Corps

Unit title/function/Company	ASC Company	PRO Kew WO 95/
Corps Troops Train	1043	4503
810 MT Company	810	4502
811 MT Company	811	4502
904 MT Company	904	4502
951 MT Company	951	4502
952 MT Company	952	4502
955 MT Company	955	4502
964 MT Company	964	4503
965 MT Company	965	4503
967 MT Company	967	4503
982 MT Company	982	4503
983 MT Company	983	4503
984 MT Company	984	4503
988 MT Company	988	4503
989 MT Company	989	4503
990 MT Company	990	4503
1 Egyptian Mobile Repair Unit	-	4503
2 Egyptian Mobile Repair Unit	-	4503

Divisions

Unit title/function/Company	ASC Company	PRO Kew WO 95/
Yeomanry Mounted Division Train	999, 1000, 1001, 1002	4505
1 Mounted Division Train	999, 1000,1001, 1002	4508
4 Cavalry Division Train	999, 1000, 1001, 1002	4512
5 Cavalry Division Train	1044, 1103, 1104, 1105	4517
Australia and New Zealand Mounted Division Train	991, 992, 993, 994	4533
Australia and New Zealand Mounted Division Train	32, 33, 34	4533
10th (Irish) Division Train	475, 476, 477, 478	4577
31 Division Train	217, 218, 219, 220	4589
42 (East Lancashire Division Train	447, 448, 449, 450	4593
52 (Lowland) Division Train	217, 218, 219, 220	4605-6
53 (Welsh) Division Train	246, 247, 248, 249	4624
54 (East Anglian) Division Train	921, 922, 923, 924	4648
60 (London) Division Train	517, 518, 519, 520	4666
74 (Yeomanry) Division Train	447, 448, 449, 450	4676
75 Division Train	925, 926, 927, 928	4687
3 (Lahore) Indian Division Train		4699
7 (Meerut) Indian Division Train		4710

Lines of Communication - Egypt

347 MT Company	347	4721
1073 MT Company	1073	4721
35 Motor Ambulance Convoy	894	4720
Field Ambulance Workshop Unit	772	4720
Motor Boat Company ASC	-	4721
35 Division Ammunition Park	303	4721
34 (L of C) Supply Company	-	4722
35 (L of C) Supply Company	-	4722
27 Field Bakery	-	4722

Lines of Communication - Palestine

Unit title/function/Company	ASC Company	PRO Kew WO 95/
347 MT Company	347	4737
493 MT Company	493	4737
963 MT Company	963	4737
988 MT Company	988	4738
990 MT Company	990	4738
1006 MT Company	1006	4738
1073 MT Company	1073	4738
2 MT Tractor Company	972	4737
23 Auxiliary HT Company	900	4737
18 (L of C) Supply Company	-	4738
19 (L of C) Supply Company	-	4738
20 (L of C) Supply Company	-	4738
21 (L of C) Supply Company	-	4738
22 (L of C) Supply Company	-	4738
18 Field Bakery	-	4738
19 Field Bakery	-	4738

SALONIKA, MACEDONIA, TURKEY, BLACK SEA, CAUCASUS AND SOUTH RUSSIA

Brigades

7 Mounted Brigade Train HT	210	4793
7 Mounted Brigade Supply Column MT	802	4793
7 Mounted Brigade Ammunition Column MT	803	4793
8 Mounted Brigade Supply Column MT	860	4793
8 Mounted Brigade Ammunition Column		4793

Army Troops

Unit title/function/Company	ASC Company	PRO Kew WO 95/
GHQ Troops Supply Column	766	4813
7 Motor Ambulance Convoy	325	4804
9 Motor Ambulance Convoy	355	4804
17 Motor Ambulance Convoy	595	4804
32 Motor Ambulance Convoy	771	4805
34 Motor Ambulance Convoy	787	4805
38 Motor Ambulance Convoy	920	4805
12 Auxiliary HT Company	208	4808
13 Auxiliary HT Company	209	4808
14 Auxiliary HT Company	238	4808
15 Auxiliary HT Company	798	4808
16 Auxiliary HT Company	799	4808
17 Auxiliary HT Company	800	4808
18 Auxiliary HT Company	163	4809
21 Auxiliary HT Company	362	4809
"A" Provisional HT Company	-	4809
854 Auxiliary Pack Company	854	4809
855 Auxiliary Pack Company	855	4809
857 Auxiliary Pack Company	857	4809
858 Auxiliary Pack Company	858	4809
29 Reserve Park HT	270	4809
38 Auxiliary MT Company	605	4810
56 Auxiliary MT Company	913	4810
89 Auxiliary MT Company	244	4810

Army Troops

Unit title/function/Company	ASC Company	PRO Kew WO 95/
90 Auxiliary MT Company	245	4811
91 Auxiliary MT Company	338	4811
92 Auxiliary MT Company	346	4811
93 Auxiliary MT Company	597	4811
94 Auxiliary MT Company	619	4811
95 Auxiliary MT Company	683	4811
96 Auxiliary MT Company	738	4811
97 Auxiliary MT Company	778	4812
98 Auxiliary MT Company	779	4812
99 Auxiliary MT Company	780	4812
100 Auxiliary MT Company	781	4812
376 MT Company	376	4812
739 MT Company	739	4812
740 MT Company	740	4812
765 MT Company	765	4813
767 MT Company	767	4813
777 MT Company	777	4813
809 MT Company	809	4813
810 MT Company	810	4813
1031 MT Company	1031	4813
1032 MT Company	1032	4813
1071 MT Company	1071	4813
1083 MT Company	1083	4813
Anti-Aircraft Workshop	919	4813
Supply Column with the Serbian Army (MT Companies ASC)	688, 689, 706, 707, 708, 709, 819, 820, 880, 881	4814

12 Corps

Corps Troops Supply Column	887	4822
Corps Ammunition Column	-	4822
26 Ammunition Park	782	4822
60 Ammunition Park	685	4822

16 Corps

Unit title/function/Company	ASC Company	PRO Kew WO 95/
Corps Ammunition Column	-	4827
Corps Troops Supply Column	801	4827

Divisions

10 (Irish) Division Train	475, 476, 477, 478	4833
22 Division Train	108, 109, 110, 111	4849
26 Division Train	112, 113, 114, 115	4868
27 Division Train	852, 853, 854, 855	4886
28 Division Train	856, 857, 858, 859	4912
60 Division Train	861, 862, 863, 864	4927

Lines of Communication Troops

19 Auxiliary HT Company	128	4942
3 Base HT Depot	573	4947
4 Advanced HT Depot	579	4947
Muleteer Base Depot	-	4948
Base MT Depot	-	4948
33 Motor Boat Section	-	4943
Heavy Repair Workshop	660	4942
Heavy Repair Workshop	910	4943
Agricultural Park ASC	-	4943
Main Supply Depot (Salonika)	-	4948
20 Field Bakery	-	4943
28 Labour Company	-	4944

Black Sea

Unit title/function/Company	ASC Company	PRO Kew WO 95/
DST/MT Information Office	-	4952

Black Sea Troops

17 Auxiliary HT Company	800	4954
99 Auxiliary HT Company	780	4954
706 MT Company	706	4954
738 MT Company	738	4954
765 MT Company	765	4954
767 MT Company	767	4954
887/766 Combined MT Company	887/766	4954
33 Motor Boat Section	-	4954
Allied Corps Troops MT Company	605	4957

Army Troops

Unit title/function/Company	ASC Company	PRO Kew WO 95/
33 Motor Ambulance Convoy	773	5003
39 Motor Ambulance Convoy	911	5003
40 Motor Ambulance Convoy	970	5004
596 MT Company	596	5005
729 MT Company	729	5005
730 MT Company	730	5005
783 MT Company	783	5005
784 MT Company	784	5005
788 MT Company	788	5005
789 MT Company	789	5005
815 MT Company	815	5005
818 MT Company	818	5006
901 MT Company	901	5006
902 MT Company	902	5006
903 MT Company	903	5006
953 MT Company	953	5006
954 MT Company	954	5006
968 MT Company	968	5006
969 MT Company	969	5006
971 MT Company	971	5006
976 MT Company	976	5006
1013 MT Company	1013	5006
1014 MT Company	1014	5006
1015 MT Company	1015	5007
1016 MT Company	1016	5007
1017 MT Company	1017	5007
1018 MT Company	1018	5007
1019 MT Company	1019	5007
1020 MT Company	1020	5007
1023 MT Company	1023	5007
1024 MT Company	1024	5008

Army Troops

Unit title/function/Company	ASC Company	PRO Kew WO 95/
1028 MT Company	1028	5008
1054 MT Company	1054	5008
1055 MT Company	1055	5008
1094 MT Company	1094	5008
1095 MT Company	1095	5008
1096 MT Company	1096	5008
1097 MT Company	1097	5008
1099 MT Company	1099	5008
1100 MT Company	1100	5008
1110 MT Company	1110	5008
1111 MT Company	1111	5008
1114 MT Company	1114	5008
1115 MT Company	1115	5008

Bushire Force MT Detachment	596	5010

EUPHRATES DEFENCE & COMMUNICATIONS

HQ & Troops

Euphrates Front Transport Section	-	5029
41 Indian Brigade Supply Column	-	5030

Advanced Base and Defences

Army Ammunition Park	-	5036
45 Motor Ambulance Convoy	1091	5036
Advanced MT Depot	-	5041

NORTH PERSIA FORCE

Indian Cavalry Division ADST	-	5082

6 Indian Cavalry Brigade

Unit title/function/Company	ASC Company	PRO Kew WO 95/
Brigade Supply Column	-	5088
Brigade Ammunition Column	-	5088

7 Indian Cavalry Brigade

Brigade Supply and Transport Company	-	5091
Brigade Ammunition Column	-	5091

3 (Lahore) Indian Division

9 Infantry Brigade Transport Company	-	5111

6 Indian Division

Attached Troops MT section	-	5119

7 (Meerut) Indian Division

Troops Supply Column	-	5135
28 Infantry Brigade Supply Column	-	5141

13 (Western) Division

217 Company ASC	217	5154
218 Company ASC	218	5154
219 Company ASC	219	5154

14 Indian Division

Troops Divisional Train	-	5173

15 Indian Division

Division Train	-	5192

42 Indian Infantry Brigade

Unit title/function/Company	ASC Company	PRO Kew WO 95/
Brigade Supply Column	-	5197
Brigade Combined Mule Transport	-	5197

18 Indian Division

Division Supply Column	-	5224
Division Train	-	5224

LINES OF COMMUNICATION

Lines of Communication Troops

23 Motor Ambulance Convoy	656	5248
596 MT Company	596	5276
1056 MT Company	1056	5276
1093 MT Company	1093	5276
1098 MT Company	1098	5276
962 Heavy Repair Workshop	-	5276
Base Ammunition Depot	-	5282
Base MT Depot	695	5284

Persian Lines of Communication

39 Motor Ambulance Convoy	911	5288

EAST AFRICA AND CAMEROONS, WEST AFRICA

Lindi Force - Ammunition Column	-	5324
Lindi Column - Ammunition Column	-	5325
1 East African Division Supply Train	-	5338
2 East African Division Senior Transport Officer	-	5342
3 East African Division Senior Supply Officer	-	5346

362

Lines of Communication

Unit title/function/Company	ASC Company	PRO Kew WO 95/
18 Motor Ambulance Convoy	618	5371
19 Motor Ambulance Convoy	626	5371
29 Motor Ambulance Convoy	699	5371
Brigade Supply Column	635	5377
Brigade Supply Column	570	5377
Base MT Depot	599	5378
1 Auxiliary MT Company	-	5378
631 MT Company	631	5378
635 MT Company	635	5378
68 Field Butchery	-	5378
1 Bullock Cart Train	-	5378
4/5 Armoured Motor Batteries Workshops	-	5378

Cameroons

581 MT Company	581	5388

INDIA AND EAST PERSIA

North-West Frontier Force - Corps Troops

1028 MT Company	1028	5390
630 MT Company	630	5390
656 MT Company	656	5390
692 MT Company	692	5390
693 MT Company	693	5390
694 MT Company	694	5390
871 MT Company	871	5390

Lines of Communication - Northern

2 MT Company	-	5393
693 MT Company	693	5393
K Company Supply Depot	-	5393

Lines of Communication - Nowshera

Unit title/function/Company	ASC Company	PRO Kew WO 95/
DAD S & T	-	5393

Waziristan Force

AD S & T	-	5393

1 Indian Division

AD S & T	-	5404

4 Indian Division

AD S & T	-	5412

16 Indian Division

AS S & T	-	5413

East Persia - L of C

Light Lorry Section	-	5418

NORTH RUSSIA & SIBERIA

GHQ

1152 Company	1152	5422

Syren Force

Base Supply Depot	-	5426

Divina Force

Divina Force	-	5430

Lines of Communication

Unit title/function/Company	ASC Company	PRO Kew WO 95/
AD S & T	-	5413
DAD S & T (Bakaritza)	-	5413

Lines of Communication - Troops

393 Depot Unit of Supply	-	5432
394 Depot Unit of Supply	-	5432
400 Depot Unit of Supply	-	5432
1123 HT Company	1123	5432
OC ASC (Kola)	-	5432
OC ASC (Petchenga)	-	5432
OC ASC (Bakaritza)	-	5432
OC Supplies (Economic)	-	5432

COLONIES AND PROTECTORATES

Aden Force: OC S & T	-	5436
Ceylon: AD S & T	-	5440
South China Command Hong Kong: AD S & T	-	5444
Malta: AD S & T	-	5448
Mauritius: OC ASC	-	5450

Unit title/function/Company	ASC Company	PRO Kew WO 95/
Home MT Depot	-	5466
2/2 South-West Mounted Brigade ASC	-	5455
South Wales Mounted Brigade	-	5461
2/1 London Mounted Brigade	-	5461
2/1 Highland Mounted Brigade	-	5461
2/1 South Midland Mounted Brigade	-	5461
63 (Northumbrian) Division Train - No 1 Company	-	5462
67 (Home Counties) Division Train	545, 546, 547, 548	5463
68 (Welsh) Division Train	-	5464
69 (East Anglian) Division Train	-	5464
3 Provisional Brigade Train	-	5458
4 Provisional Brigade train	-	5458
6 Provisional Brigade Train	-	5458
7 Provisional Brigade Train	-	5458
8 Provisional Brigade Train	-	5458
9 Provisional Brigade Train	-	5458
10 Provisional Brigade Train	839	5458
227 Mixed Brigade Train	839	5458

Troops

Unit title/function/Company	ASC Company	PRO Kew WO 95/
206 HT Company	206	5460
311 HT Company	311	5460
351 HT Company	351	5460
432 HT Company	432	5460
504 HT Company	504	5460
791 HT Company	791	5460
792 HT Company	792	5460
274 MT Company	274	5460
348 MT Company	348	5460
369 MT Company	369	5460
381 MT Company	381	5460
606 MT Company	606	5460
650 MT Company	650	5460
882 MT Company	882	5460
978 MT Company	978	5460
985 MT Company	985	5460
1124 MT Company	1124	5460

Honours and Awards

To Members of the Army Service Corps
For Service in the Great War

	1914	1915	1916	1917	1918	1919	1920	Total
BRITISH DECORATIONS								
Victoria Cross	-	-	-	-	2	-	-	2
KCB	-	-	1	1	-	-	-	2
CB	-	10	2	6	8	2	-	28
KCMG	-	1	-	-	-	2	-	3
CMG	-	14	14	12	16	26	-	82
CIE	-	-	-	1	-	-	-	1
KBE	-	-	-	-	1	3	-	4
CBE	-	-	-	-	3	69	6	78
DSO	-	10	39	115	110	3	-	277
OBE	-	-	-	-	35	472	11	518
MBE	-	-	-	-	42	223	16	281
Bar to MC	-	-	-	1	5	3	1	10
MC	-	39	60	96	232	82	3	512
Bar to DFC	-	-	-	-	-	1	-	1
DFC	-	-	-	-	-	1	-	1
AFC	-	-	-	-	2	6	-	8
Albert Medal	-	-	4	-	5	1	-	10
Bar to DCM	-	-	-	-	-	4	1	5
DCM	-	19	95	34	71	105	11	335
2nd Bar to MM	-	-	-	-	1	-	-	1
1st Bar to MM	-	-	-	-	9	10	-	19
MM	-	-	218	320	703	516	4	1,761
MSM	1	-	191	303	732	2,172	54	3,453
Medal of OBE	-	-	-	-	-	-	31	31
Mentioned in Despatches - Officers	37	188	437	963	876	808	4	3,313
Mentioned in Despatches - Other Ranks	27	189	544	956	1,424	2,497	7	5,644
Names brought to notice of Secretary of State for War - Officers	-	-	-	198	269	471	140	1,078
Names brought to notice of Secretary of State for War - Other Ranks	-	-	-	156	285	371	240	1,052
FOREIGN DECORATIONS								
Belgium								
Ordre de Leopold Commandeur	-	-	-	3	1	-	-	4
Ordre de Leopold Officier	-	-	-	2	1	-	1	4
Ordre de Leopold II Chevalier	-	-	-	-	8	5	-	13
Médaille du Roi Albert	-	-	-	-	-	-	2	2
Croix de Guerre avec Palme	-	-	-	-	-	-	1	1
Croix de Guerre Officier	-	-	-	-	12	5	-	17

	1914	1915	1916	1917	1918	1919	1920	Total
Croix de Guerre OR	-	-	-	-	91	5	-	96
Ordre de la Couronne - Commandeur	-	-	-	1	-	-	-	1
Ordre de la Couronne - Officier	-	-	-	2	3	1	-	6
Ordre de la Couronne - Chevalier	-	-	-	2	4	-	-	6
Decoration Militaire	-	-	-	2	-	3	-	5
Decoration Militaire 2nd Class	-	-	-	-	-	7	-	7
Ordre de la Couronne avec Croix de Guerre - Officier	-	-	-	-	-	1	-	1
Ordre de Leopold II avec Croix de Guerre - Chevalier	-	-	-	-	-	1	-	1
Decoration Militaire avec Croix de Guerre	-	-	-	-	-	8	-	8
Médaille Civique 1st Class	-	-	-	-	-	-	3	3
Médaille Civique 2nd Class	-	-	-	-	-	-	2	2

China

	1914	1915	1916	1917	1918	1919	1920	Total
Order of Wen-Hu 5th Class	-	-	-	-	-	-	1	1

Egypt

	1914	1915	1916	1917	1918	1919	1920	Total
Order of the Nile 3rd Class	-	-	-	1	-	1	3	5
Order of the Nile 4th Class	-	-	3	1	-	8	3	15

France – Légion d'Honneur

	1914	1915	1916	1917	1918	1919	1920	Total
Croix de Grand Officier	-	-	-	1	-	-	-	1
Croix de Commandeur	-	-	-	2	-	-	-	2
Croix d'Officier	-	-	-	5	-	3	1	9
Croix de Chevalier	-	-	7	3	2	3	3	18
Croix de Guerre avec Palme	-	-	-	-	1	-	-	1
Croix de Guerre Officiers	-	-	-	4	18	20	4	46
Croix de Guerre Other Ranks	-	-	-	11	61	41	-	113
Croix de Guerre avec Etoile en Bronze	-	-	-	-	-	1	-	1
Ordre du Mérite Agricole - Officer	-	-	-	-	-	1	2	3
Ordre du Mérite Agricole - Chevalier	-	-	-	-	-	17	5	22
Ordre d'Etoile Noire - Officer	-	-	-	-	-	1	3	4
Médaille d'Honneur avec Glaives en Vermeil	-	-	-	-	-	18	4	22
Médaille d'Honneur avec Glaives en Argent	-	-	-	-	-	35	14	49
Médaille d'Honneur avec Glaives en Bronze	-	-	-	-	-	52	30	82
Médaille d'Honneur en Argent	-	-	-	-	-	1	3	4
Médaille d'Honneur en Bronze	-	-	-	-	-	-	9	9
Médaille Militaire	-	-	26	12	10	3	4	55
Médaille de la Reconnaissance Française 3rd Class en Bronze	-	-	-	-	-	1	2	3
Oissam Alacuite - Croix d'Officier	-	-	-	-	1	-	-	1
Oissam Alacuite - Croix de Chevalier	-	-	-	-	1	-	-	1

	1914	1915	1916	1917	1918	1919	1920	Total
Ordre due Nichan Iftikhar – Officier	-	-	-	-	-	-	3	3
Palmes Academie Officier de l'Instruction Publique	-	3	-	-	-	-	-	3

Greece

	1914	1915	1916	1917	1918	1919	1920	Total
Order of the Redeemer – Commander	-	-	-	-	-	-	1	1
Order of the Redeemer – Officer	-	-	-	-	-	4	1	5
Order of the Redeemer – Chevalier	-	-	-	-	-	6	-	6
Order of the Redeemer - 4th Class	-	-	-	-	1	-	-	1
Greek Military Cross	-	-	-	-	-	3	-	3
Greek Military Cross 2nd Class	-	-	-	-	-	-	1	1
Greek Military Cross 3rd Class	-	-	-	-	-	-	2	2
Order of King George I – Officer	-	-	-	-	-	-	1	1
Silver Medal of the Order of King George I 1st Class	-	-	-	-	-	-	3	3
Medal of Order of King George I	-	-	-	-	-	2	-	2
Medal of Order of King George I 2nd Class	-	-	-	-	-	-	13	13
Medal for Military Merit 3rd Class	-	-	-	-	-	9	-	9
Medal for Military Merit 4th Class	-	-	-	-	-	3	-	3

Italy

	1914	1915	1916	1917	1918	1919	1920	Total
Order of the Crown of Italy – Commendatori	-	-	-	1	-	-	-	1
Order of the Crown Italy – Officier	-	-	-	-	1	2	-	3
Order of the Crown of Italy – Cavalieri	-	-	-	2	2	4	2	10
Order of St Maurice & St Lazarus – Officier	-	-	-	-	2	1	-	3
Order of St Maurice & St Lazarus – Cavalieri	-	-	-	-	-	1	1	2
Croci di Guerra – Officiers	-	-	-	-	2	1	1	4
Croci di Guerra - Other Ranks	-	-	-	-	1	3	1	5
Silver Medal for Military Valour	-	-	-	2	1	-	-	3
Bronze Medal for Military Valour – Officiers	-	-	-	9	2	14	-	25
Bronze Medal for Military Valour – Other Ranks	-	-	-	-	-	23	-	23

Japan

	1914	1915	1916	1917	1918	1919	1920	Total
Order of the Rising Sun 7th Class	-	-	-	-	-	1	-	1
Order of the Sacred Treasure	-	-	-	-	-	1	-	1

Montenegro

	1914	1915	1916	1917	1918	1919	1920	Total
Medal for Merit – Gold	-	-	-	2	-	-	-	2
Medal for Merit – Silver	-	-	-	2	-	-	-	2

	1914	1915	1916	1917	1918	1919	1920	Total
Panama								
Medal of La Solidaridad 3rd Class	-	-	-	-	-	-	1	1
Persia								
Order of El Nahada 3rd Class	-	-	-	-	-	-	2	2
Order of El Nahada 4th Class	-	-	-	-	-	-	7	7
Portugal								
Military Order of Avis - Commandeur	-	-	-	-	-	3	3	6
Military Order of Avis - Chevalier	-	-	-	-	-	1	1	2
Order of Tower & Sword - Chevalier	-	-	-	-	-	1	-	1
Military Medal for Good Service - Bronze	-	-	-	-	-	-	21	21
Roumania								
Order of Crown of Roumania - Officer	-	-	-	-	-	4	-	4
Medaille Barbatie si Credinta "with Swords" 2nd Class	-	-	-	-	-	-	6	6
Medaille Barbatie si Credinta 1st Class	-	-	-	-	-	4	-	4
Medaille Barbatie si Credinta 2nd Class	-	-	-	-	-	6	1	7
Medaille Barbatie si Credinta 3rd Class	-	-	-	-	-	17	3	20
Russia								
Cross of Order of St George 3rd Class	-	1	-	-	-	-	-	1
Cross of Order of St George 4th Class	-	2	-	-	-	-	-	2
Cross of St Anne 2nd Class with Swords	-	-	-	1	1	-	-	2
Cross of St Stanislaus 2nd Class	-	-	-	2	1	-	-	3
Cross of St Stanislaus 3rd Class	-	-	-	-	1	-	-	1
Medal of St George 1st Class	-	4	-	-	-	-	-	4
Medal of St George 2nd Class	-	3	-	-	-	-	-	3
Medal of St George 3rd Class	-	2	-	-	-	-	-	2
Medal of St George 4th Class	-	3	-	2	-	-	-	5
Silver Medal on Ribbon of St Stanislaus	-	-	-	4	-	-	-	4
Serbia								
Order of the White Eagle with Swords 3rd Class	-	-	-	2	1	-	-	3
Order of the White Eagle with Swords 4th Class	-	-	-	8	3	1	2	14
Order of the White Eagle with Swords 5th Class	-	-	-	3	-	-	31	34
Order of the White Eagle 4th Class	-	-	-	4	-	1	1	6
Order of the White Eagle 5th Class	-	-	-	2	11	-	1	14
Order of Karageorge 3rd Class with Swords	-	-	-	1	-	-	-	1

	1914	1915	1916	1917	1918	1919	1920	Total
Order of St Sava 4th Class	-	-	-	1	1	-	1	3
Order of St Sava 5th Class	-	-	-	5	-	1	1	7
Cross of Mercy	-	-	-	-	-	1	-	1
Cross of Karageorge 2nd Class with Swords	-	-	-	4	-	-	-	4
Cross of Karageorge (Silver Star) with Swords	-	-	-	1	-	-	-	1
Cross of Karageorge 3rd Class with Swords	-	-	-	1	-	-	-	1
Gold Medal for Merit	-	-	-	4	3	-	-	7
Silver Medal for Merit	-	-	-	10	-	-	-	10
Gold Medal for Zealous Service	-	-	-	31	10	3	39	83
Silver Medal for Zealous Service	-	-	-	20	71	2	152	245
Distinguished Service Medal	-	-	-	5	-	-	-	5
Medal for Military Virtue	-	-	-	1	1	1	-	2
United States of America								
American Distinguished Service Medal	-	-	-	-	-	1	1	2
TOTAL	64	493	1,655	3,364	5,238	8,313	929	20,057

ALBERT MEDAL

Albert Medal winners during the war were:

Lieutenant Sidney Albert Rowlandson	21 May 1916	France
Mech Staff Sergeant Thomas Michael Walton	21 May 1916	France
Private Alexander Anderson	21 May 1916	France
Private Joseph Thomas Lawrence	21 May 1916	France
Major Lewis Collingwood Bearne DSO	30 June 1918	France
Private Albert Edward Usher	30 June 1918	France
Private Arthur Johnson	30 June 1918	France
Driver Alfred Horne	30 June 1918	France
Lieutenant Geoffrey Rackham	27 October 1918	France
Private Walter Cleall (on demobilization leave)	11 August 1919	Cardiff

In October 1971 those who held the Albert Medal were able to exchange it for the George Cross, which had been instituted by HM King George VI in 1940. Only three ASC recipients were still alive at this time: Geoffrey Rackham and Walter Cleall exchanged; Thomas Walton declined.

AWARDS TO MEMBERS OF THE ARMY SERVICE CORPS

This annex contains citations, by years, for members of the ASC, the majority of which were published in the Corps Journal. Grammar, spelling etc has been retained as published, with only occasional editorial amendment.

This selection tells better than any generalized overview the sort of activity that went on all the time. In some cases, the awards resulted from routine ASC work with horse transport and mechanical transport units, even camels; in others it involved ambulances (often called 'cars'), clerical or supply work, close to the front line or back at Base depots, caterpillars, ammunition, light battery patrols or when attached to the Royal Engineers, Infantry, Tank Corps or RFC. It was all the same — the men did their best. Awards reflect more the opportunity to perform brave acts than a general level of courage (or otherwise).

1914

Distinguished Conduct Medal

Driver H J Vickers, 7th Company ASC. At Vendresse, on 14 September, when loading wounded, a bursting shell frightened the horses of the ambulance he was driving, but he kept control of them, and by his presence of mind, although the shell fire continued, he enabled the remainder of the wounded to be conveyed to a place of safety.

1915

Distinguished Conduct Medal

M2/076770 Pte J Holmes attached 23rd Field Ambulance. Private Holmes drove a motor ambulance up to bring in some wounded near Hulluch on 26th September. Although he was fired upon by the enemy, he drove the car in the reverse for 400 yards, the man beside him having been killed, till a bullet struck the carburettor. He then came up with another car, and towed his own away safely. His car was hit twenty-two times, and, but for his great bravery and resource must have been wrecked.

T/20789 Provisional Farrier Sergeant T Cussens and **TS/1067 Driver A G Hardesty.** For conspicuous gallantry and coolness on 5 November at Ypres, in extricating the horses after a shell had burst in the stables; six men and many horses were killed by the shells on this occasion.

Military Cross

Temporary Lieutenant The Honourable Eric Fox Pitt Lubbock, attached Royal Flying Corps. For conspicuous gallantry and skill on 26 October when he attacked a German Albatross machine at a height of 9,000 feet with machine-gun fire. The hostile pilot was shot, and the air-plane was brought to the ground within our line. The attack finished at a height of only 600 feet, and during an almost vertical dive, when the pilot was fully occupied, Lieutenant Lubbock fired deliberately and with effect.

Temporary Second Lieutenant Wallington Armstrong Pope, attached

170th Tunnelling Company RE, formerly ASC. For conspicuous gallantry on 16 October near the Hulluch quarries. A shaft had been discovered close to the front line of trenches, and the sentry on this shaft reported having seen two of the enemy moving along a gallery leading out of the shaft. Second Lieutenant Pope formed the opinion that the enemy must be mining, and with one man, descended the shaft by a rope ladder, fully expecting to find the enemy there. No gallery was found, but Second Lieutenant Pope's action showed courage of a high order.

1916

Distinguished Conduct Medal

S-24179 Acting Sergeant J R Boxall. For conspicuous ability, tact and zeal in the performance of his duties as Chief Clerk in the office of the Assistant Director of Supplies, Boulogne.

T-11653 Staff Sergeant Major W E Brent. For conspicuous gallantry and most excellent work as Warrant Officer in charge of a supply store. During a heavy bombardment of the town and railway station for over a fortnight he continued steadfastly at his post, until ordered to evacuate the store.

MS-287 Private T R Clements. For conspicuous gallantry since the commencement of the war, always displaying great coolness and bravery under fire. On one occasion he made fourteen journeys with signal stores through a town in flames and under heavy fire. On two occasions his car was struck by a shell and nearly buried in the debris of falling houses.

M2-022303 Serjeant J F Lloyd. For conspicuous gallantry when, night after night, he traversed roads swept with high explosives and shrapnel fire, inspiring his drivers by his bravery and example and getting his vehicles over almost impassable roads.

S-18058 Acting Staff Sergeant Major T Martin. For continuous good services throughout the campaign as Master Baker in charge of a bakery. He displayed conspicuous ability and resource in starting the bakery, and its success has been largely owing to his energy and capacity for hard work.

S-30241 Lance Corporal A Rodgers. For conspicuous gallantry throughout the bombardment. When no stretcher-bearers were available he voluntarily left shelter and offered his services to the medical officer, and continued carrying wounded officers and men to a dressing station until all were removed. The work was carried out under a heavy and continuous fire.

S-2-016366 Acting Serjeant H W Anderson. For consistent good work on the Gallipoli Peninsula from May to September 1915 when the depots and bakeries were repeatedly under shell fire.

M2-048022 Driver E McGrory. For conspicuous gallantry on 12 July 1915 on the Gallipoli Peninsula. Driver McGrory was knocked off the seat of his motor ambulance by a shell and badly wounded, but he struggled back to his seat to stop the car, thus saving the wounded patient from a serious accident.

Albert Medal of the Second Class

Lieutenant Sidney Albert Rowlandson, Mechanist Staff Sergeant Thomas Michael Walton, Private Alexander Anderson and **Private Joseph Thomas Lawrence** serving in France, in recognition of their gallantry in saving life. The exploit of the party is thus described:

On the 2nd May last, whilst a German 21 centimetre shell, in which several holes had been bored, was being "steamed" in a laboratory for the purpose of investigation, the box of shavings in which it was packed caught fire. The officer in charge of the laboratory at once sent for help to the nearest Army Service Corps fire station, ordered all persons to leave the building, and warned the inhabitants of the neighbouring houses that a serious explosion was imminent.

On receipt of the request for help Lieutenant Rowlandson, with Walton, Anderson and Lawrence, at once collected fire extinguishers and proceeded by motor to the laboratory. They entered the building, played on the fire (which had spread considerably), and after about two minutes were able to reach the burning shell, which they dragged into the yard and extinguished there. At any moment after the fire broke out the shell might have exploded with disastrous results.

Military Cross

Temporary Lieutenant Reginald Holland Fairbairns. Although wounded he led the first wave of the attack with great courage and determination. Later, when again wounded, he tried to continue, but his wounds prevented him.

Distinguished Conduct Medal

M2-102696 Private (acting Corporal) G B Shepherd. For conspicuous gallantry and skill in driving the Tank of his Section Commander throughout an action. It was entirely due to Private Shepherd's skill and courage that it reached its objective, and was successfully withdrawn.

1917

Military Cross

Second Lieutenant (temporary Lieutenant) Charles Edward Murray Pickthorn, Special Reserve and RFC. For conspicuous gallantry and devotion to duty in attacking hostile aircraft, and in carrying out difficult reconnaissances. On one occasion, although wounded, he continued his combat and brought down a hostile machine. On two other occasions he brought down hostile machines in flames.

Lieutenant (acting Captain) Thomas Buchanan Maclean Egleston, Special Reserve and Machine Gun Corps. He rendered invaluable assistance under heavy fire of every kind, in going to the assistance of several tanks and repairing them, and also attended several wounded men to safety. He exposed himself continuously for several hours.

Distinguished Conduct Medal

M2-131363 Private B Bourke. For conspicuous gallantry and ability in action. As motor cyclist scout he has been invaluable in tracking and bringing the cars into action by shortest and best routes, whereby many casualties have been inflicted on the enemy. On many occasions he has gone forward under heavy fire to discover the best route by which to come into action (Mesopotamia).

T/14586 Lance Corporal (A/Sergeant) L Makin. For conspicuous gallantry and devotion to duty. He rendered most valuable services with the Trench Tramway Detachment in taking up ammunition and supplies.

M2/119019 Private R W Stevens, attached Light Car Patrol. For conspicuous gallantry and devotion to duty. He showed great courage and skill in taking his car into action in the face of very heavy machine gun fire.

Distinguished Conduct Medal

M2-033691 Private (acting Sergeant) F V Houchen. For conspicuous gallantry and devotion to duty. He displayed great courage and determination in moving two of his guns from their position under heavy shell fire. His fine example and disregard of personal danger inspired those working with him.

T2-10777 SSM C Wassell. For conspicuous gallantry and devotion to duty when in charge of horse lines. Amidst violent explosions caused by a burning ammunition dump he remained with the horses for three hours without any assistance, preventing them from straying and keeping them under control, thereby saving many valuable animals. His fearlessness and cool persistence in a most perilous situation were most marked.

Military Cross

Second Lieutenant (temporary Lieutenant) Arthur Willoughby Falls Glenny, attached RFC. For conspicuous gallantry and devotion to duty when in co-operation with our artillery. By dint of great perseverance, skill, and very gallant flying he has accomplished splendid work under very difficult circumstances. On one occasion, during a gale of wind, he successfully ranged three of four heavy batteries upon an enemy battery, which was completely obliterated. He has consistently set a very fine example to his squadron.

Distinguished Conduct Medal

M2-132166 Private J Godfrey. For conspicuous gallantry and devotion to duty when driving his ambulance car under heavy shell fire. In spite of the intense bombardment he stopped his car to rescue three wounded officers. During this action his orderly was wounded by a shell and the radiator of his car was blown to pieces. He succeeded, however, in getting his car and the wounded into safety, showing the utmost coolness and courage throughout.

1918

Victoria Cross

Second Lieutenant Alfred Cecil Herring attached 6th Battalion The Northamptonshire Regiment 23 March 1918. For most conspicuous bravery, initiative and devotion to duty when, after severe fighting, the enemy gained a position on the south bank of the canal. His post was cut off from the troops on both flanks and surrounded. Second Lieutenant Herring, however, immediately counter-attacked, and recaptured the position together with twenty prisoners and six machine guns. During the night the post was continually attacked, but all attacks were beaten off. This was largely due to the splendid heroism displayed by Second Lieutenant Herring, who continually visited his men and cheered them up. It was entirely due to the bravery and initiative of this officer that the enemy advance was held up for eleven hours at an exceedingly critical period. His magnificent heroism, coupled with the skilful handling of his troops, were most important factors leading to success.

M2-048544 Private Richard George Masters. Bethune 9 April 1918. For most conspicuous bravery and devotion to duty. Owing to an enemy attack, communications were cut off, and wounded could not be evacuated. The road was reported impassable, but Private Masters volunteered to try to get through, and after the greatest difficulty succeeded, although he had to clear the road of all sorts of debris. He made journey after journey throughout the afternoon over a road consistently shelled and swept by machine-gun fire, and was on one occasion bombed by an aeroplane. The greater part of the wounded cleared from this area were evacuated by Private Masters, as his was the only car that got through during this particular time.

Military Cross

Lieutenant E D G Galley, ASC and RFC. Attacking on one occasion 14 enemy scouts, he shot down one of these, which was confirmed to have crashed. On a later occasion he engaged from a low altitude a large convoy on a road, and after driving down from 800 ft, fired all his ammunition into its midst. He then returned to his aerodrome for a further supply of ammunition, and again attacked transport on the same road with the most effective results. He has not only led his flight with signal success, but has on occasion led the whole squadron patrols in the most daring and efficient manner.

Temporary Lieutenant (acting Captain) R W F Self. On receipt of orders, he rushed down four lorries to the batteries, which were under machine-gun fire, to pull out the guns. It was due to his energy that, out of sixteen heavy howitzers, fourteen were saved. Throughout the period of the retreat he was untiring in keeping the batteries fed with ammunition.

Temporary Lieutenant (acting Captain) F C A Allday MC attached Tank Corps. For conspicuous gallantry and devotion to duty as a Tank battalion engineer. Owing to his untiring energy 100 per cent of tanks were always mechanically fit at their starting points. He accompanied them in action, on one occasion suffering from gas poisoning, and invariably rendered most useful assistance. His courage and technical ability in many instances enabled tanks to reach their objectives, which otherwise they would have been unable to do (MC gazetted 3 June 1918).

Distinguished Conduct Medal

M2-148078 Private R S Davies (MT) ASC. For conspicuous gallantry and devotion to duty. During an enemy attack he drove the wounded away in his motor ambulance under a heavy gas-shell bombardment and machine-gun fire. His petrol tank was twice pierced by bullets, and to keep it from emptying he got out a tin of petrol and instructed one of the wounded to keep the tank filled from it as he drove, thereby preventing the stoppage of the ambulance in an exposed position in full view of the enemy. Later, when the ambulance was bogged, with the assistance of one man he carried all the wounded 1½ miles under shell fire to a place of safety. He set a splendid example of courage and resource.

Albert Medal

Major L C Bearne DSO and Private A E Usher. On 22 October 1916, a French motor lorry loaded with 3,000 lb of aeroplane bombs, caught fire in the middle of a camp of the Serbian Army. Efforts to deal with the flames with earth proved ineffectual, and after the fire had been burning for seven or eight minutes, and the bomb cases were already involved, Major Bearne and Usher ran up with extinguishers. Both immediately crawled underneath the lorry, and eventually succeeded in extinguishing the flames, thus averting a serious disaster at the risk of their own lives. Major Bearne was severely burnt about the hands and arms.

1919

Military Cross

Temporary Captain B Holt attached 8th Battalion Somerset Light Infantry. For conspicuous gallantry and devotion to duty. His company formed the escort to four tanks detailed to clear up a village. With the assistance of the tanks he inflicted heavy losses on the enemy, and took over 200 prisoners. He showed the greatest gallantry and determination throughout.

Captain A H Mackay (TF) attached 2nd Battalion, Middlesex Regiment. For conspicuous gallantry, initiative, and determination while in command of a company during the attack on the enemy trenches east of Arleux on 27th September 1918. When all his platoon commanders had early become casualties, he at once went forward through intense enemy barrage, and personally led his platoon on, capturing all his objectives, together with two machine guns and some prisoners, and inflicting heavy losses on the enemy. When, owing to the darkness, two sections lost touch, he went back through enemy barrage and led them on to their objective. Throughout the night, under very heavy fire, he patrolled his whole outpost line, thus establishing complete communication, and giving his men confidence.

Lieutenant Temporary Captain and Acting Major G H Sargeant seconded 5th Brigade, Tank Corps. For conspicuous gallantry during operations of 8th August 1918 east of Amiens. He walked close behind the tanks with total disregard for his own safety as far as the first objective. Here he inspected all the tanks, and was instrumental in reaching several fit for action in the assault on Morcourt-Harbonnières line. On 9th and 23rd August he again followed the tanks on foot, and under severe shelling was untiring in his efforts to render them fit for action. The success of the operations was largely due to his untiring energy and fearless devotion to duty.

Temporary Second Lieutenant A Boatswain. During the attack on Pocha (North Russia) on 1 June 1919, he was with Advanced Headquarters as Supply Officer. Owing to shortage of officers he volunteered to take command of an artillery battery, and in this capacity was continuously in action with the battery under fire for forty-eight hours. He thus rendered gallant and valuable service.

Temporary Second Lieutenant W C Wannell RASC. When carrying out a reconnaissance on Lake Onega (Murmansk) on 8 July, in close touch with enemy vessels, the motor boat caught fire and a petrol tank exploded. Though badly shaken himself, he assisted three wounded mechanics on to the upper deck, and then returned to the engine room and drove the one engine which was still working, until the boat was within a mile from the shore, when a second explosion wrecked her. His pluck and devotion to duty in driving the engine, at great risk to himself, got the boat near the shore and saved lives.

1920

Military Cross

Temporary Second Lieutenant John George Oswald Ash, attached No 10 Pontoon Park, Canadian Engineers. He has shown great courage and resource, under heavy shell fire, when in charge of MT drawn pontoon and trestle wagons during recent operations. The success of the bridging operations over the Canal de l'Escault on 9 October 1918 was largely due to the excellent and speedy manner in which he got his pontoons through the barrage to the bridge site at Morenchies. He has invariably shown tireless energy under trying circumstances.

Temporary Lieutenant Jack Bowden Malthouse, attached 1/16th Battalion London Regiment. On 4 November 1918, during the attack on Sebourg, he led his company with marked gallantry. When the company was held up by machine gun fire at close range he organised a defensive position by running from man to man and arranging dispositions for them. He thus protected the bridgehead over the Aunelle river, in spite of intense shelling and a counter-attack delivered against the troops on his right.

Temporary Lieutenant Geoffrey Watt. For conspicuous gallantry and devotion to duty between Menjil and Resht Persia on 21 June 1918. He was in command of a convoy of 66 vans which was heavily attacked by hostile irregulars. Eight vans were put out of action but by his entire disregard of danger and good conduct he managed to salve them. Later, on three occasions, he went out with a small party under fire and salved four more vans which had been abandoned.

Distinguished Conduct Medal

DM-153985 Private C A Broom MM, attached 87th (West Lancashire) Field Ambulance RAMC TF (Christchurch). During the operations of 21 October and 22 October 1918 he showed great gallantry whilst engaged in the evacuation of the wounded from the RAPs in front of Banhout Bosche to a car-loading post further in the rear. Immediately after zero he brought his Ford ambulance straight to the RAP 600 yards from the line, whilst the road was being heavily shelled and he continued to remove the cases from the RAP for hours during the rush of casualties, notwithstanding heavy shelling of the road at short intervals. His fine devotion to duty saved many lives.

M2-151849 Sergeant P M Hamblin, attached 154th Siege Battery, RGA (Bath). For gallantry and devotion to duty. At Bergwijk, at about 1530, 5 November 1918 a caterpillar was knocked out by a direct hit and set on fire. Assisted by Lance Corporal Pountney, and at once realising the danger of the second caterpillar being set alight, he ran to the caterpillar and backed it down the road out of danger. Then, with assistance, stores etc were thrown clear.

T4-212961 Sergeant R Blaylock, attached Camel Transport Corps (Heaton) (Palestine). For continuous good work during the recent operations. On the evening of 19 September 1919, when two platoons of a battalion were lost near the Wadi Rabeh, he was sent out to find the camels attached to the battalion. He had to march back under fire through a very difficult part of the enemy's front, and it was due to his skill and fearless devotion to duty that the animals were safely recovered.

M2-050304 Sergeant E Gittens, MM, attached 16th Siege Battery RGA (King's Lynn). At Inchy-en-Artois on 25 September 1918, in front of Bourlon Wood, he succeeded in bringing up a 6 inch howitzer into a position 700 yards from the front line trenches. He personally drove the FWDs and guns over a bridge where, 50 yards away, an ammunition dump was on fire, and which later blew up.

M2-187702 Private E Goldfinch, attached No 7 Light Car Patrol (Folkestone) (Palestine). He has always driven the leading car in any action the patrol has taken part in, and invariably shown great gallantry. On 22 October 1918, near Khan Sebil, in pursuit of an enemy armoured car and six motor lorries of troops, he, with great coolness under close range fire, manoeuvred the open Ford van he was driving so as to enable the gunner to get into action and cause one lorry to be captured and thirty enemy to be killed or wounded.

DM2-155186 Corporal C Graham, attached 102nd AA Section (Northallerton). (Palestine). On 21 September 1918, while the position of the Jordan Valley was under very heavy hostile gun fire, he showed great courage and coolness in withdrawing the guns to a place of safety.

Meritorious Service Medal

In recognition of valuable services rendered whilst prisoners of war or interned:

Burgess, Pte H G	**M2-082579**
Pickles, Pte A	**M2-032754**

Bar to Military Cross

In recognition of gallant conduct and determination displayed in escaping or attempting to escape from captivity:

Milner, Capt J, MC (MC gazetted 14 January 1916).

Military Medal

Hand, Pte B	**M2-073450**

Tubb, Pte (acting Lance Corporal) W H

Military Cross

For conspicuous gallantry and devotion to duty in North Russia:

Second Lieutenant H B Finch. At Bolshe-Ozerki, on 1 September 1919, he showed great gallantry as guide to a patrol. They found a position unexpectedly strongly held. He stayed behind with a badly wounded man and one other man. He personally killed four enemy and wounded several more. The work of this patrol in cutting the enemy's lines of communication was instrumental in breaking up the enemy's attack on Bolshe-Ozerki.

Victoria Cross

Royal Inniskilling Fusiliers

Lance Corporal E Seaman. Western Front. For most conspicuous bravery and devotion to duty. When the right flank of his company was held up by a nest of enemy machine guns, he, with great courage and initiative, rushed forward under heavy fire with his Lewis gun, and engaged the position single-handed, capturing two machine guns and twelve prisoners, and killing one officer and two men. Later in the day he again rushed another machine gun post, capturing the gun under heavy fire. He was killed immediately after. His courage and dash were beyond all praise, and it was entirely due to the very gallant conduct of LCpl Seaman that his company was enabled to push forward to its objective and capture many prisoners.

Military Growth of the ASC During the 1914–1918 War

General and Staff Officers (late ASC)

	August 1914	*November 1918*
Major Generals	3	8
Brigadier Generals	–	20
Colonels	15	33

Strengths of Officers and Other Ranks at Home and Abroad

	Totals
August 1914	6,431
August 1915	161,414
August 1916	242,729
August 1917	323,747
August 1918	325,881

Casualties amongst ASC Officers and Other Ranks during the War

	Officers	*Other Ranks*
Killed in action	79	1,507
Died of wounds	42	967
Died (diseases etc)	159	5,713
Wounded	384	7,262
Prisoners-of-war	22	98
Total	686	15,547

Expansion of ASC Units during the Great War
1914 to 1918

	On Mobilization	November 1918
Mechanical Transport Units		
MT Companies	20	605
Mobile Repair Units	–	22
MT Depots	1	21
Australian MT Companies	–	6
	21	654
Horse Transport Units		
HT Companies	40	552
HT Depot	3	4
Australian HT Companies	–	27
Divisional Trains	6	72
Reserve Parks	6	23
Auxiliary HT Companies	–	36
Local Service Companies	–	28
	55	715
Supply Units		
Field Bakeries	6	45
Bakery Section	–	58
Field Butcheries	6	29
Railway Supply Dets	8	73
Depot Units of Supply	30	84
Line of Communication Supply Companies	–	38
Supply Depots	–	19
	50	346

Expansion of the Mechanical Transport Branch
of the ASC during the War

	Peace Establishment 1914	Balance provided on Mobilization in 1914	Total all Theatres 11 November 1918
Motor Lorries, Tractors etc	80	1,061	56,659
Motor Cars and Motor Vans	20	193	23,133
Motor Ambulances	–	–	7,045
Motor Cycles	15	116	34,865
Total	115	1,370	121,702

On the Outbreak of War, prior to Mobilization, the
ASC was responsible for feeding

	Men	Animals
At Home	120,000	23,500
Abroad	44,000	4,000
Total	164,000	27,500

The Ration Strength on 11 November 1918 was

Theatre	Men	Animals
France	2,360,400	404,000
Egypt	480,000	167,000
Salonika	385,000	120,000
East Africa	111,731	1,499
Mesopotamia	413,406	88,145
Italy	97,822	20,482
Home	1,514,993	94,644
Total	5,363,352	895,770

Formation of ASC Units
(in addition to those units which existed before the war)

Year	Month	MT		HT		Other		Total	
		Formed	Totals	Formed	Totals	Formed	Totals	Formed	Totals
1914	July	21	21	43	43	9	9	73	73
	August	27	48	106	149	68	77	201	274
	September	16	64	15	164	6	83	37	311
	October	14	78	34	198	14	97	62	373
	November	7	85	37	235	13	110	57	430
	December	2	87	21	256	20	130	43	473
Totals for 1914		**87**	**87**	**256**	**256**	**130**	**130**	**473**	**473**
1915	January	18	105	35	291	24	154	77	550
	February	13	118	9	300	39	193	61	611
	March	25	143	25	325	59	252	109	720
	April	13	156	12	337	66	318	91	811
	May	17	173	3	340	106	424	126	937
	June	17	190	1	341	26	450	44	981
	July	27	217	-	341	54	504	81	1062
	August	18	235	2	343	12	516	32	1094
	September	18	253	36	379	37	553	91	1185
	October	10	263	3	382	7	560	20	1205
	November	10	273	16	398	124	684	150	1355
	December	7	280	-	398	51	735	58	1413
Totals for 1915		**193**	**280**	**142**	**398**	**605**	**735**	**940**	**1413**
1916	January	29	309	4	402	26	761	59	1472
	February	6	315	-	402	4	765	10	1482
	March	8	323	4	406	3	768	15	1497
	April	14	337	6	412	4	772	24	1521
	May	5	342	2	414	24	796	31	1552
	June	29	371	35	449	60	856	124	1676

Year	Month	MT		HT		Other		Total	
		Formed	Totals	Formed	Totals	Formed	Totals	Formed	Totals
	July	17	388	6	455	27	883	50	1726
	August	13	401	1	456	14	897	28	1754
	September	6	407	-	456	27	924	33	1787
	October	7	413	34	490	27	951	68	1855
	November	3	417	8	498	13	964	24	1879
	December	14	431	9	507	16	980	39	1918
Totals for 1916		**151**	**431**	**109**	**507**	**245**	**980**	**505**	**1918**
1917	January	11	442	12	519	11	991	34	1952
	February	17	459	1	520	7	998	25	197
	March	7	466	-	520	5	1003	12	1989
	April	17	483	6	526	9	1012	32	2021
	May	4	487	2	528	8	1020	14	2035
	June	10	497	-	528	14	1034	24	2059
	July	10	507	2	530	2	1036	14	2073
	August	10	517	13	543	10	1046	33	2106
	September	11	528	-	543	7	1053	18	2124
	October	19	547	3	546	11	1064	33	2157
	November	8	555	6	552	4	1068	18	2175
	December	2	557	1	553	5	1073	8	2183
Totals for 1917		**126**	**557**	**46**	**553**	**93**	**1073**	**265**	**2183**
1918	January	2	559	2	555	1	1074	5	2188
	February	-	559	-	555	-	1074	-	2188
	March	14	573	-	555	-	1074	14	2202
	April	9	582	-	555	2	1076	11	2213
	May	2	584	4	559	6	1082	12	2225
	June	9	593	-	559	13	1095	22	2247
	July	14	607	2	561	5	1100	21	2268
	August	5	612	-	561	-	1100	5	2273

Year	Month	MT		HT		Other		Total	
		Formed	Totals	Formed	Totals	Formed	Totals	Formed	Totals
	September	2	614	1	562	-	1100	3	2276
	October	13	627	-	562	-	1100	13	2289
	November	2	629	1	563	3	1103	6	2295
	December	2	631	-	563	6	1109	8	2302
Totals for 1918		74	631	10	563	36	1109	120	2302

Note:

'Others' consists of a variety of units, including:

Labour units
Remount units
Tyre Press Detachments
Railhead Supply Detachments
Field Bakeries
Field Butcheries
Butchery/Bakery Sections
Depot Units of Supply
Line of Communication Supply Companies
Field Ambulance Workshops

Supply Statistics

Shipment of ASC Supplies and Stores from all Ports to the BEF in France from 9 August 1914 to 1 May 1920

	Tons
Supplies (General)	3,713,208
Petrol Case Boards	20,394
Hay	2,669,184
Oats	3,250,243
Petrol and Oil	875,598
Petrol Tins (Empty)	13,350
Coal and Fuel Wood	2,013,031
MT Stores	172,536
Total	12,727,554

Base Supply Depot Statistics

Boulogne	Highest Daily Feeding Strength	Highest Monthly Issues	
		Frozen Meat lbs	Bread lbs
1914	65,919	1,022,386	1,598,944
1915	311,242	6,826,306	7,950,682
1916	381,620	9,201,062	10,694,650
1917	692,423	17,346,498	12,776,070
1918	670,266	21,658,847	15,875,667

Rouen	Highest Daily Feeding Strength	Highest Monthly Issues		
		Fuel Tons	Petrol Gallons	Bread lbs
1914	16	-	222,011	2,406,113
1915	213	8,472	397,738	5,145,736
1916	1,056	18,423	2,956,442	8,484,687
1917	1,234	20,453	2,833,060	7,096,564
1918	1,294	14,186	4,673,024	9,073,375

Havre	Highest Daily Feeding Strength	Highest Monthly Issues			
		Frozen Meat Rations	Bread lbs	Forage Rations	Petrol Gallons
1914	214,565	165,000	1,969,325	59,000	338,091
1915	383,689	415,000	10,147,460	100,000	517,208
1916	416,958	933,000	12,113,513	182,000	909,188
1917	138,107	1,135,000	11,109,519	215,000	250,466
1918	233,005	1,230,000	9,263,930	211,000	225,610

Marseilles	Highest Daily Feeding Strength	Highest Monthly Issues of Forage lbs	Highest Monthly Receipts of Goats and Sheep
1914	27,477	1,497,360	16,537
1915	52,200	12,677,208	26,096
1916	34,150	8,989,085	6,203
1917	51,800	4,233,905	13,049
1918	58,400	4,537,396	7,833

Dieppe	Highest Local Feeding Strengths	Highest Monthly Issues		Highest Monthly Tonnage Receipts Tons
		Bread lbs	Fuel lbs	
1916	7,572	9,300,000	-	23,489
1917	11,327	15,000,000	14,636	40,415
1918	24,295	12,357,150	13,896	43,915

Calais	Highest Daily Feeding Strength	Highest Monthly Issues			
		Bread lbs	Forage lbs	Petrol Gallons	Charcoal lbs
1915	188,000	3,868,898	29,248,991	282,503	949,209
1916	361,000	8,051,760	64,300,044	2,081,650	2,985,702
1917	606,700	11,882,866	80,488,178	3,636,961	4,327,199
1918	665,110	13,146,984	132,033,992	7,918,384	825,068

St Valery	Highest Monthly Tonnage Received	Highest Daily Feeding Strength
1916	7,719	-
1917	7,160	11,617
1918	5,160	13,933

Cherbourg	Highest Monthly Tonnage Received	Highest Daily Feeding Strength
1917	461	6,047
1918	2,500	13,745

Petrol Depots

	Calais (NPD) Gallons	Rouen (SPD) Gallons
1914	-	222,011
1915	282,503	397,738
1916	2,081,650	2,956,442
1917	3,636,961	2,833,060
1918	7,918,384	4,673,024

Bakeries

	Highest Monthly Issues (lbs)				
	Boulogne	Rouen	Havre	Dieppe	Calais
1914	1,598,944	2,406,113	1,969,325	-	-
1915	7,950,682	5,145,736	10,147,460	-	3,868,898
1916	10,694,650	8,484,687	12,113,513	9,300,000	8,051,760
1917	17,346,498	7,096,564	11,109,519	15,000,000	11,882,866
1918	21,658,847	9,073,375	9,263,930	12,357,150	13,146,984

Index

Abadan, 160
Abancourt, 74
Abbeville, 47, 54, 74, 96, 110, 120, 121, 126
Aberdeen, 36
Achiet, 121
Act of Parliament, 46
Adjvasil, 168
Advanced Workshops, 104
AEC, 63, 68, 82, 85, 144
Agincourt, 102
Agricultural Company, 187
Agricultural Park ASC, 168
Agricultural work, 76
Akbunar, 166, 168
Albert, 123, 124
Albert Medal, 167, 189
Albion, 33, 63, 66, 82, 85, 146, 150, 167
Aldershot, 1, 5–10, 12–17, 22–24, 26, 29, 30, 34, 35, 37, 39, 40, 45, 47, 49, 50, 56, 69, 72, 76, 85, 91, 130, 133, 134, 138, 147, 194
Aldershot Command, 11
Aldershot Gazette, 73
Aldershot ovens, 74, 164
Aleppo, 153, 155, 156
Alexandria, 153, 155, 157, 171, 174
Allday, Capt F C A, 378
Alldays Onion lorry, 85
Allenby, Gen Sir Edmund, 153, 155, 158
Ally Sloper's Cavalry, 75
Amiens, 107, 121, 150
Amman, 155
Ancre, 108
Anderson, Pte A, 372, 375
Anderson, Chap Gen F I, 194
Anderson, Sgt H W, 374
Anderson, Capt M N G, 12, 33
Andover, 18
Anglo-Persian Company, 160
Antwerp, 67, 84
ANZAC, 154, 171, 177, 179
Anzac Cove, 171, 172, 174
Arborfield Cross, 147
Archangel, 183, 186, 187
Armentières, 61
Army Catering Corps, 29
Army Football Cup, 39
Army Motor Reserve, 21
Army & Navy Gazette, 17

Army Ordnance Corps/Department, 5, 21, 22, 24, 48, 56, 72, 79, 80, 102, 110, 147, 157
Army Postal Service, 76
Army Veterinary Corps, 46
Arquata, 151
Arras, 103, 121, 160
Arrol Johnstone, 38
Artificer Instructional School, 76
ASC Central Comforts Fund, 61
ASC Journal, 6, 8, 11, 16, 23, 26, 28, 31, 33, 34, 35, 39, 60, 77, 79, 81, 84, 186
ASC MT (Volunteers), 142
ASC Quarterly, 8, 13, 37
ASC Records, 27, 49, 104, 148
ASC School of Instruction, 23, 32
ASC Training Establishment, 22, 25, 26, 29, 45, 48
Ash, Lt J G O, 379
Asiago, 151, 152
Asiatic Petroleum Company, 95
Atcherley, Maj/Col/Hon Maj Gen L W, 12
Atvatli, 166
Aubers Ridge, 71
Austin, 63, 85, 144
Australian ASC, 23
Autocar, 63
Automobile Association, 8, 32, 50
Auxiliary Omnibus Park, 96, 97, 103, 107, 123–125
Aveling & Porter steam tractor, 85
Avonmouth, 47, 52, 53, 68, 69, 84, 85, 100, 101, 134, 135, 157
Aylesbury, 137
Aziziyeh, 162

Baghdad, 103, 159, 160, 162
Bailleul, 56, 59, 68, 123
Baizieux, 100, 124
Baker, Sgt Maj, 94
Bakeries/Bakery Sections, 38, 51, 56, 74, 87, 98
Bakers, 133
Balkans, 149, 164, 171
Band, 7, 33, 34, 75
Barber, LCpl T, 14
Barbor, Capt R D, 12
Bard, Wilkie, 142
Barlin, 74
Barnham, 102

Basingstoke,   18, 137
Basra,   159, 160
Beadon, Col R H,   1
Bearne, Maj/Lt Col L C,   167, 372, 378
Beaumont,   59
Beckenham,   143
Becket, Col,   11
Beddy, Capt D L,   33
Beersheba,   153, 155
Beirut,   155, 156
Belfast,   135
Belsize lorry,   63
Benn, Capt J A,   84
Bennett, 2nd Cpl C,   14
Berbera,   17, 33
Bergues,   137
Berliet car,   85
Bermicourt,   102, 104
Berna lorry,   144
Bernard, Capt W K,   21
Bernay,   120
Béthune,   74, 99, 126
Bicknell, Sgt O D,   112
Bingham, Capt C H M,   12
Birmingham,   16, 53, 143
Bisley,   100
Blackheath,   136, 137
Blackie, Pte John Parkinson,   125
Blangy,   68
Blaylock, Sgt R,   380
Blunt, Lt G C G,   16
Boatswain, 2Lt A,   379
Boer War,   1, 2, 7, 8, 9, 13, 25, 30, 35, 46,
     49, 67, 75, 82, 86, 94, 127
Bonfield, 2Lt W H,   112
Bonn,   130
Boulogne,   53, 54, 55, 67, 74
Bourke, Pte B,   376
Bovington,   22, 102, 103
Boxall, Sgt J R,   374
Boyce, Capt H A,   21
Boyce, Brig Gen/Maj Gen W G E,   69, 96,
     190, 191, 192, 205
Boyd, Col J A,   7
Bradburn, Cpl,   14
Bradford,   50, 133, 147
Branch Requisition Office,   51
Brander, Lt Col M C,   139
Bray-sur-Somme,   99, 101
Brent, SSM W E,   374
Bridge, Col/Brig Gen C H,   19, 46, 49,
     189, 205
Bridge, Sgt Percival,   125
Bristol,   46, 68
British Army of the Rhine,   130
British Berna,   63, 85

British Red Cross Society,   54, 55, 66, 86,
     93, 94, 172
Brockbank, Maj J G,   102
Brodrick Cap,   35
Brooke car,   14
Brooklands,   35, 36, 37, 38
Broom, Pte C A,   380
Brunton, Cpl A S,   14
Bryce, SSgt,   7
BSA motor cycle,   85, 144
Buick,   54, 63, 85, 144
Bulford,   24, 43, 72, 84, 120, 134, 135,
     162, 168, 194
Bulford Mobilization and Embarkation
     Area,   134, 135
Buller, Gen Sir Redvers,   8, 19
Buller Barracks,   24, 35, 36
Bulmer, Wagoner T,   50
Bunbury, Col/Maj Gen H N,   11–13, 33,
     189, 205
Burao,   33
Burghclere, Lady,   78
Burgess, Pte H G,   381
Burrell steam tractor,   14, 85
Burrows, Brevet Major,   21
Bus-les-Artois,   107
Busnes,   124
Butchers/Butcheries,   51, 91, 133
Butcher-Hill, Capt,   14

Cable, Maj J F,   56
Cadillac,   63, 85
Caestre,   56
Cahil, SSgt Maj J W F,   23
Cairo,   11, 153
Calais,   54, 56, 66, 67, 72, 74, 89, 94, 95,
     126–128, 137
Calder, Cpl Gilbert,   125
Camberwell,   79, 134
Cambrai,   103, 107
Camel Transport Corps,   153, 156
Cameron, Capt D C,   12
Camp, Pte John Notton,   125
Campling, Sgt Ernest Stratford,   125
Camposampiero,   150
Canadian ASC,   23
Canadian Forestry Corps,   120, 146
Canny, Lt Col J C M,   136
Canteen and Mess Co-operative Society,
     86
Cape Boys Auxiliary Horse Companies,
     90
Cape Helles,   171, 172, 174, 177, 179
Cape Town,   182
Caporetto,   150
Carden, Lt/Sir John,   104
Carden-Lloyd,   104

Cardiff, 143
Carpenter, Cpl Reginald George, 125
Carpenters, 16
Carriage Smiths, 16
Carter, Maj/Brig Gen E E, 11, 69, 190, 191, 206
Carter, LCpl, 60
Carver, Lt, 174
Caterham, 146
Catford, 134
Catterick, 147, 148
Caulers, 123
Census Branch, 79
Central London Recruiting Office, 53
Central Prisoners of War Committee, 79
Central Repair Workshop & Stores, 102, 104
Central Requisition Office, 38, 51
Central School of Instruction, 89
Chasseurs Alpins, 68
Chatfield, Lt, 181
Chatham, 10, 13, 14, 17, 24, 32
Chenard car, 85
Cherbourg, 56
Chichester, Lt Col A W, 188
Chief Inspector(ate) of MT, 22, 25, 38, 139
Chiuppano, 151
Christmas Truce, 66
Cinema Department, 87
Cippenham, 137
Clacton-on-Sea, 20, 22
Clark, Sgt Douglas, 113, 114, 134, 135
Clarke, Lt Gen Travers, 124
Clayton, Lt Col/Col/Maj Gen/Lt Gen Sir Frederick, 6, 7, 9, 11–13, 25, 69, 70, 190, 194, 206
Clayton steam tractor, 85, 144
Cleall, Pte W, 372
Clements, Pte T R, 374
Clement-Bayard, 85
Clement-Talbot, 85, 138
Clydesdale, 144
Clyno, 63, 85, 144
Cochrane, Maj, 14
Cockburn, Capt C B, 96
Cockshott, Lt Col A M, 115
Cody, Col, 16, 35
Colchester, 20, 72, 194
Colenso, 35
Cologne, 126, 130
Colonel of the ASC, 6
Comforts Fund, 76, 77, 79, 148
Commer, 63, 82, 85
Commercial Motor/Cars, 38, 77, 79
Commissariat & Transport Department, 75, 127

Commos, 74
Company signs, 115
Compiègne, 60
Conductors, 17
Connaught, HRH, Field Marshal The Duke of, 6, 7, 20, 21, 39, 148
Constantinople, 72, 167, 169, 170
Controller of Salvage, 97, 119
Cook, Cpl, T, 14
Cook, H J, Bandmaster, 7
Cooke, Capt C A, 172
Cookery School, 29
Cork, 38
Corps Club, 33
Corps Masonic Lodge, 7
Corps of Military Staff Clerks, 5
Corps Week, 6
Cossey, Sapper W, 14
Coulston, Capt, 68
Courtneidge, Cicely, 142
Cove Balloon School, 36
Cowans, Lt Gen Sir John, 43
Crawford, Lt Col H A B, 89
Crawley, Col, 186
Cricklewood, 68
Crofton Atkins, Maj/Col/Maj Gen A R, 12, 29, 137, 143, 148, 190, 192, 205
Croft Spa, 147
Croix de Guerre, 164, 167, 189
Cross, Pte James, 127
Crossley car, 85, 144
Crump, Sgt Typewriter Mechanic A, 151
Cumberlege, Capt H F C, 29, 38
Cummings, Alfred, 4
Curragh, 14, 26, 72
Curtis, Pte George, 114
Cussens, Farr Sgt, 373

Daily Mail, 68, 116, 128
Daimler, 14, 48, 63, 67, 85, 86, 144, 146, 181
Damascus, 155, 156
Darby, Pte Edward, 68
Dardanelles, 149, 171, 177
Dar-es-Salaam, 180
Dartnell, Lt Col G B, 134
Darracq, 85
Davidson, Capt A E, 38
Davidson, Wagoner R, 50
Davies, Brig Gen/Maj Gen G F, 153, 207
Davies, Lt Col J E, 169
Davies, Pte R S, 378
Day, Capt F I, 21
Deasy, 38
De Dion Bouton, 85
Deir El Belah, 155
Delage, 85

Delahaye, 85
Delauney Belleville, 85
Delavoye, Capt F J, 21
Dennis, 26, 63, 82, 85, 123, 144
Department of Tank Design, 104
Depot Units of Supply, 38, 51
Deptford, 47, 49, 76, 87, 133, 136
Derby, 16
Derby, Lord, 137
Devonport, 50, 157
Dickinson, Lt Col H, 161
Didcot, 18
Dieppe, 56, 74
Director General of Transportation, 69
Director(ate) of Labour, 97, 190
Director of Salvage, 190
Directorate of Agricultural Production, 119
Directorate of Forestry, 76, 120
Distinguished Conduct Medal, 54
District Barrack Officers, 5
Divisional Salvage Companies, 118
Dodgson, Lt Col C S, 40
Doherty, Sgt R, 14
Doiran, 164, 168
Donahue, Maj/Col W E, 16, 21, 25, 38
Dorchester, 104
Douai, 67
Douglas motor cycle, 37, 85, 144
Douglas, Pte James, 188
Doulieu, 122
Doullens, 74, 107, 124
Dover, 149
Draper, Capt C N, 162
Driving School, 16
du Cros, Arthur/Capt George/Lt W, 54
Dublin, 6, 26, 136
Duleep Singh, Prince, 100
Dülmen, 78
Dunkirk, 67
Dunne, Col W A, 11, 12, 127
Dunstable, 137

East Africa, 149, 180–182, 192
East Yorkshire Volunteer Brigade Transport
    & Supply Company, 141
Edinburgh, 17, 21, 146
Edkins, Capt B H, 102
Eglestone, Capt T B M, 376
Egypt, 11, 46, 48, 49, 90, 91, 102, 119,
    120, 149, 153, 156, 157, 160, 171, 172,
    174, 175, 177, 179
El Arish, 153, 155
El Gamli, 155
Elgin, 36
Elliott, Col W, 153
Eltham, 134, 148

Elveden, 100, 101, 102, 104
Elverdinghe, 68
Employment Companies, 119
Engine Cleaners, 16
Enfield motor cycle, 85
English, Maj W J, 183
Ermanville, 57
Erivan, 188
Es Salt, 155
Esher, 146
Esher Committee/Report, 24, 25

Establishments (Annex B and N)
    Ammunition Park 1915, 253
    Ammunition Sub Park for Divisions
        1915, 254
    Army Troops Supply Column 1916, 247
    Auxiliary Petrol Company 1916, 245
    Auxiliary Steam Company 1916, 246
    Corps Troops Supply Column , 247
    Divisional Ambulance Workshop 1915,
        257
    Divisional Ammunition Park 1915, 252
    Divisional Supply Column 1915, 248
    Divisional Train 1912, 243
    Field Ambulance 1916, 255
    Horse Transport Company 1902, 204
    Mobile Repair Unit 1915, 258
    MT for Siege Artillery Battery 1915, 249
    MT for Siege Artillery Battery 1917, (for
        Egypt and Mesopotamia) 250
    Workshop for Anti-aircraft Batteries
        1916, 256

Etaples, 74, 121
Eu, 121
Evans, Lt Col E G, 134
Expeditionary Force Canteens, 71, 74, 76,
    86, 87, 161, 162, 179

Fairbairns, Lt R H, 373
Fara, 151
Farman biplane, 35
Farnborough, 21, 35
Farriers, 16, 147
Feltham, 194
Ferguson, Pte Robert, 125
Festubert, 71
Fiat, 85, 144, 151, 160
Field Bakery, 38, 171, 172, 174
Field Butchery, 38, 171
Finch, 2Lt H B, 381
Fire Brigades, 72
First Aid Nursing Yeomanry, 94
Fitters, 16, 131
Flanders, 71, 72, 97, 103, 129, 190, 193
Flers-Courcelette, 100, 101, 104, 259

Foden, 9, 85, 144
Foot, Lt S H, 102
Forage Committee/ Department, 83
Ford, 63, 85, 144, 155, 160–162, 171, 180, 181, 188
Ford, Lt Col/Brig Gen/Maj Gen R, 34, 37, 171, 190, 207
Forestry Commission, 98
Forward Tractor Park, 112
Foster steam tractor, 85
Foster Daimler, 63, 66, 101, 144
Foster, Capt/Maj Gen H N, 16, 32, 38
Fowler steam tractor, 14, 15, 85
Fox, Sgt Charles Percy, 125
French, Gen/Field Marshal Sir John, 20, 24, 37, 41, 75, 81
Frèvent, 123, 124
Frimley, 35
Frinton, 20
FWD, 63, 113, 123

Gale, CSM, 60
Galilee, 156
Galley, Lt E D G, 377
Gallipoli, 71, 153, 169, 171, 174, 175, 177, 190
Garford lorry, 63, 85, 88
Garrett tractor, 144
Gaymer, Capt R C, 168
Gaza, 102, 153, 155, 157
Geddes, Sir Eric, 69, 82
Genoa, 150, 151
Ghent, 118
Gibb, Maj/Col/Brig Gen Evan, 97, 119, 190, 193, 194, 207
Gibbs, Capt A, 62
Gilpin, Lt Col/Brig Gen F C, 25, 69
Girdlestone-Edwards, Capt G, 188
Gittens, Sgt E, 380
Gitz-Rice, Lt, 61
Glasgow, 146
Glen Imaal, 26
Glenny, Lt A W F, 376
Gloucester, 87
Gommecourt, 124
Godfrey, Pte J, 377
Goldfinch, Pte E, 381
Graham, Cpl, C, 381
Granezza, 151
Grantham, 22, 136, 147
Grapes, Capt QM J, 49
Grattan, Lt Col, 8
Graudenz, 126
Gravesend, 14, 15
Greenwich, 136
Grimsby, 141
Groushkonsky, Pte, 174

Grove Park, 43, 67–69, 88, 102, 134, 135
Guys, 33
GWK car, 85
Gwynn, Pte, 95

Hadfield, Col/Maj Gen C A, 13, 28, 208
Haggard, Maj Arthur, 7
Haifa, 155, 156, 177
Haig, Lt Gen/Field Marshal Sir Douglas, 12, 37, 40, 125
Haldane, 21, 22, 40
Halleys, 33, 63
Hallfords, 33, 38, 63, 82, 85
Ham, 58
Hamblin, Sgt P M, 380
Hamilton, Gen Sir Ian, 15, 171, 177–179
Hampshire Company ASC, 30
Hand, Pte B, 381
Handeni, 180
Harman, Capt A E W, 11
Harris, Capt D H, 120
Harrow Weald, 137
Hartshorn, Capt A H, 56
Hastings, 32
Hayes, 137
Haylor, Capt, 59
Hayter, Capt H R, 16
Hazebrouck, 121
Hazleton, Brig Gen P O, 180
Heath, Col/Maj Gen C E, 9, 11–13, 45, 79, 208
Heavy Branch of the Machine Gun Corps, 76, 88, 100, 103, 104, 148, 259
Hell Fire Corner, 109, 151
Henley-on-Thames, 25
Herlin-le-Sec, 123
Herring, Lt Alfred, 126, 377
Hesdin, 126
Hesketh, Pte Donald, 125
Hickie, Maj G W C, 188
Hicks, Lt H H, 104
High Wood, 101
Hill, Pte, 122
Hills, Miss Christobel, 93
Hilsea, 44
Hit, 160
Hitchin, 76
HM King Edward VII, 6, 21, 40
HM King George V, 21, 37, 39, 67, 126, 128, 134, 147, 189
Hobbs, Maj Gen P E F, 208
Hoffman, Capt A R G, 168
Holbrook, Col C V, 83
Holden, Col H C L, 38, 43
Holman, Maj Gen H C, 188
Holmes, Pte J, 373
Holt, Capt B, 378

Holt caterpillar, 63, 85, 100, 101, 144, 160, 171
Home Defence Corps, 100
Homs, 155
Honourable East India Company, 23
Hook, Dvr, 54, 55
Hore-Belisha, Maj I L, 29, 190
Horne, Pte A, 372
Horniblow, Col F, 27, 49
Hornsby-Ackroyd, 22
Horse Shows, 109
Hortiacn, 166
Hotchkiss car, 85
Houchen, Sgt F V, 376
Hounslow, 49, 107, 134
Houplines, 68
Howell, Lt Col G L H, 96, 124, 126
Howitt, Lt Frank, 175
HRH The Duke of Cambridge, 127
HT School of Instruction, 187
Hughes, Capt C G E, 21
Hunt's ovens, 74
Hurley, 25
Hutchinson, Capt/Lt Col T M, 16, 26, 48

Imbercourt, 144
Imbros, 171
Imperial War Museum, 62, 126, 134, 172, 175
Indian motor cycle, 85
Inspection Branch Mechanical Transport, 138, 139
Inspectorate of MT, 21, 22, 36, 149
Inspector General, Line of Communication, 36, 69, 79, 166, 190
Inspector of Catering, 29
Inspector of Fuel Consumption, 95
Inspector of Subsidized Transport, 32, 38
Inspector of the ASC, 28
Iredell, Maj J S, 148
Iron Rations, 50
Isleworth, 134
Islington, 47
Ismailia, 177
Istanbul, 72
Italy, 149–152, 192
Iveagh, Lord, 100

Jack, LCpl, J, 14
Jackson, Cpl, Frederick Charles, 125
Jackson, Pte John, 14, 57
Jaffa, 155
Jam Stealers, 4, 74
Jeffrey Quadrant lorry, 85
Jericho, 155
Jerusalem, 103, 155, 156
John, Cpl, 60

Johnson, Pte A, 372
Johnson, Col/Maj Gen F F, 11, 208
Johnson, Pte/Lt Col P H, 104, 105
Jones, Pte David, 125
Jones, Sapper, G H, 14
Jordan, 155, 156
Jussy, 126

Kalamaria, 164, 167
Karm, 155
Karrier lorry, 63
Kasvin, 162
Kaye, Maj Sir John, 142
Kearns, Col T J, 148
Keene, Sgt Frederick Herbert, 125
Kelly lorry, 63, 85, 144
Kelsey Manor, 148
Kempton Park, 137, 138, 145
Kensington Barracks, 33, 48, 131, 140
Kettering, 147
Keys, Nelson, 142
Khan Unis, 155, 157
King, Brig Gen Sir Charles, 69, 95
King's African Rifles, 33
Kitchener, Field Marshal Lord, 9, 41, 45, 67, 70, 71, 82, 139, 171, 179, 189
Kitchfield, Asst Comm Gen E, 33
Knothe, Maj/Lt Col H O, 100, 101, 102
Knox, Capt/Maj/Lt Col/Brig Gen H O, 23, 52
Knox-Gore, Lt P, 167
Koe, Brig Gen/Maj Gen F W G, 166, 171, 177–179, 190, 209
Kola Inlet, 183
Kut el Amara, 88, 103, 159, 160, 162, 169

Labour Companies, 55, 56, 103, 106, 110, 133
Labour Corps, 97, 110, 190
Labour Directorate, 106, 110
Lacre lorry, 85
Ladysmith, 13
Laffan's Plain, 21
Lairia, 166
Lake Beshik, 166, 167
Lake Langaza, 166, 167
Lake Onega, 187
Lake Tahinos, 167
Lake Tanganyika, 181, 182
Lampwicks, 75
Lancia, 85, 138, 144
Land Transport Corps, 31, 35
Landon, Col/Brig Gen F W B, 25, 27, 39, 45, 76, 79, 209
Landon, Mrs, F W B, 76, 78, 70
Langavuk, 166, 168

Langley, Cpl, A,   14
Larkhill,   120
Lawrence, Pte T L,   372, 375
Lawrence, Col T E,   156
Leavis, Capt H,   95
Le Cateau,   51, 58, 127
Lecocq, Mme Marie,   61
Le Havre,   45, 53, 56, 58, 72, 74, 91, 92,
    95, 101
Lee Reception & Training area,   134
Lees, Maj A H,   124
Leggott, 2Lt T G,   102
Leicester,   147
Leland, Lt Col F W,   160
Lemnos,   171, 175, 177
Leon Bollee cars,   85
Lever Brothers,   83
Lever, Capt H R,   16
Leverton, Pte Benjamin,   125
Leyland,   26, 38, 63, 66, 82, 85, 182
Liddell, Capt A R,   29
Liencourt,   107
Light Railways and Crane Detachment,   76
Lille,   67
Lillers,   123
Lindsay Lloyd, Maj F L,   135
Little Caterpillar,   22
Lincoln,   102
Liverpool,   46, 53, 127, 135
Lloyd George, David,   69, 82, 135, 137
Lloyd, Lt Gen Sir Francis,   142
Lloyd, Sgt J F,   374
Lloyd, Lt V H,   104
Locomobile,   63, 85, 95
London,   7, 8, 14, 31–33, 36, 43, 45, 48,
    53, 67, 68, 70, 72, 83, 87, 88, 92, 93,
    100–102, 126, 131–134, 136, 137, 139,
    140, 142, 143, 145, 146, 149, 194
London Gazette,   19, 81, 152, 163, 169
London School of Economics,   29
Londonderry, Lady,   93
London General Omnibus Company,   26,
    29, 31, 63, 64, 67, 68, 79, 131, 134,
    144, 145
Long, Brig, A,   166, 168, 169
Long, Col/Brig Gen/Maj Gen S S,   29, 43,
    45, 46, 70, 79, 82, 83, 86, 147, 164,
    166, 171, 177, 178, 189, 190, 209
Long, Mrs S S,   77
Longfellow-Cooper, Lt Col,   171
Loos,   71, 100
Lorry and Engine Drivers,   16, 17
Lubbock, Lt The Hon E F P,   373
Ludd,   155
Lyons, Lt C S,   14, 25
Lyons Biggar, Lt Col J,   23

Macdonald, Col The Rt Hon Sir John,   19
Macedonian Mule Corps,   167
Macedonia,   169
Machine Gun Corps,   90, 96, 100–102,
    136, 137, 156
Machine Gun Training Centre,   147
Mackay, Capt A H,   379
Mackie, Lt J C,   36
Macmillan, Maj G,   21
Mademoiselle from Armentières,   61
Madrid,   11
Maidstone,   14
Major, Cpl Bertie Edwin,   125
Makin, Sgt L,   376
Makrikeuy,   169
Malthouse, Lt J B,   380
Marburg, Lt W,   54
Marcoing,   123
Market Harborough,   147
Marlborough,   16, 68
Marne,   41, 56
Marriott, Lt,   60
Marseilles,   56, 74, 120
Marshall, Cpl,   109
Marshall, Pte R,   60
Marshall, Lt Gen W R,   163
Martin, Cpl, G W,   14
Martin, SSM T,   374
Masters, Pte George,   126, 377
Matchless motor cycle,   85
Maude, Gen,   160
Maudslay,   26, 59, 63, 82, 85
Maxse, Lt Gen Sir Ivor,   115
Mayhew, Lt Col M J,   91, 21
Mbuyuni,   180
McLean, Lt,   174
McFarlane, Maj G,   7
McGrory, Dvr E,   374
McLaren & Tasker steam engine,   85
McMurdo, Col,   31
McNalty, Brevet Major, C E I,   13, 14
Mercedes car,   85, 144
Mersa Matruh,   153
Mesopotamia,   88, 149, 159, 161–163, 192
Messines Ridge,   89, 123
Metallurgique,   144
Middleton, Lt J A,   194
Midwinter, Maj W,   157
Milan,   152
Military Cross,   187, 189
Military Medal,   50, 112, 114, 124, 189
Military Train,   33, 35
Milne, General Sir George,   169
Milner, Capt J,   381
Milnes-Daimler,   9
Milnes-Marienfeldt,   14

Milnes-Neustadt, 14
Mineral Water Factories, 74, 87
Ministry of Munitions, 82, 83, 93, 143,
    144, 145, 193
Minor Repairs School, 103
Mobile Workshop, 80, 105
Model-T Ford, 86
Moins, Cpl, J C, 14
Molony, Capt W W, 12
Mombasa, 180
Mombo, 180
Monro, Gen Sir Charles, 179
Mons, 41, 56, 57, 58, 59, 61
Montgomery, Pte Frank, 125
Moore, Lt Col T C R, 183
Moores, Capt C F, 12
Morgan, Pte C E, 188
Morgan, Gen H G, 83
Morgan, Lt Col H O, 29
Morning Post, 75
Morris, Pte Arthur Andrew, 125
Morrison, Maj S W, 68
Moscow, 186
Motor Boat Company/Section, 167, 177
Motor Cycle Show, 37
Motor Union, 50
Motor Volunteer Corps, 19–21, 30, 50,
    140–142
Mount Pleasant, 145
MT Committee, 9, 10, 22, 26, 38
MT Reception Parks, 126
MT Repair Depot, 25
MT School of Instruction, 108, 187
MT Stores Depot, 16
Mucky Dozen, 14
Mudros, 171, 175, 178, 179
Mule Purchasing Commission, 49
Murmansk, 183, 187
Murray, Gen Sir Archibald, 153

Nantes, 56
Napier, 48, 63, 85, 144, 169
National Motor Volunteers, 141
National Society of Chauffeurs, 53
Nazareth, 156
Neuve Chapelle, 71
Newcastle-on-Tyne, 147
Newhaven, 52, 87, 135
New Zealand ASC, 23, 174
Newbury, 18
Newton, Lt, 145
Nicholson, Pte, 14
Nieppe, 123
Nieuport , 91, 112
Nixon, Pte H, 188
Northamptonshire Regiment, 126
Norwood, 148

Nugent, Col R A, 11
Nunq, 123

O'Dell, Col T J, 37
Odessa, 188
Old Comrades Club, 33
Old Contemptibles, 41
O'Neill, Cpl, G, 188
Order of St John of Jerusalem, 54
Orleans, 74
Ormskirk, 147
Ory, 2Lt V W, 109
Ostend, 67
Osterley Park, 43, 134, 135, 148
Ostler, SSgt F E, 23
Oughterson, Col J C, 12
Outreau, 74
Overland car, 144
Oxford, LCpl, F, 112

Packard lorry, 63, 85, 144, 161
Packers and Loaders, 133
Page, Lt Gen Sir Arthur, 32
Pagefield lorry, 82, 85, 144
Palestine, 149, 153, 174, 192
Palmer, Pte Frederick Earle, 125
Panhard car, 19, 85
Paris, 11, 41, 54, 56, 57, 63, 68, 107
Park Royal, London, 136
Parkyn, Lt Col G J, 7
Passchendaele, 87, 103, 113
Patterson, Lt Col J H, 174
Paul, Col G R C, 27, 32
Pavesi tractors, 152
'P' Corps Siege Park, 110
Peerless lorry, 63, 85, 123, 144, 160
Pelly, Lt Col E G, 161
Pennington, Maj H N, 89
Percival, Lt Col Harold Franz Passauer, 12
Perivale, 137
Perkins ovens, 74, 164
Pernes, 123
Péronne, 59
Petty, SQM, P M, 23
Phelon & Moore motor cycle, 37, 144
Phelps, Maj/Col A , 12, 39
Piave, 152
Pickles, Pte A, 381
Pickthorn, Lt C E M, 375
Pierce-Arrow lorry, 63, 85
Pigeon Lofts, 96
Pigott, Maj G E, 33
Plessis-Belleville, 59
Plevey, Cpl, Samuel, 12
Ploegsteert, 123
Plum-and-apple jam, 74
Pope, 2Lt W A, 373

Poperinghe, 55, 114
Porton, 143, 144
Portsmouth, 24, 44, 50, 120, 135, 194
Portuguese Expeditionary Force, 127
Preed, 2Lt, 113
Premier motor cycle, 37
Princess Mary boxes, 59, 66
Prisoners-of-War Fund, 57, 78, 79

Qantara, 153, 155, 157
Queen Mary's Army Auxiliary Corps, 74,
    87, 94, 144, 145, 148
Queenstown (Cork), 136

Rackham, Lt G, 372
Rafa, 153, 155, 157
Railway Labour Company, 56
Railway Supply Detachments, 38, 51
Rainsford, Col M E R, 11
Ramadi, 160
Ramscappelle, 112
Reading, 18, 68
Redhill, 147
Regent's Park, 76, 138, 145, 146
Regimental Numbers, 92
Registration Scheme, 32, 47
Reid, Cpl, 109
Reid, Capt F J, 21
Reid, Lt Col H G, 188
Reindeer Transport Corps, 183
Remount Companies, 5, 28, 43
Remount Service, 46, 162
Remount Squadron, 46
Renault, 85, 146
Rennie, Sgt Maj, 60
Resht, 162
Reynolds, Maj T W, 33
Ribecourt, 123
Richardson, Pte Leonard, 125
Richmond, 133
Riddell, Brig Gen E V, 151
Rigby, Sgt Maj, 57
Riker lorry, 85
River Struma, 167
Road Board, 76
Roadless Traction, 105
Roberts, Field Marshal Lord, 21, 53, 127
Robey, George, 142
Robinson, Lt Col A C, 194
Rochette, 151
Rodgers, LCpl, A, 374
Rolls, Hon, C S, 9, 19
Rolls-Royce, 63, 66, 85, 131, 132, 147,
    156, 169
Romani, 153
Romsey, 44, 147
Rorke's Drift, 127

Rouen, 49, 53, 63, 66, 68, 74, 89, 92, 95,
    97, 120
Rouxmesnil, 107
Rowe, Lt Col C, 151
Rowland, Sgt E C H, 57, 61
Rowlandson, Lt S A, 372, 375
Royal Army Clothing Department, 141,
    144
Royal Army Medical Corps, 44, 55, 75, 88,
    90, 146, 175, 185
Royal Artillery, 6, 9, 19, 33, 36, 155
Royal Automobile Club, 50, 53, 54, 132
Royal Dublins, 68
Royal Enfield, 144
Royal Engineers, 2, 7–10, 13, 14, 19, 30,
    50, 52, 56, 80, 88, 89, 96, 97, 102, 104,
    110, 111, 113, 123, 138, 144–146, 153,
    168, 172, 174
Royal Flying Corps, 54, 90, 91, 140
Royal Garrison Artillery, 88, 89, 135
Royal Inniskilling Fusiliers, 87
Royal Marine Labour Corps, 56
Royal Marines, 56, 67
Royal Navy & Military Tournament, 7, 34
Royal Tournament, 22, 34
Royal Waggoners, 39
Royal Waggon Train, 39
Royal Warwicks, 68
Ruaha, 181
Rudge-Whitworth motor cycle, 37, 85
Russia, 149, 183, 188

Saddlers, 147
Sailly, 122
Salisbury, 15, 44, 78, 135, 143
Salmon, Sir Isidore, 29
Salonika, 71, 72, 90, 164–169, 177–179,
    190, 192
Salvage, 118, 119
Sanderson, Lt I C, RAF, 148
Sandusky, 144
Sargeant, Maj G H, 379
Sargeant, Maj Gen H N, 209
Saunders, Lt, 14
Saurer lorry, 36, 63, 85
School of Ballooning, 16
School of Instruction in Tank Driving,
    102
Scott motor cycle, 144
Scott, Col/Brig Gen P C J, 160, 166
Scott, Capt E W W, 17
Seabrook lorry, 63, 85
Seaforth, 47
Seaforth Highlanders, 68
Seaman, LCpl E, 87, 382
Self, Capt R W F, 378
Senior MT Officer, 105

Serbia,   93
Serbian Army,   71
Service Companies,   25, 34, 43
Sheldrick, Wagoner D,   50
Sheffield Simplex,   85
Shellal,   155
Shepherd, Cpl G B,   375
Shepherd's Bush,   143, 145
Shirehampton,   147
Shoeburyness,   14, 107, 144
Shoeing Smiths,   16
Shorncliffe,   72
Shortlands,   148
Short's Gardens,   72, 137, 139
Siddeley,   15, 63, 85
Sidon,   155
Simpson, Maj G,   188
Sinai,   153, 156
Singer,   63, 85, 144
Siwa Oasis,   153
Slade Baker, Lt Col A,   38
Slough,   128, 137, 138
Smallpiece, Lt C,   73
Smiths,   16
Smith, LCpl Alec,   78
Smith, Mech Sgt Maj F R,   96
Snepp, Maj/Lt Col E,   160, 161
Snowden-Smith, Lt/Maj Gen,   35, 36
Sollum,   153
Somaliland,   17, 32, 33
Somme,   88, 96, 97, 110, 156
South African ASC,   23, 180
Southampton,   22, 52, 53, 135
Southport,   126
Special Reserve,   21, 39, 43
Special Transport Reserve,   32
Spicer-Simson, Comdr Geoffrey,   181
Squarey, Capt E M,   183
Standard Oil Company,   164, 166
'S' (Statistical) Branch,   149
St Eloi,   68, 122
St George's Church,   6
St John, 2Lt,   100
St Just,   121
St Nazaire,   56
St Omer,   54, 56, 63, 84, 89, 137
St Pol,   107, 121, 123, 124
St Quentin,   58, 59, 126
St Valéry-sur-Somme,   56, 96
St Venant,   68
Stable belt,   28
Staff College,   12, 38
Stanhope Lines,   6, 29, 34, 39
Star van,   85
Staynes, Sgt George,   125
Stayton, Frank,   98
Steedman, 2Lt H P G,   100, 102, 103

Steenwerck,   56
Stevedores,   133
Stevens, Pte R W,   376
Stevenson, Maj A G,   38
Stewart, Lt C J,   167
Stewart, Mrs Athole,   83
Stirling lorries,   17
Straker Squire,   9, 16, 63, 85
Strazeele,   56
Strickland, Maj F,   103
Striedinger, Capt/Lt Col O,   29, 164
Stringer, Lt Col F W,   43, 45, 49
Struma,   166
Studebaker,   63, 85, 144, 181
Subsidy Scheme,   32, 33, 48
Suez Canal,   71, 153, 157
Sunbeam,   63, 66, 85, 144
Sunningdale,   137
Supply Branch,   5
Supply Column,   17
Supply Company,   5, 6, 133
Supply Park,   17, 18
Supply & Transport Corps,   23, 74, 159
Suvla,   171, 172, 175, 176, 178, 179
Swabey, Brig Gen W S,   151, 152
Swann, Lt G,   167
Swanston, Capt R G,   162
Swaythling,   147
Swift car,   85
Swinton, Col E D,   104
Swiss Berna,   63
Sydenham,   134, 148
Sykes, Lt Col Sir Mark,   39
Sykes, Capt S E,   39
Syria,   153

Talbot,   63, 144
Tank Companies/Battalions/Brigades/
    Corps,   100, 104, 157
Tarver, Maj Gen W K,   210
Tasker,   14
Taylor, Lt,   122
Terry, Capt G E,   52
Thetford,   100
Thompson, Wagoner W,   50
Thornycroft,   9, 26, 36, 63, 66, 82, 144,
    146, 150, 181
Tidworth,   6, 44
Tilbury,   181
Tournai,   67
Townshend, Gen,   159, 169
Traction Engine Firemen,   16
Tractor Park,   122
Tramways (MET) Omnibus Company,   67
Transvaal,   11
Travers Barracks,   24
Trent,   151

Triggs, Pte A,   34
Tripoli,   155, 156, 177
Triumph motor cycle,   37, 85, 144
Tubb, LCpl W H,   381
Turner, Capt D M,   145
Turner, Lt QM,   102
Twickenham,   93, 134
Tyre,   155
Tyre Press Detachments,   72

Uganda Protectorate,   11
Uhlans,   57
Unic car,   85
Union Jack Club,   7
Unwin, Lt E F,   16
Usher, Pte A E,   372, 378

Vauxhall,   63, 66, 144
Vehicle Subsidy Scheme,   32, 33
Verdun,   88
Versailles,   12, 118
Vickers,   104
Vickers, Dvr H J,   373
Victoria Cross,   3, 87, 126, 127, 179, 183,
    189, 382
Vieux Berquin,   122
Villaverla,   151
Vimy Ridge,   103
Vinot lorry,   85
Vlamertinghe,   55
Voyennes,   109
Vulcan car,   38, 85, 144

WAACs,   119
Wace, Col E,   97
Wadi Ghuzze,   153
Wagoners Special Reserve,   39, 50
Walcker car,   85
Wallis & Stevens,   14, 144
Walton, MSS T M,   372, 375
Walthamstow,   68
Wannell, 2Lt W C,   379
Ward, Col Sir Edward,   7, 11, 23, 189, 210
Ward, Col E I,   49
Ward, Maj J,   188
Wardrecques,   74
Ware, Lt,   122
Warwick motor cycle,   144
Wass, CQMS J J,   23
Wassell, SSM C,   376
Waterlow, Capt C B,   168
Water tankers,   88
Watling, Capt C E,   17, 21
Watson, Capt/Maj H N G,   59, 183, 186
Watt, Lt G,   380

Way, Pte,   14
Weir, Maj P,   161
Wellbelove, CSM Albert William,   125
Wembley,   137
Weobley Company ASC,   30
Westoutre,   123
Wheater, Maj J B,   151
Wheelers,   16, 147
White, 1st Class SSgt Maj,   127
White lorry,   63, 85
White, Pte,   57
Whittingham, Col C W,   153
Wiesbaden,   130
Wilder, Maj H C,   37
Wilks, CSM C S,   77
Willys,   144
Williams, Bransby,   142
Wilson, Brig Gen/Maj Gen F M,   130, 210
Wilson, Brig Gen/Field Marshal Sir Henry,
    12, 115
Wilson, Capt F Dunbar,   115
Wilson, Woodrow, President,   118
Williams, Maj,   186
Wilton,   76
Windsor,   134
Wingate, LCpl E,   14
Wissant,   126
Witt, Capt J W,   194
Wolds Wagoners,   39
Wolseley,   14, 15, 24, 53, 63, 85, 138, 144,
    170
Women's Forage Corps,   83, 84
Women's Legion,   93, 94, 144, 145, 148
Wood, Gen Sir Evelyn,   9
Woodhams, Cpl A G,   14
Woods, Maj J C,   49
Woollcombe, Lt Gen Sir C,   148
Woolmer, Cpl,   78
Woolwich,   5, 6, 8, 16, 17, 24, 27, 34, 39,
    40, 45, 49, 91, 133, 134, 136, 143, 144,
    147, 194
Wormhoudt,   123
Wright, Lt Col E C,   86
Wulpen,   112
Wulverghem,   123

York,   39, 147, 194
Ypres,   41, 55, 67, 68, 71, 75, 81, 82, 87,
    94, 99, 103, 107, 109, 114, 151

Zenith motor cycle,   37, 85, 144
Zeppelin,   101, 136, 137
Zillebeke,   109
Zion Mule Corps,   174
Zonnebeke,   55

UNITS AND FORMATIONS

Ammunition Parks

1st–6th Divisional Ammunition Parks, 51
1 Ammunition Park,   96
3 Ammunition Park,   96
4 Divisional Ammunition Park,   57
4 GHQ Ammunition Park,   96
5th Cavalry Brigade Ammunition Park, 51
6 Ammunition Park,   96
7 GHQ Ammunition Park,   96
8 Ammunition Park,   96
Cavalry Ammunition Park,   51
GHQ Ammunition Park,   69
'B' Corps Ammunition Park,   109

Armies

1st Army,   68, 88
1st New Army,   49
2nd Army,   68, 88, 130
3rd Army,   63, 84, 88
4th Army,   63, 95, 126
5th Army,   63, 84

Army Corps

1st Army Corps,   10, 11, 12, 17, 18

Brigades

Middlesex Brigade,   71
1 Tank Brigade,   76
2nd South Midland Mounted Brigade, 31
83rd Brigade,   108

Columns

4th Divisional Ammunition Column,   57
43rd (Wessex) Column,   190
122nd Siege Battery Ammunition Column,   112
227th Siege Battery Ammunition Column
Lowland Division Transport & Supply Column,   31

Companies (See also Annexes Q and R)

1 Company,   147
4 Company,   21
5 Company,   50, 51
6 Company,   5
7 Company,   5, 64
9 Company,   5, 50, 51
10 Company,   5, 51
11 Company,   5
12 Company,   5, 44, 50, 51
13 Company,   21
14 Company,   51
15 Company,   6, 17, 33
17 Company,   5
19 Company,   5
20 Company,   50, 51
21 Company,   5
22 Company,   6, 17
24 Company,   5
25 Company,   5
26 Company,   23, 51
27 Company,   21
28 Company,   5
29 Company,   5
30 Company,   5, 50, 51
31 Company,   5
33 Company,   5
34 Company,   5, 50, 51
35 Company,   5
37 Company,   5
40 Company,   5, 21
42 Company,   5, 26
44 Company,   97
45 Company,   51
46 Company,   51
47 Company,   26, 51
48 Company,   51, 58, 190
49 Company,   51
50 Company,   51, 96
51 Company,   21, 51
52 Company,   16, 23, 38, 69, 85
53 Company,   51
54 Company,   51, 60
55 Company,   21, 51
56 Company,   51
57 Company,   26, 51
58 Company,   21, 51
59 Company,   21, 51
60 Company,   51
61 Company,   26, 51
62 Company,   51
63 Company,   51
64 Company,   51
65 Company,   51
66 Company,   26
68 Company,   6
69 Company,   6
70 Company,   6
74 Company,   100, 120
77 Company,   14, 16, 24
78 Company,   16, 24
82 Company,   91
89 Company,   91
90 Company,   68
91 Company,   68
92 Company,   68, 96
93 Company,   68
166 Company,   64
231 Company,   110

Companies *(continued)*

244 Company, 164
322 Company, 182
339 Company, 96
340 Company, 100
341 Company, 124
352 Company, 108
355 Company, 64
365 Company, 60
405 Company, 84
418 Company, 53
419 Company, 54
421 Company, 54
428 Company, 175
429 Company, 174, 175
430 Company, 175
431 Company, 175
532 Company, 141
563 Company, 84, 115
570 Company, 181
588 Company, 95
590 Company, 97, 98
596 Company, 160, 161
598 Company, 164
604 Company, 110
606 Company, 93, 143, 145
610 Company, 123
614 Company, 146
620 Company, 76, 145, 146
621 Company, 147
646 Company, 88
650 Company, 76
656 Company, 160
660 Company, 80
661 Company, 136
662 Company, 136
663 Company, 136
664 Company, 136
665 Company, 136
666 Company, 136
667 Company, 136
668 Company, 136
683 Company, 107
688 Company, 167
706 Company, 167
707 Company, 167
708 Company, 167
709 Company, 167
711 Company, 100–104
718 Company, 88
728 Company, 76
729 Company, 161
730 Company, 161
766 Company, 169
777 Company, 168
783 Company, 161
784 Company, 161

806 Company, 109
815 Company, 161
872 Company, 147
873 Company, 147
874 Company, 147
875 Company, 147
876 Company, 147
877 Company, 169
879 Company, 92
882 Company, 131, 147
905 Company, 156
906 Company, 157
918 Company, 161
953 Company, 161
954 Company, 161
961 Company, 102, 157
971 Company, 161
976 Company, 161
985 Company, 76
1013 Company, 161
1014 Company, 161
1015 Company, 161
1016 Company, 161
1018 Company, 161, 162
1020 Company, 161
1023 Company, 161, 162
1024 Company, 162
1034 Company, 151
1050 Company, 76
1053 Company, 76
1056 Company, 162
1057 Company, 120
1081 Company, 151
1085 (Steam) Company, 76
1086 Company, 76
1122 Company, 186, 187
1150 Company, 152
1152 Company, 183
1153 Company, 187
1160 Company, 187
1st Auxiliary Bus Company, 68, 125, 126
2nd Auxiliary Bus Company, 68, 96, 125
3rd Auxiliary Omnibus Company, 68, 69, 125
4th Auxiliary Omnibus Company, 68, 69, 125
15th Auxiliary Omnibus Company, 84, 96, 107, 125
16th Auxiliary Omnibus Company, 84, 96, 115, 125
18th Auxiliary Omnibus Company, 95, 96, 125
50th Auxiliary Omnibus Company, 96, 125

51st Auxiliary Omnibus Company, 96, 125, 126
2 Auxiliary HT Company, 151
54 Auxiliary Petrol Company, 156
1 Labour Company, 47
2 Labour Company, 47
51 Chinese Labour Company, 102
1 Water Tank Company, 88
2 Water Tank Company, 88
3 Water Tank Company, 88
4 Water Tank Company, 88
33 Railway Labour Company, 56
34 Railway Labour Company, 56
4 GHQ Reserve MT Company, 124
8 GHQ Reserve MT Company, 124
ASC (Naval Labour) Companies, 56
Line of Communication Supply Companies, 95
'A' Company, 147
'A' Provisional HT Company, 168
'A' Supply Company, 133
'C' Supply Company, 133
'K' Supply Company, 133

Corps
1st Corps, 89
12th Corps, 108
17th Corps, 124
18th Corps, 115
Australian Corps, 123
Canadian Corps, 122

Depots
1 Base MT Depot, 66
1 Corps Depot, 194
1 Evacuation Depot, 152
1 Reserve HT Depot, 47, 136
1 Reserve MT Depot, 134
2nd Advanced MT Depot, 60
2 Base MT Depot, 66
2 Reserve HT Depot, 47
2 Reserve MT Depot, 134, 136
5 Base Supply Depot, 74
Advanced HT Depot, 47, 151
Advanced MT Depot, 51, 66, 80, 127, 162, 180
Advanced Remount Depot, 38, 46, 51
Advanced Supply Depot, 74, 166, 171, 187
ASC Depot, 53, 56, 85, 132, 147
ASC Discharge Depot, 147
ASC MT Depot, 67
ASC Tractor Depot, 85, 135
Base Depot, 53, 72, 80, 91, 127
Base HT Depot, 51, 92, 166
Base MT Depot, 66, 89, 92, 108, 127, 137, 151, 160, 162, 167, 180

Base Remount Depot, 38, 46, 51
Base Supply Depot, 56, 151, 153, 160, 164, 187
Canadian Forestry Depot, 146
Detailed Issue Depot, 95
Field Supply Depot, 74, 133, 172
Home MT Depot, 72, 101, 139
Home Repair Depot, 139
Home Supply Depot, 90
Mechanical Warfare Supplies Depot, 102
Main Supply Depot, 165
MT Depot, 100, 148, 161
MT Mobilization Depots, 47
Petrol Depot, 56
Remount Depot, 47, 92, 147, 149, 187
Reserve Supply Personnel Depot, 134
Stationery & Printing Depot, 151
Supply Reserve Depot, 45, 49, 133
Tractor Depot, 69, 100, 101

Divisions
1st Division, 18, 21, 64
1st Cavalry Division, 63
1/1st Highland Division, 72
1st London Division, 71
1st Indian Cavalry Division, 91
1st Canadian Division , 124
2nd Division, 18, 21, 124
2nd Cavalry Division, 63
2nd London Division, 71
2nd Australian Division, 124
3rd Division, 21, 124
3rd Cavalry Division, 63
3rd Australian Division, 124
3rd Indian Division, 155
4th Division, 124
4th Cavalry Division, 63
5th Cavalry Division, 63
5th Australian Division, 124
7th Division, 97, 150
7th Indian Division, 155
8th Division, 100, 120
10th Division, 164
12th Division, 124
13th Division, 166
14th Division, 124
20th Division, 124
21st Division, 124
22nd Division, 108, 166
23rd Division, 100, 150
26th Division, 166
27th Division, 166
28th Division, 166
29th Division, 124, 164, 171, 172
31st Division, 124
31st French Infantry Division, 124

Divisions *(continued)*

32nd Division,   108
32nd French Infantry Division,   124
34th Division,   110
35th Division,   124
37th Division,   124
41st Division,   124
42nd Division,   124, 174
46th (North Midland) Division,   71
48th Division,   150, 151
50th Division,   124
51st (Highland) Division,   72, 115
52nd (Lowland) Division,   155, 174
53rd Division,   155
54th Division,   155
62nd Division,   124
Anzac Mounted Division,   155
East Lancashire Division,   71
Guards Division,   107, 130
New Zealand Division,   123
Royal Naval Division,   67, 136, 171
1st East African Division,   180
2nd East African Division,   180

Heavy Repair Shop

Heavy Repair Shop,   16, 65, 80

Field Ambulance

141st Field Ambulance,   126

Local Auxiliary Companies

23 Local Auxiliary Company,   143
831 Local Auxiliary MT Company,   104
20th Auxiliary Petrol Company,   97

Mobile Repair Units

No 1 Mobile Repair Unit,   69
Army Troops Mobile Repair Unit,   109
Mobile Repair Unit,   80

Motor Ambulance Convoys

1 Motor Ambulance Convoy,   53, 54
2 Motor Ambulance Convoy,   54
4 Motor Ambulance Convoy,   54
9 Motor Ambulance Convoy,   64
21 Motor Ambulance Convoy,   107
Motor Ambulance Convoy,   86

Repair Shops

1st Repair Shop,   63
2nd Repair Shop,   63
3rd Repair Shop,   63
Heavy Repair Shop,   110, 137, 140, 151

Reserve Parks

1st Reserve Park,   50, 51
2nd Reserve Park,   50, 51
3rd Reserve Park,   50, 51
4th Reserve Park,   50, 51
5th Reserve Park,   44, 50, 51
6th Reserve Park,   50, 51
19th Reserve Park,   64

Supply Columns

1/1st Highland Division Transport &
   Supply Column,   72
1st–6th Divisional Supply Columns,   51
5th Cavalry Brigade Supply Column,   51
5th Divisional Supply Column,   58
29th Divisional Supply Column,   164
32nd Division Supply Column,   108
Army Troops Supply Column,   51
Cavalry Supply Column,   51

Trains

Army Troops Train,   51
1st–6th Divisional Trains,   51
5th Divisional Train,   57, 190
9th Divisional Train,   99
29th Divisional Train,   171, 172
51st (Highland) Divisional Train,   72
Cavalry Divisional Train,   59
Meerut Divisional Train,   76

Armoured Motor Battery

1 (Willoughby's) Armoured Motor
   Battery,   182

Royal Engineers

1st and 2nd Bridging Trains RE,   50
171 Tunnelling Company RE,   109
267 Railway Company RE,   168